CASIAN ANTON (born July 30, 1988) Private Researcher in International Relations with concerns in the study of interdisciplinary methodology and world state. MA in *Security and International Relations* ('Lucian Blaga' University of Sibiu, Romania, 2013), BA in *International Relations and European Studies* (Petru Maior's University of Târgu Mureş, Romania, 2011), Erasmus Student to *University of Social Science and Humanities* (Warsaw, Poland, 2012-2013).

This edition was ordered as a copy for feedback. It contains errors.

Casian Anton

February 3, 2024

Revi Project 88

REVI PROJECT 88

Series *Propaganda and Mass-Media:*

1. Black and White Music: A Journey Behind the Musical Notes.
2. On the Famous Feud.
3. The Famous Feud Project

FAMOUS FEUD
THE PROJECT

—— BY ——

CASIAN ANTON

Author: Casian Anton
Cover: created inside the app Adobe Express (standard license)

Amazon Printed Edition

© 2024 CASIAN ANTON VIA REVI PROJECT 88

THE FAMOUS FEUD PROJECT, ISBN: 979-8872033752

This book is based on:

© Casian, Anton: *Black and White Music: A Journey Behind the Musical Notes*, Amazon, Second Edition, 2023
© Casian Anton: *On the Famous Feud*, Amazon, Second Edition, 2023

REVI PROJECT 88 (London, UK): *is dedicated to create knowledge and advance the understanding of various topics in the fields of Social Science & Humanities (International Relations as a specific area of study). All the activities within this project is to guide, exchange, sustain and share unique and original ideas that can help people to understand the world.*

Contact: www.reviproject88.com
Social Media: Revi Project 88 (Twitter, Facebook, Instagram, Tumblr)

FIRST EDITION

TABLE OF CONTENTS

8

FOREWORD: the never-ending feud?

In the history of human nature there are conflicts with a happy ending, or with a tragic ending. The **FAMOUS FEUD**, in general, seems to have a happy ending with one winner: Taylor Swift. However, every time fans and main players think this conflict is over and it's buried forevermore, an unpredictable event? of a player's life extends the thread of the narrative, and offers the prospect of a never-ending conflict. From my point of view, the **FAMOUS FEUD** ended in July 2016, with the publication of Taylor Swift's answer on Instagram about the short edited video of the telephone conversation between Taylor Swift and Kanye West that took place in January 2016. In June 2017, despite the presentation of a limited information package by the players, I was convinced that Taylor Swift was the victim (for the second time) of Kanye West. In October 2023, after I have updated the entire research on the **FAMOUS FEUD**, the original conclusion did not change. In December 2023, Time magazine published its list of *Person of the Year*, and Taylor Swift received a place due to the positive impact she has in the music industry globally. The inclusion in the *Person of the Year* list came with an interview in which Taylor Swift again mentioned the story behind the **FAMOUS FEUD**[1]. The side effect

of the interview was fast, and social media servers were overheated from hundreds of thousands of positive messages for Taylor Swift. In terms of the number of social media posts about Taylor Swift's interview with Time magazine and the mention of the **FAMOUS FEUD**, it shows that the version of the telephone conversation described by Taylor Swift is more widespread and accepted by users, than the version described by Kanye West and Kim Kardashian.

I created this edition to **INCLUDE EVERYTHING** I wrote about the **FAMOUS FEUD**. It is an edition for people interested in **READING THE ENTIRE FAMOUS FEUD STORY FROM A TO Z**. In contrast, the other independent editions are more for people who are either only interested in the fight to eliminate discrimination in the USA music industry, or just the conflict between Kanye West and Taylor Swift from September 2009 to March 2020.

The report has two parts:

Part 1. Music in Black and White: A Journey Behind the Musical Notes;
Part 2. On the Famous Feud.

Enjoy your reading!
CASIAN ANTON
ENGLAND, DECEMBER 2023

---

[1] Sam Lansky, 'Person of the Year: Taylor Swift', *Time*, December 6, 2023, available at: https://time.com/6342806/person-of-the-year-2023-taylor-swift/, last accessed: December 6, 2023.

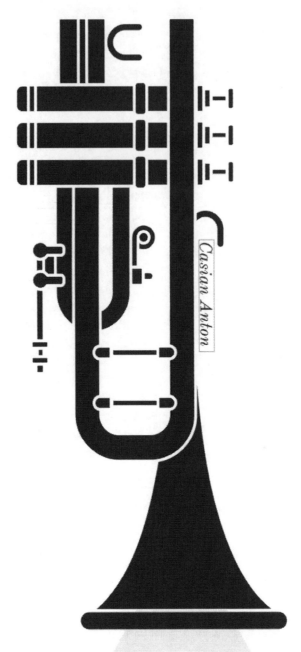

Casian Anton

BLACK
AND
WHITE
MUSIC

Dedication:

To white and black artists from this report:

'It is better to fail in originality, than to succeed in imitation.
He who has never failed somewhere, that man cannot be great.
Failure is the true test of greatness.'
Herman Melville (1850)

List of **Tables** and **Figures**

List of Tables:

List of Figures:

FOREWORD: a new FAMOUS journey

Between 2004 and 2005 *RBD* was one of the bands I listened to on the DVD bought by my older brother, Traian. During the music session, I preferred to lock the door, cover the small square windows with a thick black & red blanket, so that no light or uninvited eyes could see in. The light was turned off most of the time, and either I sat on the bed or I walked around the room. In the music of *RBD*, and later other artists (such as David Guetta, and Benny Benassi) which I discovered through tv channels, I found a path full of instruments and lyrics which enhanced my thinking skills, and allowed me to understand and develop my own personality, but also to create my own lifestyle in a colourful form.

As a child, I was hooked by the lyrics of songs, instruments and the life of my favorite artists. In Sighișoara, across the street from the Policlinică, right next to the grey cement stairs leading to the walled citadel, there was a small shop made of wood and plastic with newspapers and magazines. I don't remember the saleswoman's name, but I know that she never refused my honest request to read for free any magazines or newspapers; however, I had to follow a simple rule: 'don't bend the pages', which I nailed it everytime. In these pages, I found magnetic stories about my favorite artists, or information considered to be piquant and incognito. When the magazines were wrapped in a thin transparent plastic bag, the saleswoman used to rip off the bag for me. Most of the time, I preferred to sit alone on the weather-beaten bench near the store. However, once in a blue moon I was asked by friends to borrow other magazines than what I was habitually exploring, and I did it every time with the endorsement of the saleswoman. At this point in life, I wasn't interested in the history of music. I was pleased with participating in the school choir which, thanks to my teacher, met every year during the winter, spring and national holidays; in the beginning, we were a jam-packed group of boys and girls, but, for like 3 years, I was the only boy in the group. Around age 17 I decided to break away from the group.

Even today I am not predisposed in the history of music, but in these pages, having reached the multicultural world of England and the competition between races, cultures and religions, I decided to travel behind the musical notes of the artists used by the Western mass-media as examples of racial discrimination in the music industry of the United States of America (henceforth USA). The first version of this edition was a chapter in the research on the feud between Taylor Swift and Kanye West[2], but, in July 2021, I changed my mind and created an expanded and independent version; eventually, I incorporated extra research elements of songs and albums released by black and white artists.

I am delighted to have been able to make, I hope, a modest and all-purpose contribution to the discussion of the awards and allegations of discrimination and racism in the music industry of the USA. *Black & White Music* help us to see and understand another side of the origin and quality of the music released. *Black & White Music* can be better understood and appreciated by listening to all the albums analysed in these pages, and by reading the reviews written by experts in music.

I wish you a bright **FAMOUS** journey.

CASIAN ANTON

---

[2] Casian Anton, *On the FAMOUS Feud*, 2023.

Introduction: **music** and **white privilege**

The Recording Academy was formally established in 1957 with the purpose to recognise and award achievements in the music industry in the USA. In the last 64 years the Grammy Awards (created by the Recording Academy) have gained an impressive prestige. The number of awards have been changed over the years with categories added and removed depending on various events that have had a positive or negative impact on the music industry and the artists. The Grammy Awards is considered the most significant event in the music industry of the USA, and most of the artists nominated dream to be recognised for their music (which expresses creativity, talent, originality and value).[3]

THE NARRATIVE OF RACISM AGAINST THE RECORDING ACADEMY

Articles published in popular newspapers and magazines argue with examples in which the contribution of black artists in the music industry is not recognised and celebrated as often as it happens with the contribution of the white artists. For example, since the Grammy Awards (1957-2021) ten black artists have won the *Album of the Year* award; this number is promoted negatively (only ten) because, for black artists and their supporters, the actual number of albums that should have received this recognition is higher. Moreover, black artists have a superb presence in charts[4], for example Billboard charts in the USA, and yet the number of nominations and winnings for the Grammy Awards was lower than their presence in charts. In 2021 Samantha Hissong wrote an extensive article for the Rolling Stone with a vital point of view about the music industry in the USA:

> *'It's beyond the Grammys,' says Smith. 'The Grammy Awards are the pinnacle. But they're a part of this system that has been built with white superiority in mind, like all of our other systems in this country.'[5]*

In the last five years various articles on an resentful tone have been written about the white privilege in the music industry from USA. The main idea of these articles is the existence of a

---

[3] Tatum Herrin, 'The Grammys' Casual Racism Has Gone on for Too Long', *The Coat of Arms*, May 12, 2021, available at: https://menlocoa.org/20626/opinions/the-grammys-casual-racism-has-gone-on-for-too-long/, last accessed: July 26, 2021.
[4] It is based on the numbers of songs/albums sold every week and it is difficult to show if the higher number of sales is equal with high quality of the song/album.
[5] Samantha Hissong, 'The Crisis Behind the All-White Grammy Category', *Rolling Stone*, January 7, 2021, available at: https://www.rollingstone.com/pro/features/grammys-2021-childrens-music-controversy-1109502/, last accessed: July 25, 2021.

privilege that the white artists benefit, a privilege that lacks, or it is at a lower level for black artists and other minorities.[6] In 2015 Raquel Cepeda wrote an article for Rolling Stone:

'WHITE PEOPLE REJOICE! You've managed to cold-jack yet another awards season, and in February no less. The Oscars will be whiter than they've been since 1998, and this year the Grammy Awards promise to be a throwback to that time when Shirley Temple got down in blackface – dumb-stoopid-affected accents and all.'[7]

At the same time, another important opinion against the outcome advanced by The Recording Academy is the possible existence of an unfair intention to diminish the importance of albums promoted by black artists that, according to a visible number of specialists in music along with black artists and their supporters, had a significant cultural impact at least in the USA; there are albums that were not nominated in the categories they belong to, or they were nominated but did not win the Grammy Award. For a visible number of black artists and their supporters this attitude and position of The Recording Academy is most of the time labelled as 'racist phenomenon', 'corrupt' and 'unfair'. The first example I have is Nicki Minaj (black female artist) who in 2020 wrote on Twitter about her experience:

'Never forget the Grammys didn't give me my best new artist award when I had 7 songs simultaneously charting on billboard & bigger first week than any female rapper in the last decade- went on to inspire a generation. They gave it to the white man Bon Iver. #PinkFriday;'[8]

A second example is *The Weeknd* (black male artist) who expressed his dissatisfaction with the decision of The Recording Academy to not nominate at all ('zero nomination' to use the words spread on Twitter by his supporters) his album *After Hours* for Grammy Awards[9]:

[6] See for example: Lizzy Wan, 'Racial bias in the Grammys impacts our generation', *The Burling Game B*, April 2, 2021, available at: https://theburlingameb.org/4029/showcase/racial-bias-in-the-grammys-impacts-our-generation/, last accessed: July 25, 2021; 'Accusations of racial bias in Grammy Awards', *Wikipedia*, available at: https://en.wikipedia.org/wiki/Accusations_of_racial_bias_in_Grammy_Awards, last accessed: July 25, 2021. Natalie Harmsen, 'Goodbye, Grammys: Why Black artists think the awards show is irrelevant', *Global News*, February 24, 2021, available at: https://globalnews.ca/news/7617502/grammys-award-music-relevance/, last accessed: July 26, 2021. Cassie Owens, 'Do the Grammys have a diversity problem?', *Inquirer*, January 24, 2020, available at: https://www.inquirer.com/entertainment/inq2/grammys-2020-awards-nominees-predictions-history-lizzo-billie-eilish-20200124.html, last accessed: July 26, 2021. Jon Caramanica, '#GrammysSoWhite Came to Life. Will the Awards Face Its Race Problem?', *The New York Times*, February 13, 2017, available at: https://www.nytimes.com/2017/02/13/arts/music/grammys-adele-beyonce-black-artists-race.html, last accessed: July 26, 2021.
[7] Raquel Cepeda, 'Do the Grammys Have a Race Problem?', *Rolling Stone*, February 5, 2015, available at: https://www.rollingstone.com/music/music-news/do-the-grammys-have-a-race-problem-62956/, last accessed: July 26, 2021.
[8] Nicki Minaj, 'Message on Twitter', *Twitter*, November 24, 2020, available at: https://twitter.com/NICKIMINAJ/status/1331315767967551488?lang=en, last accessed: July 26, 2021; Elizabeth Aubrey, 'Nicki Minaj takes aim at the Grammys as she remembers her 2012 loss', *NME*, November 25, 2020, available at: https://www.nme.com/news/music/nicki-minaj-takes-aim-at-the-grammys-as-she-remembers-her-2012-loss-2824940, last accessed: July 26, 2021.
[9] *After Hours* set several records in the music industry from the USA: it topped the charts with the song *Blinding Lights* for most weeks spent in top five of the Billboard Hot 100.

'The Grammys remain corrupt. You owe me, my fans and the industry transparency…'[10]

Samantha Hissong has a clear example where black artists are not nominated in the category they belong:

'Only white artists were nominated for Best Children's Album – and three of them have asked to be taken off the ballot. Artists of color in children's music are fed up with the genre's homogeneity: 'It's like being served a baked potato with fries and hash browns on the side,' says one black artist.'

'Meanwhile, [Latin duo] 123 Andrés is over here with their flavor, we've got some Jamaican flavor, we've got hip-hop. These are different elements and aspects that bring a richness to the genre but are being systematically excluded.'[11]

A quick look at the method of deciding the winners of the Grammy Awards and the narrative about institutional racism, exposes an intrigue storyline where the true projection of the allegations of discrimination and racism are rather highlighting the voting members of the The Recording Academy: this happens because the voting members have the power to vote the winners of the Grammy Awards, and not the Co-Chairs, the Steering Committee and the Advisory Council. The Recording Academy offers the guidelines and the instructions to the voting members, for which outcome is difficult, if not impossible, to be blamed. The Recording Academy presents at the ceremony the choices voted by its members and, therefore, only the voting members can be accused of discrimination and racism against black artists, but also other minorities.

The voting members are artists from various races, cultures and religious backgrounds. After reading several articles and posts on social media (Facebook, Twitter and Reddit), I extracted four levels of the allegations of discrimination and racism advanced mostly by black artist and their supporters against The Recording Academy and its voting members:

1. the allegations of discrimination and racism are spread from black artists and their supporters, along with critics in music toward and in reference to white artists; this is completed on the assumption that black artists are not and cannot have a discriminatory or racist attitude toward and in reference to white artists;

2. there is an *absolute* and *ultimate* point of view in which the choices and the vote of black artists is to a higher extent right, and they deserve the award because the black artists expressed the opinion about it, or there is a visible endorsement by a number of experts and critics in music (outside The Recording Academy), and should be seen as the final truth; the choices and the votes of the white artists are not correct and fair,

---

[10] The Weeknd, 'Message on Twitter', *Twitter*, November 25, 2020, available at: https://twitter.com/theweeknd/status/1331394452447870977?lang=en-GB, last accessed: July 26, 2021.
[11] Samantha Hissong, 'The Crisis Behind the All-White Grammy Category'.

and are presented most of the time as being made up on the basis of discrimination and racism against black artists;

3. there is a *Spiral of Silence*[12] in favour of the contribution and the artistic merit of black artists at the expense of the contribution and the artistic merit of white artists; this is a highly wrong strategy of presentation of the issue of discrimination and racism because, whatever the contribution and artistic merit that white artists may produce, it is never good enough to earn the awards; from this point of view, the white artists are forevermore the artists who should not be awarded; subsequently, in this level, the white artists are accused of being inspired by black artists (create original music) and are taking advantage and profit from their music creation; most of the time, there is no mention of black artists being inspired and using the artistic creation of the white artists;

4. the only way for The Recording Academy to be seen and presented in good terms is to follow the outcome written by mass-media, critics outside The Recording Academy, and the opinions of black artists and their supporters.

The examples above represents a tiny part of the negative narrative about the outcome advanced against the voting members and The Recording Academy, however, I hope, it is enough for readers to create a small wave of awareness and understanding about the existent issues in the music industry in the USA.

THE LITERATURE ABOUT THE WINNERS OF THE GRAMMY AWARDS
Based on this research, there are four debate camps (from higher to lower number of supporters involved in the debates) about the winners of the Grammy Awards:

the first debate camp (higher as number of supporters): it is an *overall opinion* about who should win the award;
- in this camp the knowledge of the writer is presented as mostly being true;
- there is no specific analysis based on a specific methodology to find substantial evidence to support the opinion; in this case, the opinion advanced creates (maybe inevitable and with no direct intention) a feel of 'gaslighting' than 'enlightening', where every person of interest feel the need to say something good or bad about an artist;

---

[12] More information about The Spiral of Silence, see: 'Spiral of Silence', *Wikipedia*, available at: https://en.wikipedia.org/wiki/Spiral_of_silence#:~:text=It%20states%20that%20an%20individual%27s,others%20to%20express%20their%20opinions., last accessed: October 24, 2020; 'The Spiral of Silence Theory', *Communication Theory*, available at: https://www.communicationtheory.org/the-spiral-of-silence-theory/, last accessed: October 24, 2020.

- this camp is spread and used to a minor extent by journalists as well and, definitely more, by supporters of the artists which dream for their favourite artists to be awarded with a Grammy Award;

the second debate camp (lower as number of supporters than the first debate camp): it is based on *conclusions acquired* after *using a specific methodology* (either created and used by specialists in statistics, instruments and lyrics, or by fans and ordinary people interested in getting a in-depth understanding of the outcome);
- in this camp, the knowledge is considered to have a higher quality and version of truth than the knowledge in the first debate camp;
- the methodology is clearly stated in the opinion, and it is difficult to argue against it; however, if there is an argument against the opinion, then it is based on the methodology applied where most of the time it consist on (from high to low importance and use):

1. mathematical calculations: the artists and their supporters can be against this method due to its nature of snapshotting music in numbers (may be considered as a limited way of thinking, because *music is more than numbers*);

2. questioning the ability of the artists *to write* and *sing* the songs released: this involves opinions based on reviews of songs and albums written by experts in music, and available online in magazines with an experience in reviewing music, or close to this topic of interest; subsequently, to some extent, it includes the personal opinion of the supporter: at this point (this part of debate enters also in the first debate camp) depends on how well the opinion is formulated and if a method of research was applied;

- this camp it is used both by journalists and supporters who prefer to have better reasons to advance an argument in favour or against the decision of The Recording Academy;

the third debate camp (made only by the voting members of The Recording Academy): it is based on the *knowledge about music that the members of The Recording Academy have* and it is *self-considered as holder of the final truth* about the right winners;
- this position of the *self-holder of truth* is based directly on its *voting members* which includes 'performers, songwriters, producers, engineers, instrumentalists, and other creators currently working in the recording industry; voting members determine Grammy winners each year;[13]

---

[13] The Recording Academy, *Recording Academy Membership, Membership Types*, available at: https://members.recordingacademy.com/s/?language=en_US, last accessed: July 26, 2021.

the fourth debate camp is the critics and their reviews (lowest number among all other three debate camps; depends on the number of reviews written for an album, it can include one review to as many as possible[14]) available on various websites with content in the music industry;

- as with the third debate, this is also *self-considered as holder of the final truth* about the right winners;
- this position of the *self-holder of truth* is based directly on the *main critic* as being an expert in music, and (from the research conducted) without being an artist with proven songs and albums that are considered by other critics and artists as the best, or the worst contribution in the music industry;
- the most used platforms with reviews written by experts in music and available online are *Metacritic*[15] and *All Music*[16];
- this debate camp is used more by the second debate camp to advance their opinions with a higher value of truth.

Each year, between all these four debate camps, there is a thin line that it is crossed intentionally and unintentionally and are caught in a war of winners; the 'artistic merit war' is on three levels:

> *the first level:* it is between the first and the second debate camps; these two debate camps advance powerful opinions which are able to gaslight and uplift artists and supporters;

> *the second level:* it is between the third and the fourth debate camp: here it is a battle of artists and experts in music where sometimes the winners are not the ones predicted by critics outside The Recording Academy; this contradiction creates among supporters and artists a visible wave of untrust in both sources;

> *the third level:* it is a mix between all four debates camps to justify the outcome of the awards.

THE AIM OF THE RESEARCH
This report is in the same bubble of research with other articles and reports published about the issues of awards and allegations of discrimination and racism in the music industry in the

---

[14] I could not find a clear reason of why some artists have more reviews than others; however, I identified a pattern: to a certain level the reviews depends also on the popularity of the artists; if the artist is new in the music industry: the reviews can present the abilities of the new artist and the outcome of the album, which can support the artist to be appreciated more or less by fans and the general public.

[15] *Metacritic*, https://www.metacritic.com.

[16] *All Music*, https://www.allmusic.com.

USA. I started by mentioning few articles that can provide a better overview of this bubble of research; at the same time, I offered a reason of rejecting or accepting articles as part of my research interest. In the last part of this section, I developed the full aim of the research.

- In 2014, Aimee Cliff wrote for *The Fader* the article *10 Reasons The Grammys Are As White As You Think They Are* which are divided in two parts: *Historically* (reasons 1 to 5) and *In 2014* (reasons 6 to 10):

'1. Fewer than 20 percent of Album of the Year awards have gone to black artist; 2. It took them 10 years to recognize rap; 3. Only three Album of the Year awards have ever been given to hip-hop records; 4. Kanye hasn't been up for Album of the Year since Graduation; 5. The people picking the winners are out of touch; 6. Every Best New Artist nominee is white; 7. Every Record of the Year and Song of the Year nominee is white; 8. It's not a case of black artists not selling as much as white artists; 9. The Grammys are still using "urban" to denote "black"; 10. White artists making music influenced by black culture get treated differently.'[17]

this research is on the same line with Aimee Cliff's article: history and facts, but with a distinctive difference: Aimee focused on facts from before and until 2014, while I used data from 2003 to 2022 and investigated few white and black artists who topped the charts and are considered, by The Recording Academy and various experts in music, as one of the best artists in the music industry in the USA;

- the article written by Raquel Cepeda for Rolling Stone in 2015:

'WHITE PEOPLE REJOICE! You've managed to cold-jack yet another awards season, and in February no less. The Oscars will be whiter than they've been since 1998, and this year the Grammy Awards promise to be a throwback to that time when Shirley Temple got down in blackface – dumb-stoopid-affected accents and all.'[18]

Raquel Cepeda is entitled to her own view and strategy of presentation of the issue with black artists being less awarded in comparison with white artists, but her article does not have substantial evidence to allow her to manifest the issue with the sentence *'WHITE PEOPLE REJOICE! You've managed to cold-jack yet another awards season'*: this is a general view which implies that all white people from the USA are to blame for the outcome; this position is wrong as The Recording Academy, and other institutions in the music industry in the USA, have a number of members with experience in music; where there is the option for the general public to vote for their favourite artists, and the white artist win the award, you cannot blame the people for their choices; however, the information used in this research allowed me to create a chapter, *__What if__*, where I wrote various hypothetical and negative scenarios based on the in-depth research advanced in these pages;

---

[17] Aimee Cliff, '10 Reasons The Grammys Are As White As You Think They Are', *The Fader*, December 12, 2014, available at: https://www.thefader.com/2014/12/12/10-reasons-the-grammys-are-as-white-as-you-think-they-are, last accessed: July 25, 2021.
[18] Raquel Cepeda, 'Do the Grammys Have a Race Problem?'

- this research does not go on the line with Ira Madison III who wrote in 2018 for *The Daily Beast* an interesting point of view about the outcome in the music industry; his article is a short history of the albums included or which should be included for the Grammy Awards; however, what is lacking is the same as Raquel's article: substantial evidence achieved after using a specific methodology which allows an in-depth investigation about the music that should or should have not win the award;[19] the title has the word 'hell', but Ira Madison III spectacularly failed to actually prove that the Grammys are 'racists as hell' as the mentioning of albums, and a short comparison about the names of the albums and the race of the artists, barely scratches the surface of the award issue and discrimination and racism in The Recording Academy; all in all, I find Ira Madison III interest to be worthy of research, but his technique of approach does not help to expose a credible storyline of the allegations of discrimination and racism advanced by black artists and their supporters.

After reading various articles about the Grammy Awards (some mentioned above) in the USA's mass-media, I reached the following conclusions: the articles that I read are written from 'he said / she said' perspective, and there is a visible lack of focus on neutral articles with solid methodology to advance an in-depth and credible storyline to better support the allegations of discrimination and racism. I had no other option than to extend the research beyond USA's mass-media. I selected two articles and one report. The first two articles were published by two journalists, one from UK and one from USA; the third source is a report published in the USA by a university.

1. Chris Sweeney (from Scotland) is an author and columnist who has written for newspapers such as The Times, The Sun, the Daily Record and Nut Magazine from UK, along with several international-selling magazines: in 2020 he wrote the article 'The Grammys aren't racist, claiming so is just a cynical attempt to play the race card' for Russia Today; however, since he wrote for mass-media from the UK before and after 2020 and other international magazines, it must mean that his analysis are based on the principle of truth and honour in the field of journalism.

Chris Sweeney made few important points of view, however, I mentioned two of them, since there are good examples to support his view:

in the first example, Chris Sweeney mentioned the race of the artists nominated where 'diversity' is the main key term of The Recording Academy:

'The shortlist for the most prestigious award, Record of the Year, is really varied. Beyonce is there, along with soul duo Black Pumas, who are black singer Eric Burton and latino musician Adrian Quesada. Others

[19] Ira Madison III, 'The Grammy Awards Are Racist as Hell', *The Daily Beast*, January 28, 2018, available at: https://www.thedailybeast.com/the-grammy-awards-are-racist-as-hell, last accessed: July 25, 2021.

include; Dua Lipa (British with Kosovan heritage), Da Baby (black American), Doja Cat (Jewish American mother/South African Zulu father), Billie Eilish (white American), Megan Thee Stallion (black American from Texas) and Post Malone (white American with Italian roots).'[20]

the second example is based on statistics:

'America's population is crudely divided into; White (60 percent), Black (13 percent), Asian (6 percent), Hispanic (18 percent) and American Indian (1.3 percent). So if we go by the logic of connecting impact to race, then so-called white music and white artists would dominate.'[21]

this research is in the same bubble of research presented by Chris Sweeney, however, only from the point of view of statistics, but again with a distinctive difference: Chris Sweeney used the statistics already existent and related to population percentage, while I created statistics based on elements such as the race of the artists, songs and albums caught in the middle of the conflict about the outcome of The Recording Academy and which song/artists and album should win or not.

2. Michael McCaffrey is a freelance writer, film critic and cultural commentator. He currently resides in Los Angeles where he runs his acting coaching and media consulting business: the use of statistics and being a freelancer in the USA (with many good articles written) was a good reason for me to consider his interest as being genuine, and for the benefits of all the parts interested and involved in the research about the outcome of The Recording Academy. **Black & White Music** is in the same bubble of the research advanced by Michael McCaffrey, but with a different point of view. Michael McCafrey investigation is about finding a relations in terms of population percentage (as Chris Sweeney) and representation in awards; in his own words, he investigated:

'to see if Black artists are under-represented in awards in relation to their population percentage;'[22]

Black & White Music is an investigation about the sources and origins of the music released by 8 white and black artists. After exposing various statistics about the race of the artists nominated at the Grammy Awards and population percentage, Michael McCaffrey wrote the following conclusion:

'It is obvious upon reviewing the data that, over the last 30 years, Black artists are, in fact, substantially over-represented at the Grammys in relation to their percentage of the US population.'[23]

---

[20] Chris Sweeney, 'The Grammys aren't racist, claiming so is just a cynical attempt to play the race card', *Russia Today*, November 27, 2020, available at: https://www.rt.com/op-ed/508053-drake-weeknd-grammys-racism/, last accessed: July 25, 2021.
[21] Ibidem.
[22] Michael McCaffrey, '#GrammysSoWhite: Is White privilege really repressing Black entertainers?', *Russia Today*, February 26, 2017, available at: https://www.rt.com/op-ed/378651-grammys-oscars-favor-whites/, last accessed: July 25, 2021.
[23] Ibidem.

Finally, this research is also in the bubble of interest and research with the study conducted by *3. The USC Annenberg Inclusion from University of South Carolina: Inclusion in the Recording Studio? Gender and Race/Ethnicity of Artists, Songwriters & Producers across 900 Popular Songs from 2012-2020.* The lead researchers, Dr. Stacy L. Smith, Dr. Katherine Pieper, Marc Choueiti, Karla Hernandez & Kevin Yao, came to various conclusions, but for this research I picked one that I find to have a connection with the last two authors:

'Black performers represented about 38% of all artists on Billboard's signature chart from 2012 to 2020, yet they received only 26.7% of top Grammy nominations during the same period. Only 24% of this year's top Grammy nominees were Black'.[24]

If Chris Sweeney and Michael McCaffrey used the percentage population and representation in the awards, the *Inclusion in the Recording Studio?* used the percentage from charts and the reflection in number of nominations, **Black & White Music** used the sources and origins of the music to reach new conclusions about the awards and allegations of discrimination and racism in the music industry in the USA.

From *Inclusion in the Recording Studio?*, I understand that the right way and fairness for black artists and for The Recording Academy, it is to have the same percentage in nominations as on charts. I reached this understanding due to the overall view and conclusions on the report, but also by the keyword used in the conclusions: 'only', which for me is suggesting that the percentage should be higher.

However, *Inclusion in the Recording Studio?* does not take into consideration the quality of the music released. From this perspective, in the music industry in the USA there are various albums with high grades from critics, yet they fail to achieve and maintain top 3 or 10 in Billboard charts for long term. For example Fiona Apple's album in 2020, *Fetch the Bolt Cutters*: Fiona has one of the highest overall grade in the music industry on Metacritic with 98 out of 100 based on 28 critic reviews, but her album sold in the first week in the USA 44,000 equivalent albums unit; eventually, Fiona Apple's album was number 4 on the USA Billboard 200.[25] On the other hand, there are albums with lower grades from critics. For example Beyoncé for her debut album, *Dangerously in Love*, won five Grammy Awards even though *The Guardian* gave her album 40 points out of 100 on Metacritic, the overall grade for her album is 63 out of 100 based on 17 critic reviews[26]; for Beyoncé first-week sales in the USA

[24] The full report can be read online: Dr. Stacy L. Smith, Dr. Katherine Pieper, Marc Choueiti, Karla Hernandez & Kevin Yao, *Inclusion in the Recording Studio? Gender and Race/Ethnicity of Artists, Songwriters & Producers across 900 Popular Songs from 2012-2020*, March 2021, The USC Annenberg Inclusion, University of South Carolina, available at: https://assets.uscannenberg.org/docs/aii-inclusion-recording-studio2021.pdf, last accessed: July 26, 2021.

[25] Fiona Apple, 'Fetch the Bolt Cutters', *Wikipedia*, available at: https://en.wikipedia.org/wiki/Fetch_the_Bolt_Cutters, last accessed: July 26, 2021. 'Of that sum, 30,000 are in album sales, 13,000 are in SEA units and less than 1,000 are in TEA units'.

[26] Read: Adam Sweeting, 'Review: Beyonce Knowles: Dangerously in Love', *The Guardian*, June 27, 2003, 2 stars out of 5, available at: https://www.theguardian.com/music/2003/jun/27/popandrock.artsfeatures8, last accessed: July 26, 2021; 'Beyoncé:

was 317,000 album copies, and in the following months and years to reach over 11 millions of albums sold worldwide.[27]

Based on the information used to create Figure 1, I can identify and show the precise locations of my research in the bubble of the research interests in the music industry in the USA.

Dr. Stacy L. Smith acknowledged that popularity of a song doesn't always equate with its artistic merit.'[28] I extracted the words *artistic merit,* because this is main aim of the research in these pages. However, to be able to research the artistic merit, I have to interfere in the narrative line of other research interests in the music industry, which is the only way to *see* and *understand* the *artistic merit.*

The music industry in the USA (the figure is created using this information) is formed from individuals and organisation such as: 'lyricists, composers, singers, musicians, conductors, bandleaders who perform the music, the record labels, music publishers, recording studios, music producers, audio engineers, retail and digital music stores, performance rights organizations who create and sell recorded music and sheet music, the booking agents, promoters, music venues, road crew, and audio engineers who help organize and sell concerts;'[29] other research interests included in the music industry are the race of the musicians and other professional categories, the awarding institutions and their voting members, the conventional wisdom and critics (inside and outside The Recording Academy).

Black & White Music's research interests are in the following research interests of the music industry in the USA:

- *lyricists* (in terms of number of lyricists, including the main vocal artists length of songs written by the main vocal artists),
- *composers* (in terms of number of lyricists, including the main vocal artists),
- *singers* (black and white),
- *musicians* (black and white)[30],

Dangerously in Love', *Metacritic*, June 24, 2003, available at: https://www.metacritic.com/music/dangerously-in-love/beyonce, last accessed: July 26, 2021.

[27] Beyoncé, 'Dangerously in Love', *Wikipedia*, available at: https://en.wikipedia.org/wiki/Dangerously_in_Love, last accessed: July 26, 2021.

[28] Chauncey Alcorn, 'The Grammys rarely award chart-topping Black artists with top honors, new study finds', *CNN*, March 9, 2021, available at: https://edition.cnn.com/2021/03/09/media/grammys-diversity/index.html, last accessed: July 26, 2021.

[29] 'Music industry', *Wikipedia*, available at: https://en.wikipedia.org/wiki/Music_industry, last accessed: June 26, 2021.

[30] 'The major difference is that musicians perform using an instrument or multiple instruments, while singers perform vocal performances. This means that a musician may use the voice as one of many tools to create music, while a singer uses music as one of many tools to create vocal performances.' Climb the Ladder, *Musician vs. Singer: What Are the Differences?*, available at: https://climbtheladder.com/musician-vs-singer/#:~:text=The%20major%20difference%20is%20that,tools%20to%20create%20vocal%20performances, last accessed: March 2, 2023.

- *bandleaders* (more for Macklemore & Ryan),
- *music producers* (the number of producers in the creation of the song and the album, the main vocal artist included),
- *audio engineers* (in terms of samples),
- *performance rights organizations who create and sell recorded music and sheet music* (in terms of song and album sales),
- *the race* (the main vocal artists investigated in this report, producers and lyricists, allegations of discrimination and racism),
- *the awarding institutions and their voting members* (The Recording Academy),
- *conventional wisdom* (advanced and supported by black artists and their supporters),
- and *critics* (a short comparison based on the number of existent critics inside and outside the awarding institutions; in this part, 'critics' is also use with the meaning of 'voting member', since the voting member performed a critique, based on own abilities, about the final choices regarding the award).

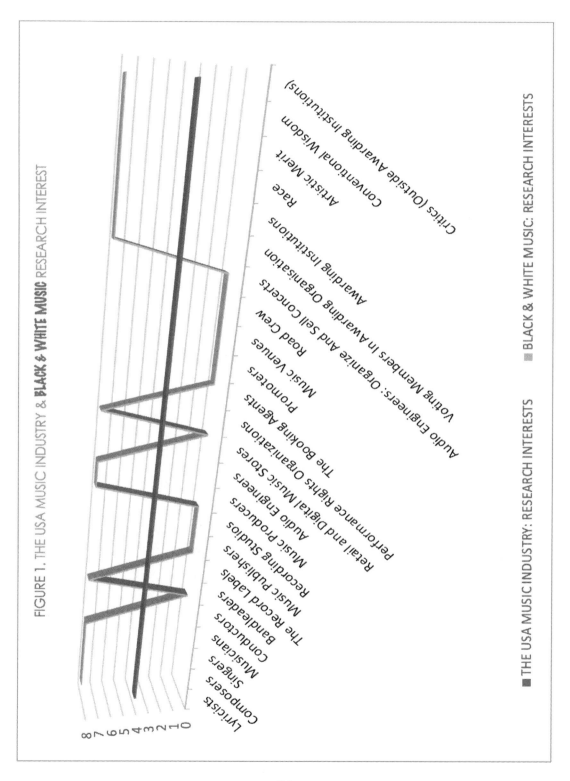

FIGURE 1. THE USA MUSIC INDUSTRY & *BLACK & WHITE MUSIC* RESEARCH INTEREST

■ THE USA MUSIC INDUSTRY: RESEARCH INTERESTS   ■ BLACK & WHITE MUSIC: RESEARCH INTERESTS

In terms of number of artists investigated (8) from total number of musicians (9603)[31], I used:

- *Black artists (3)*: Kanye West, Beyoncé, Kendrick Lamar,
- *White artists (5)*: Taylor Swift, Adele, Beck, Macklemore & Ryan (it is a group, but I calculated as sole individual);

this research investigated around 0.09% of the total number of musicians in the USA;

from the point of view of race, this research investigated around 0.03% black artists, and 0.05% white artists;

from the point of view of camp debates, *Black & White Music's* research interest is the second debate camp because the '*conclusions were acquired* after *using a specific methodology* to find new information about the artistic merit of the artists investigated';

from the point of view of 'artistic merit war', *Black & White Music's* is in the *third level*: it is a mix between all four debates camps to justify the outcome of the awards.

In *Black & White Music* report I investigated a very small part of the music industry from the USA, 0.09% musicians; more precisely, I investigated the contribution and the artistic merit (greater or lesser) of black artists (0.03%) and white artists (0.05%) in the production and writing of their albums. The artists investigated in this report are Taylor Swift, Kanye West, Beyoncé, Kendrick Lamar, Macklemore & Ryan, Adele and Beck. I selected these artists because the music produced and released by them was used by various artists and journalists as examples of allegations of discrimination and racism which takes place in the music industry in the USA. For example, Kendrick Lamar (black man) was promoted by western journalists the winner of the *Best Rap Album* days before the 2014 ceremony, but was defeated by Macklemore & Ryan (white artists), and in 2016 by Taylor Swift (white artist); Beyoncé (black artist) lost in 2015 to Beck (white artist) and in 2017 she lost to Adele (white artist from UK, but nominated for Grammy Awards in various categories); although he had one of the most recommended and positive reviewed albums of his life (*My Beautiful Dark Twisted Fantasy*) and in the music industry, Kanye West's album was not nominated for *Album of the Year*. In other words, today's music industry is caught in a difficult situation that is severely undermining The Recording Academy's credibility and the Grammy Awards.

The aim of the research is split into 2 levels:

---

[31] 'Musician Demographic and Statistics in the US', *Zippia*, available at: https://www.zippia.com/musician-jobs/demographics/#race-statistics, last accessed: August 3, 2022.

BLACK AND WHITE MUSIC: A JOURNEY BEHIND THE MUSICAL NOTES

in the first level: *I explored, analysed and created a comparative study about the contribution and the artistic merit of black and white artists in the production and writing of their albums*; to achieve this aim, I added *contribution* and *artistic merit* into one bubble of research and treated the two concepts with the same meaning, then I divided the bubble into 8 points of research that

1. created a general view of the contribution and artistic merit of the artists investigated

and **2.** granted the opportunity to observe and identify areas of the music production where one artists is greater or lesser than others;

the 8 points of research were used to show (within the limits of the information used):

1. the creativity, originality and novelty of the investigated artists;

2. the artist(s) with a greater contribution in the production and writing of a song(s) and album(s) that have been released;

3. whether the awards and recognition offered by the USA music industry are based on originality, creativity and novelty in music, or are offered based on the colour of the skin;

4. what are the differences between the music recognized by receiving an award, and the music that did not receive an award, but was nominated for the music award (either by the vote of the general public, or by the vote of the members of the jury);

5. whether the loss of the award is a direct and personal non-recognition of the black artist(s) who performed the song(s) and under whose name the song(s) and album(s) were released;

6. whether the loss of the award is a direct and personal non-recognition of the black producer(s) and lyricist(s) who created a part(s) (or full) of a song(s) and the album(s);

7. reasons that may justify why white artists received more recognition than black artists in the music industry (only the artists in this report and Grammy Awards: *Album of the Year*, *Best Rap Album*; MTV Awards: Beyoncé (*Single Ladies (Put a Ring On It), If I were a Boy*) versus Taylor Swift (*You Belong With Me, The Man*) regarding the originality of these songs;

8. in the music industry, among fans and critics there is a conventional wisdom attached and used toward and in reference to Kanye West: 'one of the greatest artists of all time'; in this point of research, I challenged this conventional wisdom attached to Kanye West; furthermore, I extended the conventional wisdom to Taylor Swift through a comparative analysis between her and Kanye West's music.

in the second level *is about using the findings from the eight points of research to offer a response to three conventional wisdom advanced by black artists and their supporters* against the rules and awards offered by The Recording Academy:

1. the higher recognition in the music industry received by the white artists is not about the quality and originality of their music, but because of the colour of their skin; in other words, the white artists received the higher recognition because the institution behind the awards is ruled by white people;[32]

2. black artists create music and white artists take advantage and profit from their creation;[33]

3. black artists need to work twice as much to get half, or the same as white artists.[34]

POTENTIAL CONTRIBUTIONS:

- this report is the first part of the research project named *The Famous Feud Project*[35]; this report it is unique and original which investigates the artistic merit of six of the best artists in the music industry of the USA; in these pages, there is an advanced

---

[32] This argument was created based on the mix of ideas from the following articles: Tatum Herrin, 'The Grammys' Casual Racism Has Gone on for Too Long'; Samantha Hissong, 'The Crisis Behind the All-White Grammy Category'; Lizzy Wan, 'Racial bias in the Grammys impacts our generation'; Natalie Harmsen, Goodbye, 'Grammys: Why Black artists think the awards show is irrelevant'; Jon Caramanica, '#GrammysSoWhite Came to Life. Will the Awards Face Its Race Problem?'.

[33] This argument was created based on the mix of ideas from the following articles: Jasmine Garsd, 'Music industry confronts calls to 'make things right' for Black artists', *Marketplac*e, August 6, 2020, available at: https://www.marketplace.org/2020/08/06/music-industry-confronts-calls-make-things-right-for-black-artists/, last accessed: July 26, 2021; Wesley Morris, 'Why is Everyone Always Stealing Black Music?, *The New York Times*, August 14, 2019, available at: https://www.nytimes.com/interactive/2019/08/14/magazine/music-black-culture-appropriation.html, last accessed: July 26, 2021; Elias Leight, 'The Music Industry Was Built on Racism. Changing It Will Take More Than Donations', *Rolling Stone*, June 5, 2020, available at: https://www.rollingstone.com/music/music-features/music-industry-racism-1010001/, last accessed: July 26, 2021; Ruka Hatua-Saar White, 'Cultural Appropriation in Music', *Take Note from Berklee Online*, February 1, 2020, available at: https://online.berklee.edu/takenote/cultural-appropriation-in-music/; last accessed: July 26, 2020; Chris Jancelewicz, 'The 'whitewashing' of Black music: A dark chapter in rock history', *Global News*, July 30, 2019, available at: https://globalnews.ca/news/4321150/black-music-whitewashing-classic-rock/, last accessed: July 26, 2021.

[34] This argument was created based on the mix of ideas from the following articles: Britni Danielle, 'Michelle Obama's 'twice as good' speech doesn't cut it with most African Americans', *The Guardian*, May 12, 2015, available at: https://www.theguardian.com/commentisfree/2015/may/12/michelle-obama-twice-as-good-african-americans-black-people, last accessed: July 26, 2021; Gillian B. White, 'Black Workers Really Do Need to Be Twice as Good', *The Atlantic*, October 7, 2015, available at: https://www.theatlantic.com/business/archive/2015/10/why-black-workers-really-do-need-to-be-twice-as-good/409276/, last accessed: July 26, 2021; Elias Leight, ''Separate and Unequal': How 'Pop' Music Holds Black Artists Back', *Rolling Stone*, June 17, 2020, available at: https://www.rollingstone.com/music/music-features/the-problem-with-pop-1013534/, last accessed: July 26, 2021; Charles Stephens, 'When Black Professionals Must Work Twice as Hard', *Advocate*, March 19, 2019, available at: https://www.advocate.com/commentary/2018/3/19/when-black-professionals-must-work-twice-hard, last accessed: July 26, 2021; Jamilah Malika Abu-Bakare, 'How Black artists use citational art to build upon one another's legacies', *CBC*, February 1, 2022, available at: https://www.cbc.ca/arts/how-black-artists-use-citational-art-to-build-upon-one-another-s-legacies-1.6329781, last accessed: July 22, 2022.

[35] The second part is Casian Anton, *On the **Famous** Feud*, 2023.

comparative analysis of the music released by famous artists that was never done before using the elements described in methodology;

- this report was born out of the urgent need to confront and challenge the three conventional wisdom advanced by black artists and their supporters who feel and promote the idea of injustice regarding the music released;
- this research provides transparent information and better-founded reasons about the decision of The Recording Academy and its voting members to award the white artists with the highest award in the music industry, respectively *Album of the Year*;
- black artists and white artists are in need of answers and this report is a meditative resource about the recognition of their contribution in the music industry;
- in this report interested people about music and awards have the space to read about it, and confront their knowledge with the investigation's findings;
- the report can be used to calm the realities of racism and provides a point of reference of the quality, originality and novelty of the music investigated in these pages;
- the report is for future artists waiting to be discovered, and what they need to expect once they are part of the music industry;
- the findings of this report are a challenge for the music industry as well, as it contributes to the wider discussion about creativity, originality and novelty of the artists and who / which artist / song / album should get the higher award;
- by no means this report is made with the intentional purpose to present the artists investigated in a negative view; I followed and interpreted raw numbers; this report has numbers and interpretation / inference of information, not reviews of the quality of the music completed by experts in instruments and lyrics.

This report has three chapters.

In the first chapter, ***the music sheet:* methodology**, I described the main research methods and the limits of the research.

In the second chapter, ***black* and *white* music**, I created a comparative study between the following artists: Taylor Swift versus Kanye West, Beyoncé versus Kendrick Lamar, Beyoncé versus Taylor Swift, Kendrick Lamar versus Taylor Swift, Beyoncé versus Adele, Beyoncé versus Beck and Macklemore & Ryan versus Kendrick Lamar; in the ***Awards*** section I investigated the originality of the songs released by Beyoncé (*Single Ladies (Put a Ring On It), If I were a Boy*) versus Taylor Swift (*You Belong With Me, The Man*).

In chapter three, ***What if***, I wrote scenarios based on the information found. These scenarios are hypothetical and negative. After writing this chapter, I decided to delete it; few minutes later, I changed my mind as I remembered that in each scenario there could be one gram of truth; maybe the hypothetical and negative scenarios in this chapter are true or partially true, and could help to create a better understanding of the unfolding events between the following artists: Kanye West, Beyoncé, Jay Z and Taylor Swift.

Finally, in **the end of the journey: *black* and *white* music**, I reformulated the aim of this report; I exposed the conclusions I reached for each of the eight points of research, and wrote a response to each conventional wisdom advanced by black artists and their supporters.

I. **the music sheet**: methodology

In this chapter I described the research methodology with the purpose to expose the contribution and artistic merit of the artists investigated.

Sample:

- 'Reuse of portion (or sample) of a sound recording in another recording, such as rhythm, melody, speech, sounds, or entire bars of music; may be layered, equalized, sped up or slowed down, repitched, looped, manipulated.[36]

Lyricist:

- 'Is a songwriter who writes lyrics – words for songs'.[37]

Lyricist (Composer Lyricist):

- 'Writes the song's music which may include but not limited to the melody, harmony, arrangement and accompaniment'.[38]

Original Song:

- 'the first and genuine form of something, from which others are derived; able to think or carry out new ideas and concepts; the way the person who sang it, wanted the song to be';[39]
- song written and performed for the first time in the world by an artist and does not contain any samples.

Creativity:

---

[36] 'Sampling (music)', *Wikipedia*, available at: https://en.m.wikipedia.org/wiki/Sampling_(music), last accessed: February 25, 2021.
[37] 'Lyricist', *Wikipedia*, available at: https://en.m.wikipedia.org/wiki/Lyricist, last accessed: February 25, 2021.
[38] *Ibidem*.
[39] This information is a mix of ideas from Quora website, and first page of results from Google with the keywords: 'what is original song'.

- the ability to create something new, making connections and observations; original ideas;
- I read the lyrics of the songs that used samples to find out the connection between the original song, and the song that sampled the original song.

Novelty:

- the quality of being new, original, unfamiliar thing or experience;
- I read the lyrics of the songs that used samples to find out the connection between the original song, and the song that sampled the original song.

General public:

- all the people, 'especially those not part of a specified group; ordinary people as opposed to officials, experts, politicians'.[40]

Conventional wisdom:

- 'the body of ideas or explanations generally accepted by the public and/or by experts in a field'.[41]

Music industry:

- it is formed from individuals and organisation such as: 'lyricists, composers, singers, musicians, conductors, bandleaders who perform the music, the record labels, music publishers, recording studios, music producers, audio engineers, retail and digital music stores, performance rights organizations who create and sell recorded music and sheet music, the booking agents, promoters, music venues, road crew, and audio engineers who help organize and sell concerts;'[42]
- in this report, the music industry investigated is from USA, but with one artist from UK, Adele (due to being part of USA's mass-media articles about allegations of discrimination and racism in the music industry of the USA).

---

[40] The Britannica Dictionary, 'general public', available at: https://www.britannica.com/dictionary/general-public#:~:text=the%20general%20public,open%20to%20the%20general%20public.; last accessed: February 25, 2021; 'general public', Cambridge Dictionary, available at: https://dictionary.cambridge.org/dictionary/english/general-public; last accessed: February 25, 2021; 'general public', Dictionary.com, available at: https://www.dictionary.com/browse/the-general-public; last accessed: February 25, 2021.
[41] 'Conventional wisdom', *Wikipedia*, available at: https://en.wikipedia.org/wiki/Conventional_wisdom, last accessed: February 25, 2021; 'Conventional wisdom', *Dictionary.com*, available at: https://www.dictionary.com/browse/conventional-wisdom, last accessed: February 25, 2021.
[42] 'Music industry', *Wikipedia*.

Artistic merit:

- it 'means evidence of some or all of the following: potential impact on the artistic and/or cultural development of a community or individuals; and/or potential to broaden access to, expand and diversify the audiences for, and/or strengthen communities through the arts';[43] the Arts Council England developed a Quality Metrics to assess the artistic merit in two groups: **1.** Self, peer and public: '*Concept*: it was an interesting idea; *Presentation*: it was well produced and presented; *Distinctiveness*: it was different from things I've experienced before; *Challenge*: it was thought-provoking; *Captivation*: it was absorbing and held my attention; *Enthusiasm*: I would come to something like this again; *Local impact*: it is important that it's happening here; *Relevance*: it has something to say about the world in which we live; *Rigour*: it was well thought through and put together'; **2.** Self and peer only: *Originality:* it was ground-breaking; *Risk*: the artists/curators really challenged themselves; *Excellence*: it is one of the best examples of its type that I have seen.'[44]

The main research methods are: mathematical calculation, interpretation / inference (deduction and induction) of information; these methods are used in terms of number of songs, albums, producers, lyricists, review grades, dates of album release, reading the lyrics of the songs, checking the sources of the samples (fame, top charts and awards), find similarities and differences between the music of the artists investigated.

Mathematical calculation of the songs written by each artist:

- sole lyricist;
- two lyricists;
- three lyricists;
- at least four lyricists;
- the number of producers and lyricists;
- the length of songs: sole and two lyricists (one is the main artists used in this report);
- the number of songs with or with no samples (percentage included).

The Average Method:

- the grades and rating on Metacritic;
- the average number of lyricists and producers for songs and albums, and total career.

---

[43] The definition it is a mix of definitions available here: 'Artistic Merit', *Law Insider*, available at: https://www.lawinsider.com/dictionary/artistic-merit#:~:text=Artistic%20merit%20is%20evaluated%20according,artists%20and%20curator%2Fs%20involved., last accessed: August 6, 2022;

[44] 'About Quality Metrics', *Arts Council England*, available at: https://www.artscouncil.org.uk/quality-metrics-pilot, last accessed: August 6, 2022.

The List of Samples:

- I collected as much as possible the sources of the samples used by artists; unfortunately, due to lack of this information on various websites, I was unable to offer information for each song.

The Fame of the Samples:

- I investigated the fame (charts, awards, popular opinion, reviews, influence and legacy) of the samples to show if there is a connection between the old and the new song, the differences and similarities between the samples used and the final songs of the artists from this report. This information is available only in a comparison table, no further explanation is written.

The Album Release Pattern:

- I used the information to find patterns that could show how artists are releasing their albums: similarities, differences, predictable and fixed release patterns, changing release patterns, surprise pattern.

The Race of the Samples:

- it is used only for the comparative study between Taylor Swift and Kanye West: I investigated only their albums released in 2010, because I wanted to discover how many black and white people inspired the artists in creating their music.

The Race of the Artists:

- *Black artists*: Kanye West, Beyoncé, Kendrick Lamar, Jay Z (only in *What If* chapter);
- *White artists*: Taylor Swift, Adele, Beck, Macklemore & Ryan.

What if:

- during the investigation my mind (based on what I read) created a few hypothetical and negative scenarios related to the artists investigated in these pages; the hypothetical and negative scenarios are reproduced in order to help, if possible, to observe the events behind the creation of the music released by the following artists: Kanye West, Beyoncé, Jay Z (only in this chapter) and Taylor Swift.

Other considerations:

- all the artists in this report had a source of inspiration, but I focused on samples as sources of inspiration, and as a method of comparison between the investigated artists;
- in this report I used only the number of lyricists and general producers, not Mixer(s), Mastering Engineer(s) and so forth;
- the information collected from the credit page was used for the rest of this report without recitation;
- the methodology is described in each chapter;
- the list of songs in this report are not used to argue that the artists infringed the copyrights of other artists, or to claim any wrongdoing from any point of view of music copyrights; this list is used *only* to *show* and *understand* the background narrative of creating music.

The Limits of the Research:

- not all the articles used in this report have the date of the last modification, or a history of modifications made by the data producer; also, not all the articles show a summary of the modifications made to see the difference between the first version and the last version of the article; from these points of view, it could exist a different opinion between readers who accessed the article before the modifications were made, and readers who accessed the last available version;
- this report was not created or revised by professionals in the music industry;
- all the information in this report should not be used as a source of final truth: only a few research ideas and the calculations of numbers under certain conditions are used to show information about the creation of music by artists, the connections between methods of creating music, similarities, differences;
- Metacritic website does not include all the reviews written about the albums; there are reviews with higher and lower grades which are not included, and, therefore, the real and the final grade could be higher or lower than what is available on Metacritic and in this report;
- the numbers and the final maths calculations used in figures were rounded to the nearest decimal; this happened because I used figure / chart option in Excel program by Microsoft, and by default the numbers are rounded to the nearest decimal; from this point of view, the percentage available in this research might have an error between 0,01% – 0.99% of the final percentage; this error depends on the algorithm behind the Excel option to create a figure / chart;
- based on the quality metrics set by Arts Council England and the methodology used, the artistic merit from this research paper does not reflect 100% of the true artistic merit of the artists investigated;

- *the lyrics and production*: I did not find the real contribution (in percentage sense: 20% or 90%, 100%) of each artist in writing and producing songs and albums and, therefore, the information in this report can be inaccurate about the real contribution and the artistic merit of the artists;
- *the length of songs and albums*: the information about the length (in minutes and seconds) on Wikipedia and Tidal are different: on Wikipedia some songs have 1 - 3 seconds more or less than what is available on Tidal, which means the length of the albums is higher or lower on both services; from this point of view, the length of the songs in this report can be misleading;
- from the album released by Taylor Swift, *1989*, we know three ways to write a song:

  1. songs based on your own life or events in the lives of the people you live around;
  2. to listen to instrumental music sent by a producer and write the lyrics;
  3. ideas born and explored during a music session;

  it is very possible that these three techniques to be valid for the other artists investigated in this report;
- the information and conclusions in this report are limited, and should be used only in terms of the information used here;
- there might be a wrong interpretation of the information used, and I could not see or think about it as a wrong way to use it;
- this report explored mostly mathematical / suggestion / interpretation / inference / correlations and does not provide / assure / guarantee all the time a clear causal link and evidence to support the findings.

II. **black** and **white** music

II.1 Taylor Swift versus Kanye West

Taylor Swift (white woman) and Kanye West (black man) are the main actors in the *Famous* feud, and for its understanding over a thousand of articles have been written by the Western mass-media.[45] For this reason, Taylor Swift and Kanye West are the best source of comparison in terms of original songs and albums, as Kanye West has often expressed his disagreement with the music released by Taylor Swift.[46]

In this chapter I investigated which artist provided the original music, needed additional support to write and produce songs, and what this support consists of. At the same time, I investigated who was the most original artist after the MTV Music Video Awards event, and the albums released in 2010, Taylor Swift or Kanye West. Finally, the information in this chapter was used to challenge the conventional wisdom attached to Kanye West ('one of the greatest artists of all time') and its extension to Taylor Swift, with the purpose to expose, through the comparative analysis, which artist has more reasons (originality, novelty, number of producers and lyricists) for a better support of the conventional wisdom in their favour.

II.1.1 Sample

II.1.1.1 Use of Sample

TABLE 1. USE OF SAMPLE: TAYLOR SWIFT & KANYE WEST	
TAYLOR SWIFT	KANYE WEST

---

[45] Read Casian Anton, *On the Famous Feud*, 2023.

[46] One example: Kanye West and Kim Kardashian are on the cover of Harper's Bazaar September issue. When asked by editor Laura Brown about their favourite Taylor Swift song, Kanye West replied, 'For me? I don't have one.' Carine Roitfeld, 'Icons: In Bed with Kim and Kanye', *Harper's Bazaar*, July 28, 2016, http://www.harpersbazaar.com/fashion/photography/a16784/kanye-west-kim-kardashian-interview/, last accessed: October 23, 2017.

Taylor Swift (Deluxe, 2006): 0 out of 14[47]	The College Dropout (2004): 11 out of 22[48]
Fearless (Platinum, 2008): 1 out of 19[49]	Late Registration (2005): 14 out of 22[50]
Speak Now (Deluxe, 2010): 0 out of 17[51]	Graduation (2007): 11 out of 14[52]
RED (Deluxe, 2012): 0 out of 19[53]	88s & Heartbreak (2008): 3 out of 12[54]
1989 (Deluxe, 2013): 0 out of 16[55]	My Beautiful Dark Twisted Fantasy (2010): 10 out of 14[56]
reputation (2017): 1 out of 15[57]	Yeezus (2013): 8 out of 10[58]
Lover (2019): 3 out of 18[59]	The Life of Pablo (2016): 15 out of 20[60]
folklore (Deluxe, 2020): 0 out of 17[61]	Ye (2018): 5 out of 7[62]
Evermore (Deluxe, 2020): 0 out of 17[63]	Jesus is King (2019): 8 out of 11[64]
Fearless (Taylor's Version, 2021): 0 out of 7	
Total: 5 out of 159 songs (3%)	*Total: 85 out of 132 songs (64%)*

[47] Taylor Swift, 'Taylor Swift Credits', *Tidal*, 2006, https://listen.tidal.com/album/116125894/credits, last accessed: September 1, 2019.

[48] Kanye West, 'The College Dropout Credits Tracks 1 -21', *Tidal*, 2004, https://listen.tidal.com/album/92099357, last accessed September 1, 2019. Track 22 from *The College Dropout*, Wikipedia, https://en.wikipedia.org/wiki/The_College_Dropout, last accessed September 1, 2019. The data collected from this credit page will be used for the rest of this report without recitation.

[49] Taylor Swift, 'Fearless (Platinum Edition) Credits', *Tidal*, 2008, https://listen.tidal.com/album/3169103/credits, last accessed: September 1, 2019. 'Forever & Always' has two versions which were included in this chart since both have a different length.

[50] Kanye West, 'Late Registration Credits', *Tidal*, 2005, https://listen.tidal.com/album/34739750, last accessed September 1, 2019. The data collected from this credit page was used for the rest of this report without recitation.

[51] Taylor Swift, 'Speak Now Credits', *Tidal*, 2010, https://listen.tidal.com/album/4726104/credits, last accessed: September 1, 2019.

[52] Kanye West, 'Graduation Credits Tracks 1 – 13', *Tidal*, https://listen.tidal.com/album/103805723, last accessed: September 1, 2019. The data collected from this credit page was used for the rest of this report without recitation.

[53] Taylor Swift, 'RED (Deluxe Edition) Credits', *Tidal*, 2012, https://listen.tidal.com/album/92138674/credits, last accessed: September 1, 2019.

[54] Kanye West, '88s & Heartbreak', *Tidal*, 2008, https://tidal.com/browse/album/63863045/credits, last accessed: September 1, 2019. '808s & Heartbreak', *Wikipedia*, https://en.wikipedia.org/wiki/808s_%26_Heartbreak, last accessed: September 1, 2019. The data collected from this credit page was used for the rest of this report without recitation.

[55] Taylor Swift, '1989 (Deluxe Edition) Credits', *Tidal*, 2014, https://listen.tidal.com/album/121444594/credits, last accessed: September 1, 2019.

[56] Kanye West, 'My Beautiful Dark Twisted Fantasy Credits Tracks 1 – 13', *Tidal*, 2010, https://listen.tidal.com/album/4875681, last accessed: September 1, 2019. Track 14 from Wikipedia, *My Beautiful Dark Twisted Fantasy*, https://en.wikipedia.org/wiki/My_Beautiful_Dark_Twisted_Fantasy, last accessed: September 1, 2019. The data collected from this credit page was used for the rest of this report without recitation.

[57] Taylor Swift, 'reputation Credits', *Tidal*, 2017, https://listen.tidal.com/album/121255042/credits, last accessed: September 1, 2019.

[58] Kanye West, 'Yeezus Credits', *Tidal*, 2013, https://listen.tidal.com/album/20753857, last accessed: September 1, 2019. The data collected from this credit page was used for the rest of this report without recitation.

[59] Taylor Swift, 'Lover Credits', *Tidal*, 2019, https://listen.tidal.com/album/116125894/credits, last accessed: September 1, 2019.

[60] Kanye West, 'The Life of Pablo Credits', *Tidal*, 2016, https://listen.tidal.com/album/57273408/credits, last accessed: September 1, 2019. The data collected from this credit page was used for the rest of this report without recitation.

[61] Taylor Swift, 'folklore (Deluxe Edition)', *Tidal*, 2020, https://listen.tidal.com/album/152246341/credits, last accessed: February 3, 2021.

[62] Kanye West, 'Ye Credits', *Tidal*, 2018, https://listen.tidal.com/album/98156343, last accessed: September 1, 2019. The data collected from this credit page was used for the rest of this report without recitation.

[63] Taylor Swift, 'Evermore (Deluxe Edition)', *Tidal*, 2020, https://listen.tidal.com/album/168101331/credits, last accessed: February 3, 2021.

[64] Kanye West, 'Jesus is King', *Tidal*, 2019, https://listen.tidal.com/album/121012112, last accessed: November 21, 2019. The data collected from this credit page was used for the rest of this report without recitation.

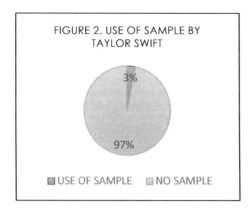

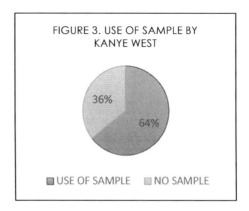

II.1.1.2 No Use of Samples

TABLE 2. ORIGINAL SONGS WITH NO SAMPLE: TAYLOR SWIFT & KANYE WEST	
TAYLOR SWIFT	KANYE WEST
Taylor Swift (Deluxe, 2006): 14 out of 14	The College Dropout (2004): 11 out of 22
Fearless (Platinum, 2008): 18 out of 19	Late Registration (2005): 7 out of 22
Speak Now (Deluxe, 2010): 17 out of 17	Graduation (2007): 4 out of 14
RED (Deluxe, 2012): 19 out of 19	88s & Heartbreak (2008): 9 out of 12
1989 (Deluxe, 2014): 16 out of 16	My Beautiful Dark Twisted Fantasy (2010): 4 out of 14
reputation (2017): 14 out of 15	Yeezus (2013): 2 out of 10
Lover (2019): 15 out of 18	The Life of Pablo (2016): 5 out of 20
folklore (Deluxe, 2020): 17 out of 17	Ye (2018): 2 out of 7
Evermore (Deluxe): 17 out of 17	Jesus is King (2019): 3 out of 11
Fearless (Taylor's Version, 2021): 7 out of 7	
Total: 154 out of 159 songs (97%)	*Total: 47 out of 132 songs (36%)*

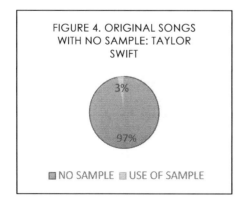

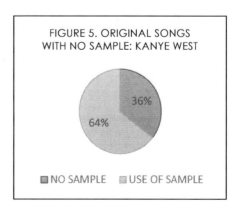

CONCLUSIONS:

- Taylor Swift has a higher number of original songs than Kanye West, with 97% of her music having no samples, while Kanye West has 36% of music with no samples;
- from the point of view of *Use of Sample*, Taylor Swift's music is 21.33(3) times more original than Kanye West's music;
- from the point of view of *No Sample*, Taylor Swift's music is 2.694(4) times more original than Kanye West's music.

II.1.2 Lyricists

II.1.2.1 Sole Lyricist

TABLE 3. ORIGINAL SONGS AS SOLE LYRICIST: TAYLOR SWIFT & KANYE WEST	
TAYLOR SWIFT	KANYE WEST
Taylor Swift (Deluxe, 2006): 3 out of 14	The College Dropout (2004): 6 out of 22[65]
Fearless (Platinum, 2008): 10 out of 19	Late Registration (2005): 1 out of 22
Speak Now (Deluxe, 2010): 16 out of 17	Graduation (2007): 0 out of 14
RED (Deluxe, 2012): 11 out of 19	88s & Heartbreak (2008): 1 out of 12[66]
1989 (Deluxe, 2014): 1 out of 16	My Beautiful Dark Twisted Fantasy (2010): 0 out of 14
reputation (2017): 0 out of 15	Yeezus (2013): 0 out of 10
Lover (2019): 3 out of 18	The Life of Pablo (2016): 0 out of 20
folklore (Deluxe, 2020): 1 out of 17	Ye (2018): 0 out of 7
Evermore (Deluxe, 2020): 1 out of 17	Jesus is King (2019): 0 out of 11
Fearless (Taylor's Version, 2021): 2 out of 7	
Total: 48 out of 159 (30%)	*Total: 8 out of 132 songs (6%)*

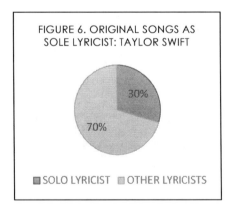

FIGURE 6. ORIGINAL SONGS AS SOLE LYRICIST: TAYLOR SWIFT

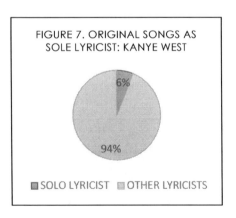

FIGURE 7. ORIGINAL SONGS AS SOLE LYRICIST: KANYE WEST

---

[65] 'Skit No. 1', 'Skit No. 2', 'Skit No. 3', 'Skit No. 4' are instrumental songs with no lyricist.
[66] The song name is 'Pinocchio Story'.

CONCLUSIONS:

- Taylor Swift has a higher percentage of songs written by herself with 30% of her catalogue, while Kanye West has 6%; however, the songs written by Kanye West are not only full songs, but also a short text spoken in *Intro, Outro* and *Skit;*
- as *Sole Lyricist,* Taylor Swift released 5 times more songs than Kanye West.

II.1.2.2 Two Lyricists

TABLE 4. ORIGINAL SONGS WITH TWO LYRICISTS: TAYLOR SWIFT & KANYE WEST	
TAYLOR SWIFT	KANYE WEST
Taylor Swift (Deluxe, 2006): 7 out of 14	The College Dropout (2004): 4 out of 22
Fearless (Platinum, 2008): 7 out of 19	Late Registration (2005): 4 out of 22
Speak Now (Deluxe, 2010): 1 out of 17	Graduation (2007): 5 out of 14
RED (Deluxe, 2012): 4 out of 19	88s & Heartbreak (2008): 1 out of 12
1989 (Deluxe, 2014): 7 out of 16	My Beautiful Dark Twisted Fantasy (2010): 0 out of 14
reputation (2017): 5 out of 15	Yeezus (2013): 0 out of 10
Lover (2019): 9 out of 18	The Life of Pablo (2016): 0 out of 20
folklore (Deluxe, 2020): 15 out of 17	Ye (2018): 0 out of 7
Evermore (Deluxe, 2020): 13 out of 17	Jesus is King (2019): 0 out of 11
Fearless (Taylor's Version, 2021): 4 out of 7	
Total: 72 out of 159 songs (45%)	*Total: 14 out of 132 songs (11%)*

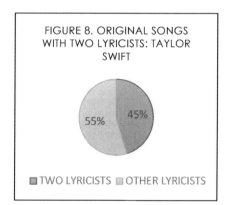

FIGURE 8. ORIGINAL SONGS WITH TWO LYRICISTS: TAYLOR SWIFT

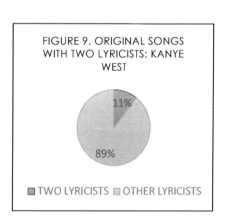

FIGURE 9. ORIGINAL SONGS WITH TWO LYRICISTS: KANYE WEST

CONCLUSION:

- Taylor Swift has a higher number of songs written in partnership with a second lyricist, which is 45% of her total songs, while Kanye West has a lower number of songs, 11%, which is 4.09(09) times lower than Taylor Swift.=

II.1.2.3 Three Lyricists

TABLE 5. ORIGINAL SONGS WITH THREE LYRICISTS: TAYLOR SWIFT & KANYE WEST	
TAYLOR SWIFT	KANYE WEST
Taylor Swift (Deluxe, 2006): 4 out of 14	The College Dropout (2004): 3 out of 22
Fearless (Platinum, 2008): 1 out of 19	Late Registration (2005): 8 out of 22
Speak Now (Deluxe, 2010): 0 out of 17	Graduation (2007): 3 out of 14
RED (Deluxe, 2012): 4 out of 19	88s & Heartbreak (2008): 1 out of 12
1989 (Deluxe, 2014): 7 out of 16	My Beautiful Dark Twisted Fantasy (2010): 1 out of 14
reputation (2017): 5 out of 15	Yeezus (2013): 0 out of 10
Lover (2019): 5 out of 18	The Life of Pablo (2016): 0 out of 20
folklore (Deluxe, 2020): 1 out of 17	Ye (2018): 0 out of 7
Evermore (Deluxe, 2020): 2 out of 17	Jesus is King (2019): 1 out of 11
Fearless (Taylor's Version, 2021): 1 out of 7	
Total: 30 out of 159 songs (19%)	*Total: 17 out of 132 songs (13%)*

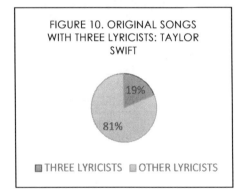

FIGURE 10. ORIGINAL SONGS WITH THREE LYRICISTS: TAYLOR SWIFT

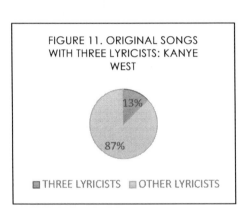

FIGURE 11. ORIGINAL SONGS WITH THREE LYRICISTS: KANYE WEST

II.1.2.4 At Least Four Lyricists

TABLE 6. ORIGINAL SONGS WITH AT LEAST FOUR LYRICISTS: TAYLOR SWIFT & KANYE WEST	
TAYLOR SWIFT	KANYE WEST
Taylor Swift (Deluxe, 2006): 0 out of 14	The College Dropout (2004): 8 out of 22[67]
Fearless (Platinum, 2008): 1 out of 19	Late Registration (2005): 4 out of 22
Speak Now (Deluxe, 2010): 0 out of 17	Graduation (2007): 8 out of 14
RED (Deluxe, 2012): 0 out of 19	88s & Heartbreak (2008): 8 out of 12
1989 (Deluxe, 2014): 1 out of 16	My Beautiful Dark Twisted Fantasy (2010): 13 out of 14
reputation (2017): 5 out of 15	Yeezus (2013): 10 out of 10

---

[67] 'I'll Fly Away' was written by Albert E. Brumley solely for Kanye West's debut album.

Lover (2019): 1 out of 18	The Life of Pablo (2016): 20 out of 20
folklore (Deluxe, 2020): 0 out of 16	Ye (2018): 7 out of 7
Evermore (Deluxe, 2020): 1 out of 17	Jesus is King (2019): 10 out of 11
Fearless (Taylor's Version, 2021): 0 out of 7	
Total: 9 out of 159 songs (6%)	*Total: 88 out of 132 songs (67%)*

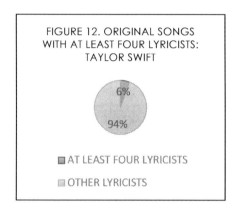

FIGURE 12. ORIGINAL SONGS WITH AT LEAST FOUR LYRICISTS: TAYLOR SWIFT

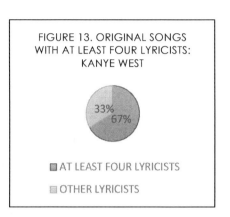

FIGURE 13. ORIGINAL SONGS WITH AT LEAST FOUR LYRICISTS: KANYE WEST

CONCLUSIONS:

- Kanye West has a higher number of songs written in partnership with at least four lyricists (67%) than Taylor Swift with 6%, which is 11.16 times higher than Taylor Swift;
- overall, Taylor Swift seems to be highly more capable than Kanye West to write her own music (full songs), while Kanye West needed highly additional support (a reason behind this high support may be due to use of samples from other songs: includes instrumental and lyrics, and adaptation of these instrumentals and lyrics into a new song with a different or close musical notes (it may be difficult to be achieved solely by Kanye West)).

II.1.3 The Origins of Music

In this subchapter I investigated the sources of the music creativity of both artists: which artist has more original ideas and brings new sounds and lyrics.

II.1.3.1 The Origins of Music for Taylor Swift

TABLE 7. THE LIST OF SAMPLES USED BY TAYLOR SWIFT	
Taylor Swift (Deluxe, 2006)	N/A

Fearless (Platinum, 2008)	'Untouchable'[68] is a reworked version of Luna Halo's 'Untouchable'[69], written by Cary Barlowe, Nathan Barlowe, and Tommy Lee James.
Speak Now (Deluxe, 2010)	N/A
RED (Deluxe, 2010)	N/A
1989 (Deluxe, 2014)	N/A
reputation (2017)	'Look What You Made Me Do'[70] contains an interpolation of the 1991 song 'I'm Too Sexy'[71] by the band Right Said Fred.
Lover (2019)	1. 'The Archer'[72] contains an interpolation of the nursery rhyme 'Humpty Dumpty'[73];
	2. 'London Boy'[74] contains a sample of 'Cold War'[75] by Cautious Clay and a snippet of James Corden interviewing Idris Elba;
	3. 'It's Nice to Have a Friend'[76] contains a sample of 'Summer in the South' by the Toronto-based Regent Park School of Music.
folklore (Deluxe, 2020)	N/A
Evermore (Deluxe, 2020)	N/A
Fearless (Taylor's Version, 2021)	N/A

CONCLUSIONS:

- Taylor Swift's sources of samples are at low level in creating her music; the first source of sample used was a full song named 'Untouchable' (modified by Taylor Swift in her

---

[68] Audio: Taylor Swift, 'Untouchable', *Youtube*, December 12, 2018, available at: https://www.youtube.com/watch?v=WR6LNojTHG0, last accessed: February 25, 2020; Lyrics: Taylor Swift, 'Untouchable Lyrics', *Genius*, available at: https://genius.com/Taylor-swift-untouchable-lyrics, last accessed: February 25, 2020.

[69] Audio: Luna Halo, 'Untouchable', *Youtube*, January 26, 2009, available at: https://www.youtube.com/watch?v=6vmVhaFDe4A, last accessed: February 25, 2020; Lyrics: Luna Halor, 'Untouchable Lyrics', *Genius*, available at: https://genius.com/Luna-halo-untouchable-lyrics, last accessed: February 25, 2020.

[70] Audio: Taylor Swift, 'Look What You Made Me Do', *Youtube*, August 28, 2017, available at: https://www.youtube.com/watch?v=3tmd-ClpJxA, last accessed: February 25, 2020; Lyrics: Taylor Swift, 'Look What You Made Me Do', *Genius*, available at: https://genius.com/Taylor-swift-look-what-you-made-me-do-lyrics, last accessed: February 25, 2020.

[71] Audio: Right Said Fred, 'I'm Too Sexy (Original Mix – 2006 Version)', *Youtube*, June 14, 2009, available at: https://www.youtube.com/watch?v=P5mtclwloEQ, last accessed: February 25, 2020. Lyrics: Right Said Fred, 'I'm Too Sexy', *Genius*, available at: https://genius.com/Right-said-fred-im-too-sexy-lyrics, last accessed: February 25, 2020.

[72] Audio: Taylor Swift, 'The Archer', *Youtube*, July 23, 2019, available at: https://www.youtube.com/watch?v=8KpKc3C9V3w, last accessed: February 25, 2020; Lyrics: Taylor Swift, 'The Archer' *Genius*, available at: https://genius.com/Taylor-swift-the-archer-lyrics, last accessed: February 25, 2020.

[73] Lyrics: Humpty, Dumpty, *Genius*, available at: https://genius.com/Children-songs-humpty-dumpty-annotated, last accessed: February 25, 2020.

[74] Audio: Taylor Swift, 'London Boy', *Youtube*, available at: https://www.youtube.com/watch?v=VsKoOH6DVys, last accessed: February 25, 2020; Lyrics: Taylor Swift, 'London Boy', *Genius*, available at: https://genius.com/Taylor-swift-london-boy-lyrics, last accessed: February 25, 2020.

[75] Audio: Cautious Clay, 'Cold War', *Youtube*, April 30, 2018, available at: https://www.youtube.com/watch?v=S1kyno4u9cQ, last accessed: February 25, 2020; Lyrics: Cautious Clay, 'Cold War', *Genius*, available at: https://genius.com/Cautious-clay-cold-war-lyrics, last accessed: February 25, 2020.

[76] Audio: Taylor Swift, 'It's Nice To have A Friend', *Youtube*, August 23, 2019, available at: https://www.youtube.com/watch?v=eaP1VswBF28, last accessed: February 25, 2020; Lyrics: Taylor Swift, 'It's Nice To have A Friend', *Genius*, available at: https://genius.com/Taylor-swift-its-nice-to-have-a-friend-lyrics, last accessed: February 25, 2020.

own musical vision), while the rest of her songs includes bits of instrumental and lyrics from other songs;

- Taylor Swift is highly capable to create her own music world with songs based on her life (from family to relationships and enemies) never heard before;
- Taylor Swift demonstrated a high level of musical imagination and ideas in the music industry.

II.1.3.2 The Origins of Music for Kanye West

In this table I also included the following albums (only to show the background work (similarities and differences) of the music by Kanye West, and which are not part of this investigation): *Watch the Throne* (2011, with Jay-Z), *Cruel Summer* (2012) and *Kids See Ghosts* (2017).

TABLE 8. THE LIST OF SAMPLES USED BY KANYE WEST	
	1. 'We Don't Care'[77] contains samples of 'I Just Wanna Stop'[78], written by Ross Vannelli and performed by The Jimmy Castor Bunch. 2. 'All Falls Down'[79] contains interpolations of 'Mystery of Iniquity'[80], written and performed by Lauryn Hill. 3. 'Spaceship'[81] contains samples of 'Distant Lover'[82], written by Marvin Gaye, Gwen Gordy Fuqua and Sandra Greene, and performed by Marvin Gaye.

---

[77] Audio: Kanye West, 'We Don't Care', *Youtube*, July 16, 2018, available at: https://www.youtube.com/watch?v=0Tdpq3FRGhY&list=OLAK5uy_l139P2p521JCZVZX8S_PuGFUKyD1brXWY&index=2, last accessed: February 25, 2020; Lyrics: Kanye West, 'We Don't Care, *Genius*, available at: https://genius.com/Kanye-west-we-dont-care-lyrics, last accessed: February 25, 2020.

[78] Audio: The Jimmy Castor Bunch, 'I Just Wanna Stop', *Youtube*, January 23, 2017, available at: https://www.youtube.com/watch?v=xf9CKTk37-I, last accessed: February 25, 2020. Lyrics: The Jimmy Castor Bunch, 'I Just Wanna Stop', *Genius*, available at: https://genius.com/The-jimmy-castor-bunch-i-just-wanna-stop-lyrics, last accessed: February 25, 2020 .

[79] Audio: Kanye West, 'All Falls Down', *Youtube*, December 24, 2009, available at: https://www.youtube.com/watch?v=8kyWDhB_Qel&list=OLAK5uy_l139P2p521JCZVZX8S_PuGFUKyD1brXWY&index=4, last accessed: February 25, 2020; Lyrics: Kanye West, 'All Falls Down', *Genius*, available at: https://genius.com/Kanye-west-all-falls-down-lyrics, last accessed: February 25, 2020.

[80] Audio: Lauryn Hill, 'Mystery of Iniquity', *Youtube*, February 2, 2012, available at: https://www.youtube.com/watch?v=BUZzW3wQg7Q, last accessed: February 25, 2020. Lyrics: Lauryn Hill, 'Mystery of Iniquity', *Genius*, available at: https://genius.com/Lauryn-hill-the-mystery-of-iniquity-lyrics, last accessed: February 25, 2020.

[81] Audio: Kanye West, 'Spaceship', *Youtube*, July 16, 2018, available at: https://www.youtube.com/watch?v=mn77gzjBl1U&list=OLAK5uy_l139P2p521JCZVZX8S_PuGFUKyD1brXWY&index=6, last accessed: February 25, 2020. Lyrics: Kanye West, 'Spaceship', *Genius*, available at: https://genius.com/Kanye-west-spaceship-lyrics, last accessed: February 25, 2020.

[82] Audio: Marvin Gaye, 'Distant Lover', *Youtube*, September 18, 2010, available at: https://www.youtube.com/watch?v=NShJXGrNotU, last accessed: February 25, 2020. Lyrics: Marvin Gaye, 'Distant Lover', *Genius*, available at: https://genius.com/Marvin-gaye-distant-lover-lyrics, last accessed: February 25, 2020.

The College Dropout (2004)	4. 'Jesus Walks'[83] contains samples of 'Walk with Me'[84], performed by The ARC Choir and '(Don't Worry) If There's a Hell Below, We're All Going to Go'[85], written and performed by Curtis Mayfield; interpolation of 'Hovi Baby (remix)'[86], written by Shawn Carter, Justin Smith and Kenneth Edmonds, and preformed by Jay Z. 5. 'Never Let Me Down'[87] contains samples of 'Maybe It's the Power of Love'[88], written by Michael Bolton and Bruce Kulick, and performed by Blackjack. 6. 'Slow Jamz'[89] contains samples of 'A House Is Not a Home'[90], written by Burt Bacharach and Hal David, and performed by Luther Vandross. 7. 'Breathe In Breathe Out'[91] contains samples of 'Precious Precious'[92], written and Performed by Jackie Moore. 8. 'School Spirit'[93] contains samples of 'Spirit in the Dark'[94], written and performed by Aretha Franklin.

---

[83] Audio: Kanye West, 'Jesus Walks', *Youtube*, December 24, 2009, available at: https://www.youtube.com/watch?v=MYF7H_fpc-g&list=OLAK5uy_l139p2p521JCZVZX8S_PuGFUKyD1brXWY&index=7, last accessed: February 25, 2020; Lyrics: Kanye West, 'Jesus Walks', *Genius*, available at: https://genius.com/Kanye-west-jesus-walks-lyrics, last accessed: February 25, 2020.

[84] Audio: The ARC Choir, 'Walk With Me', *Youtube*, November 2, 2008, available at: https://www.youtube.com/watch?v=-Ib36OXrEL8, last accessed: February 25, 2020. Lyrics: The ARC Choir, 'Walk With Me', *Genius*, available at: https://genius.com/The-arc-choir-walk-with-me-lyrics, last accessed: February 25, 2020.

[85] Audio: Curtis Mayfield, '(Don't Worry) If There's a Hell Below, We're All Going To Go', *Youtube*, June 5, 2011, available at: https://www.youtube.com/watch?v=x1xmXOP3lhM, last accessed: February 25, 2020. Lyrics: Curtis Mayfield, '(Don't Worry) If There's a Hell Below, We're All Going To Go', *Genius*, available at: https://genius.com/Curtis-mayfield-dont-worry-if-theres-a-hell-below-were-all-going-to-go-lyrics, last accessed: February 25, 2020.

[86] Audio: Blackjack, 'Maybe It's The Power Of Love', *Youtube*, March 12, 2012, available at: https://www.youtube.com/watch?v=C71EfYUIrYo, last accessed: February 25, 2020. Lyrics: Blackjack, 'Maybe It's The Power Of Love', *Genius*, available at: https://genius.com/Blackjack-maybe-its-the-power-of-love-lyrics, last accessed: February 25, 2020.

[87] Audio: Kanye West, 'Never Let Me Down', *Youtube*, July 16, 2018, available at: https://www.youtube.com/watch?v=p4NvOKy7GOU&list=OLAK5uy_l139P2p521JCZVZX8S_PuGFUKyD1brXWY&index=8, last accessed: February 25, 2020; Lyrics: Kanye West, 'Never Let Me Down', *Genius*, available at: https://genius.com/Kanye-west-never-let-me-down-lyrics, last accessed: February 25, 2020.

[88] Audio: Blackjack, 'Maybe It's The Power Of Love', *Youtube*, March 12, 2012, available at: https://www.youtube.com/watch?v=C71EfYUIrYo, last accessed: February 25, 2020. Lyrics: Blackjack, 'Maybe It's The Power Of Love', *Genius*, available at: https://genius.com/Blackjack-maybe-its-the-power-of-love-lyrics, last accessed: February 25, 2020.

[89] Audio: Kanye West, 'Slow Jamz', *Youtube*, December 12, 2012, available at: https://www.youtube.com/watch?v=jl-w4gvkCkQ&list=OLAK5uy_l139P2p521JCZVZX8S_PuGFUKyD1brXWY&index=12, last accessed: February 25, 2020; Lyrics: Kanye West, 'Slow Jamz', *Genius*, available at: https://genius.com/Twista-kanye-west-and-jamie-foxx-slow-jamz-lyrics, last accessed: February 25, 2020.

[90] Audio: Luther Vandross, 'A House Is Not a Home', *Youtube*, May 23, 2015, available at: https://www.youtube.com/watch?v=CGib6okEeZ4, last accessed: February 25, 2020. Lyrics: Luther Vandross, 'A House Is Not a Home', *Genius*, available at: https://genius.com/Luther-vandross-a-house-is-not-a-home-lyrics, last accessed: February 25, 2020.

[91] Audio: Kanye West, 'Breathe In Breathe Out', *Youtube*, July 16, 2018, available at: https://www.youtube.com/watch?v=E3dWKq3s6u0, last accessed: February 25, 2020. Lyrics: Kanye West, 'Breathe In Breathe Out', *Genius*, available at: https://genius.com/Kanye-west-breathe-in-breathe-out-lyrics, last accessed: February 25, 2020.

[92] Audio: Jackie Moore, 'Precious Precious', *Youtube*, April 23, 2013, available at: https://www.youtube.com/watch?v=dlaIRRcKkfU=, last accessed: February 25, 2020. Lyrics: Jackie Moore, 'Precious Precious', *Genius*, available at: https://genius.com/Jackie-moore-precious-precious-lyrics, last accessed: February 25, 2020.

[93] Audio: Kanye West, 'School Spirit', *Youtube*, July 16, 2018, available at: https://www.youtube.com/watch?v=-MOIPnu50O4&list=OLAK5uy_l139P2p521JCZVZX8S_PuGFUKyD1brXWY&index=15, last accessed: February 25, 2020; Lyrics: Kanye West, 'School Spirit', *Genius*, available at: https://genius.com/Kanye-west-school-spirit-lyrics, last accessed: February 25, 2020.

[94] Audio: Aretha Franklin, 'Spirit In The Dark', *Youtube*, March 7, 2011, available at: https://www.youtube.com/watch?v=qvGmbsLxF0w, last accessed: February 25, 2020. Lyrics: Aretha Franklin, 'Spirit In The Dark', *Genius*, available at: https://genius.com/Aretha-franklin-spirit-in-the-dark-lyrics, last accessed: February 25, 2020.

	9. 'Two Words'[95] contains samples of 'Peace & Love (Amani Na Mapenzi) – Movement IV (Encounter)'[96], written by Lou Wilson, Ric Wilson and Carlos Wilson, and performed by Mandrill; samples of 'The Rainmaker'[97], written by Harry Nilsson and Bill Martin and performed by The 5th Dimension. 10. 'Through the Wire'[98] contains samples of 'Through the Fire'[99], written by David Foster, Tom Keane and Cynthia Weil, and performed by Chaka Khan. 11. 'Family Business'[100] contains samples of 'Fonky Thang'[101], written by Terry Callier and Charles Stepney, and performed by The Dells; interpolations of 'Ambitionz As A Ridah'[102], written by Tupac Shakur and Delmar Arnaud and performed by 2Pac. 12. 'Last Call'[103] contains samples of 'Mr. Rockefeller'[104], written by Jerry Blatt and Bette Midler, and performed by Bette Midler; sample of 'She's Gone To Another'[105], written by Kenneth Ruffin and performed by The Whatnauts.

---

[95] Audio: Kanye West, 'Two Words', *Youtube*, June 16, 2009, available at: https://www.youtube.com/watch?v=tkFOBx6j0l8&list=OLAK5uy_l139P2p521JCZVZX8S_PuGFUKyD1brXWY&index=18, last accessed: February 25, 2020; Lyrics: Kanye West, 'Two Words', *Genius*, available at: https://genius.com/Kanye-west-two-words-lyrics, last accessed: February 25, 2020.

[96] Audio: Mandrill, 'Peace and Love (Amani Na Mapenzi) – Movement IV (Encounter)', *Youtube*, July 29, 2012, available at: https://www.youtube.com/watch?v=gXCcPAk2NBY, last accessed: February 25, 2020. Lyrics: Audio: Mandrill, 'Peace and Love (Amani Na Mapenzi) – Movement IV (Encounter)', *Genius*, available at: https://genius.com/Mandrill-peace-and-love-amani-na-mapenzi-movement-iv-encounter-lyrics, last accessed: February 25, 2020.

[97] Audio: The 5th Dimension, ,The Rainmaker', *Youtube*, September 24, 2015, available at: https://www.youtube.com/watch?v=aQ4GgAvYBpY, last accessed: February 25, 2020; Lyrics: The 5th Dimension, ,The Rainmaker', Genius, available at: https://genius.com/The-5th-dimension-time-and-love-lyrics, last accessed: February 25, 2020.

[98] Audio: Kanye West, 'Through the Wire', *Youtube*, July 16, 2018, available at: https://www.youtube.com/watch?v=AE8y25CcE6s&list=OLAK5uy_l139P2p521JCZVZX8S_PuGFUKyD1brXWY&index=19, last accessed: February 25, 2020; Lyrics: Kanye West, 'Through the Wire', *Genius*, available at: https://genius.com/Kanye-west-through-the-wire-lyrics, last accessed: February 25, 2020.

[99] Audio: Chaka Khan, 'Through The Fire', *Youtube*, February 26, 2009, available at: https://www.youtube.com/watch?v=ymuWb8xtCsc, last accessed: February 25, 2020. Lyrics: Chaka Khan, 'Through The Fire', *Genius*, available at: https://genius.com/Chaka-khan-through-the-fire-lyrics, last accessed: February 25, 2020.

[100] Audio: Kanye West, 'Family Business', *Youtube*, July 16, 2018, available at: https://www.youtube.com/watch?v=JwAjANmjajc&list=OLAK5uy_l139P2p521JCZVZX8S_PuGFUKyD1brXWY&index=20, last accessed: February 25, 2020; Lyrics: Kanye West, 'Family Business', *Genius*, available at: https://genius.com/Kanye-west-family-business-lyrics, last accessed: February 25, 2020.

[101] Audio: The Dells, 'Fonky Thang', *Youtube*, October 23, 2016, available at: https://www.youtube.com/watch?v=Rz9SLTRi_IE, last accessed: February 25, 2020. Lyrics: The Dells, 'Fonky Thang', *Genius*, available at: https://genius.com/The-dells-fonky-thang-diamond-rang-lyrics, last accessed: February 25, 2020.

[102] Audio: 2Pac, 'Mabitionz As A Ridah', *Youtube*, November 19, 201, available at: https://www.youtube.com/watch?v=cQZqPi1aHNo, last accessed: February 25, 2020; Lyrics: 2Pac, 'Mabitionz As A Ridah', *Genius*, available at: https://genius.com/2pac-ambitionz-az-a-ridah-lyrics, last accessed: February 25, 2020.

[103] Audio: Kanye West, 'Last Call', *Youtube*, July 16, 2018, available at: https://www.youtube.com/watch?v=cpbeS15sHZ0&list=OLAK5uy_l139P2p521JCZVZX8S_PuGFUKyD1brXWY&index=21, last accessed: February 25, 2020; Lyrics: Kanye West, 'Last Call', *Genius*, available at: https://genius.com/Kanye-west-last-call-lyrics, last accessed: February 25, 2020.

[104] Audio: Bette Midler, 'Mr. Rockefeller', *Youtube*, April 6, 2011, available at: https://www.youtube.com/watch?v=hao8NDTeREs, last accessed: February 25, 2020. Lyrics: Bette Midler, 'Mr. Rockefeller', *Genius*, available at: https://genius.com/Bette-midler-mr-rockefeller-lyrics, last accessed: February 25, 2020.

[105] Audio: The Whatnauts, 'She's Gone To Another', *Youtube*, May 25, 2008, available at: https://www.youtube.com/watch?v=fJXIGOizJsE, last accessed: February 25, 2020.

	1. 'Wake Up Mr. West'[106] and 'Heard Em Say'[107] both contain excerpts of 'Someone That I Used to Love'[108] as performed by Natalie Cole. 2. 'Touch the Sky'[109] contains samples of 'Move On Up'[110] as performed by Curtis Mayfield. 3. 'Gold Digger'[111] contains samples of 'I Got a Woman'[112] as performed by Ray Charles. 4. 'Drive Slow'[113] contains samples of 'Wildflower'[114] as performed by Hank Crawford. 5. 'My Way Home'[115] contains samples of 'Home Is Where the Hatred Is'[116] as performed by Gil Scott-Heron. 6. 'Crack Music'[117] contains samples of 'Since You Came in My Life'[118] as performed by New York Community Choir.

---

[106] Audio: Kanye West, 'Wake Up Mr. West', October 29, 208, *Youtube*, available at: https://www.youtube.com/watch?v=Bwyu-SZ7g_E&list=OLAK5uy_mS2sPIJinRK2fIXN9Ce756lZFRX2KT21o, last accessed: February 25, 2020; Lyrics: Kanye West, 'Wake Up Mr. West', *Genius*, available at: https://genius.com/Kanye-west-wake-up-mr-west-lyrics, last accessed: February 25, 2020.

[107] Audio: Kanye West, 'Heard Em Say', *Youtube*, June 16, 2009, available at: https://www.youtube.com/watch?v=elVF7oG0pQs&list=OLAK5uy_mS2sPIJinRK2fIXN9Ce756lZFRX2KT21o&index=2, last accessed: February 25, 2020; Lyrics: Kanye West, 'Heard Em Say', *Genius*, available at: https://genius.com/Kanye-west-heard-em-say-lyrics, last accessed: February 25, 2020.

[108] Audio: Natalie Cole, 'Someone That I Used To Love', *Youtube*, January 30, 2014, available at: https://www.youtube.com/watch?v=H89_X3v0c9g, last accessed: February 25, 2020. Lyrics: Natalie Cole, 'Someone That I Used To Love', *Genius*, available at: https://genius.com/Natalie-cole-someone-that-i-used-to-love-lyrics, last accessed: February 25, 2020.

[109] Audio: Kanye West, 'Touch The Sky', *Youtube*, June 16, 2009, available at: https://www.youtube.com/watch?v=YkwQbuAGLj4&list=OLAK5uy_mS2sPIJinRK2fIXN9Ce756lZFRX2KT21o&index=3, last accessed: February 25, 2020; Lyrics: Kanye West, 'Touch The Sky', *Genius*, available at: https://genius.com/Kanye-west-touch-the-sky-lyrics, last accessed: February 25, 2020.

[110] Audio: Curtis Mayfield, 'Move On Up', *Youtube*, December 22, 2009, available at: https://www.youtube.com/watch?v=6Z66wVo7uNw, last accessed: February 25, 2020. Lyrics: Curtis Mayfield, 'Move On Up', *Genius*, available at: https://genius.com/Curtis-mayfield-move-on-up-lyrics, last accessed: February 25, 2020.

[111] Audio: Kanye West, 'Gold Digger', *Youtube,* June 16, 2009, available at: https://www.youtube.com/watch?v=6vwNcNOTVzY&list=OLAK5uy_mS2sPIJinRK2fIXN9Ce756lZFRX2KT21o&index=4, last accessed: February 25, 2020; Lyrics: Kanye West, 'Gold Digger', *Genius*, available at: https://genius.com/Kanye-west-gold-digger-lyrics, last accessed: February 25, 2020.

[112] Audio: Ray Charles, 'I Got A Woman', *Youtube*, August 3, 2009, available at: https://www.youtube.com/watch?v=Cnl_LuCJ4Ek, last accessed: February 25, 2020. Lyrics: Ray Charles, 'I Got A Woman', *Genius*, available at: https://genius.com/Ray-charles-i-got-a-woman-lyrics, last accessed: February 25, 2020.

[113] Audio: Kanye West, 'Drive Slow', *Youtube*, October 29, 2018, available at: https://www.youtube.com/watch?v=Q1ViJEYNki4&list=OLAK5uy_mS2sPIJinRK2fIXN9Ce756lZFRX2KT21o&index=6, last accessed: February 25, 2020; Lyrics: Kanye West, 'Drive Slow', *Genius*, available at: https://genius.com/Kanye-west-drive-slow-lyrics, last accessed: February 25, 2020.

[114] Audio: Hank Crawford, 'Wildflower', *Youtube*, June 9, 2012, available at: https://www.youtube.com/watch?v=QC88dJ4KuFw, last accessed: February 25, 2020. Lyrics: Hank Crawford, 'Wildflower', *Genius*, available at: https://genius.com/Hank-crawford-wildflower-lyrics, last accessed: February 25, 2020.

[115] Audio: Kanye West, 'My Way Home', *Youtube*, October 29, 2018, available at: https://www.youtube.com/watch?v=TgAomHGqKUM&list=OLAK5uy_mS2sPIJinRK2fIXN9Ce756lZFRX2KT21o&index=7, last accessed: February 25, 2020; Lyrics: Kanye West, 'My Way Home', *Genius*, available at: https://genius.com/Kanye-west-my-way-home-lyrics, last accessed: February 25, 2020.

[116] Audio: Gil Scott-Heron, 'Home Is Where The Hatred Is', *Youtube*, August 19, 2014, available at: https://www.youtube.com/watch?v=nSpBs1ghyoo, last accessed: . Lyrics: Gil Scott-Heron, 'Home Is Where The Hatred Is', *Genius*, available at: https://genius.com/Gil-scott-heron-home-is-where-the-hatred-is-pieces-of-a-man-version-lyrics, last accessed: .

[117] Audio: Kanye West, 'Crack Music', *Youtube*, October 29, 2018, available at: https://www.youtube.com/watch?v=2tmPSK-w90o&list=OLAK5uy_mS2sPIJinRK2fIXN9Ce756lZFRX2KT21o&index=8, last accessed: February 25, 2020; Lyrics: Kanye West, 'Crack Music', *Genius*, available at: https://genius.com/Kanye-west-crack-music-lyrics, last accessed: February 25, 2020.

[118] Audio: New York Community Choir, 'Since You Came In My Life', *Youtube*, December 16, 2017, available at: https://www.youtube.com/watch?v=RRcuYBg9S8w, last accessed: February 25, 2020. Lyrics: New York Community Choir, 'Since You Came In My Life', *Genius*, available at: https://genius.com/New-york-community-choir-since-you-came-in-my-life-lyrics, last accessed: February 25, 2020.

Late Registration (2005)	7. 'Roses'[119] contains samples of 'Rosie'[120] as performed by Bill Withers. 8. 'Addiction'[121] contains elements of 'My Funny Valentine'[122] as performed by Etta James. 9. 'Diamonds from Sierra Leone'[123] contains samples of 'Diamonds Are Forever'[124] as performed by Shirley Bassey. 10. 'We Major'[125] contains samples of 'Action'[126] as performed by Orange Krush. 11. 'Hey Mama'[127] contains samples of 'Today Won't Come Again'[128] as performed by Donal Leace. 12. 'Celebration'[129] contains samples of 'Heavenly Dream'[130] as performed by The Kay-Gees.

---

[119] Audio: Kanye West, 'Roses', *Youtube*, October 29, 2018, available at: https://www.youtube.com/watch?v=Qxlnb1lEdEs&list=OLAK5uy_mS2sPIJinRK2fIXN9Ce756lZFRX2KT21o&index=9, last accessed: February 25, 2020; Lyrics: Kanye West, 'Roses', *Genius*, available at: https://genius.com/Kanye-west-roses-lyrics, last accessed: February 25, 2020.

[120] Audio: Bill Withers, 'Rosie', *Youtube*, March 22, 2013, available at: https://www.youtube.com/watch?v=TLdRoeO2OQ4, last accessed: February 25, 2020. Lyrics: Bill Withers, 'Rosie', *Genius*, available at: https://genius.com/Bill-withers-rosie-lyrics, last accessed: February 25, 2020.

[121] Audio: Kanye West, 'Addiction', *Youtube*, October 29, 2018, available at: https://www.youtube.com/watch?v=YuCwP-NbY0s&list=OLAK5uy_mS2sPIJinRK2fIXN9Ce756lZFRX2KT21o&index=11, last accessed: February 25, 2020; Lyrics: Kanye West, 'Addiction', *Genius*, available at: https://genius.com/Kanye-west-addiction-lyrics, last accessed: February 25, 2020.

[122] Audio: Etta James, 'My Funny Valentine', *Youtube*, June 20, 2008, available at: https://www.youtube.com/watch?v=Bt7eqkPXO8A, last accessed: February 25, 2020. Lyrics: Etta James, 'My Funny Valentine', *Genius*, available at: https://genius.com/Etta-james-my-funny-valentine-lyrics, last accessed: February 25, 2020.

[123] Audio: Kanye West, 'Diamonds From Sierra Leone', June 16, 2009, *Youtube*, available at: https://www.youtube.com/watch?v=92FCRmggNqQ&list=OLAK5uy_mS2sPIJinRK2fIXN9Ce756lZFRX2KT21o&index=20, last accessed: February 25, 2020; Lyrics: Kanye West, 'Diamonds From Sierra Leone', *Genius*, available at: https://genius.com/Kanye-west-diamonds-from-sierra-leone-lyrics, last accessed: February 25, 2020.

[124] Audio: Shirley Bassey, 'Diamonds Are Forever', *Youtube*, November 4, 2010, available at: https://www.youtube.com/watch?v=QFSAWiTJsjc, last accessed: February 25, 2020. Lyrics: Shirley Bassey, 'Diamonds Are Forever', *Genius*, available at: https://genius.com/Shirley-bassey-diamonds-are-forever-lyrics, last accessed: February 25, 2020.

[125] Audio: Kanye West, 'We Major', *Youtube*, October 29, 2018, available at: https://www.youtube.com/watch?v=_fr4SV4fGAw&list=OLAK5uy_mS2sPIJinRK2fIXN9Ce756lZFRX2KT21o&index=14, last accessed: February 25, 2020; Lyrics: Kanye West, 'We Major', *Genius*, available at: https://genius.com/Kanye-west-we-major-lyrics, last accessed: February 25, 2020.

[126] Audio: Orange Krush, 'Action', *Youtube*, May 26, 2011, available at: https://www.youtube.com/watch?v=fGyTxXfV4FQ, last accessed: February 25, 2020.

[127] Audio: Kanye West, 'Hey Mama', *Youtube*, October 29, 2018, available at: https://www.youtube.com/watch?v=B3NmMKfl3Ic&list=OLAK5uy_mS2sPIJinRK2fIXN9Ce756lZFRX2KT21o&index=16, last accessed: February 25, 2020; Lyrics: Kanye West, 'Hey Mama', *Genius*, available at: https://genius.com/Kanye-west-hey-mama-lyrics, last accessed: February 25, 2020.

[128] Audio: Donal Leace, 'Today Won't Come Again', *Youtube*, March 22, 2013, available at: https://www.youtube.com/watch?v=4PJ1YyCGg4k, last accessed: February 25, 2020. Lyrics: Donal Leace, 'Today Won't Come Again', *Musixmatch*, available at: https://www.musixmatch.com/lyrics/Donal-Leace/Today-Won-t-Come-Again, last accessed: February 25, 2020.

[129] Audio: Kanye West, 'Celebration', *Youtube*, October 29, 2018, available at: https://www.youtube.com/watch?v=FZjlP-N7Hl4&list=OLAK5uy_mS2sPIJinRK2fIXN9Ce756lZFRX2KT21o&index=17, last accessed: February 25, 2020; Lyrics: Kanye West, 'Celebration', *Genius*, available at: https://genius.com/Kanye-west-celebration-lyrics, last accessed: February 25, 2020.

[130] Audio: The Kay-Gees, 'Heavenly Dream', *Youtube*, September 18, 2008, available at: https://www.youtube.com/watch?v=oecXXqAPyQ0, last accessed: February 25, 2020. Lyrics: The Kay-Gees, 'Heavenly Dream', *Genius*, available at: https://genius.com/The-kay-gees-heavenly-dream-lyrics, last accessed: February 25, 2020.

	13. 'Gone'[131] contains samples of 'It's Too Late'[132] as performed by Otis Redding. 14. 'Late'[133] contains samples of 'I'll Erase Away Your Pain'[134] by The Whatnauts.
	1. 'Good Morning'[135] contains samples from 'Someone Saved My Life Tonight'[136] performed by Elton John. 2. 'Champion'[137] contains elements of 'Kid Charlemagne'[138] performed by Steely Dan. 3. 'Stronger'[139] contains a sample of 'Harder, Better, Faster, Stronger'[140] performed by Daft Punk and master use of 'Cola Bottle Baby'[141] performed by Edwin Birdsong. 4. 'I Wonder'[142] contains a sample from 'My Song'[143] performed by Labi Siffre.

---

[131] Audio: Kanye West, 'Gone', *Youtube*, October 29, 2018, available at: https://www.youtube.com/watch?v=TwPCaWQIJME&list=OLAK5uy_mS2sPIJinRK2fIXN9Ce756lZFRX2KT21o&index=19, last accessed: February 25, 2020; Lyrics: Kanye West, 'Gone', *Genius*, available at: https://genius.com/Kanye-west-gone-lyrics, last accessed: February 25, 2020.

[132] Audio: Otis Redding, 'It's Too Late', *Youtube*, November 16, 2009, available at: https://www.youtube.com/watch?v=5bbv8PYQD-0, last accessed: February 25, 2020. Lyrics: Otis Redding, 'It's Too Late', *Genius*, available at: https://genius.com/Otis-redding-its-too-late-lyrics, last accessed: February 25, 2020.

[133] Audio: Kanye West, 'Late', *Youtube*, October 29, 2018, available at: https://www.youtube.com/watch?v=YRwTaWWK3dI&list=OLAK5uy_mS2sPIJinRK2fIXN9Ce756lZFRX2KT21o&index=21, last accessed: February 25, 2020; Lyrics: Kanye West, 'Late', *Genius*, available at: https://genius.com/Kanye-west-late-lyrics, last accessed: February 25, 2020.

[134] Audio: The Whatnauts, 'I'll Erase Away Your Pain', *Youtube*, September 8, 2007, available at: https://www.youtube.com/watch?v=euSVtelwD_Q, last accessed: February 25, 2020. Lyrics: The Whatnauts, 'I'll Erase Away Your Pain', *Genius*, available at: https://genius.com/Whatnauts-ill-erase-away-your-pain-lyrics, last accessed: February 25, 2020.

[135] Audio: Kanye West, 'Good Morning', *Youtube*, December 13, 2009, available at: https://www.youtube.com/watch?v=6CHs4x2uqcQ&list=OLAK5uy_kVXQTEtfSWtL_gP_czGRaKH1KyfraNW80, last accessed: February 25, 2020; Lyrics: Kanye West, 'Good Morning', *Genius*, available at: https://genius.com/Kanye-west-good-morning-lyrics, last accessed: February 25, 2020.

[136] Audio: Elton John, 'Someone Saved My Life Tonight', *Youtube*, February 17, 2009, available at: https://www.youtube.com/watch?v=Sw2Lptf7K0E, last accessed: February 25, 2020. Lyrics: Elton John, 'Someone Saved My Life Tonight', *Genius*, available at: https://genius.com/Elton-john-someone-saved-my-life-tonight-lyrics, last accessed: February 25, 2020.

[137] Audio: Kanye West, 'Champion', *Youtube*, February 7, 2019, available at: https://www.youtube.com/watch?v=L1SEEMkc-qw&list=OLAK5uy_kVXQTEtfSWtL_gP_czGRaKH1KyfraNW80&index=2, last accessed: February 25, 2020; Lyrics: Kanye West, 'Champion', *Genius*, available at: https://genius.com/Kanye-west-champion-lyrics, last accessed: February 25, 2020.

[138] Audio: Steely Dan, 'Kid Charlemagne', *Youtube*, January 19, 2016, available at: https://www.youtube.com/watch?v=jJ9Xk-VoGqo, last accessed: February 25, 2020. Lyrics: Steely Dan, 'Kid Charlemagne', *Genius*, available at: https://genius.com/Steely-dan-kid-charlemagne-lyrics, last accessed: February 25, 2020.

[139] Audio: Kanye West, 'Stronger', *Youtube*, June 16, 2009, available at: https://www.youtube.com/watch?v=PsO6ZnUZI0g&list=OLAK5uy_kVXQTEtfSWtL_gP_czGRaKH1KyfraNW80&index=3, last accessed: February 25, 2020; Lyrics: Kanye West, 'Stronger', *Genius*, available at: https://genius.com/Kanye-west-stronger-lyrics, last accessed: February 25, 2020.

[140] Audio: Daft Punk, 'Harder, Better, Faster, Stronger', *Youtube*, February 26, 2009, available at: https://www.youtube.com/watch?v=gAjR4_CbPpQ, last accessed: February 25, 2020. Lyrics: Daft Punk, 'Harder, Better, Faster, Stronger', *Genius*, available at: https://genius.com/Daft-punk-harder-better-faster-stronger-lyrics, last accessed: February 25, 2020.

[141] Audio: Edwin Birdsong, 'Cola Bottle', *Youtube*, February 7, 2009, available at: https://www.youtube.com/watch?v=Z3AKrwna2C8, last accessed: February 25, 2020. Lyrics: Edwin Birdsong, 'Cola Bottle', *Genius*, available at: https://genius.com/Edwin-birdsong-cola-bottle-baby-lyrics, last accessed: February 25, 2020.

[142] Audio: Kanye West, 'I Wonder', *Youtube*, February 7, 2019, available at: https://www.youtube.com/watch?v=z15wKo0r-74&list=OLAK5uy_kVXQTEtfSWtL_gP_czGRaKH1KyfraNW80&index=4, last accessed: February 25, 2020; Lyrics: Kanye West, 'I Wonder', *Genius*, available at: https://genius.com/Kanye-west-i-wonder-lyrics, last accessed: February 25, 2020.

[143] Audio: Labi Siffre, 'My Song', *Youtube*, August 7, 2015, available at: https://www.youtube.com/watch?v=aBhBG5lqpzM, last accessed: February 25, 2020. Lyrics: Labi Siffre, 'My Song', *Genius*, available at: https://genius.com/Labi-siffre-my-song-lyrics, last accessed: February 25, 2020.

Graduation (2007)	5. 'Good Life'[144] contains a sample of 'P.Y.T. (Pretty Young Thing)'[145] performed by Michael Jackson. 6. 'Barry Bonds'[146] contains a sample of 'Long Red'[147] performed by Mountain. 7. 'Drunk and Hot Girls'[148] contains elements of 'Sing Swan Song'[149] performed by Can. 8. 'Everything I Am'[150] contains elements of 'If We Can't Be Lovers'[151] performed by Prince Phillip Mitchell, and 'Bring the Noise'[152] performed by Public Enemy. 9. 'The Glory'[153] contains elements of 'Save the Country'[154] performed by Laura Nyro and contains a sample of 'Long Red'[155] performed by Mountain.

---

[144] Audio: Kanye West, 'Good Life', *Youtube*, June 16, 2009, available at: https://www.youtube.com/watch?v=FEKEjpTzB0Q&list=OLAK5uy_kVXQTEtfSWtL_gP_czGRaKH1KyfraNW80&index=5, last accessed: February 25, 2020; Lyrics: Kanye West, 'Good Life', *Genius*, available at: https://genius.com/Kanye-west-good-life-lyrics, last accessed: February 25, 2020.

[145] Audio: Michael Jackson, 'P.Y.T. (Pretty Young Thing)', *Youtube*, February 20, 2017, available at: https://www.youtube.com/watch?v=1ZZQuj6htF4, last accessed: February 25, 2020. Lyrics: Michael Jackson, 'P.Y.T. (Pretty Young Thing)', *Genius*, available at: https://genius.com/Michael-jackson-pyt-pretty-young-thing-lyrics, last accessed: February 25, 2020.

[146] Audio: Kanye West, 'Barry Bonds', *Youtube*, February 7, 2019, available at: https://www.youtube.com/watch?v=6QARCF_dvWo&list=OLAK5uy_kVXQTEtfSWtL_gP_czGRaKH1KyfraNW80&index=7, last accessed: February 25, 2020; Lyrics: Kanye West, 'Barry Bonds', *Genius*, available at: https://genius.com/Kanye-west-barry-bonds-lyrics, last accessed: February 25, 2020.

[147] Audio: Mountain, 'Long Red', *Youtube*, May 21, 2015, available at: https://www.youtube.com/watch?v=a-0selX930s, last accessed: February 25, 2020. Lyrics: Mountain, 'Long Red', *Genius*, available at: https://genius.com/Mountain-long-red-lyrics, last accessed: February 25, 2020.

[148] Audio: Kanye West, 'Drunk and Hot Girls', *Youtube*, February 7, 2019, available at: https://www.youtube.com/watch?v=4UvPblbLFAc&list=OLAK5uy_kVXQTEtfSWtL_gP_czGRaKH1KyfraNW80&index=8, last accessed: February 25, 2020; Lyrics: Kanye West, 'Drunk and Hot Girls', *Genius*, available at: https://genius.com/Kanye-west-drunk-and-hot-girls-lyrics, last accessed: February 25, 2020.

[149] Audio: Can, 'Sing Swan Song', *Youtube*, March 23, 2008, available at: https://www.youtube.com/watch?v=3VmM8qRRLwU, last accessed: February 25, 2020. Lyrics: Can, 'Sing Swan Song', *Genius*, available at: https://genius.com/Can-sing-swan-song-lyrics, last accessed: February 25, 2020.

[150] Audio: Kanye West, 'Everything I am', *Youtube*, February 7, 2019, available at: https://www.youtube.com/watch?v=1ey-fHASEuQ&list=OLAK5uy_kVXQTEtfSWtL_gP_czGRaKH1KyfraNW80&index=10, last accessed: February 25, 2020; Lyrics: Kanye West, 'Everything I am', *Genius*, available at: https://genius.com/Kanye-west-everything-i-am-lyrics, last accessed: February 25, 2020.

[151] Audio: Prince Phillip Mitchell, 'If We Can't Be Lovers', *Youtube*, June 11, 2012, available at: https://www.youtube.com/watch?v=0StV8XtoO34, last accessed: February 25, 2020. Lyrics: Prince Phillip Mitchell, 'If We Can't Be Lovers', *Cifras*, available at: https://www.cifras.com.br/cifra/prince-phillip-mitchell/if-we-cant-be-lovers, last accessed: February 25, 2020.

[152] Audio: Public Enemy, ,Bring The Noise', *Youtube*, July 19, 2010 available at: https://www.youtube.com/watch?v=l_Jeyif7bB4, last accessed: February 25, 2020; Lyrics: Public Enemy, ,Bring The Noise', *Genius*, available at: https://genius.com/Public-enemy-bring-the-noise-lyrics, last accessed: February 25, 2020.

[153] Audio: Kanye West, 'The Glory', *Youtube*, February 7, 2019, available at: https://www.youtube.com/watch?v=gfj5FYaCxlA&list=OLAK5uy_kVXQTEtfSWtL_gP_czGRaKH1KyfraNW80&index=11, last accessed: February 25, 2020; Lyrics: Kanye West, 'The Glory', *Genius*, available at: https://genius.com/Kanye-west-the-glory-lyrics, last accessed: February 25, 2020.

[154] Audio: Laura Nyro, 'Save The Country', *Youtube*, May 4, 2008, available at: https://www.youtube.com/watch?v=E21KH_YOk7Y, last accessed: February 25, 2020. Lyrics: Laura Nyro, 'Save The Country', *Genius*, available at: https://genius.com/Laura-nyro-save-the-country-single-version-lyrics, last accessed: February 25, 2020.

[155] Audio: Mountain, 'Long Red', *Youtube*, May 21, 2015, available at: https://www.youtube.com/watch?v=a-0selX930s, last accessed: . Lyrics: Mountain, 'Long Red', *Genius*, available at: https://genius.com/Mountain-long-red-lyrics, last accessed: .

	10. 'Big Brother'[156] contains elements of 'It's Gonna Be Lonely'[157] performed by Prince and an interpolation of 'Hola Hovito'[158] from Jay Z, The Blueprint album. 11. 'Good Night'[159] contains elements of 'Nuff Man a Dead'[160] performed by Super Cat and 'Wake The Town'[161] performed by U-Roy. 12. 'Bittersweet Poetry'[162] interpolates 'Bittersweet'[163] performed by Chairmen of the Board.
88s & Heartbreak (2008)	1. 'RoboCop'[164] embodies portions of 'Kissing in the Rain'[165], written by Patrick Doyle. 2. 'Bad News'[166] contains a sample of the recording 'See Line Woman'[167] as performed by Nina Simone and written by George Bass

---

[156] Audio: Kanye West, 'Big Brother', *Youtube*, February 7, 2019, available at: https://www.youtube.com/watch?v=gfqmlkXjVJk, last accessed: February 25, 2020; Lyrics: Kanye West, 'Big Brother', *Genius*, available at: https://genius.com/Kanye-west-big-brother-lyrics, last accessed: February 25, 2020.

[157] Audio: Prince, 'It's Gonna Be Lonely', *Youtube*, November 7, 2014, available at: https://www.youtube.com/watch?v=csGzQep_DQc, last accessed: February 25, 2020. Lyrics: Prince, 'It's Gonna Be Lonely', *Genius*, available at: https://genius.com/Prince-its-gonna-be-lonely-lyrics, last accessed: February 25, 2020.

[158] Audio: Jay Z, 'Hola Hovito', *Youtube*, August 17, 2019, available at: https://www.youtube.com/watch?v=WNImnZ92CsM, last accessed: February 25, 2020. Lyrics: Jay Z, 'Hola Hovito', *Genius*, available at: https://genius.com/Jay-z-hola-hovito-lyrics, last accessed: February 25, 2020.

[159] Audio: Kanye West, 'Good Night', *Youtube*, July 20, 2018, available at: https://www.youtube.com/watch?v=cGkyVEpuR3o, last accessed: February 25, 2020; Lyrics: Kanye West, 'Good Night', *Genius*, available at: https://genius.com/Kanye-west-good-night-lyrics, last accessed: February 25, 2020.

[160] Audio: Super Cat, 'Nuff Man A Dead', *Youtube*, January 18, 2009, available at: https://www.youtube.com/watch?v=j7QWJXXqiOc, last accessed: February 25, 2020. Lyrics: Super Cat, 'Nuff Man A Dead', *Genius*, available at: https://genius.com/Super-cat-nuff-man-a-dead-lyrics, last accessed: February 25, 2020.

[161] Audio: U-Roy, 'Wake The Town', *Youtube*, January 23, 2020, available at: https://www.youtube.com/watch?v=w7BdFEccQ-0, last accessed: February 25, 2020. Lyrics: U-Roy, 'Wake The Town', *Genius*, available at: https://genius.com/U-roy-wake-the-town-lyrics, last accessed: February 25, 2020.

[162] Audio: Kanye West, 'Bittersweet Poetry', *Youtube*, September 21, 2007, available at: https://www.youtube.com/watch?v=35c8IW0vsSE, last accessed: February 25, 2020; Lyrics: Kanye West, 'Bittersweet Poetry', *Genius*, available at: https://genius.com/Kanye-west-bittersweet-poetry-lyrics, last accessed: February 25, 2020.

[163] Audio: Chairmen Of The Board, 'Bittersweet', *Youtube*, November 2, 2008, available at: https://www.youtube.com/watch?v=cta48KVs4bA, last accessed: February 25, 2020. Lyrics: Chairmen Of The Board, 'Bittersweet', *Genius*, available at: https://genius.com/Chairmen-of-the-board-bittersweet-lyrics, last accessed: February 25, 2020.

[164] Audio: Kanye West, 'RoboCop', *Youtube*, January 29, 2019, available at: https://www.youtube.com/watch?v=3aQQDh6N_zg&list=OLAK5uy_lxlAkj0irzRmBAbhZz3JJZRph6Crb3bCY&index=7, last accessed: February 25, 2020; Lyrics: Kanye West, 'RoboCop', *Genius*, available at: https://genius.com/Kanye-west-robocop-lyrics, last accessed: February 25, 2020.

[165] Audio: Patrick Doyle, 'Kissing The Rain', *Youtube*, July 5, 2010, available at: https://www.youtube.com/watch?v=y4fcqHVkxqE, last accessed: February 25, 2020.

[166] Audio: Kanye West, 'Bad News', *Youtube*, January 31, 2019, available at: https://www.youtube.com/watch?v=ZBeXHnxu5PA&list=OLAK5uy_lxlAkj0irzRmBAbhZz3JJZRph6Crb3bCY&index=9, last accessed: February 25, 2020; Lyrics: Kanye West, 'Bad News', *Genius*, available at: https://genius.com/Kanye-west-bad-news-lyrics, last accessed: February 25, 2020.

[167] Audio: Nina Simone, 'See Line Woman', *Youtube*, February 6, 2015, available at: https://www.youtube.com/watch?v=hVEbzdN_7n0, last accessed: February 25, 2020. Lyrics: Nina Simone, 'See Line Woman', *Genius*, available at: https://genius.com/Nina-simone-see-line-woman-lyrics, last accessed: February 25, 2020.

	3. 'Coldest Winter'[168] embodies an interpolation of 'Memories Fade'[169], written by Roland Orzabal.
My Beautiful Dark Twisted Fantasy (2010)	1. 'Dark Fantasy'[170] contains samples of 'In High Places'[171], written by Mike Oldfield and Jon Anderson, and performed by Anderson. 2. 'Gorgeous'[172] contains portions and elements of the composition 'You Showed Me'[173], written by Gene Clark and Roger McGuinn, and performed by The Turtles. 3. 'Power'[174] contains elements from 'It's Your Thing'[175], performed by Cold Grits; elements of '4. Afromerica'[176], written by Francois Bernheim, Jean-Pierre Lang, and Boris Bergman, and performed by Continent Number 6; and material sampled from '21st Century Schizoid Man'[177], composed by Robert Fripp, Michael Giles, Greg Lake, Ian McDonald, and Peter Sinfield, and performed by King Crimson. 4. 'So Appalled'[178] contains samples of 'You Are – I Am'[179], written by Manfred Mann, and performed by Manfred Mann's Earth Band.

[168] Audio: Kanye West, 'Coldest Winter', *Youtube*, February 11, 2010, available at: https://www.youtube.com/watch?v=n6rjQ9VVLDI&list=OLAK5uy_lxIAkj0irzRmBAbhZz3JJZRph6Crb3bCY&index=11, last accessed: February 25, 2020; Lyrics: Kanye West, 'Coldest Winter', *Genius*, available at: https://genius.com/Kanye-west-coldest-winter-lyrics, last accessed: February 25, 2020.

[169] Audio: Orzabal, 'Memories Fade', *Youtube*, July 31, 2018, (the song was performed by Tears for Fears), available at: https://www.youtube.com/watch?v=iuQSBr-YQYY, last accessed: February 25, 2020. Lyrics: Orzabal, 'Memories Fade', *Genius*, available at: https://genius.com/Tears-for-fears-memories-fade-lyrics, last accessed: February 25, 2020.

[170] Audio: Kanye West, 'Dark Fantasy', *Youtube*, July 12, 2011, available at: https://www.youtube.com/watch?v=PeFGaXCYktg&list=OLAK5uy_mRFuqe0IIrexXkU7JOxo4rOb0WLEcwuz8, last accessed: February 25, 2020; Lyrics: Kanye West, 'Dark Fantasy', *Genius*, available at: https://genius.com/Kanye-west-dark-fantasy-lyrics, last accessed: February 25, 2020.

[171] Audio: Mike Oldfield, 'In High Places', *Youtube*, available at: https://www.youtube.com/watch?v=AofUt0TQyf0, last accessed: February 25, 2020. Lyrics: Mike Oldfield, 'In High Places', *Genius*, available at: https://genius.com/Mike-oldfield-in-high-places-lyrics, last accessed: February 25, 2020.

[172] Audio: Kanye West, 'Gorgeous', *Youtube*, July 23, 2018, available at: https://www.youtube.com/watch?v=miJAfs7jhak&list=OLAK5uy_mRFuqe0IIrexXkU7JOxo4rOb0WLEcwuz8&index=2, last accessed: February 25, 2020; Lyrics: Kanye West, 'Gorgeous', *Genius*, available at: https://genius.com/Kanye-west-gorgeous-lyrics, last accessed: February 25, 2020.

[173] Audio: The Turtles, 'You Showed Me', *Youtube*, August 18, 2010, available at: https://www.youtube.com/watch?v=Ul3K_e-ZgiE, last accessed: February 25, 2020. Lyrics: The Turtles, 'You Showed Me', *Genius*, available at: https://genius.com/The-turtles-you-showed-me-lyrics, last accessed: February 25, 2020.

[174] Audio: Kanye West, 'Power', *Youtube*, August 5, 2010, available at: https://www.youtube.com/watch?v=L53gjP-TtGE&list=OLAK5uy_mRFuqe0IIrexXkU7JOxo4rOb0WLEcwuz8&index=3, last accessed: February 25, 2020; Lyrics: Kanye West, 'Power', *Genius*, available at: https://genius.com/Kanye-west-power-lyrics, last accessed: February 25, 2020.

[175] Audio: Cold Grits, 'It's Your Thing', *Youtube*, July 2, 2011, available at: https://www.youtube.com/watch?v=cozD75RcSRM, last accessed: February 25, 2020. Lyrics: Cold Grits, 'It's Your Thing', *Genius*, available at: https://genius.com/Cold-grits-its-your-thing-lyrics, last accessed: February 25, 2020.

[176] Audio: Continent Number 6, 'Afromerica', *Youtube*, November 25, 2008, available at: https://www.youtube.com/watch?v=e-dtwySzcQc, last accessed: February 25, 2020.

[177] Audio: King Crimson', 21st Century Schizoid Man', *Youtube*, December 7, 2019, available at: https://www.youtube.com/watch?v=t7n7KvWiCME, last accessed: February 25, 2020. Lyrics: King Crimson', 21st Century Schizoid Man', *Genius*, available at: https://genius.com/King-crimson-21st-century-schizoid-man-lyrics, last accessed: February 25, 2020.

[178] Audio: Kanye West, 'So Appalled', *Youtube*, July 23, 2018, available at: https://www.youtube.com/watch?v=0o9HzQ3zAcE&list=OLAK5uy_mRFuqe0IIrexXkU7JOxo4rOb0WLEcwuz8&index=7, last accessed: February 25, 2020; Lyrics: Kanye West, 'So Appalled', *Genius*, available at: https://genius.com/Kanye-west-so-appalled-lyrics, last accessed: February 25, 2020.

[179] Audio: Manfred Mann's Earth Band, 'You Are – I am', *Youtube*, April 8, 2010, available at: https://www.youtube.com/watch?v=cYJ0iLHeyNM, last accessed: February 25, 2020. Lyrics: Manfred Mann's Earth Band, 'You Are – I am', *Genius*, available at: https://genius.com/Manfred-manns-earth-band-you-are-i-am-lyrics, last accessed: February 25, 2020.

<table>
<tr>
<td></td>
<td>

5. 'Devil in a New Dress'[180] contains samples of 'Will You Love Me Tomorrow'[181], written by Carole King and Gerry Goffin, and performed by Smokey Robinson.

6. 'Runaway'[182] contains a sample of 'Expo 83'[183], written by J. Branch, and performed by Backyard Heavies; and excerpts from Rick James Live at Long Beach, CA, 1981.[184]

7. 'Hell of a Life'[185] contains samples of 'She's My Baby'[186], written by Sylvester Stewart, and performed by The Mojo Men; samples of 'Stud-Spider'[187] by Tony Joe White; and portions of 'Iron Man'[188], written by Terence Butler, Anthony Iommi, John Osbourne, and William Ward, and performed by Black Sabbath.

8. 'Blame Game'[189] contains elements of 'Avril 14th'[190], written by Richard James, and performed by Aphex Twin.

</td>
</tr>
</table>

[180] Audio: Kanye West, 'Devil In A New Dress', *Youtube*, July 23, 2018, available at: https://www.youtube.com/watch?v=sk3rpYkiHe8&list=OLAK5uy_mRFuqe0IIrexXkU7JOxo4rOb0WLEcwuz8&index=8, last accessed: February 25, 2020; Lyrics: Kanye West, 'Devil In A New Dress', *Genius*, available at: https://genius.com/Kanye-west-devil-in-a-new-dress-lyrics, last accessed: February 25, 2020.

[181] Audio: Smokey Robinson, 'Will You Love me Tomorrow', *Youtube*, July 31, 2018, available at: https://www.youtube.com/watch?v=p8VDWxLj5Wk, last accessed: February 25, 2020. Lyrics: Smokey Robinson, 'Will You Love me Tomorrow', *Genius*, available at: https://genius.com/Smokey-robinson-will-you-love-me-tomorrow-lyrics, last accessed: February 25, 2020.

[182] Audio: Kanye West, 'Runaway', *Youtube*, October 21, 20110, available at: https://www.youtube.com/watch?v=Bm5iA4Zupek&list=OLAK5uy_mRFuqe0IIrexXkU7JOxo4rOb0WLEcwuz8&index=9, last accessed: February 25, 2020; Lyrics: Kanye West, 'Runaway', *Genius*, available at: https://genius.com/Kanye-west-runaway-lyrics, last accessed: February 25, 2020.

[183] Audio: Backyard Heavies, 'Expo 83', *Youtube*, November 15, 2010, available at: https://www.youtube.com/watch?v=EjQ70gCx0H4, last accessed: February 25, 2020.

[184] Audio: Ricky James Live at Long Beach, CA, 1981, *Youtube*, May 27, 2011, available at: https://www.youtube.com/watch?v=Vp_Rxsat3FA&list=PLXMaLu7UP_qjn184yjcy9GmEG-J8IKmUx, last accessed: February 25, 2020.

[185] Audio: Kanye West, 'Hell Of A Life', *Youtube*, July 23, 2018, available at: https://www.youtube.com/watch?v=tJKNcI6jC6A&list=OLAK5uy_mRFuqe0IIrexXkU7JOxo4rOb0WLEcwuz8&index=10, last accessed: February 25, 2020; Lyrics: Kanye West, 'Hell Of A Life', *Genius*, available at: https://genius.com/Kanye-west-hell-of-a-life-lyrics, last accessed: February 25, 2020.

[186] Audio: The Mojo Men, 'She's My Baby', *Youtube*, October 8, 2011, available at: https://www.youtube.com/watch?v=KgLeOkSm56E, last accessed: February 25, 2020. Lyrics: The Mojo Men, 'She's My Baby', *Genius*, available at: https://genius.com/The-mojo-men-shes-my-baby-lyrics, last accessed: February 25, 2020.

[187] Audio: Tony Joe White, 'Stud-Spider', *Youtube*, February 10, 2010, available at: https://www.youtube.com/watch?v=6rkXth6pTr0, last accessed: February 25, 2020. Lyrics: Tony Joe White, 'Stud-Spider', *Genius*, available at: https://genius.com/Tony-joe-white-stud-spider-lyrics, last accessed: February 25, 2020.

[188] Audio: Black Sabbath, 'Iron Man', *Youtube*, August 14, 2012, available at: https://www.youtube.com/watch?v=8aQRq9hhekA, last accessed: February 25, 2020. Lyrics: Black Sabbath, 'Iron Man', *Genius*, available at: https://genius.com/Black-sabbath-iron-man-lyrics, last accessed: February 25, 2020.

[189] Audio: Kanye West, 'Blame Game', *Youtube*, July 23, 2018, available at: https://www.youtube.com/watch?v=6mp72xUirfs&list=OLAK5uy_mRFuqe0IIrexXkU7JOxo4rOb0WLEcwuz8&index=11, last accessed: February 25, 2020; Lyrics: Kanye West, 'Blame Game', *Genius*, available at: https://genius.com/Kanye-west-blame-game-lyrics, last accessed: February 25, 2020.

[190] Audio: Aphex Twin, 'Avril 14th', *Youtube*, May 7, 2015, available at: https://www.youtube.com/watch?v=F6dGAZTj8xA, last accessed: February 25, 2020. Lyrics: Aphex Twin, 'Avril 14th', *Genius*, available at: https://genius.com/Aphex-twin-avril-14th-lyrics, last accessed: February 25, 2020.

	9. 'Lost in the World'[191] contains portions of 'Soul Makossa'[192], written by Manu Dibango; a sample of 'Think (About It)'[193], written by James Brown, and performed by Lyn Collins; samples of 'Woods'[194], written by Justin Vernon, and performed by Bon Iver; and samples of 'Comment No. 1'[195], written and performed by Gil Scott-Heron. 10. 'Who Will Survive in America'[196] contains samples of 'Comment No. 1'[197] performed by Gil Scott-Heron.
Watch the Throne (2011)[198]	1. 'No Church in the Wild' contains samples from 'K-Scope', written and performed by Phil Manzanera; samples of 'Sunshine Help Me', written and performed by Spooky Tooth; and samples of 'Don't Tell a Lie About Me (and I Won't Tell the Truth About You)', written and performed by James Brown. 2. 'Niggas in Paris' contains samples of the Reverend W. A. Donaldson recording 'Baptizing Scene'; and dialogue between Will Ferrell and Jon Heder from the 2007 comedy film Blades of Glory. 3. 'Otis' contains samples of 'Try a Little Tenderness', written by [Jimmy Campbell and Reg Connelly, Harry M. Woods] and performed by Otis Redding; samples of 'Don't Tell a Lie About Me (and I Won't Tell the Truth About You)', written and performed by James Brown; and elements of 'Top Billin', written and performed by Audio Two. 4. 'Gotta Have It' contains elements of 'Don't Tell a Lie About Me (and I Won't Tell the Truth About You)'; samples of 'People Get Up and Drive Your Funky Soul'; and elements of 'My Thang', written and performed by James Brown. 5. 'New Day' contains samples of 'Feeling Good', written and performed by Nina Simone. 6. 'That's My Bitch' contains samples of 'Get Up, Get Into It, Get Involved', written and performed by James Brown; and samples of 'Apache', written and performed by Incredible Bongo Band. 7. 'Who Gon Stop Me' contains samples of 'I Can't Stop', written and performed by Flux Pavilion.

---

191 Audio: Kanye West, 'Lost In The World', *Youtube*, May 23, 2012, available at: https://www.youtube.com/watch?v=ofaRvNOV4SI&list=OLAK5uy_mRFuqe0IIrexXkU7JOxo4rOb0WLEcwuz8&index=12, last accessed: February 25, 2020; Lyrics: Kanye West, 'Lost In The World', *Genius*, available at: https://genius.com/Kanye-west-lost-in-the-world-lyrics, last accessed: February 25, 2020.

192 Audio: Manu Dibango, 'Soul Makossa', *Youtube*, December 31, 2015, available at: https://www.youtube.com/watch?v=o0CeFX6E2yI, last accessed: February 25, 2020. Lyrics: Manu Dibango, 'Soul Makossa', *Genius*, available at: https://genius.com/Manu-dibango-soul-makossa-lyrics, last accessed: February 25, 2020.

193 Audio: Lyn Collins, 'Think (About it)', *Youtube*, August 31, 2014, available at: https://www.youtube.com/watch?v=HKix_06L5AY, last accessed: February 25, 2020. Lyrics: Lyn Collins, 'Think (About it)', *Genius*, available at: https://genius.com/Lyn-collins-think-about-it-lyrics, last accessed: February 25, 2020.

194 Audio: Bon Iver, 'Woods', *Youtube*, October 8, 2010, available at: https://www.youtube.com/watch?v=1_cePGP6lbU, last accessed: February 25, 2020. Lyrics: Bon Iver, 'Woods', *Genius*, available at: https://genius.com/Bon-iver-woods-lyrics, last accessed: February 25, 2020.

195 Audio: Gil Scott-Heron, 'Comment No.1', *Youtube*, May 17, 2009, available at: https://www.youtube.com/watch?v=8B6DVdCzwy0, last accessed: . Lyrics: Gil Scott-Heron, 'Comment No.1', *Genius*, available at: https://genius.com/Gil-scott-heron-comment-1-annotated, last accessed: February 25, 2020.

196 Audio: Kanye West, 'Who Will Survive In America', *Youtube*, July 23, 2018, available at: https://www.youtube.com/watch?v=UB6sXiZ1ldw&list=OLAK5uy_mRFuqe0IIrexXkU7JOxo4rOb0WLEcwuz8&index=13, last accessed: February 25, 2020; Lyrics: Kanye West, 'Who Will Survive In America', *Genius*, available at: https://genius.com/Kanye-west-who-will-survive-in-america-lyrics, last accessed: February 25, 2020.

197 Audio: Gil Scott-Heron, 'Comment No.1', *Youtube*, May 17, 2009, available at: https://www.youtube.com/watch?v=8B6DVdCzwy0, last accessed: February 25, 2020. Lyrics: Gil Scott-Heron, 'Comment No.1', *Genius*, available at: https://genius.com/Gil-scott-heron-comment-1-annotated, last accessed: February 25, 2020.

198 The information for this album was retrieved from 'Watch the Throne', *Wikipedia*, available at: https://en.wikipedia.org/wiki/Watch_the_Throne, last accessed: February 25, 2020.

	8. 'Murder to Excellence' contains samples of 'LA LA LA', written and performed by The Indiggo Twins; and samples of 'Celie Shaves Mr./Scarification' from the 1985 drama film The Color Purple, written and performed by Quincy Jones. 9. 'Why I Love You' contains samples of 'I Love You So', written and performed by Cassius. 10. 'Primetime' contains samples of 'Action', written and performed by Orange Krush. 11. 'The Joy' contains samples of 'The Makings of You (Live)', written and performed by Curtis Mayfield; and elements of 'Different Strokes', written and performed by Syl Johnson. 12. Each interlude after the songs 'No Church in the Wild', 'New Day', and 'Welcome to the Jungle', as well as before 'Illest Motherfucker Alive' all contain samples of 'Tristessa', written and performed by Orchestra Njervudarov.
Cruel Summer (2012)[199]	1. 'Mercy' contains samples of the recording 'Dust a Sound Boy', written by Denzie Beagle and Winston Riley, and performed by Super Beagle; samples of the recording 'Cu-Oonuh', written by Reggie Williams and Winston Riley, and performed by Reggie Stepper; portions of the recording 'Lambo', performed by YB; and a sample of 'Tony's Theme', composed by Giorgio Moroder. 2. 'New God Flow' contains samples of the recording 'Synthetic Substitution', written by Herb Rooney, and performed by Melvin Bliss; samples of the recording 'Mighty Healthy', written by Herb Rooney, Ronald Bean, Highleigh Crizoe and Dennis Coles, and performed by Ghostface Killah; a sample of the Reverend G. I. Townsend recording 'Sermon Fragment', written and performed by Townsend; and samples from the recording 'Bôdas De Sangue', written and performed by Marcos Valle. 3. 'The Morning' contains portions of 'Get Me to the Church on Time', written and performed by Alan Jay Lerner and Frederick Loewe. 4. 'Cold' contains interpolations of 'Illegal Search', written by James T. Smith and Marlon L. Williams, and performed by LL Cool J; and 'Lookin' at Me' by Mase. 5. 'The One' contains samples of the recording 'Public Enemy No. 1', written by Carlton Ridenhour and James Boxley, and performed by Public Enemy; and samples of the recording 'Double Barrel', written by Dave Barker, Winston Riley, and Ansell George Collins, and performed by Dave and Ansell Collins. 6. 'Don't Like' contains elements of 'Under Mi Sensi', written and performed by Barrington Levy and Paul Love.
	1. 'On Sight'[200] contains an interpolation of 'Sermon (He'll Give Us What We Really Need)'[201], written by Keith Carter, Sr. 2. 'I Am a God'[202] contains samples of 'Forward Inna Dem Clothes'[203], written by Clifton Bailey III and H. Hart, performed by Capleton; and samples of 'Are Zindagi Hai Khel'[204],

---

[199] The information for this album was retrieved from 'Cruel Summer', *Wikipedia*, available at: https://en.wikipedia.org/wiki/Cruel_Summer_(GOOD_Music_album), last accessed: February 25, 2020.

[200] Audio: Kanye West, 'On Sight', *Youtube*, July 21, 2018, available at: https://www.youtube.com/watch?v=uU9Fe-WXew4&list=OLAK5uy_m6VFZd8KNhbFoHGRhtzFakGNVSkMMGvbU&index=1, last accessed: February 25, 2020; Lyrics: Kanye West, 'On Sight', *Genius*, available at: https://genius.com/Kanye-west-on-sight-lyrics, last accessed: February 25, 2020.

[201] Audio: Keith Carter, Sr., 'Sermon (He'll Give Us What We Really Need)', *Youtube*, September 7, 2013, available at: https://www.youtube.com/watch?v=vyf7f7ouzjk, last accessed: February 25, 2020.

[202] Audio: Kanye West, 'I am A God', *Youtube*, July 21, 2018, available at: https://www.youtube.com/watch?v=KuQoQgL63Xo&list=OLAK5uy_m6VFZd8KNhbFoHGRhtzFakGNVSkMMGvbU&index=3, last accessed: February 25, 2020; Lyrics: Kanye West, 'I am A God', *Genius*, available at: https://genius.com/Kanye-west-i-am-a-god-lyrics, last accessed: February 25, 2020.

[203] Audio: Capleton, 'Forward Inna Dem Clothes', *Youtube*, April 27, 2017, available at: https://www.youtube.com/watch?v=HNVY4pTj6pk, last accessed: February 25, 2020.

[204] I did not find a version that is directly linked with the title of the song.

	written by Anand Bakshi and Rahul Burman, performed by Burman, Manna Dey and Asha Bhosle.
	3. 'New Slaves'[205] contains samples of 'Gyöngyhajú lány'[206], written by Gábor Presser and Anna Adamis, performed by Omega.
	4. 'I'm In It'[207] contains samples of 'Lately'[208], written by Vidal Davis, Carvin Haggins, Andre Harris, Kenny Lattimore and Jill Scott, performed by Lattimore.
Yeezus (2013)	5. 'Blood on the Leaves'[209] contains a sample of 'Strange Fruit'[210], written by Lewis Allan, performed by Nina Simone; samples of 'R U Ready'[211], written by Ross Birchard and Lunice Pierre, performed by TNGHT.
	6. 'Guilt Trip'[212] contains interpolations of 'Chief Rocka'[213], written by Keith Elam, Kevin Hansford, Dupre Kelly, Christopher Martin, Alterick Wardrick and Marlon Williams, performed by Lords of the Underground; and a sample of 'Blocka (Ackeejuice Rockers Remix)'[214], written by Terrence Thornton and Tyree Pittman, performed by Pusha T featuring Travis Scott and Popcaan.

---

[205] Audio: Kanye West, 'New Slaves', *Youtube*, July 21, 2018, available at: https://www.youtube.com/watch?v=vQ0u09mFodw&list=OLAK5uy_m6VFZd8KNhbFoHGRhtzFakGNVSkMMGvbU&index=4, last accessed: February 25, 2020; Lyrics: Kanye West, 'New Slaves', *Genius*, available at: https://genius.com/Kanye-west-new-slaves-lyrics, last accessed: February 25, 2020.

[206] Audio: Omega, 'Gyöngyhajú lány', *Youtube*, April 12, 2007, available at: https://www.youtube.com/watch?v=CGt-rTDkMcM, last accessed: February 25, 2020. Lyrics: Omega, 'Gyöngyhajú lány', *Genius*, available at: https://genius.com/Omega-gyongyhaju-lany-lyrics, last accessed: February 25, 2020.

[207] Audio: Kanye West, 'I'am In It', *Youtube*, July 21, 2018, available at: https://www.youtube.com/watch?v=_jZuz3NEr18&list=OLAK5uy_m6VFZd8KNhbFoHGRhtzFakGNVSkMMGvbU&index=6, last accessed: February 25, 2020; Lyrics: Kanye West, 'I'am In It', *Genius*, available at: https://genius.com/Kanye-west-im-in-it-lyrics, last accessed: February 25, 2020.

[208] Audio: Lattimore, 'Lately', *Youtube*, November 8, 2014, available at: https://www.youtube.com/watch?v=mkJQzvrcBZM, last accessed: February 25, 2020. Lyrics: Lattimore, 'Lately', *Genius*, available at: https://genius.com/Kenny-lattimore-lately-lyrics, last accessed: February 25, 2020.

[209] Audio: Kanye West, 'Blood On The Leaves', *Youtube*, July 21, 2018, available at: https://www.youtube.com/watch?v=KEA0btSNkpw&list=OLAK5uy_m6VFZd8KNhbFoHGRhtzFakGNVSkMMGvbU&index=7, last accessed: February 25, 2020; Lyrics: Kanye West, 'Blood On The Leaves', *Genius*, available at: https://genius.com/Kanye-west-blood-on-the-leaves-lyrics, last accessed: February 25, 2020.

[210] Audio: Nina Simone, 'Strange Fruit', *Youtube*, July 7, 2009, available at: https://www.youtube.com/watch?v=BcCm_ySBslk, last accessed: February 25, 2020. Lyrics: Nina Simone, 'Strange Fruit', *Genius*, available at: https://genius.com/Nina-simone-strange-fruit-lyrics, last accessed: February 25, 2020.

[211] Audio: THGHT, 'R U Ready', *Youtube*, May 6, 2013, available at: https://www.youtube.com/watch?v=U_2gU4N9k3o, last accessed: February 25, 2020. Lyrics: THGHT, 'R U Ready', *Genius*, available at: https://genius.com/Tnght-r-u-ready-lyrics, last accessed: February 25, 2020.

[212] Audio: Kanye West, 'Guilt Trip', *Youtube*, July 21, 2018, available at: https://www.youtube.com/watch?v=5hthMeEqf40&list=OLAK5uy_m6VFZd8KNhbFoHGRhtzFakGNVSkMMGvbU&index=8, last accessed: February 25, 2020; Lyrics: Kanye West, 'Guilt Trip', *Genius*, available at: https://genius.com/Kanye-west-guilt-trip-lyrics, last accessed: February 25, 2020.

[213] Audio: Lords Of The Underground', 'Chief Rocka', *Youtube*, May 17, 2006, available at: https://www.youtube.com/watch?v=YFbLRZCExBk, last accessed: February 25, 2020. Lyrics: Lords Of The Underground', 'Chief Rocka', *Genius*, available at: https://genius.com/Lords-of-the-underground-chief-rocka-lyrics, last accessed: February 25, 2020.

[214] Audio: Pusha T, Travis Scott and Popcaan, 'Blocka (Ackeejuice Rockers Remix)', *Youtube*, May 30, 2013, available at: https://www.youtube.com/watch?v=OeNaX98bPE4, last accessed: February 25, 2020. Lyrics: Pusha T, Travis Scott and Popcaan, 'Blocka (Ackeejuice Rockers Remix)', *Genius*, available at: https://genius.com/Pusha-t-blocka-lyrics, last accessed: February 25, 2020.

	7. 'Send It Up'[215] contains a sample of 'Memories'[216], written by Anthony Moses Davis, Collin York and Lowell Dunbar, performed by Beenie Man. 8. 'Bound 2'[217] contains interpolations of 'Aeroplane (Reprise)'[218], written by Norman Whiteside, performed by Wee; samples of 'Bound'[219], written by Bobby Massey and Robert Dukes, performed by Ponderosa Twins Plus One; a sample of 'Sweet Nothin's'[220], written by Ronnie Self, performed by Brenda Lee.
	1. 'Ultralight Beam'[221] contains uncredited elements of the video game Counter-Strike.[222] 2. 'Father Stretch My Hands, Pt. 1'[223] contains samples of 'Father I Stretch My Hands'[224], written and performed by Pastor T. L. Barrett featuring Youth for Christ. 3. 'Pt. 2'[225] contains samples of the song 'Panda'[226], written by Sidney Selby III and Adnan Khan, and performed by Desiigner; samples of 'Father I Stretch My Hands'[227], written and

[215] Audio: Kanye West, 'Send It Up', *Youtube*, July 21, 2018, available at: https://www.youtube.com/watch?v=vUFiVwa6U_c&list=OLAK5uy_m6VFZd8KNhbFoHGRhtzFakGNVSkMMGvbU&index=9, last accessed: February 25, 2020; Lyrics: Kanye West, 'Send It Up', *Genius*, available at: https://genius.com/Kanye-west-send-it-up-lyrics, last accessed: February 25, 2020.

[216] Audio: Beenie Man, 'Memories', *Youtube*, April 17, 2013, available at: https://www.youtube.com/watch?v=-jkmmZZfK-I, last accessed: February 25, 2020. Lyrics: Beenie Man, 'Memories', *Genius*, available at: https://genius.com/Beenie-man-memories-lyrics, last accessed: February 25, 2020.

[217] Audio: Kanye West, 'Bound 2', *Youtube*, November 19, 2013, available at: https://www.youtube.com/watch?v=BBAtAM7vtgc&list=OLAK5uy_m6VFZd8KNhbFoHGRhtzFakGNVSkMMGvbU&index=10, last accessed: February 25, 2020; Lyrics: Kanye West, 'Bound 2', *Genius*, available at: https://genius.com/Kanye-west-bound-2-lyrics, last accessed: February 25, 2020.

[218] Audio: Wee, 'Aeroplane (Reprise)', *Youtube*, August 1, 2011, available at: https://www.youtube.com/watch?v=ncB65dETKlM, last accessed: February 25, 2020. Lyrics: Wee, 'Aeroplane (Reprise)', *Genius*, available at: https://genius.com/Wee-aeroplane-reprise-lyrics, last accessed: February 25, 2020.

[219] Audio: Ponderosa Twins Plus One, 'Bound', *Youtube*, August 28, 2013, available at: https://www.youtube.com/watch?v=d6mGHwHMB5s, last accessed: February 25, 2020. Lyrics: Ponderosa Twins Plus One, 'Bound', *Genius*, available at: https://genius.com/Ponderosa-twins-plus-one-bound-lyrics, last accessed: February 25, 2020.

[220] Audio: Brenda Lee, 'Sweet Nothin's', *Youtube*, March 8, 2008, available at: https://www.youtube.com/watch?v=KWgyum5fjJc, last accessed: February 25, 2020. Lyrics: Brenda Lee, 'Sweet Nothin's', *Genius*, available at: https://genius.com/Brenda-lee-sweet-nothins-lyrics, last accessed: February 25, 2020.

[221] Audio: Kanye West, 'Ultralight Beam', *Youtube*, August 24, 2018, available at: https://www.youtube.com/watch?v=6oHdAA3AqnE, last accessed: March 1, 2020. Lyrics: Kanye West, 'Ultralight Beam', *Genius*, available at: https://genius.com/Kanye-west-ultralight-beam-lyrics, last accessed: March 1, 2020.

[222] Audio: Flash Bang Ultralight Beam, *Youtube*, January 16, 2017, available at: https://www.youtube.com/watch?v=ozCsGQIM29o, last accessed: March 1, 2020

[223] Audio: Kanye West, 'Father Stretch My Hands, Pt. 1', *Youtube*, July 24, 2018, available at: https://www.youtube.com/watch?v=wuO4_P_8p-Q&list=OLAK5uy_keyJA-JsoAdfCylvyyIQMRjenzX6MzmnE&index=2, last accessed: February 25, 2020; Lyrics: Kanye West, 'Father Stretch My Hands, Pt. 1', *Genius*, available at: https://genius.com/Kanye-west-father-stretch-my-hands-pt-1-lyrics, last accessed: February 25, 2020.

[224] Audio: Pastor T.L., Youth For Christ, 'Father I Stretch My Hands', *Youtube*, July 31, 2013, available at: https://www.youtube.com/watch?v=lBYcOGkWEJY, last accessed: February 25, 2020. Lyrics: Pastor T.L., Youth For Christ, 'Father I Stretch My Hands', *Genius*, available at: https://genius.com/Pastor-tl-barrett-father-stretch-my-hands-lyrics, last accessed: February 25, 2020.

[225] Audio: Kanye West, 'Pt. 2', *Youtube*, July 24, 2018, available at: https://www.youtube.com/watch?v=xp8z7pconzw&list=OLAK5uy_keyJA-JsoAdfCylvyyIQMRjenzX6MzmnE&index=3, last accessed: February 25, 2020; Lyrics: Kanye West, 'Pt. 2', *Genius*, available at: https://genius.com/Kanye-west-pt-2-lyrics, last accessed: February 25, 2020.

[226] Audio: Desiigner, 'Panda', *Youtube*, March 6, 2006, available at: https://www.youtube.com/watch?v=4NJlUribp3c, last accessed: February 25, 2020. Lyrics: Desiigner, 'Panda', *Genius*, available at: https://genius.com/Desiigner-panda-lyrics, last accessed: February 25, 2020.

[227] Audio: Pastor T.L., Youth For Christ, 'Father I Stretch My Hands', *Youtube*, July 31, 2013, available at: https://www.youtube.com/watch?v=lBYcOGkWEJY, last accessed: February 25, 2020. Lyrics: Pastor T.L., Youth For Christ, 'Father I

	performed by Pastor T. L. Barrett featuring Youth for Christ; and contains elements of the video game Street Fighter II: The World Warrior. 4. 'Famous' [228]contains samples of 'Do What You Gotta Do'[229], written by Jimmy Webb and performed by Nina Simone; samples of 'Bam Bam'[230], written by Winston Riley and performed by Sister Nancy; and contains samples of 'Mi Sono Svegliato E… Ho Chiuso Gli Occhi'[231], written by Luis Bacalov, Sergio Bardotti, Giampiero Scalamogna, and Enzo Vita, and performed by Il Rovescio della Medaglia. 5. 'Feedback'[232] contains samples of 'Talagh'[233], written by Ardalan Sarfaraz and Manouchehr Cheshmazar, and performed by Googoosh. 6. 'Low Lights'[234] contains samples of 'So Alive (Acapella)'[235], written by Sandy Rivera and performed by Kings of Tomorrow 7. 'Freestyle 4'[236] contains samples of 'Human'[237], written by Alison Goldfrapp, William Gregory, Robert Locke, and Timothy Norfolk, and performed by Goldfrapp.
The Life of Pablo (2016)	

Stretch My Hands', *Genius,* available at: https://genius.com/Pastor-tl-barrett-father-stretch-my-hands-lyrics, last accessed: February 25, 2020.

[228] Audio: Kanye West, 'Famous', *Youtube*, July 24, 2018, available at: https://www.youtube.com/watch?v=Lq2TmRzg19k&list=OLAK5uy_keyJA-JsoAdfCylvyyIQMRjenzX6MzmnE&index=4, last accessed: February 25, 2020; Lyrics: Kanye West, 'Famous', *Genius*, available at: https://genius.com/Kanye-west-famous-lyrics, last accessed: February 25, 2020.

[229] Audio: Nina Simone, 'Do What You Gotta Do', *Youtube*, June 29, 2014, available at: https://www.youtube.com/watch?v=E4xde537g1A, last accessed: February 25, 2020. Lyrics: Nina Simone, 'Do What You Gotta Do', *Genius*, available at: https://genius.com/Nina-simone-do-what-you-gotta-do-lyrics, last accessed: February 25, 2020.

[230] Audio: Sister Nancy, 'Bam Bam', *Youtube*, September 23, 2008, available at: https://www.youtube.com/watch?v=OcaPu9JPenU, last accessed: February 25, 2020. Lyrics: Sister Nancy, 'Bam Bam', *Genius*, available at: https://genius.com/Sister-nancy-bam-bam-lyrics, last accessed: February 25, 2020.

[231] Audio: Il Rovescio della Medaglia, 'Mi Sono Svegliato E … Ho Chiuso Gli Occhi', *Youtube*, November 8, 2014, available at: https://www.youtube.com/watch?v=GrKyFS-22w8, last accessed: February 25, 2020. Lyrics: Il Rovescio della Medaglia, 'Mi Sono Svegliato E … Ho Chiuso Gli Occhi', *Genius,* available at: https://genius.com/Il-rovescio-della-medaglia-mi-sono-svegliato-e-ho-chiuso-gli-occhi-lyrics, last accessed: February 25, 2020.

[232] Audio: Kanye West, 'Feedback', *Youtube*, July 24, 2018, available at: https://www.youtube.com/watch?v=Q-fluWQ6zW8&list=OLAK5uy_keyJA-JsoAdfCylvyyIQMRjenzX6MzmnE&index=5, last accessed: February 25, 2020; Lyrics: Kanye West, 'Feedback', *Genius*, available at: https://genius.com/Kanye-west-feedback-lyrics, last accessed: February 25, 2020.

[233] Audio: Googoosh, 'Talagh', *Youtube*, July 16, 2011, available at: https://www.youtube.com/watch?v=DF2sGMjEVHo, last accessed: February 25, 2020. Lyrics: Googoosh, 'Talagh', *Genius*, available at: https://genius.com/Googoosh-talagh-lyrics, last accessed: February 25, 2020.

[234] Audio: Kanye West, 'Low Lights', *Youtube,* July 24, 2018, available at: https://www.youtube.com/watch?v=wj0C2oet2r0&list=OLAK5uy_keyJA-JsoAdfCylvyyIQMRjenzX6MzmnE&index=6, last accessed: February 25, 2020; Lyrics: Kanye West, 'Low Lights', *Genius*, available at: https://genius.com/Kanye-west-low-lights-lyrics, last accessed: February 25, 2020.

[235] Audio: King Of Tomorrow, 'So Alive', *Youtube*, June 28, 2013, available at: https://www.youtube.com/watch?v=X0YxSuWvatE, last accessed: February 25, 2020. Lyrics: King Of Tomorrow, 'So Alive', *Genius*, available at: https://genius.com/Kings-of-tomorrow-so-alive-lyrics, last accessed: February 25, 2020.

[236] Audio: Kanye West, 'Freestyle 4', *Youtube*, July 24, 2018, available at: https://www.youtube.com/watch?v=yt3rfHIijZQ&list=OLAK5uy_keyJA-JsoAdfCylvyyIQMRjenzX6MzmnE&index=8, last accessed: February 25, 2020; Lyrics: Kanye West, 'Freestyle 4', *Genius*, available at: https://genius.com/Kanye-west-freestyle-4-lyrics, last accessed: February 25, 2020.

[237] Audio: Goldfrapp, 'Human', *Youtube*, September 5, 2016, available at: https://www.youtube.com/watch?v=ZAYt7Jf4uPc, last accessed: February 25, 2020. Lyrics: Goldfrapp, 'Human', *Genius*, available at: https://genius.com/Goldfrapp-human-lyrics, last accessed: February 25, 2020.

	8. 'Waves'[238] contains samples and elements of 'Fantastic Freaks at the Dixie'[239], written by Fred Bratwaithe, Robin Diggs, Kevin Ferguson, Theodore Livingston, Darryl Mason, and James Whipper, and performed by Fantastic Freaks. 9. 'FML'[240] contains interpolations of 'Hit'[241], written by Lawrence Cassidy, Vincent Cassidy, and Paul Wiggin, and performed by Section 25. 10. 'Real Friends'[242] contains interpolations of 'Friends'[243], written by Jalil Hutchins and Lawrence Smith, and performed by Whodini. 11. 'Wolves'[244] contains samples of 'Walking Dub'[245], written and performed by Sugar Minott. 12. '30 Hours'[246] contains samples of 'Answers Me'[247], written and performed by Arthur Russell; interpolations of 'Hot in Herre'[248], written by Cornell Haynes, Pharrell Williams, and Charles Brown, and performed by Nelly; interpolations of 'EI'[249], written by Cornell

[238] Audio: Kanye West, 'Waves', *Youtube*, July 24, 2018, available at: https://www.youtube.com/watch?v=ML8Yq1Rd6I0&list=OLAK5uy_keyJA-JsoAdfCylvyyIQMRjenzX6MzmnE&index=10, last accessed: February 25, 2020; Lyrics: Kanye West, 'Waves', *Genius*, available at: https://genius.com/Kanye-west-waves-lyrics, last accessed: February 25, 2020.

[239] Audio: Fantastic Freaks, 'Fantastic Freaks At The Dixie', *Youtube*, May 25, 2012, available at: https://www.youtube.com/watch?v=94snQ9hXa7o, last accessed: February 25, 2020. Lyrics: Fantastic Freaks, 'Fantastic Freaks At The Dixie', *Genius*, available at: https://genius.com/Fantastic-freaks-fantastic-freaks-at-the-dixie-lyrics, last accessed: February 25, 2020.

[240] Audio: Kanye West, 'FML', *Youtube*, July 24, 2018, available at: https://www.youtube.com/watch?v=SHfB5HBFeTc&list=OLAK5uy_keyJA-JsoAdfCylvyyIQMRjenzX6MzmnE&index=11, last accessed: February 25, 2020; Lyrics: Kanye West, 'FML', *Genius*, available at: https://genius.com/Kanye-west-fml-lyrics, last accessed: February 25, 2020.

[241] Audio: Section 25, 'Hit', *Youtube*, June 12, 2012, available at: https://www.youtube.com/watch?v=J-IxWxbO7FI, last accessed: February 25, 2020. Lyrics: Section 25, 'Hit', *Genius*, available at: https://genius.com/Section-25-hit-lyrics, last accessed: February 25, 2020.

[242] Audio: Kanye West, 'Real Friends', *Youtube*, July 24, 2018, available at: https://www.youtube.com/watch?v=fWD9GF-Ogf4&list=OLAK5uy_keyJA-JsoAdfCylvyyIQMRjenzX6MzmnE&index=12, last accessed: February 25, 2020; Lyrics: Kanye West, 'Real Friends', *Genius*, available at: https://genius.com/Kanye-west-real-friends-lyrics, last accessed: February 25, 2020.

[243] Audio: Whodini, 'Friends', *Youtube*, February 12, 2010, available at: https://www.youtube.com/watch?v=LRn2VQWNkgA, last accessed: February 25, 2020. Lyrics: Whodini, 'Friends', *Genius*, available at: https://genius.com/Whodini-friends-lyrics, last accessed: February 25, 2020.

[244] Audio: Kanye West, 'Wolves', *Youtube*, July 29, 2016, available at: https://www.youtube.com/watch?v=LsA84bXrBZw&list=OLAK5uy_keyJA-JsoAdfCylvyyIQMRjenzX6MzmnE&index=13, last accessed: February 25, 2020; Lyrics: Kanye West, 'Wolves', *Genius*, available at: https://genius.com/Kanye-west-wolves-lyrics, last accessed: February 25, 2020.

[245] Audio: Sugar Minott, 'Walking Dub', *Youtube*, December 29, 2016, available at: https://www.youtube.com/watch?v=N3rOM-BjKEo, last accessed: February 25, 2020.

[246] Audio: Kanye West, '30 Hours', *Youtube*, July 24, 2018, available at: https://www.youtube.com/watch?v=OH3bNgA1rkE&list=OLAK5uy_keyJA-JsoAdfCylvyyIQMRjenzX6MzmnE&index=16, last accessed: February 25, 2020; Lyrics: Kanye West, '30 Hours', *Genius,* available at: https://genius.com/Kanye-west-30-hours-lyrics, last accessed: February 25, 2020.

[247] Audio: Arthur Russell, 'Answers Me', *Youtube*, November 20, 2014, available at: https://www.youtube.com/watch?v=VBJZ0t2avpI, last accessed: February 25, 2020. Lyrics: Arthur Russell, 'Answers Me', *Genius,* available at: https://genius.com/Arthur-russell-answers-me-lyrics, last accessed: February 25, 2020.

[248] Audio: Nelly, 'Hot In Herre', *Youtube*, December 24, 2009, available at: https://www.youtube.com/watch?v=GeZZr_p6vB8, last accessed: . Lyrics: Nelly, 'Hot In Herre', *Genius,* available at: https://genius.com/Nelly-hot-in-herre-lyrics, last accessed: February 25, 2020.

[249] Audio: Nelly, 'EI', *Youtube*, October 8, 2009, available at: https://www.youtube.com/watch?v=mNaMR8AyeWc, last accessed: February 25, 2020. Lyrics: Nelly, 'EI', *Genius,* available at: https://genius.com/Nelly-ei-lyrics, last accessed: February 25, 2020.

Haynes and Jason Epperson, and performed by Nelly; and samples of 'Joy'[250], written and performed by Isaac Hayes.

13. 'No More Parties in LA'[251] contains samples of 'Give Me My Love'[252], written and performed by Johnny 'Guitar' Watson; samples of 'Suzie Thundertussy'[253], written and performed by Walter 'Junie' Morrison; samples of 'Mighty Healthy'[254], written by Herbert Rooney, Ronald Bean, Highleigh Crizoe, and Dennis Coles, and performed by Ghostface Killah; and samples of 'Stand Up and Shout About Love'[255], written by Larry Graham Jr., Tina Graham, and Sam Dees, and performed by Larry Graham.

14. 'Facts (Charlie Heat Version)'[256] contains samples of 'Dirt and Grime'[257], written by Nicholas Smith and performed by Father's Children; interpolations of 'Jumpman'[258], written by Aubrey Graham, Leland T. Wayne, and Nayvadius D. Wilburn, and performed by Drake and Future; and contains elements of the video game Street Fighter II: The World Warrior.

15. 'Fade'[259] contains samples of '(I Know) I'm Losing You'[260], written by Eddie Holland, Norman Whitfield, and Cornelius Grant, and performed by Rare Earth; samples of '(I

---

[250] Audio: Isaac Hayes, 'Joy', *Youtube*, January 25, 2011, available at: https://www.youtube.com/watch?v=OmZAvAuCDn4, last accessed: February 25, 2020. Lyrics: Isaac Hayes, 'Joy', *Genius,* available at: https://genius.com/Isaac-hayes-joy-lyrics, last accessed: February 25, 2020.

[251] Audio: Kanye West, 'No More Parties In LA', *Youtube*, July 24, 2018, available at: https://www.youtube.com/watch?v=NnMuFqsmYSE&list=OLAK5uy_keyJA-JsoAdfCylvyyIQMRjenzX6MzmnE&index=17, last accessed: February 25, 2020; Lyrics: Kanye West, 'No More Parties In LA', *Genius,* available at: https://genius.com/Kanye-west-no-more-parties-in-la-lyrics, last accessed: February 25, 2020.

[252] Audio: Johnny 'Guitar' Watson, 'Give Me My Love', *Youtube*, March 9, 2013, available at: https://www.youtube.com/watch?v=jawLEK8icbw, last accessed: February 25, 2020. Lyrics: Johnny 'Guitar' Watson, 'Give Me My Love', *Genius,* available at: https://genius.com/Johnny-guitar-watson-give-me-my-love-lyrics, last accessed: February 25, 2020.

[253] Audio: Walter 'Junie' Morrison, 'Suzie Thundertussy', *Youtube*, July 22, 2011, available at: https://www.youtube.com/watch?v=CtIlZDSo2Mk, last accessed: February 25, 2020. Lyrics: Walter 'Junie' Morrison, 'Suzie Thundertussy', *Genius,* available at: https://genius.com/Junie-morrison-suzie-thundertussy-lyrics, last accessed: February 25, 2020.

[254] Audio: Ghostface Killah, 'Mighty Healthy', *Youtube*, March 26, 2011, available at: https://www.youtube.com/watch?v=KBWXgVdAJiY, last accessed: February 25, 2020. Lyrics: Ghostface Killah, 'Mighty Healthy', *Genius,* available at: https://genius.com/Ghostface-killah-mighty-healthy-lyrics, last accessed: February 25, 2020.

[255] Audio: Larry Graham, 'Stand Up And Shout About Love', *Youtube*, February 27, 2012, available at: https://www.youtube.com/watch?v=KGtT5P28MnI, last accessed: February 25, 2020. Lyrics: Larry Graham, 'Stand Up And Shout About Love', *Genius,* available at: https://genius.com/Larry-graham-stand-up-and-shout-about-love-lyrics, last accessed: February 25, 2020.

[256] Audio: Kanye West, 'Facts (Charlie Heat Version)', *Youtube*, July 24, 2018, available at: https://www.youtube.com/watch?v=yiwDWKg9AMA&list=OLAK5uy_keyJA-JsoAdfCylvyyIQMRjenzX6MzmnE&index=18, last accessed: February 25, 2020; Lyrics: Kanye West, 'Facts (Charlie Heat Version)', *Genius,* available at: https://genius.com/Kanye-west-facts-charlie-heat-version-lyrics, last accessed: February 25, 2020.

[257] Audio: Father's Children, 'Dirt And Grime', *Youtube*, July 4, 2011, available at: https://www.youtube.com/watch?v=-X6B0_xd8Mg, last accessed: February 25, 2020. Lyrics: Father's Children, 'Dirt And Grime', *Genius,* available at: https://genius.com/Fathers-children-dirt-and-grime-lyrics, last accessed: February 25, 2020.

[258] Audio: Drake, Future, 'Jumpman', *Youtube*, June 12, 2016, available at: https://www.youtube.com/watch?v=elaR1IsAGwY, last accessed: February 25, 2020. Lyrics: Drake, Future, 'Jumpman', *Genius,* available at: https://genius.com/Drake-and-future-jumpman-lyrics, last accessed: February 25, 2020.

[259] Audio: Kanye West, 'Fade', *Youtube*, September 6, 2016, available at: https://www.youtube.com/watch?v=IxGvm6btP1A&list=OLAK5uy_keyJA-JsoAdfCylvyyIQMRjenzX6MzmnE&index=19, last accessed: February 25, 2020; Lyrics: Kanye West, 'Fade', *Genius,* available at: https://genius.com/Kanye-west-fade-lyrics, last accessed: February 25, 2020.

[260] Audio: Rare Earth, '(I Know) I'm Loosing You', *Youtube*, February 17, 2011, available at: https://www.youtube.com/watch?v=F28X8--2dFU, last accessed: February 25, 2020. Lyrics: Rare Earth, '(I Know) I'm Loosing You', *Genius,* available at: https://genius.com/Rare-earth-i-know-im-losing-you-lyrics, last accessed: February 25, 2020.

	Know) I'm Losing You'[261], written by Eddie Holland, Norman Whitfield, and Cornelius Grant, and performed by The Undisputed Truth; samples of 'Mystery of Love'[262], written by Larry Heard and Robert Owens, and performed by Mr. Fingers; samples of 'Deep Inside'[263], written by Louie Vega and performed by Hardrive; samples of 'I Get Lifted (The Underground Network Mix)'[264], written by Louie Vega, Ronald Carroll, Barbara Tucker, and Harold Matthews, and performed by Barbara Tucker; and contains an interpolation of 'Rock the Boat'[265], written by Stephen Garrett, Rapture Stewart, and Eric Seats, and performed by Aaliyah. 16. 'Saint Pablo'[266] contains samples of 'Where I'm From'[267], written by Shawn Carter, Marek Manning, Deric Angelettie, Ronald Lawrence, and Norman Whitfield, and performed by Jay-Z.
	1. The original version of 'I Thought About Killing You'[268] contains an uncredited sample from 'Fr3sh'[269], as performed by Kareem Lotfy. 2. 'Yikes'[270] contains a sample from 'Kothbiro'[271], as performed by Black Savage. 3. 'Wouldn't Leave'[272] contains a sample from 'Baptizing Scene'[273], as performed by Reverend W.A. Donaldson.

[261] Audio: The Undisputed Truth, '(I Know) I'm Loosing You', *Youtube*, December 4, 2012, available at: https://www.youtube.com/watch?v=2jtnCeV3rEk, last accessed: February 25, 2020. Lyrics: The Undisputed Truth, '(I Know) I'm Loosing You', *Genius,* available at: https://www.youtube.com/watch?v=ZNoFtLGZBwk, last accessed: February 25, 2020.

[262] Audio: Mr. Fingers, 'Mystery Of Love', *Youtube*, September 20, 2013, available at: https://www.youtube.com/watch?v=CvUp3P9sLO4, last accessed: February 25, 2020. Lyrics: Mr. Fingers, 'Mystery Of Love', *Genius,* available at: https://genius.com/Mr-fingers-mystery-of-love-lyrics, last accessed: February 25, 2020.

[263] Audio: Hardrive, 'Deep Inside', *Youtube*, December 13, 2015, available at: https://www.youtube.com/watch?v=OJ0WL4TJVCg, last accessed: February 25, 2020. Lyrics: Hardrive, 'Deep Inside', *Genius,* available at: https://genius.com/Hardrive-deep-inside-lyrics, last accessed: February 25, 2020.

[264] Audio: Barbara Tucker, 'I Get Lifted (The Underground Network Mix), *Youtube*, December 19, 2008, available at: https://www.youtube.com/watch?v=4En_rYmiUMg, last accessed: February 25, 2020.

[265] Audio: Aaliyah, 'Rock The Boat', *Youtube*, August 26, 2008, available at: https://www.youtube.com/watch?v=A5AAcgtMjUI, last accessed: February 25, 2020. Lyrics: Aaliyah, 'Rock The Boat', *Genius,* available at: https://genius.com/Aaliyah-rock-the-boat-lyrics, last accessed: February 25, 2020.

[266] Audio: Kanye West, 'Saint Pablo', *Youtube*, July 24, 2018, available at: https://www.youtube.com/watch?v=w9rzz4pDFwA&list=OLAK5uy_keyJA-JsoAdfCylvyyIQMRjenzX6MzmnE&index=20, last accessed: February 25, 2020; Lyrics: Kanye West, 'Saint Pablo', *Genius,* available at: https://genius.com/Kanye-west-saint-pablo-lyrics, last accessed: February 25, 2020.

[267] Audio: Jay Z, 'Where I'm From', *Youtube*, November 12, 2018, available at: https://www.youtube.com/watch?v=UDAVDTN5zHw, last accessed: February 25, 2020. Lyrics: Jay Z, 'Where I'm From', *Genius,* available at: https://genius.com/Jay-z-where-im-from-lyrics, last accessed: February 25, 2020.

[268] Audio: Kanye West, 'I Thought About Killing You', *Youtube*, November 6, 2018, available at: https://www.youtube.com/watch?v=no1YszVVybo, last accessed: February 25, 2020; Lyrics: Kanye West, 'I Thought About Killing You', *Genius,* available at: https://genius.com/Kanye-west-i-thought-about-killing-you-lyrics, last accessed: February 25, 2020.

[269] Audio: Kareem Lotfy, 'Fr3sh', *Youtube*, March 21, 2017, available at: https://www.youtube.com/watch?v=Q0UMnxmMAZ8, last accessed: February 25, 2020. Lyrics: Kareem Lotfy, 'Fr3sh', *Genius,* available at: https://genius.com/Kareem-lotfy-fr3sh-lyrics, last accessed: February 25, 2020.

[270] Audio: Kanye West, 'Yikes', *Youtube*, November 6, 2018, available at: https://www.youtube.com/watch?v=kPPyUO6m3-4, last accessed: February 25, 2020; Lyrics: Kanye West, *Genius,* available at: https://genius.com/Kanye-west-yikes-lyrics, last accessed: February 25, 2020.

[271] Audio: Black Savage, 'Kothbiro', *Youtube*, March 25, 2016, available at: https://www.youtube.com/watch?v=btn9sV4D9tM, last accessed: February 25, 2020. Lyrics: Black Savage, 'Kothbiro', *Genius,* available at: https://genius.com/Black-savage-kothbiro-lyrics, last accessed: February 25, 2020.

[272] Audio: Kanye West, 'Wouldn't Leave', *Youtube*, November 6, 2018, available at: https://www.youtube.com/watch?v=nMkXJohQiuQ, last accessed: February 25, 2020; Lyrics: Kanye West, 'Wouldn't Leave', *Genius,* available at: https://genius.com/Kanye-west-wouldnt-leave-lyrics, last accessed: February 25, 2020.

[273] Audio: Reverend W.A. Donaldson, 'Baptizing Scene', *Youtube,* September 7, 2011, available at: https://www.youtube.com/watch?v=JpYPoMZhdyU, last accessed: February 25, 2020.

Ye (2018)	4. 'No Mistakes'[274] contains a sample from 'Children (Get Together)'[275], as performed by Edwin Hawkins Singers; and 'Hey Young World'[276], as performed by Slick Rick. 5. 'Ghost Town'[277] contain a sample from 'Take Me for a Little While'[278], as performed by The Royal Jesters; and 'Someday'[279], as performed by Shirley Ann Lee. 6. 'Violent Crimes'[280] is a reworking of the track 'Brothers'[281], produced by Irv Gotti and 7 Aurelius.
Kids See Ghosts (2017)[282]	1. 'Fire' contains a sample of 'They're Coming to Take Me Away, Ha-Haaa!', written and performed by Jerry 'Napoleon XIV' Samuels. 2. '4th Dimension' contains samples of 'What Will Santa Claus Say (When He Finds Everybody Swingin')', written and performed by Louis Prima; and an uncredited sample of 'Someday', written and performed by Shirley Ann Lee. 3. 'Freee (Ghost Town, Pt. 2)' contains samples of 'Stark', written and performed by Corin 'Mr. Chop' Littcler; an uncredited sample of a speech from Marcus Garvey; and portions of the previous 'Ghost Town'. 4. 'Cudi Montage' contains samples of 'Burn the Rain', written and performed by Kurt Cobain.
	1. 'Selah'[283] contains a cover of 'Revelation 19:1'[284] from 'Jesus Is Born', originally performed by the New Jerusalem Baptism Choir under the direction of Curtis Hayes and Jeffrey LaValley.

---

[274] Audio: Kanye West, 'No Mistakes', *Youtube*, November 6, 2018, available at: https://www.youtube.com/watch?v=4I8gDpuvZt4, last accessed: February 25, 2020; Lyrics: Kanye West, 'No Mistakes', *Genius,* available at: https://genius.com/Kanye-west-no-mistakes-lyrics, last accessed: February 25, 2020.

[275] Audio: Edwin Hawkins Singer, 'Children (Get Together)', *Youtube,* January 24, 2018, available at: https://www.youtube.com/watch?v=1f3KCCU4QUM, last accessed: February 25, 2020. Lyrics: Edwin Hawkins Singer, 'Children (Get Together)', *Genius,* available at: https://genius.com/The-edwin-hawkins-singers-children-get-together-lyrics, last accessed: February 25, 2020.

[276] Audio: Slick Rick, 'Hey Young World', *Youtube*, November 22, 2009, available at: https://www.youtube.com/watch?v=ea-ezolZq5k, last accessed: February 25, 2020. Lyrics: Slick Rick, 'Hey Young World', *Genius*, available at: https://genius.com/Slick-rick-hey-young-world-lyrics, last accessed: February 25, 2020.

[277] Audio: Kanye West, 'Ghost Town', *Youtube*, November 6, 2018, available at: https://www.youtube.com/watch?v=5S6az6odzPI, last accessed: February 25, 2020; Lyrics: Kanye West, 'Ghost Town', *Genius*, available at: https://genius.com/Kanye-west-ghost-town-lyrics, last accessed: February 25, 2020.

[278] Audio: The Royal Jesters, 'Little While', *Youtube*, June 24, 2015, available at: https://www.youtube.com/watch?v=AKG0j29VtIg, last accessed: February 25, 2020. Lyrics: The Royal Jesters, 'Little While', *Musixmatch*, available at: https://www.musixmatch.com/lyrics/The-Royal-Jesters/Take-Me-For-a-Little-While, last accessed: February 25, 2020.

[279] Audio: Shirley Ann Lee, 'Someday', *Youtube*, June 25, 2018, available at: https://www.youtube.com/watch?v=D7kSw_OFy2Y, last accessed: February 25, 2020. Lyrics: Shirley Ann Lee, 'Someday', *Genius*, available at: https://genius.com/Shirley-ann-lee-someday-lyrics, last accessed: February 25, 2020.

[280] Audio: Kanye West, 'Violent Crimes', *Youtube*, June 18, 2018, available at: https://www.youtube.com/watch?v=DSY7u8Jg9c0, last accessed: February 25, 2020; Lyrics: Kanye West, 'Violent Crimes', *Genius,* available at: https://genius.com/Kanye-west-violent-crimes-lyrics, last accessed: February 25, 2020.

[281] I did not find the original track to make a direct link with the song.

[282] The information for this album was retrieved from Kids See Ghosts, *Wikipedia*, available at: https://en.wikipedia.org/wiki/Kids_See_Ghosts_(album), last accessed: February 25, 2020.

[283] Audio: Kanye West, 'Selah', *Youtube*, October 25, 2019, available at: https://www.youtube.com/watch?v=6CNPg2IQoC0&list=OLAK5uy_nG0R7GxWTXwhsxxi_cwx8QwZe0QI1tED8&index=2, last accessed: February 25, 2020; Lyrics: Kanye West, 'Selah', *Genius*, available at: https://genius.com/Kanye-west-selah-lyrics, last accessed: February 25, 2020.

[284] Audio: New Jerusalem Baptism Choir, 'Revelation 19:1', *Youtube*, May 31, 2010, available at: https://www.youtube.com/watch?v=tF9uq9lj94s, last accessed: February 25, 2020.

Jesus is King (2019)	2. 'Follow God'[285] contains samples of 'Can You Lose By Following God'[286], written by Johnny Frieson, Curtis Eubanks, and Calvin Eubanks, and performed by Whole Truth. 3. 'Closed on Sunday'[287] contains samples of 'Martín Fierro'[288], written by Chango Farías Gómez and performed by Grupo Vocal Argentino. 4. 'On God'[289] contains samples of 'Lambo'[290], written and performed by YB; and 'Oh My God'[291], written by Jonathan Davis, Ali Shaheed Muhammad, Trevor Smith, and Malik Taylor, and performed by A Tribe Called Quest featuring Busta Rhymes. 5. 'Water'[292] contains an interpolation of 'We're All Water'[293], written by Yoko Ono and performed by Ono and John Lennon; contains samples of 'Blow Job'[294], written and performed by Bruce Haack. 6. 'God Is'[295] contains samples of 'God Is'[296], written by Robert Fryson and performed by James Cleveland and The Southern California Community Choir.

[285] Audio: Kanye West, 'Follow God', *Youtube*, November 8, 2019, available at: https://www.youtube.com/watch?v=ivCY3Ec4iaU&list=OLAK5uy_nG0R7GxWTXwhsxxi_cwx8QwZe0QI1tED8&index=3, last accessed: February 25, 2020; Lyrics: Kanye West, 'Follow God', *Genius*, available at: https://genius.com/Kanye-west-follow-god-lyrics, last accessed: February 25, 2020.

[286] Audio: Whole Truth, 'Can You Lose By Following God', *Youtube*, March 17, 2017, available at: https://www.youtube.com/watch?v=AgsK5xpzT90, last accessed: February 25, 2020. Lyrics: Whole Truth, 'Can You Lose By Following God', *Genius*, available at: https://genius.com/Whole-truth-can-you-lose-by-following-god-lyrics, last accessed: February 25, 2020.

[287] Audio: Kanye West, 'Closed On Sunday', *Youtube*, October 25, 2019, available at: https://www.youtube.com/watch?v=Lp0q1wWe6XI&list=OLAK5uy_nG0R7GxWTXwhsxxi_cwx8QwZe0QI1tED8&index=4, last accessed: February 25, 2020; Lyrics: Kanye West, 'Closed On Sunday', *Genius*, available at: https://genius.com/Kanye-west-closed-on-sunday-lyrics, last accessed: February 25, 2020.

[288] Audio: Grupo Vocal Argentino, 'Martin Fierro', *Youtube*, December 18, 2015, available at: https://www.youtube.com/watch?v=2yV1IsTE97w, last accessed: February 25, 2020. Lyrics: Grupo Vocal Argentino, 'Martin Fierro', *Genius*, available at: https://genius.com/Grupo-vocal-argentino-martin-fierro-lyrics, last accessed: February 25, 2020.

[289] Audio: Kanye West, 'On God', *Youtube*, October 25, 2019, available at: https://www.youtube.com/watch?v=AOBQkHy8_p8&list=OLAK5uy_nG0R7GxWTXwhsxxi_cwx8QwZe0QI1tED8&index=5, last accessed: February 25, 2020; Lyrics: Kanye West, 'On God', *Genius*, available at: https://genius.com/Kanye-west-on-god-lyrics, last accessed: February 25, 2020.

[290] Audio: YB, Lambo', *Youtube*, May 7, 2012, available at: https://www.youtube.com/watch?v=LcOusBxmZF0, last accessed: February 25, 2020. Lyrics: YB, Lambo', *Genius*, available at: https://genius.com/Yung-bizzle-lambo-lyrics, last accessed: February 25, 2020.

[291] Audio: A Tribe Called Quest (featuring Busta Rhymes), 'Oh My God', *Youtube*, December 5, 2012, available at: https://www.youtube.com/watch?v=Olah18jcJko, last accessed: February 25, 2020. Lyrics: A Tribe Called Quest (featuring Busta Rhymes), 'Oh My God', *Genius*, available at: https://genius.com/A-tribe-called-quest-oh-my-god-lyrics, last accessed: February 25, 2020.

[292] Audio: Kanye West, 'Water', *Youtube*, October 25, 2019, available at: https://www.youtube.com/watch?v=-YfG1Xbo4OA&list=OLAK5uy_nG0R7GxWTXwhsxxi_cwx8QwZe0QI1tED8&index=7, last accessed: February 25, 2020; Lyrics: Kanye West, 'Water', *Genius*, available at: https://genius.com/Kanye-west-water-lyrics, last accessed: February 25, 2020.

[293] Audio: Yoko Ono, John Lennon, 'We're All Water', *Youtube*, September 26, 2009, available at: https://www.youtube.com/watch?v=n_8dWTEWEKo, last accessed: February 25, 2020. Lyrics: Ono, John Lennon, 'We're All Water', *Genius*, available at: https://genius.com/Yoko-ono-were-all-water-lyrics, last accessed: February 25, 2020.

[294] Audio: Bruce Haack, 'Blow Job', *Youtube*, July 17, 2013, available at: https://www.youtube.com/watch?v=XaOwzqb1jDc, last accessed: February 25, 2020. Lyrics: Bruce Haack, 'Blow Job', *Genius*, available at: https://genius.com/Bruce-haack-blow-job-annotated, last accessed: February 25, 2020.

[295] Audio: Kanye West, 'God Is', *Youtube*, October 25, 2019, available at: https://www.youtube.com/watch?v=G8u3P7Xqlvo&list=OLAK5uy_nG0R7GxWTXwhsxxi_cwx8QwZe0QI1tED8&index=8, last accessed: February 25, 2020; Lyrics: Kanye West, 'God Is', *Genius*, available at: https://genius.com/Kanye-west-god-is-lyrics, last accessed: February 25, 2020.

[296] Audio: James Cleveland, The Southern California Community Choir, 'God Is', *Youtube*, April 13, 2014, available at: https://www.youtube.com/watch?v=dLyY8F96sfg, last accessed: February 25, 2020. Lyrics: James Cleveland, The Southern

	7. 'Use This Gospel'[297] contains samples of 'Costume Party'[298], written by Alex Trimble, Kevin Baird, and Sam Halliday and performed by Two Door Cinema Club. 8. 'Jesus Is Lord'[299] contains samples of 'Un Homme Dans La Nuit'[300], written by Claude Léveillée.

CONCLUSIONS:

- for Kanye West: from the point of view of creating music heard and used for the first time in the world, and written and released *only* by him, there is a lower level of originality and novelty brought in the music industry in comparison with Taylor Swift;
- from the point of view that musical notes and lyrics from songs already known and awarded in the music industry, and a mix of them (in any format) by Kanye West is novelty in the music industry, then Kanye West brought a high level of originality and novelty in the music industry;
- Kanye West has a high level of abilities to mix different songs in a way that few people can do it;[301]
- Kanye West's power to create music resides in listening to other songs, then to mix these songs with close or sometimes different musical notes and lyrics that can be connected, or have some meaning to the theme of the song he intends to create (to sings a lyric on a different note, you need a different lyric and the right musical note to match the sound of that lyric); there are many songs in Kanye West's catalogue where his (and other producers from his albums) intervention is the creation of a close sound around a sound used already by another artist;
- Kanye West may struggle to create his own titles of songs as he used title of songs in his catalogue which belongs to other artists (either inspired from the title of a song, or from the lyrics of the songs that he sampled).

California Community Choir, 'God Is', *Musixmatch*, available at: https://www.musixmatch.com/lyrics/James-Cleveland-The-Southern-California-Community-Choir/God-Is, last accessed: February 25, 2020.

[297] Audio: Kanye West, 'Use This Gospel', *Youtube*, October 25, 2019, available at: https://www.youtube.com/watch?v=8yQVcGkbpAc&list=OLAK5uy_nG0R7GxWTXwhsxxi_cwx8QwZe0QI1tED8&index=10, last accessed: February 25, 2020; Lyrics: Kanye West, 'Use This Gospel', *Genius*, available at: https://genius.com/Kanye-west-use-this-gospel-lyrics, last accessed: February 25, 2020.

[298] Audio: The Two Door Cinema, 'Costume Party', *Youtube*, November 14, 2009, available at: https://www.youtube.com/watch?v=sz3AL5w1Rfs, last accessed: February 25, 2020. Lyrics: The Two Door Cinema, 'Costume Party', *Genius*, available at: https://genius.com/Two-door-cinema-club-costume-party-lyrics, last accessed: February 25, 2020.

[299] Audio: Kanye West, 'Jesus Is Lord', *Youtube*, October 25, 2019, available at: https://www.youtube.com/watch?v=rns_n82HiMo&list=OLAK5uy_nG0R7GxWTXwhsxxi_cwx8QwZe0QI1tED8&index=11, last accessed: February 25, 2020; Lyrics: Kanye West, 'Jesus Is Lord', *Genius,* available at: https://genius.com/Kanye-west-jesus-is-lord-lyrics, last accessed: February 25, 2020.

[300] Audio: Claude Léveillée, *'Un Homme Dans La Nuit'*, *Youtube*, October 19, 2018, available at: https://www.youtube.com/watch?v=jVv2ummG7Xk, last accessed: February 25, 2020.

[301] This statement is based *1.* on personal comparison between the music of Kanye West and other artists based on listening Kanye West's all albums and several artists over the years; *2.* in comparison with the artists investigated in this research.

II.1.4 The Sources of the Samples

The list of songs in this table are not used to argue that Kanye West infringed the copyrights of other artists, or to claim any wrongdoing from any point of view of music (Kanye West acknowledge the sources he sampled and the wider music community is well aware of; also, there is a high number of artists which agreed (verbally and written) the use of their ideas in his music). This table is used *only* to *show* and *understand* the background narrative of creating music.

II.1.4.1 Taylor Swift

I read the lyrics of the songs that used samples to find out if there is a connection between the original song, and the song that sampled the original song.

TABLE 9. THE SOURCES OF THE SAMPLES USED BY TAYLOR SWIFT		
NAME OF THE ALBUM	NAME OF THE SONG	INSPIRATION
Taylor Swift (Deluxe, 2006)	N/A	
Fearless (Platinum, 2008)	'Untouchable'	'Untouchable'
Speak Now (Deluxe, 2010)	N/A	
RED (Deluxe, 2010)	N/A	
1989 (Deluxe, 2014)	N/A	
reputation (2017)	'Look What You Made Me Do'	'I'm Too Sexy'
Lover (2019)	'The Archer'	'Humpty Dumpty'
	'London Boy'	'Cold War'
	'It's Nice to Have a Friend'	'Summer in the South'
folklore (Deluxe, 2020)	N/A	
Evermore (Deluxe, 2020)	N/A	
Fearless (Taylor's Version, 2021)	N/A	

CONCLUSIONS:

- Taylor Swift used a lower level of music instruments and lyrics from other songs;
- overall, the theme of the songs that Taylor Swift sampled is different than the songs released under her name and lyrics; there is one exception: for *Untouchable* song, Taylor changed the speed of the song (slower) and tone of the voice (soft);
- in 2017 Taylor Swift changed the pattern of her songs by including samples, a feature that it is highly visible on Kanye West's music catalogue, and it is done on two albums: *reputation* and *Lover*, both being in close connection with Kanye West's albums: *My Beautiful Dark Twisted Fantasy* and *reputation* (dark theme) and *The Life*

of Saint Pablo with *Lover* (personal perception about family, love, friends, and enemies).[302]

II.1.4.2 Kanye West

In this table I added only the songs that I found to have some connection with Kanye West's titles and lyrics. I read the lyrics of the songs that used samples to find out the connection between the original song, and the song that sampled the original song.

TABLE 10. THE SOURCES OF THE SAMPLES USED BY KANYE WEST		
NAME OF THE ALBUM	NAME OF THE SONG	INSPIRATION
The College Dropout (2004)	'All Falls Down'	'Mystery of Iniquity'
	'Spaceship'	'Distant Lover'
	'Jesus Walks'	'Walk with Me'; '(Don't Worry) If There's a Hell Below, We're All Going to Go';
	'Never Let Me Down'	'Maybe It's the Power of Love'
	'Slow Jamz'	'A House Is Not a Home'
	'School Spirit'	'Spirit in the Dark'
	'Two Words'	'Peace & Love (Amani Na Mapenzi) – Movement IV (Encounter)'
	'Through the Wire'	'Through the Fire'
	'Family Business'	'The Rainmaker' and 'Fonky Thang'
	'Last Call'	'Mr. Rockefeller' and 'She's Gone To Another'.
Late Registration (2005)	'Wake Up, Mr. West'	'Someone That I Used to Love'
	'Touch the Sky'	'Move On Up'
	'Gold Digger'	'I Got a Woman'
	'My Way Home'	'Home Is Where the Hatred Is'
	'Roses'	'Rosie'
	'Addiction'	'My Funny Valentine'
	'Diamonds From Sierra Leone'	'Diamonds Are Forever'
	'Gone'	'It's Too Late'
	'Late'	'I'll Erase Away Your Pain'
Graduation (2007)	'Champion'	'Kid Charlemagne'
	'Stronger'	'Harder, Better, Faster, Stronger'
	'I Wonder'	'My Song'
	'Good Life'	'P.Y.T. (Pretty Young Thing)'
	'Bittersweet Poetry'	'Bittersweet'
88s & Heartbreak (2008)	'Coldest Winter'	'Memories Fade'
	'Dark Fantasy'	'In High Places'
	'Power'	'It's Your Thing' and '21st Century Schizoid Man
	'So Appalled'	'You Are – I Am'

---
[302] Read Casian Anton, *On the Famous Feud*, Chapter VI.

My Beautiful Dark Twisted Fantasy (2010)	'Who Will Survive in America'	'Comment No. 1'
Yeezus (2013)	'New Slaves'	'Gyöngyhajú lány'
	'Blood on the Leaves'	'Strange Fruit'
	'Guilt Trip'	'Chief Rocka'
	'Send it Up'	'Memories'
	'Bound 2'	'Bound'
The Life of Pablo (2016)	'Father Stretch My Hands'	'Father I Stretch My Hands'
	'Pt 2'	'Panda'
	'Famous'	'Do What You Gotta Do', 'Bam Bam' and 'Mi Sono Svegliato E... Ho Chiuso Gli Occhi'
	'So Alive'	'So Alive (Acapella)'
	'FML'	'Hit'
	'Real Friends'	'Friends'
	'30 Hours'	'Answers Me'
	'No More Parties in LA'	'Give Me My Love'
	'Facts (Charlie Version)'	'Dirt and Grime' and 'Jumpman'
	'Fade'	'(I Know) I'm Losing You', 'Mystery of Love', 'Deep Inside' and 'Rock the Boat'
	'Saint Pablo'	'Where I'm From'
Ye (2018)	'Ghost Town' from 'Take Me for a Little While'	'Take Me for a Little While'
Jesus is King (2019)	'Follow God'	'Can You Lose By Following God'
	'Water'	'We're All Water'
	'God is'	'God Is'

CONCLUSIONS:

- Kanye West's samples used in his music can be added to a good extent in the following categories:

  - *the title of the song:* used the original title of the song that he was inspired from; modified the original title with his own idea, but with close/strong meaning with the original title that he sampled; used a part of the original title as a full title for his song; the title of his song was inspired and contains lyrics from the original song sampled in his song;
  - *lyrics:* is on four levels: a. some lyrics; b. more lyrics; c. a combination of his lyrics with other artists lyrics; d. rich lyrics from other songs;
  - *theme of the songs/albums:* followed the same pattern as lyrics, but with three levels: a. some connection; b. good connection; c. strong connection with the song that he sampled (lyrics, instrumentals and order of chorus, verse, intro, outro and a mix between them);

    ○   *the structure of a song*: sometimes he used the same musical structure of the song (first Intro, Verses, Chorus, Bridge, Hook, Outro, and so forth) that he sampled; modified and changed the position of a part of the song (for example Chorus became Intro or Outro and so forth).

II.1.5 The Fame of the Samples

In this subchapter I investigated the fame of the samples used by both artists. The reason behind this investigation is to see if the samples used were already awarded, and appreciated by the wider music community and the general public and to what degree (measured in Top Charts and Awards).

II.1.5.1 The Fame of the Samples Used by Taylor Swift

The following table has only the songs that I could find information about their fame, it may be more songs which are not included here.

TABLE 11. THE FAME OF THE SAMPLES USED BY TAYLOR SWIFT		
NAME OF THE ALBUM	NAME OF THE SONG	TOP CHARTS & AWARDS
Taylor Swift (Deluxe, 2006)		N/A
Fearless (Platinum, 2008)	'Untouchable'	All Music rated the album 'Luna Halo' where the song was included with 3.5 out of 5 stars.[303]
Speak Now (Deluxe, 2010)		N/A
RED (Deluxe, 2010)		N/A
1989 (Deluxe, 2014)		N/A
reputation (2017)	'I'm Too Sexy'	'Is the debut song by British group *Right Said Fred*. The single peaked at number two on the UK Singles Chart. Outside the United Kingdom, 'I'm Too Sexy' topped the charts in six countries, including Australia, Ireland, and the United States. The song was nominated for an Ivor Novello Award for Best Selling 'A' Side. In April 2008, the song was rated No. 49 on 'The 50 Worst Songs Ever! Watch, Listen and Cringe!' by Blender. In June 2007, the song was voted No. 80 on VH1's 100 Greatest Songs of the '90s. In April 2011, it was voted No. 2 on VH1's 40 Greatest One-Hit Wonders of the '90s.'[304]

---

[303] Jared Johnson, 'Luna Halo', *All Music*, available at: https://www.allmusic.com/album/luna-halo-mw0000582485, last accessed February 27, 2020.
[304] 'I'm Too sexy', *Wikipedia*, available at: https://en.wikipedia.org/wiki/I%27m_Too_Sexy, last accessed: February 27, 2020.

Lover (2019)	'Humpty Dumpty'	Humpty Dumpty is a character in an English nursery rhyme and one of the best known in the English-speaking world. The first recorded versions of the rhyme date from late eighteenth-century England and the tune from 1870 in James William Elliott's National Nursery Rhymes and Nursery Songs. The character of Humpty Dumpty was popularised in the United States on Broadway by actor George L. Fox, where his show ran from 1868 to 1869, for a total of 483 performances, becoming the longest-running Broadway show until it was passed in 1881. As a character and literary allusion, he has appeared or been referred to in many works of literature and popular culture, particularly English author Lewis Carroll's 1871 book *Through the Looking-Glass*, in which he was described as an egg.'[305]
	'Cold War'	I did not find information about the charts and awards for this song
	'Summer in the South'	It was created by a group of students from Toronto-based Regent Park School of Music.
folklore (Deluxe, 2020)		N/A
Evermore (Deluxe, 2020)		N/A
Fearless (Taylor's Version, 2021)		N/A

CONCLUSIONS:

- the inspiration from other songs is too small to create at least a satisfactory argument that Taylor Swift's musical career is because of the samples that she used in her music, and without the samples she would not exist today as a global pop artist;
- if the title of 'the greatest artist of all time' is based on writing your own lyrics and musical notes, Taylor Swift is naturally one of the greatest artists of all time.

II.1.5.2 The Fame of the Sample Used by Kanye West

The following table has only the songs that I could find information about their fame, it may be more songs which are not included here.

TABLE 12. THE FAME OF THE SAMPLES USED BY KANYE WEST		
NAME OF THE ALBUM	NAME OF THE SONG	TOP CHARTS & AWARDS

---

[305] 'Humpty Dumpty', *Wikipedia*, available at: https://en.wikipedia.org/wiki/Humpty_Dumpty, last accessed: February 27, 2020.

	'Mystery of Iniquity'	Was nominated at the 45th Grammy Awards for Best Female Rap Solo Performance.'[306]
	'Distant Lover'	'The 1974 live version of 'Distant Lover' has been regarded as one of the greatest live performances of all time.'[307]
	'(Don't Worry) If There's a Hell Below, We're All Going to Go'	'The song earned U.S. Billboard Hot Soul Singles number 3. Also the song meant to serve as a warning regarding the state of race relations and the tempest growing in America's inner cities.'[308]
The College Dropout (2004)	'A House Is Not a Home'	'Despite its modest initial success, the song went on to achieve greater renown through frequent recordings by other artists.'[309]
	'Spirit in the Dark'	'The song reached number 3 on the U.S. R&B chart and number 23 on the Billboard Hot 100 in 1970.'[310]
	'Through the Fire'	Is a song recorded by Chaka Khan from her sixth studio album, *I Feel for You* (1984). The David Foster-produced track was the third single from the album and reached number 60 on the US Billboard Hot 100 chart and number 15 on the Hot R&B/Hip-Hop Songs charts.[311]
	'Someone That I Used to Love'	Also peaked at number 21 on the Billboard R&B chart, however, it was a single hit.'[312]
	'Move On Up'	'The song became a soul music classic over the years.'[313]
Late Registration (2005)	'I Got a Woman'	'The song would be one of the prototypes for what later became termed as 'soul music' after Charles released 'What'd I Say' nearly five years later. It was a hit—Charles' first—climbing quickly to #1 R&B in January 1955. It was later ranked No. 239 on Rolling Stone's list of the 500 Greatest Songs of All Time.'[314]
	'Wildflower'	'It became a huge soul hit before breaking out nationally and crossing over to the pop charts. Eventually 'Wildflower' spent 21 weeks on the Billboard pop chart. [...] The song proved to be extremely popular in Canada as well; it ultimately peaked at number 10 on the RPM Top Singles chart, and number 1 on the Adult Contemporary chart. Total sales of the single exceeded one million copies.'[315]

---

[306] 'MTV Unplugged', *Wikipedia*, available at: https://en.wikipedia.org/wiki/MTV_Unplugged_No._2.0, last accessed: February 27, 2020.

[307] 'Distant Lover', *Wikipedia*, available at: https://en.wikipedia.org/wiki/Distant_Lover, last accessed: February 27, 2020.

[308] '(Don't Worry) If There's a Hell Below, We're All Going to Go', *Wikipedia*, available at: https://en.wikipedia.org/wiki/(Don%27t_Worry)_If_There%27s_a_Hell_Below,_We%27re_All_Going_to_Go, last accessed: February 27, 2020.

[309] 'A House is Not a Home', *Wikipedia*, available at: https://en.wikipedia.org/wiki/A_House_Is_Not_a_Home_(song), last accessed: February 27, 2020.

[310] 'Aretha Franklin', 'Spirit in the Dark', *Music CVF*, available at: https://musicvf.com/song.php?id=2851&artist=Aretha+Franklin&title=Spirit+in+the+Dark, last accessed: February 27, 2020.

[311] 'Through the Fire', *Wikipedia*, available at: https://en.wikipedia.org/wiki/Through_the_Fire_(song), last accessed: February 27, 2020.

[312] 'Someone That I Used to Love', *Wikipedia*, available at: https://en.wikipedia.org/wiki/Someone_That_I_Used_to_Love, last accessed: February 27, 2020.

[313] 'Move On Up', *Wikipedia*, available at: https://en.wikipedia.org/wiki/Move_On_Up, last accessed: February 27, 2020.

[314] 'I Got a Woman', *Wikipedia*, available at: https://en.wikipedia.org/wiki/I_Got_a_Woman, last accessed: February 27, 2020.

[315] 'Wildflower (Skylark song)', *Wikipedia*, available at: https://en.wikipedia.org/wiki/Wildflower_(Skylark_song); Skylark Review Wildflower, https://books.google.co.uk/books?id=CQkEAAAAMBAJ&pg=PA17&dq=skylark+review+wildflower&num=100&client=firefox-a&redir_esc=y#v=onepage&q&f=true, last accessed: February 27, 2020.

	'My Funny Valentine'	'The song became a popular jazz standard, appearing on over 1300 albums performed by over 600 artists. The song first hit the charts in 1945, performed by Hal McIntyre with vocals by Ruth Gaylor. It only appeared for one week and hit #16.[316]
	'Diamonds Are Forever'	'It is the name of the one of the soundtracks of James Bond fim series, named 'Diamonds are Forever' (1971), which was a global commercial success.'[317]
	'It's Too Late'	'It reached #3 on the U.S. R&B chart in 1956.'[318]
Graduation (2007)	'Someone Saved My Life Tonight'	'It peaked on the Billboard Hot 100 chart in the U.S. at #4 and in Canada on the RPM Top Singles chart at #2. The song concludes side one of the album's narrative, chronicling the early history of John and lyricist, Bernie Taupin, and their struggles to find their place within the music industry. 319
	'Kid Charlemagne'	'Reached number 82 in the Billboard charts. The guitar solo by jazz fusion guitarist Larry Carlton was ranked #80 in the list of the 100 greatest guitar songs by Rolling Stone.[320]
	'Harder, Better, Faster, Stronger'	This version won a Grammy Award for Best Dance Recording in 2009. In October 2011, NME placed it at number 132 on its list '150 Best Tracks of the Past 15 Years'. The song is built around a 'bouncy' keyboard riff sampled from the 1979 track 'Cola Bottle Baby' [which Kanye West used in one of his songs] by the funk musician Edwin Birdsong. Kanye West's song 'Stronger' from the album Graduation prominently features a sample of 'Harder, Better, Faster, Stronger'. Two actors who wore the robotic Daft Punk costumes in the film Daft Punk's Electroma appear in the music video for 'Stronger'. It was performed live at the 2008 Grammy Awards with Daft Punk in their trademark pyramid while Kanye West was on stage rapping. Daft Punk member Guy-Manuel de Homem-Christo said that 'Stronger' was 'not a collaboration in the studio, but the vibe of the music we do separately connected in what [Kanye West] did with the song'. He later clarified that the live version was 'truly a collaboration from the start. We really did it all hand in hand.'[321]
	'P.Y.T. (Pretty Young Thing)'	'The single charted at no. 10 on the Billboard Hot 100 and no. 46 on the Hot Black Singles chart, becoming the sixth Top 10 hit from Thriller. In the United Kingdom, the song reached a peak position of 11.'[322]

---

[316] 'My Funny Valentine', *Wikipedia*, available at: https://en.wikipedia.org/wiki/My_Funny_Valentine, last accessed: February 27, 2020.

[317] 'Diamonds Are Forever (Film)', *Wikipedia*, available at: https://en.wikipedia.org/wiki/Diamonds_Are_Forever_(film), last accessed: February 27, 2020; 'Diamonds Are Forever (soundtrack)', *Wikipedia*, available at: https://en.wikipedia.org/wiki/Diamonds_Are_Forever_(soundtrack), last accessed: February 27, 2020.

[318] 'It's Too Late (Chuck Willis song)', *Wikipedia*, available at: https://en.wikipedia.org/wiki/It%27s_Too_Late_(Chuck_Willis_song), last accessed: February 27, 2020.

[319] 'Someone Saved My Life Tonight', *Wikipedia*, available at: https://en.wikipedia.org/wiki/Someone_Saved_My_Life_Tonight, last accessed: February 27, 2020.

[320] 'Kid Charlemagne', *Wikipedia*, available at: https://en.wikipedia.org/wiki/Kid_Charlemagne, last accessed: February 27, 2020.

[321] 'Harder, Better, Faster, Stronger', *Wikipedia*, available at: https://en.wikipedia.org/wiki/Harder,_Better,_Faster,_Stronger, last accessed: February 27, 2020.

[322] 'P.Y.T (Pretty Young Thing)', *Wikipedia*, available at: https://en.wikipedia.org/wiki/P.Y.T._(Pretty_Young_Thing), last accessed: February 27, 2020.

	'Bring the Noise'	'The single reached No. 56 on the Billboard Hot R&B/Hip-Hop Songs chart. It was included on the soundtrack of the 1987 film *Less Than Zero*.
	'Save the Country'	The most successful version was performed by *The 5th Dimension*. It reached #10 on the U.S. adult contemporary chart, #24 in Canada, #27 on the Billboard Hot 100, and #79 in Australia in 1970.'[323]
	'Wake the Town'	'It was U-Roy's first big hit and one of the songs that established U-Roy as the grandfather of the modern deejay phenomenon. It also helped created dancehall style in Jamaica, helped create the deejay sound.'[324]
808s & Heartbreak (2008)	'Sea Lion Woman'	'It charted through digital downloads on the Canadian Hot 100 under the title "Sea Lion Woman" and peaked #94 on the Billboard Canadian Hot 100 Chart.'[325]
My Beautiful Dark Twisted Fantasy (2010)	'In High Places'	'On the occasion of Virgin Records founder Richard Branson's launch of the then-largest hot-air balloon ever made, the song was released as a single in 1987 in the UK and Spain.'[326]
	'You Showed Me'	'The song was the group's last big hit in the U.S, U.S. Record World Weekly Chart: 1, U.S. Cash Box Top 100, weekly chart: 4.'[327]
	'It's Your Thing'	'The song quickly rose to the top of both the Billboard pop and R&B singles charts, peaking at #2 [...] and marking their first #1 hit in the latter. In February 1970 the [authors of the song] became the first former Motown act to win a Grammy Award for Best R&B Vocal Performance by a Duo or Group. The song is ranked #420 on the Rolling Stone magazine's list of The 500 Greatest Songs of All Time.'[328]
	'21st Century Schizoid Man'	'The song encompasses the heavy metal, jazz-rock and progressive rock genres, and is considered to be an influence on the development of progressive metal. The atonal solo was rated number 82 in Guitar World's list of the Top 100 Greatest Guitar Solos in 2008. Louder Sound ranked the solo at no. 56 in its '100 greatest guitar solos in rock' poll.'[329]
	'Will You Love Me Tomorrow'	'It was originally recorded in 1960 by the Shirelles, who took their single to number one on the Billboard Hot 100 chart. The song is also notable for being the first song by a black all-girl group to reach number one in the United States. It was ranked at #126 among Rolling Stone's list of The 500 Greatest Songs of All Time.

[323] 'Save the Country', *Music CVF*, available at:
https://www.musicvf.com/song.php?title=Save+the+Country+by+The+5th+Dimension&id=426, last accessed: February 27, 2020.
[324] 'Wake the Town', *Wikipedia*, available at: https://en.wikipedia.org/wiki/Wake_the_Town, last accessed: February 27, 2020.
[325] Feist, 'Sea Lion Woman', *Billboard Canadian Hot 100 Chart*, April 26, 2008, available at:
https://www.billboard.com/charts/canadian-hot-100/2008-04-26, last accessed: February 27, 2020.
[326] 'In High Places', *Wikipedia*, available at: https://en.wikipedia.org/wiki/In_High_Places_(song), last accessed: February 27, 2020.
[327] 'You Showed Me', *Wikipedia*, available at: https://en.wikipedia.org/wiki/You_Showed_Me, last accessed: February 27, 2020.
[328] 'It's Your Thing', *Wikipedia*, available at: https://en.wikipedia.org/wiki/It%27s_Your_Thing, last accessed: February 27, 2020.
[329] '21st Century Schizoid Man', *Wikipedia*, available at: https://en.wikipedia.org/wiki/21st_Century_Schizoid_Man, last accessed: February 27, 2020.

		Billboard named the song #3 on their list of 100 Greatest Girl Group Songs of All Time.'[330]
	'Iron Man'	'The song won spot number 317 in Rolling Stone's list of the 500 Greatest Songs of All Time as of 2004. VH1 ranked the song as the greatest heavy metal song of all time.'[331]
	'Soul Makossa'	'The song also became an international hit leading to even more cover versions by various groups around the world.'[332]
	'Think (About It)'	The song is very popular for its raw drumbeat dressed with tambourine and multiple background vocals, which suggest the song was recorded altogether in one take. It peaked at No. 9 on the Billboard Best Selling Soul Singles chart and No. 66 on the Hot 100. Owing to the composition, it became a fan favourite and has been featured on various compilation albums posthumously.'[333]
Yeezus (2013)	'Gyöngyhajú lány'	'The song was very popular in many countries, including Germany, Great Britain, France, Poland, Romania, Czechoslovakia, Yugoslavia and Bulgaria.'[334]
	'Strange Fruit'	'The song protested American racism, particularly the lynching of African Americans. The song was highly regarded; the 1939 recording eventually sold a million copies, in time becoming Holiday's biggest-selling recording.'[335]
	'Chief Rocka'	'It peaked at #55 on the Billboard 200, the group's highest appearance on that chart, and went to #1 on the Hot Rap Singles.'[336]
	'Sweet Nothin's'	' 'It peaked at No. 4 on the Billboard Hot 100 and No. 12 on the Hot R&B Sides chart, in 1960. The song (as Sweet Nuthin's) also charted on the UK Singles Chart in 1960, peaking at No. 4.'[337]
	'Panda'	'The single received a nomination for Best Rap Performance at the 59th Annual Grammy Awards. A music video was released on May 10, 2016. It was nominated for Best Hip Hop Video at the 2016 MTV Video Music Awards. Rolling Stone named 'Panda' one of the 30 best songs of the first half of 2016. Billboard ranked 'Panda' at number 24 on their '100 Best Pop Songs of 2016', Pitchfork listed 'Panda' on their ranking of the 100 best songs of 2016 at number 56.'[338]
	'Human'	Reached number 87 on the UK Singles Chart.[339]
	'Bam Bam'	'The song has been labeled as a 'well-known reggae anthem' arguably, one of the most sampled reggae songs ever.' [340]

[330] 'Will You Love Me Tomorrow', *Wikipedia*, available at: https://en.wikipedia.org/wiki/Will_You_Love_Me_Tomorrow, last accessed: February 27, 2020.

[331] 'Iron Man', *Wikipedia*, available at: https://en.wikipedia.org/wiki/Iron_Man_(song) , last accessed: February 27, 2020.

[332] 'Soul Makossa', *Wikipedia*, available at: https://en.wikipedia.org/wiki/Soul_Makossa, last accessed: February 27, 2020.

[333] 'Think (About It)', *Wikipedia*, available at: https://en.wikipedia.org/wiki/Think_(About_It), last accessed: February 27, 2020.

[334] 'Gyöngyhajú lány', *Wikipedia*, available at: https://en.wikipedia.org/wiki/Gyöngyhajú_lány, last accessed: February 27, 2020.

[335] 'Strange Fruit', *Wikipedia*, available at: https://en.wikipedia.org/wiki/Strange_Fruit, last accessed: February 27, 2020.

[336] 'Chief Rocka', *Wikipedia*, available at: https://en.wikipedia.org/wiki/Chief_Rocka, last accessed: February 27, 2020.

[337] 'Sweet Nothin's', *Wikipedia*, available at: https://en.wikipedia.org/wiki/Sweet_Nothin%27s, last accessed: February 27, 2020.

[338] 'Panda (song)', *Wikipedia*, available at: https://en.wikipedia.org/wiki/Panda_(song), last accessed: February 27, 2020.

[339] 'Human (Goldfrapp song)', *Wikipedia*, available at: https://en.wikipedia.org/wiki/Human_(Goldfrapp_song), last accessed: February 27, 2020.

[340] 'Bam Bam (song)', *Wikipedia*, available at: https://en.wikipedia.org/wiki/Bam_Bam_(song), last accessed: February 27, 2020.

The Life of Pablo (2016)	'Hot in Herre'	'Hot in Herre' was the inaugural winner of the Grammy Award for Best Male Rap Solo Performance at the 45th Annual Grammy Awards on February 23, 2003.'[341]
	'EI'	'It peaked at number 11 on the UK Singles Chart and 16 on the U.S. Billboard Hot 100.'[342]
	'Jumpman'	'Jumpman peaked at number 12 on the US Billboard Hot 100 chart in the week of November 7, 2015, prior to being released as a single. The song was eventually certified quadruple platinum by the Recording Industry Association of America for combined sales and streaming units of over four millions units.'[343]
	'(I Know) I'm Losing You'	'(I Know) I'm Losing You' was a No. 1 hit on the Billboard R&B singles chart, and reached No. 8 on the Billboard Pop Singles chart. In Canada the song reached No.21.'[344]
	'Rock the Boat'	'Rock the Boat' charted as an 'album cut' and peaked at number 14 on the Billboard Hot 100 in the week of January 5. The song stayed on the chart for twenty-five weeks. 'Rock the Boat' was nominated for Best Female R&B Vocal Performance at the 44th Annual Grammy Awards.'[345]
Ye (2018)	'Hey Young World'	'Hey Young World' was written and produced by Slick Rick. It was number 42 on the Hot Black Singles chart and number 17 on the Hot Rap Singles.[346]
	'Take Me For a Little While'	'Take Me For a Little While': according with a Reddit post: Kanye West sampled 75% of the original song.[347]
Jesus is King (2019)	'Oh My God'	'Oh My God' is a song from the album *Midnight Marauders*, an album included on various 'best of' lists by music writers.[348]

CONCLUSIONS:

- the inspiration from other songs is at a satisfactory level and can create at least a satisfactory argument that Kanye West's musical career is because of the samples that he used in his music; it is possible that without these samples to not have the same level of fame as rap artist and producer;

---

[341] 'Hot in Herre', *Wikipedia*, available at: https://en.wikipedia.org/wiki/Hot_in_Herre, last accessed: February 27, 2020.

[342] 'E.I. (song)', *Wikipedia*, available at: https://en.wikipedia.org/wiki/E.I._(song), last accessed: February 27, 2020.

[343] 'Jumpman', *Wikipedia*, available at: https://en.wikipedia.org/wiki/Jumpman_(song), last accessed: February 27, 2020.

[344] 'I Know I'm Losing You', *Wikipedia*, available at: https://en.wikipedia.org/wiki/(I_Know)_I%27m_Losing_You, last accessed: February 27, 2020.

[345] 'Rock the Boat (Aaliyah song)', *Wikipedia*, available at: https://en.wikipedia.org/wiki/Rock_the_Boat_(Aaliyah_song), last accessed: February 27, 2020.

[346] 'Hey Young World', *Wikipedia*, available at: https://en.wikipedia.org/wiki/Hey_Young_World, last accessed: February 25, 2020.

[347] U/hobbbz, 'Kanye's "Ghost Town" is 75% a cover of "Take Me for a little While" whose author now makes racist albums', *Reddit*, available at:
https://www.reddit.com/r/hiphopheads/comments/8r25ju/kanyes_ghost_town_is_75_a_cover_of_take_me_for_a/, last accessed: July 31, 2022.

[348] Read the list here: 'Midnight Marauders', *Wikipedia*, available at: https://en.wikipedia.org/wiki/Midnight_Marauders, last accessed: February 25, 2020.

- Kanye West linked himself to some extent and used the instruments and lyrics of songs that were highly awarded, topped the charts, and some were considered by critics the best songs of all time;
- if the title of 'the greatest artist of all time' is based on writing your own lyrics and musical notes, Kanye West (in comparison with Taylor Swift) is not the greatest artist of all time;
- if the title of 'the greatest artist of all time' is based on mixing other songs, titles (used in any formats) and lyrics that were created and belong to other artists, then Kanye West is one of the greatest artists of all time, and higher than Taylor Swift;
- Kanye West used sounds and lyrics well known in the music industry;
- Kanye West brought to life music lost in the past to a new generation, where few to no people ever listened to the songs used in his music;
- Kanye West successfully managed to give glory to songs that were not awarded, or received less appreciation than what he thinks the songs should;
- Kanye West successfully united music from various artists and genres.

Same road: Taylor Swift (for *Lover* album in 2019) used samples from 'Humpty Dumpty' which is a character in an English nursery rhyme and one of the best known in the English-speaking world;[349] Kanye West used sample in the song 'Bad News' (from the album *808s & Heartbreak*, 2008) from 'Sea Lion Woman' which is a traditional African American folk song originally used as a children's playground song.[350]

II.1.6 The Race of the Samples

II.1.6.1 The Race of the Samples Used by Taylor Swift

TABLE 13. THE RACE OF THE SAMPLES USED BY TAYLOR SWIFT		
NAME OF THE ALBUM	BLACK MALE ARTISTS	BLACK FEMALE ARTISTS
Taylor Swift (Deluxe, 2006)	N/A	
Fearless (Platinum, 2008)	N/A	
Speak Now (Deluxe, 2010)	N/A	
RED (Deluxe, 2010)	N/A	
1989 (Deluxe, 2014)	N/A	
reputation (2017)	N/A	
Lover (2019)	2	0
folklore (Deluxe, 2020)	N/A	

---

[349] Lyrics: 'Humpty, Dumpty', *Genius*, available at: https://genius.com/Children-songs-humpty-dumpty-annotated, last accessed: February 25, 2020; 'Humpty Dumpty', *Wikipedia*, available at: https://en.wikipedia.org/wiki/Humpty_Dumpty; last accessed: February 25, 2020.
[350] 'Sea Lion Woman', *Wikipedia*, available at: https://en.wikipedia.org/wiki/Sea_Lion_Woman, last accessed: February 25, 2020.

Evermore (Deluxe, 2020)	N/A
Fearless (Taylor's Version, 2021)	N/A
TOTAL: 2 Black Male Artists + A group of students from Regent Park School of Music[351]	

CONCLUSIONS:

- Taylor Swift's music includes an extremely small number of black artists in her music, and it is not enough to build at least a satisfactory argument that she is famous because she sampled songs created by black artists, and she is taking advantage of them;
- the use of samples of music created by black artists can help to promote black artists at a global level and to millions of people.

II.1.6.2 The Race of the Samples Used by Kanye West

TABLE 14. THE RACE OF THE SAMPLES USED BY KANYE WEST		
NAME OF THE ALBUM	WHITE MALE ARTISTS	WHITE FEMALE ARTISTS
The College Dropout (2004)	7 out of 15	2 out of 6
Late Registration (2005)	N/A	
Graduation (2007)	5 out of 20	1 out of 1
88s & Heartbreak (2008)	2 out of 3	N/A
My Beautiful Dark Twisted Fantasy (2010)	21 out of 25	1 out of 1
Yeezus (2013)	2 out of 25	1 out of 2
The Life of Pablo (2016)	8 out o 64	2
Ye (2018)	3 out of 6	N/A
Jesus is King (2019)	5 out of 14	N/A
TOTAL	53 out of 172	7 out of 10
TOTAL IN PERCENTAGE	31%	70%

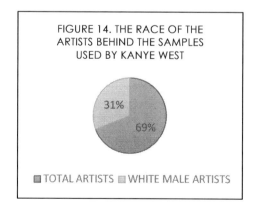

FIGURE 14. THE RACE OF THE ARTISTS BEHIND THE SAMPLES USED BY KANYE WEST

31%

69%

■ TOTAL ARTISTS ■ WHITE MALE ARTISTS

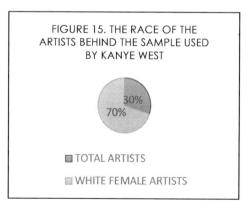

FIGURE 15. THE RACE OF THE ARTISTS BEHIND THE SAMPLE USED BY KANYE WEST

30%
70%

■ TOTAL ARTISTS

■ WHITE FEMALE ARTISTS

---

[351] I did not include the number of the students involved in making the sound that Taylor Swift used in her song, as I did not find credible information regarding the number of students and their ethnic background.

CONCLUSIONS:

- Kanye West's music contains 31% white artists in his music and there is evidence to build at least a satisfactory argument that he is famous also because he sampled songs created by white artists already known in the music industry, and maybe by the general public; however, this report found no clear evidence and link that Kanye West is taking advantage of the white artists, as the white artists allowed (to what I read, and at the time of writing this report, Kanye West is not involved in any copyrights lawsuit about the use of unauthorized samples in his songs) Kanye West to use their music in the format that he wanted;
- the high number of white artists in the music of a black artist shows a high level of intellectual abilities of Kanye West to create music based on various lyrics, instruments and genres;
- the use of samples of music created by white artists was a new strategy of global promotion of their songs, and their early success continued also with Kanye West and his version of their songs.

II.1.7 The Length of Songs

In this section of the chapter I investigated the length of songs released by Kanye West and Taylor Swift to show which artist has a higher number of minutes of music based purely on their own writing abilities.

II.1.7.1 The Length of Songs as Sole Lyricist: Taylor Swift

TABLE 15. THE LENGTH OF SONGS AS SOLE LYRICIST: TAYLOR SWIFT[352]		
NAME OF THE ALBUM	NAME OF THE SONG	LENGTH (MINUTES)
Taylor Swift (Deluxe, 2006)	The Outside	3:27
	Should've Said No	4:02
	Our Song	3:21
	Total: 10:50 minutes	
Fearless (Platinum, 2008)	Jump Then Fall: 3:57	3:57
	Forever & Always (piano version)	4:27
	The Other Side of the Door	3:58
	Fifteen	4:54
	Love Story	3:55
	Hey Stephen	4:14
	You're Not Sorry	4:22
	Forever & Always	3:45
	The Best Day	4:05
	Change	4:41
	Total: 42:18 minutes	

[352] On *Wikipedia* the songs have with 2 to 4 seconds more than on *Tidal*.

	Mine	3:50
	Sparks Fly	4:20
	Back to December	4:53
	Speak Now	4:00
	Dear John	6:53
	Mean	3:57
	The Story of Us	4:25
	Never Grow Up	4:50
Speak Now (Deluxe, 2010)[353]	Enchanted	5:52
	Better than Revenge	3:37
	Innocent	5:02
	Haunted	4:02
	Last Kiss	6:07
	Long Live	5:17
	Ours	3:58
	Superman	4:36
	Total: 75:29 minutes	
	State of Grace	4:55
	Red	3:43
	I Almost Do	4:04
	Stay Stay Stay	3:25
	Holy Ground	3:22
	Sad Beautiful Tragic	4:44
RED (Deluxe, 2012)	The Lucky One	4:00
	Starlight	3:40
	Begin Again	3:59
	The Moment I Knew	4:46
	Girl at Home	3:40
	Total: 44:18 minutes	
1989 (Deluxe, 2014)	This Love	4:10
	Total: 4:10 minutes	
reputation (2017)	N/A	
	Lover	3:41
Lover (2019)	Cornelia Street	4:47
	Daylight	4:53
	Total: 13:21 minutes	
folklore (Deluxe, 2020)	My Tears Ricochet	4:16
	Total: 4:16 minutes	
Evermore (Deluxe, 2020)	No Body, No Crime	3:35
	Total: 3:35 minutes	
	Today Was a Fairytale	4:01
Fearless (Taylor's Version, 2021)	Mr. Perfectly Fine	4:37
	Total: 8:38 minutes	
Total (songs/length)	*Songs: 48; Length: 206:55 minutes*	

---

[353] The length of the songs 'Our Song' and 'Superman' was taken from Wikipedia.
https://en.wikipedia.org/wiki/Fearless_(Taylor_Swift_album)#Track_listing, last accessed: February 25, 2020.

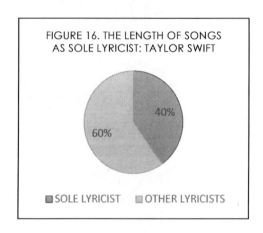

FIGURE 16. THE LENGTH OF SONGS
AS SOLE LYRICIST: TAYLOR SWIFT

II.1.7.2 The Length of Songs as Sole Lyricists: Kanye West

TABLE 16. THE LENGTH OF SONGS AS SOLE LYRICIST: KANYE WEST		
NAME OF THE ALBUM	NAME OF THE SONG	LENGTH (MINUTES)
The College Dropout (2004)	Intro (Skit)	0:19
	Workout Plan (Skit)	0:46
	School Spirit (Skit 1)	1:18
	School Spirit (Skit 2)	0:43
	Lil Jimmy (Skit)	0:53
	Family Business	4:38
	Total: 8:57 minutes	
Late Registration (2005)	Celebration	3:18
	Total: 3:18 minutes	
Graduation (2007)	N/A	
808s & Heartbreak (2008)	Pinocchio Story	6:01
	Total: 6:01 minutes	
My Beautiful Dark Twisted Fantasy (2010)	N/A	
Yeezus (2013)	N/A	
The Life of Pablo (2016)	N/A	
Ye (2018)	N/A	
Jesus is King (2019)	N/A	
Total (songs/length)	*Songs: With Intro and Skit: 8; Without Intro and Skit: 3*	
	Minutes: With Intro and Skit: 18:16; Without Intro and Skit: 13:57	

| TABLE 17. THE LENGTH OF SONGS AS SOLE LYRICIST: TAYLOR SWIFT & KANYE WEST ||
TAYLOR SWIFT	KANYE WEST
Taylor Swift (Deluxe, 2006): 10:50 out of 51:14 minutes	The College Dropout (2004): 8:57 out of 76:11 minutes
Fearless (Platinum, 2008): 42:18 out of 79:32 minutes	Late Registration (2005): 3:18 out of 73:52 minutes
Speak Now (Deluxe, 2010): 75:29 out of 79:23 minutes	Graduation (2007): 0 out of 54:30 minutes
RED (Deluxe, 2012): 44:18 out of 77:27 minutes	88s & Heartbreak (2008): 6:01 out of 52:05 minutes
1989 (Deluxe, 2014): 4:10 out of 61:11 minutes	My Beautiful Dark Twisted Fantasy (2010): 0 out of 68:44 minutes
reputation (2017): 0 out of 55:44 minutes	Yeezus (2013): 0 out of 40:03 minutes
Lover (2019): 13:21 out of 61:48 minutes	The Life of Pablo (2016): 0 out of 66:01 minutes
folklore (Deluxe, 2020): 4:16 out of 67:01 minutes	Ye (2018): 0 out of 23:45 minutes
Evermore (Deluxe, 2020): 3:35 out of 69:08 minutes	Jesus is King (2019): 0 out of 27:04 minutes
Fearless (Taylor's Version, 2021): 8:38 out of 23:00 minutes	
Total minutes: 206:55 out of 625:37 minutes	*Total minutes: 18:16 out of 492:03 minutes (With Intro & Skit); 13:57 out of 492:03 minutes (Without Intro & Skit)*

FIGURE 17. THE LENGTH OF SONGS AS SOLE LYRICIST: KANYE WEST (WITH INTRO & SKIT)

4%

96%

■ SOLE LYRICIST ■ OTHER LYRICISTS

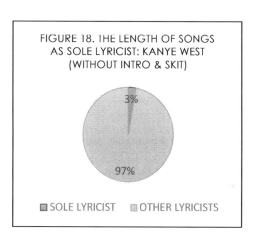

FIGURE 18. THE LENGTH OF SONGS AS SOLE LYRICIST: KANYE WEST (WITHOUT INTRO & SKIT)

3%

97%

■ SOLE LYRICIST ■ OTHER LYRICISTS

CONCLUSIONS:

- Taylor Swift wrote alone at least 11 times (includes Intro & Skit by Kanye West) and at least 14 times (without Intro & Outro by Kanye West) more minutes of music than Kanye West;
- Taylor Swift wrote at least 6 (includes *Intro & Outro* by Kanye West) and 16 times (does not include *Intro & Outro* by Kanye West) more songs than Kanye West.

II.1.7.3 The Length of Songs with Two Lyricists for Taylor Swift

TABLE 18. THE LENGTH OF SONGS WITH TWO LYRICISTS: TAYLOR SWIFT		
NAME OF THE ALBUM	NAME OF THE SONG	LENGTH (MINUTES)
Taylor Swift (Deluxe, 2006)	Tim McGraw	3:54
	Picture to Burn	2:55
	Teardrops on my Guitar	3:55
	Cold as You	4:01
	Tied Together with a Smile	4:11
	Stay Beautiful	3:58
	Invisible	3:26
	Total: 26:20 minutes	
Fearless (Platinum, 2008)	White Horse	3:54
	You Belong with Me	3:51
	Breathe	4:23
	Tell Me Why	3:20
	The Way I Loved You	4:04
	Come in the Rain	3:58
	Superstar	3:26
	Total: 27:51 minutes	
Speak Now (Deluxe, 2010)[354]	If This Was a Movie	3:54
	Total: 3:54 minutes	
RED (Deluxe, 2012)	Treacherous	4:02
	All Too Well	5:29
	Everything Has Changed	4:05
	Come Back … Be Here	3:42
	Total: 17:18 minutes	
1989 (Deluxe, 2014)	Welcome to New York	3:32
	Out of the Woods	3:55
	All You Had To Do Was Stay	3:13
	I Wish You Would	3:27
	I Know Places	3:15
	Clean	4:30
	You Are In Love	4:27
	Total: 26:19 minutes	
reputation (2017)	Getaway Car	3:53
	Dress	3:50
	This is Why We Can't Have Nice Things	3:27
	Call It What You Want	3:23
	New Year's Day	3:55
	Total: 18:28 minutes	
	The Man	3:10
	The Archer	3:31
	I Think He Knows	2:53

---

[354] The length of the songs 'Our Song' and 'Superman' was taken from Wikipedia.

Lover (2019)	Miss Americana & The Heartbreak Prince	3:54
	Paper Rings	3:42
	Death by a Thousand Cuts	3:19
	Soon You'll Get Better	3:22
	False God	3:20
	You Need To Calm Down	2:51
	Total: 30:02 minutes	
folklore (Deluxe, 2020)	the 1	3:30
	cardigan	3:59
	the last great American dynasty	3:51
	my tears ricochet	4:15
	mirrorball	3:29
	seven	3:28
	august	4:21
	this is me trying	3:15
	illicit affairs	3:10
	invisible string	4:12
	mad woman	3:57
	epiphany	4:49
	betty	4:54
	peace	3:54
	hoax	3:40
	Total: 58:44 minutes	
Evermore (Deluxe, 2020)	Willow	3:34
	Champagne Problems	4:04
	Gold Rush	3:05
	Tis the Damn Season	3:49
	Tolerate It	4:05
	Happiness	5:15
	Dorothea	3:45
	Cowboy Like Me	4:35
	Long Story Short	3:35
	Marjorie	4:17
	Closure	3:00
	Right Were You Left Me	4:05
	It's Time to Go	4:15
	Total: 51:24 minutes	
Fearless (Taylor's Version, 2021)	You All Over Me	3:40
	We Were Happy	4:04
	Don't You	3:28
	Bye Bye Baby	4:02
	Total: 15:14 minutes	
Total (songs/length)	*Songs: 72; Length: 275:34 minutes*	

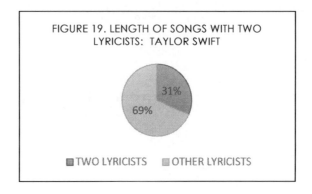

FIGURE 19. LENGTH OF SONGS WITH TWO LYRICISTS: TAYLOR SWIFT

II.1.7.4 The Length of Songs with Two Lyricists for Kanye West

TABLE 19. THE LENGTH OF SONGS WITH TWO LYRICISTS: KANYE WEST		
NAME OF THE ALBUM	NAME OF THE SONG	LENGTH (MINUTES)
The College Dropout (2004)	'All Falls Down'	3:43
	'Breathe In Breathe Out'	4:06
	'School Spirit'	3:02
	Total: 10:51 minutes	
Late Registration (2005)	'Roses': 4:05	'Roses': 4:05
	'Bring Me Down': 3:18	'Bring Me Down': 3:18
	'Hey Mama': 5:05	'Hey Mama': 5:05
	Total: 12:28 minutes	
Graduation (2007)	'I Wonder'	4:03
	'Can't Tell Me Nothing'	4:31
	'Flashing Lights'	3:57
	'Big Brother'	4:47
	Total: 17:18 minutes	
808s & Heartbreak (2008)	'Bad News'	3:58
	Total: 3:58 minutes	
My Beautiful Dark Twisted Fantasy (2010)	N/A	
Yeezus (2013)	N/A	
The Life of Pablo (2016)	N/A	
Ye (2018)	N/A	
Jesus is King (2019)	N/A	
Total (songs/length)	*Songs: 11; Length: 44:35 minutes.*	

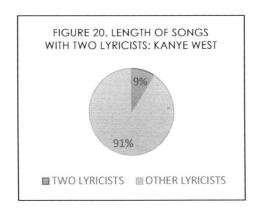

FIGURE 20. LENGTH OF SONGS WITH TWO LYRICISTS: KANYE WEST

TABLE 20. THE LENGTH OF SONGS WITH TWO LYRICISTS: TAYLOR SWIFT AND KANYE WEST	
TAYLOR SWIFT	KANYE WEST
Taylor Swift (Deluxe, 2006): 26:20 out of 51:14 minutes	The College Dropout (2004): 10:51 out of 76:11 minutes
Fearless (Platinum, 2008): 27:51 out of 79:32 minutes	Late Registration (2005): 12:28 out of 73:52 minutes
Speak Now (Deluxe, 2010): 3:54 out of 79:23 minutes	Graduation (2007): 17:18 out of 54:30 minutes
RED (Deluxe, 2012): 17:18 out of 77:27 minutes	88s & Heartbreak (2008): 3:58 out of 61:53 minutes
1989 (Deluxe, 2014): 26:19 out of 61:11 minutes	My Beautiful Dark Twisted Fantasy (2010): 0 out of 68:44 minutes
reputation (2017): 18:28 out of 55:44 minutes	Yeezus (2013): 0 out of 40:03 minutes
Lover (2019): 30:02 out of 61:48 minutes	The Life of Pablo (2016): 0 out of 66:01 minutes
folklore (Deluxe, 2020): 58:44 out of 67:01 minutes	Ye (2018): 0 out of 23:45 minutes
Evermore (Deluxe, 2020): 51:24 out of 69:08 minutes	Jesus is King (2019): 0 out of 27:04 minutes
Fearless (Taylor's Version, 2021): 15:14 out of 23:00 minutes	
Total length: 275:34 out of 625:37 minutes	*Total length: 44:35 out of 492:03 minutes*

CONCLUSION:

- Taylor Swift has written at least 6 times more songs in partnership with a second lyricist than Kanye West, and 6 times more minutes of music than Kanye West.

II.1.7.5 Number of Songs Produced Only by Kanye West

TABLE 21. NUMBER OF SONGS PRODUCED ONLY BY KANYE WEST
The College Dropout (2004): 19 out of 22
Late Registration (2005): 4 out of 22
Graduation (2007): 3 out of 14
88s & Heartbreak (2008): 3 out of 12

My Beautiful Dark Twisted Fantasy (2010): 0 out of 14
Watch the Throne Deluxe (2011): 1 out of 16
Cruel Summer (2012): 0 out of 12
Yeezus (2013): 0 out of 10
The Life of Pablo (2016): 0 out of 20
Ye (2018): 0 out of 7
Kids See Ghosts (2018): 0 out of 7
Jesus is King (2019): 0 out of 11
Total songs: 30 out of 167

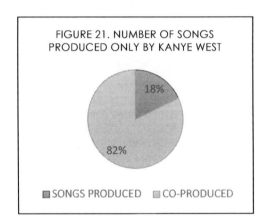

FIGURE 21. NUMBER OF SONGS PRODUCED ONLY BY KANYE WEST

CONCLUSIONS:

- Kanye West sole production is 18% of his songs, and Taylor Swift 0%;
- Kanye West's abilities seems to be limited when he has to actually play live at piano and with a guitar: I did not find a video with Kanye West singing in full one of his songs at a piano, or with a guitar; Taylor Swift, on the other hand, has good, maybe advanced, skills in using musical instruments such as piano and guitar, and also plays live using both instruments successfully with positive praise.[355]

II.1.7.6 Length of Music Produced Only by Kanye West

TABLE 22. LENGTH OF MUSIC PRODUCED ONLY BY KANYE WEST
The College Dropout (2004): 8:57 out of 76:11 minutes

---

[355] Christina Nunn, 'Taylor Swift Proves She's a Musical Genius But Doesn't Recognize Her Own Hit Song', *Cheat Sheet*, October 5, 2019, available at: https://www.cheatsheet.com/entertainment/taylor-swift-proves-shes-a-musical-genius-but-doesnt-recognize-her-own-hit-song.html/, last accessed: February 20, 2020.

Late Registration (2005): 3:18 out of 73:52 minutes
Graduation (2007): 0 out of 54:30 minutes
88s & Heartbreak (2008): 6:01 out of 52:05 minutes
My Beautiful Dark Twisted Fantasy (2010): 0 out of 68:44 minutes
Watch the Throne Deluxe (2011): 0 out of 64:50 minutes
Cruel Summer (2012): 0 out of 54:34 minutes[356]
Yeezus (2013): 0 out of 40:03 minutes
The Life of Pablo (2016): 0 out of 66:01 minutes
Ye (2018): 0 out of 23:45 minutes
Kids See Ghosts (2018): 0 out of 23:53 minutes[357]
Jesus is King (2019): 0 out of 27:04 minutes
Total lengths: 18:16 out of 536:49 minutes (around 3.1%)

Taylor Swift does not have songs produced only by herself, but in partnership with at least one producer.

II.1.8 The Rabbit Hat: Fame, Originality and Creativity After VMA 2009

In this section of the chapter I investigated the roots of the new album released a year after the MTV scene that is the music released by both artists in the autumn of 2010, first Taylor Swift then Kanye West.[358]

TABLE 23. THE RABBIT HAT: TAYLOR SWIFT AND KANYE WEST		
CATEGORY	TAYLOR SWIFT: *SPEAK NOW (DELUXE, 2010)*	KANYE WEST: *MY BEAUTIFUL DARK TWISTED FANTASY (2010)*
FIRST WEEK SALES	HIGH INCREASE	HIGH DECREASE
OVERALL ALBUM SALES	HIGH NUMBER OF SALES ON LONG TERM	MODERATE NUMBER OF SALES WITH TRACKS OF SLOW SALES ON LONG TERM
USE OF SAMPLE	0%	10 OUT OF 14 SONGS
ORIGINAL SONGS WITH NO SAMPLE	17 SONGS (100%)	4 OUT OF 14 SONGS
ORIGINAL SONG AS SOLE LYRICIST	16 OUT OF 17 SONGS	0 SONGS (0%)
ORIGINAL SONG WITH TWO LYRICISTS	1 OUT OF 17 SONGS	0 OUT OF 14 SONGS (0%)
ORIGINAL SONG WITH THREE LYRICISTS	0 SONGS	1 OUT OF 14 SONGS
ORIGINAL SONG WITH AT LEAST FOUR LYRICICTS	0 SONGS	13 OUT OF 14 SONGS

---

[356] Kanye West, 'Kanye West Presents Good Music Cruel Summer', *Tidal,* available alt: https://listen.tidal.com/album/17078868, last accessed: February 20, 2020.

[357] Kanye West, 'Kids See Ghosts Credits', *Tidal*, available at: https://listen.tidal.com/album/90151605, last accessed: February 20, 2020.

[358] Read Casian Anton, *On the Famous Feud.*

DIRECT INSPIRATION FROM OTHER SONGS	NO	YES
TOP CHARTS & AWARDS OF THE SONG SAMPLED	NO	YES
DIRECT WHITE MALE INSPIRATION	N/A	21 OUT OF 25
DIRECT WHITE FEMALE INSPIRATION	N/A	1 OUT OF 1
DIRECT BLACK MALE INSPIRATION	N/A	4 out of 25
DIRECT BLACK FEMALE INSPIRATION	N/A	
METACRITIC RATING	77	94
LENGTH OF SONG AS SOLE LYRICIST	75:29 MINUTES	0 MINUTES
LENGTH OF SONG WITH TWO LYRICISTS	3:54	0 MINUTES (THERE IS A HIGHER NUMBER OF MINUTES ONLY TO SONGS WITH AT LEAST 4 SONGWRITERS)
LYRICS	OWN LYRICS	LYRICS FROM OTHER ARTISTS
THE ORIGINS OF TITLE SONGS	OWN TITLES	FROM OTHER TITLES OF SONGS AND LYRICS OF SONGS SAMPLED IN HIS MUSIC
PATTERN OF MUSIC RELEASE	2006: October 24 2008: November 11 2010: October 25	2004: February 10 2005: August 30 2007: September 11 2008: November 24 2010: November 22
	The following date are written to observe the full pattern of music release of both artists.	
	2012: October 22 2014: October 27 2017: November 10 2019: August 23 2020: July 24 2020: December 11	2013: June 18 2016: February 14 2018: June 1 2019: October 25

CONCLUSIONS:

- *Taylor Swift*:

    o came with traces of global success;
    o came with her own lyrics;
    o released an album with original songs never heard before in the music industry;
    o the length of the music written by herself for *Standard Edition* is 100% of the album, for *Deluxe Edition* she has one song written in partnership with another lyricist;
    o released the music following October – November pattern;

- *Kanye West*:

  o Kanye West has 0% as sole lyricist;
  o came with lyrics written in partnership with other artists and instruments already created and used by other artists in the music industry;
  o 13 out of 14 songs were written in partnership with at least 4 lyricists;
  o it is inspired by the music written by white male artists, 21 out of 25 male artists;
  o overall, his album was rated on Metacritic with a higher grade (94) than Taylor Swift (77);
  o changed the pattern of music release and interfered for a second time in Taylor Swift's pattern of album release: one album in each year for two years and in total for four albums: the first two albums: 2004 and 2005, the next two albums: 2007 and 2008; since 2008 Kanye West changed the season and released his album in the same month as Taylor Swift, but two weeks later: Taylor Swift on November 11, 2008 and Kanye West on November 24; *in 2010*: Taylor Swift released the album on October 25 (she released her first album in October 24, 2006), then Kanye West later in November 22, keeping the release date connected with the last release, which is the first and last time when Kanye West followed this release pattern; the following albums were released in different seasons, only to be changed to October 25, 2019 with *Jesus is King*, the same release date as Taylor Swift with *Speak Now* in 2010.

- *Album reviews*: Kanye West received higher reviews and grades than Taylor Swift, but given the sources of his songs, the following questions arise: do the reviews also include an analysis of his voice? online critics argue that his singing skills are either weak, or he does not know how to sing[359]; did the reviewers perform a genuine analysis of his voice? if this argument is true, how did he manage to get such a high score? Kanye West used samples (title, lyrics, instruments) from other artists, basically what is Kanye West's original contribution in his album? are the reviews and grades received based only on his work, or the final song that contains samples? are reviewers able to make the difference between Kanye West's original part and the samples part? if we take the samples from Kanye's album, what remains written and produced by him alone is worth grades 9 and 10? Taylor Swift got the grades based

---

[359] 'How Well Does Kanye West Really Sing', *Quora*, available at: https://www.quora.com/How-well-does-Kanye-West-really-sing, last accessed: February 25, 2020; 'Why is Kanye West considered to be a great artist? I have listened to his music, and it sounds like every other song on the radio. Am I missing something?', *Quora*, available at: https://www.quora.com/Why-is-Kanye-West-considered-to-be-a-great-artist-I-have-listened-to-his-music-and-it-sounds-like-every-other-song-on-the-radio-Am-I-missing-something, last accessed: February 25, 2020; 'David Crosby: Kanye West can neither sing, nor write, nor play', *The Guardian*, October 28, 2016, available at: https://www.theguardian.com/music/2016/oct/28/david-crosby-kanye-west, last accessed: February 25, 2020.

on her own lyrics and 50% participation as producer of her album, and were 7 and 8 in the eyes of the reviewers; Kanye got 9 and 10 with the help of more lyricists and producers than Taylor Swift, but we do not know for sure how much is Kanye's contribution in the lyrics of the songs and production; are the reviews real or have they been exaggerated to the detriment of the music industry, but also of the white artist Taylor Swift to prove that black artists have better music than white artists, and Kanye West was right to point out that Taylor Swift did not deserve the award from 2009?

II.1.9 Producers and Lyricists

In the following pages I created figures with the number of producers and lyricists in partnership with both artists. Indeed, Kanye West has a better start in comparison with Taylor Swift, however, the overall conclusion is that Taylor Swift partnered with less producers and lyricists to create and sell millions of songs and albums than Kanye West.

II.1.9.1 Number of Producers: Kanye West and Taylor Swift

In this section of the chapter I created figures to compare the number of producers in partnership with Kanye West and Taylor Swift on different layers. The *first layer* is a comparison of the number of producers at the start of their careers; the *second layer* is a comparison of the number of producers of albums released in the same year; the *third layer* is a comparison of the number of producers of albums released in different years; the *fourth layer* are figures with the number of producers only about the albums released by Kanye West.

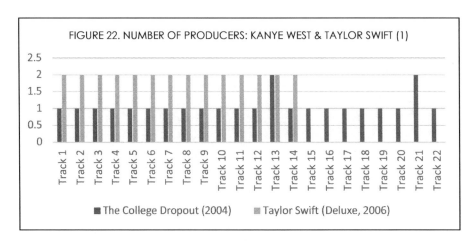

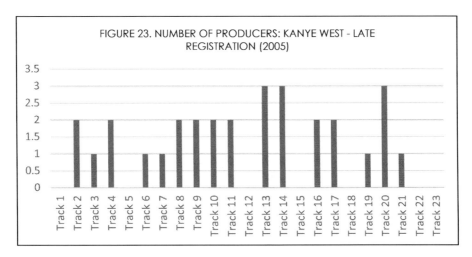

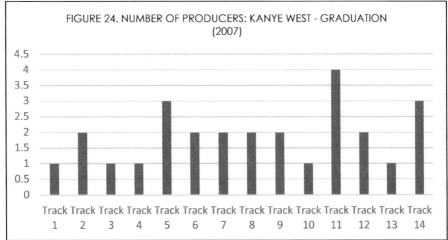

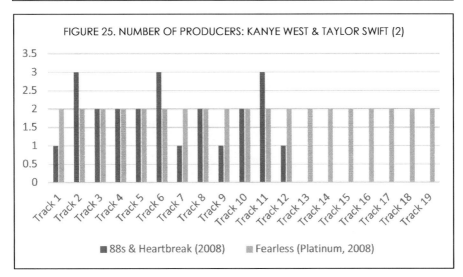

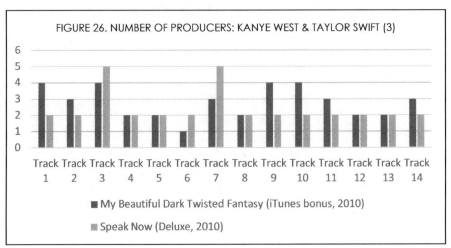

FIGURE 26. NUMBER OF PRODUCERS: KANYE WEST & TAYLOR SWIFT (3)

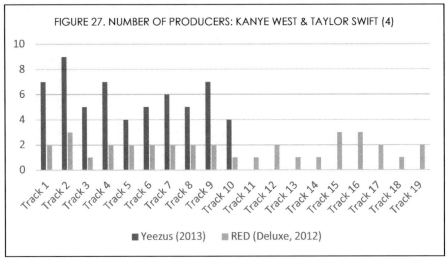

FIGURE 27. NUMBER OF PRODUCERS: KANYE WEST & TAYLOR SWIFT (4)

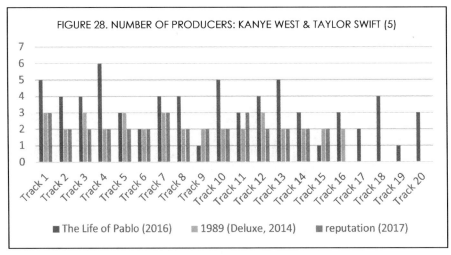

FIGURE 28. NUMBER OF PRODUCERS: KANYE WEST & TAYLOR SWIFT (5)

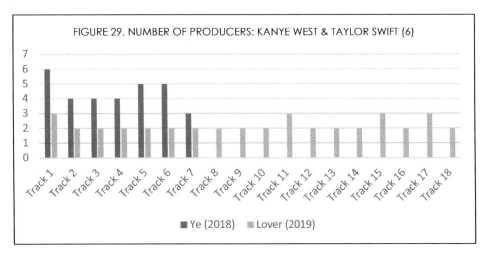

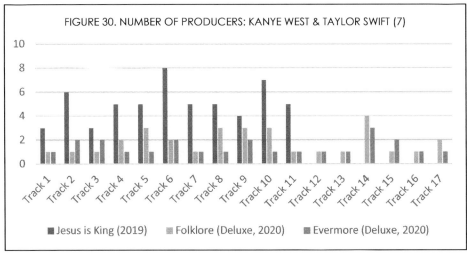

II.1.9.2 Number of Lyricists: Kanye West and Taylor Swift

In this section of the chapter I used the same strategy (on four layers) as with the number of producers, but with focus on the number of lyricists in partnership with Kanye West and Taylor Swift.

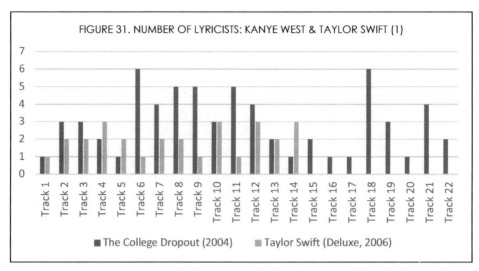

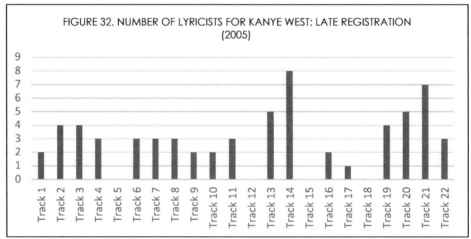

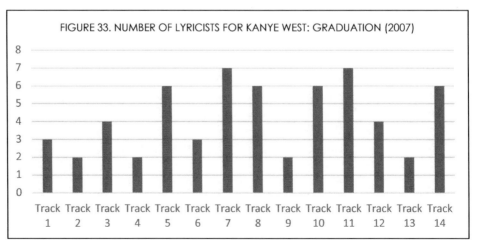

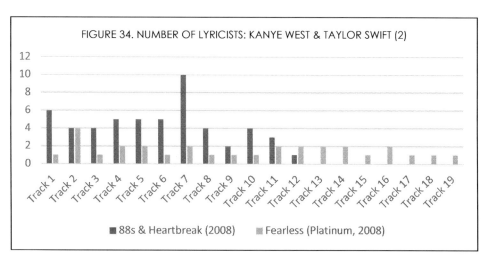

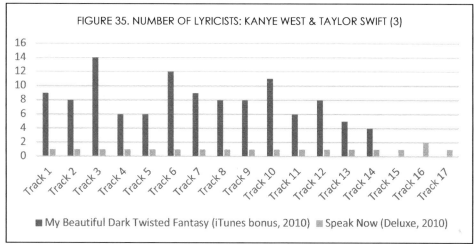

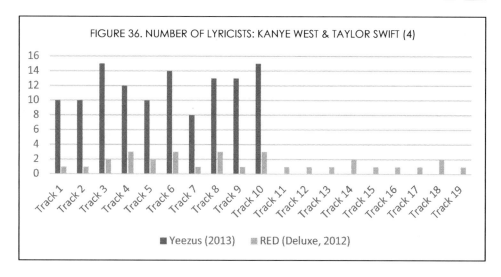

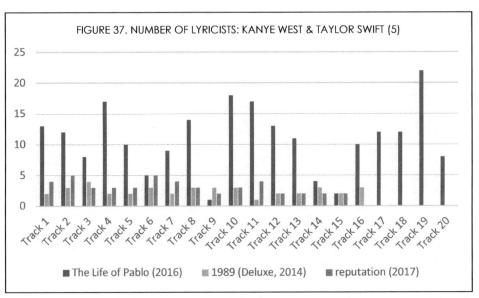

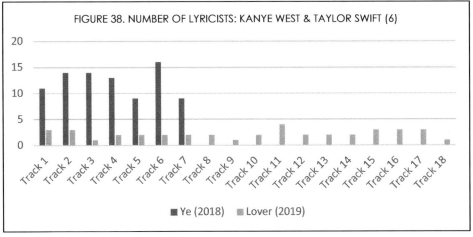

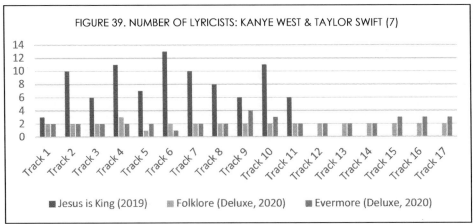

II.1.10 The Rating on Metacritic

TABLE 24. THE ALBUM RATINGS ON METACRITIC: TAYLOR SWIFT & KANYE WEST	
TAYLOR SWIFT[360]	KANYE WEST[361]
Taylor Swift (Deluxe, 2006): not on Metacritic	The College Dropout (2004): 87
Fearless (Platinum, 2008): 73	Late Registration (2005): 85
Speak Now (Deluxe, 2010): 77	Graduation (2007): 79
RED (Deluxe, 2012): 77	88s & Heartbreak (2008): 75
1989 (Deluxe, 2014): 76	My Beautiful Dark Twisted Fantasy (2010): 94
reputation (2017): 71	Yeezus (2013): 84
Lover (2019): 79	The Life of Pablo (2016): 75
folklore (Deluxe, 2020): 88	Ye (2018): 64
Evermore (Deluxe, 2020): 85	Jesus is King (2019): 55
Fearless (Taylor's Version, 2021): 82	
Total average: 78.66	*Total average: 77.55*

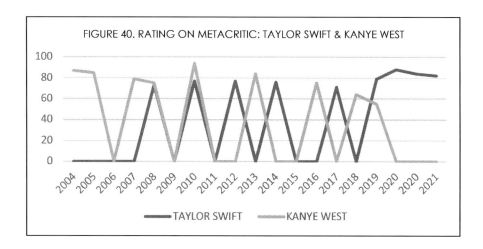

FIGURE 40. RATING ON METACRITIC: TAYLOR SWIFT & KANYE WEST

CONCLUSIONS:

- *Taylor Swift*:

  - the grades received for each album are based on the work and ideas of the artist, but also to a considerable extent of other artists and producers she

[360] Taylor Swift, *Metacritic*, available at: https://www.metacritic.com/person/taylor-swift, last accessed: July 1, 2021.
[361] Kanye West, *Metacritic*, available at: https://www.metacritic.com/person/kanye-west?filter-options=music&sort_options=date&num_items=30, last accessed: July 1, 2021.

worked with (see the producers of *folklore* and *Evermore*, most of them is one producer, Aaron Dessner or Jack Antonoff);
- o male producers are the constant base of her musical career;
- o compared to Kanye West and Metacritic, the grades received is close to 8, where they increase and decrease over the years;
- o a significant percentage of the grade received is based purely on her ability to write and compose unheard songs; in her music catalogue there are lots of songs that were written shortly after she heard the instruments, and were hits on the radio and charts;
- o Metacritic does not include all the reviews written about her albums, there are reviews with higher and lower grades which are not included; it is highly possible that the final grade to be over 80.

- *Kanye West*:

  - o the grades received for each album are based on the work and ideas of the artist, but also to a considerable extent of other artists from whom he sampled; also, for lyricists and producers who contributed to his songs;
  - o compared to Taylor Swift (the grades increased, and before the age 30 she has one of the highest reviewed album in her life, *folklore*), he received a high grade, 87 and then decreased (for 3 albums), then raised to the highest grade (94); for the last albums, the grades decreased, and for the last album the final grade is 55;
  - o parts of his grades belong to white artists as well;
  - o Metacritic does not include all the reviews written about his albums; there are reviews with higher and lower grades which are not included; it is highly possible that the final grade to be over 80.

II.2 Beyoncé versus Kendrick Lamar

In the following section of chapter II, I investigated the music released by Beyoncé (black woman) and Kendrick Lamar (black man). I applied the same research methods used for Kanye West and Taylor Swift.

The idea of this chapter is to see similarities and differences between the black artists.

The information from this chapter was used to compare the black artists (Beyoncé and Kendrick Lamar) with the white artists (Adele, Beck, Taylor Swift and Macklemore & Ryan).

II.2.1 Samples

II.2.1.1 Use of Sample

TABLE 25. USE OF SAMPLE: BEYONCÉ & KENDRICK LAMAR	
BEYONCÉ	KENDRICK LAMAR
Dangerously in Love (2003): 8 out of 16[362]	Section.80 (2011): 8 out of 16[363]
B'Day (Deluxe, 2006): 3 out of 17[364]	good kid, m.A.A.d. City (Deluxe, 2012): 8 out of 17[365]
I am...Sasha Fierce (Platinum, 2008): 0 out of 20[366]	To Pimp a Butterfly (2015): 6 out of 16[367]
4 (2011): 4 out of 14[368]	Damn (2017): 10 out of 14[369]
Beyoncé (Platinum, 2013): 4 out of 16[370]	
Lemonade (2016): 6 out of 12[371]	

[362] Beyoncé, 'Dangerously In Love Credits', 2003, *Tidal*, available at: https://listen.tidal.com/album/2859862, last accessed: July 1, 2021.

[363] Kendrick Lamar, 'Section.80', 2011, *Tidal*, available at: https://listen.tidal.com/album/114492492, last accessed: July 1, 2021.

[364] Beyoncé, 'B'Day (Deluxe Edition) Credits', 2006, *Tidal*, available at: https://listen.tidal.com/album/3347090, from Volume 2 only Amor Gitano is included as the rest of the songs are Spanish (one song is mixed with Spanish and English) and remixes of songs from volume 1; last accessed: July 1, 2021.

[365] Kendrick Lamar, 'good kid, m.A.A.d. city (Deluxe Edition) Credits', 2012, *Tidal* available at: https://listen.tidal.com/album/20556792, last accessed: July 1, 2021.

[366] Beyoncé, 'I am...Sasha Fierce (Platinum Edition) Credits', *Tidal*, available at: https://listen.tidal.com/album/3147463, last accessed: July 1, 2021. The songs included in this study are: Standard Edition (11 songs), International (1), Deluxe (6): in total 18 songs.

[367] Kendrick Lamar, 'To Pimp a Butterfly', 2015, *Tidal*, available at: https://listen.tidal.com/album/77703636, last accessed: July 1, 2021.

[368] Beyoncé, '4 Credits', 2011, *Tidal*, available at: https://listen.tidal.com/album/19646520, last accessed: July 1, 2021. Tracks '7/11' and 'Ring Off' were not included in this table.

[369] Kendrick Lamar, 'Damn Credits', 2017, *Tidal*, available at: https://listen.tidal.com/album/72694579, last accessed: July 1, 2021.

[370] Beyoncé, 'Beyoncé (Platinum Edition) Credits', 2014, *Tidal*, available at: https://listen.tidal.com/album/37936030, last accessed: July 1, 2021. From Volume 2 I included only '7/11' and 'Ring Off' as part of the total number of songs, but the sample from 'Ring Off' was not included since it was a portion of a speech, and not a genuine song.

[371] Beyoncé, 'Lemonade Credits', 2016, *Tidal*, available at: https://listen.tidal.com/album/108043414, last accessed: July 1, 2021. Tracks 'Sorry (Original Demo)', 'Formation (Choreography Video)' and 'Lemonade Film' were not listed in this table.

| Total: 25 out of 95 songs (26%) | Total: 32 out of 63 songs (51%) |

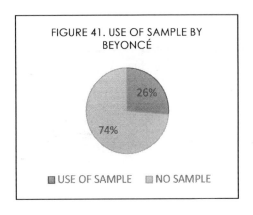

FIGURE 41. USE OF SAMPLE BY BEYONCÉ

26%

74%

■ USE OF SAMPLE   ■ NO SAMPLE

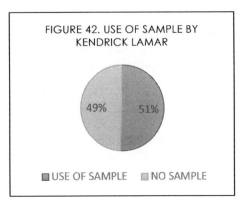

FIGURE 42. USE OF SAMPLE BY KENDRICK LAMAR

49%   51%

■ USE OF SAMPLE   ■ NO SAMPLE

CONCLUSION:

- both artists used samples, but Kendrick Lamar more than Beyoncé, more precisely, almost double.

II.2.1.2 No Use of Sample

TABLE 26. NO USE OF SAMPLE: BEYONCÉ & KENDRICK LAMAR	
BEYONCÉ	KENDRICK LAMAR
Dangerously in Love (2003): 8 out of 16	Section.80 (2011): 8 out of 16
B'Day (Deluxe, 2006): 14 out of 17	good kid, m.A.A.d. City (Deluxe, 2012): 9 out of 17
I am...Sasha Fierce (Platinum, 2008): 20 out of 20	To Pimp a Butterfly (2015): 10 out of 16
4 (2011): 10 out of 14	Damn (2017): 4 out of 14
Beyoncé (Platinum, 2013): 12 out of 16	
Lemonade (2016): 6 out of 12	
Total: 70 out of 95 songs (74%)	*Total: 31 out of 63 songs (closed to 50%)*

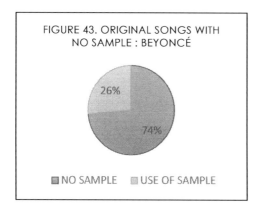

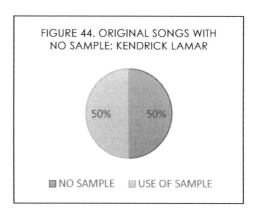

II.2.2 Lyricists

II.2.2.1 Sole Lyricist

TABLE 27. ORIGINAL SONGS AS SOLE LYRICIST: BEYONCÉ & KENDRICK LAMAR	
BEYONCÉ	KENDRICK LAMAR
Dangerously in Love (2003): 1 out of 16[372]	Section.80 (2011): 0 out of 16
B'Day (Deluxe, 2006): 0 out of 17	good kid, m.A.A.d. City (Deluxe, 2012): 0 out of 17
I am...Sasha Fierce (Platinum, 2008): 1 out of 20[373]	To Pimp a Butterfly (2015): 0 out of 16
4 (2011): 1 out of 14[374]	Damn (2017): 0 out of 14
Beyoncé (Platinum, 2013): 0 out of 16	
Lemonade (2016): 0 out of 12	
Total: 3 out of 95 songs (3%)	Total: 0 out of 63 songs (0%)

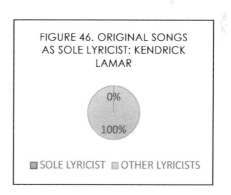

---

[372] 'Interlude': it is not a full song; it has 16 seconds and it is the only song written solely by Beyoncé in her entire discography.
[373] The song 'Honesty': was solely written by Billy Joel.
[374] The song 'I Was Here': was solely written by Diana Eve Warren.

II.2.2.2 Two Lyricists

TABLE 28. ORIGINAL SONGS WITH TWO LYRICISTS: BEYONCÉ & KENDRICK LAMAR	
BEYONCÉ	KENDRICK LAMAR
Dangerously in Love (2003): 4 out of 16	Section.80 (2011): 10 out of 16
B'Day (Deluxe, 2006): 0 out of 17	good kid, m.A.A.d. City (Deluxe, 2012): 4 out of 17
I am...Sasha Fierce (Platinum, 2008): 1 out of 20	To Pimp a Butterfly (2015): 1 out of 16
4 (2011): 0 out of 14	Damn (2017): 4 out of 14
Beyoncé (Platinum, 2013): 3 out of 16	
Lemonade (2016): 1 out of 12	
Total: 9 out of 95 songs (9%)	*Total: 19 out of 63 songs (30%)*

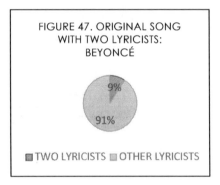

FIGURE 47. ORIGINAL SONG
WITH TWO LYRICISTS:
BEYONCÉ

9%
91%

■ TWO LYRICISTS ■ OTHER LYRICISTS

FIGURE 48. ORIGINAL SONG
WITH TWO LYRICISTS:
KENDRICK LAMAR

30%
70%

■ TWO LYRICISTS ■ OTHER LYRICISTS

CONCLUSION:

- Beyoncé has fewer original songs written with two lyricists (herself included) than Kendrick Lamar.

II.2.2.3 Three Lyricists

TABLE 29. ORIGINAL SONGS WITH THREE LYRICISTS: BEYONCÉ & KENDRICK LAMAR	
BEYONCÉ	KENDRICK LAMAR
Dangerously in Love (2003): 4 out of 16	Section.80 (2011): 6 out of 16
B'Day (Deluxe, 2006): 6 out of 17	good kid, m.A.A.d. City (Deluxe, 2012): 5 out of 17
I am...Sasha Fierce (Platinum, 2008): 5 out of 20	To Pimp a Butterfly (2015): 3 out of 16
4 (2011): 8 out of 14	Damn (2017): 1 out of 14
Beyoncé (Platinum, 2013): 4 out of 16	
Lemonade (2016): 3 out of 12	
Total: 30 out of 95 songs (32%)	*Total: 15 out of 63 songs (24%)*

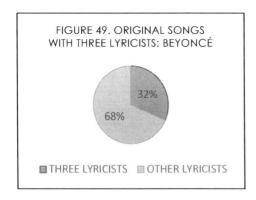

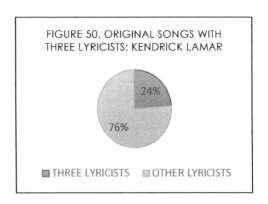

II.2.2.4 At Least Four Lyricists

| TABLE 30. ORIGINAL SONGS WITH AT LEAST FOUR LYRICISTS: BEYONCÉ & KENDRICK LAMAR ||
BEYONCÉ	KENDRICK LAMAR
Dangerously in Love (2003): 7 out of 16	Section.80 (2011): 0 out of 16
B'Day (Deluxe, 2006): 11 out of 17	good kid, m.A.A.d. City (2Deluxe, 012): 8 out of 17
I am...Sasha Fierce (Platinum, 2008): 13 out of 20	To Pimp a Butterfly (2015): 12 out of 16
4 (2011): 5 out of 14	Damn (2017): 9 out of 14
Beyoncé (Platinum, 2013): 9 out of 16	
Lemonade (2016): 8 out of 12	
Total: 53 out of 95 songs (56%)	Total: 29 out of 63 songs (46%)

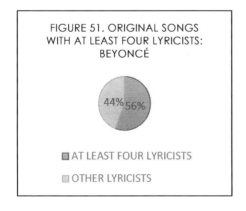

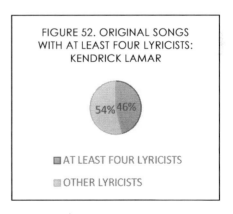

CONCLUSION:

- both artists partnered with at least four lyricists, Beyoncé 12% more than Kendrick Lamar.

II.2.3 The List of Samples

II.2.3.1 The List of Samples Used by Beyoncé

TABLE 31. THE LIST OF SAMPLES USED BY BEYONCÉ	
NAME OF THE ALBUM	**SAMPLES**
Dangerously in Love (2003)	1. 'Crazy in Love' samples 'Are You My Woman (Tell Me So)' (1970) by the Chi-Lites 2. 'Naughty Girl' contains interpolations from 'Love to Love You Baby' (1975) by Donna Summer 3. 'Baby Boy' contains interpolations from 'Hot Stepper' (1990) by Ini Kamoze. 4. 'Be with You' samples 'Ain't Nothing I Can Do' (1979) Tyrone Davis and contains interpolations from 'I'd Rather Be with You' (1976) by Bootsy's Rubber Band and 'Strawberry Letter 23' (1977) by the Brothers Johnson. 5. 'That's How You Like It' contains interpolations from 'I Like It' (1982) by DeBarge 6. 'Gift from Virgo' samples 'Rainy Day' (1974) by Shuggie Otis. 7. '03 Bonnie & Clyde' contains interpolations from 'If I Was Your Girlfriend' (1987) by Prince and samples of 'Me and My Girlfriend' (1996) by 2Pac. 8. 'What's It Gonna Be' samples 'Do It Roger' (1981) by Roger Troutman.
B'Day (Deluxe, 2006)	1. 'Suga Mama' samples 'Searching for Soul' by Jake Wade and the Soul Searchers. 2. 'Upgrade U' samples 'Girls Can't Do What the Guys Do' by Betty Wright. 3. 'Resentment' samples 'Think (Instrumental)' by Curtis Mayfield.
I Am... Sasha Fierce (Platinum, 2008)	N/A
4 (2011)	1. 'Party' contains a sample of 'La Di Da Di' as performed by Doug E. Fresh and the Get Fresh Crew featuring MC Ricky D. and written by Douglas Davis and Ricky Walters. 2. 'Countdown' contains a sample of 'Uhh Ahh' as performed by Boyz II Men and written by Michael Bivins, Nathan Morris and Wanya Morris. 3. 'End of Time' contains an uncredited sample of 'BTSTU' as performed and written by Jai Paul. 4. 'Run the World (Girls)' contains a sample 'Pon de Floor' as performed by Major Lazer and written by Afrojack, Vybz Cartel, Diplo and Switch.
4 (2011)	N/A
Beyoncé (Platinum, 2013)	1. 'Partition' contains an interpolation of the French-dubbed version of the 1998 film *The Big Lebowski*, performed by Hajiba Fahmy.

	2. 'Flawless' contains portions of the speech 'We should all be feminists', written and delivered by Chimamanda Ngozi Adichie. 3. 'Heaven' contains portions of 'The Lord's Prayer' in Spanish, performed by Melissa Vargas.
Lemonade (2016)	1. 'Hold Up'[375] contains elements of 'Can't Get Used to Losing You'[376], written by Doc Pomus and Mort Shuman, performed by Andy Williams; portions of 'Turn My Swag On'[377], written and performed by Soulja Boy, Antonio Randolph, Kelvin McConnell and elements of 'Maps'[378], written and performed by Yeah Yeah Yeahs (Brian Chase, Karen O and Nick Zinner). 2. 'Don't Hurt Yourself'[379] contains samples of 'When the Levee Breaks'[380], written by Memphis Minnie and Led Zeppelin, performed by Led Zeppelin (Jimmy Page, Robert Plant, John Paul Jones, John Bonham). 3. '6 Inch'[381] contains samples of 'Walk On By'[382], written by Burt Bacharach and Hal David, performed by Isaac Hayes; and an interpolation of 'My Girls'[383], written by Avey Tare (Dave Portner), Panda Bear (Noah Lennox) and Geologist (Brian Weitz), performed by Animal Collective.

---

[375] Audio: Beyoncé, 'Hold Up', *Youtube*, September 4, 2016, available at: https://www.youtube.com/watch?v=PeonBmeFR8o&list=OLAK5uy_m9dO997hqyquaE-xTYmZUqhm2pyKbQj-k&index=2, last accessed February 26, 2020; Lyrics: Beyoncé, 'Hold Up', *Genius*, available at: https://genius.com/BEYONCÉ-hold-up-lyrics, last accessed: February 26, 2020.

[376] Audio: Andy, Williams, 'Can't Get Used To Losing You', *Youtube*, May 25, 2013, available at: https://www.youtube.com/watch?v=kO_vKrVxGJM, last accessed: February 26, 2020. Lyrics: *Genius*, available at: https://genius.com/Andy-williams-cant-get-used-to-losing-you-lyrics, last accessed: February 26, 2020.

[377] Soulja Boy Tell'em, 'Turn My Swag On', *Youtube*, December 14, 2009, available at: https://www.youtube.com/watch?v=9yRme0C2pmI, last accessed: last accessed: February 26, 2020; Lyrics: Soulja Boy Tell'em, 'Turn My Swag On', *Genius*, available at: https://genius.com/Soulja-boy-tell-em-turn-my-swag-on-lyrics, last accessed: February 26, 2020.

[378] Yeah, Yeah, Yeahs, 'Maps', *Youtube*, June 17, 2009, available at: https://www.youtube.com/watch?v=oIlxlgcuQRU, last accessed: February 26, 2020; Lyrics: Yeah, Yeah, Yeahs, 'Maps', *Genius*, available at: https://genius.com/Yeah-yeah-yeahs-maps-lyrics, last accessed: February 26, 2020.

[379] Audio: Beyoncé, 'Don't Hurt Yourself', *Youtube*, April 22, 2019, available at: https://www.youtube.com/watch?v=xnMnZURoztQ&list=OLAK5uy_m9dO997hqyquaE-xTYmZUqhm2pyKbQj-k&index=3, last accessed February 26, 2020; Lyrics: Beyoncé, 'Don't Hurt Yourself', *Genius*, available at: https://genius.com/BEYONCÉ-dont-hurt-yourself-lyrics, last accessed: February 26, 2020.

[380] Audio: Led Zeppelin, 'When the Levee Breaks', *Youtube*, January 25, 2017, available at: https://www.youtube.com/watch?v=uwiTs60VoTM, last accessed: last accessed: February 26, 2020. Lyrics: Led Zeppelin, 'When the Levee Breaks', *Genius*, available at: https://genius.com/Led-zeppelin-when-the-levee-breaks-lyrics, last accessed: February 26, 2020.

[381] Audio: Beyoncé, '6 Inch', *Youtube*, April 22, 2019, available at: https://www.youtube.com/watch?v=UKMmfBkrhtY&list=OLAK5uy_m9dO997hqyquaE-xTYmZUqhm2pyKbQj-k&index=5, last accessed February 26, 2020; Lyrics: Beyoncé, '6 Inch', *Genius*, available at: https://genius.com/BEYONCÉ-6-inch-lyrics, last accessed: February 26, 2020.

[382] Audio: Isaac Hayes, 'Walk On By', *Youtube*, December 30, 2010, available at: https://www.youtube.com/watch?v=iqR4CZj0mJQ, last accessed: February 26, 2020. Lyrics: Isaac Hayes, 'Walk On By', *Genius*, available at: https://genius.com/Isaac-hayes-walk-on-by-lyrics, last accessed: February 26, 2020.

[383] Audio: Animal Collective, 'My Girls', January 14, 2009, *Youtube*, available at: https://www.youtube.com/watch?v=zol2MJf6XNE, last accessed: February 26, 2020. Lyrics: Animal Collective, 'My Girls', *Genius*, available at: https://genius.com/Animal-collective-my-girls-lyrics, last accessed: February 26, 2020.

	4. 'Freedom'[384] contains samples of 'Yeah'[385] performed by Jojo Simmons; also contains samples of 'Let Me Try'[386], written by Frank Tirado, performed by Kaleidoscope; samples of 'Collection Speech/Unidentified Lining Hymn'[387], recorded by Alan Lomax in 1959, performed by Reverend R.C. Crenshaw; and samples of 'Stewball'[388], recorded by Alan Lomax and John Lomax, Sr. in 1947, performed by Prisoner '22' at Mississippi State Penitentiary at Parchman. 5. 'All Night'[389] contains a sample of 'SpottieOttieDopaliscious'[390], written by OutKast (André Benjamin, Antwan Patton) and Sleepy Brown (Patrick Brown), performed by OutKast. 6. 'Lemonade' contains a sample of 'The Court of the Crimson King'[391], performed by King Crimson, written by Ian McDonald and Peter Sinfield. 7. 'Sorry (Original Demo)'[392] interpolates 'Young, Wild & Free'[393], as performed by Snoop Dogg, Wiz Khalifa and Bruno Mars.

CONCLUSION:

- Beyoncé used an extensive list of samples.

---

[384] Audio: Beyoncé, 'Freedom', *Youtube*, April 22, 2019, available at: https://www.youtube.com/watch?v=7FWF9375hUA&list=OLAK5uy_m9dO997hqyquaE-xTYmZUqhm2pyKbQj-k&index=10, last accessed February 26, 2020; Lyrics: Beyoncé, 'Freedom', *Genius*, available at: https://genius.com/BEYONCÉ-freedom-lyrics, last accessed: February 26, 2020.

[385] I have not found the audio and the lyrics.

[386] Audio: Kaleidoscope, 'Let me try', *Youtube*, January 15, 2020, available at: https://www.youtube.com/watch?v=KhyDmEb1L_Y, last accessed: February 26, 2020; Kaleidoscope, 'Let Me Try (BEYONCÉ - Freedom *Story Behind the Beat*)', *Youtube*, available at: https://www.youtube.com/watch?v=9BdTjPSV0p8Lyrics: Kaleidoscope, 'Let me try', *Genius*, available at: https://genius.com/Kaleidoscope-let-me-try-lyrics, last accessed: February 26, 2020.

[387] Audio: Alan Lomax, 'Collection Speech/Unidentified Lining Hymn', *Youtube*, April 25, 2016, available at: https://www.youtube.com/watch?v=f2dRRkUjVnw, last accessed: February 26, 2020.

[388] Audio: Alan Lomax and John Lomax, 'Stewball', (recorded in 1947), *Youtube*, November 7, 2009, available at: https://www.youtube.com/watch?v=SYq0EPX8mS0, last accessed: February 26, 2020.

[389] Audio: Beyoncé, 'All Night', *Youtube*, November 30, 2016, available at: https://www.youtube.com/watch?v=gM89Q5Eng_M&list=OLAK5uy_m9dO997hqyquaE-xTYmZUqhm2pyKbQj-k&index=11, last accessed February 26, 2020; Lyrics: Beyoncé, 'All Night', *Genius*, available at: https://genius.com/BEYONCÉ-all-night-lyrics, last accessed: February 26, 2020.

[390] Audio: OutKast, 'SpottieOttieDopaliscious', *Youtube*, January 1, 2008, available at: https://www.youtube.com/watch?v=vXmqauitBkM, last accessed: February 26, 2020. Lyrics: OutKast, 'SpottieOttieDopaliscious', *Genius*, available at: https://genius.com/Outkast-spottieottiedopaliscious-lyrics, last accessed: February 26, 2020.

[391] The Court of the Crimson King, *Wikipedia*, available at: https://en.wikipedia.org/wiki/The_Court_of_the_Crimson_King, last accessed: February 26, 2020.

[392] Audio: Beyoncé, 'Sorry (Original Demo), *Youtube*, April 22, 2019, available at: https://www.youtube.com/watch?v=c8hhQHnJWzE&list=OLAK5uy_m9dO997hqyquaE-xTYmZUqhm2pyKbQj-k&index=13, last accessed February 26, 2020; Lyrics: Beyoncé, 'Sorry (Original Demo), *Genius*, available at: https://genius.com/BEYONCÉ-sorry-original-demo-lyrics, last accessed: February 26, 2020.

[393] Audio: Snoop Dogg, Wiz Khalifa, Bruno Mars, 'Young, Wild & Free', *Youtube*, available at: https://www.youtube.com/watch?v=Wa5B22KAkEk, last accessed: February 26, 2020. Lyrics: Snoop Dogg, Wiz Khalifa, Bruno Mars, 'Young, Wild & Free', *Genius*, available at: https://genius.com/Snoop-dogg-and-wiz-khalifa-young-wild-and-free-lyrics, last accessed: February 26, 2020.

II.2.3.2 The List of Sample Used by Kendrick Lamar

TABLE 32. THE LIST OF SAMPLES USED BY KENDRICK LAMAR	
NAME OF THE ALBUM	SAMPLE
Section.80 (2011)	1. 'Hol' Up' contains a sample of 'Shifting Sands of Sound', as performed by Dick Walter. 2. 'Tammy's Song (Her Evils)' contains a sample of 'Alfie', as performed by Dick Hyman. 3. 'Chapter Six' contains a sample of 'Hey', as performed by King. 4. 'Poe Mans Dreams (His Vice)' contains a sample of 'Peace Go With You, Brother', as performed by Gil Scott-Heron. 5. 'The Spiteful Chant' contains a sample of 'Iron', as performed by Woodkid. 6. 'Keisha's Song (Her Pain)' contains a sample of 'Old and Wise', as performed by The Alan Parsons Project. 7. 'Rigamortis' contains a sample of 'The Thorn', as performed by Willie Jones III. 8. 'Blow My High (Members Only)' contains samples of '4 Page Letter', as performed by Aaliyah; 'Voyager', as performed by Dexter Wansel; and 'Big Pimpin', as performed by Jay-Z featuring UGK.
good kid, m.A.A.d. City (Deluxe, 2012)	1. 'Bitch, Don't Kill My Vibe'[394] contains portions of 'Tiden Flyver'[395], as performed by Boom Clap Bachelors. 2. 'Backseat Freestyle'[396] contains a sample of 'Yo Soy Cubano'[397], as performed by The Chakachas. 3. 'The Art of Peer Pressure'[398] contains a sample of 'Helt Alene'[399], as performed by Suspekt.

[394] Audio: Kendrick Lamar, 'Bitch, Don't Kill My Vibe', *Youtube*, May 13, 2013, available at: https://www.youtube.com/watch?v=GF8aaTu2kg0&list=OLAK5uy_mhYMgh1v0LpLuS0FqC693tfVkyVZK9WSQ&index=2, last accessed February 26, 2020; Lyrics: Kendrick Lamar, 'Bitch, Don't Kill My Vibe', *Genius*, available at: https://genius.com/Kendrick-lamar-bitch-dont-kill-my-vibe-lyrics, last accessed: February 26, 2020.

[395] Audio: Boom Clap Bachelors, 'Tiden Flyer', *Youtube*, November 3, 2013, available at: https://www.youtube.com/watch?v=ZrHNlRLh-ps, last accessed: February 26, 2020. Lyrics: Boom Clap Bachelors, 'Tiden Flyer', *Genius*, available at: https://genius.com/Boom-clap-bachelors-tiden-flyver-lyrics, last accessed: February 26, 2020.

[396] Audio: Kendrick Lamar, 'Backseat Freestyle', *Youtube*, January 7, 2013, available at: https://www.youtube.com/watch?v=EZW7et3tPuQ&list=OLAK5uy_mhYMgh1v0LpLuS0FqC693tfVkyVZK9WSQ&index=3, last accessed February 26, 2020; Lyrics: Kendrick Lamar, Backseat Freestyle, *Genius*, available at: https://genius.com/Kendrick-lamar-backseat-freestyle-lyrics, last accessed: February 26, 2020.

[397] Audio: The Chakachas, 'Yo Soy Cubano', *Youtube*, February 21, 2015, available at: https://www.youtube.com/watch?v=mNTH-isTTiU, last accessed: February 26, 2020. Lyrics: The Chakachas, 'Yo Soy Cubano', *Metrolyrics*, available at: https://www.metrolyrics.com/yo-soy-cubano-lyrics-chakachas.html, last accessed: February 26, 2020.

[398] Audio: Kendrick Lamar, 'The Art of Peer Pressure', *Youtube*, July 26, 2018, available at: https://www.youtube.com/watch?v=t93uK0DKvEk&list=OLAK5uy_mhYMgh1v0LpLuS0FqC693tfVkyVZK9WSQ&index=4, last accessed February 26, 2020; Lyrics: Kendrick Lamar, 'The Art of Peer Pressure', *Genius*, available at: https://genius.com/Kendrick-lamar-the-art-of-peer-pressure-lyrics, last accessed: February 26, 2020.

[399] Audio: Suspekt, Tina Dickow, 'Helt Alene', *Youtube*, January 23, 2012, available at: https://www.youtube.com/watch?v=Oj7F14vITFk, last accessed: February 26, 2020. Lyrics: Suspekt, 'Helt Alene', *Genius*, available at: https://genius.com/Suspekt-helt-alene-lyrics, last accessed: February 26, 2020.

	4. 'Money Trees'[400] contains a sample of 'Silver Soul'[401], as performed by Beach House. 5. 'Poetic Justice'[402] contains excerpts from 'Any Time, Any Place'[403], as performed by Janet Jackson. 6. 'm.A.A.d city'[404] contains samples of 'Don't Change Your Love'[405], as performed by The Five Stairsteps; 'Funky Worm'[406], as performed by Ohio Players; 'A Bird In The Hand'[407] as performed by Ice Cube; 7. 'Sing About Me, I'm Dying of Thirst'[408] contains a sample of 'Maybe Tomorrow'[409], as performed by Grant Green; 'I'm Glad Your Mine'[410], as performed by Al Green; sampled 'Use Me'[411], as performed by Bill Whither; sampled 'My Romance'[412], as performed by The Singers Unlimited.

[400] Audio: Kendrick Lamar, 'Money Trees', *Youtube*, July 26, 2018, available at: https://www.youtube.com/watch?v=ly-dJwHVX84&list=OLAK5uy_mhYMgh1v0LpLuS0FqC693tfVkyVZK9WSQ&index=5, last accessed: February 26, 2020; Lyrics: Kendrick Lamar, 'Money Trees', *Genius*, available at: https://genius.com/Kendrick-lamar-money-trees-lyrics, last accessed: .

[401] Audio: Beach House, 'Silver Soul', *Youtube*, March 4, 2010, available at: https://www.youtube.com/watch?v=njbmwfndFH4, last accessed: February 26, 2020. Lyrics: Beach House, 'Silver Soul', *Genius*, available at: https://genius.com/Beach-house-silver-soul-lyrics, last accessed: February 26, 2020.

[402] Audio: Kendrick Lamar, 'Poetic Justice', *Youtube*, February 22, 2013, available at: https://www.youtube.com/watch?v=yyr2gEouEMM&list=OLAK5uy_mhYMgh1v0LpLuS0FqC693tfVkyVZK9WSQ&index=6, last accessed February 26, 2020; Lyrics: Kendrick Lamar, 'Poetic Justice', *Genius*, available at: https://genius.com/Kendrick-lamar-poetic-justice-lyrics, last accessed: February 26, 2020.

[403] Audio: Janet Jackson, 'Any Time, Any Place', *Youtube*, November, 16, 2010, available at: https://www.youtube.com/watch?v=3HO9H1VMMOk, last accessed: February 26, 2020. Lyrics: Janet Jackson, 'Any Time, Any Place', *Genius*, available at: https://genius.com/Janet-jackson-any-time-any-place-lyrics, last accessed: February 26, 2020.

[404] Audio: Kendrick Lamar, 'm.A.A.d city', *Youtube*, July 24, 2018, available at: https://www.youtube.com/watch?v=KKCSwOVudMo, last accessed February 26, 2020; Lyrics: Kendrick Lamar, 'm.A.A.d. city', *Genius*, available at: https://genius.com/Kendrick-lamar-maad-city-lyrics, last accessed: February 26, 2020.

[405] Audio: The Five Stairsteps, 'Don't Change Your Love', *Youtube*, March 13, 2011, available at: https://www.youtube.com/watch?v=zzLfR2Cn56s, last accessed: February 26, 2020. Lyrics: The Five Stairsteps, 'Don't Change Your Love', *Genius*, available at: https://genius.com/Ice-cube-a-bird-in-the-hand-lyrics, last accessed: February 26, 2020.

[406] Audio: Ohio Players, 'Funky Worm', *Youtube*, November 21, 2009, available at: https://www.youtube.com/watch?v=bSIb4T5vu9E, last accessed: February 26, 2020. Lyrics: Ohio Players, 'Funky Worm', *Genius*, available at: https://genius.com/Ohio-players-funky-worm-lyrics, last accessed: February 26, 2020.

[407] Audio: Ice Cube, 'A Bird In The Hand', *Youtube*, June 28, 2012, available at: https://www.youtube.com/watch?v=QQU8lazOsKc, last accessed: February 26, 2020. Lyrics: Ice Cube, 'A Bird In The Hand', *Genius*, available at: https://genius.com/Ice-cube-a-bird-in-the-hand-lyrics, last accessed: February 26, 2020.

[408] Audio: Kendrick Lamar, 'Sing About Me, I'm Dying Of Thirst', *Youtube*, July 26, 2018, available at: https://www.youtube.com/watch?v=75wmW7xjyog&list=OLAK5uy_mhYMgh1v0LpLuS0FqC693tfVkyVZK9WSQ&index=10, last accessed February 26, 2020; Lyrics: Kendrick Lamar, 'Sing About Me, I'm Dying Of Thirst', *Genius*, available at: https://genius.com/Kendrick-lamar-sing-about-me-im-dying-of-thirst-lyrics, last accessed: February 26, 2020.

[409] Audio: Grant Green, 'Maybe Tomorrow', *Youtube*, September 10, 2007, available at: https://www.youtube.com/watch?v=k9oNHowrg4w, last accessed: February 26, 2020. Lyrics: Grant Green, 'Maybe Tomorrow', *Genius*, available at: https://genius.com/Grant-green-maybe-tomorrow-lyrics, last accessed: February 26, 2020.

[410] Audio: Al Green, 'I'm Glad Your Mine', *Youtube*, February 16, 2010, available at: https://www.youtube.com/watch?v=QzAL59zslSM, last accessed: February 26, 2020. Lyrics: Al Green, 'I'm Glad Your Mine', *Genius*, available at: https://genius.com/Al-green-im-glad-youre-mine-lyrics, last accessed: February 26, 2020.

[411] Audio: Bill Whiters, 'Use Me', *Youtube*, February 17, 2008, available at: https://www.youtube.com/watch?v=g3hBYTkI-sE, last accessed: February 26, 2020. Lyrics: Bill Whiters, 'Use Me', *Genius*, available at: https://genius.com/Bill-withers-use-me-lyrics, last accessed: February 26, 2020.

[412] Audio: The Singers Unlimited, 'My Romance', *Youtube*, January 29, 2014, available at: https://www.youtube.com/watch?v=DOQCsLsyTBU, last accessed: February 26, 2020. Lyrics: The Singers Unlimited, 'My Romance', *Flashlyrics*, available at: https://www.flashlyrics.com/lyrics/the-singers-unlimited/my-romance-23, last accessed: February 26, 2020.

	8. 'Compton'[413] contains excerpts from 'What's This World Coming To'[414], as performed by Formula IV. 9. 'The Recipe'[415] contains a sample of 'Meet the Frownies'[416], as performed by Twin Sister.
	1. 'Wesley's Theory'[417] contains elements of 'Every Nigger is a Star'[418], written and performed by Boris Gardiner. 2. 'King Kunta'[419] contains interpolations of 'Get Nekkid'[420], written by Johnny Burns and performed by Mausberg; resung lyrics from 'Smooth Criminal'[421], written and performed by Michael Jackson; elements of 'The Payback'[422], written by James Brown, Fred Wesley and John Starks, and performed by James Brown; and samples of 'We Want the Funk'[423], written and performed by Ahmad Lewis.
To Pimp a Butterfly (2015)	

---

[413] Audio: Kendrick Lamar, 'Compton', *Youtube*, July 26, 2018, available at: https://www.youtube.com/watch?v=9PovU-C2osU&list=OLAK5uy_mhYMgh1v0LpLuS0FqC693tfVkyVZK9WSQ&index=12, last accessed February 26, 2020; Lyrics: Kendrick Lamar, 'Compton', *Genius*, available at: https://genius.com/Kendrick-lamar-compton-lyrics, last accessed: February 26, 2020.

[414] Audio: Formula IV, 'What's This World Coming To', *Youtube*, October, 24, 2012, available at: https://www.youtube.com/watch?v=JyEF0Drogjo, last accessed: February 26, 2020.

[415] Audio: Kendrick Lamar, 'The Recipe', *Youtube*, April 23, 2012, available at: https://www.youtube.com/watch?v=YpugK0RpEaU, last accessed February 26, 2020; Lyrics: Kendrick Lamar, 'The Recipe', *Genius*, available at: https://genius.com/Kendrick-lamar-the-recipe-lyrics, last accessed: February 26, 2020.

[416] Audio: Twin Sister, 'Meet The Frownies', *Youtube*, October 13, 2010, available at: https://www.youtube.com/watch?v=P-F7AS-Xhus, last accessed: February 26, 2020. Lyrics: Twin Sister, 'Meet The Frownies', *Genius*, available at: https://genius.com/Boris-gardiner-every-nigger-is-a-star-lyrics, last accessed: February 26, 2020.

[417] Audio: Kendrick Lamar, 'Wesley's Theory', *Youtube*, December 12, 2018, available at: https://www.youtube.com/watch?v=l9fN-8Njrvl&list=OLAK5uy_n_dmtzA0lWImBN3fbUBUl_WgD-YSaMZaI, last accessed February 26, 2020; Lyrics: Kendrick Lamar, 'Wesley's Theory', *Genius*, available at: https://genius.com/Kendrick-lamar-wesleys-theory-lyrics, last accessed: February 26, 2020.

[418] Audio: Boris Gardiner, 'Every Nigger Is A Star', *Youtube*, January 21, 2011, available at: https://www.youtube.com/watch?v=mYnenlWZjwE, last accessed: February 26, 2020. Lyrics: Boris Gardiner, 'Every Nigger Is A Star', *Genius*, available at: https://genius.com/Boris-gardiner-every-nigger-is-a-star-lyrics, last accessed: February 26, 2020.

[419] Audio: Kendrick Lamar, 'King Kunta', *Youtube*, April 1, 2015, available at: https://www.youtube.com/watch?v=hRK7PVJFbS8&list=OLAK5uy_n_dmtzA0lWImBN3fbUBUl_WgD-YSaMZaI&index=3, last accessed February 26, 2020; Lyrics: Kendrick Lamar, 'King Kunta', *Genius*, available at: https://genius.com/Kendrick-lamar-king-kunta-lyrics, last accessed: February 26, 2020.

[420] Audio: Mausberg, 'Get Nekkid', *Youtube*, April 10, 2011, available at: https://www.youtube.com/watch?v=cvZCs27gg70, last accessed: February 26, 2020. Lyrics: Mausberg, 'Get Nekkid', *Genius*, available at: https://genius.com/Mausberg-get-nekkid-lyrics, last accessed: February 26, 2020.

[421] Audio: Michael Jackson, 'Smooth Criminal', *Youtube*, November 19, 2010, available at: https://www.youtube.com/watch?v=h_D3VFfhvs4, last accessed: February 26, 2020. Lyrics: Michael Jackson, 'Smooth Criminal', *Genius*, available at: https://genius.com/Michael-jackson-smooth-criminal-lyrics, last accessed: February 26, 2020.

[422] Audio: James Brown, 'The Payback', *Youtube*, May 2, 2011, available at: https://www.youtube.com/watch?v=istJXUJJP0g, last accessed: February 26, 2020. Lyrics: James Brown, 'The Payback', *Genius*, available at: https://genius.com/James-brown-the-payback-lyrics, last accessed: February 26, 2020.

[423] Audio: Ahmad Lewis, 'We Want The Funk', *Youtube*, November 6, 2010, available at: https://www.youtube.com/watch?v=NyaP1B1AypE, last accessed: February 26, 2020. Lyrics: Ahmed Lewis, 'We Want The Funk', *Metrolyrics*, available at: https://www.metrolyrics.com/we-want-the-funk-lyrics-ahmad.html, last accessed: February 26, 2020.

	3. 'Momma'[424] contains elements of 'Wishful Thinkin''[425] written by Sylvester Stone and performed by Sly and the Family Stone; and elements of 'On Your Own'[426], written and performed by Lalah Hathaway; sampled 'So[rt]'[427], by Knxwledge; sampled 'Control (HOF)'[428], as performed by Big Sean, Kendrick Lamar and Jay Electronica. 4. 'Hood Politics'[429] contains a sample of 'All for Myself'[430], written and performed by Sufjan Stevens. 5. 'i'[431] contains a sample of 'That Lady'[432], written by Ronald Isley, O'Kelly Isley, Jr., Ernie Isley, Marvin Isley, Rudolph Isley and Christopher Jasper, and performed by The Isley Brothers. 6. 'Mortal Man'[433] contains excerpts from 'I No Get Eye for Back'[434], written by Fela Anikulapo Kuti and performed by Houston Person; and a sample of music journalist Mats Nileskar's November 1994 interview with Tupac Shakur for P3 Soul Broadcasting Corporation.
	1. 'Blood' and 'DNA' contain elements of Fox News commentators Eric Bolling, Kimberly Guilfoyle and Geraldo Rivera criticizing Lamar's 2015 BET Awards performance' 'DNA' also contains a sample from a live recording of 'Mary Jane', as written and performed by Rick James, from the album Come Get It!.

[424] Audio: Kendrick Lamar, 'Momma', *Youtube*, December 12, 2018, available at: https://www.youtube.com/watch?v=q1AOP6NtGuc&list=OLAK5uy_n_dmtzA0IWImBN3fbUBUl_WgD-YSaMZaI&index=9, last accessed February 26, 2020; Lyrics: Kendrick Lamar, 'Momma', *Genius*, available at: https://genius.com/Kendrick-lamar-momma-lyrics, last accessed: February 26, 2020.

[425] Audio: Sly & The Family Stone, 'Wishful Thinkin', *Youtube*, November 8, 2014, available at: https://www.youtube.com/watch?v=HUICXLAKUX4, last accessed: February 26, 2020. Lyrics: Sly & The Family Stone, 'Wishful Thinkin', *Genius*, available at: https://genius.com/Sly-and-the-family-stone-wishful-thinkin-lyrics, last accessed: February 26, 2020.

[426] Audio: Lalah Hathaway, 'On Your Own', *Youtube*, July 26, 2018, available at: https://www.youtube.com/watch?v=jhZ6nuO5uos, last accessed: February 26, 2020. Lyrics: Lalah Hathaway, 'On Your Own', *Genius*, available at: https://genius.com/Lalah-hathaway-on-your-own-lyrics, last accessed: February 26, 2020.

[427] Audio: Knxwledge, 'So[rt]', *Youtube*, December 12, 2017, available at: https://www.youtube.com/watch?v=fPaZTF1kJrs, last accessed: February 26, 2020.

[428] Audio: Big Sean, Kendrick Lamar, Jay Electronica, 'Control', *Youtube*, August 13, 2013, available at: https://www.youtube.com/watch?v=xufJHc2EdBA, last accessed: February 26, 2020. Lyrics: Big Sean, Kendrick Lamar, Jay Electronica, 'Control', *Genius*, available at: https://genius.com/Big-sean-control-lyrics, last accessed: February 26, 2020.

[429] Audio: Kendrick Lamar, 'Hood Politics', *Youtube*, December 12, 2018, available at: https://www.youtube.com/watch?v=iIsHg3BHpB0&list=OLAK5uy_n_dmtzA0IWImBN3fbUBUl_WgD-YSaMZaI&index=10, last accessed February 26, 2020; Lyrics: Kendrick Lamar, 'Hard Politics', *Genius*, available at: https://genius.com/Kendrick-lamar-hood-politics-lyrics, last accessed: February 26, 2020.

[430] Audio: Sufjan Stevens, 'All For Myself', *Youtube*, September 10, 2010, available at: https://www.youtube.com/watch?v=5zlxFUlRgdg, last accessed: February 26, 2020. Lyrics: Sufjan Stevens, 'All For Myself', *Genius*, available at: https://genius.com/Sufjan-stevens-all-for-myself-lyrics, last accessed: February 26, 2020.

[431] Audio: Kendrick Lamar, 'i', *Youtube*, December 12, 2018, available at: https://www.youtube.com/watch?v=tt2-GsPA9kk&list=OLAK5uy_n_dmtzA0IWImBN3fbUBUl_WgD-YSaMZaI&index=15, last accessed February 26, 2020; Lyrics: Kendrick Lamar, 'i', *Genius*, available at: https://genius.com/Kendrick-lamar-i-album-version-lyrics, last accessed: February 26, 2020.

[432] Audio: The Isley Brothers, 'That Lady', *Youtube*, July 31, 2015, available at: https://www.youtube.com/watch?v=S1Mvy3E8P2U, last accessed: February 26, 2020. Lyrics: The Isley Brothers, 'That Lady', *Genius*, available at: https://genius.com/The-isley-brothers-that-lady-pt-1-and-2-lyrics, last accessed: February 26, 2020.

[433] Audio: Kendrick Lamar, 'Mortal Man', *Youtube*, December 12, 2018, available at: https://www.youtube.com/watch?v=axwpgn3GRMs&list=OLAK5uy_n_dmtzA0IWImBN3fbUBUl_WgD-YSaMZaI&index=16, last accessed February 26, 2020; Lyrics: Kendrick Lamar, 'Mortal Man', *Genius*, available at: https://genius.com/Kendrick-lamar-mortal-man-lyrics, last accessed: February 26, 2020.

[434] Audio: Houston Person, 'I No get Eye For Back', *Youtube*, December 5, 2011, available at: https://www.youtube.com/watch?v=DhClaL03Ec4, last accessed: February 26, 2020.

Damn (2017)	2. 'Yah' contains elements from 'How Good Is Your Game', performed by Billy Paul. 3. 'Element' contains pieces from 'Ha', as written by Terius Gray and Byron O. Thomas, and performed by Juvenile, from the album 400 Degreez. 4. 'Feel' contains a sample of 'Stormy', as written and performed by O. C. Smith, from the album For Once in My Life; and an interpolation from 'Don't Let Me Down', as written and performed by Fleurie, from the album Love and War. 5. 'Loyalty' contains samples of '24K Magic', as written by Bruno Mars, Christopher Brody Brown and Philip Lawrence, and performed by Bruno Mars, from the album 24K Magic; 'Shimmy Shimmy Ya', as written by Russell Jones and Robert Diggs, and performed by Ol' Dirty Bastard, from the album Return to the 36 Chambers: The Dirty Version; and 'Get Your Mind Right Mami', as written by Shawn Carter, Cordozar Calvin Broadus, Jr., Gerrell Gaddis and Malik Cox, and performed by Jay-Z featuring Snoop Dogg, Rell and Memphis Bleek, from the album The Dynasty: Roc La Familia. 6. 'Lust' contains a sample of 'Knock Knock Knock', as written and performed by Rat Boy, from the album Neighbourhood Watch. 7. 'Fear' contains a sample of 'Poverty's Paradise', as written by Dale Warren and performed by 24-Carat Black, from the album Ghetto: Misfortune's Wealth. 8. 'XXX' contains samples of 'Get Up Offa That Thing', as written by Deanna Brown, Diedra Brown and Yamma Brown, and performed by James Brown, from the album Get Up Offa' That Thing; 'Fugue', as written and performed by Foals, from the album Total Life Forever; and 'Wah Wah Man', performed by Young-Holt Unlimited. 9. 'God' contains a sample of 'End of the World', as written and performed by Illmind, from the album #BoomTrap Vol. 2. 10. 'Duckworth' contains samples of 'Atari', as written by Nai Palm and performed by Hiatus Kaiyote; 'Be Ever Wonderful', as written by Don Robey and Joe Scott, and performed by Ted Taylor, from the album Keepin' My Head Above Water; 'Ostavi Trag', as written by September, from the album Zadnja Avantura; and 'Let the Drums Speak', as written by Bill Curtis and performed by the Fatback Band, from the album Yum Yum.

CONCLUSION:

- Kendrick Lamar has a list of samples more generous than Beyoncé, but less than Kanye West.

II.2.4 The Sources of the Samples

I read the lyrics of the songs that used samples to find out the connection between the original song, and the song that sampled the original song.

TABLE 33. THE SOURCES OF THE SAMPLES USED BY BEYONCÉ AND KENDRICK LAMAR

NAME OF THE ALBUM	NAME OF THE SONG	INSPIRATION
Beyoncé (Lemonade, 2016)	*'Hold Up'*	Good connection with the theme of the song (relationships, cheating, losing someone) 'Can't Get Used to Losing You' and use of lyrics from 'Turn My Swag On' and 'Maps'. Some lyrics of this song 'Can't Get Used to Losing You' are being used to create a visual representation in the music video, which is also genuine similar with the video of the Swiss visual artist Pipilotti Rist's project 'Ever Is Over All'.[435] On the album *Aquemini* (contains the word 'aque' acronymous for 'aqua' which translates as 'water' (which is one of the main themes and visuals of the album *Lemonade*), from which Beyoncé samples the song 'SpottieOttieDopaliscious', has the introductory song named 'Hold On, Be Strong.'[436]
	'Don't Hurt Yourself'	'When the Levee Breaks': good connection with the song's theme and use of lyrics. The song is a reflection of the experience during the upheaval caused by the Great Mississippi Flood of 1927, which is linked with Beyoncé's visual album with floods (water) in Formation and other videos which represents the real world and the negative side effects of tornadoes, hurricanes from the USA.
	'6 Inch'	Title and lyrics connection with 'My Girls'.
	'Freedom'	Some connection with 'Let Me Try'.
	'All Night'	Some connection with the theme of the song (events from a night) 'SpottieOttieDopaliscious'. However, there is strong connection between the whole album of Lemonade (visual and lyrics themes) and the whole album named Aquemini ('SpottieOttieDopaliscious' is one of the songs included in this album), released in 1998 by the hip-hop duo Outkast. Lyrically, much of Aquemini features introspection about the desolation of the human condition (strong theme in Lemonade), which include precarious relationships (Lemonade: between her and her husband, Jay Z), freedom from self-inflicted struggles (Lemonade: between her and her husband, Jay Z), also one of Beyoncé songs from Lemonade is named Freedom. If Aquemini is about a shift between science – fiction inspired topics combined with the harsh reality of urban life, Lemonade is showing in her videos the harsh reality of the country and urban life of black people. In the end, the similarity between the two albums is the experimentation of delivery styles on the record, using relaxed, hyper, distorted, speedy and conversational presentations.'[437]
	'Sorry (Original Demo)'	Use of lyrics from the title 'Young, Wild & Free' and chorus.
	'm.A.A.d. City'	Some connection with 'Don't Change Your Love' and 'A Bird In The Hand.'

---

[435] Phil Maphela, 'Here We Go Again BEYONCÉ Accused of Stealing Hold Up Music Video B Scott lovebscottcom', *Youtube*, May 3, 2016, https://www.youtube.com/watch?v=2V7tQwnJQEo, last accessed: February 26, 2020.
[436] 'Aquemini', *Wikipedia*, available at: https://en.wikipedia.org/wiki/Aquemini, last accessed: February 27, 2020.
[437] *Ibidem*.

good kid, m.A.A.d City (Deluxe, 2012)	*'The Art of Peer Pressure'*	'Helt Alene': it was the main sample for this track.
	'Poetic Justice'	'It used heavily sample from the song 'Any Time, Any Place' co-written and performed by Janet Jackson.'
	'The Receipe'	Some lyrics from 'Meet the Frownies.'
To Pimp a Butterfly (2015)	'Wesley's Theory'	Lyrics from 'Every Nigger is a Star.'
	'King Kunta'	Lyrics from 'Smooth Criminal' and 'We Want the Funk.'
	'Momma'	Some connection with 'On Your Own' and some lyrics from 'Control (HOF).'

II.2.5 The Fame of the Samples

TABLE 34. THE FAME OF THE SAMPLES USED BY BEYONCÉ AND KENDRICK LAMAR		
NAME OF THE ALBUM	NAME OF THE SONGS	TOP CHARTS & AWARDS
	'Can't Get Used to Losing You' (1963)	'The song was number 2 in both the US and the UK'. [438]
	'Maps' (2004)	'The song was US Rap Songs (Billboard) weekly charts number 3, US Pop 100 (Billboard) weekly charts number 39, US Hot R&B/Hip Hop Songs (Billboard) weekly charts number 3.'[439] 'The music video received extensive play on MTV, it reached number 9 on Billboard's Alternative Songs chart and was included in popular video game Rock Band.' Other success includes: 'NME best alternative love song in 2009; number 6 on Pitchfork Media's top 500 songs of the 2000s; Roling Stone ranked it number 386 on their list of the 500 Greatest Songs of All Time; in 2011 NME placed the song at number 55 on its list '150 Best Tracks of the Past 150 Years'; NME ranked the song at number 1 on their list of 'Indie Weddings Songs: 20 Tracks Perfect For Your First Dance'.[440]
	'When the Levee Breaks' (1929)	'It is a wide loved country blue song'.[441]
	'My Girls' (2009)	'The lyrics of the song are about the desire of the artist on a basic level to own my own place and kind of provide a safe house for my family and the people I care about.' Other success include: Pitchfork named the song number 1 of 2009 and also number 9 on their Top 500 Tracks of the 2000s; NME named the 5th best song of 2009; Slant Magazine named the best song of 2009; The Village Voice name the third best song of 2009; NME in 2011 place it at number 91

---

[438] 'Can't get Used to Losing You', *Wikipedia*, available at: https://en.wikipedia.org/wiki/Can%27t_Get_Used_to_Losing_You, last accessed: February 27, 2020.

[439] 'Turn My Swag On', *Wikipedia*, available at: https://en.wikipedia.org/wiki/Turn_My_Swag_On, last accessed: February 27, 2020.

[440] 'Maps (Yeah, Yeah, Yeah)', *Wikipedia*, available at: https://en.wikipedia.org/wiki/Maps_(Yeah_Yeah_Yeahs_song), last accessed: February 27, 2020.

[441] 'When the Levee Breaks', *Wikipedia*, available at:
https://en.wikipedia.org/wiki/When_the_Levee_Breaks#Led_Zeppelin_version, last accessed: February 27, 2020.

Beyoncé (Lemonade, 2016)		on their list '150 Best Tracks of the Past 15 Years'; NME in 2014 named the 248th best song of all time.'[442]
	'*Walk On By' (1963)*	'The song peaked at number 6 on the US Billboard Hot 100 and number 1 on the Cash Box Rhythm and Blues Chart in June 1964; also, it was nominated for a 1965 Grammy Award for the Best Rhythm and Blues Recording.'[443]
	'*SpottieOttieDopaliscious'*	'It is a song from the album *Aquemini* which is the third studio album of the American hip hop duo Outkast. Aquemini received highly widespread acclaim from critics with most the grade being one 3,5 out of 4 stars from USA Today and Chicago Sun-Times, to 5 out of 5 stars from Q, to A- from Christgau's Consumer Guide, to A from Entertainment Weekly. Los Angeles Times gave 4 stars out of 4, Rolling Stone 4 out of 5 stars. In the end the album was included in several publication's best album lists such as: in 2003 Rolling Stone ranked it on their 500 Greatest Albums of All Time and number 11 on the list '100 best Albums of the Nineties'; Paste called it 'the best Atlanta hip-hop album of all time'; Pitchfork ranked it number 50 on their 'Top 100 Albums of the 1990's'; Spin ranked it number 35 on the '90 Greatest Albums of the '90' and number 3 on the 'Top 20 Albums of '98'; the lead single 'Rosa Park' was nominated in the category Grammy Award for Best Rap Performance by a Duo or Group at the 1999 Grammy Awards; in the end the song 'SpottieOttieDopaliscious' was ranked at number 16 on Pitchfork Media's list of the top 200 tracks of the 1990s.' The legacy of this album is virtuosic masterpiece, a landmark hip-hop, artistic success, brilliant, avant-garde, sonic ideas, new sounds, ravenous as ever which is in direct line with the reviews received by Beyoncé for *Lemonade*, her highest rated album yet.[444]
	'*Don't Change Your Love'*	Album inspiration from *Aquemini*: record production and aesthetic.[445]
good kid, m.A.A.d City (Deluxe, 2012)	'*Any Time, Any Place'*	'The song reached number 2 on the US Billboard Hot 100 and became an R&B chart-topper. Also, it held the number-one position on the Billboard Hot R&B/Hip-Hop Songs for ten weeks and was Janet Jackson's biggest hit on the chart.'[446]
	'*Smooth Criminal'*	'The song was number 7 on the Billboard Hot 100, number 2 on the Billboard Hot Black Singles chart.'[447]
To Pimp a Butterfly (2015)	'*The Payback'*	'Samples from this song was heavily used in popular games and movies.'[448]

---

[442] 'My Girls (Animal Collective Song)', *Wikipedia*, available at: https://en.wikipedia.org/wiki/My_Girls_(Animal_Collective_song), last accessed: February 27, 2020.

[443] 'Walk On By', *Wikipedia*, available at: https://en.wikipedia.org/wiki/Walk_On_By_(song), last accessed: February 27, 2020.

[444] Aquemini.

[445] ibidem.

[446] 'Any Time, Any Place', *Wikipedia*, available at: https://en.wikipedia.org/wiki/Any_Time,_Any_Place, last accessed: February 27, 2020.

[447] 'Smooth Criminal', *Wikipedia*, available at: https://en.wikipedia.org/wiki/Smooth_Criminal, last accessed: February 27, 2020.

[448] 'The Payback', *Wikipedia*, available at: https://en.wikipedia.org/wiki/The_Payback_(song), last accessed: February 27, 2020.

	'That Lady'	'The song is ranked number 357 on Rolling Stone's list of the 500 Greatest Songs of All Time.'[449]

CONCLUSION:

- as with Kanye West, the samples used by Kendrick Lamar and Beyoncé were already included and charted in the music industry and, therefore, to some extent the outcome from critics and fans belongs to the original artists of the samples.

II.2.6 The Rating on Metacritic

TABLE 35. THE ALBUM RATINGS: BEYONCÉ & KENDRICK LAMAR	
BEYONCÉ	**KENDRICK LAMAR**
Dangerously in Love (2003): 63	Section.80 (2011): 80
B'Day (Deluxe, 2006): 70	good kid, m.A.A.d. City (Deluxe, 2012): 91
I am...Sasha Fierce (Platinum, 2008): 62	To Pimp a Butterfly (2015): 96
4 (2011): 73	Damn (2017): 95
Beyoncé (Platinum, 2013): 85	
Lemonade (2016): 92	
Total average: 74.16	*Total average: 90.5*

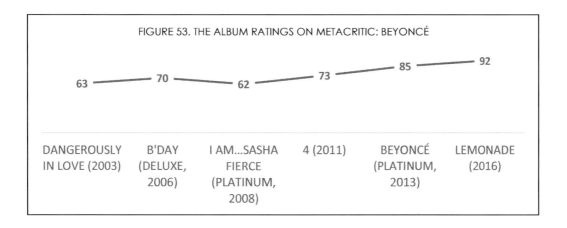

FIGURE 53. THE ALBUM RATINGS ON METACRITIC: BEYONCÉ

63 — 70 — 62 — 73 — 85 — 92

| DANGEROUSLY IN LOVE (2003) | B'DAY (DELUXE, 2006) | I AM...SASHA FIERCE (PLATINUM, 2008) | 4 (2011) | BEYONCÉ (PLATINUM, 2013) | LEMONADE (2016) |

---

[449] 'That Lady (song)', *Wikipedia*, available at: https://en.wikipedia.org/wiki/That_Lady_(song), last accessed: February 27, 2020.

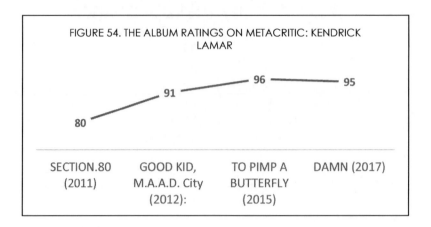

FIGURE 54. THE ALBUM RATINGS ON METACRITIC: KENDRICK LAMAR

CONCLUSIONS:

- overall, Kendrick Lamar has better reviews on Metacritic than Beyoncé;
- there is a common point: over the years both artists received better grades (based on better music) in comparison with the last album released, except for a slight decrease of 1 point for Kendrick Lamar (from 2015 to 2017).

II.3 Beyoncé versus Taylor Swift

In this part of the chapter I used the information presented in the last pages about both artists with no recitation. This section completed a comparative analysis of the music released by Beyoncé.

II.3.1 Use of Sample

TABLE 36. USE OF SAMPLE: BEYONCÉ & TAYLOR SWIFT	
TAYLOR SWIFT	BEYONCÉ
Taylor Swift (Deluxe, 2006): 0 out of 14	Dangerously in Love (2003): 8 out of 16
Fearless (Platinum, 2008): 1 out of 19	B'Day (Deluxe, 2006): 3 out of 17
Speak Now (Deluxe, 2010): 0 out of 17	I am...Sasha Fierce (Platinum, 2008): 0 out of 20
RED (Deluxe, 2012): 0 out of 19	4 (2011): 4 out of 14
1989 (Deluxe, 2013): 0 out of 16	Beyoncé (Platinum, 2013): 4 out of 16
reputation (2017): 1 out of 15	Lemonade (2016): 6 out of 12
Lover (2019): 3 out of 18	
folklore (Deluxe, 2020): 0 out of 17	
Evermore (Deluxe, 2020): 0 out of 17	
Fearless (Taylor's Version, 2021): 0 out of 7	
Total: 5 out of 159 songs (3%)	*Total: 25 out of 95 songs (26%)*

CONCLUSION:

- Beyoncé used 5 times more samples in her songs than Taylor Swift.

II.3.2 No Use of Sample

TABLE 37. NO USE OF SAMPLE: BEYONCÉ & TAYLOR SWIFT	
TAYLOR SWIFT	BEYONCÉ
Taylor Swift (Deluxe, 2006): 14 out of 14	Dangerously in Love (2003): 8 out of 16
Fearless (Platinum, 2008): 18 out of 19	B'Day (Deluxe, 2006): 14 out of 17
Speak Now (Deluxe, 2010): 17 out of 17	I am...Sasha Fierce (Platinum, 2008): 20 out of 20
RED (Deluxe, 2012): 19 out of 19	4 (2011): 10 out of 14
1989 (Deluxe, 2014): 16 out of 16	Beyoncé (Platinum, 2013): 12 out of 16
reputation (2017): 14 out of 15	Lemonade (2016): 6 out of 12
Lover (2019): 15 out of 18	
folklore (Deluxe, 2020): 17 out of 17	
Evermore (Deluxe): 17 out of 17	
Fearless (Taylor's Version, 2021): 7 out of 7	
Total: 154 out of 159 songs (97%)	*Total: 70 out of 95 songs (74%)*

CONCLUSION:

- Taylor Swift has more than double the number of songs with no samples than Beyoncé.

II.3.3 Original Songs as Sole Lyricist

TABLE 38. ORIGINAL SONGS AS SOLE LYRICIST: BEYONCÉ & TAYLOR SWIFT	
TAYLOR SWIFT	BEYONCÉ
Taylor Swift (Deluxe, 2006): 3 out of 14	Dangerously in Love (2003): 1 out of 16[450]
Fearless (Platinum, 2008): 10 out of 19	B'Day (Deluxe, 2006): 0 out of 17
Speak Now (Deluxe, 2010): 16 out of 17	I am...Sasha Fierce (Platinum, 2008): 1 out of 20
RED (Deluxe, 2012): 11 out of 19	4 (2011): 1 out of 14
1989 (Deluxe, 2014): 1 out of 16	Beyoncé (Platinum, 2013): 0 out of 16
reputation (2017): 0 out of 15	Lemonade (2016): 0 out of 12
Lover (2019): 3 out of 18	
folklore (Deluxe, 2020): 1 out of 17	
Evermore (Deluxe, 2020): 1 out of 17	
Fearless (Taylor's Version, 2021): 2 out of 7	
Total: 48 out of 159 songs (30%)	*Total: 3 out of 95 songs (3%)*

CONCLUSION:

- Taylor wrote 48 times more songs as sole lyricists than Beyoncé.

II.3.4 The Length of Original Songs as Sole Lyricist

TABLE 39. THE LENGTH OF ORIGINAL SONG AS SOLE LYRICIST: BEYONCÉ & TAYLOR SWIFT
TAYLOR SWIFT: 206:55 minutes
BEYONCÉ: 16 seconds

CONCLUSION:

---

[450] 'Interlude': it is not a full song; it has 16 seconds and it is the only song written solely by Beyoncé in her entire discography. The conclusion '48 times' was made based solely on Beyoncé's lyrics from 'Interlude.'

- Taylor Swift single-handedly wrote 775.93 times more seconds of music than Beyoncé.

II.3.5 Original Songs with Two Lyricists

TABLE 40. ORIGINAL SONGS WITH TWO LYRICISTS: BEYONCÉ & TAYLOR SWIFT	
TAYLOR SWIFT	BEYONCÉ
Taylor Swift (Deluxe, 2006): 7 out of 14	Dangerously in Love (2003): 4 out of 16
Fearless (Platinum, 2008): 7 out of 19	B'Day (Deluxe, 2006): 0 out of 17
Speak Now (Deluxe, 2010): 1 out of 17	I am...Sasha Fierce (Platinum, 2008): 1 out of 20
RED (Deluxe, 2012): 4 out of 19	4 (2011): 0 out of 14
1989 (Deluxe, 2014): 7 out of 16	Beyoncé (Platinum, 2013): 3 out of 16
reputation (2017): 5 out of 15	Lemonade (2016): 1 out of 12
Lover (2019): 9 out of 18	
folklore (Deluxe, 2020): 15 out of 17	
Evermore (Deluxe, 2020): 13 out of 17	
Fearless (Taylor's Version, 2021): 4 out of 7	
Total: 72 out of 159 songs (45%)	*Total: 9 out of 95 songs (9%)*

CONCLUSION:

- with the help of a second lyricist, Taylor Swift wrote 9 times more songs than Beyoncé.

II.3.6 Original Songs with Three Lyricists

TABLE 41. ORIGINAL SONGS WITH THREE LYRICISTS: BEYONCÉ & TAYLOR SWIFT	
TAYLOR SWIFT	BEYONCÉ
Taylor Swift (Deluxe, 2006): 4 out of 14	Dangerously in Love (2003): 4 out of 16
Fearless (Platinum, 2008): 1 out of 19	B'Day (Deluxe, 2006): 6 out of 17
Speak Now (Deluxe, 2010): 0 out of 17	I am...Sasha Fierce (Platinum, 2008): 5 out of 20
RED (Deluxe, 2012): 4 out of 19	4 (2011): 8 out of 14
1989 (Deluxe, 2014): 7 out of 16	Beyoncé (Platinum, 2013): 4 out of 16
reputation (2017): 5 out of 15	Lemonade (2016): 3 out of 12
Lover (2019): 5 out of 18	
folklore (Deluxe, 2020): 1 out of 17	
Evermore (Deluxe, 2020): 2 out of 17	
Fearless (Taylor's Version, 2021): 1 out of 7	
Total: 30 out of 159 songs (19%)	*Total: 30 out of 95 songs (32%)*

CONCLUSION:

- both artists have the same number of songs written in partnership with two extra lyricists.

II.3.7 Original Songs with at Least Four Lyricists

TABLE 42. ORIGINAL SONGS WITH AT LEAST FOUR LYRICISTS: BEYONCÉ & TAYLOR SWIFT	
TAYLOR SWIFT	BEYONCÉ
Taylor Swift (Deluxe, 2006): 0 out of 14	Dangerously in Love (2003): 7 out of 16
Fearless (Platinum, 2008): 1 out of 19	B'Day (Deluxe, 2006): 11 out of 17
Speak Now (Deluxe, 2010): 0 out of 17	I am...Sasha Fierce (Platinum, 2008): 13 out of 20
RED (Deluxe, 2012): 0 out of 19	4 (2011): 5 out of 14
1989 (Deluxe, 2014): 1 out of 16	Beyoncé (Platinum, 2013): 9 out of 16
reputation (2017): 5 out of 15	Lemonade (2016): 8 out of 12
Lover (2019): 1 out of 18	
folklore (Deluxe, 2020): 0 out of 16	
Evermore (Deluxe, 2020): 1 out of 17	
Fearless (Taylor's Version, 2021): 0 out of 7	
Total: 9 out of 159 songs (6%)	Total: 53 out of 95 songs (56%)

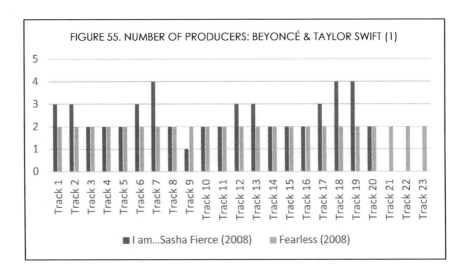

FIGURE 55. NUMBER OF PRODUCERS: BEYONCÉ & TAYLOR SWIFT (1)

CONCLUSION:

- Beyoncé partnered with almost 6 times more lyricists than Taylor Swift.

II.3.8 Number of Producers

The following figures show the number of producers in partnership with Beyoncé and Taylor Swift. The conclusion is: Taylor Swift partnered with less producers than Beyoncé.

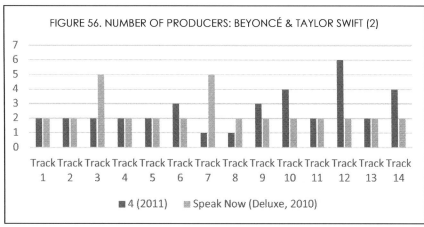

FIGURE 56. NUMBER OF PRODUCERS: BEYONCÉ & TAYLOR SWIFT (2)

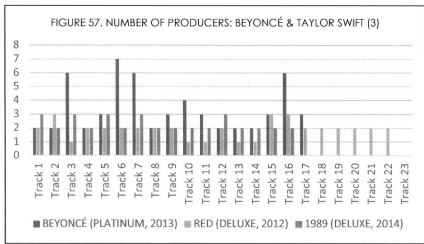

FIGURE 57. NUMBER OF PRODUCERS: BEYONCÉ & TAYLOR SWIFT (3)

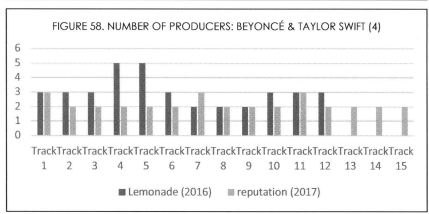

FIGURE 58. NUMBER OF PRODUCERS: BEYONCÉ & TAYLOR SWIFT (4)

II.3.9 Number of Lyricists

The following figures show the number of lyricists in partnership with Beyoncé and Taylor Swift. The conclusion is: Taylor Swift partnered with less lyricists than Beyoncé.

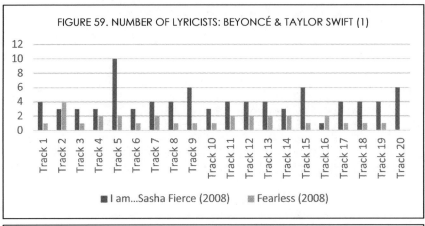

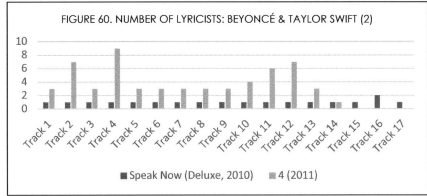

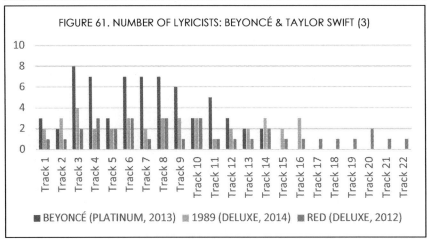

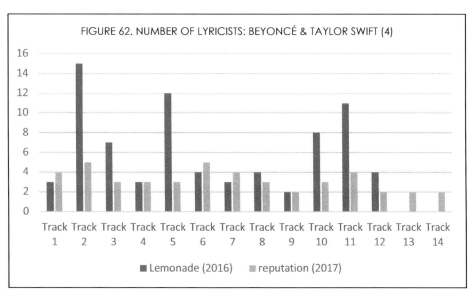

FIGURE 62. NUMBER OF LYRICISTS: BEYONCÉ & TAYLOR SWIFT (4)

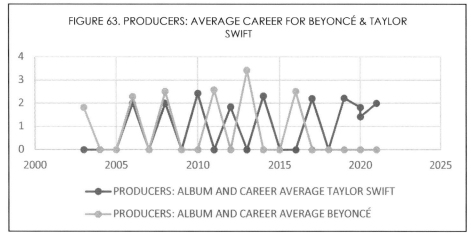

FIGURE 63. PRODUCERS: AVERAGE CAREER FOR BEYONCÉ & TAYLOR SWIFT

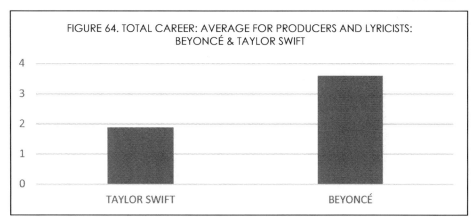

FIGURE 64. TOTAL CAREER: AVERAGE FOR PRODUCERS AND LYRICISTS: BEYONCÉ & TAYLOR SWIFT

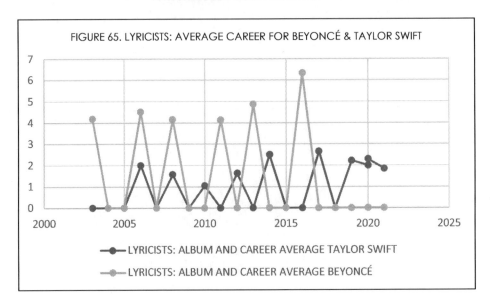

FIGURE 65. LYRICISTS: AVERAGE CAREER FOR BEYONCÉ & TAYLOR SWIFT

LYRICISTS: ALBUM AND CAREER AVERAGE TAYLOR SWIFT

LYRICISTS: ALBUM AND CAREER AVERAGE BEYONCÉ

II.3.10 The Rating on Metacritic

From the point of view of linking the number of producers and lyricists with the grades received based on music review, there is the following conclusion: Beyoncé's grades increased after the involvement of more producers and lyricists; in contrast, Taylor Swift's grades increased with a low number of producers and lyricists.

TABLE 43. THE RATING ON METACRITIC: BEYONCÉ & TAYLOR SWIFT	
BEYONCÉ	TAYLOR SWIFT
Dangerously in Love (2003): 63	Fearless (Platinum, 2008): 73
B'Day (Deluxe, 2006): 70	Speak Now (Deluxe, 2010): 77
I am...Sasha Fierce (Platinum, 2008): 62	RED (Deluxe, 2012): 77
4 (2011): 73	1989 (Deluxe, 2014): 76
Beyoncé (Platinum, 2013): 85	reputation (2017): 71
Lemonade (2016): 92	*Lover* (2019): 79
	folklore (Deluxe, 2020): 88
	Evermore (Deluxe, 2020): 85
	Fearless (Taylor's Version, 2021): 82
Total average: 74.16	*Total average: 78.66*

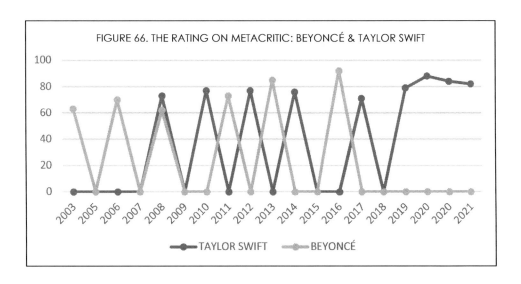

FIGURE 66. THE RATING ON METACRITIC: BEYONCÉ & TAYLOR SWIFT

II.3.11 The Album Release

In this section of the chapter I explored the *album release dates* with the purpose *to find patterns* that may show new information about how artists promote their music.

TABLE 44. THE ALBUM RELEASE DATES: TAYLOR SWIFT & BEYONCÉ		
ARTIST	TAYLOR SWIFT	BEYONCÉ
NAME OF THE ALBUM	*FEARLESS (PLATINUM, 2008)*	*I AM... SASHA FIERCE (2008)*
THEME	'This album is called *Fearless*, and I guess I'd like to clarify why we chose that as the title. To me, *Fearless* is not the absence of fear. It's not being completely unafraid. To me, *Fearless* is having fears, *Fearless* is having doubts. Lots of them. To me, *Fearless* is living in spite of those things that scare you to death. *Fearless* is falling madly in love again, even though you've been hurt before. *Fearless* is walking into your freshman year of high school at fifteen. *Fearless* is getting back up and fighting for what you want over and over again... even though every time you've tried before, you've lost. It's *Fearless* to have faith that someday things will change. *Fearless* is having the courage to say goodbye to someone who only hurts you, even though you can't breathe without them. I think it's *Fearless* to fall for your best friend, even though he's in love with someone else. And when someone	'I'm in a very good place right now. I'm very happy. I'm growing up, and I'm really comfortable with myself. I'm getting wiser and smarter. Hopefully my fans have grown with me, because some of the things that I loved, I don't love so much anymore, and I love new things. That's a part of life. I know that people see celebrities, and they seem like they're so perfect — they seem like their life is so great, and they have money and fame. But I'm a human being. I cry. I'm very passionate and sensitive. My feelings get hurt. I get scared and nervous like everyone else. And I wanted to show that about myself. It's about love. That's what this album is all about. It's about love.'

	apologizes to you enough times for things they'll never stop doing, I think it's *Fearless* to stop believing them. It's *Fearless* to say "you're NOT sorry". I think loving someone despite what people think is *Fearless*. I think allowing yourself to cry on the bathroom floor is *Fearless*. Letting go is Fearless. Then, moving on and being alright... That's *Fearless* too. But no matter what love throws at you, you have to believe in it. You have to believe in love stories and prince charmings and happily ever after. That's why I write these songs. Because I think love is *Fearless*.[451]	'You know, I'm a woman, I'm married, and this portion of my life is all in the album. It's a lot more personal. I'm very private and I don't talk about a lot of things, but there are certain songs that are on the album that are very personal. It's my diary. It's my story.'
		'Young women listen to my album when they need encouragement, and when they are going through tough times, or when they need to forget about what their tough times are, and they just want to have fun and put on their sexy dresses and go dance with their friends, or when they need the strength to be out of a bad relationship, they listen to my album in the car. So I still have my album of fun songs.[452]
RELEASE DATE USA	November 11, 2008	November 18, 2008
RELEASE DATE OTHER COUNTRIES	*November 11, 2008*: Canada; *November 15, 2008*: Australia; Platinum edition was announced on September 10, 2009 and released on October 26, 2009.	*November 12, 2008*: Japan *November 14, 2008*: Australia and Germany; *November 17, 2008*: France and United Kingdom; Platinum edition was released in September – October (depends on country) 2009.
METACRITIC	73	62
PATTERN OF MUSIC RELEASE	2006: October 24 2008: November 11, 15.	2003: June 17 2006: September 4 2008: November 12, 14, 17, 18
	The following dates are written to observe the full pattern of music release by both artists.	
	2010: October 25 2012: October 22 2014: October 27 2017: November 10 2019: August 23 2020: July 24 2020: December 11	2011: June 24 2013: December 13 2016: April 23

[451] Taylor Swift, *Fearless* (Platinum Edition, 2009).
[452] I do not know if this is the good source to explain the theme of the album, but it is the best information that I could find about Beyoncé and her message about her album.

AWARDS	Winner of the Album of the Year at the 52nd Annual Grammy Awards. The most awarded album in the history of country music.	At the 52nd Annual Grammy Awards ceremony she was awarded with five Grammys with a lower grade from critics, and eventually collecting a record setting six wins—the most awards won in one night by a female artist.

CONCLUSIONS:

Beyoncé's album release patterns are:

> *fixed pattern*: June 2003 and 2011;
> *surprise pattern*: 2013 and 2016 (in 2013 the album release dates interfered in Taylor Swift's narrative line as it was released on her birthday, 13 December 2013; in 2016, after Kanye West's song *Famous*, Taylor has a negative image because of the lyrics of the song *Famous* and the line 'that bitch';

- on the contrary, Taylor Swift follows *long term fixed pattern*: autumn for 6 albums; however, after *Lover* (2019) the pattern changed: *Lover* was released following a different pattern: August 23, 2019: two years since the announcement of the *reputation* album (2017); for Taylor Swift is like ending a cycle of two albums: *reputation* first part, and *Lover* as second and final part; in the end, Taylor created a *surprise pattern* like Beyoncé: with two albums, *folklore* (July 2020) and *Evermore* (December 2020);
- Taylor Swift: *folklore* and *Evermore* are two sister albums; Beyoncé: *I Am... Sasha Fierce*: an album with two discs: first disc name is *I Am...* while the second disc name is *Sasha Fierce*;
- *the strange element in 2008*: the keyword and theme of both artists is *fear*;
- *the strange element in 2009*: the albums released in 2008 were in direct competition at the MTV VMA 2009.

TABLE 45. THE ALBUM RELEASE DATES: TAYLOR SWIFT, BEYONCÉ & KANYE WEST			
ARTIST	TAYLOR SWIFT	BEYONCÉ	KANYE WEST
ALBUM	*FEARLESS (PLATINUM, 2008)*	*I AM... SASHA FIERCE (2008)*	*808s & HEARTHBREAK (2008)*
RELEASE DATE USA	November 11, 2008	November 18, 2008	November 24, 2008
PATTERN OF MUSIC RELEASE	2006: October 24 2008: November 11 2010: October 25 2012: October 22 2014: October 27 2017: November 10	2003: June 17 2006: September 4 2008: November 12 2011: June 24 2013: December 13	2004: February 10 2005: August 30 2007: September 11 2008: November 24 2010: November 22 2013: June 18

	2019: August 23 2020: July 24 2020: December 11	2016: April 23	2016: February 14 2018: June 1 2019: October 25

CONCLUSIONS:

- Beyoncé album release (November 12, 2008 in Japan) is in the same month as Taylor Swift: November 11, which is the second day after Taylor Swift; however, the full release in the USA by Beyoncé is on next week, November 18, 2008, a week before Kanye West's album: November 24, 2008;

- Kanye West changed the pattern of music release and interfered for a second time in Taylor Swift's pattern of album release: one album in each year for two years, and in total for four albums: 2004 and 2005, the next two albums: 2007 and 2008; since 2008 Kanye West changed the season and released his album in the same month as Taylor Swift, but two weeks later: Taylor Swift on November 11, 2008 and Kanye West on November 24; *in 2010*: Taylor Swift released the album on October 25 (she released her first album in October 24, 2006), then Kanye West later in November 22 which was connected with the last release (November 2008), and is the first and the last time when Kanye West followed this release pattern; the following albums were released in different seasons, only to be changed to October 25, 2019 with *Jesus is King*, the same release date as Taylor Swift with *Speak Now* in 2010;

- Kanye West (change of release pattern) and Beyoncé (fixed pattern: June 2003 and 2011; surprise pattern: 2013 and 2016) changed the album release date and both artists released their albums in the same month as Taylor Swift (fixed pattern until *Lover* album 2019), then for the next album Kanye West and Beyoncé changed the release month again; strangely, in 2009 all the artists found themselves (with the generous help of Kanye West) involved into one of the most famous feuds of all time in the music industry, with the starting point at the MTV Music Awards for the Video Music Awards (September 13, 2009), and based on the albums released by Taylor Swift and Beyoncé in the same month of November 2008;

- The MTV Video Music Awards were presented on September 13, 2009: the lucky number of Taylor Swift (or not so lucky for this day) where Kanye West showed his lack of manners in front of the entire world.[453]

---

[453] This statement is based on the conclusions from *On the **Famous** Feud*.

II.4 Kendrick Lamar versus Taylor Swift

In this section of the chapter I investigated the music released by Taylor Swift in 2014 (the album *1989*) and Kendrick Lamar (*To Pimp a Butterfly)* in 2015. These albums were in direct competition for the *Album of the Year* at the Grammy Awards in 2016, and for which Kanye West said that Kendrick Lamar should have won because his album is better.

II.4.1 No Use of Sample

TABLE 46. NO USE OF SAMPLES: TAYLOR SWIFT & KENDRICK LAMAR
TAYLOR SWIFT: 1989 (Deluxe, 2014): N/A
KENDRICK LAMAR: To Pimp a Butterfly (2015): 10 out of 16

CONCLUSION:

- Kendrick Lamar used samples for his songs, while Taylor Swift did not, which makes her album more original in comparison with him.

II.4.2 Original Songs as Sole Lyricist

TABLE 47. ORIGINAL SONGS AS SOLE LYRICIST: TAYLOR SWIFT & KENDRICK LAMAR
TAYLOR SWIFT: 1989 (Deluxe, 2014): 1 out of 16
KENDRICK LAMAR: To Pimp a Butterfly (2015): 0 out of 16

CONCLUSION:

- Taylor Swift released a song written by herself, while Kendrick Lamar none.

II.4.3 The Length of Original Songs as Sole Lyricist

TABLE 48. THE LENGTH OF SONGS AS SOLE LYRICIST: TAYLOR SWIFT & KENDRICK LAMAR
TAYLOR SWIFT: 1989 (Deluxe, 2014): This Love with 4:10 minutes
KENDRICK LAMAR: To Pimp a Butterfly (2015): 0 minutes

CONCLUSION:

- Taylor Swift has 4:10 minutes of music written by herself, while Kendrick Lamar has 0 minutes; this show the ability and courage of Taylor Swift to bet on the power of her abilities to write music.

II.4.4 Original Songs with Two Lyricists

TABLE 49. ORIGINAL SONGS WITH TWO LYRICISTS: TAYLOR SWIFT & KENDRICK LAMAR
TAYLOR SWIFT: 1989 (Deluxe, 2014): 7 out of 16
KENDRICK LAMAR: To Pimp a Butterfly (2015): 1 out of 16

CONCLUSION:

- almost half of the songs from her album are written in partnership with another lyricists, while Kendrick Lamar partnered with one lyricist.

II.4.5 The Length of Original Songs with Two Lyricists

TABLE 50. THE LENGTH OF ORIGINAL SONGS WITH TWO LYRICISTS: TAYLOR SWIFT & KENDRICK LAMAR
TAYLOR SWIFT: 1989 (Deluxe, 2014): 26:19 minutes
KENDRICK LAMAR: To Pimp a Butterfly (2015): 4:51

CONCLUSION:

- Taylor Swift has at least 5 times more minutes of music written in partnership with a second lyricists than Kendrick Lamar.

II.4.6 The Sources of the Samples

TABLE 51. THE SOURCES OF SAMPLES: TAYLOR SWIFT & KENDRICK LAMAR	
ARTIST & ALBUM	SOURCE OF SAMPLES
TAYLOR SWIFT: 1989 (Deluxe, 2014)	N/A

KENDRICK LAMAR: To Pimp a Butterfly (2015)	1. 'Wesley's Theory' contains elements of 'Every Nigger is a Star', written and performed by Boris Gardiner. 2. 'King Kunta' contains interpolations of 'Get Nekkid', written by Johnny Burns and performed by Mausberg; resung lyrics from 'Smooth Criminal', written and performed by Michael Jackson; elements of 'The Payback', written by James Brown, Fred Wesley and John Starks, and performed by James Brown; and samples of 'We Want the Funk', written and performed by Ahmad Lewis. 3. 'Momma' contains elements of 'Wishful Thinkin' written by Sylvester Stone and performed by Sly and the Family Stone; and elements of 'On Your Own', written and performed by Lalah Hathaway; sampled 'So[rt]', by Knxwledge; sampled 'Control (HOF)', as performed by Big Sean, Kendrick Lamar and Jay Electronica. 4. 'Hood Politics' contains a sample of 'All for Myself', written and performed by Sufjan Stevens. 5. 'i' contains a sample of 'That Lady', written by Ronald Isley, O'Kelly Isley, Jr., Ernie Isley, Marvin Isley, Rudolph Isley and Christopher Jasper, and performed by The Isley Brothers. 6. 'Mortal Man' contains excerpts from 'I No Get Eye for Back', written by Fela Anikulapo Kuti and performed by Houston Person; and a sample of music journalist Mats Nileskar's November 1994 interview with Tupac Shakur for P3 Soul Broadcasting Corporation.

CONCLUSION:

- the songs released by Kendrick Lamar contain samples from various songs and artists; Taylor Swift did not use samples.

II.4.7 The Fame of The Samples

TABLE 52. THE FAME OF THE SAMPLES: TAYLOR SWIFT & KENDRICK LAMAR	
TAYLOR SWIFT: 1989 (Deluxe, 2014)	N/A
KENDRICK LAMAR: To Pimp a Butterfly (2015)	1. 'Smooth Criminal': 'The song was number 7 on the Billboard Hot 100, number 2 on the Billboard Hot Black Singles chart.' 2. 'The Payback': 'Samples from this song was heavily used in popular games and movies.' 3. 'That Lady': 'The song is ranked number 357 on Rolling Stone's list of the 500 Greatest Songs of All Time.'

CONCLUSION:

- some of the samples used by Kendrick Lamar were already known in the music industry, and included on charts.

II.4.8 Producers and Lyricists

TABLE 53. PRODUCERS AND LYRICISTS: TAYLOR SWIFT & KENDRICK LAMAR
TAYLOR SWIFT: 1989 (Deluxe, 2014): ***Producers***: Max Martin, Taylor Swift, Jack Antonoff, Nathan Chapman, Imogen Heap, Mattman & Robin, Ali Payami, Shellback, Ryan Tedder, Noel Zancanella. ***Lyricists***: between one to four, most of the songs have two and three lyricists.
KENDRICK LAMAR: To Pimp a Butterfly (Deluxe, 2015): ***Producers***: Boi-1da, Flippa, Flying Lotus, Knxwledge, KOZ, Larrance Dopson, LoveDragon, Pharrell Williams, Rahki, Sounwave, Tae Beast, Taz Arnold, Terrace Martin, Thundercat, Tommy Black, Whoarei. ***Lyricists***: from two to eight.

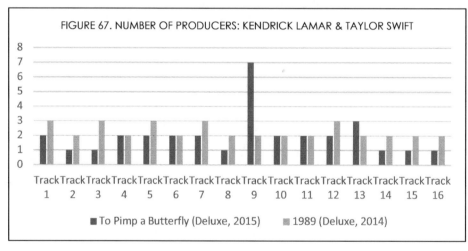

FIGURE 67. NUMBER OF PRODUCERS: KENDRICK LAMAR & TAYLOR SWIFT

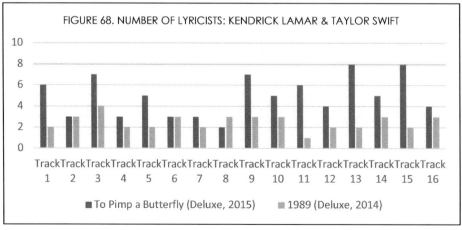

FIGURE 68. NUMBER OF LYRICISTS: KENDRICK LAMAR & TAYLOR SWIFT

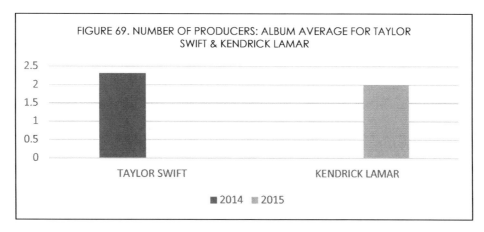

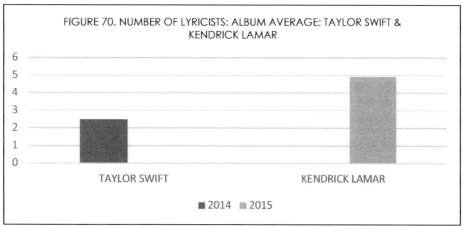

CONCLUSIONS:

- overall, the album by Kendrick Lamar was in partnership with more lyricists than Taylor Swift, but with less producers than Taylor Swift;
- Taylor Swift partnered with less lyricists to create the album, and has a higher level of originality because her sounds and lyrics are not based on other songs, as it happens to some extent with Kendrick Lamar;
- Taylor Swift is part of the producers, but Kendrick Lamar is not;
- perhaps because of these conclusions the voting members of The Recording Academy decided that Taylor Swift has a higher genuine reason than Kendrick Lamar to be awarded with the *Album of the Year*, and less because she is white and her album sold millions of copies in the world in the last two years, since the release of the album (2014) and the award ceremony (2016).

II.4.9 The Album Ratings

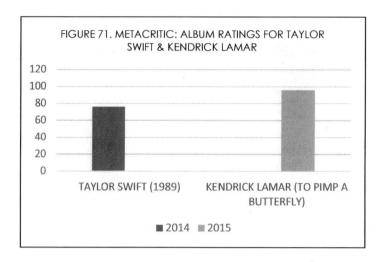

FIGURE 71. METACRITIC: ALBUM RATINGS FOR TAYLOR SWIFT & KENDRICK LAMAR

CONCLUSIONS:

- Taylor Swift's grades (76) are based on her clean music, while Kendrick Lamar's grades (96) are based also to some extent on the samples used;
- the comparative analysis reveals a thin line of the quality and originality of the music released by both artists; Taylor Swift's album is clean and belongs to a greater extent to herself and the producers and lyricists;
- another different feature between these albums is the language design: Kendrick Lamar has a rich vulgar and offensive language, where this is missing in Taylor Swift's album.

II.5 Beyoncé versus Beck

In the next section of this chapter I investigated the album released by Beyoncé (black woman) in 2013 and Beck (white man) in 2014, to find why Beyoncé lost the *Album of the Year* at the Grammy Awards in 2015.

II.5.1 Use of Sample

TABLE 54. ORIGINAL SONGS WITH SAMPLE: BEYONCÉ & BECK
BEYONCÉ: Beyoncé (Platinum, 2013): 4 out of 16
BECK: Morning Phase (2014): 0 out of 13[454]

CONCLUSION:

- all of Beck's songs contain no sample, while Beyoncé has 3 songs with samples.

II.5.2 Original Songs as Sole Lyricist

TABLE 55. ORIGINAL SONGS AS SOLE LYRICIST: BEYONCÉ & BECK
BEYONCÉ: Beyoncé (Platinum, 2013): 0 out of 16
BECK: Morning Phase (2014): 13 out of 13

CONCLUSION:

- Beck is the sole lyricist of the songs included in his album, while Beyoncé does not have songs written solely by herself.

II.5.3 The Length of Songs as Sole Lyricists

TABLE 56. THE LENGTH OF SONGS AS SOLE LYRICIST: BEYONCÉ & BECK
BEYONCÉ: Beyoncé (Platinum, 2013): 0 minutes
BECK: Morning Phase (2014): 47:03 minutes (100%)

---

[454] Beck, 'Morning Phase Credits', *Tidal,* 2014, available at: https://listen.tidal.com/album/77668770/credits, last accessed: February 25, 2020. This source it is used for the rest of the section of this chapter.

CONCLUSION:

- Beck has 47:03 minutes of music based only on his lyrics, while Beyoncé has 0 minutes of music written only by herself.

II.5.4 The Sources of the Samples

TABLE 57. THE SOURCES OF THE SAMPLES: BEYONCÉ & BECK	
BEYONCÉ: Beyoncé (Platinum, 2013):	*BECK*: Morning Phase (2014):
1. 'Partition' contains an interpolation of the French-dubbed version of the 1998 film The Big Lebowski, performed by Hajiba Fahmy.	own musical mind.
2. 'Flawless' contains portions of the speech 'We should all be feminists', written and delivered by Chimamanda Ngozi Adichie.	
3. 'Heaven' contains portions of 'The Lord's Prayer' in Spanish, performed by Melissa Vargas.	

CONCLUSION:

- Beyoncé's songs contain samples, but only one song, *Partition*, contain sample from other song; the other two songs contain sample from sources outside music.

II.5.5 The Fame of The Samples

TABLE 58. THE FAME OF THE SAMPLES: BEYONCÉ & BECK	
NAME OF THE ALBUM	SAMPLES
BEYONCÉ: Beyoncé (Platinum, 2013)	*1. The Big Lebowski:* become a cult classic. An annual festival, Lebowski Fest, which expanded to several other cities and countries. Various publications included this film in different charts: Entertainment Weekly ranked it 8th on their Funniest Movies of the Past 25 Years list, also was ranked No. 34 on their list of 'The Top 50 Cult Films' and ranked No. 15 on the magazine's 'The Cult 25: The Essential Left-Field Movie Hits Since '83' list. The film was also nominated for the prestigious Grand Prix of the Belgian Film Critics Association. The Big Lebowski was voted as the 10th best film set in Los Angeles in the last 25 years by a group of Los Angeles Times writers and editors with two criteria: 'The movie had to communicate some inherent truth about the L.A. experience, and only one film

	per director was allowed on the list.' Roger Ebert added The Big Lebowski to his list of 'Great Movies' in March 2010.[455]
	2. We Should All Be Feminists': it was a speech that later was extended into a book 'which received overwhelmingly positive reviews.' Rupert Hawksley said: 'it just might be the most important book you read all year" in The Telegraph. The Independent selected it as a book of the year'.[456]
	3. 'The Lord's Prayer', also called the *Our Father* (Latin: Pater Noster), is a central Christian prayer which, according to the New Testament, Jesus taught as the way to pray.
BECK: Morning Phase (2014)	N/A

CONCLUSION:

- the sample used by Beyoncé existed already in the music industry, but it is at a lower level.

II.5.6 Producers and Lyricists

In this section I created figures with the number of producers and lyricists for Beyoncé and Taylor Swift. The figures are used to find which artist was in partnership with more and less producers and lyricists.

TABLE 59. PRODUCERS AND LYRICISTS: BEYONCÉ & BECK	
BEYONCÉ: Beyoncé (Platinum, 2013): *Producers:* Beyoncé (also exec.) 40, Ammo Boots, Brian Soko, Caroline Polachek, Detail, Dre Moon, HazeBanga, Hit-Boy, J-Roc, Justin Timberlake, Key Wane, Majid Jordan, Mike Dean, Omen, Patrick Wimberly, Pharrell Williams, Rasool Ricardo Diaz, Rey Reel, Ryan Tedder, The-Dream, Timbaland. *Lyricists*: from two to ten.	*BECK*: Morning Phase (2014): *Producer*: Beck *Lyricist*: Beck

---

[455] 'The Big Lebowski', *Wikipedia*, available at: https://en.wikipedia.org/wiki/The_Big_Lebowski#Legacy, last accessed: February 25, 2020.

[456] 'We Should All Be Feminists', *Wikipedia*, available at: https://en.wikipedia.org/wiki/We_Should_All_Be_Feminists, last accessed: February 25, 2020.

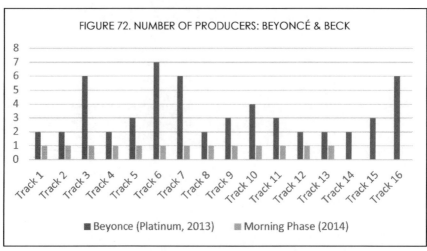

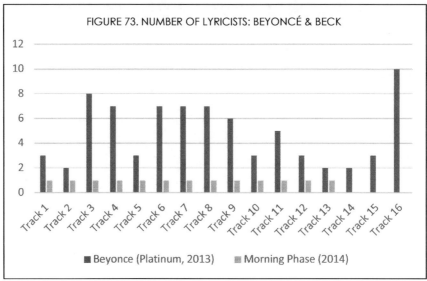

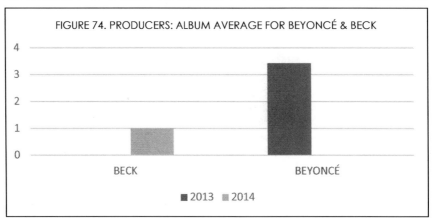

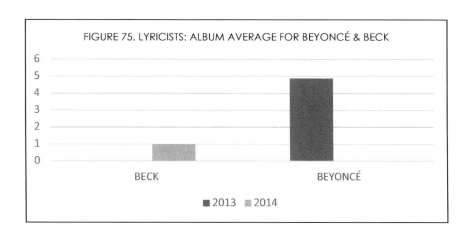

FIGURE 75. LYRICISTS: ALBUM AVERAGE FOR BEYONCÉ & BECK

CONCLUSION:

- Beck is the sole producer and lyricist of his album and maybe this is a genuine argument for being the winner of the *Album of the Year,* and not Beyoncé, and the producers and lyricists which contributed to her album. It seems that number 13 (also the lucky number of Taylor Swift) was a lucky number for Beck's number of songs (13), but bad luck for Beyoncé which released her self-titled album on December 13, 2013 (the birthday of Taylor Swift; at that time Taylor Swift already won the *Album of the Year* in 2009 with *Fearless,* and won again in 2016 for the album *1989* (the standard edition has 13 songs).

II.5.7 The Album Ratings

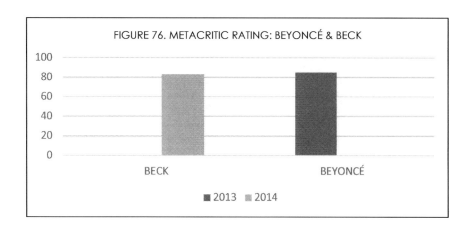

FIGURE 76. METACRITIC RATING: BEYONCÉ & BECK

CONCLUSION:

- Beck's final review grade (83) is based on his personal contribution, while Beyoncé's final review grade (85) is based on her personal contribution, but to a considerable extent to other producers and lyricists.

II.6 Beyoncé versus Adele

In this subchapter I investigated the album released by Beyoncé (black woman) in 2016 and Adele (white woman) in 2015 to find a possible answer to a highly important question spread worldwide: why Beyoncé did not win the *Album of the Year* at the Grammy Awards in 2017?

II.6.1 No Use of Sample

TABLE 60. ORIGINAL SONGS WITH NO SAMPLE: BEYONCÉ & ADELE
BEYONCÉ: Lemonade (2016): 6 out of 12
ADELE: 25 (Target, 2015): 14 out of 14[457]

CONCLUSION:

- all of Adele's songs contain no samples, while Beyoncé has six songs with no samples.

II.6.2 Original Songs as Sole Lyricist

TABLE 61. ORIGINAL SONGS AS SOLE LYRICIST: BEYONCÉ & ADELE
BEYONCÉ: Lemonade (2016): 0 out of 12
ADELE: 25 (Target, 2015): 14 out of 14

CONCLUSIONS:

- based on the following statement 'Adele is credited on *Tidal* as sole lyricist, but on the *Composer Lyricists* her songs are credited with a second lyricist; in this report, I used only *Lyricist* as Adele (this is the raw version of the song, the main idea that later was transformed into a song)', Adele may be the sole lyricist of her songs;
- Beyoncé has no single with her as the sole lyricist.

II.6.3 The Length of the Original Songs as Sole Lyricist

---

[457] Adele, '25 Credits', *Tidal*, 2015, available at: https://listen.tidal.com/album/62300892/credits, last accessed: February 25, 2020. The songs from the version *25 (Target Edition)* were taken from Wikipedia, available at: https://en.wikipedia.org/wiki/25_(Adele_album), last accessed: February 25, 2020. This source it is used for the rest of the section of this chapter.

TABLE 62. THE LENGTH OF THE ORIGINAL SONGS AS SOLE LYRICIST: BEYONCÉ & ADELE
BEYONCÉ: Lemonade (2016): 0 minutes
ADELE: 25 (Target, 2015): 60:12 minutes

CONCLUSIONS:

- based on the following statement 'Adele is credited on *Tidal* as sole lyricist, but on the *Composer Lyricists* her songs are credited with a second lyricist; in this report, I used only *Lyricist* as Adele (this is the raw version of the song, the main idea that later was transformed into a song)', Adele may have the full album as sole lyricist;
- Beyoncé has 0 minutes of music as the sole lyricist.

II.6.4 The Sources of the Samples

TABLE 63. THE SOURCES OF THE SAMPLES: BEYONCÉ & ADELE	
ARTIST & ALBUM	SOURCE OF SAMPLES
BEYONCÉ: Lemonade (2016)	1. *'Hold Up'*: Good connection with the theme of the song (relationships, cheating, losing someone) 'Can't Get Used to Losing You' and use of lyrics from 'Turn My Swag On' and 'Maps'. Some lyrics of this song 'Can't Get Used to Losing You' are being used to create a visual representation in the music video, which is also genuinely similar with the video of the Swiss visual artist Pipilotti Rist's project 'Ever Is Over All'. On the album Aquemini (contains the word 'aque' acronymous for 'aqua' which translates as 'water' (which is one of the main themes and visuals of the album Lemonade), from which Beyoncé samples the song 'SpottieOttieDopaliscious', has the introductory song named 'Hold On, Be Strong.' 2. *Don't Hurt Yourself'*: 'When the Levee Breaks': good connection with the song's theme and use of lyrics. The song is a reflection of the experience during the upheaval caused by the Great Mississippi Flood of 1927, which is linked with Beyoncé's visual album with floods (water) in Formation and other videos which represents the real world and the negative side effects of tornadoes, hurricanes from the United States of America. 3. *'6 inch'*: Title and lyrics connection with 'My Girls'. 4. *'Freedom'*: Some connection with 'Let Me Try'. 5. *'All Night'*: Some connection with the theme of the song (events from a night) 'SpottieOttieDopaliscious'. However, there is strong connection between the whole album of Lemonade (visual and lyrics themes) and the whole album named Aquemini ('SpottieOttieDopaliscious' is one of the songs included in this album), released in 1998 by the hip-hop duo Outkast. Lyrically, much of Aquemini features introspection about the desolation of the human condition (strong theme in Lemonade), which include precarious relationships (Lemonade: between her and Jay Z), freedom from self-inflicted struggles (Lemonade: between her and Mr. Carter), also one of Beyoncé songs from Lemonade is named Freedom. If Aquemini is about a shift between science – fiction inspired topics combined with the harsh reality of urban life, Lemonade is showing in her videos the harsh reality of the country and urban life of black people. In the end, the similarity between the two albums is the experimentation of delivery styles on the record, using relaxed, hyper, distorted, speedy and conversational presentations.'

	6. *'Sorry (Original Demo)'*: Use of lyrics from the title 'Young, Wild & Free' and chorus.
ADELE: 25 (Target, 2015)	N/A as she did not use samples in her music. Adele was accused of ripping off an artist from Turkey.[458]

CONCLUSION:

- Beyoncé's song contains samples from various songs and artists.

II.6.5 The Fame of The Samples

TABLE 64. THE FAME OF THE SAMPLES USED: BEYONCÉ & ADELE	
ARTIST & ALBUM	THE FAME OF THE SAMPLES
BEYONCÉ: Lemonade (2016)	1. *'Turn My Swag On'*: 'The song was US Rap Songs (Billboard) weekly charts number 3, US Pop 100 (Billboard) weekly charts number 39, US Hot R&B/Hip Hop Songs (Billboard) weekly charts number 3.' 2. *'Maps'*: The music video received extensive play on MTV, it reached number 9 on Billboard's Alternative Songs chart and was included in popular video game Rock Band.' Other success includes: 'NME best alternative love song in 2009; number 6 on Pitchfork Media's top 500 songs of the 2000s; Rolling Stone ranked it number 386 on their list of the 500 Greatest Songs of All Time; in 2011 NME placed the song at number 55 on its list '150 Best Tracks of the Past 150 Years'; NME ranked the song at number 1 on their list of 'Indie Weddings Songs: 20 Tracks Perfect For Your First Dance' 3. *When the Levee Breaks'*: 'It is a wide loved country blue song'. 4. *'My Girls'*: 'The lyrics of the song is about the desire of the artist on a basic level to own my own place and kind of provide a safe house for my family and the people I care about.' Other success include: Pitchfork named the song number 1 of 2009 and also number 9 on their Top 500 Tracks of the 2000s; NME named the 5th best song of 2009; Slant Magazine named the best song of 2009; The Village Voice name the third best song of 2009; NME in 2011 place it at number 91 on their list '150 Best Tracks of the Past 15 Years'; NME in 2014 named the 248th best song of all time'. 5. *'Walk On By'*: 'The song peaked at number 6 on the US Billboard Hot 100 and number 1 on the Cash Box Rhythm and Blues Chart in June 1964; also, it was nominated for a 1965 Grammy Award for the Best Rhythm and Blues Recording.' 6. *'SpottieOttieDopaliscious'*: 'It is a song from the album Aquemini which is the third studio album of the American hip hop duo Outkast. Aquemini received highly widespread acclaim from critics with most the grade being one 3,5 out of 4 stars from USA Today and Chicago Sun-Times, to 5 out of 5 stars from Q, to A- from Christgau's Consumer Guide, to A from Entertainment Weekly. Los Angeles Times gave 4 stars out of 4, Rolling Stone 4 out of 5 stars. In the end the album was included in several publication's best album lists such as: in 2003, Rolling Stone ranked it on their 500 Greatest Albums of All Time and number 11 on the list '100 best Albums of the Nineties'; Paste called it 'the best Atlanta hip-hop album of all time'; Pitchfork ranked it number 50 on their 'Top 100 Albums of the 1990s'; Spin ranked

---

[458] Paul Gallagher, 'Adele accused by 'stealing' Kuridsh singer's 1985 song for new album', *The Independent*, December 7, 2015, available at: https://www.independent.co.uk/arts-entertainment/music/news/adele-accused-of-stealing-kurdish-singer-s-1985-song-for-her-new-album-25-a6764041.html, last accessed: February 25, 2020.

	it number 35 on the '90 Greatest Albums of the '90' and number 3 on the 'Top 20 Albums of '98'; the lead single 'Rosa Park' was nominated in the category Grammy Award for Best Rap Performance by a Duo or Group at the 1999 Grammy Awards; in the end the song 'SpottieOttieDopaliscious' was ranked at number 16 on Pitchfork Media's list of the top 200 tracks of the 1990s.' The legacy of this album is virtuosic masterpiece, a landmark hip-hop, artistic success, brilliant, avant-garde, sonic ideas, new sounds, ravenous as ever which is in direct line with the reviews received by Beyoncé for Lemonade, her highest rated album yet. 7. *'Young, Wild & Free'*: 'The song peaked at number 7 on the Billboard Hot 100. The song was praised for standing out stylistically from the rest of the soundtrack with hip-hop drums and a piano back. It was a commercial success and by April 16, 2013 was certified 3 times Platinum by the Recording Industry Association of America and before Lemonade release, around 4 times platinum. The song was nominated for Best Rap Song at the 2013 Grammy Awards'.
ADELE: 25 (Target, 2015)	N/A as she did not used samples in her music. Adele was accused of ripping off an artist from Turkey.[459]

CONCLUSIONS:

- the samples used by Beyoncé were part of the music industry, included in charts and awarded before the release of her songs with the samples included;
- there is a good and visible connection between Beyoncé's songs and the songs sampled in her songs.

II.6.6 Producers and Lyricists

25 (Target, 14 songs) has 3 songs more than the standard edition (11 songs), for Target Edition (extra 3 songs) I used Wikipedia as source for *Lyricists* and the number is 2 per song; however, considering *Tidal* credits for standard edition, it is possible that the main *Lyricist* to be Adele, while the *Composer Lyricists* to be Adele, and a second lyricist as it happens with the standard edition.

TABLE 65. PRODUCERS AND LYRICISTS: BEYONCÉ & ADELE	
BEYONCÉ: Lemonade (2016)	*ADELE*: 25 (Target, 2015):
Producers: Beyoncé (also exec.), Beyoncé, Diplo, Kevin Garret, Ezra Koenig, Jack White, MeLo-X, Dina Gordon, Boots, DannyBoyStyles, Mike Dean, Vincent Berry II, James Blake, Jonathan Coffer, Just Blaze, Mike Will Made It.	*Producers*: Danger Mouse, Samuel Dixon, Paul Epworth, Greg Kurstin, Max Martin, Linda Perry, Ariel Rechtshaid, Mark Ronson, Shellback, The Smeezingtons, Ryan Tedder.

---

[459] *Ibidem.*

Lyricists: between two to fifteen.	**Lyricists**: one, Adele (Composer Lyricist: most of the songs have two).

The average for *Producers* and *Lyricists* used in the figure is based on *25 (Target)* with 14 songs.

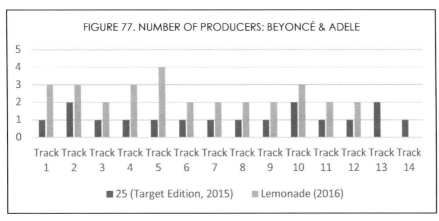

FIGURE 77. NUMBER OF PRODUCERS: BEYONCÉ & ADELE

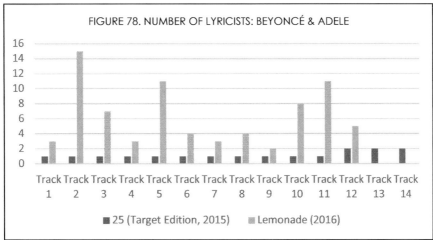

FIGURE 78. NUMBER OF LYRICISTS: BEYONCÉ & ADELE

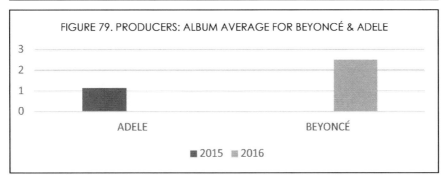

FIGURE 79. PRODUCERS: ALBUM AVERAGE FOR BEYONCÉ & ADELE

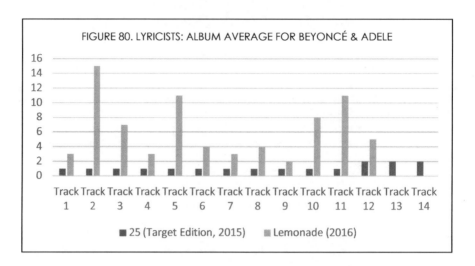

FIGURE 80. LYRICISTS: ALBUM AVERAGE FOR BEYONCÉ & ADELE

CONCLUSIONS:

- Adele partnered with less producers and lyricists than Beyoncé (partnered with a high number of producers; inspirations with sounds, themes and lyrics of other songs already known, included in charts and awarded in the music industry);
- Adele is the sole lyricist of her music, but with a second lyricist for *Composer Lyricist*;
- the figures available in this report reveal evidence to build a good argument that Adele has a better musical dossier of high personal involvement in the making of her album, and maybe this is the reason why she was awarded with the *Album of the Year*.

II.6.7 The Album Ratings

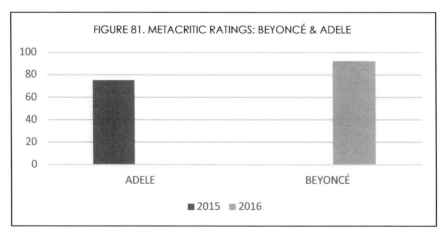

FIGURE 81. METACRITIC RATINGS: BEYONCÉ & ADELE

CONCLUSION:

- Adele's final review grade (75) is based on her personal contribution at high level, while Beyoncé's final review grade (92) is based on her personal contribution, but to a considerable extent to other producers, lyricists and samples.

II.7 Macklemore & Ryan versus Kendrick Lamar

On January 26, 2014, Macklemore & Ryan Lewis won the Grammy Award for *Best Rap Album*. According to K.B. Denis, 'Macklemore & Ryan were criticised and a good number of people within the music industry felt that Kendrick Lamar was cheated. Strangely, Macklemore & Ryan Lewis considered Kendrick Lamar as the right winner and offered an apology; there were news which presented the award to Macklemore & Ryan Lewis as a controversial turn of events where Kendrick Lamar was seen as the right winner; another criticism was that Macklemore & Ryan Lewis are white and their whiteness lift and granted them the Grammy which has also made a habit of over-rewarding white rappers; Macklemore & Ryan Lewis are very much aware of their white privilege and how it is has given them advantages in life and career.'[460]

In this section I investigated the origin of Macklemore & Ryan Lewis and Kendrick Lamar's music albums that were in direct competition for the *Best Rap Album of the Year* at the Grammy Awards in 2014.

II.7.1 No Use of Sample

TABLE 66. ORIGINAL SONGS WITH NO SAMPLE: MACKLEMORE & RYAN LEWIS & KENDRICK LAMAR
MACKLEMORE & RYAN LEWIS: The Heist (Deluxe, 2012): 0 out of 18[461]
KENDRICK LAMAR: good city, m.A.A.d. city (Deluxe, 2012): 9 out of 18

CONCLUSION:

- all of Macklemore & Ryan's songs contain no sample, while Kendrick Lamar used sample in 9 (50%) of his songs.

II.7.2 Original Songs as Sole Lyricist

---

[460] The idea of this paragraph existed before the publication of K.B. Denis's article, but it was changed to contain more from his article, read: K.B. Denis, 'Grammy Rewind: 6 Years Later, How Did Macklemore Beat Out Kendrick Lamar at the Grammys?', *Awardswatch*, July 10, 2020, available at: https://awardswatch.com/grammy-rewind-6-years-later-how-did-macklemore-beat-out-kendrick-lamar-at-the-grammys/, last accessed: July 11, 2020.
[461] Macklemore & Ryan, 'The Heist (Deluxe, 2021) Credits', *Tidal,* available at: https://listen.tidal.com/album/23374211/credits, last accessed: February 25, 2020. This source it is used for the rest of the section of this chapter.

TABLE 67. ORIGINAL SONGS AS SOLE LYRICIST: MACKLEMORE & RYAN LEWIS & KENDRICK LAMAR
MACKLEMORE & RYAN LEWIS: The Heist (Deluxe, 2012): 1 out of 18 (by Ryan Lewis)
KENDRICK LAMAR: good city, m.A.A.d. city (Deluxe, 2012): 0 out of 18

CONCLUSION:

- Kendrick Lamar does not have a song written only by himself, however, Ryan has one song.

II.7.3 Original Songs with Two Lyricists

TABLE 68. ORIGINAL SONGS WITH TWO LYRICISTS: MACKLEMORE & RYAN LEWIS & KENDRICK LAMAR
MACKLEMORE & RYAN LEWIS: The Heist (Deluxe, 2012): 5 out of 18 (Written by Macklemore & Ryan Lewis)
KENDRICK LAMAR: good city, m.A.A.d. city (Deluxe, 2012): 5 out of 18

CONCLUSION:

- both artist's albums contain songs with two lyricists, however, Macklemore & Ryan are the main artists in writing and singing their songs as group.

II.7.4 The Length of Songs as Sole Lyricist

TABLE 69. THE LENGTH OF SONGS AS SOLE LYRICIST: MACKLEMORE & RYAN LEWIS & KENDRICK LAMAR
MACKLEMORE & RYAN LEWIS: The Heist (Deluxe, 2012): 4:55 minutes out of 76:18 minutes
KENDRICK LAMAR: good city, m.A.A.d. city (Deluxe, 2012): 0 minutes out of 100:03 minutes

CONCLUSION:

- Ryan is the sole lyricist of a song included in the album, while all of Kendrick Lamar's songs are written in partnership with at least a second lyricist.

II.7.5 The Length of Songs with Two Lyricists

TABLE 70. THE LENGTH OF SONGS WITH TWO LYRICISTS: MACKLEMORE & RYAN LEWIS & KENDRICK LAMAR
MACKLEMORE & RYAN LEWIS: The Heist (Deluxe, 2012): 19:49 minutes out of 76:18 minutes
KENDRICK LAMAR: good city, m.A.A.d. city (Deluxe, 2012): 23:49 minutes out of 100:03 minutes

CONCLUSION:

- Kendrick Lamar has more minutes of music in partnership with a second lyricist than Macklemore & Ryan.

II.7.6 The Sources of the Samples

TABLE 71. THE SOURCES OF THE SAMPLES: MACKLEMORE & RYAN LEWIS & KENDRICK LAMAR	
MACKLEMORE & RYAN LEWIS: The Heist (Deluxe, 2012)	N/A as they did not use samples in their music.
KENDRICK LAMAR: good city, m.A.A.d. city (Deluxe, 2012)	While Kendrick Lamar used samples, I found these songs to be used more than the others: 1. 'The Art of Peer Pressure': 'Helt Alene': it was the main sample for this track. 2. 'Poetic Justice': 'It used heavily sample from the song 'Any Time, Any Place' co-written and performed by Janet Jackson.' 3. 'The Receipe': Some lyrics from 'Meet the Frownies.'

CONCLUSION:

- Kendrick Lamar's album has more samples from other songs than Macklemore & Ryan, which opted for their own musical ear.

II.7.7 The Fame of the Sample

TABLE 72. THE FAME OF THE SAMPLES: MACKLEMORE & RYAN LEWIS & KENDRICK LAMAR	
MACKLEMORE & RYAN LEWIS: The Heist (Deluxe, 2012)	N/A as they did not use samples in their music.
	1. 'Smooth Criminal': 'The song was number 7 on the Billboard Hot 100, number 2 on the Billboard Hot Black Singles chart.'

KENDRICK LAMAR: good city, m.A.A.d. city (Deluxe, 2012)	2. 'The Payback': 'Samples from this song was heavily used in popular games and movies.' 3. 'That Lady': 'The song is ranked number 357 on Rolling Stone's list of the 500 Greatest Songs of All Time.'

CONCLUSIONS:

- the samples used by Kendrick Lamar were already included in charts, awarded and recognized in the music industry;
- Macklemore & Ryan came with their own album and got recognition; their songs were included in various charts, and awarded for the first time in the music industry.

II.7.8 Producers and Lyricists

TABLE 73. PRODUCERS AND LYRICISTS: MACKLEMORE & RYAN LEWIS & KENDRICK LAMAR	
***MACKLEMORE & RYAN LEWIS:** The Heist (Deluxe, 2012):* **Producer:** Ryan Lewis **Lyricists:** the average number of lyricists per song is 2.72; all songs are written by Macklemore & Ryan Lewis with support for a second and third lyricist.	***KENDRICK LAMAR:** good city, m.A.A.d. city (Deluxe, 2012):* **Producer:** DJ Dahi, Hit-Boy, Just Blaze, Like, Pharrell Williams, Rahki, Scoop DeVille, Skhye Hutch, Sounwave, T-Minus, Tabu, Terrace Martin, THC, Tha Bizness; most of the song is credited with one producer, however, Kendrick Lamar is not credited as producer for his songs. **Lyricists:** the average number of lyricists per song is 3.77.

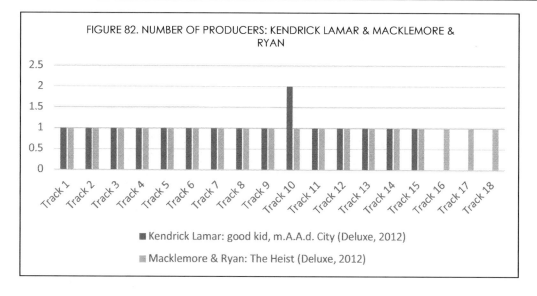

FIGURE 82. NUMBER OF PRODUCERS: KENDRICK LAMAR & MACKLEMORE & RYAN

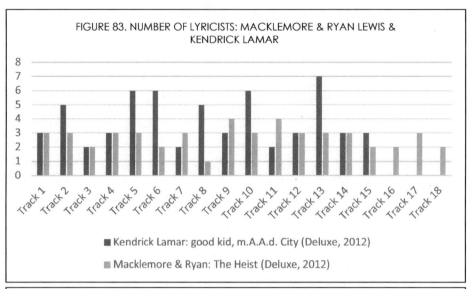

FIGURE 83. NUMBER OF LYRICISTS: MACKLEMORE & RYAN LEWIS & KENDRICK LAMAR

■ Kendrick Lamar: good kid, m.A.A.d. City (Deluxe, 2012)

■ Macklemore & Ryan: The Heist (Deluxe, 2012)

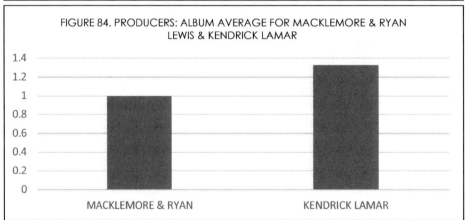

FIGURE 84. PRODUCERS: ALBUM AVERAGE FOR MACKLEMORE & RYAN LEWIS & KENDRICK LAMAR

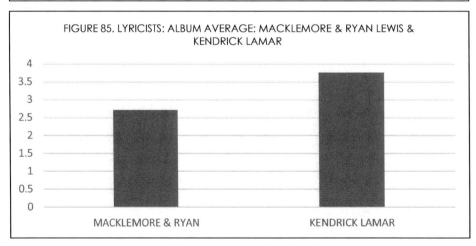

FIGURE 85. LYRICISTS: ALBUM AVERAGE: MACKLEMORE & RYAN LEWIS & KENDRICK LAMAR

CONCLUSIONS:

- Ryan Lewis is the artist and the sole producer of his album;
- from the information that I had access: Kendrick Lamar has no credit as producer for this album;
- overall, Macklemore & Ryan partnered with less lyricists than Kendrick Lamar.

II.7.9 The Album Ratings

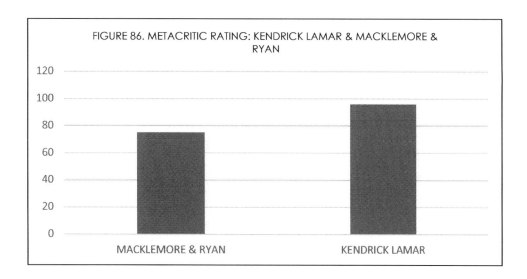

FIGURE 86. METACRITIC RATING: KENDRICK LAMAR & MACKLEMORE & RYAN

CONCLUSIONS:

- Macklemore & Ryan[462] final review grade (75) is based on a higher personal contribution in their own album, while Kendrick Lamar's[463] final review grade (96) is based on his personal contribution, but to a considerable extent to other producers, lyricists, samples with music already existent in the music industry, included in charts and awarded;
- Macklemore & Ryan have a higher level of their own musical notes and lyrics, maybe they can rap faster than Kendrick Lamar, and maybe these are the reasons to be awarded with the *Best Rap Album*.

---

[462] Macklemore & Ryan, 'The Heist (Deluxe, 2012)', *Metacritic*, available at: https://www.metacritic.com/music/the-heist/ryan-lewis, last accessed: February 25, 2020.

[463] Kendrick Lamar, 'good kid, m.A.A.d. city (Deluxe, 2012)', *Metacritic*, available at: https://www.metacritic.com/music/good-kid-maad-city/kendrick-lamar, last accessed: February 25, 2020.

II.8 Awards

II.8.1 'Single Ladies' *versus* 'You Belong with Me' for MTV: Origins

In this section I investigated which artist is more original regarding the song and the video sent for consideration to *MTV Music Video Awards,* for which Kanye West interrupted Taylor Swift during the ceremony of this event in 2009.

TABLE 74. 'SINGLE LADIES' VERSUS 'YOU BELONG WITH ME': ORIGINS		
ARTIST	BEYONCÉ	TAYLOR SWIFT
NAME OF THE SONG	*SINGLE LADIES (PUT A RING ON IT)*	*YOU BELONG WITH ME*
VIDEO INSPIRATION	From 1969 Bob Fosse routine entitled 'Mexican Breakfast' seen on The Ed Sullivan Show, which featured Fosse's wife, Gwen Verdon, dancing with two other women. The 'Mexican Breakfast' was an Internet viral sensation the previous summer after Unk's 'Walk It Out' was dubbed over the original mix. The choreography of 'Single Ladies' was liberally adapted from 'Mexican Breakfast'. Beyoncé said: 'I saw a video on YouTube [...] had a plain background and it was shot on the crane; it was 360 degrees, they could move around. And I said, 'This is genius.'[464]	Traditional love game: a girl likes a guy that she knows, but he is in a sort of complicated relationship with another girl and, in the end, by remaining true to herself, she gets the guy. The video followed the traditional love scene of a girl who likes a guy who plays rugby, the popular game in the USA.
LYRICS	Beyoncé, Terius 'The-Dream' Nash, Thaddis 'Kuk' Harrell, and Christopher 'Tricky' Stewart	Taylor Swift & Liz Rose

CONCLUSIONS:

- Taylor Swift wrote the song with another lyricist, while Beyoncé was in partnership with extra three lyricists;
- Taylor Swift released a song that was more hers than *Single Ladies* for Beyoncé;
- Beyoncé used the choreography of a song that was an internet sensation a year before her video release, while Taylor Swift used the traditional scene of a girl who

---

[464] 'Beyoncé's Infectious Moves', *NPR*, November 22, 2008, https://www.npr.org/templates/story/story.php?storyId=97356053&singlePage=true&t=1595868492327, last accessed: February 26, 2020.

likes a guy that plays rugby, which has no novelty as the scenes are set in already well-known environment; however, it could be novelty for Taylor Swift and her fans;

- perhaps the reason why more people considered that Taylor Swift's video was the best among all the nominations is because of the themes of the song: love, dreams and pain, while Beyoncé's dancing scenes are repetitive: herself and dancers are spinning around the camera for most of the whole video, and few people could see themselves/identify in her narrative?
- Taylor Swift's video is a dynamic and emotional love story with a narrative line where the characters evolve from sadness to happiness, and it leads to the idea of whether she will be able to express her feeling for him, and if they will end up together; Beyoncé's video is more emotional static with repetitive scenes which makes you wonder how she did it, what kind of camera tricks she used to show a dance in 360 degrees; furthermore, other people already knew that Beyoncé used a choreography scene that was famous a year before her video;
- Taylor Swift used her own lyrics, while Beyoncé used another artist choreography.

II.8.2 'If I Were a Boy' *versus* 'The Man': Origins

In 2019 Taylor Swift was accused online (Twitter, Facebook, Reddit) by various users of copying and ripping-off Beyoncé's music video *If I Were a Boy* with her new song *The Man* for the album *Lover*.[465] In this section I investigated this allegation.

TABLE 75. 'IF I WERE A BOY' VERSUS 'THE MAN': ORIGINS		
ARTIST	BEYONCÉ	TAYLOR SWIFT
NAME OF THE SONG	IF I WERE A BOY	THE MAN
VIDEO INSPIRATION	The song was not written by Beyoncé but by BC Jean and Toby Gad, 'who also handled its production alongside Beyoncé. [...] The song was initially recorded by Jean, whose record company rejected it, then later Beyoncé recorded her own version. Jean was upset when she learned that Beyoncé was releasing it as a single, but eventually, they reached an agreement'.[466]	Personal experience relate to private life, but also the public life and events from the *Famous* feud.
LYRICS	BC Jean & Toby Gad	Taylor Swift & Joel Little

---

[465] This allegation was made mostly on social media (Twitter, Facebook and Reddit). However, there are few online sources writing about similarities between the songs investigated in this section of the chapter. Spencer Kornhaber, 'Why Taylor Swift Wants to Be 'The Man'', *The Atlantic*, August 29, 2019, available at: https://www.theatlantic.com/entertainment/archive/2019/08/taylor-swifts-man-follows-beyonce-and-other-divas/597061/, last accessed: February 26, 2020; 'Taylor Swift's New Song 'The Man' Already Has Big 'If I Were a Boy' Vibes', *Head Topics*, August 8, 2019, available at: https://headtopics.com/us/taylor-swift-s-new-song-the-man-already-has-big-if-i-were-a-boy-vibes-7417996, last accessed: February 26, 2020.

[466] 'If I Were a Boy', *Wikipedia*, available at: https://en.wikipedia.org/wiki/If_I_Were_a_Boy, last accessed: February 26, 2020.

CONCLUSIONS:

- Taylor Swift wrote the song with another lyricist, while Beyoncé had no role in writing the song;
- Taylor Swift's song is her own view about being a man, for which she is credited for lyrics and as producer; lyrically, Beyoncé's song is the view of a different artist that had the bad luck to be rejected by her company producer which offered a chance to Beyoncé;
- Taylor Swift did not copied or ripped-off Beyoncé's song as she is not the artists that composed the song in the first place, the core idea belongs to another artist; also BC Jean, then Beyoncé through her song, is not the first female in the world to imagine herself as a man: this association is hundreds, if not thousands, of years old in the mind of women around the planet, it is nothing new and no intellectual property to get permission to use it; maybe women on this planet don't need BC Jean, Beyoncé, Taylor Swift, or other artists, to inspire them to imagine their lives from a man's point of view, maybe it happens naturally.

II.8.3 Grammy Awards

In the last section I investigated the overall origin of the music released only by Taylor Swift, Kendrick Lamar, Kanye West and Beyoncé as this group of artists are more on the news, and I already have the right information collected for their whole career. First, I exposed tables and figures, then I interpreted the results.

TABLE 76. THE BEAUTIFUL MIND OF MUSIC IN THE BACKGROUND				
ARTISTS	TAYLOR SWIFT	KANYE WEST	BEYONCÉ	KENDRICK LAMAR
Use of sample	3%	64%	26%	51%
Songs with no sample	97%	36%	74%	Close to 50%
Songs as sole lyricist	30%	6%	3%	0%
Songs with two lyricists	45%	11%	9%	30%
Songs with three lyricists	19%	13%	32%	24%
Songs with at least 4 lyricists	6%	67%	56%	46%
Length as sole lyricists (minutes)	206:55 minutes	18:16 minutes (Intro & Skit) 13:57 minutes (Without Intro & Skit)	16 Seconds	0 seconds

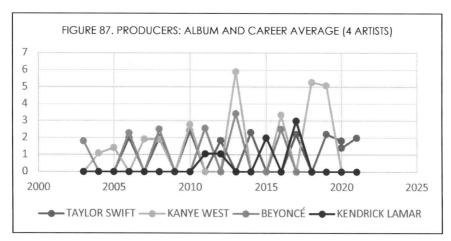

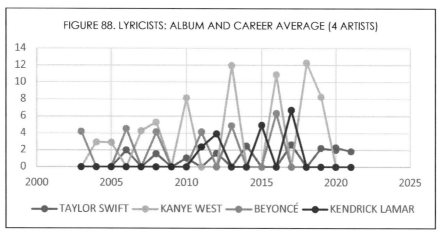

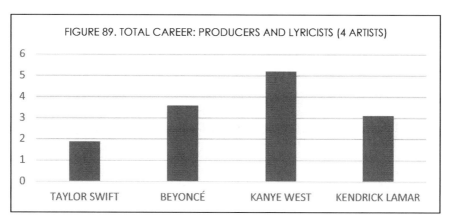

The next table contains only the albums released solely by Kanye West, no share producer for other albums.

TABLE 77. PRODUCERS AND LYRICISTS: ALBUM AND CAREER AVERAGE (4 ARTISTS)								
YEAR / ARTIST	TAYLOR SWIFT		KANYE WEST		BEYONCÉ		KENDRICK LAMAR	
	Producers	Lyricists	Producers	Lyricists	Producers	Lyricists	Producers	Lyricists
2003	-	-	-	-	1.81	4.18	-	-
2004	-	-	1.09	2.95	-	-	-	-
2005	-	-	1.42[467]	2.90	-	-	-	-
2006	2	2	-	-	2.29	4.52	-	-
2007	-	-	1.92	4.28	-	-	-	-
2008	2	1.57	1.91	5.3	2.5	4.15	-	-
2009	-	-	-	-	-	-	-	-
2010	2.42	1.05	2.78	8.14	-	-	-	-
2011	-	-	-	-	2.57	4.14	1.06	2.37
2012	1.84	1.63	-	-	-	-	1.06	3.93
2013	-	-	5.9	12	3.43	4.87	-	-
2014	2.31	2.5	-	-	-	-	-	-
2015	-	-	-	-	-	-	2	4.93
2016	-	-	3.35	10.9	2.5	6.33	-	-
2017	2.2	2.66	-	-	-	-	3	6.71
2018	-	-	5.28	12.28	-	-	-	-
2019	2.22	2.22	5.09	8.27	-	-	-	-
2020	1.82	2	-	-	-	-	-	-
2020	1.41	2.29	-	-	-	-	-	-
2021	2[468]	1.85[469]	-	-	-	-	-	-
TOTAL	2.02	1.77	2.98	7.44	2.51	4.69	1.78	4.48
TOTAL CAREER (P+L)	1.89		5.21		3.60		3.13	

CONCLUSIONS:

- overall, the information from this section reveal Taylor Swift as the artist with a higher level of originality and own lyrics than the artists from this section and report;
- as regard to specific albums that were in competition for awards between the artists investigated in this section, we can see, from the tables above, that a strong reason that could have convinced the voting members of The Recording Academy to vote and award Taylor Swift with the *Album of the Year,* is for her abilities to write songs and released them at the level of abilities she really has, no matter the negative conclusions written by the critics outside The Recording Academy (for example critical reviews available on Metacritic, All Music and other online platforms);
- more and less, Kanye West, Beyoncé and Kendrick Lamar used samples from other songs, and maybe this is the reason for not receiving the award; the music of the white artists is cleaner and new compared to the music of the black artists who used

---

[467] The songs with 0 producers and lyricists are not part of this average.
[468] Only the songs 'From the Vault' were included in this table, in total 7 songs were considered.
[469] *Ibidem*.

samples from other songs that existed, awarded and included in charts; it seems that black artists, with the endorsement of their supporters, want to be recognized at a high level for parts of songs that belong to other producers and lyricists for which royalties and copyrights were paid; in addition, the samples have an owner which is not included on the main list with producers and lyricists of the new album; in other words, the artists, producers and lyricists behind the samples used are not mentioned in the award certificate and neither by the main vocal artists while being on the stage holding the award and speaking about the award received; definitely, the samples are a part of the song and album where there is an impact (given by instruments and lyrics) that has the ability to influence the final decision of the voting members of The Recording Academy to award the best song, album and artist.

II.8.4 MUSIC REVIEW: an unfinished comparative study

Shortly after I finished this report, I decided to continue with a new chapter, *Music Review*: a comparative analysis between Taylor Swift, Kanye West, Beyoncé and Kendrick Lamar's music reviews written by various news agencies and published on Metacritic. For this chapter, I read:

- all the reviews for all the artists in a word document: 410 pages;
- the lyrics written by Taylor Swift, Kanye West, Beyoncé and Kendrick Lamar from their albums included in this report (250 pages);
- the most negative articles written in the media about Taylor Swift (99 pages);
- a number of over 500 articles written in the mass media in the UK, USA, Australia and New Zealand (over 500 from 1175 articles gathered with name of the news agency and link with the articles).

In the end, I simply did not have the energy to continue. The negative articles written about Taylor Swift, and the lack of Western mass-media to link the events between the artists and expose the truth (Taylor Swift a victim of Kanye West's dark twisted game), plus I got tired of the feud, kept me away from continuing this type of analysis. However, I present two ideas that are presented in the Western mass-media, and I offer two examples for *reputation* and *Lover*: money and originality.

Money: today music experts are mind readers as well, they just seem to know exactly what the artist think and want, and they are here to tell their truth:

Consequence of Sound, Geoff Nelson: 'Besides, she, like so many before her, has a voice that sounds like money'.

The Guardian, Alexis Petridis: 'The big problem with Lover is that it's too long, the suspicion being that Swift is trying to reassert her commercial dominance by spread-betting.'

Originality:

Paste Magazine, Clare Martin (rating 5.8 out of 10):

'Originality has never been Swift's strong suit':

- Paste Magazine reviewed many albums released by Kanye West, Beyoncé and Kendrick Lamar and, although their music is based on samples already awarded and included in charts in the music industry, their reviews are more generous compared to Taylor Swift's music which contains her own lyrics and musical notes; Taylor Swift has an album written by herself and created by her, Kanye West struggles to create his own song titles, Beyoncé works with an army of lyricists and producers, yet they received higher grades than Taylor Swift;

'and the pulsating synth of 'Cruel Summer' (thank you, St. Vincent) are particular standouts':

- in the case of Kanye West, Beyoncé (less than Kanye West) and Kendrick Lamar (to some extent), you can say this phrase to many songs from their catalogues with samples from other artists; for Kanye West is 'thank you' for at least 60% of his music to many artists, producers and lyricists; Beyoncé for less than Kanye West, but is still there.

III. What if...

In this chapter I wrote few hypothetical and negative scenarios related to the artists investigated in these pages. The hypothetical and negative scenarios are reproduced in order to help, if possible, to observe the events behind the creation of the music released by the following artists: Kanye West, Beyoncé, Jay Z (only in this chapter) and Taylor Swift.

The existence of more negative scenarios about Kanye West and Beyoncé is because of their shifting pattern of the album release date in Taylor Swift's fixed pattern. Subsequently, because of the dynamic of the events from the life of Kanye West, Beyoncé and Taylor Swift.

Why black artists are being promoted as the right winners before the award ceremony? Maybe because this a trick to put pressure on the public (to vote for them as they will win anyway, and better to be already on the side of the winner) and the voting members (who can decide the winner) to award them: the public (with the help of the mass-media) is aware before the ceremony who the winner should be and, if there is no black winner (the one that mass-media is presenting as being the right winner), then it must be a rigged ceremony that refused to rightly award the black artists; what if this is a trick to put pressure on the music institutions to award black artists, otherwise the black artists and their supporters will label the institutions as being racists and supporters of the white supremacy movement?

What if Beyoncé and Jay Z were part of the plan in 2009 for the MTV Awards?

What if Kanye West and Jay Z developed the plan for MTV Awards in 2009 without Beyoncé's knowledge?

What if Kanye West played The Bad Man (interrupted the speech) and Beyoncé the Good Woman (offered the chance to Taylor Swift to thank the fans for the award) at the MTV Awards? And if that was the plan, let's see how it could have been done in practice:

- *Step 1*. Kanye West (black man) entered the stage and interrupted Taylor Swift's speech (white woman) on the reason that she does not deserve the award, even if it was voted by the public, and that Beyoncé deserved the award;

- *Step 2*. Taylor Swift does not end the speech to thank her fans;

- *Step 3*. Beyoncé (black woman) fixed the narrative and gave Taylor Swift (white woman) her time to finish the speech (time that she received because she won *Video of the Year*), but first she mentioned her success: 'I remember being 17 years old, up for my first MTV Award with Destiny's Child, and it was one of the most exciting moments in my life, so, I'd like for Taylor to come out and have her moment '; this is a situation where the black artist, with the award of the year, offered the opportunity to the white artist (with the negative image that she does not deserve the award) to finish her speech; what if the staff behind the curtain knew that Beyoncé will get the award, and the plan was set up before the award ceremony?

What if Taylor Swift's career and progress was closely watched by Kanye West and Jay Z (probably with other people in their circle), and came to the conclusion that Taylor Swift would be the next famous pop artist in the USA and in the world (because she has the power to write her songs), and interfered in her narrative to destroy it, or to insert in the audience's memory that Taylor Swift could not have been a successful artist without a black artist (through Kanye West)?

What if the release of Beyoncé's album on November 12 was her idea, but also Jay Z and Kanye West were involved in making this decision (the day after the release of Taylor Swift's album, *Fearless*) and then November 18 (in the USA)?

What if Kanye West's album release pattern (November 24, 2008) was made in order to block Taylor Swift (November 11) to reach number 1 for several weeks, to reduce the popularity she enjoyed and grew every year since her debut in 2006?

What if Beyoncé (maybe got an idea from her husband Jay Z) changed her album name and included the word *Fierce*, which has a similar meaning to *Fearless*, and entered into direct and planned competition with Taylor Swift? in 2008 both artists used the same theme, *fear*, and in 2009 both artists competed for an award at the MTV VMA.

What if the albums released by Beyoncé (*I Am… Sasha Fierce*) a week later after Taylor Swift, then Kanye West (*808s & Heartbreak*) two weeks later than Taylor Swift and one week later than Beyoncé, were made in order to advance three strategies of promotion:

1. to block Taylor Swift to create and have a strong influence in top charts around the USA for at least two weeks after her album release;

2. Kanye West interfered in Taylor Swift's album release pattern a year earlier (2007), and then again with the next album (2008), which might have created

(intentional or unintentional) a racial comparison: Kanye West (black man) received better reviews than Taylor Swift (white woman); Beyoncé interfered in Taylor Swift's album release pattern for the first time, but her high number of fans blocked Taylor Swift to reach number 1 for the second week, and Kanye West's fans blocked Taylor Swift on the third week;

3. to create a sense of *leave Taylor in the past*, now focus on Beyoncé and Kanye West;

however, if these 3 strategies of promotion for their album were actually put into practice, on long term they failed: Taylor Swift came with her own lyrics, and in 2008 had stronger albums sales in the USA than Beyoncé and Kanye West.[470]

What if Beyoncé released the surprise album, *Beyoncé*, intentionally on Taylor Swift's birthday (December 13, 2013) as a sublime message: look who Beyoncé is and I'm coming after you (she did not win the Grammy Awards for the *Album of the Year*);

What if Taylor Swift came up with the *1989* album (the year of her birth) to complete Beyoncé's cycle, to reply and show who she is: an original lyricist and her first pure pop album, which eventually won the *Album of the Year* at the Grammy Awards?

What if Kanye West and Jay Z knew Taylor Swift is the winner of the *Best Female Video Award* before the ceremony, and Kanye West decided to bring a bottle of alcohol with him to cover his plan?[471] just as he probably knew Taylor Swift wrote a song for him, and said that he also wrote a song for her (I did not find information that he really wrote a song for Taylor Swift (maybe he said it as a marketing strategy, to not to be lower than Taylor Swift in the eyes of the general public)), and may have known some of the lyrics: CBS[472] wrote an article with content from Kanye West published on his Twitter account: 'When I woke up from the crazy nightmare I looked in the mirror and said GROW UP KANYE... '; after few days Taylor Swift sang the lyrics of the song *Innocent* written for Kanye West and played at the MTV Awards: '32 and still growin'up now'; what are the chances for Kanye West to use words so close to Taylor Swift's lyrics? if there was a leak about the lyrics written by Taylor Swift for Kanye West, who provided the information?

---

[470] Randy Lewis, Taylor Swift, 'Lil Wayne led music sales in 2008', *Seattle Times*, January 22, 2009, available at: https://www.seattletimes.com/entertainment/taylor-swift-lil-wayne-led-music-sales-in-2008/, last accessed: February 25, 2021.
[471] Atlien, '2009 MTV VMAs: Kanye West ~ Blame it on the ALCOHOL!', *Straight From the A*, September 14, 2009, available at: https://straightfromthea.com/2009/09/14/2009-mtv-vmas-kanye-west-blame-it-on-the-alcohol/, last accessed: February 25, 2021; Lauren McIver, 'KIM'S HELL Kanye West admits he was an 'alcoholic' who drank 'Grey Goose and orange juice' in the morning- but no longer drinks', *The Sun*, April 15, 2020, available at: https://www.thesun.co.uk/tvandshowbiz/11404128/kanye-west-alcoholic-drank-grey-goose-morning-no-longer/, last accessed: February 25, 2021; James Robertson, 'Kanye West: I needed God, booze and lots of sex after Taylor Swift scandal', *Mirror*, January 21, 2014, available at: https://www.mirror.co.uk/3am/celebrity-news/kanye-west-needed-sex-alcohol-3042866, last accessed: February 25, 2021.
[472] Devon Thomas, 'Kanye West Writes Song in Honor of Taylor Swift', *CBS*, September 7, 2010, available at: https:// www. cbsnews.com/news/kanye-west-writes-song-in-honor-of-taylor-swift/, last accessed: February 25, 2021.

What if the release of the album by Kanye West and Beyoncé in 2008, then the disagreement with the MTV award in 2009, and finally the release of the album in 2010 (for Kanye West), respectively in 2011 (for Beyoncé), was actually a long-term plan in order to present themselves as better than the white artist Taylor Swift, to diminish her popularity and creativity in the music industry?

What if Beyoncé's *Lemonade* album (including Jay Z) were part of Kanye West's strategy against Taylor Swift in 2016? and if this was the plan, let's see how it could have been carried out in practice:

Step 1: Kanye West released the song *Famous* (The Life of Pablo) where Taylor Swift is called 'that bitch'; Taylor entered the narrative created and promoted by Kanye by writing the truth: she did not know the lyrics in which she was called 'that bitch';

Step 2: Taylor was assailed by negative comments on social media, and the preferred term to address and label her character was 'bitch';

Step 3: Kanye promised that his album, *The Life of Pablo*, will be available exclusively on the *Tidal* platform (the platform owned also by Jay Z); however, on April 1, 2016, his album was made available on *Apple Music*, which led to the accusation that he cheated the audience, according to an article in Variety: 'By the time Mr. West changed course and broadly released 'The Life of Pablo,' the deceptive marketing ploy had served its purpose: Tidal's subscriber numbers had tripled, streaming numbers were through the roof, and Tidal had collected the personal information, credit card numbers, and social media information of millions of deceived consumers [...] Instead, they just wanted to boost Tidal's subscriber numbers – which indeed did get a big bump from the release. Tidal may have signed up as many as two million new subscribers thanks to the album, claims the lawsuit, arguing that this could have added as much as $84 million to Tidal's valuation;'[473]

Step 4: Beyoncé released the surprise album *Lemonade* on April 23, 2016; Taylor Swift was caught in the negative narrative created and promoted by Kanye West; *Lemonade* enjoyed success from critics being considered the best album released by Beyoncé; on Tidal, *Lemonade* was streamed 115 million times, setting a record for the most-streamed album in a single week by a female artist; what if Kanye West, through the exclusivity strategy of his album, plus the use of Taylor in his song, spread the narrative that in his album there could be something more about Taylor, which led to the growth of curious users and, in the end, some users decided to stay on the platform? at the same time, maybe the new number of users

---

[473] Janko Roettgers, 'Kanye West Tricked Fans Into Subscribing to Tidal, Lawsuit Claims', *Variety*, April 18, 2016, available at: https://variety.com/2016/digital/news/kanye-west-tricked-fans-into-subscribing-to-tidal-lawsuit-claims-1201755580/, last accessed: February 25, 2021.

were used to justify the record number of streaming of his album, *The Life of Pablo*, and Beyoncé's *Lemonade*?

Step 5: in July 2016, the positive popular opinion is on Kanye's side, especially after Kim Kardashian (Kanye's wife at the time of the event) published edited parts of the phone conversation between Kanye and Taylor; the conclusion of the published videos is that Taylor knew about everything; at this time, the public image of Taylor Swift is negative;

Step 6: based on her previous pattern release, Taylor releases the first song in August or September but, the *Famous* feud and the negative image obtained as a result of Kanye's song, her strategy and public image do not allow her to release a new song every two years (the last album released was in the fall of 2014, so the next album should have been in the fall of 2016), and, therefore, Beyoncé has no competition and has a positive image, while Taylor does not release a new song and album and has a negative image;

Step 7 (unexpected shift of the plan and not possible to change the course of their plan): although *Lemonade* received the most positive reviews in her career, Beyoncé does not win the *Album of the Year* (although she has 12 songs on the album, this number was not lucky) and lost in favour of the white artist, Adele;

Step 8 (unexpected shift of the plan and not possible to change the course of their plan): in 2018 Tidal was accused of intentionally falsifying the streaming number of *The Life of Pablo* and *Lemonade*, according to Variety: 'Tidal, which has rarely shared its data publicly, had a streaming exclusive on West's album for its first six weeks of release and continues to be the exclusive streamer for Beyoncé's album. It claimed that West's album had been streamed 250 million times in its first 10 days of release in February of 2016, while claiming it had just 3 million subscribers – a claim that would have meant every subscriber played the album an average of eight times per day; and that Beyoncé's album was streamed 306 million times in its first 15 days of release in April of 2016.' […] 'Today's report, according to MBW's translation, says that 'Beyoncé's and Kanye West's listener numbers on Tidal have been manipulated to the tune of several hundred million false plays… which has generated massive royalty payouts at the expense of other artists;[474]' what if Kanye West and Jay Z's strategy to use Taylor Swift was also to increase the number of users? what if Kanye West and Jay Z used the new subscribers to falsify the numbers of plays to make more money? let's not forget that in the conversation with Taylor Kanye admitted having big debts (millions of dollars); what if the false plays was done in order to increase Beyoncé's profile and the records obtained? what if the false plays were made this route as on the other streaming platforms (Apple and Spotify) Beyoncé would not make the numbers to have new records to

---

[474] Jem Aswad, 'Tidal Accused of Falsifying Beyoncé and Kanye West Streaming Numbers'; Andy Cush, 'Tidal Accused of Generating 300 Million Fake Streams for Kanye and Beyoncé'; Tim Ingham, 'Tidal 'Fake Streams': Criminal Investigation Underway Over Potential Data Fraud In Norway, *Music Business Worldwide*.

celebrate, and maintain relevance in the music industry as Taylor Swift does? what if the false plays and the exclusive availability of her album, *Lemonade*, on Tidal was made to show the world that she is so loved that her fans follow her on the new platform, and set new records in the music industry? what if Tidal is being used to justify a false point of view that black artists are not safe on other platforms because they are ruled by white people? what if Kanye, Jay Z and Beyoncé used Tidal for their own benefit, therefore, cheating the music industry and their fans?

What if Jay Z and Kanye West are actually fighting Taylor Swift's influence over people and the music industry, in which they do not accept her records, and do whatever it takes to keep Beyoncé on top?

What if Jay Z is willing to do whatever it takes to make sure Beyoncé is on top with each album release?

What if Kanye West, Jay Z and Beyoncé are too desperate to win the awards and be recognized more than they are in reality? What if they create all sorts of plans that in the end do not work, create more damage for themselves, and blame and create a negative image of white people?

What if Kanye West accused Taylor Swift of doing what he did in order to cover his track, and other artists that he is supporting by creating a negative view about her? the end of this strategy is to create a negative wave about Taylor Swift, hoping that her fans will get sick of the negative stories that she is involved too often, and switch to his favourite artists, such as Beyoncé, because there are no negative stories about her?

In 2017 the relationship between Kanye West and Jay Z was not so good, however, in 2019 it was reported that they are again on good terms[475]; what if this tension between them is false and was created as a solution to change the focus on a different topic considering *Tidal* was the platform where Kanye exclusively released his song with lyrics that put him and Taylor Swift in difficulty, also about the Tidal false plays? what if the new better terms of the relationship between Kanye and Jay Z (from December 2019) happened as a sublime and reply message to Taylor Swift, which she could have a line about their bad relationship in one of her songs from *reputation*, *This Is Why We Can't Have Nice Things*: 'but I'm not the only friend you've lost lately/if only you weren't so shady'?

What if Kanye and Jay Z are behind the feud and everything that the album patterns show in this report?

---

[475] Rianne Addo, 'Kanye West and Jay-Z are back on friendly terms two years after Tidal lawsuit left their complicated relationship on the rocks', *MailOnline*, December 17, 2019, available at: https://www.dailymail.co.uk/tvshowbiz/article-7800777/Kanye-West-Jay-Z-friendly-terms-two-years-Tidal-lawsuit.html, last accessed: February 25, 2021.

What if Beyoncé has no idea about the tricks behind the curtains, even if it benefits her by having a positive image because of Kanye and Jay Z's intentional involvement?

What if the the prediction of the album sales for Kanye West in 2013, *Yeezus*, of 500,000 copies sold in the first week[476] was made with the purpose to encourage people to buy it as it will be popular anyway? what if the prediction of the album sales for Taylor Swift in 2014 (album *1989*), of 600,000 to 750,000 copies sold in the first week[477] was made with the purpose to discourage people to buy it as is a lower number than the last album, and as subtle message that she lost her fans and popularity, so there is no need to bother with her album? if we look at the number of sales in the first week, before 2013 and 2014, Kanye West had a lower number of albums sales in 2010, 2011 and 2012 with below 500,000 albums in the first week[478], and yet in 2013 the prediction increased to half a million albums sold first week; for Taylor Swift is the opposite: in 2010 and 2012 the number of album sales was over one million[479], yet in 2014 the prediction decreased to half of the last number of albums from 2012: to 600,000 to 750,000. The common point of the two predictions is that both were not true: in 2013 Kanye West's final album sales was below the prediction (327.000[480]), while in 2014 Taylor's the albums sales were higher than the prediction (1.287.000[481]); the failed prediction for the first week sales happened first with Kanye West in 2005 when his album, *Late Registration*, was predicted to sale over 1.6 million copies in the first week, however, it sold over half of the prediction, 860,000 copies[482]; what if there are people who intentionally play with the prediction (maybe a person of interest (maybe from Kanye's team or Taylor's team; or unrelated to them), but could profit somehow from the outcome) paid the source of the prediction to write it according to a specific interest, such as to modify fans' intentions and get lower and higher album sales?

What if an unknown number of songs, and maybe even the name of the albums released by Kanye West, Beyoncé and Taylor Swift, it is a subtle/behind the curtain message to each others; what if the information we already know about the pattern of the album release, and

[476] Edna Gundersen, 'Kanye West's 'Yeezus' could debut with 500K copies', *USA Today*, June 13, 2013, available at: https://eu.usatoday.com/story/life/music/2013/06/13/kanye-west-yeezus-expected-to-sell-half-million-copies-first-week/2420829/#:~:text=Kanye%20West%27s%20Yeezus%2C%20out%20Tuesday,associate%20director%20of%20charts%2Fretail, last accessed: October 23, 2017.
[477] Steve Knopper, 'Can Taylor Swift's '1989' Save Ailing Music Industry?', *Rolling Stone*, October 21, 2014, available at: https://www.rollingstone.com/music/music-news/can-taylor-swifts-1989-save-ailing-music-industry-170217/, last accessed: October 21, 2014.
[478] Hao Nguyen, 'Can't Tell Me Nothing: Ranking Kanye West First Week Album Sales'.
[479] Ed Christmas, 'What Taylor Swift's Million-Selling Album Means for Music'; Keith Caulfield, 'Taylor Swift's 'Red' Sells 1.21 Million; Biggest Sales Week for an Album Since 2002'; Keith Caulfield, 'Official: Taylor Swift's '1989' Debuts With 1.287 Million Sold In First Week'.
[480] Hao Nguyen, idem.
[481] Keith Caulfield, 'Official: Taylor Swift's '1989' Debuts With 1.287 Million Sold In First Week'.
[482] Hao Nguyen, idem.

the interference in Taylor Swift's pattern, is the real evidence available to confirm the subtle messages?

What if *Lemonade* and *4:44* (Jay Z album) were produced on false statements about cheating in order to justify the albums and the world tour Part II (On the Run)?

What if only Kanye West is to blame for Beyoncé's pattern: maybe he knew the release date of the album and planned everything on his own and set it in motion, and Beyoncé and Jay Z were as surprised as Taylor Swift and the rest of the world?

What if Kanye West thinks he is superior to white artists and, instead of creating his sounds, titles and lyrics, he used samples to promote the idea that white artists are lucky and should be honoured because he used their music?

What if Kanye presents himself with such great creative powers that he does not bother using them to create new music, as white producers do not have the intelligence to understand his music, so, instead, uses samples from their music to show that he is still superior?

What if the black artists in this report, perhaps others outside this report, present themselves as victims of white-led music institutions to hide their lower level of originality and creativity in the music industry?

What if the reviews of the black artists are exaggerated and overrated as a strategy to change the shift of good music from the white artists to black artists, and the voting members of The Recording Academy are aware of it, and this is why black artists have a lower number of nominations and awards, which in the end is the reason of the high contrast between what mass-media is writing about who the winner should be (articles bought in newspapers?) and who is the real winner (based on originality and talent)?

What if Kanye West used the positive reviews received from the critics in the music industry, also the high number of awards from The Recording Academy (on behalf of the voting members) to redirect his own negative side of creating music in a negative strategy toward and in reference to Taylor Swift's abilities to create music?

In the following figure and table, I found a pattern that is happening in 2008, 2009 and 2016 and involves Taylor Swift, Kanye West and Beyoncé.

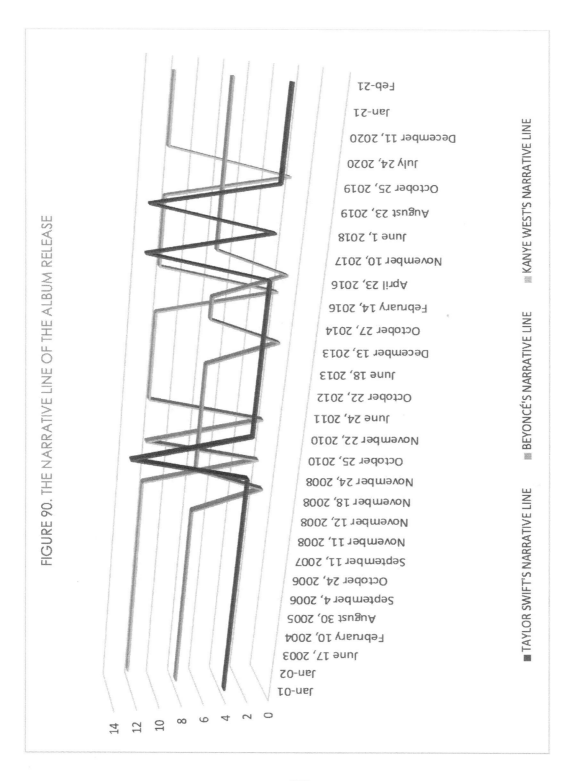

FIGURE 90. THE NARRATIVE LINE OF THE ALBUM RELEASE

TABLE 78. A **FAMOUS** ATTACK ON TAYLOR SWIFT?			
EVENT/ *NAME OF THE ARTIST:*	TAYLOR SWIFT	BEYONCÉ	KANYE WEST
RELEASE PATTERN	Fixed pattern	Fixed pattern Changing pattern Surprise pattern	Fixed pattern Changing pattern
ALBUM RELEASE NARRATIVE LINE	2008: She followed her fixed pattern and released her album in November 2008. 2016: Taylor releases the first song in August or September, but the *Famous* feud did not allow her to release a new song every two years (the last album released was in the fall of 2014, so the next album should have been in the fall of 2016). The *Famous* feud ruined Taylor's album release pattern.	2008: She released the album in the same month as Taylor Swift, the second day and a week after Taylor Swift; she followed this release pattern one time. 2016: Surprise album like in 2013 (December 13, Taylor Swift birthday); released exclusively on Tidal.	2008: A year before (2007), he changed his pattern and released the album in the same month as Taylor Swift; in 2008 he followed the new pattern for the last time. 2016: Released the album a couple of days before the Grammy Awards ceremony.
THE PUBLIC IMAGE NARRATIVE LINE	2008 - 2009: Positive before the MTV award ceremony from 2009; a little bit negative after the ceremony from 2009: Kanye told the whole world that she does not deserve the award, Beyoncé is better. 2016: Positive before the song *Famous* was released; she walked to Grammy Awards while being called in Kanye's song 'that bitch'; Negative at high level after the release by his wife, Kim, of edited parts of the telephone conversation between her and Kanye.	2008 - 2009: Positive, and also seen (through free promotion by Kanye West) as an artist that deserved the award won by Taylor Swift; the MTV ceremony was unfair with her talent and creativity. 2016: Positive at high levels, she received the highest reviews in life for her album *Lemonade*.	2008 - 2009: Positive image before the MTV award ceremony from 2009; Negative image after MTV award ceremony from 2009 because of his view about the 'true' winner of the MTV award. 2016: Little negative image, and more negative after the release of the song *Famous*, but with positive changes after the release by Kim Kardashian of edited parts of the telephone conversation between him and Taylor.
AWARDS LINE	Taylor's music was nominated for MTV, in 2010 she won the Grammy Award for the *Album of the Year* for *Fearless,* in 2016 she won the Grammy Award for *Album of the Year* for		

	1989). In both years Kanye West interfered in her narrative with a negative view about her music and character.

Discussion about another pattern: personal meaning of the album

In 2013 Beyoncé and Kanye West released their albums (*Beyoncé* album by Beyoncé, and Kanye West with *Yeezus* (which is a combination of his last two letters 'Ye' with 'Jesus' (*Yeezus* from Kanye: himself, people in his circle and fans around the world call him 'Ye') to promote himself as 'Ye' (Kanye) the Jesus (God) = Yeezus as sort of God of rap music. In 2014 Taylor Swift released her album *1989* (year of birthday). What if these albums are actually connected and Beyoncé and Kanye West, through their albums, took a shot at Taylor Swift, while Taylor Swift with her year of birth, *1989*, is her response to Beyoncé and Kanye West? Beyoncé took the shot by releasing her surprise album on Taylor Swift's birthday (December 13, 2013), while Kanye West few days before the release of his album *Yeezus,* in June 2013, in a *New York Times* interview stated about Taylor Swift VMA's moment that he doesn't have any regret about his interruption, and that it was a situation where he gave into peer pressure to apologize. When asked if he'd take back the original action or the apology, if given the choice, he answered, 'You know what? I can answer that, but I'm – I'm just -- not afraid, but I know that would be such a distraction. It's such a strong thing, and people have such a strong feeling about it. *My Beautiful Dark Twisted Fantasy* was my long, backhanded apology. You know how people give a backhanded compliment? It was a backhanded apology. It was like, all these raps, all these sonic acrobatics. I was like: 'Let me show you guys what I can do, and please accept me back. You want to have me on your shelves.'[483]

CONCLUSIONS based on the pattern *A Famous Attack on Taylor Swift?*:

- Kanye West interfered in the narrative line of Taylor Swift with a negative story about her character, while Beyoncé has a positive image about her skills and character;
- Kanye West is behind the negative stories about Taylor Swift's character and skills in 2009 and in 2016;
- Kanye West in 2016 interfered in Taylor Swift's narrative line with a negative story, while Beyoncé's narrative line is involved in releasing a new album;
- Kanye West negative behaviour toward Taylor Swift is after Beyoncé released an album (2008) and before (2016, *Lemonade*) she is out with a new album.

What if Taylor Swift used samples in her songs (*reputation* in 2017 and *Lover* in 2019) to prove to Kanye West that she can do it too, it is not something hard, she does it better and has a higher popularity than him?

---

[483] Jon Caramanica, 'Behind Kanye's Mask', *New York Times*, June 11, 2013, https://www.nytimes.com/2013/06/16/arts/music/kanye-west-talks-about-his-career-and-album-yeezus.html?_r=0, last accessed: May 28, 2018.

What if the mole in Taylor Swift's team leaked the lyrics *Dear John* to Kanye West (dark twisted games) and he decided to use them to name his album *My Beautiful Dark Twisted Fantasy* and, therefore, a strong connection was made between their albums, where the audience could compare their music, because both used identical words in their music?

What if Taylor Swift found out the name of Kanye West's album and she decided to use it slightly differently in her song *Dear John,* with the purpose to remind her fans of the person who ruined her moment, therefore, positioning herself as a long-term white victim of a black man?

What if by awarding the *Best Contemporary Christian Music Album*, the voting members of The Recording Academy lost their credibility because Kanye West's album used samples (even modified song titles that originally does not belong to Kanye West) and the album cover, and not because they awarded clean music from white artists such as Beck, Adele and Taylor Swift? Here the original source of the album does not belong to Kanye West, but to the artists he sampled.

What if Kanye West and Beyoncé didn't get the Grammy Award for *Album of the Year* because of the negative strategies presented in this report to get the highest and often recognition possible in the music industry? What if the voting members of The Recording Academy found out every time and, by nominating their songs and albums but not winning the category, it was the warning signal that it was not good for them to follow that path, that the award and the institution should not be used as a bridge for personal attacks against artists and the category of music they belong to? Maybe the voting members of The Recording Academy did it also with Taylor Swift: she released the album *reputation* in 2017, considered by fans and Western mass-media as a response to Kanye West's negative attitude against her: it was nominated in one category, *Pop Vocal Album*, but did not win.

What if Kanye West uses the music of white producers to humiliate the white producers after he was awarded with a Grammy based on their music, while they did not get even a nomination?

What if Kanye West wants to prove that only himself can play the music of the white artists to a level that the white artists cannot? What if for these very reasons the voting members of The Recording Academy did not nominate all of Kanye West's albums for *Album of the Year* and, when was nominated, did not win the *Album of the Year*?

The end of the journey: **black** and **white** music

In *Black & White Music* report I investigated a very small part of the music industry from the USA, 0.09% musicians; more precisely, I investigated the contribution and the artistic merit (greater or lesser) of black artists (0.03%) and white artists (0.05%) in the production and writing of their albums. The artists investigated in this report are Taylor Swift, Kanye West, Beyoncé, Kendrick Lamar, Macklemore & Ryan, Adele and Beck.

In the first level I explored, analysed and created a comparative study about the contribution and the artistic merit of black and white artists in the production and writing of their albums; to achieve this aim, I added contribution and artistic merit into one bubble of research and treated the two concepts with the same meaning, then I divided the bubble into 8 points of research that **1.** created a general view of the contribution and artistic merit of the artists investigated and **2.** granted the opportunity to observe and identify areas of the music production where one artists is greater or lesser than others;

Below are the conclusions I reached for the first level of the research:

1. *the creativity and originality of the investigated artists*:

- the artists investigated in this report demonstrated creativity and originality;
- based on the information used in this report and the interpretations made: white artists are more creative, original and have a higher level of novelty than black artists;

2. *the artist(s) with a greater contribution in the production and writing of a song(s) and album (s) that have been released*:

- in terms of the number of songs and the length of minutes written by a single artist, Taylor Swift has the highest level of creativity, originality and novelty; in terms of writing and producing a solo album, Beck has the highest level of creativity and originality (Beck may be even more creative and original than Taylor Swift due to other albums released, but not part of this investigation);

3. *whether the awards and recognition offered by the USA music industry are based on originality, creativity and novelty in music, or are offered based on the colour of the skin*:

- based on the information in this report and the methods used, the white artists were awarded for their originality, creativity and novelty in the music industry;
- unfortunately, this report does not have the information necessary to determine whether the colour of the skin is the primary condition for receiving a higher recognition for the artistic merit and contribution in the USA music industry;

4. *what are the differences between the music recognized by receiving an award, and the music that did not receive an award, but was nominated for the music award (either by the vote of the general public, or by the vote of the members of the jury):*

- the white artists (main vocal artist) wrote and produced songs based on their own musical imagination, which is in high contrast with the music of the black artists who used their own mind to create songs, lyrics and titles, but also to some extent were inspired by and sampled songs, lyrics and titles (more Kanye West) that have been awarded, charted and included in lists with the best songs in the music industry; furthermore, the black artists (main vocal artist) worked in partnership with more producers and lyricists, which to some extent their final songs and albums belongs also to other producers and lyricists; this extended partnership has an effective impact on the percentage of contribution and the artistic merit: for black artists (main vocal artist) it simply drops to a lower level than for white artists (main vocal artist);
- despite the lower grades received by the white artists (main vocal artist), the music belongs to them to a greater extent compared to black artists (main vocal artist);

5. *whether the loss of the award is a direct and personal non-recognition of the black artist(s) who performed the song(s) and under whose name the song(s) and album(s) were released:*

- for Beyoncé, Kanye West and Kendrick Lamar (the artists who were and were not nominated for the *Album of the Year* and lost to white artists) there is evidence to create at least a satisfactory argument that there is a direct and personal non-recognition of their contribution in the music industry, but at the same time they used samples and were supported by many lyricists and producers in creating songs and albums; from this point of view is difficult, by the methods used in this research, to demonstrate and support at least a satisfactory argument of intentional act of racism against these artists from the voting members of The Recording Academy; Kanye West used titles of songs from other artists; maybe the non-recognition is not as high to claim that the lack of the award is because of the colour of their skin, and due to institutional racism;
- the black artists from this report and the reviews written based on their albums, are also to a considerable extent on the work and samples of other artists, lyricists and producers; while reading the reviews in magazines, the lyrics of the songs, the

number of producers and lyricists for Beyoncé and Kanye West, this idea came in my mind: are they primary artists (because of the high number of people involved in the creation of the music released under their name), or participated in the music released and promoted by using their names?

- for Kanye West, the rewards and recognition is also because of the music created by white people and used in his music and, therefore, also white people's music was not awarded and recognized with the *Album of the Year*;
- from the point of view of the

number of album reviews available online on Metacritic, All Music and *additional album reviews*[484] (in numbers it could be between 1 and up to 60-70 reviews),

the number of the voting members of The Recording Academy (for all categories, around 12,000; the number of the voting members per category is definitely lower than the total number of the voting members, but definitely higher than the number of experts in music who wrote and published online or only in print a review about an album):

and *the status of the voting members of The Recording Academy*, which includes 'performers, songwriters, producers, engineers, instrumentalists, and other creators currently working in the recording industry', and also the race of the voting members (which includes white, black etc) and various cultural and religious background:

it is greatly difficult, if not impossible, to create at least a satisfactory argument to support the allegations of discrimination and racism against the voting members and The Recording Academy of the existence of a direct and personal non-recognition of the black artists, and the producers and lyricists they partnered with for the songs and albums released, and under the name of a black artist;

6. *whether the loss of the award is a direct and personal non-recognition of the black producer(s) and lyricist(s) who created a part(s) (or full) of a song(s) and the album(s):*

- for the producers and lyricists who worked with Kanye West, Beyoncé and Kendrick Lamar, there is strong evidence that can create at least a good argument of a direct and personal non-recognition: the songs and albums released, under the name of a black artist, received a higher level of appreciation and grades from critics on Metacritic in comparison with the music created and released by the white artists;
- same conclusion as in *point of research 5:* from the point of view of the

---

[484] Based on average results made by the author of this report: the number of available reviews on Metacritic and All Music + the online reviews not available on Metacritic and All Music + possible to exists other online reviews that I did not search for + possible reviews written in various magazines and journals available only in printed version, and not accessed by the author of this report.

number of album reviews available online on Metacritic, All Music and *additional album reviews*[485] (in numbers it could be between 1 and up to 60-70 reviews),

the number of the voting members of The Recording Academy (for all categories, around 12,000; the number of the voting members per category is definitely lower than the total number of the voting members, but definitely higher than the number of experts in music who wrote and published online or only in print a review about an album):

and *the status of the voting members of The Recording Academy*, which includes 'performers, songwriters, producers, engineers, instrumentalists, and other creators currently working in the recording industry', and also the race of the voting members (which includes white, black etc) and various cultural and religious background:

it is greatly difficult, if not impossible, to create at least a satisfactory argument to support the allegations of discrimination and racism against the voting members and The Recording Academy of the existence of a direct and personal non-recognition of the black artists and the producers and lyricists they partnered with for the songs and albums released, and under the name of a black artist;

7. reasons that may justify why white artists received more recognition than black artists in the music industry (only the artists in this report and Grammy Awards: *Album of the Year*, *Best Rap Album*; MTV Awards: Beyoncé (*Single Ladies (Put a Ring On It)*, *If I were a Boy*) versus Taylor Swift (*You Belong With Me*, *The Man*) regarding the originality of these songs*:*

- maybe the white artists won the *Album of the Year*, other awards and enjoy a higher support of the general public, because they bet more on their musical ear and imagination than the black artists investigated in this report; maybe this is the way to win the *Album of the Year,* other awards and the high support of the general public: to believe in your own lyrics and instruments even if your reviews are poor, average or high, but they are truly yours, to be authentic no matter what the critics outside The Recording Academy consider the best and worst song(s) and album(s);
- the voting members of The Recording Academy seem to appreciate:

    1. the music composed with real instruments than the music created with samples that were already included, and awarded to some extent in the music industry;

---

[485] Ibidem.

2. the artists who can create strong roots (writing and composition) of their own songs and albums;

3. the artists who can perform on the stage songs own to a good extent by the main vocal artist;

- at the same time, the white population in the USA is definitely higher than the black population: this fact can have a visible impact on the outcome of music awards, since the white population is in the position to vote possibly more in favour of white artists; when it comes to the voting members of The Recording Academy: since the white population is higher than the black population, then it is possible to have more white artists as voting members than black artists (it depends on the quality metrics used by The Recording Academy to determine the guidelines for artists to be selected as voting members); it is possible that the white population and white artists to vote in favour of white artists, or it could be a mix of votes: from white people and black people in favour of the white artists, and vice versa; white and black people artists might vote in favour of an white or black artist when the music is not as good as the main vocal artists wants to believe; different studies needs to be pursued to be able to find a better understanding of the intention to vote for white and black artists, and credible reasons and examples of why and how this happens;

8. *in the music industry, among fans and critics there is a conventional wisdom attached and used toward and in reference to Kanye West: 'one of the greatest artists of all time'; in this point of research, I challenged this conventional wisdom attached to Kanye West; furthermore, I extend the conventional wisdom to Taylor Swift through a comparative analysis between her and Kanye West's music*[486]:

- based on the conclusions from chapter *II.1 Taylor Swift versus Kanye West*, the conventional wisdom attached and used toward and in reference to Kanye West exists in better and transparent terms if I add the conditional *if*, which is based on three metrics[487]:

  1. genuine originality, creativity and novelty brought for the first time into the music industry;

---

[486] I wrote the point of research as mentioned in *Introduction*, however, there is no other and new comparative analysis performed in this section; to find the answers to this point of research: I used the results from the comparative analysis between Taylor Swift and Kanye West completed in the first part of chapter *II.1 Taylor Swift versus Kanye West.*
[487] The metrics to create the *conditional if* could be different from the perspective of other experts in the methods of social research and music research. I used the metrics based on the research ideas that I had, and was able to interpret the information used in this research.

2. based on a high level and participation in writing your own lyrics and musical notes (the songs and albums belong to a good to higher extent to the main vocal artist);

3. based on mixing other songs, titles (used in any formats) and lyrics that were created and belong to other artists, then mix them with your own ideas:

> **if** the title of 'one the greatest artist of all time' *is based on genuine originality, creativity and novelty brought for the first time into the music industry*, Kanye West is not 'one of the greatest artists of all time', and it is lower than Taylor Swift; Taylor Swift has more genuine reason to be 'one the greatest artists of all time';

> **if** the title of 'one the greatest artist of all time' *is based on a high level and participation in writing your own lyrics and musical notes (the songs and albums belong to a good to higher extent to the main vocal artist)*, Taylor Swift is naturally 'one of the greatest artists of all time'; Kanye West is not 'one of the greatest artist of all time';

> **if** the title of 'one the greatest artist of all time' *is based on mixing other songs, titles* (used in any formats) *and lyrics* that were *created and belong to other artists*, then *mix them with your own ideas*, then Kanye West is 'one of the greatest artists of all time', and higher than Taylor Swift.

In *Introduction* I wrote that *'the second level is about using the findings from the eight points of research to offer a response to three conventional wisdom by black artists and their supporters'* against the rules and awards offered by The Recording Academy. Based on the findings for all eight points of research, this report can provide answers for each conventional wisdom:

1. *the higher recognition in the music industry received by the white artists is not about the quality and originality of their music, but because of the colour of their skin; in other words, the white artists received the higher recognition because the institution behind the awards is ruled by white people*:

- unfortunately, this report does not have the information necessary to determine whether the colour of the skin is the primary condition for receiving a higher recognition for the artistic merit and contribution in the USA music industry;
- the music released by the black artists in this report received a higher appreciation from critics on Metacritic; however, from my research and based on the information in this report, it seems that The Recording Academy does not take the reviews available on Metacritic into consideration, and maybe because the system is based

on the voting members who have their own views and critics about the winning song(s), album(s) and artist(s), since includes 'performers, songwriters, producers, engineers, instrumentalists, and other creators currently working in the recording industry';

2. *black artists create music and white artists take advantage and profit from their creation*:

- for the white artists from this report there is not enough evidence to create at least a satisfactory accusation of them taking advantage and profit from the creation of black artists;
- the black artists from this report (in the following order, from higher to lower level: Kanye West, Beyoncé and Kendrick Lamar) used the creation of other artists (white artists included for Kanye West, maybe more than what I was able to show in this report; maybe for Beyoncé too); Kanye West used even titles of other songs, the cover of the album *Jesus is King* is inspired and very similar with an album cover from 1970[488]; moreover, Kanye West's album, *My Beautiful Dark Twisted Fantasy*, it is inspired by the music written by white male artists (21 out of 25 male artists), so is more appropriate to say that a black artist used music created by the white artists; however, this report cannot offer a clear causal link to accuse Kanye West of taking advantage of their music; on the other hand, because the samples used (which are based on the creation of white artists) and were at the base of his album, I can suggest that Kanye West's reviews were based also on the contribution of the white artists that he sampled; it is possible that, without the samples of the music created by white artists, his recognition to not be at a higher level; furthermore, it is possible for Kanye West to profit from the music created by white artists: he sampled their music which could have encouraged the fans of the white artists (who may be interested in listening his songs and how their favourite songs were used) to purchase his albums; furthermore, Kanye West could profit from using the music of the white artists by dragging the white artists and fans on both camps in his narrative to create a mix community and, therefore, improving his image as an artist among white people;
- it is more appropriate to say that black artists from this report used other people music and, to an extent, took advantage and profit from other artists creation: they had already a strong base of musical instruments, lyrics, theme of the song and the structure of the song from where to begin their music (which to some extent, contained samples of the music created by other artists with their own fan base);

[488] Tara C. Mahadevan, 'Mystery Behind Kanye's 'Jesus Is King' Album Cover Art Solved by Third Man Records', *Complex*, November 1, 2019, available at: https://www.complex.com/music/2019/11/mystery-behind-kanyes-jesus-is-king-album-cover-art-solved-by-third-man-records, last accessed: February 27, 2021.

- it is more appropriate to say that Beyoncé and Kanye West acted like sort of curators of other people's ideas, and used the knowledge found in the music of other artists (for which they were awarded at high level);

3. *black artists need to work twice as much to get half, or the same as white artists:*

- I find this conventional wisdom to be true to some extent in the case of Beyoncé and Kanye West, and less for Kendrick Lamar: because of their inspiration and samples from other songs, which includes instruments, titles and lyrics and adaptation of these into a new song with a different or close musical notes, definitely cannot be achieved solely; creating a new song based on other songs is a hard work, which requires experts in music to create and modify the structures of the songs sampled; this looks like a curse for using other artist's work;
- the black artists in this report already had a strong base to start from, the next step for them was to think how to mix and arrange what is already created by other artists, producers and lyricists;
- the rewards for black artists using other people's work are smaller too; the white artists from this report took the shot for new songs, and got the higher reward; it is like the black artists from this report want to be recognised for other people's work;
- do black artists from this report try to cheat the fans and the music industry by using other people's music as their own, and want to be highly recognized for it as being the best music because they used it?

Other conclusions:

- overall, Taylor Swift is highly more capable than Beyoncé, Kanye West and Kendrick Lamar to write and compose her own music;
- Beyoncé and Kanye West's power to create music resides to a certain level in listening to other songs, then to mix these songs with close or sometimes different musical notes and lyrics that can be connected or have some meaning to the theme of the song they intend to create (if they sing a lyric on a different note, they need a different and the right musical note to match the sound of that lyric); there are songs in their music dossier where their (and other producers from their albums) intervention is the creation of a close sound around a sound used already by another artist;
- from the point of view of creating a song with lyrics and musical notes never heard before, Kanye West and Beyoncé have a lower level of originality, creativity and novelty than Taylor Swift;
- Kanye West and Beyoncé seems to have difficulties, (lack of musical imagination?) when it comes to solely compose and write lyrics for a full clean song never heard before, and of course to achieve highly desired global musical recognition by

themselves, as Taylor Swift successfully managed to achieve at global level since the start of her career;

- from this research, Kanye West, Beyoncé, Kendrick Lamar do not have the ability or struggle (Kanye West) to play live a full song using a piano or a guitar, while Taylor Swift has good, maybe advanced, skills in using them with positive praise;

- the white artists partnered with less producers and lyricists to create music, while black artists partnered with more lyricists and producers to create music;

- the black artists review grades are based on their own work, but also to a considerable extent on the creativity and musical ear of the artists they sampled in their songs, and the partnership with producers and lyricists;

- black artists can shout 'unfair' only to the songs written and produced by their own mind, and which exist for the first time in the music industry; for the songs they used samples (title, lyrics, instruments and work in partnership with lots of lyricists and producers) they cannot shout 'unfair': the success of the song and the album is given by the level of creativity of the original artist, producers and lyricists;

- Kanye West is on the side of Beyoncé, Kendrick Lamar, Drake and Jay Z and the reason may be the following: all of them are using samples with music already known, awarded and charted in the music industry, and partnered with more producers and lyricists; Kanye West is acting like a person that does not like original music, and we already know he doesn't like the original music of Taylor Swift (see Harper's Bazaar interview from 2016); Kanye West's expectation of the general public and juries that award songs and albums is to prefer and love more songs that are not his own, while rejecting Taylor Swift's original lyrics and musical compositions;

- Beyoncé was rewarded in the early of her career with Grammy awards while having less favorable reviews and grades than Taylor Swift (for her debut album, *Dangerously in Love*, she won five Grammys even though *The Guardian* gave her album 40 points out of 100 on Metacritic); subsequently, her albums earned a higher number of awards and grades from critics after she used a higher number of samples, cooperated with a higher number of lyricists and producers; Taylor Swift earned them with less to no samples, partnered with less lyricists and producers, received various awards on her own songs; from this point of view: black artists and their supporters are not against the decision to award a black artists even if the review grades received are lower than expected, but not happy when an white artists is awarded with higher or lower review grades;

- if there are double standards of the reasons to be awarded at high level by the voting members of The Recording Academy, then there is more evidence to create at least a satisfactory argument that black artists and their supporters are more in favour to change the reasons to be awarded according with their own desire, and less based on the artistic merit of the main vocal artist;

- the black artists from this report forgot to mention on the stage the contribution of the artists that they sampled, and have a song and album to promote as their own, while Taylor Swift was blamed by Ellie Woodward for being the only female on the stage at the Grammy Award in 2016 despite promoting feminism[489] (for Beyoncé there is no mention in a bad light of her being the only female on the stage while using samples from various artists, in partnership with other producers and lyricists);

- this report can show information that I could not see, and maybe it can help to understand and fight against institutional racism;

- there are rumours that Taylor Swift writes music for money, but black artists from this report paid copyrights and royalties to have music to release;

- this report also exposed that a visible number of black artists, producers and lyricists are involved in making music, and get better grades than the white artists; if the black artists, producers and lyricists are indeed (behind the curtain) cut their success and awards, then this report has the number of black artists, producers and lyricists who were not awarded the right recognition;

- Beyoncé and Taylor Swift about the release of their albums in 2008: I could not find information about the album's first announcement titles for both artists: I wanted to see which artist used first 'fear' to describe the theme of the album; this information is important as it can show if Beyoncé (fixed, changing and surprise pattern) entered in the same album release pattern with Taylor Swift (fixed pattern: autumn) to possible create direct competition; using same theme, *fear*, both artists expressed their own view about it, and could have encouraged people to create a comparative analysis between the two artists; however, even if Taylor Swift used 'fear' first, then later Beyoncé, it is not an evidence to support the idea that Beyoncé copied Taylor Swift (from the information that I had accessed: Taylor Swift wrote the song *Fearless* while on tour, and was ready before Beyoncé's announcement of the name of her future album); even if Beyoncé used 'fear' first, is still not an evidence to support the idea that Taylor Swift copied Beyoncé (the only way for Beyoncé to know Taylor's Swift's album name is through the existence of a mole inside Taylor's team, maybe the same person that possibly leaked the lyrics of *Innocent* to Kanye West?, or maybe when the production of the CD started and a person involved in the production informed Kanye West, Jay Z and Beyoncé?);

- the music created by the white artists (lyricists and producers; main artist of the album) is truly theirs at a higher level than the music created by the black artists (lyricists and producers, main artist of the album);

- based on this research, it is super hard, if not impossible, to demonstrate that black artists did not get the desired and highly requested music recognition because of the colour of their skin; the only way to demonstrate this allegation is to hear or record (audio and video) a voting member of The Recording Academy with the power to decide the award that he/she is not going to give the award to a black artist because

---

[489] Ellie Woodward, 'How Taylor Swift Played The Victim For A Decade And Made Her Entire Career', *Buzzfeed,* January 31, 2017, available at: https://www.buzzfeed.com/elliewoodward/how-taylor-swift-played-the-victim-and-made-her-entire-caree?utm_term=.eqJNKE2B6#.kiP4wEOYB, last accessed: June 26, 2022.

he/she does not like the skin colour, or another reason which show intentional discrimination and racism;

- *after Grammy*:

Jay Z called out the Grammys for his 2017 album, *4:44*, winning no awards, despite being a leading nominee: 'Tell the Grammys fuck that 0 for 8 shit/ Have you ever seen the crowd goin' apeshit?'[490]

Kanye West shared a video on Twitter of himself(?) urinating on one of the 21 Grammys he's won;[491]

on what reasons both artists justified their behaviour? Jay Z's album (12 out of 13 songs) used samples; Kanye's Grammy Award (not know for which category and the name of the award) most probably is based also on the use of samples with lots of producers and lyricists, so, through his behaviour or the person that did it, it was a huge disrespect to people whose music imagination was used in making and earning that award, even if he use it allegedly to protest against the company who owns his masters;[492]

in the case of Jay Z, the lyrics from his song *Apeshit*, are for his own contribution, or for the samples he used? on what reasons Jay Z can decide if the samples that he used should have been good enough to give him a Grammy? and, because he did not win an award, Jay Z is entitled and justified on good reasons to use lyrics against the institution? what if his album was good, but not good enough to win an award? or maybe he was betrayed by the samples used, where the original artist had a lower level of musical imagination and Jay Z paid the price? isn't it better to bet on your own imagination? just because he is a black artist it does not mean that he must receive an award, the award is also about quality, creativity, novelty and a high personal contribution which is lacking to a certain level in his album *4:44*;

in the case of Kanye, what is the link between the Grammy Award and the company who owns his masters? The Recording Academy awards music, it does not hold the

[490] Ashley Iasimone, 'Beyonce and Jay-Z Call Out the Super Bowl and Grammys in 'Apes—t' Video', *The Hollywood Report*, June 16, 2018, available at: https://www.hollywoodreporter.com/news/music-news/beyonce-jay-zs-apeshit-video-calls-super-bowl-grammys-1120746/, last accessed: February 25, 2020.

[491] Alicia Adejobi, 'LL Cool J drags Kanye West for urinating on Grammy Award: 'Pee in those Yeezys'', *Metro*, October 4, 2020, available at: https://metro.co.uk/2020/10/04/ll-cool-j-slams-kanye-west-urinating-grammy-award-13369300/, last accessed: February 27, 2021.

[492] Andrew Court, Frances Mulraney, 'Kanye URINATES on Grammy, declares 'Black Masters Matter' and says he 'can't be muted or canceled' after comparing the music industry to a slave ship and vowing not to release songs until he's freed from Universal and Sony contracts', *Daily Mail*, September 16, 2020, available at: https://www.dailymail.co.uk/news/article-8739833/Kanye-West-shares-clip-urinating-Grammy-Award-amid-fight-music-labels.html, last accessed: February 27, 2021.

copyrights of his music, so his disrespect toward the awarding institution is not justified;

- Kanye West and Taylor Swift are caught in an awkward position: Taylor Swift sings her songs, but does not have the best voice in the pop industry, and rumours has it she struggles to sing her own songs[493]; Kanye West is a producer, but rumours has it he does not know how to sing, or his singing abilities are a low performance in comparison with Taylor Swift[494]; from this perspective: we have a lyricist who struggle to sing her songs, and a producer who used multiple samples from other artists, struggles to create his *own* music, titles for his own songs, and possible lack of singing skills as the final blow; maybe the lack of a 'voice to sing' is the real reason of Kanye West being against Taylor Swift: he does not like to see a talentless side of his own reflection; maybe Kanye West is against Taylor Swift as a decoy strategy to redirect his critics and own lack of singing skills toward another person who struggles to sing her songs;

- it is possible that the low grades and reviews of the latest albums by Kanye West to show that he used already all the best samples available for his creative mind, or for which he could hear a new song; at the moment, and better for Kanye West, the only safe place to find something new is his own mind; it is time for Kanye West to show that he can also be a 'yenius' with his own lyrics, own voice and own production heard for the first time in the world, as he is way behind Taylor Swift;

- by using samples, the black and the white artists offered a reheated soup, why should they receive the highest recognition for this strategy?

- there are rumours that black artists want to put pressure on the music industry to change the rules[495]; however, persons of interest in the music industry must investigate this pressure, and see if it follows to celebrate pure creativity, originality and novelty in the music industry, or is an attempt to celebrate the power of sampling; if everybody samples, then who creates the samples? for black artists and white artists the final aim should be quality and high personal contribution, not pressure for a larger freedom to use someone else music, and shame the institution when the music is not nominated and awarded;

- owning the masters of the song is important for artists, but also it is important to check the correct contribution of the artist in a song and album, and see if the specific song and the album is made solely on the artists contribution, or were paid

---

[493] Marc Hirsh, 'Hey, Has Anybody Noticed That Taylor Swift Can't Sing?', *NPR*, November 28, 2008, available at: https://www.npr.org/2008/11/28/97583296/hey-has-anybody-noticed-that-taylor-swift-cant-sing, last accessed: February 27, 2021; 'Is Taylor Swift actually a good singer?', *Discover Music*, April 26, 2019, available at: https://www.classicfm.com/discover-music/music-theory/taylor-swift-good-singer/, last accessed: February 27, 2021.

[494] Luke Morgan Britton, 'David Crosby: 'Kanye West can't write, sing or play'', *NME*, June 27, 2015, available at: https://www.nme.com/news/music/kanye-west-321-1225032, last accessed: February 27, 2021.

[495] This statement is based on the articles about black artists and the racists allegations against The Recording Academy used in this research.

copyrights and royalties to be able to have a song and album to release; artists should not own other artists masters just for the sake to shake it off with the sounds and lyrics created by other artists / lyricists and producers, to cheat the music industry, themselves and the fans;

- Kanye West used lots of samples and paid copyrights to use it; also, is possible to pay royalties (monthly) for the samples used, so his case to own the masters of the albums is complicated; from my understanding it seems that the artists he sampled need to renounce to a part of their music in Kanye's favour; the artists that Kanye West sampled need to accept that another artists bought their music, so Kanye West can enjoy 100% ownership of his and their music; why the original artists and the owning company should abandon their creation for Kanye West, if Kanye West does not bother to create his own music, showed lack of manners and disrespected the artists, producers and lyricists in his music, and which contributed to his Grammy Awards?

- strangely, Kanye West does not mention anything about the Grammys received by Drake and Jay Z: their albums are based on the same strategy: samples and many lyricists and producers; Kanye West is focused on saying something negative about Taylor Swift;

- Kanye West presence at the Grammy Awards before 2016: was present and happy when his music (based on samples from other artists, and partnership with various producers, lyricists and artists) was awarded, but definitely did not like the idea when Taylor Swift was awarded for the music she wrote and existed for the first time in the music industry; it looks like Kanye West is against originality and ownership of your own work;

- after the Famous events from February 2016: Kanye West had a more negative attitude toward and in reference to Grammy Awards and Taylor Swift: by this time he was awarded with 21 Grammy Awards, while Taylor Swift had 10 Grammy Awards;

- for a better understanding and the general view of the good support toward the artists in the USA, The Recording Academy must come with an explanation about the winning song, album and artist;

- if the black artists, producers and lyricists know that The Recording Academy does not accept samples of songs to be awarded the *Album of the Year*, why they do not produce an album without samples?

- can the black artists from this report write and produce clean and unheard music from their own mind, sell millions of copies, use at least the same number of lyricists and producers, and receive the *Album of the Year* three times each?

- on Apple Music Taylor Swift has only *1989* as essential album and yet *Lover* (79 on Metacritic), *folklore* (88) and *Evermore* (85) are not included, even though they have higher positive reviews with the last two albums being considered a genuine change of genre for the artist; *folklore* and *Fearless (Taylor's Version)* (82) or the old version with 73) should be included as essential albums for receiving the *Album of the Year*, the highest award in the USA music industry and the highest recognition of the artist;

the high impact for country music in the USA, and around the planet, should be considered in order to make the albums available in the essential list; Kanye West (*The Life of Pablo*: 75; *Graduation*: 79), Rihanna (*Loud*: 67; *ANTI*: 73), Beyoncé (*Dangerously in Love*: 63; *I am... Sasha Fierce*: 62), Lady Gaga (*The Fame Monster Deluxe*: 78; *Born This Way*: 71), Drake (*Take Care Deluxe*: 78; *Nothing Was the Same Deluxe*: 79; *If You're Reading This It's Too Late*: 78; *Views*: 69) have their albums as *Essential* even if the review grade is close or lower than Taylor Swift's; moreover, the album sales of Taylor Swift are higher than the artists in this paragraph, which exposes a high level of popularity; it is time for Apple Music to be more fair with Taylor Swift's music, and her recognition in the music industry should be available on the streaming platform as well;

- from what I read, it seems that Taylor Swift is not allowed to be successful; Taylor Swift is downgraded despite having more original songs than the black artists from this report; the universities should study Taylor Swift more than Beyoncé: Taylor Swift is more original, creative, brings novelty and has more songs solely written and released by her; Taylor Swift has a higher impact on the American music culture and people, and the numbers of album sales and concerts is the evidence of how she can connect and leave a mark in the music culture of the USA on long term; is not strange that Beyoncé is being promoted as the black artist that has the higher impact in the USA music culture, yet people do not bother to buy and listen her albums as much as they do with Taylor Swift? Now the impact in the music culture is made by people who sell less music? How a person or community can be influenced by someone, if they do not consume the product of that someone? Adele was accused that she received the Grammy Award because of the high number of albums sales and changed the American music culture[496], yet with Taylor Swift and Beyoncé we have other rules; the impact in the music culture is not only in the eyes of the beholder (artists included), but also in the wallets of the people ready to use their money and time to purchase the music of the artist, use it to live and make their own life choices, which definitely create an impact in the environment of families, friends and society in the end;

- in 2021 Taylor Swift started her long term project to own her old music; the first album re-recorded was *Fearless (Taylor's Version)*: in this album Taylor Swift came with six more songs written many years ago, but only now they have been made public; the new songs helped Taylor to improve her value and contribution in the music industry; after the re-release of her old albums (*Red* (November 2021), *1989,*

---

[496] Alexandra Topping, 'Adele can change how music industry markets female acts, says label boss', *The Guardian*, May 29, 2011, available at: https://www.theguardian.com/music/2011/may/29/adele-change-women-music-business, last accessed: June 16, 2022; 'Adele's success will be measured in cultural impact – not sales', *Music Industry Blog*, October 15, 2021, available at: https://musicindustryblog.wordpress.com/2021/10/15/adeles-success-will-be-measured-in-cultural-impact-not-sales/#:~:text=Adele%20bucked%20the%20prevailing%20industry%20trends.&text=Fast%20forward%20to%202021%20and,in%20which%2025%20was%20released., last accessed: June 16, 2022.

Speak Now, *Taylor Swift* and *reputation*) the number of songs written by herself may increase significantly, and a visible part of the figures and data used in this report will change; the same effect is going to happen with the new music released by black artists; however, after the publication of this report, the future albums released by the artists from this report will not be investigated;

- despite all the information used in this research, I was unable to find genuine evidence with strong reasons that can justify the look-like-planned-hate-and-mean-strategies-and-feedback from Kanye West toward and in reference to Taylor Swift; why Kanye West was so deep involved in negative plans to advance a negative view about Taylor Swift's skills and character? we need an answer, considering that Kanye West presents himself as a man in the service of God;[497]

- black and white artists who would like to take more awards from The Recording Academy, according with the findings in this report, should try the final strategy:

  to write and compose music by themselves; to keep the number of producers and lyricists as low as possible, and then submit the album for consideration and reviews from critics and fans;

- definitely, further in-depth analysis, beyond the use of mathematical calculations and interpretations / inferences available here, must be pursued to find in stronger and transparent terms if the colour of the artists is the main catalyst of being awarded at a higher level, or if the main vocal artists are rewarded due to being born with abilities to write, compose songs and albums that belongs to a greater extent by oneself, and heard for the first time in the music industry.

---

[497] This statement is based on Kanye West's participation on long term for Sunday Service. Read for example: Jordan Darville, 'What exactly is Kanye West's Sunday Service?', *The Fader*, September 24, 2019, available at: https://www.thefader.com/2019/09/24/a-history-of-sunday-service-kanye-west, last accessed: March 26, 2020.

Casian Anton

On The Famous Feud

★

Probably the most advanced analysis

...

To Kanye West, Kim Kardashian West, Taylor Swift, Katy Perry and Western Mass-Media:

'This goes out to all you people going bed with
a ten and waking up with a two.'
(Katy Perry, *This Is How We Do*, 'Prism,' 2013)

'We think we know someone, but the truth
is that we only know the version of them
that they've chosen to show us.'
(Taylor Swift, *reputation*, volume 1, 2017)

'A wise man should be humble enough to admit
when he's wrong and change his
mind based on new information.'
(Kanye West, *Twitter*, February 2016)

'Cause all of my enemies started out friends.'
(Taylor Swift, 'The Archer', *Lover*, 2019)

'You play stupid games, you win stupid prizes'
(Taylor Swift, 'Miss Americana & The Heartbreak Prince', *Lover*, 2019)

'Lifelike, this is what your life like, try to live
your life right, People really know you,
push your buttons like typewrite'
(Kanye West, 'Follow God', *Jesus is King*, 2010)

'Use this gospel for protection, It's a hard road to Heaven'
(Kanye West, 'Use this Gospel', *Jesus is King*, 2019)

'I just wanted you to know'
(Kanye West, 'Famous', *The Life of Pablo*, 2016)

'[…] Just thought you should know'
(Taylor Swift, 'Miss Americana & The Heartbreak Prince', *Lover*, 2019)

'If you wanna see the true character of person watch
the way they treat someone who can't do anything for them.
Question everything, Follow the innate feelings inside you,
Free to take ideas and update them at your will,
Truth is my goal'
(Kanye West, *Tweets from Twitter*, 2018)

LIST OF **Tables, Diagrams** AND **Figures**

FOREWORD: the end of the **FAMOUS** journey

The first research task was set by my English teacher in year 11 at Grup Şcolar Agricol in Sighişoara, Romania. The research was about a planet in the solar system. For many days I spent my afternoons in the reading room at the 'Zaharia Boiu' Municipal Library in Sighişoara; here, a tall gentleman with grey moustache and thick glasses (never knew his name) was always calm and willing to search books that I wanted to explore. One keyword was enough for him to arrive with a pack of rusted books where I could find exactly what I needed. Since early stages of the research, I was determined to create the best poster in the group about planet Earth; later, same week, I completed the whole solar system (9 pages). Each paragraph with information was new for me and I wanted to know and understand as much as I could write on the A3 pages. The last stage of the posters was to translate the information from Romanian into English, which I did with a dictionary; in the end, my classmate Ovidiu Răzăilă decided to help me with the final translation. The posters were a phenomenal success. At the same time, my naturally? enthusiasm was still at high level as at the start of the research, and I continued to visit the library's reading room (mostly during rainy days), where I explored W.I.T.C.H. magazines and DC Comics books (Justice League as favourite).

In the first year at Petru Maior University of Târgu Mureş, I had access for the first time and non-stop to a PC; until this point in time, I only used the computer from 'Zaharia Boiu' Library and an internet cafe in Sighişoara. Myself and Ovidiu, now both students at the same university, decided to buy the PC, and my sister, Lucia-Garofiţa, contributed with half of the cost. It took me a couple of months to improve my ICT skills. The first PowerPoint presentation for the course *Introduction in International Relations* had 65 slides, compared to classmates who came with 10-12 slides, full of colour, short and clear ideas.

During free time Ovidiu was busy with reading news about famous people in cinema, music, fashion etc. In high school we used to speak mostly about books and movies, and at university Ovidiu was deeply engaged in a research between himself and famous people born on the same day as him; later that year, he also told me about famous people born on the same day as me. What a sparkling life they have!

Surprisingly, more than a decade later, I found myself interested in one of the famous feuds of all time: Taylor Swift versus Kanye West. The first idea for a research report about the **Famous** feud arrived in my mind somewhere in September 2016 after reading few negative articles about Taylor Swift. At this time, I heard one song from her catalogue, Red.[498]

On the **Famous** *Feud* ends the **Famous** journey that lasted six years. Under normal conditions, I need about 6-10 months to finish a project, but in this case it didn't happen. Every time I wanted to publish the version I considered final, an event in my personal life and feud prevented me. In 2021, while on vacation, I decided to return to this research and published the first part, *Black and White Music*[499]. Today, I am happy that I have finished this project, and I hope that is well received by readers interested in the feud between artists, the idea of analysing this feud from the point of view of the narrative line, along with the identification of patterns which reveal the character, the strategies of communication and interpretation of the main players, but also the role of the Western mass-media in presenting the feud to fans and to the general public.

For me, **Famous** was the first productive and profound journey in the music industry and famous artists, but at the same time it is the last research of this type. Moving forward, I have to travel only in the round circle of the world state, the matrix world of structures of explanation, and stories created over the years. I hope your life journey is not as **Famous** as the one in these pages, but better.

CASIAN ANTON
England

---

[498] I discovered the song in the spring of 2014 from a post on Facebook, and while I was involved in the *Laboratory of Politics and International Relations*.

[499] Casian Anton, *Black and White Music: A Journey Behind the Musical Notes*, 2021, Amazon. 2022 for printed edition.

Introduction: on the **FAMOUS** feud

THE **FAMOUS** PROBLEM

21 months after the release of her multi-platinum and blockbuster album, namely *1989*, Taylor Swift was one of the most famous pop artist in the world and was named the 21st century Pop Princess, America's Sweetheart[500], an innocent and clean model for the young female generation of the Western world, but also for other parts of the world. However, a video posted in July 2016, on the Snapchat account of the famous Kim Kardashian[501], changed the narrative line of Taylor Swift and her positive image around the world. The video contained heavily edited parts of the telephone conversation from January 2016 between Kanye West and Taylor Swift, and the background narrative of the creation of the controversial song *Famous*. In February 2016 Taylor Swift rejected the story of the events revealed by Kanye West on his Twitter account. However, hours later, Kanye West tweeted that Taylor Swift gave her blessing about the song. In July 2016, in the video posted by Kim Kardashian, Taylor Swift's voice confirmed Kanye West's side of the story by saying over the telephone conversation: 'Umm, yeah I mean go with whatever line you think is better. It's obviously very tongue in cheek either way. And I really appreciate you telling me about it, that's really nice.' […] 'And you know, if people ask me about it I think it would be great for me to be like,' Look, he called me and told me the line before it came out. Jokes on you guys, We're fine.' […] 'You guys want to call this a feud; you want to call this throwing shade but right after the song comes out I'm going to be on a GRAMMYs red carpet and they're going to ask me about it and I'll be like, 'He called me.' The telephone conversation from January 2016, the release of the song *Famous* in February 2016, and the different views of the actual telephone conversation published by Taylor Swift and Kanye West, were the catalyst and the start of the second part of the feud (the first part was in September 2009). The Western mass-media, fans of both sides and ordinary people reacted with negative and positive comments

---

[500] Spencer Cain, 'Taylor Swift: Has America's Sweetheart Become Overexposed?', *Stylecaster*, August 24, 2012, available at: https://stylecaster.com/entertainment/entertainment/152897/taylor-swift-americas-sweetheart-overexposed/, last accessed: June 26, 2022; Alice Vincent, 'Taylor Swift: the rise, fall and re-invention of America's sweetheart', *Telegraph*, January 25, 2020, available at: https://www.telegraph.co.uk/music/artists/taylor-swift-rise-fall-re-invention-americas-sweetheart/, last accessed: June 26, 2022; Joanna Buoniconti, 'From "America's sweetheart" to "Miss Americana," Taylor Swift is at her most vulnerable in latest Netflix documentary', *Amherst Wire*, February 7, 2020, available at: https://amherstwire.com/32221/tvmovies/from-americas-sweetheart-to-miss-americana-taylor-swift-is-at-her-most-vulnerable-in-latest-netflix-documentary/, last accessed: June 26, 2022.

[501] The ex-wife of the famous rap artist Kanye West; in June 2016, a month before the videos published by Kim Kardashian, there was already a trailer of an interview with GQ magazine in which she announced the existence of a video evidence showing a different character of Taylor Swift.

and memes; also, in June and July 2016 two social forces were created by fans on both camps: the social force of Kim Kardashian and Kanye West, and the social force of Taylor Swift.[502]

Kim Kardashian and Kanye West's social force have declared the release of a small edited part of the telephone conversation as a final blow to Taylor Swift; according to Ellie Woodward, Kim Kardashian, through one short video posted on Snapchat, successfully demonstrated a white female character with two faces, and the role of the false white victim she played throughout her entire career.[503]

In July 2016, hours after Kim's video from Snapchat, Taylor Swift published her response with a screenshot (on Instagram) suggesting that it was written before Kim Kardashian's revelation. Taylor Swift's post on Instagram did not help her side of the story, but reinforced the idea that she knew there was evidence of her involvement in the song *Famous*, which she declined to confirm it as expected by Kanye West, Kim Kardashian and a minor number of Western mass-media journalists and bloggers.

Taylor Swift's social force rejected Kanye's version of the telephone conversation, and continued to support Taylor Swift's point of view: she heard the song for the first time at the same time as the general public, and did not approve the lyrics used by Kanye West in the song *Famous*: 'I feel like me and Taylor might still have sex / Why? I made that bitch famous (God damn) / I made that bitch famous.' Taylor Swift replied: 'Where is the video of Kanye telling me he was going to call me 'that bitch' in his song? It doesn't exist because it never happened. You don't get to control someone's emotional response to being called 'that bitch' in front of the entire world. Of course I wanted to like the song. I wanted to believe Kanye when he told me that I would love the song. I wanted us to have a friendly relationship. He promised to play the song for me, but he never did. While I wanted to be supportive of Kanye on the phone call, you can't 'approve' a song you haven't heard. Being falsely painted as a liar when I was never given the full story or played any part of the song is character assassination. I would very much like to be excluded from this narrative, one that I have never asked to be a part of, since 2009.'[504]

---

[502] Various parts from this report were also used in *Black and White Music: A Journey Behind the Musical Notes*, August 2022, Amazon (printed edition). The reason behind this use is simple: it was a single report in two parts: 1. *On the Famous Feud* and the 2. *Music of the Famous Feud* (a comparison research of the music released by Kanye West and Taylor Swift, then later extended to other artists). In this chapter some of the reasons are used from *Black and White Music: A Journey Behind the Musical Notes,* but modified to accommodate specific explanations and needs for this report.

[503] Ellie Woodward, 'How Taylor Swift Played The Victim For A Decade And Made Her Entire Career', *Buzzfeed,* January 31, 2017, available at: https://www.buzzfeed.com/elliewoodward/how-taylor-swift-played-the-victim-and-made-her-entire-caree?utm_term=.eqJNKE2B6#.kiP4wEOYB, last accessed: June 26, 2022.

[504] Gina Mei, 'Taylor Swift Just Responded to Kim Kardashian's "Famous" Call Out', *Cosmopolitan*, July 18, 2016, available at: https://www.cosmopolitan.com/entertainment/celebs/news/a61476/taylor-swift-responds-kim-kardashian-famous-call-out-kanye/, last accessed: June 26, 2022.

The feud between the three celebrities is important because it covers a major topic in the USA: the allegations made by black people about the persistent racism of the white people against them, and other minorities. In the **Famous** case, between Taylor Swift (the 'privileged white woman': a concept and movement advanced by various activists (including by Black Lives Matter) that is describing the benefits and the positive outcome for white women, which are in high contrast with the negative outcome for black women) and Kanye West (the black man persecuted by white people, including by Taylor Swift by refusing to confirm and accept his narrative about the background details of the song).

In some Western mass-media agencies and the social force of Kim Kardashian and Kanye West, Taylor Swift's response was unconvincing leading to several articles about the causes and reasons for the feud between them. In July 2016, the popular opinion agreed with Kanye West and Kim Kardashian's side of the story. The mechanisms for interpreting the parties involved in the *Famous* feud are multiple, and there is still a great interest in debating the perpetrators and the victims of the feud.

THE LITERATURE OF THE **FAMOUS** FEUD

There is a rich literature of articles written and promoted by Western mass-media. In the first stage of the research I gathered in a word document 1175 articles; the articles were arranged in two categories: United States of America (henceforth USA) and United Kingdom (henceforth UK) with the name of the news agency and a link to the website source, so I can access it anytime. I gathered links about the *Famous* feud from the following news agencies (available in the USA, UK and Australia): Slate Magazine, People, Vanity Fair, Cosmopolitan, Glamour Magazine, Elle, Vulture, Marie Claire, Forbes, Ok! UK, Radar Online, GQ, The Sun, Metro, Evening Standard, Telegraph, Daily Star, The Guardian, The Independent, Express, AOL.co.uk, Mirror, Huffington Post, Daily Mail, Pagesix, Billboard, CBS News, Business Insider, Bazaar, New York Daily, Gossip Cop[505], Rolling Stone, People, E Online, Lifestyle, The Atlantic, TMZ, W Magazine, Latinpost, Daily Beast, Buzzfeed, Los Angeles Time, US Magazine, TIME. I managed to read over 500 articles, then I got bored and did not want to continue this research.

Based on this research, there are three debate camps (from higher to lower number of people involved in the debates) about the **Famous** Feud:

the first debate camp (high as number of supporters, and includes mostly random people, but also a very low number of fans and journalists): it is an ***overall opinion*** about which player of the feud is saying the truth, or is lying about the storyline of an event from the feud;

---

[505] The best source for accuracy: I gathered 33 links about the feud; the articles are not available at time of publishing this report, they were deleted from the website.

- in this camp the knowledge and intuition of the random person about the players of the feud is presented with a feeling of 'mostly being true';
- to reach a conclusion about a player, the random person does not use a specific analysis based on a specific methodology to find substantial evidence to support the player(s) of the feud;
- in this camp, the opinion (based on the need to say something good or bad about the players) advanced by a random person creates (maybe inevitable and with no direct intention) a feel of 'gaslighting' than 'enlightening';

the second debate camp (high as number of genuine fans): it is based on **conclusions acquired** after **using a specific methodology** (either created and used by genuine fans interested in getting an in-depth understanding of the events of the feud, or one that exists in the literature about methods of research);

- in this camp, the knowledge is considered to have a higher quality and version of truth than the knowledge in the first debate camp;
- the methodology is clearly stated in the opinion, and it is difficult to argue against it; however, if there is an argument against the opinion, then it is based on the methodology applied by fans where most of the time it consist on:

  questioning the character of the player of the feud in describing the full storyline of the event that caused or advanced the feud; where there is a lack of information about the whole or parts of the event (which can support or reject a logical order and outcome of the event), fans prefer to side with their personal favourite player of the feud;

the third debate camp (formed only by journalists): it is based on two levels: **1.** the **knowledge gathered over the years by journalists about the whole narrative of the feud,** and **2.** about **other events from the life of the players of the feud** (these events are being used to advance and support an argument from level 1);

- this camp is **self-considered as holder of the final truth** and mostly neutral about the conclusions of the feud;
- it does not engage in deciding who is the victim and who is the perpetrator;
- the history of the feud and the *character* of the players of the feud is promoted and remembered to a higher extent, and possible forevermore, by the journalists in the third debate;

Between all three debate camps, there is a thin line that is crossed intentionally and unintentionally by all persons of interest about their favourite artists.

During a new event in the feud, all three debate camps are caught in a war for justice for the players of the feud, which is on three levels:

the first level: it is between the first and the second debate camps; these two debate camps have a high power to gaslight and uplift artists and supporters;

the second level: it is between the second and the third debate camp: it is a battle of genuine fans and journalists and the methodology used to acquire logical and fair conclusions about the players of the feud;

the third level: it is a mix between all three debates camps and used in a way to justify the conclusions of the feud; the existence of different conclusions acquired by journalists, which are in visible contrast with the conclusions acquired by genuine fans, creates a visible wave of untrust in mass-media; this contradiction encourage genuine fans to create and promote *look-like-an-ultimate-support* for the victim of the feud: fans never believe the narrative written and promoted by mass-media (even if it is true to some extent), and continue to support the player of the feud at the highest level possible (can be measured in the number of songs played on streaming platforms, pure album and song sales, number of tickets sold for concerts etc).

Overall, this report is in the same bubble of research of the feud as with the investigations released by various Western mass-media news agencies.[506] However, I exposed the difference between the existent literature written and published by Western mass-media and used in this report, and my own strategy of presentation of the feud.

- ***Differences***:

    - if Western mass-media created and presented a neutral timeline of the events of the feud, I **used the timeline** of the events written by Western mass-media

        - *a.* to find the key moments of the feud; *c.* what is missing from the feud;
        - to observe, identify and extract patterns of behaviour:

            a. Kanye West's behaviour toward and in reference to Taylor Swift;
            b. Taylor Swift's behaviour toward and in reference to Kanye West;
            c. Kim Kardashian's behaviour toward and in reference to Taylor Swift;
            d. Taylor Swift's behaviour toward and in reference to Kim Kardashian;

    - if Western mass-media mentioned and analysed at low level the knowledge of Taylor Swift about the song **Famous**,

---

[506] For the full list of articles connected to this report, see chapter *V.1 The Famous Feud in Western Mass Media.*

- I assessed three points of view:

  1. Kanye West about the permission from Taylor Swift to use the lyrics in the song Famous;
  2. Kim Kardashian saying that Taylor Swift knew everything about the song;
  3. Taylor Swift about her part in making the song and the character assassination;

- I analysed:

  4. Taylor Swift's knowledge (general and in percentage) about the song *Famous*;

- I **investigated:** the **song** and **albums sales** that are part of the feud; **the impact** of the feud on song and albums sales; the **number of producers** and **lyricists** of the songs from the feud; the **sources of inspiration** and **originality** of the albums released in 2010 by Kanye West and Taylor Swift; the **rating** on Metacritic, and the **connection** between the feud of **Kanye West** and **Taylor Swift**, and **Katy Perry** and Taylor Swift.

- if Western mass-media mentioned and presented the events of the feud, sometimes with more explanations around the events of the feud and the players,

  - I **explored mechanisms** and **strategies** of **interpretation** and **communication** of the feud used by Kanye West, Kim Kardashian, Taylor Swift and the Western mass-media;

- if Western mass-media wrote over a thousand articles about the feud, including theories about the background narrative and reasons to support the feud by the players of the feud,

  - I selected and arranged key information about the feud, and other information existent in mass-media but not connected yet with the feud;
  - I created a chapter where I wrote various hypothetical and negative reasons as possible answers to the following question: why *Famous* feud was created and supported for more than 10 years? the

> hypothetical reasons and answers are based on the information used in this report;
> - I created a comparative analysis of the album release dates; I found an original and unique pattern of album release that is happening in 2008, 2009 and 2016 and involves Taylor Swift, Kanye West and Beyoncé; at time of publishing, and based on the research conducted, this pattern was not described by the Western mass-media, or fans on both camps.

THE AIM OF THE FAMOUS RESEARCH

In this report I investigated the *Famous* feud between Kim Kardashian, Kanye West and Taylor Swift from 10 points of research:

1. to expose, to extract, to understand the role of the Western mass-media about: **a.** the key moments of the *Famous* feud; **b.** specific information about the events from the *Famous* feud; **c.** to find what is missing from the *Famous* feud timeline;
2. to analyse the narrative line of the feud in order to identify patterns of behaviour: Kanye West's behaviour toward and in reference to Taylor Swift; Taylor Swift's behaviour toward and in reference to Kanye West; Kim Kardashian's behaviour toward and in reference to Taylor Swift; Taylor Swift's behaviour toward and in reference to Kim Kardashian;
3. to assess three points of view made by Kanye West, Kim Kardashian and Taylor Swift:

> **3.1 *Kanye West wrote on Twitter***: '3rd thing I called Taylor and had a hour long convo with her about the line and she thought it was funny and gave her blessings';
>
> **3.2 *Kim Kardashian in the interview with GQ magazine* from 16 June 2016** and during her show *Keeping Up with The Kardashians* (season 12, episode 11): 'She totally approved that. […] 'She totally knew that that was coming out;'
>
> **3.3 *the affirmation made by Taylor Swift in July 2016***: 'Being falsely painted as a liar when I was never given the full story *or played any part of the song* (underline by author) is character assassination';

4. to analyse the *song Famous* to see how much in percentage Taylor Swift knew about the song before its release;
5. to analyse the impact of the *Famous* feud on the albums sales and songs for Kanye West, Taylor Swift and Katy Perry;

6. to identify and expose the mechanisms and strategies of interpretation and communication used by Kim Kardashian, Kanye West, Taylor Swift and the Western mass-media;
7. to explore possible reasons for creating, supporting and promoting the *Famous* feud by Kim Kardashian, Kanye West, Taylor Swift and the Western mass-media;
8. to analyse the core argument of the 'false white victimhood' attributed to Taylor Swift;
9. to analyse the core argument of Ellie Woodward about the existence of a false worldview attributed to Kanye West which is that of a: 'black man terrorising the 'innocent' white woman', because of Taylor Swift;
10. to find out who is the victim and who is the perpetrator of the *Famous* feud.

POTENTIAL FAMOUS CONTRIBUTIONS:

- this report was born out of the urgent need to provide clearer, more transparent information and better-founded examples to explain the *Famous* feud in a different way than what Kim Kardashian, Kanye West and Taylor Swift offered through music, interviews and other media content;
- black and white people are in need of answers, and this report is a meditative resource about the *Famous* feud;
- in this report interested fans and members of the general public about Taylor Swift, Kanye West and Kim Kardashian will find the space to read about it and confront their knowledge with the investigation's findings;
- the report can be used to calm the realities of racism, and can provide a point of reference in future discussions and evolutions of this feud;
- this report explored the background strategies of Kanye West, Kim Kardashian and Taylor Swift to maintain popularity and fame in an ever-changing world: sacrifices, intelligence, methods of communications, side effects and a minimal view of the efficiency of their strategies in the long term;
- by no means this report is made with the intentional purpose to present the players of the feud in a negative light; I followed and interpreted raw numbers, analysed interviews by Kanye West, Kim Kardashian, Taylor Swift and articles written by journalists and bloggers;
- *'On the Famous feud'* report it is a unique and original investigation, there is no other research which explores this feud on various levels; at the time of publishing, this report is the most advanced analysis of the *Famous* feud.

THE JOURNEY OF THE **FAMOUS** RESEARCH

September 2016	I had the first idea of the report after reading few negative articles about Taylor Swift (including the interview of Kanye West and Kim Kardashian West for Harper's Bazaar); this happened at a time when I heard one song from her catalogue, named *Red*;
November 2016	by the end of the month, I was able to outline and finish the plan of the research;
December 2016	I bought the first album in my life, *1989*, with the purpose to create a comparison between Kanye West and Taylor Swift's music; I decided to make my own playlists with favourite songs from Kanye West and Taylor Swift's discography;
June 2017	the first version of this report; I planned to release it on same day with the album *Witness* by Katy Perry (June 9, 2017), for the world to 'witness' this report, but Taylor Swift decided to release her music on all streaming platforms and ruined my plan; I had to plan a new release date;
August 30, 2017	the next date of publication was on the one-year anniversary of Kanye West's speech at the MTV Music Awards; I considered this day a symbol and a suitable reaction to create a balance of the feud; however, on August 21, 2017 Taylor Swift decided to return with a new album, *reputation*; I decided that it was better to wait for Taylor Swift to make her own move, given that she was the main target of the West family (Kanye West and Kim Kardashian West were married at the time);
August 2018	in August 2018 I started a new job and, unfortunately, I did not have time to revisit the report and publish it; from this moment, I let the report to rest in the folder;
April 2019	in April 2019 I returned to the report and decided that it is better to include more information about the feud; for this reason, the information used in this report include various sources from different years, 2016-2022; the new information in the report can be observed by checking the 'date of publication', and the date with 'last accessed' of the online sources used;
Middle of March 2020	in the middle of March 2020, the side effects on a large scale of the Covid 19 pandemic changed my daily routine and I had time to revise the report's findings; I added new information and planned to publish the report on July 16: the symbol day of the *Famous* feud;
July 2020	news were pouring on Twitter about Kanye West's decision to announce and release a new album: I wanted to listen to his album hoping to find information that could change the report's conclusions; however, on July 23, Taylor Swift announced *folklore* album and, again, I postponed the release date of the report for another day;
Summer 2020	I added *folklore* in the report and set a release date for late August 2020, but Kanye West decided to push the announcement for *Donda* album; again, I waited for this album, so I can offer Kanye West the same treatment as I did with Taylor Swift's *folklore*; at the same time, the volume of work increased, and I had to find a new release date;
December 2020	Taylor Swift decided to release her second surprise album, *Evermore*, which I included in the report; at this point I decided not to plan further release date, to delete the report, and to deal with other important research ideas;
July 2021	in July 2021, while on vacation, after listening to the new version of the song *The Lakes (Original Version)*, I remembered the report and came up with the plan to divide it: the first part to be *On the Famous Feud*: an analysis of the feud and events

	between Kanye West and Taylor Swift (around 200 pages); the second part about black and white artists and the source of their music (around 200 pages);
August 2021	I changed the order of the report, and published the first part with the name *Black and White Music: A Journey Behind the Musical Notes*; I also added new points of research;
April 2022	I decided that *Black and White Music* had enough time and space for publicity, to be read by fans and the general public; at this time, I did not plan any release date for the second part of the report;
July 2022	the decision to release the second part of the report, *On the **Famous** Feud*, was made on my way back home; few hours later was available online.

In the first chapter, ***THE PLAYERS AND THE METHODOLOGY OF THE FAMOUS FEUD***, I described the main research methods and the limits of the research.

In the first part of the second chapter, ***THE FAMOUS FEUD TIMELINE***, I investigated the timeline of the *Famous* feud in the Western mass-media from three points of view:

a) the key moments of the *Famous* feud,
b) specific information about the events from the *Famous* feud,
c) what is missing from the *Famous* feud timeline.

To achieve this purpose, I created a

1. *General timeline of the Famous feud in the Western mass-media*: UK, USA; Australia is not part of Western mass-media, but I decided to include it as an optional view of the *Famous* feud presented in a country outside what is considered 'Western world';

2. *I analysed the events of the timeline* for each research target (USA, UK, Australia),

3. *then I compared the results between the research targets* to create a general view of Western mass-media from the three points of view written above. The final results were added in a table and in the form of a figure, and were used as an extra source of information to analyse and compare the events of the feud in the Western mass-media.

In the second part of this chapter, I wrote the details of the events from the *Famous* feud. This timeline includes only the conversations and interviews of Kanye West, Kim Kardashian and Taylor Swift. The **events of the feud were used to investigate** the narrative line of the relationship between Kanye West and Taylor Swift from September 2009 (MTV Music Awards) to November 2017 (the release of Taylor Swift's *reputation* album) and between Kim Kardashian and Taylor Swift (from June 2016 to March 2020), **with the purpose to find patterns of behaviour** that either may show unknown information, or what we know already can be presented in a new way that may be use for an in-depth, yet enlightening, understanding of the feud.

In chapter three, ***HOW MUCH TAYLOR SWIFT KNEW ABOUT THE SONG*** **FAMOUS**, I assessed three points of view:

1. ***Kanye West wrote on Twitter***: '3rd thing I called Taylor and had a hour long convo with her about the line and she thought it was funny and gave her blessings';
2. ***Kim Kardashian in the interview with GQ magazine from 16 June 2016 and during her show 'Keeping Up With The Kardashians'*** (season 12, episode 11): 'She totally approved that. […] 'She totally knew that was coming out;'
3. ***the affirmation made by Taylor Swift in July 2016***: 'Being falsely painted as a liar when I was never given the full story *or played any part of the song* (underline by author) is character assassination';

and analysed:

4. ***Taylor Swift's general knowledge of the song Famous in percentage***: the content of this section was created with the purpose to check in percentage how much Taylor Swift knew about the *song Famous*.

The information presented in chapter three is also for lovers of details, numbers and charts.

In chapter four, ***THE IMPACT OF THE*** **FAMOUS** ***FEUD***, I investigated:

1. the impact of the ***Famous*** feud on music album sales: the first week in the USA between Taylor Swift and Kanye West;
2. global sales of the songs that are the cause of the feud: ***Famous*** for Kanye West, *Look What You Made Me Do* for Taylor Swift, and *Swish, Swish* for Katy Perry;
3. the impact of the ***Bad Blood – Swish, Swish*** feud on global album sales between Taylor Swift and Katy Perry;
4. the number of producers and lyricists of the songs involved in the ***Famous*** feud: ***Famous*** for Kanye West, *Look What You Made Me Do* for Taylor Swift;
5. the sources of inspiration and originality of the albums released after the MTV VMA event in 2009: Taylor Swift's album: *Speak Now*, and Kanye West's album: *My Beautiful Dark Twisted Fantasy*;
6. the rating available on Metacritic;
7. the connection between the ***Famous*** feud and the ***Bad Blood – Swish, Swish*** feud, Taylor Swift versus Katy Perry.

Although being presented as a feud of Taylor Swift with Katy Perry, actually this feud is linked to some extent with the *Famous* feud; this *link* is explored in the final part of the chapter.

Chapter five, **FAMOUS** *FEUD:* ***STRATEGIES OF INTERPRETATION AND COMMUNICATION*** is about revealing the mechanisms and strategies of interpretation and communication of the *Famous* feud used by Kanye West, Kim Kardashian, Taylor Swift and the Western mass-media. There is strong evidence in favour of Taylor Swift, however, various journalists came to conclusions about Taylor Swift that shocked me, for example Amy Zimmerman in her article published by *The Daily Beast* wrote about Taylor Swift: 'has been tapping into virginal white victim tropes her entire career.'[507] After reading this article, I decided to explore more news sources to see how Taylor Swift is presented by various journalists. I found over one thousand articles written about the feud; I arranged the articles in two categories: USA and UK with the name of the news agency and a link to the website source. I gathered links about the *Famous* feud from the following news agencies: Slate Magazine, People, Vanity Fair, Cosmopolitan, Glamour Magazine, Elle, Vulture, Marie Claire, Forbes, Ok! UK, Radar Online, GQ, The Sun, Metro, Evening Standard, Telegraph, Daily Star, The Guardian, The Independent, Express, AOL.co.uk, Mirror, Huffington Post, Daily Mail, Pagesix, Billboard, CBS News, Business Insider, Harper's Bazaar, New York Daily, Gossip Cop, Rolling Stone, People, E Online, Lifestyle, The Atlantic, TMZ, W Magazine, Latinpost, Daily Beast, Buzzfeed, Los Angeles Time, US Magazine and TIME.

From over one thousand articles, I managed to read over 500 articles. Simply put: I got bored of the drama, and I could not read anymore. The statements released by Taylor Swift and her management team, regarding her involvement in the *song Famous* released by Kanye West, are also analysed. This text analysis is done with the purpose to expose the inability of journalists and bloggers to follow and understand the logical flow of Taylor Swift's statements, and reach logical conclusions regarding this feud. After the text analysis, I created a table with a list of the negative content written by various journalists (names included) and published in popular and highly acclaimed news agencies in the USA and in the UK (name of the news agencies, title and date of publication is included). In the end, I offered snap-shots with negative representation of Taylor Swift by various journalists through their articles about the *Famous* feud, despite missing in-depth and clear evidence of her true involvement in the creation of the *song Famous*.

In chapter six, **FAMOUS** *REASONS FOR A* **FAMOUS** *FEUD*, I wrote various hypothetical and negative reasons as possible answers to the following question: why *Famous* feud was created and supported for more than 10 years? The hypothetical reasons and answers are based on the information used in this report. Furthermore, the hypothetical and negative reasons can provide a better understanding of the strategies used to fuel voluntarily and involuntarily the feud by Kanye West, Kim Kardashian, Taylor Swift and the Western mass-

---

[507] Amy Zimmerman, 'Taylor Swift's History of Suing Friends, Fans, and Foes—and Now Kimye?', *The Daily Beast*, July 23, 2016, available at: https://www.thedailybeast.com/taylor-swifts-history-of-suing-friends-fans-and-foesand-now-kimye, last accessed: June 26, 2022.

media. Maybe there is a possibility that these hypothetical and negative reasons to have some truth and could help in making a better understanding of the events between Kanye West, Kim Kardashian and Taylor Swift. There are more negative reasons for Kanye West because he started the feud. Also, in this chapter, I found an intriguing pattern that is happening in 2008, 2009 and 2016 and involves Taylor Swift, Kanye West and Beyoncé.

Finally, *WHO IS THE* **FAMOUS** *VICTIM AND WHO IS THE* **FAMOUS** *PERPETRATOR*, I reformulated the purpose of this report, and the conclusions I reached for each point of research.

I. The players and the methodology of the **FAMOUS** feud

I.1 The players of the **FAMOUS** feud

I.1.1 Ye (Kanye West in this report)[508]

Kanye West is Grammy Award-winning (24) rapper, record producer, entrepreneur, fashion designer and one of the greatest and most influential hip hop musicians of all time. Kanye West's views about the music industry, politics, race and personal life received significant media coverage being a frequent source of controversy.[509] In October 2013, Kanye West was officially engaged to Kim Kardashian, a few months later they married in Florence, Italy. On February 19, 2021, Kim Kardashian filed for divorce and was declared legally single on March 2, 2022.[510]

I.1.2 Kim Kardashian[511]

Kim Kardashian is the star of the reality show 'Keeping Up with the Kardashians', model, media personality and businesswoman (creating brands such as KKW Beauty, KKW Fragrance and SKIMS). Kim Kardashian was under the loop of the Western mass-media and news coverage before she met Kanye West (engaged in October 2013), for example her friendship with Paris Hilton. However, the mass-media attention grew higher than before in 2007 due to a video leaked online showing her sexual intercourse with former boyfriend, rapper Ray J.[512] However, the high leap into the Hollywood world was not because of this video, but more to her ability to adapt to fashion trends, the marriage to Kanye West and, mostly, her vision to identify opportunities for women in the USA; currently she is involved in a four-year law apprenticeship that is supervised by the legal nonprofit #cut50 to become a

---

[508] Born Kanye Omari West; June 8, 1977. I decided to keep the former name because the information in this report happened when his name was Kanye West and not the current name, Ye. For more information, read Guardian Staff and Agencies, 'Kanye West officially changes name to Ye', *The Guardian*, October 19, 2021, available at: https://www.theguardian.com/music/2021/oct/19/kanye-west-changes-name-ye, last accessed: June 26, 2022.

[509] Kanye West, *Wikipedia*, available at: https://en.wikipedia.org/wiki/Kanye_West, last accessed: June 26, 2022.

[510] Nancy Dillon, 'Kim Kardashian Declared Legally Single From Kanye West: 'Thank You So Much', *Rolling Stone*, March 2, 2022, available at: https://www.rollingstone.com/music/music-news/kim-kardashian-kanye-west-divorce-final-1315042/, last accessed: June 26, 2022.

[511] Born Kimberly Noel Kardashian (formerly West; born October 21, 1980). I decided to keep the former name because the information in this report happened when her name was Kim Kardashian West and not the current name.

[512] Kim Kardashian, *Wikipedia*, available at: https://en.wikipedia.org/wiki/Kim_Kardashian, last accessed: June 26, 2022.

lawyer with the purpose to improve the prison system in the USA.[513]

I.1.3 Taylor Swift[514]

Taylor Swift is one of the best-selling musicians of all time (more than 200 million records sold worldwide), her concert tours are some of the highest-grossing in history; received 11 Grammy Awards (including three *Album of the Year*, first woman in the history to win this award for a third time), an Emmy Award, 34 American Music Awards (the most for an artist), 29 Billboard Music Awards (the most for a woman), Woman of the Decade and Artist of the Decade. Like Kanye West, Taylor Swift has received critical praise and widespread media coverage; however, for Taylor, the media coverage was also due to being involved in various relationships that did not end well all the time, and a highly number of songs from her catalogue are considered by fans (some songs by Taylor Swift) her side of the story.[515]

I.1.4 '**Famous** Feud': a definition

'Famous feud': is the long-term dispute, conflict, bitter disagreement due to different views about awards for music recognition, events behind recorded phone calls, forced interference in the narrative line of Kanye West (from September 2009 until present), Taylor Swift (from September 2009) and Kim Kardashian (from spring 2016 until present).

The 'Famous feud' concept was coined by Western mass-media starting with February 2016 and the release of the song *Famous* by Kanye West in which he used the following lyrics in reference to Taylor Swift: 'I feel like me and Taylor might still have sex / Why? I made that bitch famous (God damn) / I made that bitch famous.'

In this report, I used 'Famous feud' to describe all the events between Kanye West, Taylor Swift and Kim Kardashian.

I.1.5 Western Mass-Media: a definition

I define 'Western Mass-Media': news agencies / blogs / magazines (online and printed) from English-speaking countries: United States of America (USA), United Kingdom (UK) and Australia; it includes journalists and bloggers from these countries.

In terms of specific 'Western Mass-Media', I included the following news agencies / blogs / magazines (online and printed): Slate Magazine, People, Vanity Fair, Cosmopolitan, Glamour Magazine, Elle, Vulture, Marie Claire, Forbes, Ok! UK, Radar Online, GQ, The Sun, Metro, Evening Standard, Telegraph, Daily Star, The Guardian, The Independent, Express, AOL.co.uk, Mirror, Huffington Post, Daily Mail, Pagesix, Billboard, CBS News, Business Insider, Harper's Bazaar, New York Daily, Gossip

---

[513] Sara Bliss, 'Kim Kardashian Is Becoming A Lawyer: What Her Move Can Teach You About Making A Career Leap', *Forbes,* April 18, 2019, available at: https://www.forbes.com/sites/sarabliss/2019/04/18/kim-kardashian-is-becoming-a-lawyer-what-her-move-can-teach-you-about-making-a-career-leap/, last accessed: June 26, 2022.

[514] Taylor Alison Swift (born December 13, 1989).

[515] Taylor Swift, *Wikipedia*, available at: https://en.wikipedia.org/wiki/Taylor_Swift, last accessed: June 26, 2022.

Cop, Rolling Stone, People, E Online, Lifestyle, The Atlantic, TMZ, W Magazine, Latinpost, Daily Beast, Buzzfeed, Los Angeles Time, US Magazine, TIME.

1.1.5 General public: a definition

All the people, 'especially those not part of a specified group; ordinary people as opposed to officials, experts, politicians'.[516]

I.2 The methodology of the **FAMOUS** feud

In this subchapter I described the research methodology used in this report.

To find the existence of patterns:

- I used key dates of the *Famous* feud (based on the precise date (day, month, year) when the events happened) available in the table with the *Famous* feud timeline; the dates were used to create a figure with a 3D narrative line which shows the dynamic between the players of the *Famous* feud; the creation of one large figure (Figure 8) allowed me to see the whole narrative line of the main players of the feud; the starting point of the patterns is in September 2009 with Kanye West and Taylor Swift; for Kim Kardashian and Taylor Swift: I used information about their feud from June 2016 to March 2020; the narrative line of the feud continue as of today even if the figure does not contain information about the feud after November 2017, respectively after March 2020;

- I linked and compared the events from Kanye West's life with the events from Taylor Swift's life; in other words, what events existed in Taylor Swift's narrative line when Kanye West interfered in her narrative line; I used the same method of research with Kim Kardashian and Taylor Swift;

- surprisingly, Taylor Swift is not the only artist which has to deal with Kanye West's interference in the narrative line, he does it with other people[517] as well.

- the information collected from the credit page is used for the rest of this report without recitation.

The main research methods are:

- four arithmetic operations: addition, division, multiplication and subtraction;
- conversion into percentage;
- the average method;
- interpretation / inference of information.

The Album Release Dates:

---

[516] The Britannica Dictionary, 'general public', available at: https://www.britannica.com/dictionary/general-public#:~:text=the%20general%20public,open%20to%20the%20general%20public.; last accessed: February 25, 2021; Cambridge Dictionary, 'general public', available at: https://dictionary.cambridge.org/dictionary/english/general-public; last accessed: February 25, 2021; Dictionary.com, 'general public', available at: https://www.dictionary.com/browse/the-general-public; last accessed: February 25, 2021.

[517] I used 'people' instead of artists, because I'm not sure if all the information collected and the people involved in it can be added in the 'artist' category.

- I used the information to find patterns that could show how artists are releasing their albums: similarities, differences and patterns (predictable, fixed, changing and surprise);
- I used the findings to see if there is a positive and negative interference in the narrative line of the album release between Kanye West, Taylor Swift and Beyoncé.

Famous Reasons for a Famous Feud:

- I wrote reasons to justify the strategies used to fuel voluntarily and involuntarily the feud by Kanye West, Kim Kardashian, Taylor Swift and the Western mass-media; all the reasons are hypothetical and mostly negative.

The Race of the Samples:

- this is used only for the comparative study between Taylor Swift and Kanye West: I investigated only their albums released in 2010; I shared the information about how many black and white people inspired the artists in creating their music.

The Limits of the Research:

- not all the articles used in this report have the date of the last modification, or a history of modifications made by the data producer; also, not all the articles show a summary of the modifications made to see the difference between the first version and the last version of the article: it could exist a different opinion between readers who accessed the article before the modifications were made, and readers who accessed the last available version;
- all the information in this report should not be used as a source of final truth: only a few research ideas under certain conditions were used to show new information about the background narrative and strategies of interpretation and communication (connections, similarities, differences) used by the players of the feud;
- Metacritic website does not include all the reviews written about the albums, there are reviews with higher and lower grades which are not included and, therefore, the final grade could be higher or lower than what is available on Metacritic and in this report;
- the conclusions advanced are limited, and should be used only in terms of the information used in this report;
- the numbers and the final maths calculations used in figures from chapter ***III.*** *How much Taylor Swift knew about the song* **FAMOUS?** were rounded to the nearest decimal; this happened because I used Figure / Chart option in Excel program by Microsoft, and by default the numbers are rounded to the nearest decimal; from this point of view, the percentage available in this chapter

might have an error between 0,01% – 0.99% of the final percentage; this error depends on the algorithm behind the Excel option to create a figure / chart; also, this error might influence other figures used in this report;

- readers should use 'maybe', 'suggest' and 'allegedly' as strategy of interpretation regarding the content of this report even if the specific keywords ('maybe', 'suggest', 'allegedly') are not found in the text all the time;
- in this report some information was updated with news from 2022, other with news from 2021, and some left as first date used in 2017; for a better clarification, read the footnotes to find out the date when the information was collected and verified for the last time;
- the conclusions of this reports are based on the evidence available at the time of publishing, and based on what I was capable to collect and interpret; however, it is possible that in reality, in the full conversation between Kanye West and Taylor Swift (might be more than 25 minutes as we have today on Youtube), to be more information that can reject, approve, or reject and accept different parts of the findings;
- some examples are used multiple times because it can help to expose several patterns and strategies of interpretation and communication of the players in the feud; this method provides a better view of the threads

of the network of the feud, and the ability of an example to expose several and different faces of the patterns and strategies found and part of the feud; at the same time, the use of the same examples in multiple situations has two negative points: *1.* it might decrease the credibility of the identified patterns of behaviour and strategies of interpretation and communication, and *2.* it might lead to the creation of an exaggerated impression of the number of patterns of behaviour, and strategies of interpretation and communication used (intentionally or unintentionally) by the players;

- it might be a wrong interpretation of the information used, and I could not see or think about it as a wrong way to use it;
- this report explored mostly interpretation / inference / comparison / mathematical / maybe / suggestion / correlations / allegation and cannot provide / assure / guarantee all the time a clear causal evidence and link to support the findings.

II. The **FAMOUS** feud timeline

In this chapter I investigated the timeline of the *Famous* feud in the Western mass-media from three points of view:

a) the key moments of the *Famous* feud,
b) specific information about the events from the *Famous* feud,
c) what is missing from the *Famous* feud timeline.

To achieve this purpose:

1. I created *A general timeline of the Famous feud in the Western mass-media*: UK, USA; Australia is not part of Western mass-media, but I decided to include it as an optional view of the *Famous* feud presented in a country outside what is considered 'Western world';

2. *I analysed the events of the timeline* for each research target (USA, UK, Australia);

3. *I compared the results between the research targets* to create a general view of Western mass-media from three points of view written above.

The general methodology of this chapter is described below:

- I searched on Google.com the keywords: 'taylor swift Kanye west timeline';
- I accessed articles written only in newspapers in the United Kingdom, the United States and Australia;
- I collected the key dates of the *Famous* feud written in the Western mass-media from February 11, 2016 (the beginning of the feud) until November 10, 2017 (on the day Taylor Swift released the album *reputation* considered by the Western mass-media and fans as a response to Kanye West and Kim Kardashian for revealing to the general public an edited part of the telephone conversation between her and Kanye West, but also to Katy Perry (she wrote a song named *Swish, Swish* (2017) which is considered by Taylor Swift and Katy Perry's fans as a possible response to Taylor Swift's 2014 song *Bad Blood*);

- the final results were added in a table and in the form of a figure, and were used as an extra source of information to analyse and compare the events of the feud in the Western mass-media.

II.1 The '**Famous** Feud' Timeline in the Western Mass-Media

II.1.1 United Kingdom

TABLE 1. THE FAMOUS FEUD TIMELINE IN THE UNITED KINGDOM NEWS

NEWS	AUTHOR	TITLE WITH LINK	DATE OF PUBLICATION	LAST ACCESSED
THE INDEPENDENT	Olivia Blair	Taylor Swift and Kanye West Feud: A Brief History of the Pair's Relationship	16/07/2016	24/09/2017
MIRROR	Rebecca Pocklington	Kanye West and Taylor Swift's Feud From The Start: A Timeline Of Their Biggest Rows Over The Years	18/07/2016	24/09/2017
HUFFINGTON POST	Julia Brucculieri	A Comprehensive Outline Of Everything That Just Went Down In The Kimye-Taylor Swift Feud	18/07/2016	24/09/2017
FEMALE FIRST UK	Daniel Falconer	The Taylor Swift and Kanye West Feud (featuring Kim Kardashian) – A Timeline	18/07/2016	24/09/2017
VOGUE UK	Lucy Hutchings	Taylor Swift Vs. Kim and Kanye: A Timeline	18/07/2016	24/09/2017
OK! MAGAZINE UK	Hayley Kadrou	Taylor Swift and Kanye West: A Timeline of Their On-Off Feud	18/07/2016	24/09/2017
Elle UK	Unsah Malik	Taylor Swift Vs. Kimye: A Timeline Of Everything	02/08/2016	24/09/2017
METRO	Emma Kelly	A Brief History Of Taylor Swift And The 'Snakes' – Who Will Be Targeted On Reputation?	24/08/2017	24/09/2017
COSMOPOLITAN	Emma Dibdin	A Timeline of Taylor Swift and Kanye West's Feud	28/08/2017	24/09/2017
POPSUGAR UK	Ryan Roschke	A Timeline Of The Drama Between Kanye West And Taylor Swift	30/08/2017 – updated 3/09/2017	24/09/2017

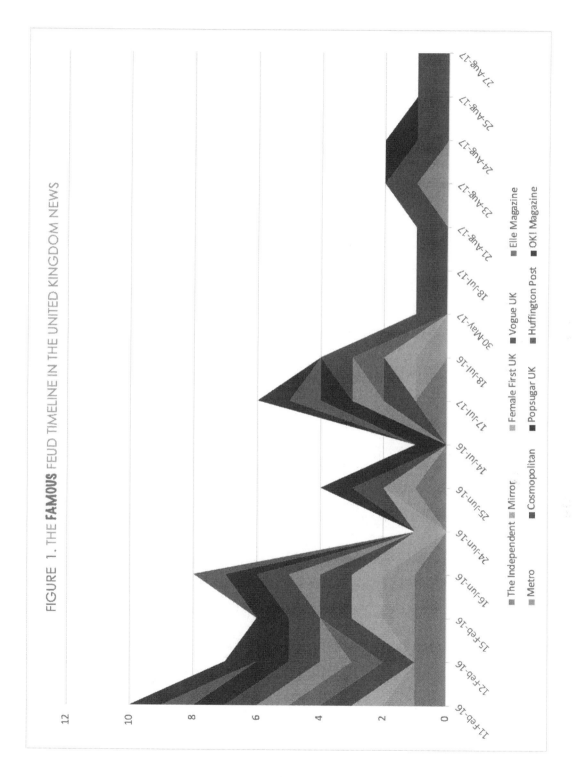

FIGURE 1. THE **FAMOUS** FEUD TIMELINE IN THE UNITED KINGDOM NEWS

II.1.2 United States of America

TABLE 2. THE **FAMOUS** FEUD TIMELINE IN THE UNITED STATES OF AMERICA NEWS

NEWS	AUTHOR	TITLE WITH LINK	DATE OF PUBLICATION	LAST ACCESSED
BILLBOARD	Erin Strecker Adelle Platon	Kanye West & Taylor Swift: A Complete Timeline of Their Relationship	9/08/2015 – updated until July 17, 2016	24/09/2017
CBS NEWS	-	Kanye West vs. Taylor Swift: A Timeline	16/02/2016	24/09/2017
ROLLING STONE	Keith Harris	Taylor Swift vs. Kanye West: A Beef History	16/02/2016 – updated August 2017	24/09/2017
BUZZFEED	Jemima Skelley	The Whole Kanye And Taylor Mess Just Got Even Worse	18/07/2016	24/09/2017
BUZZFEED	Sam Stryker	We Have All The Receipts In The Feud Between Taylor Swift, Kim Kardashian, And Kanye West	18/07/2016	24/09/2017
BUZZFEED	Ellie Bate	The Kim-Kanye-Taylor Feud, Explained For People Who Don't Know What The Hell Is Going On	18/07/2016	24/09/2017
TELL TALES ONLINE	-	Kanye West And Taylor Swift: A Timeline Of Their Feud	24/02/2016 – updated August 2017	24/09/2017
TEEN VOGUE	De Elizabeth	Taylor Swift and Kanye West Feud: A Breakdown of Every Event	18/07/2016	24/09/2017
US MAGAZINE	Nicholas Hautman	Kanye West and Taylor Swift's Tumultuous Relationship: A Timeline of Their Ups and Downs	18/07/2016	24/09/2017
HOLLYWOOD LIFE	Chris Rogers	Taylor Swift Vs. Kimye: Everything You Need To Know About Explosive Feud — Timeline	18/07/2016	24/09/2017
THE ODYSSEY	Jolie Delia	A Timeline Of Every Taylor Swift Feud Ever	18/07/2016	24/09/2017
WIRED	Brian Raftery	Buckle Up: The Kanye West/Taylor Swift Feud Will Continue Until the End of Time	18/07/2016	24/09/2017
ESQUIRE	Matt Miller	A Very Brief Recap of the New Twist in the Kanye West / Taylor Swift Feud	18/07/2016	24/09/2017
NME	Helen Thomas	Taylor Swift and Kanye West: The Good, The Bad, And The Ugly In Their Long-Standing Feud	18/07/2016	24/09/2017
THE WRAP	Rasha Ali	Taylor Swift and Kanye West: A Timeline of the Epic Feud (Photos)	18/07/2016	24/09/2017
THRILLIST	Dan Jackson	Why Kim Kardashian Annihilated Taylor Swift On Snapchat	18/07/2016	24/09/2017
COMPLEX	Complex	A Timeline of Kanye West and Taylor Swift's Feud Over the „Famous' Lyric	18/07/2016	24/09/2017

THE FADER	David Renshaw	A Brief History Of The Kanye West And Taylor Swift 'Famous' Rift	18/07/2016	24/09/2017
MOVIEPILOT	Varia Fedko-Blake	Kimye Vs. Taylor Swift: A Full Rundown Of The Rockiest Relationship In The Business	18/07/2016	24/09/2017
TIME	Cady Lang	A Comprehensive Guide to the Kanye West-Taylor Swift-Kim Kardashian West Feud	19/07/2016 – updated 29/07/2016	24/09/2017
LA TIMES	Christie D'Zurilla	Kanye West vs. Taylor Swift: A Timeline Of The Drama, Which Now Includes Kim Kardashian West	19/07/2016	24/09/2017
HARPER'S BAZAAR	Emma Dibdin	The Complete Timeline of Kanye West and Taylor Swift's Feud	19/07/2016	24/09/2017
CAPITAL FM	-	Watch: A Complete Timeline Of The Taylor Vs Kanye & Kim Beef (Just As It's Getting So Complicated)	19/07/2016	24/09/2017
HFG	copa0077	A Timeline Of Taylor Swift And Kanye West's Feud	31/05/2017	24/09/2017
PEOPLE	Grace Gavilanes	Taylor Swift and Kanye West's Rocky History: A Timeline	Updated 24/08/2017	24/09/2017
PEOPLE	Laura Cohen	A Timeline of the Complicated Relationship Between Taylor Swift and Kim Kardashian West	Posted 25/08/2017	24/09/2017
GLAMOUR MAGAZINE	Carolina Nicolao	Taylor Swift vs Kanye West: A Timeline Of Their Ongoing Feud	25/08/2017	24/09/2017
BUSTLE	Sabienna Bowman	A Timeline of Kanye West & Taylor Swift's Feud To Help You Process 'Look What You Made Me Do'	It does not have a publication date, however at the moment of data collection the publication date was 'a month ago'	24/09/2017
FOX NEWS	-	Taylor Swift's Celebrity Feud History: From Kanye West to Katy Perry, And Beyond	25/08/2017	24/09/2017
POPSUGAR	Ryan Roschke	A Timeline Of The Drama Between Kanye West And Taylor Swift	30/08/2017 – updated 3/09/2017	24/09/2017
NEW YORK DAILY NEWS	-	A Timeline Of The Drama Between Kanye West And Taylor Swift		24/09/2017
WIX	Brenda Santana	Kanye West v. Taylor Swift: A Historical Timeline	No date of publication	24/09/2017
HELLO! MAGAZINE	-	A Timeline Of Taylor Swift, Kanye West and Kim Kardashian's Rocky Relationship	No date of publication	24/09/2017

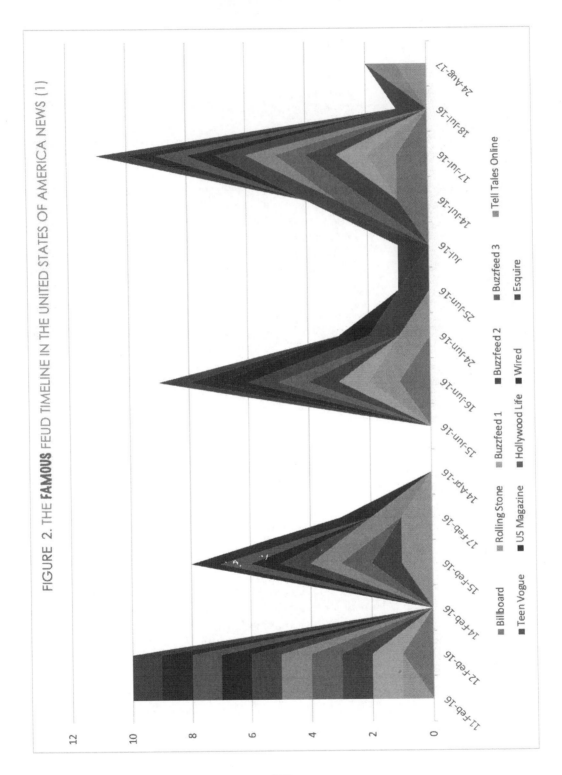

FIGURE 2. THE **FAMOUS** FEUD TIMELINE IN THE UNITED STATES OF AMERICA NEWS (1)

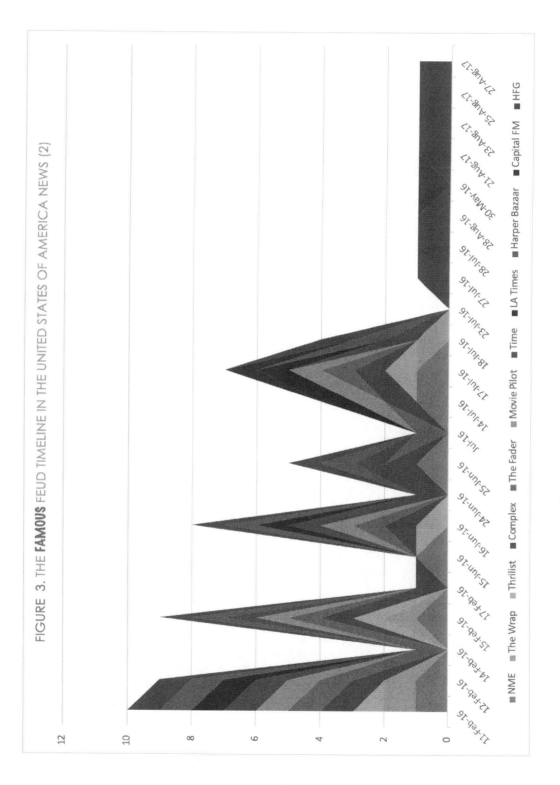

FIGURE 3. THE **FAMOUS** FEUD TIMELINE IN THE UNITED STATES OF AMERICA NEWS (2)

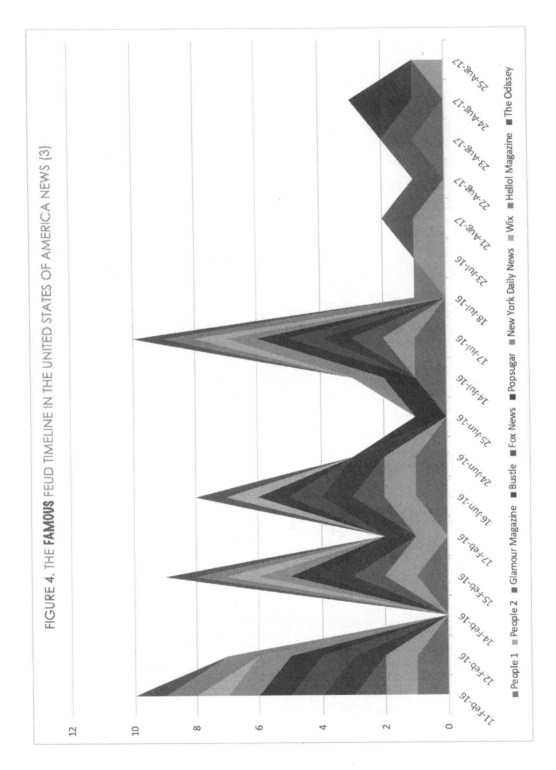

FIGURE 4. THE **FAMOUS** FEUD TIMELINE IN THE UNITED STATES OF AMERICA NEWS (3)

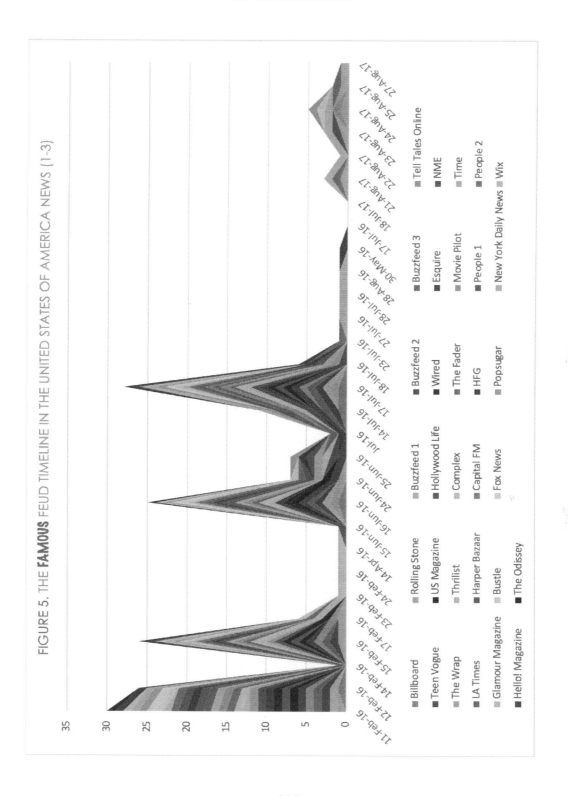

FIGURE 5. THE **FAMOUS** FEUD TIMELINE IN THE UNITED STATES OF AMERICA NEWS (1-3)

II.1.3 Australia

TABLE 3. THE FAMOUS FEUD TIMELINE IN AUSTRALIA NEWS

NEWS SOURCE	AUTHOR	TITLE WITH THE LINK	DATE OF PUBLICATION	LAST ACCESSED
POPSUGAR AUSTRALIA	Ryan Roschke	How Did We Get Here? A Timeline of the Taylor Swift and Kanye West Drama	19/07/2016	24/09/2017
YAHOO AUSTRALIA	Sarah Norton	A Timeline Of The Tumultuous Kanye West vs Taylor Swift Feud	19/07/2016	24/09/2017
VOGUE AUSTRALIA	Vogue Staff	Frenemies: A Complete Timeline Of Kanye West And Taylor Swift's Friendship	28/08/2017	24/09/2017

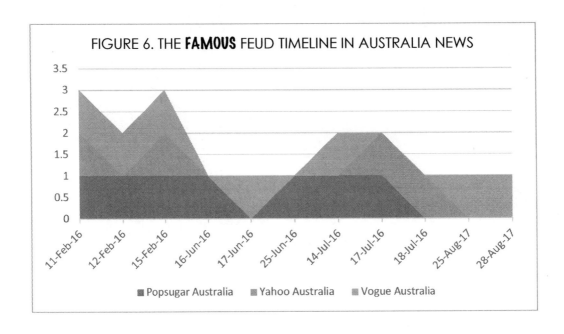

FIGURE 6. THE **FAMOUS** FEUD TIMELINE IN AUSTRALIA NEWS

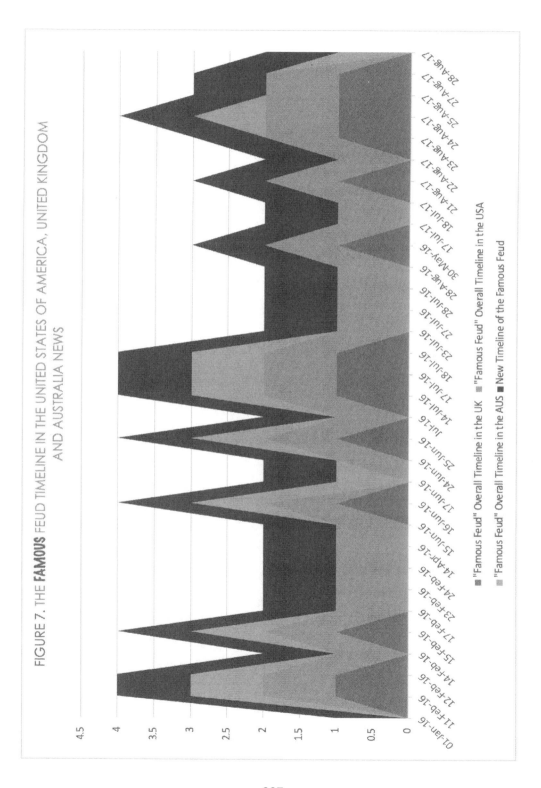

FIGURE 7. THE **FAMOUS** FEUD TIMELINE IN THE UNITED STATES OF AMERICA, UNITED KINGDOM AND AUSTRALIA NEWS

■ "Famous Feud" Overall Timeline in the UK   ■ "Famous Feud" Overall Timeline in the USA

■ "Famous Feud" Overall Timeline in the AUS   ■ New Timeline of the Famous Feud

II.1.4 Western Mass-Media Timeline: Conclusions

The conclusions of the timeline presented by the Western mass-media (general, not specific to each news source) are written for each purpose detailed in the methodology written at the beginning of the chapter.

a. *key moments of the* ***Famous*** *feud:*

- the Western mass-media focused on the important elements of the feud, respectively the confession of Kanye West about the involvement of Taylor Swift in making the song and her negation of the storyline presented by Kanye West(February 2016);
- presented the edited video as evidence of the telephone conversation (July 2016), and wrote that Taylor Swift knew Kanye West had a song that she knew and accepted it, except the word 'bitch' and the line 'I made that bitch famous';

b. *specific information about the events from the* ***Famous*** *feud:*

- each newspaper exposed the two key moments (accusation and proof), but the difference between the news sources is the following: some news sources exposed the timeline in the smallest details (for example *Complex* is the only news source which includes Taylor Swift's response from April 2016 to the *Famous* feud in 2016), or focused on only three key important events such as Thrillist (from February, June, and July 2016);
- among the news sources with a detailed and updated timeline for 2017 I found for example Rolling Stone, Popsugar, Time, Bustle, Glamour Magazine and People;
- some news sources collected and added in the timeline the dates of a feud event when new information was provided by Kanye West, Kim Kardashian or Taylor Swift (for example *Rolling Stone* wrote the release of the video of the *song Famous* on June 24, 2016 when it was published on Tidal; *Time* wrote June 25, 2016 (probably on this date the journalist watched the video), *The Fader* has July 1, 2016 (the release date on Youtube));
- the timeline presented by mass-media in a different format (either all events, the important events, or the association of an event from the feud with the day when the journalists collected the information about an event from the feud) can be confusing for readers, especially for readers who access multiple news sources to verify the information; however, this presentation of information about the players in the feud does not change the finding: high neutrality about the feud;

c. *what is missing from the* ***Famous*** *timeline:*

- Taylor Swift's response from April 2016 (she refused to add more information) to the *Famous* feud in 2016 in the timeline of all the news agency (except Complex);
- the wrong position of the telephone conversation between the artists from January 2016 to July 2016: all the timelines used in this report wrote the telephone conversation from January 2016 in July 2016 because in this month the telephone conversation was made public; for a better view of the dynamic between the artists involved, the conversation should be changed to its original place, January 2016; this aspect is important as it accurately reproduces the order of events, and help to identify the communication strategy of the two artists: who started the feud and who misled first.

II.2 The '**Famous** Feud' Timeline

In this chapter I wrote the events of the *Famous* feud from 2009 to 2017. Because both artists have deleted the public content on their social media pages (Twitter, Instagram, Facebook), readers are sent via footnotes to news sources where evidence is still to be found. This timeline includes only the conversations between Kanye West, Kim Kardashian and Taylor Swift. The conclusions of this section are written after the table and the figure with the *Famous* timeline.

TABLE 4. **FAMOUS** FEUD TIMELINE 2009 - 2020

SEPTEMBER 13, 2009	
TAYLOR SWIFT	**KANYE WEST**
-	While Taylor Swift was giving her acceptance speech for Best Female Video *You Belong with Me* at MTV Video Music Awards, Kanye West got onto the stage and interrupted her; he took her microphone, saying: 'Yo, Taylor, I'm really happy for you and I'mma let you finish, but Beyoncé had one of the best videos of all time! One of the best videos of all time!' (Kanye West was referring to the music video for 'Single Ladies (Put a Ring on It)'. He then handed the microphone back to Taylor Swift. Kanye West posted an apology on his blog.[518]

---

[518] Jayson Rodriguez, 'Kanye West Crashes VMA Stage During Taylor Swift's Award Speech', *MTV*, September 13, 2009, http://www.mtv.com/news/1621389/kanye-west-crashes-vma-stage-during-taylor-swifts-award-speech/, last accessed: October 24, 2017; Daniel Kreps, 'Kanye West Storms the VMAs Stage During Taylor Swift's Speech', *Rolling Stone*, September 13, 2009,

SEPTEMBER 14, 2009

TAYLOR SWIFT	KANYE WEST
The interview with E Online News after the MTV show: 'I was standing on stage and I was really excited because I had just won the award and then I was really excited because Kanye West was on the stage,' […] 'And then I wasn't so excited anymore after that.' The reporter asked Taylor Swift if she has hard feelings about Kanye West. Taylor responded: 'I don't know him and I've never met him.' The reporter continued asking Taylor if she was a fan before the event from the stage. Taylor responded: 'Yeah, It's Kanye West.' The reporter continued asking Taylor if she is still a fan and 'I take a no?' Taylor responded: 'You know I just… I don't know him and I don't want to start anything because I just, you know, I had a great night tonight.'[519]	Kanye West posted a second apology on his blog; he appeared on The Jay Leno Show later that night, where he delivered another apology to Taylor Swift: 'Dealing with the fact that I hurt someone or took anything away, you know, from a talented artist – or from anyone – because I only wanted to help people.' '…My entire life, I've only wanted to do and give something that I felt was right and I immediately knew in this situation that it was wrong.'[520]

SEPTEMBER 15, 2009

TAYLOR SWIFT	KANYE WEST
On September 15, 2009, two days after the outburst, Swift talked about the matter on The View. Asked what she was thinking the moment it happened, she stated: 'Well, I think my overall thought process was something like, 'Wow, I can't believe I won, this is awesome, don't trip and fall, I'm gonna get to thank the fans, this is so cool. Oh, Kanye West is	Following Taylor Swift's appearance on *The View* show, Kanye West contacted her to apologize personally. Taylor Swift accepted his apology.

https://www.rollingstone.com/music/news/kanye-west-storMs.-the-vmas-stage-during-taylor-swifts-speech-20090913?rand=84857, last accessed: October 24, 2017.

[519] Breanne L. Heldman, 'Kanye West Steals Taylor Swift's Thunder…but Not for Long', *E Online*, September 14, 2009, available at: https://www.eonline.com/news/143965/kanye-west-steals-taylor-swift-s-thunder-but-not-for-long, last accessed: October 23, 2017.

[520] Jayson Rodriguez, 'Kanye West Tells Jay Leno He's 'Ashamed' of VMA Outburst', *MTV*, September 14, 2009, http://www.mtv.com/news/1621529/kanye-west-tells-jay-leno-hes-ashamed-of-vma-outburst/, last accessed: October 24, 2017.

here. Cool haircut. What are you doing there?' And then, 'Ouch.' And then, 'I guess I'm not gonna get to thank the fans'[521]

Taylor Swift (after The View) told ABC News Radio: 'Kanye did call me and he was very sincere in his apology, and I accepted that apology.'[522]

SEPTEMBER 4, 2010

TAYLOR SWIFT	KANYE WEST
-	Kanye West wrote a series of tweets addressed to Taylor Swift and VMA incident: 'It starts with this… I'm sorry Taylor.' 'I wrote a song for Taylor Swift that's so beautiful and I want her to have it. If she won't take it then I'll perform it for her.' 'She had nothing to do with my issues with award shows. She had no idea what hit her. She's just a lil girl with dreaMs. like the rest of us.' 'She deserves the apology more than anyone… Who am I to run on stage? I would never ever again in a million years do that. Sorry to let you down. It is distasteful to cut people off as a general rule. What's the point of dressing tastefully if I'm going to act the complete opposite? Yes I was that guy. A 32 year old child. When I woke up from the crazy nightmare I looked in the mirror and said GROW UP KANYE … I take the responsibility for my actions. Beyoncé didn't need that. MTV didn't need that and Taylor and her family friends and fans definitely didn't want or need that.'[523]

SEPTEMBER 12, 2010

[521] Jocelyn Vena, 'Taylor Swift Tells 'The View' Kanye West Hasn't Contacted Her', *MTV*, September 15, 2009, http://www.mtv.com/news/1621550/taylor-swift-tells-the-view-kanye-west-hasnt-contacted-her/, last accessed: October 23, 2017.

[522] Sheila Marikar, 'Taylor Swift: Kanye West Called, 'Was Very Sincere in His Apology', *ABC News*, September 15, 2009, http://abcnews.go.com/Entertainment/FallConcert/taylor-swift-talks-kanye-west-vmas-view/story?id=8580064, last accessed: October 23, 2017.

[523] Monica Herrera, 'Kanye West Bares All on Twitter: 'I Wrote a Song for Taylor Swift',' *Billboard*, September 4, 2010, https://www.billboard.com/articles/news/956495/kanye-west-bares-all-on-twitter-i-wrote-a-song-for-taylor-swift, last accessed: October 24, 2017; Daniel Kreps, 'Kanye Unveils New Track, Offers Song to Taylor Swift', *Rolling Stone*, September 7, 2010, http://www.rollingstone.com/music/news/kanye-unveils-new-track-offers-song-to-taylor-swift-20100907, last accessed: October 24, 2017.

TAYLOR SWIFT	KANYE WEST
During MTV VMAs, Taylor Swift sang 'Innocent', a song widely believed (mass media and fans of Taylor Swift and Kanye West) to be about Kanye West and her forgiveness for what Kanye West did to her a year ago: 'It's alright, just wait and see Your string of lights is still bright to me You're still an innocent Lives change like the weather It's okay, life is a tough crowd 32 and still growin' up now I hope you remember Today is never too late to Be brand new.'[524]	-

OCTOBER 19, 2010

TAYLOR SWIFT	KANYE WEST
-	Appearing on *The Ellen Show*, Kanye West said that following the oversized reaction to 'the Taylor Swift incident,' he had to leave the country, living overseas for a while. *Ellen DeGeneres:* 'Why?' *Kanye West:* 'I feel in some ways I'm a soldier of culture. And I realize no one wants that to be my job. I'll never go onstage again, I'll never sit at an award show again, but will I feel feuded about things that meant something to culture that constantly get denied for years and years and years? I'm sorry, I will. I cannot lie about it in order to sell records.'[525]

OCTOBER 20, 2010

TAYLOR SWIFT	KANYE WEST
-	Kanye West had an interview with *Access Hollywood*: *Kanye West:* 'Why are the last four Albums of the Year: Taylor Swift, Dixie Chicks, Ray Charles and

[524] Taylor Swift, 'Innocent', *Genius*, https://genius.com/Taylor-swift-innocent-lyrics, last accessed: October 24, 2017.
[525] The Ellen Show, 'Kanye West Talks About the Taylor Swift Incident', *Youtube*, October 19, 2010, https://www.youtube.com/watch?v=rej2Ts_TpwQ, last accessed: October 24, 2017.

Herbie Hancock? Like, you know, with all due respect… that's inaccurate.'[526]

NOVEMBER 5, 2010

TAYLOR SWIFT

KANYE WEST
Kanye West had an interview with the radio station KDWB:

Kanye West: 'My moment with Taylor, 12 years old, eighteen year old girl me um cutting her off it show like a lack of compassion with everything she went to to deserve this one moment that shouldn't you know that [inaudible] have 100 magazine covers and sell a million first week, but um um that shouldn't even categorize with the greatest living artists that we have to date even be put in the same category you know it's it's just it's just disrespectful was retarded and I for me you can see the amount of work that we put into this.'

Kanye West: 'It's like, what's so arrogant about that moment? If anything, it's selfless. I'm walking around now with half an arm, trying to sell albums and having to walk in rooms and be afraid of my food getting spat in, like people going 'I lost all total respect for you,' and nobody wants to just sit and look at the reality.'

Kanye West: 'The audacity of it losing anything … I guarantee if it was the other way around, and Taylor Swift was 15, 12, 15 years into the game, and on her 40th video or 50th video, and she made the video of her career, do you think she would have lost to a brand new artist? Hell no!'[527]

NOVEMBER 24, 2010

TAYLOR SWIFT

KANYE WEST
During a secret show slash release party at the Bowery Ballroom in New York City last night, 1.00 am, Kanye West continued his rant by

---

[526] Simon Vozick-Levinson, 'Kanye West says Taylor Swift, Dixie Chicks, Ray Charles didn't deserve Grammys', *Entertainment Weekly*, October 21, 2017, http://www.ew.com/article/2010/10/21/kanye-west-grammys-taylor-swift/, last accessed: October 24, 2017; see here the official interview: *Access Hollywood*, 'Kanye West Talks Grammys, Hopes For Wider Artist Recognition', October 24, 2010, http://www.accesshollywood.com/articles/kanye-west-talks-grammys-hopes-for-wider-artist-recognition-91822/, last accessed: 24 October 2017.
[527] Sneakerhut37, 'New Interview - Kanye West speaks his mind November 5, 2010 (Part 1)', *Youtube*, November 8, 2010, https://www.youtube.com/watch?v=Uq3W-E782kc, last accessed: May 28, 2010.

-

expressing his continued issues with singer Taylor Swift and said: 'Taylor never came to my defense at any interview. ... And rode the waves and rode it and rode it.'[528]

JUNE 11, 2013

TAYLOR SWIFT	KANYE WEST

KANYE WEST

In a *New York Times* interview Kanye West stated about Taylor Swift VMA's moment that he doesn't have any regret about his interruption and that it was a situation where he gave into peer pressure to apologize. When asked if he'd take back the original action or the apology, if given the choice, he answered, 'You know what? I can answer that, but I'm – I'm just -- not afraid, but I know that would be such a distraction. It's such a strong thing, and people have such a strong feeling about it. *My Beautiful Dark Twisted Fantasy* was my long, backhanded apology. You know how people give a backhanded compliment? It was a backhanded apology. It was like, all these raps, all these sonic acrobatics. I was like: 'Let me show you guys what I can do, and please accept me back. You want to have me on your shelves.'[529]

-

FEBRUARY 8, 2015

TAYLOR SWIFT	KANYE WEST
Taylor was at the Grammy Awards and Kanye West was present as well.	Kanye West was present at the Grammy Awards. Kanye West said in a telephone interview with Ryan Seacrest about Taylor Swift: 'She wants to get in the studio and we're definitely going to go in', [...] 'I don't have an elitism about music, I don't discriminate.'[530]

APRIL 29, 2015

TAYLOR SWIFT	KANYE WEST

[528] Jason, 'Kanye Blasts Taylor Swift & Matt Lauer (Video)', *Rap Basement*, November 24, 2010, http://www.rapbasement.com/kanye-west/112410-kanye-west-blasts-taylor-swift-and-matt-lauer-during-secret-show-in-new-york-city-watch-here.html, last accessed: May 28, 2010; *Post Staff Report*, 'Rapper Kanye West disses Taylor Swift ... again: Report', November 24, 2010, https://nypost.com/2010/11/24/rapper-kanye-west-disses-taylor-swift-again-report/, last accessed: May 28, 2010; *US Weekly Staff*, 'Kanye West SlaTaylor Swift Again', November 24, 2010, https://www.usmagazine.com/entertainment/news/kanye-west-slaMs.-taylor-swift-again-20102411/, last accessed: May 28, 2010.

[529] Jon Caramanica, 'Behind Kanye's Mask', *New York Times*, June 11, 2013, https://www.nytimes.com/2013/06/16/arts/music/kanye-west-talks-about-his-career-and-album-yeezus.html?_r=0, last accessed: May 28, 2018.

[530] On Air with Ryan Seacrest, 'Kanye West Explains Grammys Stunt, Plans to Work With Taylor Swift', *Youtube*, February 11, 2015, https://www.youtube.com/watch?v=Qg1hZ329eCU, last accessed: October 23, 2017.

In an interview with *Entertainment Tonight*, Cameron Mathison asked Taylor Swift about the rumoured collaboration between her and Kanye West. Taylor Swift answered: 'He has said that… We're never been in the studio together, but he's got a lot of amazing ideas, he's one of those people who's just like idea, idea, idea, like what you think of this, what you think of that, he's very creative and like I've think we've talked about it but we've also about so many other things, I think I completely respect his vision as a producer, so that's all I know now, I have no idea how the next album is gonna be though.'[531]

AUGUST 11, 2015

TAYLOR SWIFT	KANYE WEST
During a cover interview with *Vanity Fair*, Taylor Swift said about Kanye West:	
'I feel like I wasn't ready to be friends with him until I felt like he had some sort of respect for me, and he wasn't ready to be friends with me until he had some sort of respect for me – so it was the same issue, and we both reached the same place at the same time' […] And then Kanye and I both reached a place where he would say really nice things about my music and what I've accomplished, and I could ask him how his kid doing. … We haven't planned [a collaboration, added by the author] … But hey, I like him as a person. And that's a really good, nice first step, a nice place for us to be.'[532]	

BEFORE THE MTV VMA AWARDS AUGUST 2015

TAYLOR SWIFT	KANYE WEST
In an interview for Rolling Stone, September 2019, Taylor Swift said:	
'But the 2015 VMAs come around. He's getting the Vanguard Award. He called me up beforehand – I didn't illegally record it, so I can't play it for you.	

[531] Entertainment Tonight, 'Taylor Swift on Rumored Kanye West Collaboration: 'He's Got a Lot of Amazing Ideas', *Youtube*, April 29, 2015, https://www.youtube.com/watch?v=WsqOI5ZGFZs, last accessed: October 23, 2017. Bruna Nessif, 'Is This Taylor Swift and Kanye West Collaboration Happening or What?! Watch Now', *EOnline*, April 30, 2015, https://www.eonline.com/news/652354/is-this-taylor-swift-and-kanye-west-collaboration-happening-or-what-watch-now, last accessed: October 23, 2017.
[532] Josh Duboff, 'Taylor Swift: Apple Crusader, #GirlSquad Captain, and the Most Influential 25-Year-Old in America', *Vanity Fair*, August 11, 2015, https://www.vanityfair.com/style/2015/08/taylor-swift-cover-mario-testino-apple-music, last accessed: October 23, 2017.

But he called me up, maybe a week or so before the event, and we had maybe over an hourlong conversation, and he's like, 'I really, really would like for you to present this Vanguard Award to me, this would mean so much to me,' and went into all the reasons why it means so much, because he can be so sweet. He can be the sweetest. And I was so stoked that he asked me that.'[533]

-

AUGUST 30, 2015

TAYLOR SWIFT	KANYE WEST
Taylor Swift presented the Video Vanguard Award for Kanye West and invoked the original incident in her speech: 'I first met Kanye West six years ago — at this show, actually! [..] *The College Dropout* was the very first album my brother and I bought on iTunes when I was 12 years old…I've been a fan of his for as long as I can remember because Kanye defines what it means to be a creative force in music, fashion and, well, life. So, I guess I have to say to all the other winners tonight: I'm really happy for you, and imma let you finish, but Kanye West has had one of the greatest careers of all time.'[534] After the show, Kanye West sent to Taylor Swift a huge flower arrangement.	During the acceptance speech, Kanye West said: 'First of all, thank you Taylor for being so gracious and giving me this award this evening. I often think back to the first day I met you, also. I think about when I'm in the grocery store with my daughter and I have a really great conversation about fresh juice and at the end, they say, 'Oh, you're not that bad after all. […] You know how many times MTV ran that footage again? Because it got them more ratings. You know how many times they announced Taylor was going to give me the award. Because it got them more ratings.'[535]

JANUARY 2016

TAYLOR SWIFT	KANYE WEST

Kanye West calls Taylor Swift.

Kanye West: '[To someone outside room] Lock that door and then stand on the other side of it until I knock for you … No, lock the doors up.'

---

[533] Brian Hiatt, 'The Rolling Stone Interview Taylor Swift', *Rolling Stone*, September 18, 2019, available at: https://www.rollingstone.com/music/music-features/taylor-swift-rolling-stone-interview-880794/, last accessed: October 21, 2019.

[534] Cady Lang, 'A Comprehensive Guide to the Kanye West-Taylor Swift-Kim Kardashian West Feud', *Time*, July 19, 2016, updated: July 29, 2016, https://time.com/4411055/kanye-west-taylor-swift-kim-kardashian-feud/, last accessed: October 23, 2017.

[535] Rolling Stone, 'Read Kanye West's Blunt, Poignant VMA Video Vanguard Award Speech', August 31, 2015, https://www.rollingstone.com/music/music-news/read-kanye-wests-blunt-poignant-vma-video-vanguard-award-speech-42495/, last accessed: October 23, 2017.

Kanye West: '[Resuming a conversation in progress with Swift, her end initially unintelligible.] …old school s—, yeah. I'm doing great. I feel so awesome about the music. The album's coming out February 11, I'm doing the fashion show February 11 at Madison Square Garden, we're dropping the album February 12th that morning. It's like…'

Taylor Swift: '[Inaudible.]'

Kanye West: 'Oh, thank you so, so much. Yeah. It feels good. It feels like real Ye, Apple, Steve Jobs-type music. So my next single, I wanted you to tweet it. It's a good Friday to drop it. It's a good Friday song. So that's why I'm calling you, that I wanted you to put the song out.'

Taylor Swift: 'Oh, wow. Like, um, what would people… I guess it would just be, people would be like, 'Whyyyy is this happening?' They would think I had something to do with it, probably.'

Kanye West: 'Well, the reason why it will be happening is because it has a very controversial line at the beginning of the song about you.'

Taylor Swift: '[Apprehensively.] What does it say?'

Kanye West: 'So it says… and the song is so, so dope. And I've literally sat with my wife, with my whole management team, with everything and tried to rework this line. I've thought about this line for eight months. I've had this line and I've tried to rework it every which way. And the original way that I thought about it is the best way, but it's the most controversial way. So it's gonna go Eminem a little bit, so can you brace yourself for a second?'

Taylor Swift: '[Sounding resigned.] Yeah.'

Kanye West: 'Okay. All right. Wait a second, you sound sad.'

Taylor Swift: 'Well, is it gonna be mean?'

Kanye West: 'No, I don't think it's mean.'

Taylor Swift: 'Okay, then, let me hear it.'

Kanye West: 'Okay. It says, um,… and the funny thing is, when I first played it and my wife heard it, she was like, 'Huh? What? That's too crazy,' blah, blah, blah. And then like when Ninja from Die Atwoord heard it, he was like, 'Oh my God, this is the craziest s—. This is why I love Kanye,' blah, blah, blah, that kind of thing. And now it's like my wife's favourite f—ing line. I just wanted to give you some premise of that. Right?'

Taylor Swift: 'Okay.'

Kanye West: 'So it says 'To all my Southside [N-word] that know me best, I feel like Taylor Swift might owe me sex.'

Taylor Swift: '[Laughs, relieved.] That's not mean.'

Kanye West: 'Okay. Well, this is the thing where I'm calling you, because you're got an army. You own a country of mother–ing 2 billion people, basically, that if you felt that it's funny and cool and like hip-hop, and felt like just 'The College Dropout' and the artist like Ye that you love, then I think that people would be like way into it. And that's why I think it's super-genius to have you be the one that says, 'Oh, I like this song a lot. Like, yeah, whatever, this is cool, whatever.' It's like, I got like s– on my album where I'm like, 'I bet me and Ray J would be friends, if we ain't love the same bitch'.'

Taylor Swift: 'Oh my God! I mean, I need to think about it, because you know, when you hear something for the first time, you just need to think about it. Because it is absolutely crazy. I'm glad it's not mean, though. It doesn't feel mean. But oh my God, the buildup you gave it, I thought it was going to be like, 'That stupid, dumb bitch.' But it's not. So I don't know. I mean, the launch thing, I think it would be kind of confusing to people. But I definitely like… I definitely think that when I'm asked about it, of course I'll be like, 'Yeah, I love that. I think it's hilarious.' But, um, I need to think about it.'

Kanye West: 'You don't have to do the launching and tweet. That was just an extra idea I had. But if you think that that's cool, then it's cool. If not… I mean, we are launching the s– like on just good Fridays on SoundCloud, on the site, s– like that.'

Taylor Swift: 'You know, the thing about me is, anything that I do becomes like a feminist think-piece. And if I launch it, they're going to be like, wow, like, they'll just turn into something that… I think if I launch it, honestly, I think it'll be less cool. Because I think if I launch it, it adds this level of criticism. Because having that many followers and having that many eyeballs on me right now, people are just looking for me to do something dumb or stupid or lame. And I don't know. I kind of feel like people would try to make it negative if it came from me, do you know what I mean? I think I'm very self-aware about where I am, and I feel like right now I'm like this close to overexposure.'

Kanye West: 'Oh. Well, this one, I think this is a really cool thing to have.'

Taylor Swift: 'I know, I mean, it's like a compliment, kind of. [Chuckles.]'

Kanye West: 'I have this line where I said… And my wife really didn't like this one, because we tried to make it nicer. So I say 'For all my Southside [N-word] that know me best, I feel like me and Taylor might still have sex.' And my wife was really not with that one. She was way more into the 'She owes you sex.' But then the 'owe' part was like the feminist group-type shit that I was like, ahhhhh.'

Taylor Swift: 'That's the part that I was kind of… I mean, they 're both really edgy, but that's the only thing about that line is that it's like, then the feminists are going to come out. But I mean, you don't give a f–. So…'

Kanye West: 'Yeah, basically. Well, what I give a f— about is just you as a person, as a friend….'

Taylor Swift: 'That's sweet.'

Kanye West: 'I want things that make you feel good. I don't want to do rap that makes people feel bad. Like of course, like I'm mad at Nike, so people think, 'Oh, he's a bully. He ran on stage with Taylor. He's bullying Nike now,' this $50 billion company.'

Taylor Swift: 'Why are people saying you're bullying Nike?'

Kanye West: 'Because on 'Facts,' like, I say, 'Yeezy, Yeezy, Yeezy, they line up for days / Nike out here bad, they can't give s— away.'

Taylor Swift: 'Yeah, yeah, yeah. I mean, that's just what you do, though. I mean, I wouldn't say that it's possible to bully a company like Nike. But I mean… um, yeah, I mean, go with whatever line you think is better. It's obviously very tongue-in-cheek either way. And I really appreciate you telling me about it. That's really nice.'

Kanye West: 'Oh, yeah. I just had a responsibility to you as a friend. I mean, thanks for being like so cool about it.'

Taylor Swift: 'Thanks. Yeah, I really appreciate it. The heads-up is so nice. You'd be surprised how many people just do things without even asking or seeing if I'd be okay with it, and I just really appreciate it. I never would have expected you to tell me about a line in one of your songs. That's really nice that you did.'

Kanye West: 'You mean like unexpected s— like you taking the time to give someone a really, really valuable award and then they completely run for president right afterwards? Like unexpected in that kind of way? [Laughs.] [A few months earlier, at the 2015 MTV Awards, Swift presented West with his lifetime achievement award, followed by a rambling speech in which he acknowledged he had smoked pot beforehand and was going to run for president.]'

Taylor Swift: '[Laughs.] We have not talked about what happened.'

Kanye West: 'I just thought that was wavy. It was vibey. The funny thing is, I thought about the weed and the president, both of those things I thought about in the shower the day before and just started laughing like crazy. I was like, I gotta say that I had just smoked some weed and then say I'm gonna run for president… So those are my bases of… I knew I wanted to say the thing about going to like the Dodgers game with my daughter and like getting booed and that being scary, and I knew I wanted to say like me changing and thinking about people more since I had a daughter. And then I wanted to say the weed thing. And then I wanted to say the president thing. And everything else was just like off the cuff.'

Taylor Swift: 'Oh my God. It was definitely like it stole the show… And then the flowers that you sent me. I Instagrammed a picture of them and it's the most Instagram likes I've ever gotten. It was like 2.7 million likes on that picture of the flowers you sent me. Crazy.'

Kanye West: 'It's some connection or something that I think is really important about that moment when we met on stage. There's something that I think is really important about that, and where humanity is going, or now where me and Kim are, and having a family and just everything, the way things are landing. So it's always… Relationships are more important than punchlines, you know.'

Taylor Swift: 'Yeah, I mean, I don't think anybody would listen to that and be like, 'Oh, that's a real diss' – like, 'She must be crying about that line.' And I think because of how crazy and strange and fateful the way we met was, I think we have to pick our moments to do stuff together and make sure it's only really cool stuff.'

Kanye West: 'Yeah, exactly. We can't have it like be somebody else's idea that gets in front and they're like… Because if you're like a really true, creative, visceral, vibey type person, it's probably hard for you to work at a corporation. So how can you give a creative ideas and you're working in a house of non-creativity? It's like this weird… So whenever we talk directly… Okay, now what if later in the song I was also to have said, uh… 'I made her famous'? Is that a…'

Taylor Swift: '[Apprehensively.] Did you say that?'

Kanye West: 'Yes, it might've happened. [Laughs.]'

Taylor Swift: 'Well, what am I going to do about it?'

Kanye West: 'Uh, like, do the hair flip?'

Taylor Swift: 'Yeah. I mean… Um… It's just kind of like, whatever, at this point. But I mean, you've got to tell the story the way that it happened to you and the way that you've experienced it. Like, you honestly didn't know who I was before that. Like, it doesn't matter if I sold 7 million of that album ['Fearless'] before you did that, which is what happened. You didn't know who I was before that. It's fine. But, um, yeah. I can't wait to hear it.'

Kanye West: 'I mean, it's fun. It's definitely… You're ready to trend. That's all I can say.'

Taylor Swift: 'Uh, what's the song called?'

Kanye West: 'Uh, it might be called 'Hood Famous.'

Taylor Swift: 'Oh, cool. Is it going to be like a single-single, or is it going to be a SoundCloud release? What are you doing?'

Kanye West: 'Oh, this one right here is like f—ing Song of the Year-type territory.'

Taylor Swift: 'Oh my God. Amazing. That's crazy. Oh my God. Speaking of Song of the Year, are you going to the Grammys?'

Kanye West: 'Uh, you know what? I was thinking to not do it. But I think that this song… You know what? I'm going to send you the song and send you the exact wording and everything about it, right? And then we could sit and talk through it. But if the song goes and f—ing just…'

'[The video goes out momentarily, as the filmer's phone battery apparently dies. When it resumes, they are still discussing whether West might attend the Grammys.]'

Taylor Swift: '… they just look at us and go… [Unintelligible] …Even if we've made an incredible achievement, it's harder for people to write down our names for some reason. That's just human nature. It's envy. It's asking people in our industry to vote for the people who are already killing it.'

Kanye West: 'Yeah. It's like so many people wanted Meek Mills (sic) to win because Drake was just killing it for so long, and they were just like, 'We just need, like, Meek Mills (sic) to, like…' But I think, you know, okay… So that has my mind going through a lot of places to problem-solve. I was talking to Ben Horowitz – do you know this guy? He's a VC. Ben Horowitz out of San Fran. But he's down with that.'

Taylor Swift: 'I know that name. I don't know him.'

Kanye West: 'It's just like the San Fran clique, you know, that type of thing, like he stays down the street from Mark Zuckerberg and s— like that. So I was talking to him and I was like, 'Bro'… Like me, I'm in personal debt. I'm in debt by a good like 20, 30 million, ever since the fashion, and still have not made it out of it. So that's part of the reason why I had to go to Roc Nation and the touring deals evolved, and it allowed the whole town to try to feel like they could control Kanye or even talk to me like I'm regular or have agents do it, but they saw they couldn't. It's like even in debt, he moves around like he's like a billionaire. I'm like, yeah, I'm a cultural trillionaire! I might have financial debts. So I told Ben Horowitz, I was like, 'You guys, you, Mark Zuckerberg or whoever, Tim Cook, you guys have to clean that up.' So I'm sending Ben Horowitz my current balance. That means that I'm not up 50, not up 100 million, not up 200 million, not up 300 million. No —negative 20 million, currently. I, Kanye West, the guy who created the genre of music that is the Weeknd, that is Drake – the guy who created… Every single person that makes music right now, favourite album is 'The College Dropout.' Every single person that makes music. But I'm rich enough… Like, I went into debt to my wife by 6 million working on a f—ing house, less than like a few months ago, and I was able to pay her back before Christmas and s— like that. So, you know, when I talk about Nike, the idea that they wouldn't give me a percentage, that I could make something that was so tangible, when Drake was just rapping me into the motherf—ing trashcan, that I could have something that was tangible that showed my creativity and expressed myself, that also could be a business that I could have a five-times multiple on and actually be able to sell it for like a hundred million, 200 million or a billion dollars, that was very serious. Every conversation, every time I'd scream at Charlemagne (Tha God) or scream at (radio host) Sway, that was really, really, really serious. And it also was with my family. I felt like, look, if I'm just the angry black guy with some cool red shoes from Nike five years ago, I was going to be visiting my daughter, as opposed to be living with her. It would've been like, enough is enough. It wouldn't have been cool anymore, because it would have been a group of people, including my wife, that all had at least like 500, 400 million in their account. And then you get the angry black man at the party talking about 'I'm the one that put Kim in the dress! I'm the one that did this!' But it never realized itself. So that's one of the things I just talked to.Ben... And I talk about it on the album. Talk about personal debt and s–. Just the idea like, 'Oh s–, this dude with this f–ing Maybach that makes f–ing $50 million a tour still hasn't lined it up or came out of the point when AEG and Live Nation wouldn't give him a deal.' The debt started after 'Watch the Throne' [West's joint album with Jay-Z], because I got no deal. But I still was doing my creative projects on my own, shooting a film, doing a fashion show, just trying to be very Disney, be very visceral, be creative. And...'

Taylor Swift: 'I mean, I'm sure you've thought about this up and down, but I mean, is there a way to monetize these in a way that you thought would still feel authentic but make them into a multibillion dollar company?'

Kanye West: 'Well, that's what we're going to do. That's what we're in the plans of. I'm 100% going to be like a multi, multi, multi-billionaire. I think it's fun that I can like be like Charlie Sheen and be like, 'Hey, like, I got AIDS.' You know, like.... To me, I told Drake that the other night. I was like, 'Yo, Drake, I'm in personal debt.' And for me to tell Drake, the f–ing number one bachelor in the world that can f–ing rap anybody into a trashcan, that lives four blocks down the street from my wife and like basically f–s all of her friends, that I'm in personal debt, it's such a like putting down the sword or putting down the hand or opening, showing the hand. That I don't have my poker face on with any of you guys. I'm just me. I'm just a creative. You know, everything I did, even when it was mistimed, whatever it might've been from a... It's always like from a good place, and I know that I'll overcome it and I know that the world will overcome it. Because, like, I'm going to change the world. I'm going to make it... I'm gonna make people's lives better on some post-Steve Jobs, Howard Hughes-type shit. Like, I'm going to do things with education. I'm going to do things that help to calm down murders in Chicago or across the globe. Things that help to calm down police brutality, to equalize the wealth amidst the class system. Because there's a bunch of classes of wealthy people that hate Obama because he's more social and he wants the people who don't have anything to have everything. And in my little way, by learning how to design, design is something that's only given to the rich currently. The exact color palette that Hermes uses versus the color palette that Forever 21 uses — a color palette is extremely important. Color is important. You know, the knowledge of proportions... you know, the size of our house versus the size of someone else's houses, and just the dynamics of that proportion. Like, I don't want this conversation to go too, too long, but I wanted to give you a bit of where I'm at and the perspective that I'm at and the way... the fact that I am the microprocessor of our culture. Meaning like, I can figure out how to give Rihanna a Mary J. Blige-type album. I can figure out how to get the fashion world to accept my wife, and thus the whole family. I can figure out a lot of impossible... I can figure out how to make something that you're wearing to the airport, five years after the entire globe was like, 'Hang that [N-word] alive and f– him, and let's watch him die, slowly, publicly.' So, it's a lot. I figured that out for myself, so it's a lot of s– that we collectively, with the power that you have and your fans, the power my wife has, the power that I have, that we can do to really make it where it's not just the rich getting richer, but… You know, make it not just a f—ing charity, not singing for Africa, but change things in a way that people can experience s— themselves, a piece of the good life. You know?'

Taylor Swift: 'Yeah. I mean, they're amazing ideas and amazing concepts, and I definitely would love to talk to you more about it. I know you have to do something right now, but I love that that's where you're headed. And it's been like that. I mean, when we went to dinner, there were the rumblings of those ideas. I like that you're always thinking outward. And over the last six, seven, eight years, however long it's been since that happened, I haven't always liked you, but I've always respected you. And I think that's what you're saying when you say like, you know, 'I might be in debt, but I can make these things happen, and I have the ideas to do it, and I can create these things or these concepts.' Like, I'm always going to respect you. And I'm really glad that you had the respect to call me and tell me that as a friend about the song, and it's a really cool thing to do, and a really good show of friendship. So thank you.'

Kanye West: 'Oh, thank you too.'

Taylor Swift: 'And you know, if people ask me about it, look, I think it would be great for me to be like, 'Look, he called me and told me the line before it came out. Like, the joke's on you guys - we're fine.'

Kanye West: 'Yeah. Yeah. Okay. I think that's pretty much the switch right there.'

Taylor Swift: 'Yeah. Like, you guys want to call this a feud, you want to call this throwing shade, but you know, right after the song comes out, I'm gonna be on a Grammy red carpet, and they're gonna ask me about it and I'll be like, 'He called me and sent me the song before it came out.' So I think we're good.'

Kanye West: 'Okay. I'm gonna go lay this verse, and I'm gonna send it to you right now.'

Taylor Swift: '[Taken aback.] Oh, you just… you haven't recorded it yet?'

Kanye West: 'I recorded it. I'm nuancing the lines – like the last version of it says, 'Me and Taylor might still have sex.' And then my wife was like, 'That doesn't sound as hard!'

Taylor Swift: 'Well, I mean, she's saying that honestly because she's your wife, and like, um… So I think whatever one you think is actually better. I mean, obviously do what's best for your relationship, too. I think 'owes me sex,' it says different things. It says… 'Owes me sex' means like 'Look, I made her what she is. She actually owes me.' Which is going to split people, because people who like me are going to be like, 'She doesn't owe him s–.' But then people who like thought it was bad-ass and crazy and awesome that you're so outspoken are going to be like, 'Yeah, she does. It made her famous.' So it's more provocative to say 'still have sex,' because no one would see that coming. They're both crazy. Do what you want. They're both going to get every single headline in the world. 'Owes me sex' is a little bit more like throwing shade, and the other one's more flirtatious. It just depends on what you want to accomplish with it.'

Kanye West: 'Yeah, I feel like with my wife, that she probably didn't like the 'might still have sex' because it would be like, what if she was on a TV show and said 'Me and Tom Brady might still have sex' or something?'

Taylor Swift: 'You have to protect your relationship. Do what's best. You just had a kid. You're in the best place of your life. I wouldn't ever advise you to f— with that. Just pick whatever… It's cause and effect. One is gonna make people feel a certain way, and it's gonna be a slightly different emotion for the other. But it's not… It doesn't matter to me. There's not one that hurts my feelings and the other doesn't.'

Kanye West: 'Yeah. It's just, when I'm pointing this gun, what I tried to do differently than two years ago, is like when I shoot a gun, I try to point it away from my face. So one is a little bit more flirtatious and easier… I think, so really, that means the conversation is really: One is like a little bit better for the public and a little bit less good for the relationship. One is a little bit worse for the public and better for the relationship.'

Taylor Swift: 'Yeah. I can hear it. But it's your goals, really. I mean, you always just go with your gut — obviously. But, um, amazing. Send it to me. I'm excited.'

Kanye West: 'All right, cool. Thanks so much.'

Taylor Swift: 'Awesome. I'll talk to you later.'

Kany West: 'All right, cool. Peace. Bye.'

Kanye West: '[To cameraman.] We had to get that on the record.'

Cameraman: '[About interruption.] I'm sorry. The battery on this thing died.'

Kanye West: 'It's just when it dies… You get some s— like Kanye talking to Taylor Swift explaining that line? There's gotta be three cameras on that one. We can't miss one element.'[536]

FEBRUARY 11, 2016

TAYLOR SWIFT	KANYE WEST
-	On February 11, 2016 Kanye West debuted his musical album *The Life of Pablo* at his Yeezy Season 3 show at Madison Square Garden, New York. In one of his songs, 'Famous,' he raps 'I feel like me and Taylor might still have sex /

[536] Pandoras Box, 'Leaked 2016 Kanye West / Taylor Swift Conversation re: Famous', *Youtube*, March 21, 2020, https://www.youtube.com/watch?v=-OjyJD3pxD4, last accessed: July 1, 2021.

	Why? I made that bitch famous (God damn) / I made that bitch famous.'

FEBRUARY 12, 2016

TAYLOR SWIFT	KANYE WEST
	Kanye West wrote a few tweets (now deleted) on his Twitter account:
	'I did not diss Taylor Swift and I've never dissed her… — KANYE WEST (@kanyewest) February 12, 2016'
	'First thing is I'm an artist and as an artist I will express how I feel with no censorship — KANYE WEST (@kanyewest) February 12, 2016'
Taylor Swift camp replied:	'2nd thing I asked my wife for her blessings and she was cool with it — KANYE WEST (@kanyewest) February 12, 2016'
'Kanye did not call for approval, but to ask Taylor to release his single „Famous' on her Twitter account. She declined and cautioned him about releasing a song with such a strong misogynistic message. Taylor was never made aware of the actual lyric, „I made that bitch famous.'[537]	'3rd thing I called Taylor and had a hour long convo with her about the line and she thought it was funny and gave her blessings — KANYE WEST (@kanyewest) February 12, 2016'
	'4th Bitch is an endearing term in hip hop like the word Nigga — KANYE WEST (@kanyewest) February 12, 2016'
	'5th thing I'm not even gone take credit for the idea… it's actually something Taylor came up with … — KANYE WEST (@kanyewest) February 12, 2016'
	'I can't be mad at Kanye because he made me famous! #FACTS

---

[537] Melody Chiu, Karen Mizoguchi, 'Kanye West Did Not Call Taylor Swift for Approval Over 'B----' Lyric, Singer Cautioned Him Against Releasing 'Strong Misogynistic Message' Rep Says', *People*, February 12, 2016, https://people.com/celebrity/kanye-west-did-not-call-taylor-swift-for-approval-over-bitch-lyric/, last accessed: October 23, 2017.

– KANYE WEST (@kanyewest) February 12, 2016'

'6th Stop trying to demonize real artist
Stop trying to compromise art
– KANYE WEST (@kanyewest) February 12, 2016'

'That's why music is so fucking watered down right now I miss that DMX feeling
– KANYE WEST (@kanyewest) February 12, 2016'

'7th I miss that feeling so that's what I want to help restore
– KANYE WEST (@kanyewest) February 12, 2016'

'8th They want to control us with money and perception and mute the culture
– KANYE WEST (@kanyewest) February 12, 2016.'

FEBRUARY 14, 2016

TAYLOR SWIFT	KANYE WEST
-	1. Kanye West said in the backstage of Saturday Night Live on 14 February:

'Look at that shit, they took my fucking stage off a 'SNL' without asking me. Now I'm bummed. That and Taylor Swift, fake ass.'

'Now I ain't gonna do this, we're breaking the motherfucking internet.' 'I went through six years of this fucking shit. Let's get to it, bro. Let's get to it, bro.'

'Are they fucking crazy, bro? By 50 percent. Stanley Kubrick, Apostle Paul, Picasso... fucking Picasso and Escobar. By 50 percent, more influential than any other human being.'

	'Don't fuck with me. Don't fuck with me. Don't fuck with me. By 50 percent, dead or alive, by 50 percent for the next thousand years. Stanley Kubrick. Ye.'[538]
	2. 'The Life of Pablo' and *song Famous* are officially released via Tidal. The song would arrive on Spotify and Apple Music on April 1. 'Famous' is the lead single of his album.[539]

FEBRUARY 15, 2016

TAYLOR SWIFT	KANYE WEST
While accepting Album of the Year award at the GRAMMYs, Taylor Swift addressed what is believed to be about the infamous Kanye West lyrics about her: 'I want to thank the fans for the last 10 years, and the recording academy for giving us this unbelievable honor. I want to thank all of the collaborators that you see on this stage. Mostly, I want to thank my co-executive producer Max Martin, who has deserved to be up here for 25 years. And as the first woman to win album of the year at the Grammy's twice, I want to say to all the young women out there, there are going to be people along the way who, will try to undercut your success or take credit for your accomplishments or your fame. But if you just focus on the work and you don't let those people sidetrack you, someday when you get where you're going, you will know it was you and the people who love you who put you there, and that will be the greatest feeling in the world. Thank you for this moment.'[540]	-

FEBRUARY 17, 2016

TAYLOR SWIFT	KANYE WEST

[538] ABC News, 'Kanye West 'SNL' Meltdown Leaked', *Youtube*, February 18, 2016, https://www.youtube.com/watch?v=cN4Gnzo9z4c, last accessed: October 23, 2017.

[539] Jazz Monroe, 'Kanye West's The Life of Pablo Is Out Now', *Pitchfork*, February 14, 2016, https://pitchfork.com/news/63408-kanye-wests-the-life-of-pablo-is-out-now/, last accessed: October 23, 2017.

[540] Taylor Swift, 'Taylor Swift, Album of the Year Acceptance Speech (Grammys 2016)', *Genius*, February 15, 2016, https://genius.com/Taylor-swift-album-of-the-year-acceptance-speech-grammys-2016-annotated, last accessed: October 23, 2017.

-	1. Two days after Taylor Swift's Grammy win, *Page Six* posted the audio record with Kanye West in the backstage at SNL on 14 February 2016.[541] 2. Paparazzi at *LAX Kanye* questioned Kanye West about his 'Famous' lyric. He answered: 'It's like, I want the best for that person, but there's people going through real issues out here. There's people out of work. There's people in debt that can't make it out of the debt. There's people that's in debt that don't have a shoe. There's people that are in debt that don't have a hit album out also. The media tried to make this an ongoing story and everything for hits and blah blah. I don't think people care about me or her in that way. People care about their families, their kids. If you like my music, listen to it. If you like her music, listen to it.'[542]

FEBRUARY 23, 2016

TAYLOR SWIFT	KANYE WEST
-	Kanye West wrote a few tweets (now deleted) on his Twitter account: 'I made Dark Fantasy and Watch the Throne in one year and wasn't nominated for either and you know who has 2 albums of the year.' — KANYE WEST (@kanyewest) February 23, 2016

FEBRUARY 24, 2016

TAYLOR SWIFT	KANYE WEST
-	At Yo Gotti's album release party at the 1OAK nightclub in Hollywood, Kanye West reiterates he told Taylor Swift about the 'Famous' lyric and said 'She

---

[541] Emily Smith, 'Don't f–k with me': Hear Kanye's uncensored 'SNL' meltdown', *Page Six*, February 17, 2016, https://pagesix.com/2016/02/17/dont-f-k-with-me-hear-kanyes-uncensored-snl-meltdown/, last accessed: October 23, 2017.
[542] Ted Simmons, 'Kanye West Tells Paparazzi He Wants the Best for Taylor Swift', *XXL Magazine*, February 18, 2016, http://www.xxlmag.com/news/2016/02/kanye-west-talks-taylor-swift-to-paparazzi/, last accessed: October, 23,2017.

	had two seconds to be cool and she fucked it up!'[543]

APRIL 14, 2016

TAYLOR SWIFT	KANYE WEST
In an interview with Vogue, Taylor Swift addressed her acceptance speech at Grammy Awards and Kanye West: 'I think the world is bored with the saga. I don't want to add anything to it, because then there's just more... I guess what I wanted to call attention to in my speech at the Grammys was how it's going to be difficult if you're a woman who wants to achieve something in her life - no matter what.'[544]	-

JUNE 16, 2016

TAYLOR SWIFT	KIM KARDASHIAN WEST
	In a GQ interview for July new issue, Kim Kardashian spoked about Taylor Swift and her implication in the song 'Famous':
Taylor Swift camp, after Kim Kardashian's interview with GQ, issued a statement to GQ: 'Taylor does not hold anything against Kim Kardashian as she recognizes the pressure Kim must be under and that she is only repeating what she has been told by Kanye West. However, that does not change the fact that much of what Kim is saying is incorrect. Kanye West and Taylor only spoke once on the phone while she was on vacation with her family in January of 2016 and they have never spoken since. Taylor has never denied that conversation took place. It was on that phone call that Kanye West also asked her to release the song on her Twitter account, which she declined to do. Kanye West never told Taylor he was going to use the term 'that bitch' in referencing her. A song cannot be approved if it was never heard. Kanye West never played the song for Taylor Swift. Taylor heard it for the first	'She totally approved that.' […] 'She totally knew that that was coming out. She wanted to all of a sudden act like she didn't. I swear, my husband gets so much shit for things he really was doing proper protocol and even called to get it approved.' […] 'What rapper would call a girl that he was rapping a line about to get approval?' 'I don't know why she just, you know, flipped all of a sudden.… It was funny because said, 'When I get on the Grammy red carpet, all the media is going to think that I'm so against this, and I'll just laugh and say, 'The joke's on you, guys. I was in on it the whole time.' And I'm like, wait, but your Grammy speech, you completely dissed my husband just to play the victim again.'

[543] Complex, *A Timeline of Kanye West and Taylor Swift's Feud Over the 'Famous' Lyric*, July 18, 2016, http://www.complex.com/music/2016/07/kanye-west-taylor-swift-famous-lyric-timeline, last accessed: October 23, 2017.
[544] Jason Gay, 'Taylor Swift As You've Never Seen Her Before', *Vogue*, April 14, 2016, https://www.vogue.com/article/taylor-swift-may-cover-maid-of-honor-dating-personal-style, last accessed: October 23, 2017.

time when everyone else did and was humiliated. Kim Kardashian's claim that Taylor and her team were aware of being recorded is not true, and Taylor cannot understand why Kanye West, and now Kim Kardashian, will not just leave her alone.'[545]

GQ reporter: 'Were they in touch after that?'

Kim Kardashian: 'No. Maybe an attorney's letter she sent saying, 'Don't ever let that footage come out of me saying that. Destroy it.'

GQ reporter: 'She sent one?'

Kim Kardashian: 'Yeah.'

Kim Kardashian: 'And then they sent an attorney's letter like, 'Don't you dare do anything with that footage,' and asking us to destroy it.' She pauses. 'When you shoot something, you don't stop every two seconds and be like, 'Oh wait, we're shooting this for my documentary.' You just film everything, and whatever makes the edit, then you see, then you send out releases. It's like what we do for our show.'[546]

JUNE 24, 2016

TAYLOR SWIFT	KANYE WEST
-	'Famous' official music video is released exclusive on Tidal and at the event 'The Forum' in Inglewood, California.[547]

JULY 1, 2016

TAYLOR SWIFT	KANYE WEST
-	'Famous' official music video is released on Kanye West Vevo Youtube account.[548]

JULY 14, 2016

TAYLOR SWIFT	KIM KARDASHIAN WEST
	A trailer with Kim Kardashian with a scene from the upcoming episode

[545] Caity Weaver, 'Kanye and Taylor Swift, What's in O.J.'s Bag, and Understanding Caitlyn', *GQ*, June 16, 2016, https://www.gq.com/story/kim-kardashian-west-gq-cover-story, last accessed: October 23, 2017.

[546] *Ibidem*.

[547] Colin Stutz, 'Kanye West Nuzzles Naked Taylor Swift, Donald Trump & Bill Cosby in 'Famous' Video', *Billboard*, June 25, 2016, https://www.billboard.com/articles/columns/hip-hop/7416556/kanye-west-naked-taylor-swift-donald-trump-famous-video-premiere, last accessed: October 23, 2017.

[548] KanyeWestVevo, 'Kanye West Famous', *Youtube*, July 1, 2016, https://www.youtube.com/watch?v=p7FCgw_GlWc, last accessed: October 23, 2017.

TAYLOR SWIFT	KIM KARDASHIAN WEST & KANYE WEST
-	*Keeping Up with the Kardashians* is released. In it Kim Kardashian speaks again about Taylor Swift and her implication in the song 'Famous'.[549]

JULY 17, 2016

TAYLOR SWIFT	KIM KARDASHIAN WEST & KANYE WEST
	1. Kim Kardashian wrote on her Twitter account:
	'Wait it's legit National Snake Day?!?!? They have holidays for everybody, I mean everything these days!'

	Soon after the post with the phone conversation between Kanye West and Taylor Swift, people posted snakes on Taylor Swift Instagram, Twitter and Facebook account.[551]
Taylor Swift responded to Kim Kardashian's Snapchat videos on her Instagram and Twitter account (now the picture with her response is deleted):	2. After the episode from her tv show, *Keeping Up with the Kardashians*, Kim Kardashian posted a series of videos on her Snapchat account. The videos show Kanye West speaking on the phone with Taylor Swift. It is a small part of the conversation they had it in January 2016.
'That moment when Kanye West secretly records your phone call, then Kim posts it on the Internet.'	
'Where is the video of Kanye telling me he was going to call me 'that bitch' in his song? It doesn't exist because it never happened. You don't get to control someone's emotional response to being called 'that bitch' in front of the entire world. Of course I wanted to like the song. I wanted to believe Kanye when he told me that I would love	**Kanye West:** 'You still got the Nashville number?'
	Taylor Swift: 'I still have the Nashville umm area code, but I had to change it.'
	[video cuts off]

[549] E! Entertainment, 'KUWTK, Kim Kardashian Has 'Had It' With Kanye Haters', *Youtube*, July 14, 2016, https://www.youtube.com/watch?v=p7FCgw_GlWc, last accessed: October 23, 2017.
[551] Kim Kardashian West, 'Wait it's legit National Snake Day?!?,' *Twitter*, July 17, 2016, https://twitter.com/kimkardashian/status/754818471465287680?lang=en, last accessed: October 23, 2017.

the song. I wanted us to have a friendly relationship. He promised to play the song for me, but he never did. While I wanted to be supportive of Kanye on the phone call, you cannot 'approve' a song you haven't heard. Being falsely painted as a liar when I was never given the full story or played any part of the song is character assassination. I would very much like to be excluded from this narrative, one that I have never asked to be a part of, since 2009.'[550]

Kanye West: 'To all my southside niggas that know me best, I feel like me and Taylor might still have sex.'

Taylor Swift: 'I'm like this close to overexposure.'

Kanye West: 'Oh, well this I think this a really cool thing to have.'

Taylor Swift: 'I know, I mean it's like a compliment, kind of.'

[video cuts off]

Kanye West: 'All I give a fuck about is you as a person and as a friend, I want things that make you feel good.'

Taylor Swift: 'That's sweet.'

Kanye West: 'I don't want to do rap that makes people feel bad.'

[video cuts off]

Taylor Swift: 'Umm, yeah I mean go with whatever line you think is better. It's obviously very tongue in cheek either way. And I really appreciate you telling me about it, that's really nice.'

[video cuts off]

Kanye West: 'Oh yeah, I just had a responsibility to you as a friend you know, and I mean thanks for being so cool about it.'

Taylor Swift: 'Aw thanks. Um yeah I really appreciate it, like the heads up is so nice.'

[550] The photo with her reply is now deleted from her Facebook, Twitter and Instagram account. You can find written evidence here: Jemima Skelley, 'Taylor Swift Just Called Out Kanye West On Instagram', *BuzzFeed*, July 18, 2016, https://www.buzzfeed.com/jemimaskelley/shoulda-chose-the-rose-garden-over-madison-square, last accessed: October 23, 2017.

[inaudible]

'Even asking or seeing if I would be okay with it and I just really appreciate it. Like I would never expect you to like tell me about a line in one of your songs.'

Kanye West: 'It's pretty crazy.'

Taylor Swift: 'And then the flowers that you sent me, I like Instagrammed a picture of them and it's like the most Instagram likes I've ever gotten. It was like 2.7 millions.'

[video cuts off]

Kanye West: 'Relationships are more important than punch lines, ya know?'

Taylor Swift: 'I don't think anyone would listen to that and be like that's a real diss she must be crying. You've gotta tell the story the way that it happened to you and the way that you experienced it, like you honestly didn't know who I was before that.'

[video cuts off]

Taylor Swift: 'It doesn't matter that I sold 7 million of that album before you did that which is what happened, you didn't know who I was before that. It's fine.'

[video cuts off]

Taylor Swift: 'I might be in debt, but I can make these things happen. I have the ideas to do it and I create these things and concepts. I'm always going to respect you. I'm really glad that you have the respect to call me and tell me that as a friend about the song. It's a really cool thing to do and a really good show of friendship so thank you.'

Kanye West: 'Thank you, too.'

[video cuts off]

Taylor Swift: 'And you know, if people ask me about it I think it would be great for me to be like, 'Look, he called me and told me the line before it came out. Jokes on you guys, We're fine.'

[video cuts off]

'You guys want to call this a feud; you want to call this throwing shade but right after the song comes out I'm going to be on a GRAMMYs red carpet and they're going to ask me about it and I'll be like, 'He called me.'

[video cuts off]

'It's awesome that you're so outspoken about this and be like, 'Yeah, she does. It made her famous.' It's more provocative to say 'might still have sex…' It's doesn't matter to me. There's not like one [line] that hurts my feelings and one that doesn't.'[552]

JULY 24, 2016

TAYLOR SWIFT	KIM KARDASHIAN WEST & KANYE WEST
-	Kim Kardashian, during her night at Hakkasan nightclub in the MGM Grand in Las Vegas, shared a video of herself and friend Carla DiBello dancing and singing along to Kanye West's lyric of the song 'Famous,' specifically where Kanye West raps: 'I feel like me and Taylor might still have sex. Why? I made that

---

[552] Kylizzle Snapchizzle, 'Kanye West Phone Call to Taylor Swift about Famous (Full) Via Kim's Snapchat', *Youtube*, July 18, 2016, https://www.youtube.com/watch?v=tlN-2LDGm3A, last accessed: October 23, 2017.

	JULY 27, 2016
TAYLOR SWIFT	bitch famous. I made that bitch famous.'[553]
	KANYE WEST
-	Kanye West makes a guest appearance at Drake's concert in Chicago, and speaks out about Taylor Swift. Kanye West told his fans, 'All I gotta say is, I am so glad my wife has Snapchat!', 'Now y'all can know the truth and can't nobody talk s–t about 'Ye no more.' After his words, he performed the song 'Famous'.[554]

JULY 28, 2016	
TAYLOR SWIFT	**KANYE WEST & KIM KARDASHIAN WEST**
-	Kanye West and Kim Kardashian are on the cover of Harper's Bazaar September issue. When asked by editor Laura Brown about their favourite Taylor Swift song, Kanye West replied, 'For me? I don't have one.' Kim Kardashian replied: 'I was such a fan of hers.'[555]

AUGUST 28, 2016	
TAYLOR SWIFT	**KANYE WEST**
-	Kanye West takes the stage at the 2016 MTV Video Music Awards. He received 6 minutes to do what he wants. He addressed the song 'Famous' and Taylor Swift by saying that he's a 'lover of all,' which is 'why I called her.'[556]

AUGUST 25, 2017	
TAYLOR SWIFT	**KANYE WEST**
Taylor Swift released a new song 'Look What You Made Me Do' with lyrics possible related to Kanye West: 'I don't like your little games/ I don't like	-

---

[553] Blake Bakkila, 'Kim Kardashian Raps Along to THAT Kanye Lyric About Taylor Swift After Epic Feud', *People*, July 24, 2016, http://people.com/celebrity/kim-kardashian-sings-along-to-famous-after-taylor-swift-feud/, last accessed: October 23, 2017.

[554] Elias Leight, 'Kanye West on Taylor Swift: 'I'm So Glad My Wife Has Snapchat', *Rolling Stone*, July 28, 2016, http://www.rollingstone.com/music/news/kanye-west-on-taylor-swift-im-glad-my-wife-has-snapchat-w431395, last accessed: October 23, 2017. D, 'Kanye came and dragged Taylor more', *Twitter*, July 27, 2016, https://twitter.com/holyspearits/status/758516526190321664, last accessed: October 23, 2017.

[555] Carine Roitfeld, 'Icons: In Bed with Kim and Kanye', *Harper's Bazaar*, July 28, 2016, http://www.Harper's Bazaarbazaar.com/fashion/photography/a16784/kanye-west-kim-kardashian-interview/, last accessed: October 23, 2017.

[556] MTV, 'Kanye West's Moment, 2016 Video Music Awards', *Youtube*, August 28, 2016, https://www.youtube.com/watch?v=ycnTPgp3DY8, last accessed: October 23, 2017.

your tilted stage.' Kanye West used an elevated tilted stage during his Saint Pablo tour.[557]

AUGUST 27, 2017

TAYLOR SWIFT	KANYE WEST & KIM KARDASHIAN WEST
Taylor Swift released the music video of 'Look What You Made Me Do' which possibly contains coded references to Kanye West and Kim Kardashian: snake imagery (see page and the table *The New and Complete Timeline* 17 July 2016), imitation of Kim Kardashian and the Paris robbery (Kim Kardashian was caught in a bath tub and threaten with a gun), makes selfies then telling the others that she's 'getting receipts' so that she can 'edit them later,' at the end of the video says: 'I would like very much like to be excluded from this narrative' (is the last part of her reply to Kim Kardashian's videos on her Snapchat account with the phone conversation between her and Kanye West).[558]	-

NOVEMBER 10, 2017

TAYLOR SWIFT	KANYE WEST & KIM KARDASHIAN WEST FAN CAMP
Taylor Swift released her newest musical album entitled *reputation*, which includes another song, *This Is Why We Can't Have Nice Things*, which is believed to be about Kanye West. The lyrics are: 'It was so nice being friends again, there I was giving you a second chance, but you stabbed me in the back without shaking my hand'; 'therein lies the issues, friends don't try to trick you, get you on the phone and mind twist you.'[559] Taylor Swift's Team denied the speculation regardin the releasing date of her album and the 10th anniversary of Donda West (Kanye West mother).[560]	Kanye and Kim's fan camp accused Taylor Swift on social media (Twitter, Facebook, Instagram) that the release of *reputation* album on this day is connected to the 10th anniversary of the death of Kanye West's mother, Donda West.[561]

---

[557] Taylor Swift, 'Out Now', *Instagram*, August 25, 2017, https://www.instagram.com/p/BYM6v4FH9Bo/?taken-by=taylorswift, last accessed: 23 October 2017. Taylor Swift, 'Look What You Made Me Do Lyrics', *Genius*, https://genius.com/Taylor-swift-look-what-you-made-me-do-lyrics, last accessed: October 23, 2017.

[558] TaylorSwiftVevo, 'Look What You Made Me Do', *Youtube*, August 27, 2017, https://www.youtube.com/watch?v=3tmd-ClpJxA, last accessed: October 23, 2017.

[559] Taylor Swift, 'This Is Why We Can't Have Nice Things', *Genius*, November 10, 2017, https://genius.com/Taylor-swift-this-is-why-we-cant-have-nice-things-lyrics, last accessed: November 10, 2017.

[560] Roisin O'Connor, 'Taylor Swift: Reputation release date coinciding with anniversary of Donda West death is a 'coincidence', *The Independent*, August 26, 2017, https://www.independent.co.uk/arts-entertainment/music/news/taylor-swift-donda-west-reputation-release-date-kanye-kim-kardashian-album-tour-dates-a7914191.html, last accessed: October 23, 2017.

[561] Eddie Fu, 'Taylor Swift denies Reputation release date is connected to the anniversary of the death of Kanye West's mother', *Consequence of Sound*, August 25, 2017, https://conequenceofsound.net/2017/08/taylor-swift-denies-reputation-release-date-is-connected-to-the-anniversary-of-the-death-of-kanye-wests-mother/ , last accessed: October 23, 2017.

MARCH 2020

TAYLOR SWIFT	KIM KARDASHIAN
In June and July 2016, and in March 2020 (but without mentioning Kim Kardashian's name):	In March 2020, Kim Kardashian replied to the leak of the telephone conversation with the following statement:
'Instead of answering those who are asking how I feel about the video footage that leaked, proving that I was telling the truth the whole time about *that call* (you know, the one that was illegally recorded, that somebody edited and manipulated in order to frame me and put me, my family, and fans through hell for 4 years)… SWIPE up to see what really matters.'[562]	'@taylorswift13 has chosen to reignite an old exchange - that at this point in time feels very self-serving given the suffering millions of real victims are facing right now. I didn't feel the need to comment a few days ago, and I'm actually really embarrassed and mortified to be doing it right now, but because she continues to speak on it, I feel I'm left without a choice but to respond because she is actually lying. To be clear, the only issue I ever had around the situation was that Taylor lied through her publicist who stated that 'Kanye never called to ask for permission…' They clearly spoke so I let you all see that. Nobody ever denied the word 'bitch' was used without her permission. At the time when they spoke the song had not been fully written yet, but as everyone can see in the video, she manipulated the truth of their actual conversation in her statement when her team said she 'declined and cautioned him about releasing a song with such a strong misogynistic message.' The lie was never about the word bitch, It was always whether there was a call or not and the tone of the conversation. To add, Kanye as an artist has every right to document his musical journey and process, just like she recently did through her documentary. Kanye has documented the making of all of his albums for his personal archive, however has never released any of it for public consumption & the call between the two of them would have remained private or

[562] Nick Reilly, 'Taylor Swift says she was "framed" as 2016 phone call with Kanye West leaks online', *NME*, March 24, 2020, available online: https://www.nme.com/news/music/taylor-swift-says-she-was-framed-as-2016-phone-call-with-kanye-west-leaks-online-2633977; last accessed: July 1, 2021.

> would have gone in the trash had she
> not lied & forced me to defend him. This
> will be the last time I speak on this
> because honestly, nobody cares. Sorry
> to bore you all with this. I know you are
> all dealing with more serious and
> important matters'.[563]

The Conclusions of the *Famous* timeline are based on the evidence available; however, it is possible, that in the full conversation between Kanye West and Taylor Swift (maybe more than 25 minutes as we have today on Youtube) to exist more information that can reject, approve, or reject and accept different parts of the following conclusions:

Kanye West:

- said the truth about calling Taylor Swift and having a telephone conversation about his song and lyrics: Taylor Swift knew Kanye West's intention to make a song that includes lyrics about her: 'You guys want to call this a feud; you want to call this throwing shade but right after the song comes out I'm going to be on a GRAMMYs red carpet and they're going to ask me about it and I'll be like, 'He called me';[564]
- half presented that Taylor Swift came (as whole) with the idea of the lyrics: Kanye West tweeted in February 2016: 'I'm not even gone take credit for the idea… it's actually something Taylor came up with'[565]); indeed, Kanye West read the lyrics to Taylor Swift to which she replied: 'Yeah, she does. It made her famous.' It's more provocative to say 'might still have sex…' It doesn't matter to me. There's not like one that hurts my feelings and one that doesn't'[566], but it was only *a part* of the lyrics, not *all* the lyrics and the song as Kanye West ('That's why I called her') and Kim Kardashian wanted the world to believe ('She totally approved that.' […] 'She totally knew that that was coming out. She wanted to all of a sudden act like she didn't'[567]);
- maybe used the telephone agreement to justify the lyrics about Taylor Swift in his song (Taylor Swift: 'Umm, yeah I mean go with whatever line you think is better. It's obviously very tongue in cheek either way. And I really appreciate you telling me about it, that's really nice. […] You've gotta tell the story the way that it happened to

[563] Tatiana Tenreyro, 'Kim Kardashian Responded To Taylor Swift's Statement About The Leaked Kanye West Phone Call', *Buzzfeed*, March 24, 2020, available at: https://www.buzzfeed.com/tatianatenreyrowhitlock/kim-kardashian-speaks-about-kanye-west-phone-call-with, last accessed: July 1, 2021.
[564] Kylizzle Snapchizzle, idem.
[565] Kanye West, A tweet on Twitter, February 2016.
[566] Kylizzle Snapchizzle, idem.
[567] Caity Weaver, 'Kanye and Taylor Swift, What's in O.J.'s Bag, and Understanding Caitlyn'.

you, and the way that you experienced it[568]') and added a new line in the lyrics of the song, namely 'I made that bitch famous';

- didn't disclose to the general public that during the telephone conversation he didn't inform Taylor Swift about the word 'bitch' and the full line 'I made that bitch famous', and that it was his only decision to add the word 'bitch' and the line in the lyrics of the song;
- wrongly presented to the world the song's lyrics from the perspective that Taylor Swift knew about it, including the word 'bitch' and the line 'I made that bitch famous';
- the use of the word 'bitch' by Taylor Swift during the telephone conversation might be the link that Kanye West tried to explain in relation with Taylor Swift approving his song: 'I thought it was going to be like, 'That stupid, dumb bitch.' But it's not. So I don't know.'; maybe he used this part as a strategy of confirmation received from Taylor Swift, and used as a scapegoat strategy in case his fans, the general public and mass-media are questioning him;
- the song *Famous* was released in the week that happened to be one of the most important events in Taylor Swift's career: the Grammy Awards (she received the Grammy Award for the *Album of the Year* for the second time, which is a global record);
- presented the telephone conversation:

a. *in pieces* (in February 2016: in news as rumours and possible evidence of a telephone conversation recorded between him and Taylor Swift; in July 2016: in heavily edited video of the telephone conversation posted by Kim Kardashian on her Snapchat account) ***and not the full conversation at the same time in the same day***, so that the general public to know exactly the context of the telephone conversation;

b. *doesn't include the fact that he added the line 'I made that bitch famous' without Taylor Swift's knowledge;*

c. *when are in motion events that are part of the promotion of his album, The Life of Pablo*:

c.1 *on the cover of his album is a picture with 'look like a white girl'* (there is no evidence to support a clear causal link that the model if definitely a white person) wearing a bath suit and a black family which depicts a matrimony; also, on the cover is written 'Which/One[569]', the general meaning that readers may have is choosing between the white girl (which is lonely in the picture) or the black family; before the

---

[568] Kylizzle Snapchizzle, idem.
[569] Google, *The Life of Pablo album cover*, https://www.google.com/search?q=the+life+of+pablo+album+cover&newwindow=1&safe=active&client=safari&rls=en&source=lnMs.&tbm=isch&sa=X&ved=0ahUKEwjunYH8rpzkAhUFPFAKHQ7-BogQ_AUIESgB&biw=1440&bih=812, last accessed: 23 October 2017.

release of the album's cover, Kanye West released the song with the infamous line 'I made that bitch famous' about Taylor Swift (she is white and according with her dress style in music videos and private life -where there are pictures published on different websites about her in private life- is in opposition with the picture from Kanye West's album cover; Taylor Swift never pictured herself in the way that the white girl (?) is pictured on Kanye West's album cover); maybe the 'look like a white girl' picture on the album cover is a metaphor and artistic representation of Taylor Swift; maybe it's an alternate reality that exists in Kanye West's mind, meaning, to him, that Taylor Swift is just a 'bitch'; maybe it's Kanye West's way of saying about Taylor Swift that in reality she is different from what she promotes to the general public, and he managed to demonstrate her true personality;

c.2 Kim Kardashian, in an interview with GQ magazine, talked about the existence of a telephone conversation between Kanye West and Taylor Swift; Kim Kardashian: 'She totally approved that.' […] 'She totally knew that that was coming out. She wanted to all of a sudden act like she didn't[570]': this interview (June 16, 2016) happened in the week that Kanye West started to sale tickets (June 14 for American Express cardholders and June 16 for Tidal members, June 18 for general public[571]) to his music tour named *Saint Pablo Tour*;

c.3 Kim Kardashian presented a heavily edited video telephone conversation between Kanye West and Taylor Swift at a month after the start of Kanye West's sale of tickets for his music tour; in the video listeners can hear Taylor Swift agreeing with the lyrics, *but not the line* 'I made that bitch famous'; also, a month before the start of *Saint Pablo Tour*, Kanye West and Kim Kardashian were on the cover of *Harper's Bazaar* for the September issue: when they were asked by editor Laura Brown about the favourite Taylor Swift song, Kanye West replied, 'For me? I don't have one.' Kim Kardashian replied: 'I was such a fan of hers'[572];

- used the song and the lyrics about Taylor Swift in his concerts (from August 2016 to November 2016 and at the MTV VMA Awards 2016), and presented Taylor Swift as being a liar, while he is telling the whole truth;
- Kanye West had (has as of today) lots of opportunities to say that it was his decision to add the line 'I made that bitch famous' in the lyrics of the song; that Taylor Swift didn't know the whole lyrics, and she found out at the same time as the rest of the world;

[570] Caity Weaver, 'Kanye and Taylor Swift, What's in O.J.'s Bag, and Understanding Caitlyn'.
[571] Fionna Agomuoh, 'Kanye West Tour Dates 2016: 'Saint Pablo' Tickets, Prices And Schedule Released', *Player*, June 14, 2016, https://www.player.one/kanye-west-tour-dates-2016-saint-pablo-tickets-prices-and-schedule-released-540277, last accessed: October 23, 2017.
[572] Carine Roitfeld, 'Icons: In Bed with Kim and Kanye'.

- used the lyrics of the song to take credit for Taylor Swift's fame and to justify his actions 'I made that bitch famous', but also in a tweet, 'I can't be mad at Kanye because he made me famous! #FACTS';
- Kanye West during the telephone conversation with Taylor Swift said to her: 'Relationships are more important than punchlines, ya know?', however, the fact that he failed (even today) to recognize that he added a new line in the lyrics that Taylor Swift wasn't aware of, and then saying to the general public that Taylor Swift knew the full *song Famous* and the line 'I made that bitch famous', is a pure 'punch line' and definitely not friendly relationship;
- Kanye West and Kim Kardashian's treatment and behaviour toward Taylor Swift on social media, interviews in magazines and mostly during Kanye West music tour, *Saint Pablo Tour*, in the USA is negative, unfair, mean and wrong: the song and the lyrics encouraged people to send thousands of inappropriate comments on Taylor Swift's social media pages (Facebook, Instagram, Twitter); the words 'bitch', 'snake' and 'liar' were one of the favourite words in reference to Taylor Swift;
- Kanye West and Kim Kardashian had the opportunity to stop the feud at any moment after the release of the full song (with recognizing what each side knows about the lyrics of the song) , but they decided to keep the public attention for at least 5 months on themselves, therefore making people and mass-media extremely curious about the existence, or not of the evidence to incriminate Taylor Swift; this decision maybe it was intentional, but it was delivered to the general public under Kim and Kanye's terms;
- Kanye West and Kim Kardashian were fully aware of Taylor Swift's involvement in the lyrics of the song and they continued (and continue as of today) to present Taylor Swift in a bad light, and that she is to blame for everything bad that followed after; Kim Kardashian recorded a snapchat video listening to *song Famous* which intentionally underlined and recorded the part of the song where her husband Kanye West raps the lyrics: 'I made that bitch famous';
- Kanye West is to blame for starting the *Famous* feud, and all the reactions from people toward him and Taylor Swift;
- there is evidence to support theories (but not to be considered as genuine true) that Kanye West used Taylor Swift's involvement as source of controversy to spin the public interest around his new musical album, to promote his album, *The Life of Pablo* and his music tour *Saint Pablo Tour* (by adding new lyrics; informed the general public that Taylor Swift knew about it, when in fact she did not; the album cover 'looks like a white girl'? and Taylor Swift is a white girl; the release of information regarding Taylor Swift's involvement in the song, and not all at the same time; when events are in motion which are part of the promotion of the album and his music tour); the contradiction between West's version and Swift's version of the telephone conversation resulted in over a thousand articles being written by the Western mass-media, and hundreds of thousands (quite possibly over a million) of comments

written by fans on both camps; in the end, a high number of online posts about both artists were shared on social media by users around the planet, where the main focus was Kanye West's new music album and tour;

- there is evidence to support theories (but not to be considered as genuine true) that West family planned in rich details to use Taylor Swift as scapegoat for their own use (for example increase and maintain popularity on social media and music genre), and to falsely paint Taylor Swift as a 'liar', not the victim, but the perpetrator and to be blame for the bad things that happens in Kanye and Kim's narrative line;
- it is difficult to agree and prove that Kanye West (even maybe due to a misunderstanding of the freedom of creativity, or his intentional interpretation of the phone call as a freedom of creativity from Taylor Swift) took advantage of Taylor Swift's replies in the phone call to present her in a negative light with all-purpose to destroy Taylor Swift's reputation;
- the behaviour and the press releases by Kanye and Kim, regarding Taylor Swift's involvement in the song Famous, are misleading and biased;
- Kanye West was the first who misled and offered biased information to the general public about Taylor Swift's involvement in the song Famous, second was Kim Kardashian;
- there is evidence to suggest that Kanye West created an effective trap against Taylor Swift by creating a negative image;
- Kanye West said that he made Taylor Swift famous, but he asked her to release his song Famous on her Twitter account; he asked Taylor to present the song in a positive view because she 'owns 2 billion people and if she is ok with the song, then the 2 billion people will be ok as well': this is a contradiction of the fame power that Kanye promoted over the years, and in his song ('I made that bitch famous') about Taylor Swift and this world; however, from another corner there is the following perspective: Kanye West promoted the idea that Taylor Swift became famous because he interfered in her narrative line during the MTV Awards in 2009, and more people were interested in her songs; in 2016 maybe he wanted to use Taylor Swift's fame created through his help in his favour, to be rewarded for his interference (this perspective has a weak point because, according to rumours spread by fans on social platforms such as Twitter and Reddit, prior to September 2009 Taylor Swift experienced a strong increase in album sales in countries and places where Kanye West failed to sell as much as Taylor Swift and, because of her, Kanye West managed to enter into the music mind of people who never heard of him before, or were not interested);
- from February 2016 until today, Kanye West and Kim Kardashian were the first (and the last) and most interested in keeping their own narrative alive in mass-media and public thoughts through misleading and biased information about Taylor Swift's involvement in the creation of the song Famous;

- accused Taylor Swift of what he did: manipulation, misleading and biased information presented to the general public;
- there is evidence to support the theory that the song *Fade* performed by Teyana Taylor (born a year later than Taylor Swift: December 10, 1990) is a metaphor, but also a revelation of the effect of his lie: Taylor Swift lost the love of the world and he earned it; the song was released at the MTV VMAs in August 2016.

Kim Kardashian:

- was in partnership and decided to offer total support for her husband, Kanye West;
- presented and promoted a biased and misleading view of the creation of the song *Famous*, and about the character of Taylor Swift;
- published on her Snapchat account an edited video with the telephone conversation between Kanye West and Taylor Swift, where the context of the discussion is distorted and Taylor Swift is presented in the wrong role;
- sharing the edited video of the telephone conversation on her social media account, encouraged people to address on online social platforms malicious words toward and in reference to Taylor Swift, the most preferred word was 'bitch';[573]
- failed to show substantial evidence of the existence of the attorney's letter (Kim Kardashian: 'Don't you dare do anything with that footage,' and asking us to destroy it') sent by Taylor Swift's lawyers to Kim Kardashian about the deletion of the video recording of the telephone conversation between Kanye West and Taylor Swift.

Taylor Swift:

- said the truth from the following two perspectives: **1.** she heard the full *song Famous* as presented and released by Kanye West at the same time with the general public; **2.** she was not aware of the line 'I made that bitch famous';
- **can be accused of being a liar from the following perspectives:**

  1. she didn't inform the public right after the song release (February 2016) in more details exactly what she knows about it and her involvement in the lyrics: the lack of this information confused people and fans, and may have encouraged Western mass-media to come with their own version of truth in a visible number of negative articles published online;

---

[573] This word 'bitch' was also use toward and in reference to Kim Kardashian after the release of the video tape of the sexual intercourse between herself and her boyfriend; strangely, years later Kim Kardashian used it wrongly to an innocent woman.

2. Taylor Swift failed to bring strong evidence that 'She declined and cautioned him about releasing a song with such a strong misogynistic message' as the evidence (video of the telephone conversation published on Youtube, 25 minutes) doesn't mention anything about the word 'misogynistic'; however, Taylor Swift warned Kanye West about 'feminist' and maybe this is the connection with the misogynistic message:

Taylor Swift: 'You know, the thing about me is, anything that I do becomes like a feminist think-piece. And if I launch it, they're going to be like, wow, like, they'll just turn into something that… I think if I launch it, honestly, I think it'll be less cool. Because I think if I launch it, it adds this level of criticism. Because having that many followers and having that many eyeballs on me right now, people are just looking for me to do something dumb or stupid or lame. And I don't know. I kind of feel like people would try to make it negative if it came from me, do you know what I mean? I think I'm very self-aware about where I am, and I feel like right now I'm like this close to overexposure.'

Kanye West: 'I have this line where I said… And my wife really didn't like this one, because we tried to make it nicer. So I say 'For all my Southside [N-word] that know me best, I feel like me and Taylor might still have sex.' And my wife was really not with that one. She was way more into the 'She owes you sex.' But then the 'owe' part was like the feminist group-type shit that I was like, ahhhhh.'

Taylor Swift: 'That's the part that I was kind of… I mean, they 're both really edgy, but that's the only thing about that line is that it's like, then the feminists are going to come out. But I mean, you don't give a f—. So…'

Kanye West: 'Yeah, basically. Well, what I give a f— about is just you as a person, as a friend….'

3. Taylor Swift had a poor strategy of communication that couldn't match Kanye and Kim's strategy and that's because they had the evidence of the telephone conversation, and they used it how they wanted (edited the video of the recording with parts that they want the public to know), and what time they wanted the public to hear and watch it;

4. In her reply from July 2016 she wrote: 'I was never given the full story or **played any part of the song is character assassination'**, however, Taylor did play a part in the song:

Taylor Swift: 'Well, I mean, she's saying that honestly because she's your wife, and like, um… So I think whatever one you think is actually better. I mean, obviously do what's best for your relationship, too. I think 'owes me sex,' it says different things. It says… 'Owes me sex' means like 'Look, I made her what she is. She actually owes me.' Which is going to split people, because people who like me are going to be like, 'She doesn't owe him s—.' But then people who like thought it was bad-ass and crazy and awesome that you're so outspoken are going to be like, 'Yeah, she does. It made her famous.' So it's more provocative to say 'still have sex,' because no one would see that coming. They're both crazy. Do what you want. They're both going to get every single headline in the world. 'Owes me sex' is a little bit

264

more like throwing shade, and the other one's more flirtatious. It just depends on what you want to accomplish with it,'

but still there is no evidence for a dominant argument that Taylor played a part because she *really wanted,* or because she was involved in a phone conversation and *wanted to be nice and supportive* with Kanye West; Taylor Swift told Kanye West that she would think about the song, Kanye West instead said he would send her the song, but he never did; in the end, Taylor Swift didn't know that Kanye West would use the phone conversation as an implied agreement to her polite advice and suggestion to promote the song without hearing the final version, and then follow through on what she told Kanye West:

Taylor Swift: 'And you know, if people ask me about it, look, I think it would be great for me to be like, 'Look, he called me and told me the line before it came out. Like, the joke's on you guys – we're fine.'

[...]

Taylor Swift: 'Yeah. Like, you guys want to call this a feud, you want to call this throwing shade, but you know, right after the song comes out, I'm gonna be on a Grammy red carpet, and they're gonna ask me about it and I'll be like, 'He called me and sent me the song before it came out.' So I think we're good.'

Kanye West: 'Okay. I'm gonna go lay this verse, and I'm gonna send it to you right now.'

Taylor Swift: '[Taken aback.] Oh, you just... you haven't recorded it yet?'

Kanye West: 'I recorded it. I'm nuancing the lines – like the last version of it says, 'Me and Taylor might still have sex.' And then my wife was like, 'That doesn't sound as hard!'

- **_never denied that a phone conversation took place_**[574]: *February 2016*: Team Taylor replied after the release of the song: 'Kanye did not call for approval, but to ask Taylor to release his single 'Famous' on her Twitter account'[575]; *in June 2016*: 'It was on that phone call that Kanye West also asked her to release the song on her Twitter account, which she declined to do[576]'; *July 2016*: 'Of course I wanted to like the song. I wanted to believe Kanye when he told me that I would love the song. I wanted us to have a friendly relationship. He promised to play the song for me, but he never did. While I wanted to be supportive of Kanye on the phone call, you cannot 'approve' a song you haven't heard[577];'
- disagreed with Kanye West regarding her fame:

---

[574] Caity Weaver, 'Kanye and Taylor Swift, What's in O.J.'s Bag, and Understanding Caitlyn'.
[575] Melody Chiu, Karen Mizoguchi, 'Kanye West Did Not Call Taylor Swift for Approval Over 'B----' Lyric, Singer Cautioned Him Against Releasing 'Strong Misogynistic Message' Rep Says'.
[576] Caity Weaver, *idem*.
[577] The photo with Taylor Swift reply is now deleted from her Facebook, Twitter and Instagram account.

Kanye West: 'Yeah, exactly. We can't have it like be somebody else's idea that gets in front and they're like… Because if you're like a really true, creative, visceral, vibey type person, it's probably hard for you to work at a corporation. So how can you give a creative ideas and you're working in a house of non-creativity? It's like this weird… So whenever we talk directly… Okay, now what if later in the song I was also to have said, uh… 'I made her famous'? Is that a…'

Taylor Swift: '[Apprehensively.] Did you say that?'

Kanye West: 'Yes, it might've happened. [Laughs.]'

Taylor Swift: 'Well, what am I going to do about it?'

Kanye West: 'Uh, like, do the hair flip?'

Taylor Swift: 'Yeah. I mean… Um… It's just kind of like, whatever, at this point. But I mean, you've got to tell the story the way that it happened to you and the way that you've experienced it. Like, you honestly didn't know who I was before that. Like, it doesn't matter if I sold 7 million of that album ['Fearless'] before you did that, which is what happened. You didn't know who I was before that. It's fine. But, um, yeah. I can't wait to hear it.'

- Taylor Swift warned Kanye West about her negative thought regarding the content of the lyrics:

    Kanye West: 'Okay. All right. Wait a second, you sound sad.'

    Taylor Swift: 'Well, is it gonna be mean?'

    Kanye West: 'No, I don't think it's mean.'

    Taylor Swift: 'Okay, then, let me hear it.'

Kanye West: 'Okay. It says, um,… and the funny thing is, when I first played it and my wife heard it, she was like, 'Huh? What? That's too crazy,' blah, blah, blah. And then like when Ninja from Die Atwoord heard it, he was like, 'Oh my God, this is the craziest s–. This is why I love Kanye,' blah, blah, blah, that kind of thing. And now it's like my wife's favourite f–ing line. I just wanted to give you some premise of that. Right?'

Taylor Swift: 'Okay.'

Kanye West: 'So it says 'To all my Southside [N-word] that know me best, I feel like Taylor Swift might owe me sex.'

Taylor Swift: '[Laughs, relieved.] That's not mean.'

on the **FAMOUS** feud

Taylor Swift: 'Oh my God! I mean, I need to think about it, because you know, when you hear something for the first time, you just need to think about it. Because it is absolutely crazy. I'm glad it's not mean, though. It doesn't feel mean. But oh my God, the buildup you gave it, I thought it was going to be like, 'That stupid, dumb bitch.' But it's not. So I don't know. I mean, the launch thing, I think it would be kind of confusing to people. But I definitely like… I definitely think that when I'm asked about it, of course I'll be like, 'Yeah, I love that. I think it's hilarious.' But, um, I need to think about it.'

- offered space for Kanye and Kim to present their story in the way they wanted and under their terms;
- Taylor presented a more truthful side of the storyline of the *Famous* narrative, *only after* Kim and Kanye presented new information in regard to her involvement in the making of the song;
- she interfered only to rightfully defend herself from Kanye and Kim's accusations of being a liar, and that she knew everything about the song;
- was caught in Kanye West's wrong presentation to the general public of her involvement in the song;
- there is strong evidence that can support a good argument that Taylor Swift it is a victim of Kanye and Kim's misleading and biased information about her involvement in the creation of song **Famous**.

Both artists:

- failed to share all the details of what happened during the telephone conversation from January 2016;
- based on the current evidence: Kanye West misled and presented a biased story of Taylor Swift's involvement in the creation of the song, while Taylor Swift told a more truthful side of her involvement in the creation of the song, and the background narrative of the telephone conversation;
- the reaction of the public opinion was excessively huge with hundreds of thousands of comments and distribution of the content with Kanye West, Kim Kardashian and Taylor Swift; overall, the balance of neutrality of the Western mass-media is high, but there are articles in favour of Kanye and Kim with Taylor Swift being portrayed as the perpetrator, while Kanye and Kim as the victims of Taylor Swift[578];
- the addition of the telephone conversation from January 2016 in the chronological line of January 2016, and then its repetition in July (when the online evidence was released by Kim Kardashian on Snapchat) help to highlight the following facts: Kanye West misinformed the general public about the real contribution of Taylor Swift in the

[578] For example: Nate Jones, 'When Did the Media Turn Against Taylor Swift?', *Vulture*, July 21, 2016, https://www.vulture.com/2016/07/when-did-the-media-turn-against-taylor-swift.html, last accessed: October 23, 2017; The Ringer Staff, 'When Did You First Realize Taylor Swift Was Lying to You?', *The Ringer*, July 12, 2016, https://www.theringer.com/2016/7/12/16039240/when-did-you-first-realize-taylor-swift-was-lying-to-you-bb5a00a32b65#.paejv7bn2, last accessed: October 23, 2017. More examples in chapter V.

making of the *song Famous,* and he is the perpetrator of the feud; Taylor Swift is the victim who is not being told the whole story, but she is presented by Kanye West and Kim Kardashian as she knows everything; Taylor Swift's refusal to admit the accusations advanced by Kim and Kanye is ignored by them; Kanye and Kim refused to accept the negative consequences of the general public toward and in reference to Taylor Swift that followed after they set the path of the negative narrative; Kim and Kanye's negative narrative about Taylor Swift was largely distributed by the Western mass-media online, and also through print editions of newspapers and magazines.

II.2.1 A New Face of the '**Famous** Feud' Timeline

In this subchapter I investigated the narrative line of the relationship between Kanye West and Taylor Swift from September 2009 (MTV Music Awards) to November 2017 (the release of Taylor Swift's album *reputation*), and between Kim Kardashian and Taylor Swift from June 2016 to March 2020, with the aim of finding patterns that could present unknown information, or what we already know can be presented in a new way that could be used for a better and easier understanding of the feud.

To find the existence of patterns:

- I used the key dates of the *Famous* feud (based on the precise date (day, month, year) when the events happened) available in the table with the *Famous* feud timeline; the dates were used to create a figure with a 3D narrative line which exposes the dynamic between the players of the *Famous* feud; the creation of one large figure allowed me to see the whole narrative line.

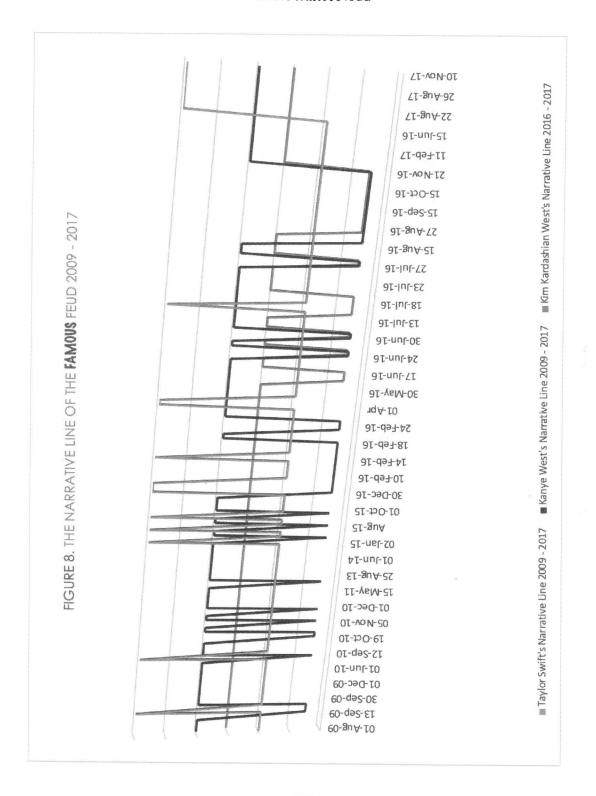

FIGURE 8. THE NARRATIVE LINE OF THE **FAMOUS** FEUD 2009 - 2017

■ Taylor Swift's Narrative Line 2009 - 2017   ■ Kanye West's Narrative Line 2009 - 2017   ■ Kim Kardashian West's Narrative Line 2016 - 2017

II.2.1.1 The Analysis of the **Famous** Feud Timeline 2009 – 2020

Based on Figure 8, I discovered few patterns of behaviour between Kanye West and Taylor Swift; the starting point of the patterns is in September 2009 with Kanye West and Taylor Swift, and between Kim Kardashian and Taylor Swift. For Kanye West and Taylor Swift the narrative line is from September 2009 to November 2017, and for Kim Kardashian and Taylor Swift the narrative is from June 2016 to March 2020.

The patterns were discovered based on the following method: I linked and compared the events from Kanye West's life with the events from Taylor Swift's life; in other words, what events existed in Taylor Swift's narrative line when Kanye West interfered in her narrative line.

TABLE 5. KANYE WEST'S PATTERNS OF THE FAMOUS FEUD TIMELINE 2009 – 2017
PATTERN 1. Interfered in Taylor Swift's key moments from her life: recognition at high level by the music industry and attendance at the awards ceremonies.

Events from Kanye West's Narrative Line	*Events from Taylor Swift's Narrative Line*
September 13, 2009:	*September 13, 2009:*
Kanye West got onto the stage of the MTV VMA and interrupted Taylor Swift speech for acceptance of the award for the Best Female Video (You Belong with Me).	Taylor Swift was nominated for the first time for the Best Female Video and she won, but was interrupted by Kanye West and was not able to finish her speech.
February 11, 2016:	*February 15, 2016:*
Kanye West debuted his musical album *The Life of Pablo* at his Yeezy Season 3 show at Madison Square Garden, New York. In one of his songs, 'Famous,' he raps 'I feel like me and Taylor might still have sex / Why? I made that bitch famous (God damn) / I made that bitch famous.' Kanye West told the public that he has the approval from Taylor Swift, in return Taylor Swift's Team replied that she cautioned Kanye West about the song and that Taylor Swift was never aware of the line 'I made that bitch famous'.	It was in the week (four days until the ceremony) before the Grammy Awards (the highest award in the USA music industry) and Taylor Swift presented to the awards with the label 'that bitch' and that her fame is because of Kanye West. Taylor Swift was the winner of the *Album of the Year* for the second time (the first woman in the music industry).

PATTERN 2. Interfered in Taylor's narrative line with a negative view about her character and skills while key events from his life are in motion: such as releasing a new album, tickets for sale for a tour and promoting a musical tour.

Before the release of his album My Beautiful Dark Twisted Fantasy in 2010:

October 20, 2010:

Kanye West had an interview with Access Hollywood:

Kanye West: 'Why are the last four Albums of the Year: Taylor Swift, Dixie Chicks, Ray Charles and Herbie Hancock? Like, you know, with all due respect… that's inaccurate.'

November 5, 2010:

Kanye West had an interview with the radio station KDWB:

Kanye West: 'My moment with Taylor, 12 years old, eighteen year old girl me um cutting her off it show like a lack of compassion with everything she went to to deserve this one moment that shouldn't you know that [inaudible] have 100 magazine covers and sell a million first week, but um um that shouldn't even categorize with the greatest living artists that we have to date even be put in the same category you know it's it's just it's just disrespectful was retarded and I for me you can see the amount of work that we put into this.'

Kanye West: 'It's like, what's so arrogant about that moment? If anything, it's selfless. I'm walking around now with half an arm, trying to sell albums and having to walk in rooms and be afraid of my food getting spat in, like people going 'I lost all total respect for you,' and nobody wants to just sit and look at the reality.'

Kanye West: 'The audacity of it losing anything … I guarantee if it was the other way around, and Taylor Swift was 15, 12, 15 years into the game, and on her 40th video or 50th video, and she made the video of her career, do you think she would have lost to a brand new artist? Hell no!'

During a secret show slash release party at the Bowery Ballroom in New York City last night, 1.00 am, Kanye West continued his rant by expressing his continued issues with singer Taylor Swift and said: 'Taylor never came to my defense at any interview. … And rode the waves and rode it and rode it.'

Before the release of his album Yeezus in 2013:

Seven days before the release of his album, June 11, 2013: In a *New York Times* interview Kanye West stated about Taylor Swift VMA's moment that he doesn't have any regret about his interruption and that it was a situation where he gave into peer pressure to apologize. When asked if he'd take back the original action or the apology, if given the choice, he answered, 'You know what? I can answer that, but I'm – I'm just -- not afraid, but I know that would be such a distraction. It's such a strong thing, and people have such a strong feeling about it. *My Beautiful*

Dark Twisted Fantasy was my long, backhanded apology. You know how people give a backhanded compliment? It was a backhanded apology. It was like, all these raps, all these sonic acrobatics. I was like: 'Let me show you guys what I can do, and please accept me back. You want to have me on your shelves.'

Before the release of his album The Life of Pablo in 2016:

On February 11, 2016 Kanye West debuted his musical album *The Life of Pablo* at his Yeezy Season 3 show at Madison Square Garden, New York. In one of his songs, 'Famous,' he raps 'I feel like me and Taylor might still have sex / Why? I made that bitch famous (God damn) / I made that bitch famous.'

In a GQ interview (June 16, 2016) for July new issue, Kim Kardashian spoked about Taylor Swift and her implication in the song 'Famous'. Two days before this interview Kanye West started to sale tickets (June 14 for American Express cardholders and June 16 for Tidal members, June 18 for general public) to his music tour named *Saint Pablo Tour*.

Before Saint Pablo Tour in 2016:

Kanye West and Kim Kardashian are on the cover of Harper's Bazaar September issue. When asked by editor Laura Brown about their favourite Taylor Swift song, Kanye West replied, 'For me? I don't have one.' Kim Kardashian replied: 'I was such a fan of hers.'

PATTERN 3. Disagreed and shared negative views about Taylor Swift's music and achievements.

SEPTEMBER 13, 2009:

While Taylor Swift was giving her acceptance speech for Best Female Video *You Belong with Me* at MTV Video Music Awards, Kanye West got onto the stage and interrupted her; he took her microphone, saying: 'Yo, Taylor, I'm really happy for you and I'mma let you finish, but Beyoncé had one of the best videos of all time! One of the best videos of all time!' (Kanye West was referring to the music video for 'Single Ladies (Put a Ring on It)'. He then handed the microphone back to Taylor Swift.

OCTOBER 20, 2010:

Kanye West had an interview with *Access Hollywood*:
Kanye West: 'Why are the last four Albums of the Year: Taylor Swift, Dixie Chicks, Ray Charles and Herbie Hancock? Like, you know, with all due respect… that's inaccurate.'

NOVEMBER 5, 2010:

Kanye West had an interview with the radio station KDWB:

Kanye West: 'My moment with Taylor, 12 years old, eighteen year old girl me um cutting her off it show like a lack of compassion with everything she went to to deserve this one moment that shouldn't you know that [inaudible] have 100 magazine covers and sell a million first week, but um um that shouldn't even categorize with the greatest living artists that we have to date even be put in the same category you know it's it's just it's just disrespectful was retarded and I for me you can see the amount of work that we put into this.'

Kanye West: 'The audacity of it losing anything ... I guarantee if it was the other way around, and Taylor Swift was 15, 12, 15 years into the game, and on her 40th video or 50th video, and she made the video of her career, do you think she would have lost to a brand new artist? Hell no!'

FEBRUARY 11, 2016:

On 11 February 2016 Kanye West debuted his musical album *The Life of Pablo* at his Yeezy Season 3 show at Madison Square Garden, New York. In one of his songs, 'Famous,' he raps 'I feel like me and Taylor might still have sex / Why? I made that bitch famous (God damn) / I made that bitch famous.'

FEBRUARY 23, 2016:

Kanye West wrote a few tweets in now deleted (deactivated?) Twitter account:
'I made Dark Fantasy and Watch the Throne in one year and wasn't nominated for either and you know who has 2 albums of the year.'
– KANYE WEST (@kanyewest) February 23, 2016

JULY 28, 2016:

Kanye West and Kim Kardashian are on the cover of Harper's Bazaar September issue. When asked by editor Laura Brown about their favourite Taylor Swift song, Kanye West replied, 'For me? I don't have one.'

PATTERN 4: Refused to take responsibility for his negative and inappropriate behaviour against Taylor Swift.

NOVEMBER 5, 2010:

Kanye West had an interview with the radio station KDWB:
Kanye West: 'It's like, what's so arrogant about that moment? If anything, it's selfless. I'm walking around now with half an arm, trying to sell albums and having to walk in rooms and be afraid of my food getting spat in, like people going 'I lost all total respect for you,' and nobody wants to just sit and look at the reality.'

JUNE 11, 2013:

In a *New York Times* interview Kanye West stated about Taylor Swift VMA's moment that he doesn't have any regret about his interruption and that it was a situation where he gave into peer pressure to apologize. When asked if he'd take back the original action or the apology, if given the choice, he answered, 'You know what? I can answer that, but I'm – I'm just -- not afraid, but I know that would be such a distraction. It's such a strong thing, and people have such a strong feeling about it. *My Beautiful Dark Twisted Fantasy* was my long, backhanded apology. You know how people give a backhanded compliment? It was a backhanded apology. It was like, all these raps, all these sonic acrobatics. I was like: 'Let me show you guys what I can do, and please accept me back. You want to have me on your shelves.'

FEBRUARY 24, 2016:

At Yo Gotti's album release party at the 1OAK nightclub in Hollywood, Kanye West reiterates he told Taylor Swift about the 'Famous' lyric and said 'She had two seconds to be cool and she fucked it up!'

JULY 27, 2016:

Kanye West makes a guest appearance at Drake's concert in Chicago, and speaks out about Taylor Swift. Kanye West told his fans, 'All I gotta say is, I am so glad my wife has Snapchat!', 'Now y'all can know the truth and can't nobody talk s–t about 'Ye no more.' After his words, he performed the song 'Famous'.

AUGUST 28, 2016:

Kanye West takes the stage at the 2016 MTV Video Music Awards. He received 6 minutes to do what he wants. He addressed the song 'Famous' and Taylor Swift by saying that he's a 'lover of all,' which is 'why I called her.'

During the music concert tour, Saint Pablo Tour, presented the *song Famous* with Taylor Swift as the negative character of the song, and encouraged people to shout 'bitch' when referencing to Taylor Swift.

PATTERN 5. He does not want to be a truly friend of Taylor Swift.

Interrupted her speech in 2009, negative views about her music in 2010, 2011, 2013 and 2016; added new lyrics in the *song Famous* and presented those lyrics as Taylor Swift knew about it; encouraged people to shout 'bitch' in referencing Taylor Swift at his concerts in 2016.

PATTERN 6. Cannot move on and let Taylor Swift alone.

From 2010 to present: 1. refuses to admit his wrongdoing; 2. to apologize to Taylor Swift for not sending her the final version of the song; 3. did not confirmed to the general public the truth that Taylor did not know the line she disputed.

PATTERN 7. Created, maintained and supported the Famous feud according with his needs.

From 2009 to present through various events created and promoted by him (songs and album release, tour tickets available and during the tours across USA, interview).

PATTERN 8. It is solely responsible for the negative opinion of the general public toward and in reference to Taylor Swift.

In 2009 by himself and from 2016 onwards with Kim Kardashian.

PATTERN 9. Presented biased information regarding Taylor Swift's involvement in the song Famous from 2016.

From February 2016, June and July 2016 until today.

PATTERN 10. Created and maintained a negative image about Taylor Swift.

In September 2009 while interrupting her speech with the reason that she did not deserve the award; in 2010 through interviews; in February, June and July 2016: through tweets and Kim Kardashian parts of the telephone conversation; from September 2016 until October 2016 through the concert Saint Pablo Tour where his song and his live interpretation of the song encouraged people to shout 'bitch' in referencing Taylor Swift.

In the table above, I wrote the following text: 'During a secret show slash release party at the Bowery Ballroom in New York City last night, 1.00 am, Kanye West continued his rant by expressing his continued issues with singer Taylor Swift and said: 'Taylor never came to my defense at any interview. … And rode the waves and rode it and rode it.' However, there is evidence to show that Taylor Swift did not 'rode the waves and rode it and rode it', and that she tried to stop the feud: during an interview on the radio programme MJ's Morning Show, Taylor Swift refused to talk about Kanye West: 'I'm just honestly trying not to make it into a bigger deal than it already is' […] It's kind of become more of a big deal than I ever thought it would be.' […] 'I just, you know, it happened on TV, so everybody saw what happened. I just would like to move on maybe a little bit.' […] 'I really would appreciate it if we could talk about something else, because I've asked you three times now, and I'm trying to be nice about it.' […] 'It just isn't something we need to spend this whole interview talking about.'[579] Overall, Kanye West has talked more negatively about Taylor Swift since September 2009 until the publication of this report.

If each album represents the life of the artist, then *The Life of Pablo* is the life of a man who sacrificed a life that does not belong to him, does not take responsibility for his negative actions, is against a person who can write and sing her own lyrics and titles of songs.[580]

TABLE 6. TAYLOR SWIFT'S PATTERNS OF THE **FAMOUS** FEUD TIMELINE 2009 – 2017
PATTERN 1. *Interfered in the narrative line of the feud to defend herself from Kanye West's negative behaviour about her character and skills.*

SEPTEMBER 14, 2009:

The interview with E Online News after the MTV show:

'I was standing on stage and I was really excited because I had just won the award and then I was really excited because Kanye West was on the stage,' […] 'And then I wasn't so excited anymore after that.'

The reporter asked Taylor Swift if she has hard feelings about Kanye West. Taylor responded:

'I don't know him and I've never met him.'

The reporter continued asking Taylor if she was a fan before the event from the stage. Taylor responded:

'Yeah, It's Kanye West.'

The reporter continued asking Taylor if she is still a fan and 'I take a no?' Taylor responded:

'You know I just… I don't know him and I don't want to start anything because I just, you know, I had a great night tonight.'

SEPTEMBER 15, 2009:

Taylor Swift (after The View) told ABC News Radio: 'Kanye did call me and he was very sincere in his apology, and I accepted that apology.'

---

[579] Catriona Wightman, 'Swift 'Refuses to Talk About Kanye'', *Digital Spy*, September 19, 2009, available at: https://www.digitalspy.com/showbiz/a178162/swift-refuses-to-talk-about-kanye/, last accessed: May 25, 2018.
[580] Read Casian Anton, *Black and White Music*.

SEPTEMBER 12, 2010:

During MTV VMAs, Taylor Swift sang 'Innocent', a song widely believed (mass media and fans of Taylor Swift and Kanye West) to be about Kanye West and her forgiveness for what Kanye West did to her a year later:

'It's alright, just wait and see
Your string of lights is still bright to me
You're still an innocent
Lives change like the weather
It's okay, life is a tough crowd
32 and still growin' up now
I hope you remember
Today is never too late to
Be brand new.'

FEBRUARY 12, 2016:

Taylor Swift camp replied:

'Kanye did not call for approval, but to ask Taylor to release his single „Famous' on her Twitter account. She declined and cautioned him about releasing a song with such a strong misogynistic message. Taylor was never made aware of the actual lyric, „I made that bitch famous.'

FEBRUARY 15, 2016:

While accepting Album of the Year award at the GRAMMYs, Taylor Swift addressed what is believed to be about the infamous Kanye West lyrics about her:

'I want to thank the fans for the last 10 years, and the recording academy for giving us this unbelievable honor. I want to thank all of the collaborators that you see on this stage. Mostly, I want to thank my co-executive producer Max Martin, who has deserved to be up here for 25 years. And as the first woman to win album of the year at the Grammy's twice, I want to say to all the young women out there, there are going to be people along the way who, will try to undercut your success or take credit for your accomplishments or your fame. But if you just focus on the work and you don't let those people sidetrack you, someday when you get where you're going, you will know it was you and the people who love you who put you there, and that will be the greatest feeling in the world. Thank you for this moment.'

JUNE 16, 2016:

Taylor Swift camp, after Kim Kardashian's interview with GQ, issued a statement to GQ:

'Taylor does not hold anything against Kim Kardashian as she recognizes the pressure Kim must be under and that she is only repeating what she has been told by Kanye West. However, that does not change the fact that much of what Kim is saying is incorrect. Kanye West and Taylor only spoke once on the phone while she was on vacation with her family in January of 2016 and they have never spoken since. Taylor has never denied that conversation took place. It was on that phone call that Kanye West also asked her to release the song on her Twitter account, which she declined to do. Kanye West never told Taylor he was going to use the term 'that bitch' in referencing her. A song cannot be approved if it was never heard. Kanye West never played the song for Taylor Swift. Taylor heard it for the first time when everyone else did and was humiliated. Kim Kardashian's claim that Taylor and her team were aware of being recorded is not true, and Taylor cannot understand why Kanye West, and now Kim Kardashian, will not just leave her alone.'

JULY 17, 2016:

Taylor Swift responded to Kim Kardashian's Snapchat videos on her Instagram and Twitter account (now the picture with her response is deleted):

'That moment when Kanye West secretly records your phone call, then Kim posts it on the Internet.'

'Where is the video of Kanye telling me he was going to call me 'that bitch' in his song? It doesn't exist because it never happened. You don't get to control someone's emotional response to being called 'that bitch' in front of the entire world. Of course I wanted to like the song. I wanted to believe Kanye when he told me that I would love the song. I wanted us to have a friendly relationship. He promised to play the song for me, but he never did. While I wanted to be supportive of Kanye on the phone call, you cannot 'approve' a song you haven't heard. Being falsely painted as a liar when I was never given the full story or played any part of the song is character assassination. I would very much like to be excluded from this narrative, one that I have never asked to be a part of, since 2009.'

AUGUST 25, 2017:

Taylor Swift released a new song 'Look What You Made Me Do' with lyrics possible related to Kanye West: 'I don't like your little games/ I don't like your tilted stage.' Kanye West used an elevated tilted stage during his Saint Pablo tour.

AUGUST 27, 2017:

Taylor Swift released the music video of 'Look What You Made Me Do' which possibly contains coded references to Kanye West and Kim Kardashian: snake imagery (see page and the table *The New and Complete Timeline* July 17, 2016), imitation of Kim Kardashian and the Paris robbery (Kim Kardashian was caught in a bath tub and threaten with a gun), makes selfies then telling the others that she's 'getting receipts' so that she can 'edit them later,' at the end of the video says: 'I would like very much like to be excluded from this narrative' (is the last part of her reply to Kim Kardashian's videos on her Snapchat account with the phone conversation between her and Kanye West).

10 NOVEMBER 2017:

Taylor Swift released her newest musical album entitled *reputation*, which includes another song, *This Is Why We Can't Have Nice Things*, which is believed to be about Kanye West. The lyrics are: 'It was so nice being friends again, there I was giving you a second chance, but you stabbed me in the back without shaking my hand'; 'therein lies the issues, friends don't try to trick you, get you on the phone and mind twist you.' Taylor Swift's Team denied the speculation regarding the releasing date of her album and the 10th anniversary of Donda West (Kanye West mother).

PATTERN 2. Shared positive views about Kanye West's music and achievements.

SEPTEMBER 14, 2009:

The interview with E Online News after the MTV show:

'I was standing on stage and I was really excited because I had just won the award and then I was really excited because Kanye West was on the stage,' […] 'And then I wasn't so excited anymore after that.'

The reporter asked Taylor Swift if she has hard feelings about Kanye West. Taylor responded:

'I don't know him and I've never met him.'

The reporter continued asking Taylor if she was a fan before the event from the stage. Taylor responded:

'Yeah, It's Kanye West.'

The reporter continued asking Taylor if she is still a fan and 'I take a no?' Taylor responded:

'You know I just… I don't know him and I don't want to start anything because I just, you know, I had a great night tonight.'

APRIL 25, 2015:

In an interview with *Entertainment Tonight*, Cameron Mathison asked Taylor Swift about the possibility of a collaboration between her and Kanye West. Taylor Swift answered: 'He has said that… We're never been in the studio together, but he's got a lot of amazing ideas, he's one of those people who's just like idea, idea, idea, like what you think of this, what you think of that, he's very creative and like I've think we've talked about it but we've also about so many other things, I think I completely respect his vision as a producer, so that's all I know now, I have no idea how the next album is gonna be though.'

APRIL 30, 2015:

In an interview with *E! News*, Jason Kennedy asked Taylor Swift about the about the possibility of a collaboration between her and Kanye West. Taylor Swift answered: 'Everybody is saying that […]

He did said that […] We've hung out, gone to dinner, talked and he's one of those people who's always throwing out ideas, so that was one of the ideas that was thrown out. There were lots of other ideas he has, you can imagine. But no creative decision has been made up about the next record.'[581]

AUGUST 11, 2015:

During a cover interview with *Vanity Fair*, Taylor Swift said about Kanye West:

'I feel like I wasn't ready to be friends with him until I felt like he had some sort of respect for me, and he wasn't ready to be friends with me until he had some sort of respect for me – so it was the same issue, and we both reached the same place at the same time' […] And then Kanye and I both reached a place where he would say really nice things about my music and what I've accomplished, and I could ask him how his kid doing. … We haven't planned [a collaboration, added by the author] … But hey, I like him as a person. And that's a really good, nice first step, a nice place for us to be.'

AUGUST 30, 2015:

Taylor Swift accepted Kanye West's request to be the person to give him the Video Vanguard Award at the MTV from 2015 and invoked the original incident in her speech:

'I first met Kanye West six years ago – at this show, actually! [..] *The College Dropout* was the very first album my brother and I bought on iTunes when I was 12 years old…I've been a fan of his for as long as I can remember because Kanye defines what it means to be a creative force in music, fashion and, well, life. So, I guess I have to say to all the other winners tonight: I'm really happy for you, and imma let you finish, but Kanye West has had one of the greatest careers of all time.'

PATTERN 3. *Tried to forgive Kanye West and move on.*

Taylor wrote the song 'Innocent' for Kanye West; despite the negative views about her by Kanye West in 2010 and 2013, in 2015 she accepted his invitation to hand him the MTV Vanguard Award; during the telephone conversation from January 2016, she supported Kanye's song and was nice on the phone. In April 2016 she refused to talk about the *song Famous*.

PATTERN 4. *Used same methods to reply as Kanye West: through interviews, official statements and music.*

---

[581] Bruna Nessif, 'Is This Taylor Swift and Kanye West Collaboration Happening or What?! Watch Now', *EOnline*, April 30, 2015, https://www.eonline.com/news/652354/is-this-taylor-swift-and-kanye-west-collaboration-happening-or-what-watch-now, last accessed: October 23, 2017.

September 2009 (interviews); September 2010 though 'Innocent'; October 2010 (the song 'Innocent' was included on her album *Speak Now*); June and July 2016 through official statement; August 2017 - November 2017 through music.

PATTERN 5. She wanted to have a positive relationship with Kanye West.

SEPTEMBER 14, 2009:

The interview with E Online News after the MTV show:

The reporter asked Taylor Swift if she has hard feelings about Kanye West. Taylor responded:

'I don't know him and I've never met him.'

The reporter continued asking Taylor if she is still a fan and 'I take a no?' Taylor responded:

'You know I just... I don't know him and I don't want to start anything because I just, you know, I had a great night tonight.'

SEPTEMBER 15, 2009:

Taylor Swift (after The View) told ABC News Radio: 'Kanye did call me and he was very sincere in his apology, and I accepted that apology.'

SEPTEMBER 12, 2010:

During MTV VMAs, Taylor Swift sang 'Innocent', a song widely believed (mass media and fans of Taylor Swift and Kanye West) to be about Kanye West and her forgiveness for what Kanye West did to her a year later:

'It's alright, just wait and see
Your string of lights is still bright to me
You're still an innocent
Lives change like the weather
It's okay, life is a tough crowd
32 and still growin' up now
I hope you remember
Today is never too late to
Be brand new.'

APRIL 29, 2015:

In an interview with *Entertainment Tonight*, Cameron Mathison asked Taylor Swift about the rumoured collaboration between her and Kanye West. Taylor Swift answered: 'He has said that... We're never been in the studio together, but he's got a lot of amazing ideas, he's one of those people who's just like idea, idea, idea, like what you think of this, what you think of that, he's very creative and like I've think we've talked about it but we've also about so many other things, I think I completely respect his vision as a producer, so that's all I know now, I have no idea how the next album is gonna be though.'

APRIL 30, 2015:

In an interview with *E! News*, Jason Kennedy asked Taylor Swift about the rumoured collaboration between her and Kanye West. Taylor Swift answered: 'Everybody is saying that [...] He did said that [...] We've hung out, gone to dinner, talked and he's one of those people who's always throwing out ideas, so that was one of the ideas that was thrown out. There were lots of other ideas he has, you can imagine. But no creative decision has been made up about the next record.'[582]

AUGUST 11, 2015:

During a cover interview with *Vanity Fair*, Taylor Swift said about Kanye West:

'I feel like I wasn't ready to be friends with him until I felt like he had some sort of respect for me, and he wasn't ready to be friends with me until he had some sort of respect for me – so it was the same issue, and we both reached the same place at the same time' [...] And then Kanye and I both reached a place where he would say really nice things about my music and what I've accomplished, and I could ask him how his kid doing. ... We haven't planned [a collaboration, added by the author] ... But hey, I like him as a person. And that's a really good, nice first step, a nice place for us to be.'

AUGUST 30, 2015:

Taylor Swift accepted Kanye West's request to be the person to give him the Video Vanguard Award at the MTV from 2015 and invoked the original incident in her speech:

'I first met Kanye West six years ago – at this show, actually! [..] *The College Dropout* was the very first album my brother and I bought on iTunes when I was 12 years old...I've been a fan of his for as long as I can remember because Kanye defines what it means to be a creative force in music, fashion and, well, life. So, I guess I have to say to all the other winners tonight: I'm really happy for you, and imma let you finish, but Kanye West has had one of the greatest careers of all time.'

PATTERN 6. Maintained and supported the feud as side effect of her defence mechanism from Kanye West.

---

[582] Bruna Nessif, 'Is This Taylor Swift and Kanye West Collaboration Happening or What?! Watch Now', *EOnline*, April 30, 2015, https://www.eonline.com/news/652354/is-this-taylor-swift-and-kanye-west-collaboration-happening-or-what-watch-now, last accessed: October 23, 2017.

September 2009; September 2010; February, June and July 2016; August 2017 to November 2017.

PATTERN 7. Does not want to be a part of the Famous feud since 2009.

SEPTEMBER 14, 2009:

The interview with E Online News after the MTV show:

'I was standing on stage and I was really excited because I had just won the award and then I was really excited because Kanye West was on the stage,' […] 'And then I wasn't so excited anymore after that.'

The reporter asked Taylor Swift if she has hard feelings about Kanye West. Taylor responded:

'I don't know him and I've never met him.'

The reporter continued asking Taylor if she was a fan before the event from the stage. Taylor responded:

'Yeah, It's Kanye West.'

The reporter continued asking Taylor if she is still a fan and 'I take a no?' Taylor responded:

'You know I just… I don't know him and I don't want to start anything because I just, you know, I had a great night tonight.'

SEPTEMBER 19, 2009:

During an interview on the radio programme MJ's Morning Show, the host asked Taylor Swift about Kanye West and she replied:

'I'm just honestly trying not to make it into a bigger deal than it already is' […] It's kind of become more of a big deal than I ever thought it would be.'

'I just, you know, it happened on TV, so everybody saw what happened. I just would like to move on maybe a little bit.'

'I didn't know what to think, but I think that we should maybe talk about something else, because I've talked about this in one interview, and that was going to be it'. […] 'It's not something I feel like we need to keep talking about.'

'I really would appreciate it if we could talk about something else, because I've asked you three times now, and I'm trying to be nice about it.'

'It just isn't something we need to spend this whole interview talking about.'

In the end, the host insisted more about Kanye West, however, Taylor Swift decided to stop the interview[583].

APRIL 14, 2016:

In an interview with Vogue, Taylor Swift addressed her acceptance speech at Grammy Awards and Kanye West:

'I think the world is bored with the saga. I don't want to add anything to it, because then there's just more... I guess what I wanted to call attention to in my speech at the Grammys was how it's going to be difficult if you're a woman who wants to achieve something in her life - no matter what.'

JUNE 16, 2016:

Taylor Swift camp, after Kim Kardashian's interview with GQ, issued a statement to GQ:

'Taylor does not hold anything against Kim Kardashian as she recognizes the pressure Kim must be under and that she is only repeating what she has been told by Kanye West. However, that does not change the fact that much of what Kim is saying is incorrect. Kanye West and Taylor only spoke once on the phone while she was on vacation with her family in January of 2016 and they have never spoken since. Taylor has never denied that conversation took place. It was on that phone call that Kanye West also asked her to release the song on her Twitter account, which she declined to do. Kanye West never told Taylor he was going to use the term 'that bitch' in referencing her. A song cannot be approved if it was never heard. Kanye West never played the song for Taylor Swift. Taylor heard it for the first time when everyone else did and was humiliated. Kim Kardashian's claim that Taylor and her team were aware of being recorded is not true, and Taylor cannot understand why Kanye West, and now Kim Kardashian, will not just leave her alone.'

JULY 17, 2016:

Taylor Swift responded to Kim Kardashian's Snapchat videos on her Instagram and Twitter account (now the picture with her response is deleted):

'That moment when Kanye West secretly records your phone call, then Kim posts it on the Internet.'

'Where is the video of Kanye telling me he was going to call me 'that bitch' in his song? It doesn't exist because it never happened. You don't get to control someone's emotional response to being called 'that bitch' in front of the entire world. Of course I wanted to like the song. I wanted to believe Kanye when he told me that I would love the song. I wanted us to have a friendly relationship. He promised to play the song for me, but he never did. While I wanted to be supportive of Kanye on the phone call, you cannot 'approve' a song you haven't heard. Being falsely painted as a liar when I was never given the full story or played any part of the song is

---

[583] Catriona Wightman, 'Swift 'Refuses to Talk About Kanye'.

character assassination. I would very much like to be excluded from this narrative, one that I have never asked to be a part of, since 2009.'

PATTERN 8. Promoted a more truthful version of the events.

September 2009 and 2010; February, June and July 2016; August – November 2017; Present day.

Surprisingly, Taylor Swift is not the only artist which had to deal with Kanye West's interference in the narrative line. In the following section I wrote examples of the marketing strategy? of Kanye West from the point of view of one pattern (shortly modified, but the essence is the same):

Pattern: *interference in the narrative line of other people while events from his life are in motion, this time with the release of a new album, **ye**, from 2018.*

Kanye West[584] met with Rick Rubin, the executive producer on Kanye West's previous two albums, *Yeezus* (2013) and *The Life of Pablo* (2016).[585] Later that month, Kanye West met with and previewed the album for radio host Charlamagne Tha God (Mr. Lenard McKelvey as real name).[586]

On April 13, Kanye West was back on social media. Following his return, Kanye West was super active, his first retweet being about the Ferguson Shootings (which involved protests and riots that began the day after the fatal shooting of Michael Brown by the white police officer Darren Wilson on August 9, 2014, in Ferguson, Missouri[587]). Due to a high numbers of tweets, I created a list with the main topics explored by Kanye West.

- Saint Pablo (memories and two tattoo designs with the word 'saint');

- philosophical statements;
- new shoes prototypes;

---

[584] In *April 2018* section: all the information (except where there is a footnote) was collected from Kanye West's Twitter account.
[585] Eddie Fu, 'Kanye West spotted with Rick Rubin at Calabasas office', *Consequence of Sound*, April 3, 2018, https://consequenceofsound.net/2018/04/kanye-west-spotted-at-rick-rubins-recording-studio/, last accessed: May 28, 2018.
[586] Nerisha Penrose, 'Kanye West Previewed His New Album For, *Billboard*, April 19, 2018, https://www.billboard.com/articles/columns/hip-hop/8350853/kanye-west-previewed-new-album-charlamagne-tha-god, last accessed: May 28, 2018; 'NEW ALBUM'S OUT
But Only for Charlamagne', *TMZ*, April 19, 2018, http://www.tmz.com/2018/04/19/kanye-west-charlamagne-tha-god-new-album/, last accessed: May 25, 2018; Danielle Harling, 'Charlamagne Tha God Details Secret Kanye West Meeting', *Hiphopdx*, April 19, 2018, https://hiphopdx.com/news/id.46551/title.charlamagne-tha-god-details-secret-kanye-west-meeting#, last accessed: May 25, 2018.
[587] 'Killing of Michael Brown', *Wikipedia*, available at: https://en.wikipedia.org/wiki/Killing_of_Michael_Brown, last accessed: June 23, 2018.

- he is writing a book in real time on Twitter;
- video: Lauren Hill 20 years of relevance;
- announced his new album of 7 songs: June 1st, me and Kudi June 8th and its called Kids See Ghosts, Teyana Taylor June 22, Pusha T May 25;
- he likes the thinking of Candance Owens;
- doesn't subscribe to the term and concept of God fearing;
- David Hammos, Bliz-aard Ball Sale. Elena Filipovic;
- David: Higher Goals;
- Slavery (a sensible topic in the USA);
- Jospeh Beuys;
- Tesla and Elon Musk;
- retweets videos made a person named Scott Adams about Kanye West and his power to change minds, takes us in the Golden Age, he advocates for African Americans, racism and has good credential;
- Donald Glover is a free thinker;
- Prince;
- Michael Jackson;
- earns more than Michael Jordan, exposes fake news about Yeezy;
- I'm this generation Ford Hughes Jobs Disney;
- TMZ fake news;
- People magazine fake news;
- Charlamagne interview: 10 million offer for his album;
- Yeezy prices;
- partnership with Adidas;
- Presidency;
- Final tribe album should have won the grammys;
- turn the grammys into yammys;
- Rocky ASAP: album release;
- Mr. Trump: both dragon energy, he is my brother;
- Kids See Ghosts: short film shot by: Dexter Navy;
- Google;
- Wants to meet with Lary from Google;
- we got love: hat MAGA signed;
- Peter Thiel;
- picture Kanye president 2024;
- retweet of president Donal Trump reply to his MAGA tweet;
- Scooter Braun;
- Irving;
- David Joseph Frank Bridgman Oliver Nusse;
- Need Hypes William for Nas movie;
- wants to meet with Tom Cook;
- wants to see a tour with Nici Minaj and Cardi B;
- about what his fans are and should be;
- black people don't need to be democrats;
- Claudio Silverstein;
- Claudio, Chance and Kanye to build new homes in Chicago;
- Obama was in office 8 years and nothing changed in Chicago;
- Cook and Trump: favourite people;
- retweet president Donald Trump retweet of his tweet with signed MAGA;
- dialogue with John Legend;

- retweet with his philosophical statements in cartoon;
- *Yeezy* pictures behind the backstage;
- *Lift Yourself* song is released;
- John Legend;
- a conversation with a person named ‚Wes' about his album cover: Kanye West decided to put as cover a picture with plastic surgeon Jan Adams (he performed his mother last surgery); Kanye West asked ‚Wes' for an idea as a cover album, ‚Wes' replied: ‚LOVE EVERYONE', Kanye West replied back: ‚I love that';
- asked people to ‚contact a person with whom you haven't spoken in years, tell them that you love them';
- *Ye vs the people* song is released;
- Emma Gonzalez inspired Kanye West with her personality and thinking, he cut his hair as a way to identify himself with Emma Gonzalez (his hair was painted blonde);
- J Cole;
- retweet Ali post about him;
- project Ashley Morgan Hastings;
- retweet John Durant;
- statements about love;
- Disney and Apple designers;
- picture with sketch about new *Yeezy* products;
- youth and their role in the world;
- Candace Owens:
- Axel Vervoordt the globe;
- Adi Shankar;
- update: I said I was the greatest artist, but we all are great artists;
- open letter from Jan Adams (mother surgeon) to Kanye West and his desire that Kanye West to not use a picture with him as cover for his new musical album.

Due to a high numbers of tweets, I wrote a list with the main topics of Kanye West's Twitter content from May 2018[588]:

- wegotlove.com website;
- The interview with Charlamagne is available on his Youtube channel: the key topics are about Mr. Donald Trump and Kanye West support because Mr. Trump proved anything is possible in the USA; his hospitalization; Jay Z; Beyoncé; Taylor Swift; he wants an apology from Barack Obama; Kim Kardashian's robbery; Harriet Tubman and his face on the $20 bill, he wants Michael Jordan on the bill; *Yeezy* company, racism and slavery[589];
- he stopped by TMZ to share his thoughts on politics and freedom; there, he said the following controversial quote that shook the world to its core: 'When you hear

---

[588] In *May 2018* section: all the information (except where there is a footnote) was collected from Kanye West's Twitter account.
[589] Kanye West, 'kanye west / charlamagne interview', *Youtube*, May 1, 2018, https://www.youtube.com/watch?v=zxwfDlhJIpw, last accessed: May 2, 2018; Luke Morgan Britton, 'A quest to understand Kanye West: The biggest revelations in Ye's Charlamagne interview', *NME*, May 1, 2018, http://www.nme.com/blogs/nme-blogs/kanye-west-charlamagne-interview-biggest-revelations-2306236#a4pssa1bPShD2rg4.99, last accessed: May 2, 2018.

about slavery for 400 years. For 400 years?! That sounds like a choice'[590];

- TMZ life with Harvey and Candance Owens;
- Retweet an article about the open letter from Jan Adams;
- TMZ article about him and his drugs; http://www.tmz.com/2018/05/01/kanye-west-opioids-liposuction/
- Magic Johnson;
- retweet a message about love with a biblical quotation;
- Learns about love;
- Tesla and Elon Musk;
- shared This is America music video;
- SNL video: Kanye world;
- google search with names;
- Ricki and Morti show;
- UN sustainable development goals in 2015 to transform the world in 2030
- short video with the new music, two tracks from his album;
- we need hugs, Amma Mata had given over 32 millions of hugs;
- Phone addiction and advice how to use it;
- Google dopamine;
- Video youtube: Basically Sigmund Freud's nephew Edward Bernays capitalized off of his uncle's

philosophies and created modern day consumerism, the century of self: https://www.youtube.com/watch?v=eJ3RzGoQC4s;

- Daytona Pusha T cover work from Houston bathroom;
- download the app Wav Media to see live from his album release;
- In an interview with Kanye West[591] conducted during the June 1st listening party, Kanye West said he „redid the whole album after TMZ', alluding to an interview with TMZ on May 1st and suggesting that the entire album was re-recorded in a month;
- Kanye West explained the album title, which is a diminutive of his own name commonly used in his songs, by stating: „I believe Ye is the most commonly used word in the Bible, and in the Bible it means ‚you'. So I'm you, I'm us, it's us. It went from Kanye, which means ‚the only one', to just Ye – just being a reflection of our good, our bad, our confused, everything. The album is more of a reflection of who we are.'[592]

As with *April 2018* and *May 2018* sections, due to a high numbers of tweets, I wrote a

---

[590] Matt Bardon, 'Slavery Is A Choice' Kanye West FULL Interview on TMZ Live', *Youtube*, May 1, 2018, https://www.youtube.com/watch?v=IWJBWU7asEg, last accessed: May 28, 2018.

[591] In *June 2018* section: all the information (except where there is a footnote) was collected from Kanye West's Twitter account. Due to a possible (future, past?)

intervention of Kanye West, some information from this section could be deleted or changed.

[592] Trupti Rami, 'Kanye West on Being 'Diagnosed With a Mental Condition' and Redoing Ye After Crashing TMZ', *Vulture*, June 3, 2018, https://www.vulture.com/2018/06/kanye-west-on-ye-being-diagnosed-with-a-mental-condition.html, last accessed: June 4, 2018.

list with the main topics of Kanye West's Twitter content from June 2018:

- the album title: 'ye' not 'Love everyone';
- shop link to his website and the new merchandise;
- links with his album to Apple, Spotify, it was deleted, people reacted negatively;
- picture with the final tracks from 'ye' (it does not include the two tracks showed few days before the album release) and 'Kids See Ghosts';
- 'ye' cover generator[593];
- pictures with his success;
- picture with Kate Spade and her suicide, she was suffering from maniac depression;
- 'Kids See Ghosts' cover work of the album;
- retweets with success of his wife Mrs. Kim Kardashian West battle for the release from the prison of Mrs. Alice Marie Johnson (a first-time nonviolent drug offender who was given a life sentence without parole, plus 25 years); after months of work behind the scenes, the final step was for Kim Kardashian West was a face to face meeting with president Donald Trump in the Oval Office the result being a clemency granted from the president and her release from the prison[594];
- Tyler, the Creator: retweet;
- Nas *Nasir* album;
- retweet of a tweet posted by Billboard and his musical success;
- shared stories about other cases of people who tried to commit suicide;
- thanked to all the people who supported his album for number 1, he says 'our album';
- tweet an article written by CNN: he was not abandoned by his fans, his songs are in top[595];
- Deadpool soundtrack, tracks that sound like his music; I would have cleared my music for Deadpool;
- Wegotlove.com website and three videos about album release party, his interview with Charlamagne and a conversation about evolution and the song Ye vs. the people[596];
- pictures with his new shoes and clothes;
- tweeted Nas album *Nasir* tracklist, then link to his album;
- retweet of a person who suffers from bipolarity and how his music inspired people;

[593] Ye Cover generator, https://yenerator.com/, last accessed: June 25, 2018.
[594] Jake Horowit, Kendall Ciesemier, 'President Donald Trump grants clemency to Alice Johnson after Kim Kardashian West involvement', *Mic*, June 6, 2018, https://mic.com/articles/189663/exclusive-president-trump-grants-clemency-to-alice-johnson-after-kim-kardashian-west-involvement#.8s6qxOIuT, last accessed: June 25, 2018.

[595] Lisa Respers France , 'Kanye West's entire album hits the Top 40', *CNN*, June 12, 2018, https://edition.cnn.com/2018/06/12/entertainment/kanye-west-album-charts/index.html, last accessed: June 25, 2018.
[596] Kanye West, https://wegotlove.com/, last accessed: June 25, 2018.

- Kim Kardashian West meeting with president Donald Trump and the release of Alice;
- he killed his ego, is only 'Ye';

- tweets about Teyana Taylor album release party and link to listen the album.

Below I have the patterns of behaviour of Kim Kardashian and Taylor Swift from June 2016 until March 2020. For both players I included three years more than I did with Kanye West (2009-2017): the events between them are rare and I needed more examples to support a stronger credibility of the patterns identified. I started with Kim Kardashian and I finished with Taylor Swift. No further explanations are given.

TABLE 7. KIM KARDASHIAN'S PATTERNS OF THE **FAMOUS** FEUD TIMELINE 2016 – 2020
PATTERN 1. Interfered in Taylor Swift's narrative line with a misleading and biased response about her implication in the creation of the song **FAMOUS**

JUNE 16, 2016:

In a GQ interview for July new issue, Kim Kardashian spoked about Taylor Swift and her implication in the song 'Famous':

'She totally approved that.' […] 'She totally knew that that was coming out. She wanted to all of a sudden act like she didn't. I swear, my husband gets so much shit for things he really was doing proper protocol and even called to get it approved.' […] 'What rapper would call a girl that he was rapping a line about to get approval?'

MARCH 2020:

In March 2020, Kim Kardashian replied to the leak of the telephone conversation with the following statement:

'@taylorswift13 has chosen to reignite an old exchange - that at this point in time feels very self-serving given the suffering millions of real victims are facing right now. I didn't feel the need to comment a few days ago, and I'm actually really embarrassed and mortified to be doing it right now, but because she continues to speak on it, I feel I'm left without a choice but to respond because she is actually lying. To be clear, the only issue I ever had around the situation was that Taylor lied through her publicist who stated that 'Kanye never called to ask for permission...' They clearly spoke so I let you all see that. Nobody ever denied the word 'bitch' was used without her permission. At the time when they spoke the song had not been fully written yet, but as everyone can see in the video, she manipulated the truth of their actual conversation in her statement when her team said she 'declined and cautioned him about releasing a song with such a strong misogynistic message.' The lie was never about the word bitch, It was always whether there was a call or not and the tone of the conversation. To add, Kanye as an artist has every right to document his musical journey and process, just like she recently did through her documentary. Kanye has documented the making of all of his albums for his personal archive, however has never released any of it for public consumption & the call between the two of them would have remained private or would have gone in the trash had she not lied & forced me to defend him. This will be the last time I speak on this because honestly, nobody cares. Sorry to bore you all with this. I know you are all dealing with more serious and important matters'.

PATTERN 2. Interfered in Taylor Swift's narrative line with a negative view about her character while key events from her life (but also events from the life of her husband, Kanye West), are in motion: such as releasing a new album, tickets for sale for a tour, promoting a musical tour, and own show Keeping Up with the Kardashians.

For Kanye West: the examples were used in Table 5. *For Kim Kardashian*:

JULY 14, 2016:

A trailer with Kim Kardashian with a scene from the upcoming episode *Keeping Up with the Kardashians* is released. In it Kim Kardashian speaks again about Taylor Swift and her implication in the song 'Famous'.

JULY 17, 2016:

Kim Kardashian wrote on her Twitter account:

"Wait it's legit National Snake Day?!?!? They have holidays for everybody, I mean everything these days!"

Soon after the post with the phone conversation between Kanye West and Taylor Swift, people posted snakes on Taylor Swift Instagram, Twitter and Facebook account.

JULY 24, 2016:

Kim Kardashian, during her night at Hakkasan nightclub in the MGM Grand in Las Vegas, shared a video of herself and friend Carla DiBello dancing and singing along to Kanye West's lyric of the song 'Famous,' specifically where Kanye West raps: 'I feel like me and Taylor might still have sex. Why? I made that bitch famous. I made that bitch famous.'

JULY 28, 2016:

Kim Kardashian was on the cover of Harper's Bazaar September issue. When asked by editor Laura Brown about her favourite Taylor Swift song, Kim Kardashian replied: 'I was such a fan of hers.'

PATTERN 3: *Advanced a negative wave of responses from the general public, from her own fan camp, from her husband fan camp against Taylor Swift and her fan camp.*

JULY 17, 2016:

Kim Kardashian wrote on her Twitter account:

"Wait it's legit National Snake Day?!?!? They have holidays for everybody, I mean everything these days!"

JULY 24, 2016:

Kim Kardashian, during her night at Hakkasan nightclub in the MGM Grand in Las Vegas, shared a video of herself and friend Carla DiBello dancing and singing along to Kanye West's lyric of the song 'Famous,' specifically where Kanye West raps: 'I feel like me and Taylor might still have sex. Why? I made that bitch famous. I made that bitch famous.'

Before the events around the song *Famous*, Kim Kardashian was the biggest fan of Taylor Swift;[597] after her marriage with Kanye West, the release of the song *Famous*, Kim Kardashian was no more a fan of Taylor Swift.

PATTERN 4. *She does not want to be a truly friend of Taylor Swift.*

Fully supported her husband Kanye West in his negative presentation of Taylor Swift.

PATTERN 5. *Maintained and supported the FAMOUS feud according with her own needs, and her husband needs.*

JUNE 16, 2016:

In the interview for GQ magazine, Kim Kardashian talked about the existence of a telephone conversation between Kanye West and Taylor Swift; Kim Kardashian: 'She totally approved that.' […] 'She totally knew that that was coming out. She wanted to all of a sudden act like she didn't': this interview happened in the week that Kanye West started to sale tickets (June 14 for American Express cardholders and June 16 for Tidal members, June 18 for general public) to her husband Kanye West and his music tour named *Saint Pablo Tour*.

---

[597] Entertainment Tonight, 'FLASHBACK: Kim Kardashian Was Taylor Swift's Self-Proclaimed 'Biggest Fan' in 2009 -- Watch!', *Youtube*, August 30, 2017, available at: https://www.youtube.com/watch?v=YrYHkfB8DY4, last accessed: October 26, 2017.

And in the statement from *MARCH 2020.*

PATTERN 6. She is one of the persons who are responsible for the negative opinion of the general public and fans on all camps toward and in reference to Taylor Swift.

In the statements released in June and July 2016, and in March 2020.

PATTERN 7. Maintained a negative image about Taylor Swift.

In the statements released in June and July 2016, and in March 2020.

TABLE 8. TAYLOR SWIFT'S PATTERNS OF THE **FAMOUS** FEUD TIMELINE 2016 – 2020
PATTERN 1. Interfered in the narrative line of the feud to defend herself from Kim Kardashian's negative view about her character.

JUNE 16, 2016:

Taylor Swift camp, after Kim Kardashian's interview with GQ, issued a statement to GQ:

'Taylor does not hold anything against Kim Kardashian as she recognizes the pressure Kim must be under and that she is only repeating what she has been told by Kanye West. However, that does not change the fact that much of what Kim is saying is incorrect. Kanye West and Taylor only spoke once on the phone while she was on vacation with her family in January of 2016 and they have never spoken since. Taylor has never denied that conversation took place. It was on that phone call that Kanye West also asked her to release the song on her Twitter account, which she declined to do. Kanye West never told Taylor he was going to use the term 'that bitch' in referencing her. A song cannot be approved if it was never heard. Kanye West never played the song for Taylor Swift. Taylor heard it for the first time when everyone else did and was humiliated. Kim Kardashian's claim that Taylor and her team were aware of being recorded is not true, and Taylor cannot understand why Kanye West, and now Kim Kardashian, will not just leave her alone.'

JULY 17, 2016:

Taylor Swift responded to Kim Kardashian's Snapchat videos on her Instagram and Twitter account (now the picture with her response is deleted):

'That moment when Kanye West secretly records your phone call, then Kim posts it on the Internet.'

'Where is the video of Kanye telling me he was going to call me 'that bitch' in his song? It doesn't exist because it never happened. You don't get to control someone's emotional response to being called 'that bitch' in front of the entire world. Of course I wanted to like the song. I wanted to believe Kanye when he told me that I would love the song. I wanted us to have a friendly relationship. He promised to play the song for me, but he never did. While I wanted to be supportive of Kanye on the phone call, you cannot 'approve' a song you haven't heard. Being falsely painted as a liar when I was never given the full story or played any part of the song is character assassination. I would very much like to be excluded from this narrative, one that I have never asked to be a part of, since 2009.'

PATTERN 2. Tried to make Kim Kardashian to understand her point of view about the creation of the song *FAMOUS.*

The statements released in June 2016 and July 2016.

PATTERN 3. Used same methods to reply as Kim Kardashian: through online statements.

In June and July 2016, and in March 2020 (but without mentioning Kim Kardashian's name):

'Instead of answering those who are asking how I feel about the video footage that leaked, proving that I was telling the truth the whole time about *that call* (you know, the one that was illegally recorded, that somebody edited and manipulated in order to frame me and put me, my family, and fans through hell for 4 years)… SWIPE up to see what really matters.'

PATTERN 4. She wanted and tried to have a positive relationship with Kim Kardashian.

AUGUST 30, 2015:

Taylor Swift accepted Kanye West's request to present him the award; sat next to Kim Kardashian while Kanye West delivered the speech; in her replies, Taylor Swift focused only on the allegations against her made by Kanye West and Kim Kardashian.

PATTERN 5. Maintained and supported the feud as side effect of her defence mechanism from Kim Kardashian.

In the statements released in June and July 2016. In 2017, in the music video of *Look What You Made Me Do*, Taylor Swift used the scene of Kim Kardashian's robbery from Paris in 2016, which is the worst event from Kim's life.

PATTERN 6. Does not want to be a part of the Famous feud even after Kim Kardashian's self-invitation, or pressured by Kanye West.

JUNE 16, 2016:

Taylor Swift camp, after Kim Kardashian's interview with GQ, issued a statement to GQ:

'Kim Kardashian's claim that Taylor and her team were aware of being recorded is not true, and Taylor cannot understand why Kanye West, and now Kim Kardashian, will not just leave her alone.'

JULY 17, 2016:

Taylor Swift responded to Kim Kardashian's Snapchat videos on her Instagram and Twitter account (now the picture with her response is deleted):

'I would very much like to be excluded from this narrative, one that I have never asked to be a part of, since 2009.'

PATTERN 7. Promoted a more truthful version of the events.

In the statements released in June and July 2016, and in March 2020.

III. How much Taylor Swift knew about the song **FAMOUS**?

This chapter was written for Kim Kardashian to support her interest in becoming a lawyer. The work of a lawyer requires attention to details, and this chapter is all about that. The content of this chapter is a way to check in percentage (details) to see how much Taylor Swift knew about the *song Famous*. The information presented below is also for lovers of details, numbers and percentages. This chapter is not an analysis to confirm Taylor's genuine intention in the creation of the song, and her refusal to accept the final version because she wanted to put Kanye West in a bad light. In this chapter I explored the dynamics of the feud through numbers and statements. For Kim Kardashian this chapter is another source of how to work with information to prove the veracity of a statement.

Now we know that Taylor Swift was aware of a song produced by Kanye West and knew parts of the lyrics, but not the line 'I made that bitch famous'.

In this chapter I assessed, for accuracy of information, the following affirmations to find out how much Taylor Swift 'played any part' in the *song Famous* before the release to the general public:

a. Kanye West wrote on Twitter: '3rd thing I called Taylor and had a hour long convo with her about the line and she thought it was funny and gave her blessings';

b. Kim Kardashian in the interview with GQ magazine from 16 June 2016 and during her show 'Keeping Up With The Kardashians' (season 12, episode 11): 'She totally approved that. […] 'She totally knew that that was coming out;'

c. the affirmation made by Taylor Swift in July 2016: 'Being falsely painted as a liar when I was never given the full story *or played any part of the song* (underline by author) is character assassination';

and I analysed:

d. the general knowledge of the song Famous in percentage.

a. Kanye West wrote on Twitter: ***'3rd thing I called Taylor and had a hour long convo with her about the line and she thought it was funny and gave her blessings'***: this information is partial true: the leak of the conversation is around 25 minutes (maybe there is more); *the conversation was funny and gave her blessing for the lyrics that she was aware*, but not for the new line, 'I made that bitch famous', added by Kanye West for which Taylor was not aware, but presented as being aware from the beginning; Taylor Swift knew 50% of the title of the song: Kanye West told Taylor Swift the first title of the song: *Hood Famous*, however, the final title was **FAMOUS**, which is half of the first title and converts into 50%;

b. Kim Kardashian in the interview with GQ magazine from June 16, 2016 and during her show *Keeping Up with The Kardashians* (season 12, episode 11): **'She totally approved that. [...] 'She totally knew that was coming out'**: this information is biased and misleading as there is evidence of Taylor Swift not being aware of the full version of the song, lyrics and instrumentals and, therefore, she did not know what was all and exactly coming out; Taylor Swift did not approve *totally* of what Kanye West released to the general public, and supported by Kim Kardashian's affirmation during her interview and TV show: Taylor Swift thanked Kanye West for letting her know about his intention, parts of the lyrics, and *she will think about it,* which is not approval;

c. the affirmation made by Taylor Swift in July 2016: 'Being falsely painted as a liar when I was never given the full story or played any part of the song (underline by author) is character assassination': this information is mostly true and based on the new recordings of the conversation leaked on Youtube in March 2020; **Taylor Swift was never given the full story of the song, *but did played a part of the song***: she knew some lyrics and even suggested a change of the lyrics, but still there is no evidence for a genuine argument that Taylor played a part because she *really wanted,* or because she was involved in a phone conversation, and *wanted to be nice* and *supportive* with Kanye West; based on Taylor Swift's statement she wasn't aware that Kanye West is going to use the telephone conversation as implicit agreement of her polite advice and suggestion; the last part: **'character assassination'** is true: Kanye West and Kim Kardashian presented to the general public biased, misleading and partial information about Taylor's involvement in the song that suited their agenda of blaming Taylor Swift for the song's evolution, and the reaction of the general public; the character assassination is true as of today; Kim and Kanye refuse to take responsibility and to acknowledge that they did not presented the information from the telephone conversation as it happened; for Kanye West and Kim Kardashian, Taylor Swift is the perpetrator for everything that happened after the release of the song;

d. general knowledge of the song Famous in percentage: I decided to explore the truth in numbers and percentage as a method to show, as accurate as possible, Taylor Swift's knowledge of the *song* **FAMOUS**.

The first part of the research method is simple: I divided the *song Famous* in independent elements according with the *Credits* of the *song Famous* found on Kanye West and Genius's website[598]: production, co-production, additional production, engineering, recording vocals, mix, songwriters (lyricists), name of the song, lyrics, publishing rights, sample, the complete *song Famous*[599].

The second part of the research method is also simple:

each author/participant in making the song = 1 point;

the 1 point for each author/participant was added, and the result was divided between the total points and the numbers of the authors/participants in the creation of the song;

the result of this simple maths was 1. converted into percentage, then 2. the percentage for Kanye West (because Taylor Swift had the telephone conversation only with Kanye West, where is the case and according with each independent element of the song) was considered for how much Taylor Swift knew about the song *Famous* before its public release.

III.1 Production

TABLE 9. PRODUCTION

Author/Participant	Kanye West	Havoc
Points	1	1
Taylor Swift Knows	1	0
Taylor Swift Knows in Percentage	50%	

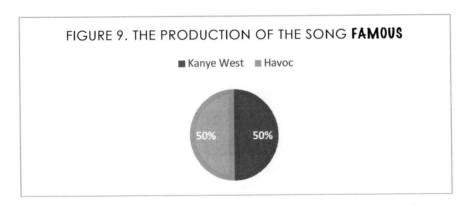

FIGURE 9. THE PRODUCTION OF THE SONG **FAMOUS**

■ Kanye West ■ Havoc

50%   50%

---

[598] Kanye West, 'Famous Credits', *The Life of Pablo*, https://www.kanyewest.com/credits/, last accessed: September 24, 2017; Kanye West, 'The Life of Pablo [Credits]', *Genius*, https://genius.com/Kanye-west-the-life-of-pablo-credits-annotated, last accessed: October 23, 2017.
[599] This element was proposed by myself in this report and is not found on Credits.

III.2 Co-Production

TABLE 10. CO-PRODUCTION

Author/Participant	Noah Goldstein for ARK Productions, INC	Charlie Heat for Very GOOD Beats, INC	Andrew Dawson
Points	1	1	1
Taylor Swift Knows	0	0	0
Taylor Swift Knows in Percentage		0%	

III.3 Additional Production

TABLE 11. ADDITIONAL PRODUCTION

Participant	Husdon Mohawke	Mike Dean #MWA for Dean's List Productions	Plain Pat
Points	1	1	1
Taylor Swift Knows	0	0	0
Taylor Swift Knows in Percentage		0%	

III.4 Engineering

TABLE 12. ENGINEERING

Author/Participant	Noah Goldstein	Andrew Dawson	Anthony Kilhoffer	Mike Dean
Points	1	1	1	1
Taylor Swift Knows	0	0	0	0
Taylor Swift Knows in Percentage		0%		

III.5 Rihanna Vocals Recording

TABLE 13. RIHANNA VOCALS RECORDING

Author/Participant	Marcos Tovar
Points	1
Taylor Swift Knows	0
Taylor Swift Knows in Percentage	0%

III.6 Rihanna Vocals Assistance

TABLE 14. RIHANNA VOCALS ASSISTANCE

Author/Participant	Jose Balaguer
Points	1
Taylor Swift Knows	0
Taylor Swift Knows in Percentage	0%

III.7 Rihanna Vocal Production

TABLE 15. RIHANNA VOCAL PRODUCTION

Author/Participant	Kuk Harrel
Points	1
Taylor Swift Knows	0
Taylor Swift Knows in Percentage	0%

III.8 Swizz Vocals Recording

TABLE 16. SWIZZ VOCALS RECORDING

Author/Participant	Zeke Mishanec
Points	1
Taylor Swift Knows	0
Taylor Swift Knows in Percentage	0%

III.9 Mix

TABLE 17. MIX

Author/Participant	Manny Marroquin
Points	1
Taylor Swift Knows	0
Taylor Swift Knows in Percentage	0%

III.10 Mix Assisted

TABLE 18. MIX ASSISTED

Author/Participant	Chris Galland	Ike Schultz	Jeff Jackson
Points	1	1	1
Taylor Swift Knows	0	0	0
Taylor Swift Knows in Percentage		0%	

III.11 Vocals

TABLE 19. VOCALS

Author/Participant	Kanye West	Rihanna	Swizz
Points	1	1	1
Taylor Swift Knows	1	0	0
Taylor Swift Knows in Percentage		34%	

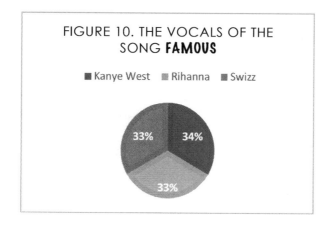

FIGURE 10. THE VOCALS OF THE SONG **FAMOUS**

■ Kanye West   ▨ Rihanna   ▨ Swizz

33%   34%   33%

III.12 Lyricists

TABLE 20. THE LYRICISTS OF FAMOUS AS CREDITS FROM WIKIPEDIA[600]

AUTHOR/PARTICIPANT	POINTS	TAYLOR SWIFT KNOWS	TAYLOR SWIFT KNOWS IN PERCENTAGE

---

[600] This list was made based on Credit page of the song *Famous* from Wikipedia, 'Famous (Kanye West song)', https://en.wikipedia.org/wiki/Famous_(Kanye_West_song), last accessed: October 23, 2017; Kanye West website: *The Life of Pablo, Credits*, https://www.kanyewest.com/credits/, last accessed: October 23, 2017; Tidal, 'The Life of Pablo', *Credits*, https://listen.tidal.com/album/57273408, last accessed: October 23, 2017.

Kanye West	1	1
Cydel Young	1	0
Kejuan Muchita	1	0
Noah Goldstein	1	0
Andrew Dawson	1	0
Mike Dean	1	0
Chancelor Bennett	1	0
Kasseem Dean	1	0
Ernest Brown	1	0
Ross Birchard	1	0
Pat Reynolds	1	0
Jimmy Webb	1	0
Winston Riley	1	0
Luis Enriquez Bacalov	1	0
Enzo Vita	1	0
Sergio Bardotti	1	0
Giampiero Scalamogna	1	0

6% (rounded as in the *Figure*, but 5.88% as maths result).[601]

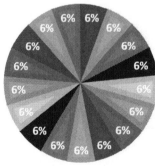

FIGURE 11. THE LYRICISTS OF THE SONG **FAMOUS**

- KANYE WEST
- CYDEL YOUNG
- KEJUAN MUCHITA
- NOAH GOLDSTEIN
- ANDREW DAWSON
- MIKE DEAN
- CHANCELOR BENNETT
- KASSEEM DEAN
- ERNEST BROWN
- ROSS BIRCHARD
- PAT REYNOLDS
- JIMMY WEBB
- WINSTON RILEY
- LUIS ENRIQUEZ BACALOV
- ENZO VITA
- SERGIO BARDOTTI
- GIAMPIERO SCALAMOGNA

[601] In the final maths calculation, I used the rounded 6%, and not the 5.88%.

III.13 Name of the Song

TABLE 21. NAME OF THE SONG (HOOD **FAMOUS**)

Author/Participant	Kanye West
Points	1
Taylor Swift Knows	0.5
Taylor Swift Knows in Percentage	50%

III.14 The Lyrics of the song **FAMOUS**[602]

For this section I used the following mathematical formulas:

Subtraction (any combination of the following information):

- total lyrics without the chorus and outro (Rihanna and Swizz)
- total lyrics without the chorus (Rihanna and Swizz)
- total lyrics as the song is played
- lyrics known by Taylor Swift
- without 'bam'
- without 'dilla'
- without 'ey'
- without 'I just wanted you to know'.

Percentage conversion: the results were converted in percentage; it was used for all the independent elements of the song.

Average: the percentage result from each independent element of the song was calculated using the average method understood as: dividing the total numbers of lyrics (taken as 6 types of lyrics described in *Subtraction*) by the total number of independent elements of the lyrics (6 for total, but was also used as **1** or **2** depending on the purpose of each section of the calculation for lyrics known by Taylor Swift) or the song (18 independent elements available in the last section of this chapter). The results from the *song Famous* and *Lyrics* section were used to find out how much in percentage Taylor Swift knew from the full version of the song *Famous*.

---

[602] This section is based on the lyrics of the *song Famous* as published and the format used by Genius website. The calculation of the number of lyrics was done by using Pages app from Apple and the option of *Word count*.

TABLE 22. THE LYRICS OF THE SONG **FAMOUS**

Total lyrics as the song is played	552
Lyrics Known by Taylor Swift	19
'Bam'	67
'I Wanted You To Know'	6 (as full line numbers of words for each line) and 36 words
Intro	43
Outro	35
Chorus 1	42
Chorus 2	8
Verse 1	97
Verse 2	82
Bridge	245
'Ey'	56
'Dilla'	8
Lyrics known by Kanye West	552

III.14.1 The Lyrics of **FAMOUS** as the Song is Played

TABLE 23. THE LYRICS OF **FAMOUS** AS THE SONG IS PLAYED

Lyrics As The Song Is Played	552
Taylor Swift	19
Taylor Swift Knows in Percentage	3%

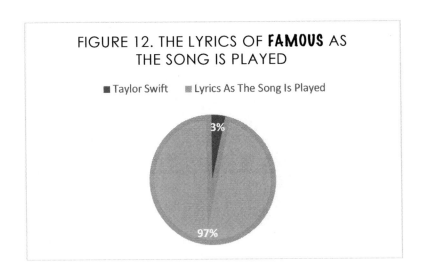

FIGURE 12. THE LYRICS OF **FAMOUS** AS THE SONG IS PLAYED

■ Taylor Swift   ■ Lyrics As The Song Is Played

3%

97%

III.14.2 The Lyrics of **FAMOUS** Without 'Bam'

TABLE 24. THE LYRICS OF FAMOUS WITHOUT 'BAM'

Lyrics As The Song Is Played	552
Taylor Swift	19
Without 'Bam'	67
Taylor Swift Knows in Percentage	4%

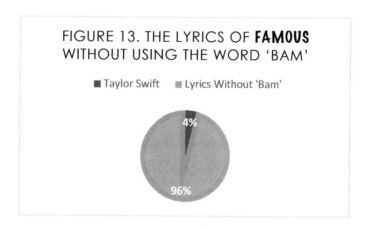

FIGURE 13. THE LYRICS OF **FAMOUS** WITHOUT USING THE WORD 'BAM'

■ Taylor Swift   ■ Lyrics Without 'Bam'

III.14.3 The Lyrics of **FAMOUS** Without 'Ey'

TABLE 25. THE LYRICS OF FAMOUS WITHOUT 'EY'

Lyrics As The Song Is Played	552
Taylor Swift	19
Without 'Ey'	56
Taylor Swift Knows in Percentage	4%

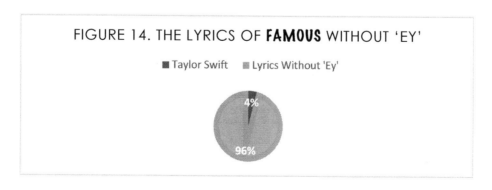

FIGURE 14. THE LYRICS OF **FAMOUS** WITHOUT 'EY'

■ Taylor Swift   ■ Lyrics Without 'Ey'

III.14.4 The Lyrics of **FAMOUS** Without the Line 'I Just Wanted You To Know'

TABLE 26. THE LYRICS OF FAMOUS WITHOUT 'I JUST WANTED YOU TO KNOW'

Lyrics As The Song Is Played	552
Without 'I just Wanted you to know'	36
Taylor Swift	19
Taylor Swift Knows in Percentage	4%

FIGURE 15. THE LYRICS OF **FAMOUS** WITHOUT 'I JUST WANTED YOU TO KNOW'

■ Taylor Swift   ■ Lyrics Without 'I Just Wanted You To Know'

III.14.5 The Lyrics of **FAMOUS** Without 'Dilla'

TABLE 27. THE LYRICS OF FAMOUS WITHOUT 'DILLA'

Lyrics As The Song Is Played	552
Without 'Dilla'	8
Taylor Swift	19
Taylor Swift Knows in Percentage	3%

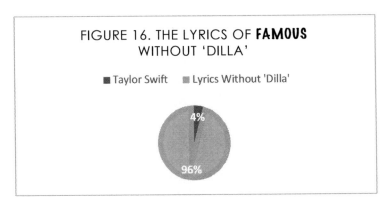

FIGURE 16. THE LYRICS OF **FAMOUS** WITHOUT 'DILLA'

■ Taylor Swift   ■ Lyrics Without 'Dilla'

III.14.6 The Lyrics of **FAMOUS** Without 'Bam', 'Ey', 'Dilla', 'I Just Wanted You To Know'

TABLE 28. THE LYRICS OF FAMOUS WITHOUT 'BAM', 'EY', 'DILLA', 'I JUST WANTED YOU TO KNOW'

Lyrics As The Song Is Played	552
Without 'Bam'	67
Without 'Ey'	56
Without 'I Just Wanted You To Without Know'	36
Without 'Dilla'	8
Taylor Swift	19
Taylor Swift Knows in Percentage	5%

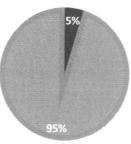

FIGURE 17. THE LYRICS OF **FAMOUS** WITHOUT 'BAM', 'EY', 'DILLA' AND 'I JUST WANTED YOU TO KNOW'

■ Taylor Swift ▨ Lyrics Without 'Bam', 'Ey', 'Dilla', 'I Just Wanted You To Know'

5%

95%

III.14.7 The Lyrics of **FAMOUS** Without Intro and Outro

TABLE 29. THE LYRICS OF FAMOUS WITHOUT 'INTRO' AND 'OUTRO'

Lyrics As The Song Is Played	552
Without Intro	43
Without Outro	35
Taylor Swift	19
Taylor Swift Knows in Percentage	5%

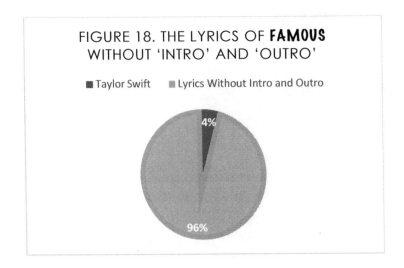

FIGURE 18. THE LYRICS OF **FAMOUS** WITHOUT 'INTRO' AND 'OUTRO'

III.14.8 The Lyrics of **FAMOUS** Without Chorus (Rihanna & Swizz 1&2)

TABLE 30. THE LYRICS OF FAMOUS WITHOUT CHORUS (RIHANNA & SWIZZ 1&2)

Lyrics As The Song Is Played	552
Without Chorus 1	42
Without Chorus 2	8
Taylor Swift	19
Taylor Swift Knows in Percentage	4%

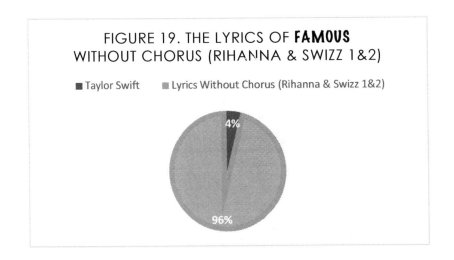

FIGURE 19. THE LYRICS OF **FAMOUS** WITHOUT CHORUS (RIHANNA & SWIZZ 1&2)

III.14.9 The Lyrics of **FAMOUS** Without Repeating Same Words

The repeated words are: 'to', 'be', 'the', 'they', 'try', 'you', 'your', 'free', 'in', 'see', 'just', 'air', 'her', 'we', 'I', 'wanted', 'know', 'made', 'that', 'bitch', 'famous', 'this', 'for', 'us', 'best', 'goddamn', 'Kanye', 'West', 'all', 'but', 'hood', 'oh', 'don't', 'blame', 'much', 'wanting', 'up', 'whoo!', 'never', 'gonna', 'die', 'bam', 'dilla', 'ey', 'let', 'me', 'what', 'me', 'how', 'feelin', 'my', 'motherfucker', 'can't', 'is', 'woo', 'man', 'too', 'stop', 'talk', 'late', 'it's', 'way'.[603] I decided to keep Taylor Swift's numbers of known lyrics, because Kanye West shared them with her during the telephone conversation.

TABLE 31. THE LYRICS OF **FAMOUS** WITHOUT REPEATING SAME WORDS

Lyrics As The Song Is Played	552
Lyrics Without Repeating Same Words	205
Taylor Swift	19
Taylor Swift Knows in Percentage	5%

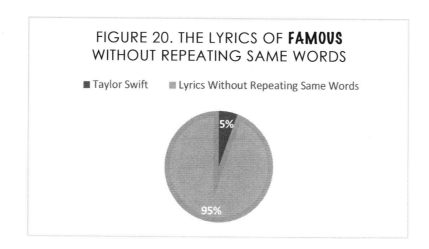

FIGURE 20. THE LYRICS OF **FAMOUS** WITHOUT REPEATING SAME WORDS

■ Taylor Swift   ■ Lyrics Without Repeating Same Words

5%

95%

TABLE 32. THE MATHS OF LYRICS OF THE SONG **FAMOUS**

Independent methods of calculations of the lyrics	Taylor Swift knew about each independent element of the lyrics in percentage
Lyrics As The Song Is Played	3%
Lyrics Without 'Bam'	4%
Lyrics Without 'Ey'	4%

---

[603] It is possible to omit words, which is unintended.

Lyrics Without The Line 'I Just Wanted You To Know'	4%
Lyrics Without 'Dilla'	3%
Lyrics Without 'Bam', 'Ey', 'Dilla', 'I Just Wanted You To Know'	5%
Lyrics Without 'Intro' and 'Outro'	5%
Lyrics Without Chorus (Rihanna & Swizz 1&2)	4%
Lyrics Without Repeating Same Words	5%

The Average Method:

In total, there are 9 independent methods of calculations of the lyrics, and I have the following maths calculation:

first: I added the percentage of each independent methods of calculations of the lyrics:

3% + 4% + 4% + 4% + 3% + 5% + 5% + 4% + 5% = 37%

second: the result was divided with the total number of independent methods of calculations of the lyrics (9):
37% / 9 = **4,11(11)%.**

Conclusion:

Overall, based on the mathematical formulas used above, Taylor Swift knew an average of **4.11(11)% lyrics of the song Famous**.

III.15 Publishing Rights

TABLE 33. PUBLISHING RIGHTS

Author/Participant	Publishing Rights
Points	1
Taylor Swift Knows	0%
Taylor Swift Knows in Percentage	0%

III.16 Sample 1

TABLE 34. SAMPLE 1

Author/Participant	Sample 1: 'Do what you gotta do', Performed by Nina Simon
Points	1
Taylor Swift Knows	0
Taylor Swift Knows in Percentage	0%

III.17 Sample 2

TABLE 35. SAMPLE 2

Author/Participant	Sample 2: 'Bam Bam' Performed by Sister Nancy
Points	1
Taylor Swift Knows	0
Taylor Swift Knows in Percentage	0%

III.18 Sample 3

TABLE 36. SAMPLE 3

Author/Participant	Sample 3: 'Mi Sono Svegliato E.. Ho Chiuso Gli Occhi' Performed by Il Rovescio Della Medgalia
Points	1
Taylor Swift Knows	0
Taylor Swift Knows in Percentage	0%

III.19 The Song **'FAMOUS'**

TABLE 37. HOW MUCH TAYLOR SWIFT KNEW ABOUT THE SONG FAMOUS?

Independent elements of the *song Famous*	Taylor Swift knew about each independent element of the *song Famous* in percentage
Production	50%
Co-Production	0%
Additional Production	0%
Engineering	0%
Vocals	34%
Lyricists	6%
Name Of The Song	50%
Rihanna Vocals Recording	0%
Rihanna Vocal Assistance	0%
Rihanna Vocal Production	0%
Swizz Vocals Recording	0%

	Mix	0%
	Mix Assisted	0%
	Publishing Rights	0%
	Sample 1	0%
	Sample 2	0%
	Sample 3	0%
Lyrics	**1.** Lyrics As The Song Is Played	3%
	2. Lyrics Without Repeating Same Words	5%

I selected these methods to calculate the lyrics because option **1** has the lowest percentage and is representing the whole song, and **2** has the highest percentage and does not contain repeated words, which has a better representation of the original lyrics. Below, I used two different methods of calculation to check and see, accurately as possible through this method, if there are any differences and similarities which can provide a different picture of Taylor Swift's level of knowledge about the song *Famous*.

The Average Method:

In total, there are 18 independent elements of the song, and I have the following maths calculation:

- *If I use **1. Lyrics as the song is played (3%)** and Taylor Swift knew the name of the song (50%):*

first: I added each independent element of the song:

50% + 0% + 0% + 0% + 34% + 6% + 50% + 0% + 0% + 0% + 0% + 0% + 0% + 0% + 0% + 0% + 0% + **3%** = 143%

second: I divided 143% with the total number of independent elements of the song (18): 143% / 18 = **7.94(44)%.**

- *If I use **2. Lyrics without repeating same words (5%)** and Taylor Swift knew the name of the song (50%):*

first: I added each independent element of the song:

50% + 0% + 0% + 0% + 34% + 6% + 50% + 0% + 0% + 0% + 0% + 0% + 0% + 0% + 0% + 0% + 0% + **5%** = 145%

second: I divided 145% with the total number of independent elements of the song (18): 145% / 18 = **8,05(22)%.**

CONCLUSIONS:

- due to multiple maths calculation, **Taylor Swift knew between 4.11(11)% to 7.94(44)%, respectively 8.05(22)% about the *song Famous*,**
- however, despite this evidence, Taylor Swift said to Kanye West that she will think about it; Taylor Swift did not receive the final song; Taylor Swift found out the final version of the song at the same time with the general public; Kanye West did not give Taylor the chance to hear the final version of the song and, therefore, to receive her final approval.

IV. The impact of the **FAMOUS** feud

In this chapter I created a comparative analysis of

1. the impact of the *Famous* feud on music album sales: the first week in the USA between Taylor Swift and Kanye West;
2. global sales of the songs that are the cause of the feud: *Famous* for Kanye West, *Look What You Made Me Do* for Taylor Swift, and *Swish, Swish* for Katy Perry;
3. the impact of the *Bad Blood – Swish, Swish* feud on global album sales between Taylor Swift and Katy Perry;
4. the number of producers and lyricists of the songs involved in the *Famous* feud: *Famous* for Kanye West, *Look What You Made Me Do* for Taylor Swift;
5. the sources of inspiration and originality of the albums released after the MTV VMA event in 2009: Taylor Swift's album: *Speak Now*, and Kanye West's album: *My Beautiful Dark Twisted Fantasy*;
6. the rating available on Metacritic;
7. the connection between the *Famous* feud and the *Bad Blood – Swish, Swish* feud, Taylor Swift versus Katy Perry.

IV.1 Kanye West versus Taylor Swift

IV.1.1 First Week Sales in the USA (Solo Album)

TABLE 38. TAYLOR SWIFT AND KANYE WEST FIRST WEEK SALES IN THE USA (SOLO ALBUM)

YEAR / ARTIST	TAYLOR SWIFT	KANYE WEST
2004	–	441.000[604]
2005	–	860.000[605]

---

[604] Hao Nguyen, 'Can't Tell Me Nothing: Ranking Kanye West First Week Album Sales', *Stop The Breaks*, December 15, 2013, https://www.stopthebreaks.com/first-week-album-sales/kanye-west-first-week-album-sales/, last accessed: October 23, 2017.
[605] Ibidem,

2006	40.000[606]	-
2007	-	957.000[607]
2008	592.000[608]	450.455[609]
2010	1.047.000[610]	496.000[611]
2012	1.208.000[612]	-
2013	-	327.000[613]
2014	1.287.000[614]	-
2016	-	28.000[615]
2017	1.216.000[616]	-
2018	-	85.000[617]
2019	679.000[618] 715.000[619]	109,000[620]
2020	615.000[621] 627.000[622]	-

[606] Billboard, *'Hannah Montana' Trumps My Chem, Legend At No. 1*, November 1, 2006, https://www.billboard.com/articles/news/56784/hannah-montana-trumps-my-chem-legend-at-no-1, last accessed: October 23, 2017.

[607] Hao Nguyen, idem.

[608] Jonathan Cohen, 'Taylor Swift Soars To No. 1 Debut', *Billboard*, November 19, 2008, https://www.billboard.com/articles/news/1043458/taylor-swift-soars-to-no-1-debut, last accessed: October 23, 2017.

[609] Hao Nguyen, idem.

[610] Ed Christmas, 'What Taylor Swift's Million-Selling Album Means for Music', *Billboard*, November 5, 2010, https://www.billboard.com/articles/news/951633/what-taylor-swifts-million-selling-album-means-for-music, last accessed: October 23, 2017.

[611] Hao Nguyen, idem.

[612] Keith Caulfield, 'Taylor Swift's 'Red' Sells 1.21 Million; Biggest Sales Week for an Album Since 2002', *Billboard*, October 30, 2012, https://www.billboard.com/articles/news/474400/taylor-swifts-red-sells-121-million-biggest-sales-week-for-an-album-since-2002, last accessed: October 23, 2017.

[613] Hao Nguyen, idem.

[614] Keith Caulfield, 'Official: Taylor Swift's '1989' Debuts With 1.287 Million Sold In First Week', *Billboard*, November 4, 2014, https://www.billboard.com/articles/columns/chart-beat/6304536/official-taylor-swifts-1989-debuts-with-1287-million-sold-in, last accessed: October 23, 2017.

[615] Keith Caulfield, 'Kanye West's 'The Life of Pablo' Debuts at No. 1 on Billboard 200 Chart', *Billboard*, April 10, 2016, https://www.billboard.com/articles/columns/chart-beat/7326493/kanye-wests-the-life-of-pablo-debuts-at-no-1-on-billboard-200, last accessed: October 23, 2017.

[616] Keith Caulfield, 'Taylor Swift's 'Reputation' Debuts at No. 1 on Billboard 200 Albums Chart', *Billboard*, November 20, 2017, https://www.billboard.com/articles/columns/chart-beat/8039679/taylor-swift-reputation-debuts-no-1-billboard-200-albums, last accessed: August 25, 2019.

[617] Keith Caulfield, 'Kanye West Earns Eighth No. 1 Album on Billboard 200 Chart With 'Ye', *Billboard*, June 10, 2018, https://www.billboard.com/articles/columns/chart-beat/8460189/kanye-west-eighth-no-1-album-billboard-200-ye, last accessed: October 23, 2018.

[618] Keith Caulfield, 'Official: Taylor Swift's 'Lover' Debuts at No. 1 on Billboard 200 Chart With 867,000 Units Earned in First Week in U.S.', *Billboard*, September 1, 2019, https://www.billboard.com/articles/business/chart-beat/8528870/taylor-swift-lover-album-debuts-at-no-1-on-billboard-200-chart, last accessed: September 1, 2019.

[619] RS Charts, RS Charts: Taylor Swift's 'Lover' Takes Number One By a Landslide, *Rolling Stone*, September 4, 2019, https://www.rollingstone.com/music/music-news/charts-taylor-swift-lover-albums-879502/, last accessed: November 6, 2019.

[620] Keith Caulfield, 'Kanye West's 'Jesus Is King' Arrives as His Record-Tying Ninth Consecutive No. 1 Debut on Billboard 200 Chart', *Billboard*, November 3, 2019, https://www.billboard.com/articles/business/chart-beat/8542364/kanye-west-jesus-is-king-billboard-200-debut-no-1, last accessed: November 6, 2019.

[621] Kevin Rutherford, 'Taylor Swift's 'Folklore' Debuts at No. 1 on Alternative Albums, 'Cardigan' Starts Atop Hot Rock & Alternative Songs', *Billboard*, https://www.billboard.com/articles/business/chart-beat/9428748/taylor-swift-folklore-alternative-albums-cardigan-hot-rock-alternative-songs, last accessed: August 7, 2020.

[622] RS Charts, *Taylor Swift's 'Folklore' Sees the Biggest Debut of 2020, and It Isn't Even Close*, August 2, 2020, available at: https://www.rollingstone.com/music/music-news/taylor-swift-folklore-debut-charts-1037919/, last accessed: August 7, 2020.

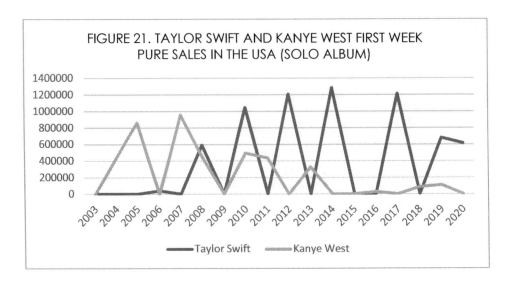

FIGURE 21. TAYLOR SWIFT AND KANYE WEST FIRST WEEK PURE SALES IN THE USA (SOLO ALBUM)

CONCLUSIONS:

- by 2009, for Taylor Swift there was a strong increase in popularity and it is shown by the increase of the album sales of her albums; overall, Taylor Swift was a global phenomenon before she met Kanye West, which is also confirmed in the telephone conversation with Kanye West; Taylor Swift said 'I sold 7 million of that album before you did that which is what happened';
- after September 2009 Taylor Swift's presence continued to increase achieving world records until 2014 (album *1989*), then to decrease in 2017 (album *reputation*) with around 6% (by using *Billboard* numbers), and more decrease in 2019 when the sales in the first week were around 44% (by using Billboard numbers) less than the last album (*reputation*, 2017); with Rolling Stone Charts the decrease of the album sales from 2017 to 2019 is around 41%; from the point of view of album-equivalent sales in the first week (Billboard reported 867.000[623], while Rolling Stone Charts 998.100[624]) the decrease is lower: around 18% from Rolling Stone and around 29% from Billboard; overall, it took 10 years for Taylor Swift to know a high decrease of lower sales in the first week;
- Kanye West's popularity and album sales decreased around 53% a year before he met Taylor Swift at MTV Awards in September 2009: in 2007 he sold 957.000 copies in the first week, while in 2008 he sold 450.455 copies in the first week; this decrease

---

[623] Keith Caulfield, *Official: Taylor Swift's 'Lover' Debuts at No. 1 on Billboard 200 Chart With 867,000 Units Earned in First Week in U.S.*
[624] RS Charts, *RS Charts: Taylor Swift's 'Lover' Takes Number One By a Landslide.*

is still valid as of today, the lowest one being the album *The Life of Pablo* with 28.000 copies;

- Kanye West lost half of his popularity in first week pure sales in 1 year (from 2007 to 2008) and after three successful albums and high increase) and remained low (in comparison with the first three albums) as of today; Taylor Swift lost 44% (from Billboard) and 41% (from Rolling Stone Charts) in two years (*reputation* in 2017 and *Lover* in 2019); from the point of view of a combination of pure sales and album-equivalent sales, Taylor Swift lost 27.5%[625] of her popularity in first week sales in 5 years (from album *1989*- the highest number of sales in the first week- to album *Lover* in 2019);

- Kanye West has the highest decrease in selling albums in the first week, however, he also had an increase of sales in the last 2 years: in 2016 he sold 28.000 copies, in 2018 sold 85.000 copies and in 2019 sold 109.000 copies; it is possible that behind this increase of fans to be the effect of an 'consumed feud' by the general public and a return of the lost fans (forgiveness?), perhaps even new fans (Christians? because of the album *Jesus is King*?);

- it is difficult to say that the decrease of Taylor Swift's *Lover* album could be related only to loss of fans (around 41% - 44% and only in the first week) as the album was her first to be available on digital platforms such as Spotify and Youtube; on these platforms users were able to listen her music for free, therefore selling less albums;

- due to different methods of calculation of the final charts, it is highly possible, that despite the decrease of pure album sales in the first week, Taylor Swift to still have one million fans and this is based on pure sales and streaming (paid and free) as released by Billboard (867.000) and Rolling Stone numbers (991.800)[626];

- on long term, Kanye West successfully managed to maintain a good number of fans on various digital platforms, which helped his albums to remain popular in charts (with other even to achieve and stay in top 10, in the US Top Gospel Albums (*Jesus in King* (2019) became number 1; however, Taylor Swift definitely has a higher number of fans, and she is more popular in charts than Kanye West;

- in 2017 (*reputation*, an album considered by both camps of the feud, and maybe by the wider general audience as a possible response to Kanye West song *Famous,* and his album *The Life of Pablo*) Taylor Swift sold in the first week a little bit over 43 more pure albums (1.216.000) than Kanye West' album, *The Life of Pablo* (28.000; 2016);

---

[625] The average result is based on the Billboard and Rolling Stone Chart for the first week sales: Billboard: 6% + 44% and 29% + Rolling Stone: 41% + 18% = 132 divided by 5 charts results (three from Billboard and two from Rolling Stone) = 27.5% average decrease. If we calculate: 6% + 44% + 41+ = 91 divided by 3 = 30.33(3)% decrease from the point of view of pure sales. If we calculate 6% + 18% + 29% = 53 divided by 3 = 17.66(6)% decrease from the point of view of pure sales (album *1989*) and album-equivalent sales (*reputation* and *Lover*).

[626] According to RIAA: *The Album Award counts album sales, song sales and on-demand audio and/or video song streams at the formula of 1,500 on-demand audio and/or video song streams = 10 track sales = 1 album sale.* Available here: https://www.riaa.com/gold-platinum/about-awards/#:~:text=RIAA%20GOLD%20%26%20PLATINUM%20AWARDS,-Certification&text=It%20counts%20album%20sales%2C%20song,track%20sales%20%3D%201%20album%20sale; last accessed: August 10, 2022.

- the decrease of the album sales is not something that happens only to Kanye West and Taylor Swift, but with other artists as well, such as Beyoncé, Rihanna, Lady Gaga, Rihanna, Katy Perry and many others; however, Kanye West's decrease is the lowest amongst all the artists written above; based on the above evidence, Kanye West's decrease (and other artists) followed a natural pattern: most artists (95-99%) have a high increase in popularity, fame and albums sales in the first two-three-four (rarely) albums of their career, then a decrease as they are in competition with other new artists with new songs, other strategies of promotion and themes of the music; in the end, the loss of popularity may be because people lose interest for the same artist (one reason can be linked to the public behaviour of the artist, and the perception of the general public of the consequences of that behaviour); in the case of Taylor Swift, it seems that she makes a different sort of music and promotion that keep fans closed and albums sales higher than many other artists (99%?);

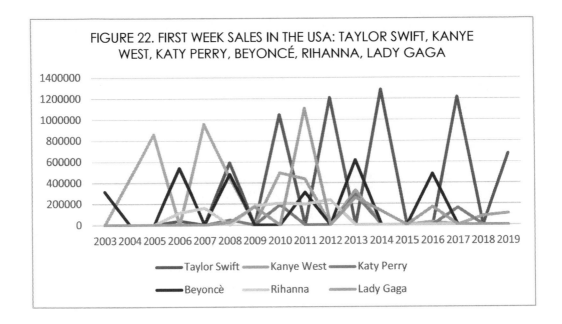

FIGURE 22. FIRST WEEK SALES IN THE USA: TAYLOR SWIFT, KANYE WEST, KATY PERRY, BEYONCÉ, RIHANNA, LADY GAGA

- during September 2009 (the start of the feud) Taylor Swift was on the natural path of increasing as global pop artist, while Kanye West was decreasing as global rap artist, therefore, it is wrong to a good extent to say that Taylor Swift became famous because Kanye West rudely interrupted her speech for an award that people voted in favour of Taylor Swift, not Beyoncé; Kanye West, over the years, promoted various artists that none of them managed to stay on the same line of popularity as Taylor Swift did; Kanye West did not managed to write and compose songs to maintain his own popularity on long term and at high levels as Taylor Swift, but also the popularity of the promoted artists for long term: his artists and the songs came and left the charts faster than you can say sabotage; Taylor Swift managed to be famous and maintain the fame earned for long term, mostly because of her ability to write songs about her life and other people in a country, pop and alternative form loved by millions of people and good reviews; Kanye West, while Taylor Swift was involved in the process of creating music, did not move a single finger, or spoken more positive sentences to make it better for her; Kanye West put in motions at least in two occasions (MTV in 2009; in February 2016, before the Grammy Awards), and to a good extent, almost-like-public-and-intentional-plan-of-negative-attacks against Taylor Swift's abilities as lyricist, and good character as pop artist;

- despite Kanye West's strategy of promotion of the *song Famous*, *The Life of Pablo* album, Saint Pablo Tour and Taylor Swift intentional implication by Kanye West in his song, Taylor Swift kept her position in top of the music industry; Kanye West highly decreased with a slow increase, but still below Taylor Swift;

- based on the above evidence (first week pure album sales) there is a higher negative impact on the long term for Kanye West than for Taylor Swift.

IV.1.2 Worldwide Sales of Songs from **Famous** Feud

TABLE 39. WORLDWIDE SALES OF SONGS FROM **FAMOUS** FEUD

TAYLOR SWIFT	KANYE WEST
Look What You Made Me Do (August 2017): 6.026.666.[627]	*Famous (February 2016):* 2.585.000.[628]

CONCLUSIONS:

- Taylor Swift's song sold with 64% more copies than Kanye West in a time where her reputation was associated with the words 'bitch' (from the lyrics of *song Famous*, the fans singing at Kanye West's concerts 'I made that bitch famous'; on Facebook and Twitter there was a visible number of posts with the caption 'rePUTAtion', highlighting the word 'puta' (translated from Spanish into English means 'bitch')), 'snake' and 'liar'; all these words, and more negative words, where highly promoted on social media for long term, even as of today; the reputation of a 'liar' was spread even in mass-

---

[627] The numbers are based on certification of sales from various countries, see Taylor Swift, *Look What You Made Me Do*, https://en.wikipedia.org/wiki/Look_What_You_Made_Me_Do#Commercial_performance, last accessed: February 21, 2020.
[628] The numbers are based on certification of sales from various countries, see Kanye West, *Famous*, https://en.wikipedia.org/wiki/Famous_(Kanye_West_song)#Certifications, last accessed: February 21, 2020.

media through various articles, though there was not enough evidence to accuse her of genuine wrongdoing and intentional manipulation of the feud in her favour; apparently, hundreds of thousands of fans disagreed with the negative narrative of Kanye West and the Western mass-media, and decided to trust Taylor's story by buying and listening to her music;

- the high sales of albums show a high interest of the fans for petty songs, the love for drama between artists, which artist is more famous after a feud, and which artist has a strong and genuine fanbase.

IV.1.3 Producers and Lyricists of Songs from **Famous** Feud

TABLE 40. PRODUCERS AND LYRICISTS OF SONGS FROM **FAMOUS** FEUD

TAYLOR SWIFT	KANYE WEST
Look What You Made Me Do:	***Famous:***
***Producers** (2):* Jack Antonoff, Taylor Swift;	***Producers** (6):* Andrew Dawson, Charlie Heat, Havoc, Kanye West, Kuk Harrell, Noah Goldstein;
***Lyricists** (5):* Fred Fairbrass, Jack Antonoff, Richard Fairbrass, Rob Manzoli, Taylor Swift.[629]	***Lyricists** (17):* Andrew Dawson, Chancelor Bennett, Cydel Young, Enzo Vita, Ernest Brown, Giampiero Scalamogna, Jimmy Webb, Kanye West, Kasseem Dean, Kejuan Muchita, Luis Enriquez Bacalov, Mike Dean, Noah Goldstein, Patrick Reynolds, Ross Birchard, Sergio Bardotti, Winston Riley.[630]

Conclusion:

Taylor Swift used less producers and lyricists, and her song was more popular in sales than Kanye West's army of lyricists and producers.

IV.1.4 The Rabbit Hat: Fame, Originality and Creativity After VMA 2009[631]

---

[629] Taylor Swift,'reputation Credits', *Tidal*, https://listen.tidal.com/artist/3557299, last accessed: August 25, 2019.
[630] Kanye West, 'The Life of Pablo Credits', *Tidal*, https://listen.tidal.com/album/57273408, last accessed: October 23, 2017.
[631] This section was also included in Casian Anton, *Black and White Music*.

In this chapter I investigated the roots of the new album released a year after the MTV scene, that is the music released by both artists in the autumn of 2010, first Taylor Swift then Kanye West.

TABLE 41. THE RABBIT HAT: TAYLOR SWIFT AND KANYE WEST

CATEGORY	TAYLOR SWIFT: *SPEAK NOW* (DELUXE, 2010)	KANYE WEST: *MY BEAUTIFUL DARK TWISTED FANTASY* (2010)
FIRST WEEK SALES	HIGH INCREASE	HIGH DECREASE
OVERALL ALBUM SALES	HIGH NUMBER OF SALES ON LONG TERM	MODERATE NUMBER OF SALES WITH TRACKS OF SLOW SALES ON LONG TERM
USE OF SAMPLE	0%	10 OUT OF 14 SONGS
ORIGINAL SONGS WITH NO SAMPLE	17 SONGS (100%)	4 OUT OF 14 SONGS
ORIGINAL SONG AS SOLE LYRICIST	16 OUT OF 17 SONGS	0 SONGS (0%)
ORIGINAL SONG WITH TWO LYRICISTS	1 OUT OF 17 SONGS	0 OUT OF 14 SONGS (0%)
ORIGINAL SONG WITH THREE LYRICISTS	0 SONGS	1 OUT OF 14 SONGS
ORIGINAL SONG WITH AT LEAST FOUR LYRICISTS	0 SONGS	13 OUT OF 14 SONGS
DIRECT INSPIRATION FROM OTHER SONGS	NO	YES
TOP CHARTS & AWARDS OF THE SONG SAMPLED	NO	YES
DIRECT WHITE MALE INSPIRATION	N/A	21 OUT OF 25
DIRECT WHITE FEMALE INSPIRATION	N/A	1 OUT OF 1
DIRECT BLACK MALE INSPIRATION	N/A	4 out of 25
DIRECT BLACK FEMALE INSPIRATION	N/A	
METACRITIC RATING	77	94
LENGTH OF SONG AS SOLE LYRICIST	75:29 MINUTES	0 MINUTES
LENGTH OF SONG WITH TWO LYRICISTS	3:54	0 MINUTES (THERE IS A HIGHER NUMBER OF MINUTES ONLY TO SONGS WITH AT LEAST 4 LYRICISTS)
LYRICS	OWN LYRICS	LYRICS FROM OTHER ARTISTS
THE ORIGINS OF TITLE SONGS	OWN TITLES	FROM OTHER TITLE SONGS AND LYRICS OF SONGS SAMPLED IN HIS MUSIC
PATTERN OF MUSIC RELEASE	2006: October 24 2008: November 11 2010: October 25	2004: February 10 2005: August 30 2007: September 11 2008: November 24 2010: November 22
	The following date are written to observe the full pattern of music release of both artists.	
	2012: October 22 2014: October 27 2017: November 10 2019: August 23 2020: July 24 2020: December 11	2013: June 18 2016: February 14 2018: June 1 2019: October 25

CONCLUSIONS:

- *Taylor Swift*:

  o came with traces of global success;
  o came with her own lyrics;
  o released an album with original songs never heard before in the music industry;
  o the length of the music written by herself for *Standard Edition* is 100% of the album, for *Deluxe Edition* she has one song written in partnership with another lyricist; Kanye West has 0% as sole lyricist;
  o released the music following October – November pattern;

- *Kanye West*:

  o came with lyrics written in partnership with other artists and instruments already created and used by other artists in the music industry;
  o 13 out of 14 songs were written in partnership with at least 4 lyricists;
  o it is inspired by the music written by white male artists, 21 out of 25 male artists;
  o overall, his album was rated on Metacritic with a higher grade (94) than Taylor Swift (77);
  o changed the pattern of music release and interfered for a second time in Taylor Swift's pattern of album release: one album in each year for two years and in total for four albums: the first two albums: 2004 and 2005, the next two albums: 2007 and 2008; since 2008 Kanye West changed the season and released his album in the same month as Taylor Swift, but two weeks later: Taylor Swift on November 11, 2008 and Kanye West on November 24; *in 2010*: Taylor Swift released the album on October 25 (she released her first album in October 24, 2006), then Kanye West later in November 22, keeping the release date connected with the last release, which is the first and last time when Kanye West followed this release pattern; the following albums were released in different seasons, only to be changed to October 25, 2019 with *Jesus is King*, the same release date as Taylor Swift with *Speak Now* in 2010;

- **Album reviews**: Kanye West received higher reviews and grades than Taylor Swift, but given the sources of his songs, the following questions arise: do the reviews also include an analysis of his voice? online critics argue that his singing skills are either weak, or he does not know how to sing[632]; did the reviewers perform a genuine analysis of his voice? if this argument is true, how did he manage to get such a high score? Kanye West used samples (title, lyrics, instruments) from other artists, basically what is Kanye West's original contribution in his album? are the reviews and grades received based only on his work, or the final song that contains samples? are reviewers able to make the difference between Kanye West's original part and the samples part? if we take the samples from Kanye's album, what remains written and produced by him alone is worth grades 9 and 10? Taylor Swift got the grades based on her own lyrics and 50% participation as producer of her album, and were 7 and 8 in the eyes of the reviewers; Kanye got 9 and 10 with the help of more lyricists and producers than Taylor Swift, but we do not know for sure how much is Kanye's contribution in the lyrics of the songs and production; are the reviews real or have they been exaggerated to the detriment of the music industry, but also of the white artist Taylor Swift to prove that black artists have better music than white artists, and Kanye West was right to point out that Taylor Swift did not deserve the award from 2009?

IV.1.5 The Rating on Metacritic[633]

TABLE 42. THE ALBUM RATINGS ON METACRITIC

TAYLOR SWIFT[634]	KANYE WEST[635]
Taylor Swift (Deluxe, 2006): not on Metacritic	The College Dropout (2004): 87
Fearless (Platinum, 2008): 73	Late Registration (2005): 85
Speak Now (Deluxe, 2010): 77	Graduation (2007): 79
RED (Deluxe, 2012): 77	88s & Heartbreak (2008): 75
1989 (Deluxe, 2014): 76	My Beautiful Dark Twisted Fantasy (2010): 94
reputation (2017): 71	Yeezus (2013): 84
Lover (2019): 79	The Life of Pablo (2016): 75
folklore (Deluxe, 2020): 88	Ye (2018): 64
Evermore (Deluxe, 2020): 85	Jesus is King (2019): 53
Fearless (Taylor's Version, 2021): 82	Donda (2021): 53

[632] 'How Well Does Kanye West Really Sing', *Quora*, available at: https://www.quora.com/How-well-does-Kanye-West-really-sing, last accessed: February 25, 2020; 'Why is Kanye West considered to be a great artist? I have listened to his music, and it sounds like every other song on the radio. Am I missing something?', *Quora*, available at: https://www.quora.com/Why-is-Kanye-West-considered-to-be-a-great-artist-I-have-listened-to-his-music-and-it-sounds-like-every-other-song-on-the-radio-Am-I-missing-something, last accessed: February 25, 2020; 'David Crosby: Kanye West can neither sing, nor write, nor play', *The Guardian*, October 28, 2016, available at: https://www.theguardian.com/music/2016/oct/28/david-crosby-kanye-west, last accessed: February 25, 2020.

[633] This section was also included in Casian Anton, *Black and White Music*.

[634] Metacritic, *Taylor Swift,* https://www.metacritic.com/person/taylor-swift, last accessed: January 7, 2022.

[635] Metacritic, *Kanye West,* https://www.metacritic.com/person/kanye-west?filter-options=music&sort_options=date&num_items=30, last accessed: January 7, 2022.

Red (Taylor's Version, 2021): 91	
Total average by albums in this table: 79.99	Total average by albums in this table: 74.9
Total average by Metacritic: 80	Total average by Metacritic: 74

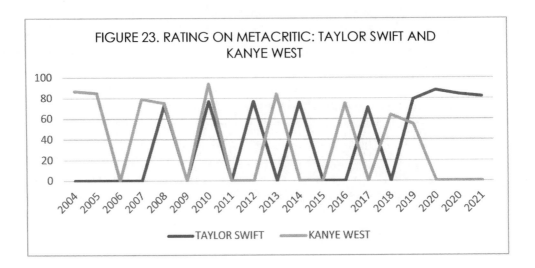

FIGURE 23. RATING ON METACRITIC: TAYLOR SWIFT AND KANYE WEST

CONCLUSIONS:

- *Taylor Swift*:

    o the grades received for each album are based on the work and ideas of the artist, but also to a considerable extent of other artists and producers she worked with (see the producers of *folklore* and *Evermore*, most of them is one producer, Aaron Dessner or Jack Antonoff);

    o male producers are the constant base of her musical career;

    o compared to Kanye West and Metacritic, the grades received is close to 8, where they increase and decrease over the years;

    o a significant percentage of the grade received is based purely on her ability to write and compose unheard songs; in her music catalogue there are lots of songs that were written shortly after she heard the instruments, and were hits on the radio and charts;

    o Metacritic does not include all the reviews written about her albums, there are reviews with higher and lower grades which are not included; it is highly possible that the final grade to be over 80.

- *Kanye West*:

- the grades received for each album are based on the work and ideas of the artist, but also to a considerable extent of other artists from whom he sampled; also, for lyricists and producers who contributed to his songs;
- compared to Taylor Swift (the grades increased, and before the age 30 she has one of the highest reviewed album in her life, *folklore*), he received a high grade, 87 and then decreased (for 3 albums), then raised to the highest grade (94); for the last albums, the grades decreased, and for the last album the final grade is 55;
- parts of his grades belong to white artists as well;
- Metacritic does not include all the reviews written about his albums; there are reviews with higher and lower grades which are not included; it is highly possible that the final grade to be over 80.

IV.2 **Bad Blood – Swish, Swish** Feud

Although being presented as a feud between Taylor Swift and Katy Perry, actually this feud is linked with the *Famous* feud. In this section I explored and set the narrative line of the feud between Taylor Swift and Katy Perry. I also showed the connection of this feud with the *Famous* feud and Kanye West.

IV.2.1 **Bad Blood – Swish, Swish** Feud Narrative Line[636]

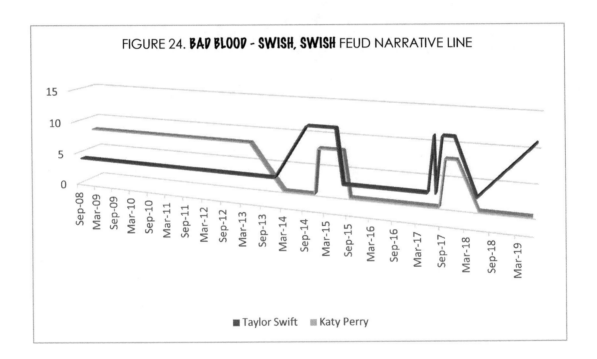

FIGURE 24. **BAD BLOOD - SWISH, SWISH** FEUD NARRATIVE LINE

CONCLUSIONS:

- during the *Carpool Karaoke Primetime Special*, Katy Perry discussed the *Bad Blood – Swish, Swish* feud with James Corden by saying: *'Honestly, it's really like she started it and it's time for her to finish it'*, however, this affirmation is not true as the narrative line

---

[636] Eliza Thompson, 'Why Were Katy Perry and Taylor Swift Even Fighting in the First Place?' *Cosmopolitan*, July 10, 2020, https://www.cosmopolitan.com/entertainment/celebs/news/a61450/taylor-swift-katy-perry-feud-timeline/, last accessed: August 6, 2020.

indicates that Katy Perry started the feud, and she is the perpetrator of the feud when she decided to interfere in the music business of Taylor Swift: few dancers from Katy Perry's team got a job with Taylor Swift's *Red Tour*; months later, Katy Perry wanted them back to join her *Prismatic Tour*, which the dancers agreed; Katy Perry wanted to hire her former dancers, but did not share this intention with Taylor Swift *before* the start of Red Tour, but only *after* the dancers were fired by Taylor's team; *'She basically tried to sabotage an entire arena tour. She tried to hire a bunch of people out from under me,'* answered Taylor Swift[637]; Katy Perry said, according to American Songwriter:

'Honestly, [Swift] started it, and it's time for her to finish it.' […] 'It's about backing dancers. It's so crazy,' she continued. 'There [are] three backing dancers that went on tour with her tour, and they asked me before they went on tour if they could go. I was like, 'Yeah, of course. I'm not on a record cycle. Get the work. She's great. But I will be on a record cycle, probably, in about a year, so be sure to put a 30-day contingency in your contract so you can get out if you wanna join me when I say I'm going back on.' So that year came up, and I texted all of them because I'm very close with them. I said, 'Look, just FYI: I'm about to start. I want to put the word out there.' They said, 'Okay. We're gonna go talk to management about it.' They did, and they got fired. I tried to talk to [Swift] about it, and she wouldn't speak to me.' […] 'I do the right thing anytime that it feels like a fumble. It was a full shutdown, and then she writes a song about me. And I'm like 'Okay, cool, cool. That's how you wanna do it? Karma.'[638]

- it is considered by fans on both camps that Taylor Swift got involved in the feud only to reply to Katy Perry's idea with the thing that Katy Perry decided to mess with: Taylor Swift's tour;[639] maybe Taylor Swift wrote the song *Bad Blood* as a reply mechanism to Katy Perry: the attempt to sabotage her music tour = wrote a song from her musical mind; *Bad Blood's* lyric 'If you live like that, you live with ghosts' and 'Ghost' is a song from Katy Perry's album called *Prism* (released in 2013); *Bad Blood* was awarded with the *Video of the Year* and the *Best Collaboration* at the MTV Video Music Awards in 2015, won the *Best Music Video* at the 58th Grammy Awards; in March 2020 it was certified 6× Platinum by the Recording Industry Association of America (RIAA);
- Taylor Swift interfered negatively in the narrative line of Katy Perry *only after* Katy interfered first negatively in her narrative line.

IV.2.2 The Link with the **FAMOUS** Feud and Kanye West

---

[637] Ibidem.

[638] Catherine Walthall, 'Behind the Beef: Katy Perry and Taylor Swift's Feud Explained Blow By Blow', *American Songwriter*, available at: https://americansongwriter.com/katy-perry-taylor-swift-feud-explained/, last accessed: October 2022.

[639] Abby Gardner, 'Katy Perry Just Announced a New Song, and Fans Are Convinced It's With Taylor Swift', *Glamour*, May 11, 2020, available at: https://www.glamour.com/story/katy-perry-just-announced-a-new-song-and-fans-are-convinced-its-with-taylor-swift, last accessed: October 20, 2020.

TABLE 43. THE LINK OF KATY PERRY WITH THE **FAMOUS** FEUD AND KANYE WEST

KANYE WEST	KATY PERRY
NAME OF THE ALBUM	*SONG & VIDEO*
	Swish, Swish (featuring Nicki Minaj)

Despite the evidence that Kanye West did not inform Taylor Swift about the line 'I made that bitch famous', Katy Perry decided to name her song *Swish, Swish*, and to include the word 'bish' allegedly to criticise negatively Taylor Swift's abilities as a pop artist.

'Initially Kanye West announced a new album entitled *So Help Me God* slated for a 2014 release; in March 2015 Kanye West announced that the album would instead be tentatively called *SWISH*. Later in January 2016, Kanye West announced that *SWISH* would be released on February 11. On January 26, 2016, Kanye West revealed he had renamed the album from *SWISH* to *Waves*[640]. Several days ahead of its release, Kanye West again changed the title for the last time: *The Life of Pablo*.'[641]

Katy Perry released a song with the words *Swish, Swish* which was one of the titles Kanye West had announced for his forthcoming album, *SWISH*; however, Kanye West later changed the name to *The Life of Pablo*. In 2016, Kanye West included the word 'bitch' in the lyrics of the song *Famous*; in the song Katy Perry used the word 'bish': 'Swish, swish, bish'. 'Swish' is a word close to pronunciation and writing style with the artist's name: Swift; 'Bish' is a word close to pronunciation and writing style with the term 'bitch'.

Maybe for Katy Perry the idea for the song released is a version of truth. Through the title of the song and the lyrics, there is a possibility that Katy Perry sided with Kanye West's story about the involvement of Taylor Swift in the song *Famous*.

Nicki Minaj joined Katy Perry in the song and the music video of *Swish, Swish*. Before this song, Nicki had her own short feud moment with Taylor Swift. Nicki Minaj tweeted about the MTV VMA nominations in 2015: 'If your video celebrates women with very slim bodies, you will be nominated for vid of the year.'[642] Taylor Swift replied to Nicki Minaj on Twitter: 'I've done nothing but love & support you. It's unlike you to pit women against each other. Maybe one of the men took your slot.'[643] This was the starting point of the feud. Nicki Minaj in return specified that she was talking about the music industry and nominations of the artist, and not about her. In the end, Taylor Swift wrote back to Nicky Minaj: 'I thought I was being called out. I missed the point, I misunderstood, then misspoke. I'm sorry, Nicki.'[644] Nicki Minaj accepted the apology. Later in 2015 at the MTV VMA, Taylor Swift and Nicki Minaj

---

[640] Matthew Strauss, 'Kanye West Announces New Album Title, Shares Final Tracklist', *Pitchfork*, February 10, 2016, https://pitchfork.com/news/63468-kanye-west-announces-new-album-title-shares-final-tracklist/, last accessed: October 25, 2017.

[641] Mitchell Peters, 'Kanye West Announces Name Change of His New Album on Twitter', *Billboard*, March 5, 2015, https://www.billboard.com/articles/columns/the-juice/6553812/kanye-west-announces-name-change-of-his-new-album-on-twitter-swish-so-help-me-god, last accessed: October 25, 2017.

[642] Nicki Minaj, 'Message on Twitter', *Twitter*, July 21, 2015, available at: https://twitter.com/NICKIMINAJ/status/623608271774072832, last accessed: October 25, 2017.

[643] Spencer Kornhaber, 'Taylor Swift and the Silencing of Nicki Minaj', *The Atlantic*, July 22, 2015, available at: https://www.theatlantic.com/entertainment/archive/2015/07/taylor-swift-silencing-nicki-minaj-vmas-twitter-bad-blood-anaconda/399164/, last accessed: October 25, 2017.

[644] Nolan Feeney, 'Taylor Swift Apologizes to Nicki Minaj: 'I Missed the Point'', *Time*, July 23, 2015, available at: https://time.com/3969778/taylor-swift-nicki-minaj/, last accessed: October 25, 2017.

performed two songs: *Bad Blood* from Taylor Swift, and *The Night Is Still Young* from Nicki Minaj.[645]

In 2017, maybe Nicki Minaj decided to be on Katy Perry's side by singing negative lyrics possibly about Taylor Swift:

'I already despise you (yeah)
All that fake love you showin'
Couldn't even disguise you, yo, yo
Ran? When? Nicki gettin' tan
Mirror mirror who's the fairest bitch in all the land?'
'I only rock with queens, so I'm makin' hits with Katy'.[646]

The lyrics 'All that fake love you showin' is to a good extent in the same theme and world with Kanye West's lyrics from the song *Fade*: 'Your love is fadin'.[647]

It is possible that these lyrics to be a reference where Nicki Minaj consider Katy Perry to be a queen (like her and the name of her future album *Queen*, 2018), and decided to diss Taylor Swift. Nicki also used the word 'bitch' to address a woman. Further, these lyrics can be related to Taylor Swift's *Bad Blood* music video: in her video she invited friends which happens to be famous people in the music, fashion and tv industry; Katy Perry decided to sing along with a famous female rapper, which happens to have already a short feud with Taylor Swift. Another common element between Taylor Swift and Katy Perry is the involvement of a rap artist in songs possibly dedicated to the feud: Taylor Swift released the music video *Bad Blood* (2015 from the album *1989*) with Kendrick Lamar (black artist), and Katy Perry released the song *Swish, Swish* with Nicki Minaj (black artist, 2017).

Katy Perry said her song is an anti-bullying anthem. During a performance, Katy Perry made a slight change to the song switching out the line 'Don't you come for me' with 'God bless you on your journey, oh baby girl'. This is another example to support the allegation that *Swish, Swish* song is about Taylor Swift.

Surprisingly, Katy Perry rejected fans speculations that the song is about Taylor Swift, by saying 'No, it's not about anyone in particular' […] 'And I've said that on the record.'[648]

The reply mechanism of Taylor Swift:

[645] Taylor Swift World, 'Taylor Swift & Nicki Minaj Perform 'The Night is Still Young + Bad Blood' at MTV VMAs 2015', *Youtube*, May 21, 2021, available at: https://www.youtube.com/watch?v=qrW5YCjbXDQ, last accessed: June 26, 2022.

[646] Katy Perry, 'Swish, Swish Lyrics', *Genius*, available at: https://genius.com/Katy-perry-swish-swish-lyrics, last accessed: March 27, 2020.

[647] Kanye West, 'Fade', *Musicmatch*, available at: https://www.musixmatch.com/lyrics/Kanye-West/Fade, last accessed: October 24, 2020.

[648] Cady Lang, 'Katy Perry Just Changed the Lyrics to 'Swish Swish' After Saying She Wants to End Feud With Taylor Swift', *Times Magazine*, June 13, 2017, available at: https://time.com/4816737/katy-perry-changes-lyrics-swish-swish-feud-taylor-swift/, last accessed: August 6, 2020.

1. *on the day of Katy Perry's album release (June 9, 2017), named Witness,* the world witnessed Taylor Swift's decision to release her entire music catalogue on streaming services for the first time: 'In celebration of 1989 selling over 10 million albums worldwide and the RIAA's 100 million song certification announcement, Taylor wants to thank her fans by making her entire catalogue available to all streaming services tonight at midnight';[649]

overall, Taylor Swift's music outperformed Katy Perry's music despite releasing a new musical album;[650] it seems that Taylor Swift refused to listen to Katy Perry's lyric 'Don't you come for me', 'No, not today (woah)' and she did came after Katy Perry on the big day album release, which it seems that Taylor Swift is as Katy Perry said: 'You're calculated';

regarding the evolution of both artists: the outperformance of Taylor Swift's music (and few month later the *reputation* album) on Spotify and other streaming services over Katy Perry, it is a strong evidence that Taylor Swift is not a joker, and *she is a killer queen* as Katy Perry sings in *Swish, Swish*: 'And I'm a courtside killer queen', 'Cause I stay winning', 'Your game is tired', 'You should retire'; Taylor Swift's music outperformed Katy Perry's music on the streaming services, and each album makes more history on charts than Katy Perry's music; overall, Katy Perry has more reasons to retire than Taylor Swift;

Katy Perry on *Swish, Swish's* lyrics: 'And you will kiss the ring, You best believe': in the end it was the other way around: Katy Perry decided to stop speaking negatively about Taylor Swift: 'I'm ready to let it go' […] 'Absolutely, 100 percent. I forgive her and I'm sorry for anything I ever did, and I hope the same from her and I think it's actually… I think it's time' […] There are bigger fish to fry and there are bigger problems in the world. I love her and I want the best for her, and I think she's a fantastic songwriter and, like, I think that if we both, her and I, can be representatives of strong women that come together despite their differences, I think the whole world is going to go, like 'Yeah we can do this';[651] in August 2017, Taylor Swift, despite the decision of Katy Perry to forgive and leave her alone, decided to go on with the release of *Look What You Made Me Do* with possible references to Katy Perry.
Taylor Swift did not mention publicly Katy Perry; while touring in 2018, Taylor Swift received from Katy Perry an olive tree (a symbol of peace)[652]; this moment was captured in a picture and shared by Taylor Swift on her Instagram account with the text: 'Thank you, Katy.'[653]

2. *she released the song Look What You Made Me Do* in August 2017 which might contain possible references to Katy Perry and Kanye West, but not about Nicki Minaj.[654]

---

[649] Taylor Nation, *Instagram*, available at: https://www.instagram.com/p/BVGMtjZA18r/, last accessed: August 6, 2020.
[650] Rihan Daly, 'Taylor Swift's back catalogue is currently outperforming Katy Perry's 'Witness' on Spotify', *NME*, June 11, 2017, available at: https://www.nme.com/news/music/taylor-swifts-back-catalogue-currently-outperforming-katy-perrys-witness-spotify-2087235, last accessed: August 6, 2020.
[651] Ibidem.
[652] Ben Beaumont-Thomas, 'No more bad blood? Katy Perry sends Taylor Swift actual olive branch to end feud', *The Guardian*, May 9, 2018, available at: https://www.theguardian.com/music/2018/may/09/katy-perry-taylor-swift-olive-branch#:~:text=Swift%20posted%20a%20video%20of,room%20and%20found%20this%20actual, last accessed: August 6, 2020.
[653] Ibidem
[654] I watched the video several times, but I could not find possible references about Nicki Minaj.

IV.2.3 The Impact of the **'Bad Blood – Swish, Swish'** Feud

In the following table I investigated the impact of the *Bad Blood – Swish, Swish* feud between Taylor Swift and Katy Perry.

TABLE 44. THE IMPACT OF THE **FAMOUS** FEUD ON WORLDWIDE ALBUM SALES

YEAR	TAYLOR SWIFT	KATY PERRY
2006	Taylor Swift: 7.000.000 albums as December 2017.	-
2008	*Fearless*: 10.000.000 albums as December 2017.	*One of the Boys:* 7.000.000 as August 2010.
2010	*Speak Now*: 6.000.000 albums as December 2017.	*Teenage Dreams*: 6.000.000 as July 2013.
2012	*RED*: 7.000.000 albums as July 2018.	-
2013	-	*Prism*: more than 4.000.000 album as August 2015.
2014	*1989:* 11.300.000 as of December 2019.	-
2017	*reputation:* 5.100.000 as of December 2019.	*Witness:* over 840.000 album as of January 2018.
2019	*Lover (2019):* more than 5.000.000 as of January 2020.	-
2020	*folklore (2020):* over 2.000.000 as August 6, 2020.[655]	*Smile (2020):* 402.000 as March 21, 2021.[656]

---

[655] Taylor Swift, 'Fearless', *RIAA*, December 11, 2017, https://www.riaa.com/gold-platinum/?tab_active=default-award&ar=Taylor+Swift&ti=Speak+Now#search_section, last accessed: December 21, 2019; Taylor Swift, 'Speak Now', *RIAA*, December 11, 2017, https://www.riaa.com/gold-platinum/?tab_active=default-award&ar=Taylor+Swift&ti=Speak+Now#search_section, last accessed: December 21, 2019; Taylor Swift, 'RED', *RIAA*, July 23, 2019, https://www.riaa.com/gold-platinum/?tab_active=default-award&se=taylor+swift#search_section, last accessed: December 21, 2019; United World Charts, 'Decade Album Chart', *Media Traffic*, http://www.mediatraffic.de/2010-2019-album-chart.htm, last accessed: January 6, 2020. RIAA certified 9.000.000 albums in December 11, 2017, https://www.riaa.com/gold-platinum/?tab_active=default-award&se=taylor+swift#search_section, last accessed: December 21, 2019; Eli Countryman, 'Taylor Swift's 'Folklore' Sells Over 2 Million Copies in First Week', *Variety*, July 31, 2020, available at: https://variety.com/2020/music/news/taylor-swift-folklore-first-week-sales-worldwide-1234722530/, last accessed: August 6, 2020.

[656] Gil Kaufman, 'Katy Perry, Fantasia Look to Unseat Eminem on Charts', *MTV*, August 26, 2010, http://www.mtv.com/news/1646527/katy-perry-fantasia-look-to-unseat-eminem-on-charts/, last accessed: November 6, 2019; Colin Stutz, 'Katy Perry Planning Las Vegas Residency at Brand-New Casino', *Billboard*, March 19, 2021, available at: https://www.billboard.com/articles/business/touring/9543635/katy-perry-las-vegas-residency-aeg-resorts-world, last accessed: July 25, 2021; Sean Michaels, 'Katy Perry announces new album, Prism, on side of golden lorry', *The Guardian*, July 30., 2013, https://www.theguardian.com/music/2013/jul/30/katy-perry-new-album-prism-lorry, last accessed: November 6, 2019; Chris Willman, 'Taylor Swift Moves to Universal Music Publishing Group with New Pact', *Variety*, February 6, 2020, https://variety.com/2020/music/news/taylor-swift-signs-umpg-publishing-deal-1203484798/, last accessed: February 18, 2020; All Access, 'Third Annual Capitol Congress Presents New Projects', *Media Notables*, August 6, 2015, https://www.allaccess.com/net-news/archive/story/144283/third-annual-capitol-congress-presents-new-project, last accessed: November 6, 2019; Shirley Halperin, 'Capitol's Steve Barnett on Five Years at the Tower, 'Plan' for Katy Perry, 'Beloved' Niall Horan', *Variety*, January 12, 2018, https://variety.com/2018/music/news/steve-barnett-capitol-interview-katy-perry-niall-horan-1202660297/, last accessed: August 25, 2019.

TABLE 45. WORLDWIDE SALES OF SONGS SWIFT & PERRY FEUD

TAYLOR SWIFT	KATY PERRY
Bad Blood: 6.057.500. *Look What You Made Me Do*: 6.026.666.[657]	*Swish, Swish*: 1.000.000 as January 2018[658]

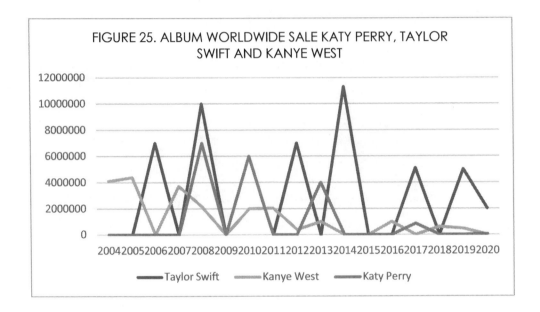

FIGURE 25. ALBUM WORLDWIDE SALE KATY PERRY, TAYLOR SWIFT AND KANYE WEST

CONCLUSIONS:

- on long term, Taylor Swift sold more albums than Katy Perry;
- the feud does not seem to stop Taylor Swift selling more songs and albums than Katy Perry; this positive side effect is due to loyal fans that Taylor Swift earned in the last years;
- Taylor Swift's power sale seems to not know the end: *Bad Blood* from 2014 sold at least 6 times more copies than Katy Perry's *Swish, Swish* from 2017; Taylor Swift' song, *Look What You Made Me Do* from 2017, sold also at least 6 times more copies than Katy Perry's song, *Swish, Swish*; making a full maths of both songs: Taylor Swift sold 12 times more songs than Katy Perry;
- Taylor Swift has definitely more loyal fans than Katy Perry.

---

[657] The numbers are based on certification of sales from different countries, see Taylor Swift, *Bad Blood*, https://en.wikipedia.org/wiki/Bad_Blood_(Taylor_Swift_song)#Chart_performance, last accessed: February 21, 2020; The numbers are based on certification of sales from different countries, see Taylor Swift, 'Look What You Made Me Do', *Wikipedia*, https://en.wikipedia.org/wiki/Look_What_You_Made_Me_Do#Commercial_performance, last accessed: February 21, 2020.
[658] Katy Perry, 'Swish, Swish', *RIAA*, January 19, 2018, https://www.riaa.com/gold-platinum/?tab_active=default-award&se=swish+swish#search_section, last accessed: August 25, 2019.

V. The **FAMOUS** feud: strategies of interpretation and communication

During the events from the *Famous* feud, the Western mass-media was one of the main source of the narrative for the outsiders.[659] A second main source was the main players of the feud, and their explanations published on their social media accounts, or through other publications, about the storyline of the events that caused or advanced the feud.[660] After reading about 10 articles, I noticed that the explanations offered by journalists are absurd and mean to Taylor Swift, for example Amy Zimmerman in her article published in *The Daily Beast,* wrote that Taylor Swift: 'has been tapping into virginal white victim tropes her entire career.'[661] Ellie Woodward used the same approach 'whole career' as Amy Zimmerman: she presented Taylor Swift as playing the role of the false white victim throughout her entire career.[662] For Amy Zimmerman and Ellie Woodward, a phone call in which you are not told the whole story (but you are accused of knowing everything from the beginning, small and edited parts of the conversation are published online) was enough to conclude that *all her life* Taylor Swift played the role of a 'false victim'. Following this conclusion, I decided to look further on the new path of the *Famous* feud: to find journalists and articles with various techniques of approach and explanation of the feud.

Following the research, I gathered in a word document 1175 articles; the articles were arranged in two categories: USA and UK with the name of the news agency and a link to the website source, so I can access it anytime. I gathered links about the *Famous* feud from the following news agencies (available in the USA, UK and Australia): Slate Magazine, People, Vanity Fair, Cosmopolitan, Glamour Magazine, Elle, Vulture, Marie Claire, Forbes, Ok! UK, Radar Online, GQ, The Sun, Metro, Evening Standard, Telegraph, Daily Star, The Guardian, The Independent, Express, AOL.co.uk, Mirror, Huffington Post, Daily Mail, Pagesix, Billboard, CBS News, Business Insider, Bazaar, New York Daily, Gossip Cop, Rolling Stone, People, E

---

[659] 'Outsiders': I define *outsiders*, as all the people who are not self-considered fans of Taylor Swift. This category of people read the news about Taylor Swift and Kanye West, but do not engage and complete in-depth research about the storyline of the events as genuine fans do, or private researchers as myself.

[660] In this position, the category of people involved are to a high extent, if not fully, made by genuine fans of the players of the feud.

[661] For a full list of the articles about the Famous feud written by Amy Zimmerman and other journalist, see Table 45.

[662] Ellie Woodward, 'How Taylor Swift Played The Victim For A Decade And Made Her Entire Career'.

Online, Lifestyle, The Atlantic, TMZ, W Magazine, Latinpost, Daily Beast, Buzzfeed, Los Angeles Time, US Magazine, TIME.

I read over 500 articles, then I got bored and did not want to continue this research; being in this state of mind, I decided to delete the articles and, while deleting some of them, I had another idea: to use the articles and see if the timeline of the feud is correct in all the newspapers that were not deleted. Western mass-media (used in this report) and their role in spreading the *Famous* feud was mostly neutral toward the narrative of the events, even if the timeline is written and presented in short, long and complex articles. In the next pages of this chapter, I created an analysis of Taylor Swift's statements. I also extracted and presented negative views about Taylor Swift written and published in news agencies from the USA and the UK.

In the table below I analysed the statements released by Taylor Swift and her management team regarding her involvement in the *song Famous* released by Kanye West. Taylor Swift was criticised negatively based on the statements below. The text analysis is done with the purpose to expose the inability of journalists and bloggers to follow and understand the logical flow of Taylor Swift's statements, and reach logical conclusions regarding this feud. After the text analysis, I presented the list of the negative content written by various journalists, and published in popular and highly acclaimed news agencies in the USA and the UK.

TABLE 46. THE STATEMENTS OF TAYLOR SWIFT FOR THE INVOLVEMENT IN THE SONG FAMOUS

STATEMENTS	CONCLUSIONS
1. February 2016: after the release of the song Famous: Taylor Swift camp replied: 'Kanye did not call for approval, but to ask Taylor to release his single 'Famous' on her Twitter account. She declined and cautioned him about releasing a song with such a strong misogynistic message. Taylor was never made aware of the actual lyric, 'I made that bitch famous.'[663]	At the start of the feud, in February 2016, Taylor Swift admitted that there was a telephone call between her and Kanye West regarding the *song Famous*. I extracted the keywords from her statement to show she did not lie about the telephone call: 'Kanye […] call […] to ask Taylor to release his single 'Famous' on her Twitter account.' 'She declined and cautioned him about releasing a song': Taylor Swift declined (could) him only during the telephone call.

---

[663] Melody Chiu, Karen Mizoguchi, 'Kanye West Did Not Call Taylor Swift for Approval Over 'B----' Lyric, Singer Cautioned Him Against Releasing 'Strong Misogynistic Message' Rep Says', *People*, February 12, 2016, https://people.com/celebrity/kanye-west-did-not-call-taylor-swift-for-approval-over-bitch-lyric/, last accessed: October 23, 2017.

2. *February 2016: during the Grammy Awards ceremony:*

While accepting Album of the Year award at the GRAMMYs, Taylor Swift addressed what is believed to be about the infamous Kanye West lyrics about her:

'I want to thank the fans for the last 10 years, and the recording academy for giving us this unbelievable honor. I want to thank all of the collaborators that you see on this stage. Mostly, I want to thank my co-executive producer Max Martin, who has deserved to be up here for 25 years. And as the first woman to win album of the year at the Grammy's twice, I want to say to all the young women out there, there are going to be people along the way who, will try to undercut your success or take credit for your accomplishments or your fame. But if you just focus on the work and you don't let those people sidetrack you, someday when you get where you're going, you will know it was you and the people who love you who put you there, and that will be the greatest feeling in the world. Thank you for this moment.'[664]

3. *In an interview with Vogue in April 2016, Taylor Swift addressed her acceptance speech at Grammy Awards and Kanye West:*

'I think the world is bored with the saga. I don't want to add anything to it, because then there's just more... I guess what I wanted to call attention to in my speech at the Grammys was how it's going to be difficult if you're a woman who wants to achieve something in her life - no matter what.'[665]

4. *Taylor Swift camp (June 2016), after Kim Kardashian's interview with GQ, issued a statement to GQ:*

'Taylor does not hold anything against Kim Kardashian as she recognizes the pressure Kim must be under and that she is only repeating what she has been told by Kanye West. However, that does not change the fact that much of what Kim is saying is incorrect. Kanye West and Taylor only spoke once on the phone while she was on vacation

For a second time in June 2016, before the release of the edited videos by Kim Kardashian on Snapchat in

[664] Taylor Swift, 'Taylor Swift, Album of the Year Acceptance Speech (Grammys 2016)', *Genius*, February 15, 2016, https://genius.com/Taylor-swift-album-of-the-year-acceptance-speech-grammys-2016-annotated, last accessed: October 23, 2017.

[665] Jason Gay, 'Taylor Swift As You've Never Seen Her Before', *Vogue*, April 14, 2016, https://www.vogue.com/article/taylor-swift-may-cover-maid-of-honor-dating-personal-style, last accessed: October 23, 2017.

with her family in January of 2016 and they have never spoken since. Taylor has never denied that conversation took place. It was on that phone call that Kanye West also asked her to release the song on her Twitter account, which she declined to do. Kanye West never told Taylor he was going to use the term 'that bitch' in referencing her. A song cannot be approved if it was never heard. Kanye West never played the song for Taylor Swift. Taylor heard it for the first time when everyone else did and was humiliated. Kim Kardashian's claim that Taylor and her team were aware of being recorded is not true, and Taylor cannot understand why Kanye West, and now Kim Kardashian, will not just leave her alone.'[666]

July 2016, Taylor Swift admitted that indeed she talked with Kanye West about the *song* Famous:

'Kanye West and Taylor only spoke once on the phone while she was on vacation with her family in January of 2016 and they have never spoken since. Taylor has never denied that conversation took place. It was on that phone call that Kanye West also asked her to release the song on her Twitter account, which she declined to do.'

---

5. *Taylor Swift (July 2016) responded to Kim Kardashian's Snapchat videos on her Instagram and Twitter account* (now the picture with her response is deleted on both platforms):

'That moment when Kanye West secretly records your phone call, then Kim posts it on the Internet.'

'Where is the video of Kanye telling me he was going to call me 'that bitch' in his song? It doesn't exist because it never happened. You don't get to control someone's emotional response to being called 'that bitch' in front of the entire world. Of course I wanted to like the song. I wanted to believe Kanye when he told me that I would love the song. I wanted us to have a friendly relationship. He promised to play the song for me, but he never did. While I wanted to be supportive of Kanye on the phone call, you cannot 'approve' a song you haven't heard. Being falsely painted as a liar when I was never given the full story or played any part of the song is character assassination. I would very much like to be excluded from this narrative, one that I have never asked to be a part of, since 2009.'[667]

For a third time, this time in July 2016, after the release of the edited videos by Kim Kardashian on Snapchat, Taylor Swift admitted that indeed she talked with Kanye West about the *song* Famous:

'I wanted to believe Kanye when he told me that I would love the song.'

'While I wanted to be supportive of Kanye on the phone call […]'

Final conclusions:

Taylor Swift admitted twice that she spoke on the phone with Kanye West, in February and June 2016, therefore before the videos posted by Kim Kardashian on her Snapchat account in July 2016.

---

[666] Caity Weaver, 'Kanye and Taylor Swift, What's in O.J.'s Bag, and Understanding Caitlyn', *GQ*, June 16, 2016, https://www.gq.com/story/kim-kardashian-west-gq-cover-story, last accessed: October 23, 2017.

[667] The photo with her reply is now deleted from her Facebook, Twitter and Instagram account. You can find written evidence here: Jemima Skelley, 'Taylor Swift Just Called Out Kanye West On Instagram', *BuzzFeed*, July 18, 2016, https://www.buzzfeed.com/jemimaskelley/shoulda-chose-the-rose-garden-over-madison-square, last accessed: October 23, 2017.

Taylor Swift cautioned Kanye West about feminists (possible to be linked with the misogynist).
Taylor Swift told Kanye West that she was famous before the event from September 2009.

In March 2020, after the leak of the video conversation (around 25 minutes), between Kanye West and Taylor Swift, the only new element was: the extended telephone conversation (from couple of minutes shared by Kim Kardashian on her Snapchat account, to around 25 minutes); however, it does not change anything about Taylor Swift's side of the story: she told the truth since February 2016, repeated in June and July 2016: was not aware of the line 'I made that bitch famous', she talked and warned Kanye West about feminists coming after him (possible linked with the misogynistic message of her reply), she was supportive with Kanye West over the phone for the lyrics she knew about it (and her reply for making her famous: 'I sold 7 million albums before' the events from September 2009; she did not approve the song as Kanye promised her to send it over for a final consideration, which never happened; Taylor heard the *song Famous* at the same time with the general public.

Back in 2020, Kim Kardashian replied on March 24 to the leak with the following statement:

'**@taylorswift13 has chosen to reignite an old exchange** - that at this point in time feels very self-serving given the suffering millions of real victims are facing right now. I didn't feel the need to comment a few days ago, and I'm actually really embarrassed and mortified to be doing it right now, but because she continues to speak on it, I feel I'm left without a choice but to respond **because she is actually lying. To be clear, the only issue I ever had around the situation was that Taylor lied through her publicist who stated that 'Kanye never called to ask for permission**...' They clearly spoke so I let you all see that. Nobody ever denied the word 'bitch' was used without her permission. At the time when they spoke the song had not been fully written yet, but as everyone can see in the video, **she manipulated the truth of their actual conversation in her statement when her team said she 'declined and cautioned him about releasing a song with such a strong misogynistic message.' The lie was** never about the word bitch, It was **always whether there was a call or not and the tone of the conversation**. To add, Kanye as an artist has every right to document his musical journey and process, just like she recently did through her documentary. Kanye has documented the making of all of his albums for his personal archive, however has never released any of it for public consumption & **the call between the two of them would have remained private or would have gone in the trash had she not lied & forced me to defend him**. This will be the last time I speak on this because honestly, nobody cares. Sorry to bore you all with this. I know you are all dealing with more serious and important matters'.[668]

Conclusions based on Kim Kardashian reply after the leak of the telephone conversation:

---

[668] Tatiana Tenreyro, 'Kim Kardashian Responded To Taylor Swift's Statement About The Leaked Kanye West Phone Call', *Buzzfeed*, March 24, 2020, available at: https://www.buzzfeed.com/tatianatenreyrowhitlock/kim-kardashian-speaks-about-kanye-west-phone-call-with, last accessed: July 1, 2021.

- failed to follow the logic flow of the statements released by Taylor Swift from February to July 2016: she did not deny the phone conversation, cautioned Kanye West about feminists (linked with the misogynistic message), told him that she was already famous when they met to MTV ceremony in September 2009; was not aware of the full song; Kanye promised her to send the song which he never did; Taylor Swift told Kanye West that she will think about the song, and waited for him to send her the *song Famous*;

- either Kim Kardashian is not capable of understanding a statement, to analyse a statement and follow the logic flow of it, or she is playing the role of a silly character (based on this research: watching online videos about her, she is capable of logical reasoning) to get away with the unfamous role she played in June and July 2016, the biased information she presented in those months, and she continued the same story in 2020 through her statement; maybe the end of playing the role of a silly character is to stop fans and haters going after her (such as unfollow her on social media, refusal to buy her products, which means losing popularity and profit), as she was exposed as a person who is presenting biased and misleading information where we need to follow logic; in the end, maybe she got the wrong advice: to continue her side of the story in order to advance her side of the story: she was right since June and July 2016, and Taylor Swift is lying since February 2016 until today, and forever (since this is her last statement on the issue with the background narrative of song);

- **'@taylorswift13 has chosen to reignite an old exchange':** in fact, Taylor Swift **responded *after*** and **to the leak** of around 25 minutes of the telephone conversation between her and Kanye West; Taylor Swift wrote on Instagram story:

'Instead of answering those who are asking how I feel about the video footage that leaked, proving that I was telling the truth the whole time about *that call* (you know, the one that was illegally recorded, that somebody edited and manipulated in order to frame me and put me, my family, and fans through hell for 4 years)... SWIPE up to see what really matters.'[669]

Taylor Swift was in her right to respond to the leak, since she was the main negative target of the telephone conversation; furthermore, Taylor Swift could answer only by rightly pointing out the part she knew, and that the video published by Kim Kardashian on her Snapchat account was manipulated to project a distorted reality of the discussions about the song *Famous*;

Kim Kardashian reignited the issue directly with Taylor Swift by adding her name (on Twitter message) in the response to the leak, a feature that Taylor Swift did not use;

---

[669] Nick Reilly, 'Taylor Swift says she was "framed" as 2016 phone call with Kanye West leaks online'.

'an old exchange': in the matters of truth the *old exchange* does not expire, but it is forevermore alive until the victim gets justice; Taylor Swift, through her statement and the leak available, pointed out that she was right from the beginning of the *exchange*, and not the old and twisted version created and spread by Kim Kardashian and Kanye West to the general public;

- **'tone of the conversation':** the tone was friendly on both sides, however, Kanye added a new line which Taylor disagreed, and told the world that she knew about it ('That's why I called her'); also, Kanye West failed to keep his side of the bargain: to send the final version of the song to Taylor; **Taylor's tone of the conversation changed because Kanye's tone *changed first*, after he released the final version of the song with new lyrics that Taylor did not know, but accused by him** ('That's why I called her') **and Kim** (Taylor 'knew everything about what was coming out'); Kanye West and Kim Kardashian's tone of the conversation in front to the general public was negative about Taylor Swift, despite having the full video with the conversation; let's see how the tone of the conversation was changed by Kanye West:

January 2016:

'Kanye West: 'So it says… and the song is so, so dope. And I've literally sat with my wife, with my whole management team, with everything and tried to rework this line. I've thought about this line for eight months. I've had this line and I've tried to rework it every which way. And the original way that I thought about it is the best way, but it's the most controversial way. So it's gonna go Eminem a little bit, so can you brace yourself for a second?'

Taylor Swift: '[Sounding resigned.] Yeah.'

Kanye West: 'Okay. All right. Wait a second, you sound sad.'

Taylor Swift: 'Well, is it gonna be mean?'

Kanye West: 'No, I don't think it's mean.'

Taylor Swift: 'Okay, then, let me hear it.'

Kanye West: 'Okay. It says, um,… and the funny thing is, when I first played it and my wife heard it, she was like, 'Huh? What? That's too crazy,' blah, blah, blah. And then like when Ninja from Die Atwoord heard it, he was like, 'Oh my God, this is the craziest s—. This is why I love Kanye,' blah, blah, blah, that kind of thing. And now it's like my wife's favourite f—ing line. I just wanted to give you some premise of that. Right?'

Taylor Swift: 'Okay.'

Kanye West: 'So it says 'To all my Southside [N-word] that know me best, I feel like Taylor Swift might owe me sex.'

Taylor Swift: '[Laughs, relieved.] That's not mean.''

February 2016:

On February 11, 2016 Kanye West debuted his musical album The Life of Pablo at his Yeezy Season 3 show at Madison Square Garden, New York. In one of his songs, 'Famous,' he raps 'I feel like me and Taylor might still have sex / Why? I made that bitch famous (God damn) / I made that bitch famous.'

Kanye West wrote a few tweets on his Twitter account:

'I did not diss Taylor Swift and I've never dissed her…
– KANYE WEST (@kanyewest) February 12, 2016'

'First thing is I'm an artist and as an artist I will express how I feel with no censorship
– KANYE WEST (@kanyewest) February 12, 2016'

'2nd thing I asked my wife for her blessings and she was cool with it
– KANYE WEST (@kanyewest) February 12, 2016'

'3rd thing I called Taylor and had a hour long convo with her about the line and she thought it was funny and gave her blessings
– KANYE WEST (@kanyewest) February 12, 2016'

'4th Bitch is an endearing term in hip hop like the word Nigga
– KANYE WEST (@kanyewest) February 12, 2016'

'5th thing I'm not even gone take credit for the idea… it's actually something Taylor came up with …
– KANYE WEST (@kanyewest) February 12, 2016'

At Yo Gotti's album release party at the 1OAK nightclub in Hollywood, Kanye West reiterates he told Taylor Swift about the 'Famous' lyric and said 'She had two seconds to be cool and she fucked it up!'

Kanye West makes a guest appearance at Drake's concert in Chicago, and speaks out about Taylor Swift. Kanye West told his fans, 'All I gotta say is, I am so glad my wife has Snapchat!', 'Now y'all can know the truth and can't nobody talk s–t about 'Ye no more.' After his words, he performed the song 'Famous'.

Kanye West and Kim Kardashian are on the cover of Harper's Bazaar September issue. When asked by editor Laura Brown about their favourite Taylor Swift song, Kanye West replied, 'For me? I don't have one.' Kim Kardashian replied: 'I was such a fan of hers.'

Kanye West takes the stage at the 2016 MTV Video Music Awards. He received 6 minutes to do what he wants. He addressed the song 'Famous' and Taylor Swift by saying that he's a 'lover of all,' which is 'why I called her.'

- **'the call between the two of them would have remained private or would have gone in the trash'**: then why was Kanye desperate to record the telephone conversation with Taylor without her knowledge? and, after the release of the final version of the song in February 2016, he refused to publicly acknowledge that Taylor didn't know the new line that he added, that Taylor has the right to challenge the line 'I made that bitch famous'? Why Kanye West did not publish an extensive description with the exact parts that he discussed with Taylor, so that the general public to understand the background narrative of the song, *because Kanye West told them*, especially the part where Taylor was not aware of the line 'I made that bitch famous'?

   Kanye West: 'It's just when it dies… You get some s— like Kanye talking to Taylor Swift explaining that line? There's gotta be three cameras on that one. We can't miss one element.'

If Kanye and Kim wanted the world to be aware of what Taylor Swift knew, why did Kim posted only parts of the recording in which there is a visible lack of the context regarding Taylor's answers? Why did Kanye and Kim refused to show everything they had about Taylor Swift, if their intention was good from the beginning? Why go to interviews with bits of information in which they incriminate Taylor, while keeping the whole video hidden? Why was there a leak instead of Kanye and Kim showing the whole video? Why having concerts made in good faith for the truth in which Kanye, Kim and fans shouted / spoke / sang multiple times and locations (included Nashville, the city where Taylor's career began) 'bitch' in reference to Taylor, if you have the whole video showing that Taylor was not aware of the line 'I made that bitch famous' for which she publicly challenged? Why these half-truths, biased and misleading information about Taylor Swift when you have the video showing a different view of the telephone conversation?

The theories advanced by Taylor Swift's fans may be true: there is no video in which Taylor agreed with the final lyrics and the song, otherwise Kanye and Kim would have used it on the next minute after Taylor's statement in February 2016.

- the best strategy for Kim Kardashian to get out clean was to say: 'I was given only the edited parts that I posted on Snapchat in 2016, and I was convinced that they were true; I was angry about it and felt the need to defend my husband, which I did. However, after the leak of the conversation (I watched it at the same time with the world as I did not have access to it, because I'm not part of the filming team), I was able to see the truth, and Taylor Swift was right about the line 'I made that bitch famous'. I'm sorry for the mess I made.' Kim Kardashian had the chance to make it right for her, in the first place, then for Taylor Swift, her fans and Taylor Swift's fans. Of course, her image has not changed since the leak of the telephone conversation and the fans still love her, and she is still famous. However, in the present and future conversations about the *Famous* feud, Kim Kardashian is seen as a liar and guilty by association and complicity with Kanye West (he dragged her first in his dark narrative about Taylor Swift); in the end, after the leak of the telephone conversation, the Western mass-media wrote about the vindication of Taylor Swift;[670] this is a logic exercise for Kim Kardashian as a future lawyer: if Taylor Swift is vindicated about her implication in the *song Famous*, then who are the perpetrators?

In the following table I have the names of the news agencies, journalists and titles with negative content about Taylor Swift's involvement in the *song Famous*; remember: the articles are based on Taylor Swift's statements from February to July 2016.

V.1 The **FAMOUS** Feud in Western Mass-Media

TABLE 47. LIST OF NEWS SOURCE WITH NEGATIVE / SHADY VIEWS ABOUT TAYLOR SWIFT IN THE **FAMOUS** FEUD

SOURCE	AUTHOR	TITLE	DATE OF PUBLICATION	LAST ACCESSED
ROLLING STONE	BRITANNY SPANOS	Hear Taylor Swift Approve Kanye West's 'Famous' Lyrics	JULY 18, 2016	SEPTEMBER 2, 2019
ROLLING STONE	ELISABETH SHERMAN	Why Taylor Swift's 'Famous' Objection Still Rings True	JULY 18, 2016	SEPTEMBER 2, 2019
SEVENTEEN	HANNAH ORENSTEIN	People Are Celebrating the Anniversary of Kim Kardashian and Taylor Swift's Drama Today'	JULY 17, 2017	SEPTEMBER 2, 2019
BUZZFEED	ELLIE WOODWARD	How Taylor Swift Played The Victim For A Decade And Made Her Entire Career	JANUARY 31, 2017	SEPTEMBER 2, 2019

[670] Jordan Hoffman, 'Vindication for Taylor Swift With Newly Leaked Kanye West Call Video', *Vanity Fair*, March 21, 2020, https://www.vanityfair.com/style/2020/03/vindication-for-taylor-swift-with-newly-leaked-kayne-west-call-video, last accessed: July 1, 2021; Lucy Buckland, 'Vindicated Taylor Swift refuses to break silence over Kanye West phone call leak', *Mirror*, March 22, 2020, https://www.mirror.co.uk/3am/celebrity-news/vindicated-taylor-swift-refuses-break-21733388, last accessed: July 1, 2021; Rachel Kiley, 'Taylor Swift Vindicated After Full 2016 Kanye West Phone Call Leaks', *Pride*, March 21, 2020, https://www.pride.com/celebrities/2020/3/21/taylor-swift-vindicated-after-full-2016-kanye-west-phone-call-leaks, last accessed: July 1, 2021; Nate Jones, 'Now That No One Cares Anymore, Who Was Right in the Kanye-Taylor Feud?', *Vulture*, March 28, 2020, https://www.vulture.com/2020/03/taylor-swift-kanye-west-who-was-right.html, last accessed: July 1, 2021; Verity Sulway, 'Kim Kardashian and Kanye West's lies in full as Taylor Swift is vindicated at last', *Mirror*, March 23, 2020, https://www.irishmirror.ie/showbiz/celebrity-news/kim-kardashian-kanye-wests-lies-21739005#comments-wrapper, last accessed: July 1, 2021; Bryan Rolli, 'Kanye West Needs Taylor Swift', *Forbes*, March 24, 2020, https://www.forbes.com/sites/bryanrolli/2020/03/24/kanye-west-needs-taylor-swift/, last accessed: July 1, 2021; Jen McDonnell, 'Taylor Swift Vindicated as Leaked Kanye West Tape Surfaces', *Dose*, March 22, 2020, http://dose.ca/2020/03/22/taylor-swift-kanye-west-leak-phone/, last accessed: July 1, 2021; Alex Clark, '4 Years Later Swifties Are Finally Vindicated: Taylor Swift Did Tell The Truth About Kanye West', *Evie Magazine*, March 23, 2020, https://www.eviemagazine.com/post/4-years-later-swifties-are-finally-vindicated-taylor-swift-did-tell-the, last accessed: July 1, 2021.

THE DAILY BEAST	AMY ZIMMERMAN	How Kim Kardashian Beat Taylor Swift at Her Own Game	JULY 18, 2016	SEPTEMBER 2, 2019
THE DAILY BEAST	AMY ZIMMERMAN	Taylor Swift's History of Suing Friends, Fans, and Foes—and Now Kimye?	JULY 23, 2016	SEPTEMBER 2, 2019
THE DAILY BEAST	AMY ZIMMERMAN	Kim Kardashian and Kanye West Are Rich, in Love, and Mourning Taylor Swift: 'I Was Such a Fan of Hers'	JULY 28, 2016	SEPTEMBER 2, 2019
THE DAILY BEAST	KEVIN FALLON	Can Taylor Swift Survive Kim Kardashian's Snapchat Burial?	JULY 18, 2016	SEPTEMBER 2, 2019
THE DAILY BEAST	AMY ZIMMERMAN	Taylor Swift Hasn't Shed Her Old Skin. She's Still Playing the Victim	AUGUST 25, 2017	SEPTEMBER 2, 2019
NEW STATESMAN	ANNA LESZKIEWICZ	Kim Kardashian vs Taylor Swift: a battle of two PR styles	JULY 18, 2016	SEPTEMBER 2, 2019
NEW STATESMAN	ANNA LESZKIEWICZ	Taylor Swift's troubled relationship with revenge	SEPTEMBER 1, 2017	SEPTEMBER 2, 2019
BILLBOARD	ASHLEY MONAE	Kanye & Kim or Taylor Swift: Who Won the Feud? Media Critics Weigh In	JULY 19, 2016	SEPTEMBER 2, 2019
POPFRONT	ADMIN8	Swiftly to the alt-right: Taylor subtly gets the lower case kkk in formation	SEPTEMBER 5, 2017	SEPTEMBER 2, 2019
POPFRONT	ADMIN8	Taylor Swift tries to silence Popfront with cease and desist letter	NOVEMBER 6, 2017	SEPTEMBER 2, 2019
COMPLEX	NOLAOJOMU	Taylor Swift Has a Long History of Omitting Facts to Fit Her Own Narrative	JULY 2, 2019	SEPTEMBER 2, 2019
COMPLEX	LAUREN M. JACKSON	The Delicious, Blinkered Hypocrisy of Taylor Swift's "Look What You Made Me Do"	AUGUST 30, 2017	SEPTEMBER 2, 2019
MADAME NOIRE	VERONICA WELLS	Taylor Swift, Kanye West And The Perpetuation Of The 'Intimidating Black Man' Myth	JULY 18, 2016	SEPTEMBER 2, 2019
TENNESSEAN	BEAU DAVIDSON	It's time to call out Taylor Swift's hypocrisy and privilege	Opinion	DECEMBER 28, 2019	JULY 25, 2021
THE DAILY BEAST	AMY ZIMMERMAN	It's Time for Taylor Swift to Denounce Her Neo-Nazi Admirers	AUGUST 6, 2017	SEPTEMBER 2, 2019
SEVENTEEN	HANNAH ORENSTEIN	People Are Celebrating the Anniversary of Kim Kardashian and Taylor Swift's Drama Today	JULY 17, 2017	SEPTEMBER 2, 2019
NEW YORK TIMES	JON CARAMANICA	Kim Kardashian West and Kanye West Reignite Feud With Taylor Swift	JULY 18, 2016	SEPTEMBER 2, 2019
JUNKEE	JARED RICHARDS	Taylor Swift, You Need To Calm Down, Because Pride Isn't About Straight People	JUNE 18, 2019	SEPTEMBER 2, 2019
TELL TALES	NO NAME	https://www.telltalesonline.com/20889/taylor-swift-liar-kanye-west-famous: the link does not work, it was replaced with the link of the articles written in the next column. However, I saved the context of the article and it was used in this report.	DUE TO LACK OF ACCESS TO THIS ARTICLE, THERE IS NO DATE AVAILABLE	SEPTEMBER 2, 2019
TELL TALES	ANGELA STEPHANOU	Kanye West and Taylor Swift: A Timeline of Their Feud	FEBRUARY 24, 2016, Updated later with information about the feud until August 25, 2017	SEPTEMBER 2, 2019
THE WASHINGTON POST	EMILY YAHR	Is Taylor Swift a hypocrite or just a really savvy songwriter?	JULY 20, 2016	SEPTEMBER 2, 2019

FSUNEWS	MACKENZIE JAMIESON	Look what you made me write, Taylor Swift	NO DATE AVAILABLE IN THE ARTICLE, HOWEVER THE CONTENT SHOWS THAT THE ARTICLE MIGHT HAVE BEEN PUBLISHED AT THE END OF AUGUST 2017	SEPTEMBER 2, 2019
ELLE	ANGELICA JADE BASTIÉN	In Kimye Vs. Taylor, No One Wins	JULY 22, 2016	SEPTEMBER 2, 2019
VICE	GRACE MEDFORD	Criticizing Taylor Swift Isn't About Negativity Towards Successful Women, It's About Vindication	JULY 20, 2016	SEPTEMBER 2, 2019
VICE	RICHARD S. HE	*Taylor Swift Isn't Like Other Celebrities, She's Worse*: this title at some points was not available on their page, however, I saved the article. You can find the original article ere. I do not know if the new link and page is the original article that I read in 2016.	JULY 2016	SEPTEMBER 2, 2019
VICE	SADY DOYLE	The Depressingly Predictable Downfall Of Taylor Swift	AUGUST 31, 2017	SEPTEMBER 2, 2019
NEWS.COM. AU	JAMES WEIR	Taylor Swifts reign comes crashing down: Has she caught a case of the Anne Hathaways?	JULY 15, 2016	SEPTEMBER 2, 2019
THE GUARDIAN	BRIDIE JABOUR	Taylor Swift's 'downfall': what the online celebrations really say	JULY 18, 2016	SEPTEMBER 2, 2019
VULTURE	NATE JONES	When Did the Media Turn Against Taylor Swift?	JULY 21, 2016	SEPTEMBER 2, 2019
THE CUT	FRANK GUAN	Now That Taylor Swift Is Definitely Less Innocent Than She Pretends to Be, What's Next?	JULY 19, 2016	SEPTEMBER 2, 2019
NEW YORK POST	HARDEEP PHULL	Why Taylor Swift needs to disappear for her own good	JULY 18, 2016	SEPTEMBER 2, 2019
NEW YORK POST	HARDEEP PHULL	Why is Taylor Swift ghosting the world?	NOVEMBER 9, 2017	SEPTEMBER 2, 2019
THE ATLANTIC	SPENCER KORNHABER	The War Over 'That Bitch'	JULY 18, 2016	SEPTEMBER 2, 2019
SLATE	HEATHER SCHWEDEL	What Do Kim Kardashian's Snapchat 'Receipts' Actually Prove About Taylor Swift and Kanye?	JULY 18, 2016	SEPTEMBER 2, 2019
SLATE	KATHRYN VANARENDONK	How Keeping Up With the Kardashians Helps Kim Tell a Better Story Than Taylor	JULY 20, 2016	SEPTEMBER 2, 2019
FORBES	DANI DI PLACIDO	Taylor Swift's Carefully Cultivated Image Is Starting To Crack	JULY 18, 2016	SEPTEMBER 2, 2019
VOX	CONSTANCE GRADY	Taylor Swift is cold-blooded and calculating. That's what makes her a great pop star.	JULY 19, 2016	SEPTEMBER 2, 2019
VOX	CONSTANCE GRADY	A unified theory of Taylor Swift's reputation	MAY 7, 2018	SEPTEMBER 2, 2019
THE VERGE	KAITLYN TIFFANY	Taylor Swift's internet rulebook	AUGUST 27, 2017	SEPTEMBER 2, 2019
MICHIGAN DAILY	CHRISTIAN KENNEDY	The danger of Taylor Swift's privileged pop	AUGUST 27, 2017	SEPTEMBER 2, 2019

THE DAILY FREE PRESS	NASHID FULCHER	FULCHER: Taylor Swift is creating trash, and we're letting it happen	SEPTEMBER 28, 2017	SEPTEMBER 2, 2019
CNET	DANIEL VAN BOOM	How Taylor Swift carefully manipulates her 'Reputation' online	SEPTEMBER 1, 2017	SEPTEMBER 2, 2019
CONSEQUENCE OF SOUND	ALEX YOUNG	Taylor Swift won't stop talking about Kanye West	NOVEMBER 10, 2017	SEPTEMBER 2, 2019
HIP HOP DX	KYLE EUSTICE	Why is Taylor Swift still obsessed with Kanye West?	NOVEMBER 11, 2017	SEPTEMBER 2, 2019
NYLON	HAYDEN MANDERS	What is Taylor Swift's reputation anyway?	NO DATE FOUND IN THE ARTICLE, MOST PROBABLY IT WAS WRITTEN AFTER THE ANNOUNCEMENT OF REPUTATION ALBUM IN AUGUST 2017.	SEPTEMBER 2, 2019
LOYOLA PHOENIX	GIANNI KULLE	Taylor Swift's New 'Reputation' Feels Manufactured	NOVEMBER 15, 2017	SEPTEMBER 2, 2019
THE REBEL HEART	NO AUTHOR	Taylor Swift is not done taking shots at Kanye West	NOVEMBER 10, 2017	SEPTEMBER 2, 2019
THE STANFORD DAILY	UGUR DURSUN	The business of Taylor Swift's 'Reputation'	NOVEMBER 17, 2017	SEPTEMBER 2, 2019
THE IRISH TIMES	JENNIFER GANNON	Taylor Swift: Why is it so difficult to support her?	JUNE 9, 2018	SEPTEMBER 2, 2019
MEDIUM	DEVON MALONEY	Just Like Us: The Rise, Fall, and Future of Taylor Swift, America's Relatable Sweetheart	OCTOBER 6, 2017	SEPTEMBER 2, 2019

In the table below I have extracted, from the articles published above, the most negative, biased and misleading information in explaining the truth of the events of the *Famous* feud. There are also positive parts in these articles, however, I focused on the negative parts because it can support the investigation by exposing a balanced side of the feud: high neutrality discovered in the first chapter, and the negative side of the feud presented and spread by few journalists part of the Western mass-media.

The conclusions I have reached are set out below. The journalists from the articles used in this report:

- exaggerated with absurd, manipulative and sleazy interpretations that portrayed the wrong role of Taylor Swift in the *Famous* feud;
- don't bother to explain why Kanye West and Kim Kardashian would not publish the part where the line 'I made that bitch famous' was mentioned;
- are not a source of accuracy of events and rational conclusions;

- omitted facts and created a narrative where Taylor Swift is presented as a false victim of the feud;
- sided with the perpetrators, Kanye West and Kim Kardashian, and forgot the mission of a genuine journalist: neutrality;
- wrote the articles from the perspective of the invisible witness that saw and listened to everything, like they were there holding the candle;
- failed to follow the exact moments of the narrative and a neutral presentation of the conclusions based on the available information from the players of the feud;
- presented and played the race card where the white woman (Taylor) is trying to harm a black man (Kanye);
- promoted Kanye and Kim's narrative as the only truth;
- draw final conclusions while the feud was in motion, and with big gaps in the narrative where all the main players failed to say exactly (the details that mass-media was waiting, for other people Taylor Swift's statements were enough) what happened;
- played the judge and executioner of Taylor Swift;
- passionate haters of Taylor Swift?
- failed to hold Kanye and Kim accountable rightly at the same level they did wrongly with Taylor Swift;
- acted and presented the feud as self-entitled to know everything Taylor Swift knows and, in the absence of this information directly from her, justified the negative views written about her;
- the journalists/bloggers forgot or did not want to consider the following option: Taylor Swift has the right to decide what information is out on her own terms; just because she does not confirm all the theories online, it does not mean that she is guilty; the journalists from this report is not the supreme court to decide that lack of information from a feud give them the right to decide who is the perpetrator and the victim.

It is highly possible to exist more negative and positive articles about the feud that were not used in this report.

The information you are about to read on the following pages was extracted only with the purpose to research the feud from the perspective of the logical mind of a few journalists from various news agencies. Again, remember: the articles are based on Taylor Swift's statements from February to July 2016.

TABLE 48. LIST OF NEWS SOURCE WITH BIASED AND MISLEADING INFORMATION ABOUT TAYLOR SWIFT IN THE FAMOUS FEUD

SOURCE	TITLE OF THE ARTICLE AND SPECIFIC CONTENT

ROLLING STONE ELISABETH SHERMAN	*Hear Taylor Swift Approve Kanye West's 'Famous' Lyrics*
	'Taylor Swift has denied any knowledge of the lyrics prior to the song's official release.'

	People Are Celebrating the Anniversary of Kim Kardashian and Taylor Swift's Drama Today
SEVENTEEN HANNAH ORENSTEIN	'In case you need a refresher, Kim proved that Kanye asked for Taylor's blessing before including a vulgar lyric about her in his song "Famous." The news dropped like a bombshell — previously, Taylor had acted as if she was upset by the line. And the Snapchats proved that Taylor had planned to act surprised by the lyric the entire time. In one swift Snapchat — pun intended — Kim exposed Taylor's lie and played the trump card in the old Kanye/Taylor feud'. [...] 'Or to quote Taylor's other rival, swish, swish, bish.'

	How Taylor Swift Played The Victim For A Decade And Made Her Entire Career
	'Swift had witnessed the negative reaction to 'Famous." Her spokesperson said she was never made aware of the lyric: "I made that bitch famous." She reverted back to a well-practised posture: that of victim.'
	'Swift's speech at the Grammys was arguably the catalyst for West's wife, Kim Kardashian, stepping in. Three months after the awards ceremony, she told GQ that she believed the speech was a deliberate attempt to 'diss' West after he'd done nothing but 'follow protocol'. She went on to claim that not only had Swift 'totally approved' the lyrics in 'Famous', but that there was also video footage to prove it.'
	'The dominant reaction, however, was a reflection of what the world has been conditioned to see: the 'threat' of an 'angry" black man terrorising the 'innocent" white woman. Even their clothes reflected the racially fuelled victim/villain framework that would define the incident: The image of West, wearing dark shades and an entirely black outfit, accosting sweet Swift in her white and silver party dress, remains an iconic one.'
	'Swift, on the other hand, was able to capitalise on the stereotype of the 'angry black man', an archetype that has been described as a 'figment of the white imagination', used to incarcerate and oppress black men. For Swift, it was PR gold.'
	'It may seem that Swift's posture of victimhood is founded on her relationship with West. But it can, in fact, be traced back to the very beginning of her decade-long career.'
BUZZFEED ELLIE WOODWARD	'But by the time 1989 came to fruition, Swift had arguably overplayed her hand. In repeating the same narrative with each relationship, she had failed to tread the line between fascination and overexposure. So, ahead of the album's release, she assigned responsibility for the fascination with her love life to the media. By presenting herself as a victim of their coverage, Swift provided a competing and more compelling narrative to counter the increasingly negative rhetoric surrounding her love life.'
	'A similar result arose from what became a second strand of PR strategy – the publicity from befriending vulnerable fans online. She gave advice to teens being bullied, thoughtful words and a playlist to a fan experiencing a breakup, a cheque for $1,989 to help pay back a student's loan. But at the heart of this was a shared sense of victimhood, exemplified in a

comment she left for a bullied fan: 'We go through life with a list of names we've been called. (I have a feeling mine is longer than yours ;)) But it doesn't mean those things are true and it doesn't mean we have to let those terrible names define us in any way, you lovely, BEAUTIFUL girl.''

'The result was twofold: In giving fans advice and inserting herself into their narrative, she encouraged them to connect with the messages she proffered, to buy her albums and pay for her tour tickets, fuelling the Taylor Swift brand. And each time Swift bonded with fans through victimhood, it also resulted in a wealth of positive press attention.'

'In fact, her fragile white femininity is merely a reflection of her privilege. That she felt so acutely victimised by Minaj's tweets and West calling her 'that bitch' is proof of her never having experienced oppression.'

'Yet, the image that provoked Kardashian to expose Swift was the one of her standing onstage at the Grammys, using her white feminine fragility to compound the well-worn narrative of her as victim and West as villain, while simultaneously imploring young women to work hard. But, as she stood, flanked by all the people who helped create her Grammy award-winning album, there was not a single other woman onstage.'

'The question is, however, after being exposed playing the victim in plain sight for over a decade, will anyone believe it?'

How Kim Kardashian Beat Taylor Swift at Her Own Game

'In what many are calling the second Lemonade of 2016, Kim Kardashian and Kanye West have totally turned on Taylor Swift. It only took three platforms—print media, reality TV, and Snapchat—to out Swift as two-faced.'

'The final nail in Swift's 'Famous' coffin came via Kim Kardashian's Sunday night Snapstory, where she finally leaked the much-hyped footage of hubby Kanye West running his 'Famous' lyrics ('I feel like me and Taylor might still have sex / Why? I made that bitch famous') by Swift, who voices her approval. These clips are pretty damning, since Swift has packaged herself as a victim of the explicit track, even referencing it in her Grammys acceptance speech and releasing a statement that she 'heard it for the first time when everyone else did and was humiliated.''

THE DAILY
BEAST
AMY
ZIMMERMAN

'It's a pretty convincing argument—until you remember Swift's first public reaction to 'Famous,' in which she basically called Kanye out for undercutting her success and taking credit for her accomplishments. Her current insistence that being called a 'bitch' was the difference between her recorded consent and her public disapproval is undermined by that initial speech, where she's clearly chastising Kanye based on the concept of his lyrics, not his cuss words.'

'Swift had to search for this note among the many on her phone, giving the impression that she knew the truth would eventually come out and had already worked overtime to craft the most convincing spin.'

'Take her Katy Perry feud; just like with Kanye, Swift publicly painted Perry as the instigator, all but outing the pop star in interviews as the shady friend who inspired her song 'Bad Blood.''

Taylor Swift's History of Suing Friends, Fans, and Foes—and Now Kimye?

'Swift, who low-key (but maybe high-key?) has been tapping into virginal white victim tropes her entire career, allegedly threw Kanye under the bus for favorable press.'

'Thank you, Chloë, Miranda, Katy, Calvin, and miscellaneous squad members. It truly takes a village.'

'If Taylor was truly unaware of being on speakerphone—which many think is an outright lie, given Rick Rubin's presence in the room.'

THE DAILY BEAST
AMY ZIMMERMAN

'Back in 2015, Swift was first outed by her own childhood guitar teacher. … Ronnie worked with her for six hours a week, at $32 an hour. Still, he understands why that story never gets told: ‚It's just that their publicity team, that doesn't sell as good> a 36-year-old bald guy taught her. That ain't gonna work.'

'But while Ronnie waited years to share his side of the story, Swift's team didn't waste any time taking him to task. About a month after his testimony went public, Cremer received a letter from T(aylor) A(lison) S(wift) Rights Management, threatening to sue him for purchasing the domain name itaughttaylorswift.com. Given the proliferation of Taylor Swift fan sites, it's clear that what Swift was really protecting was her brand as a self-taught songwriting whiz kid. Shockingly, going after the man who taught her her first guitar chords isn't Swift's legal team at its most heartless.'

Can Taylor Swift Survive Kim Kardashian's Snapchat Burial?

'So reads the meme tombstone memorializing the music industry's Empress With No Clothes, stripped naked of her self-victimizing media manipulations by reality TV's Mad Queen.'

'The wife of Kanye West provided video proof that her husband had, indeed, called Swift for her approval to refer to her in the 'I feel like me and Taylor might still have sex / Why? I made that bitch famous' lyric in his song 'Famous,' though Swift's publicist had claimed he never did.'

THE DAILY BEAST
KEVIN FALLON

'Kardashian's videos, however, shone a spotlight—albeit a grainy and at times questionably edited one—on how Swift and her camp manipulate the press and the public, going so far as to even fabricate narratives (cough, Hiddleswift, cough).'

'As The Daily Beast's Amy Zimmerman wrote, Kardashian beat Swift at her own game. Using celebrity power, a PR machine, immeasurable cultural influence, and media masterminding she refocused a spinning, potentially damaging narrative to not just 'set the record straight'— once the singular concern in a celebrity controversy, now second to public perception and goodwill—but recast herself as the victimized hero. Swift? Now she's the mean girl.'

Taylor Swift Hasn't Shed Her Old Skin. She's Still Playing the Victim

'While TayTay tried to do damage control, her subsequent statement was fairly unconvincing.'

'Like Donald Trump before her, Swift is clearly trying to turn negative press coverage to her own advantage, placing the blame for her own bad reputation on a third party.'

'The real scandal was the way in which Swift, despite having the heard the song prior to its release, proceeded to play the victim, publicly shaming the rapper for trying to take credit for a young woman's success. Whether or not you agree with Kanye's claim that he made Taylor famous, it's clear Swift only took objection to the sentiment when she saw an opportunity to manipulate the storyline, reframing the entire controversy around her performative feminist agenda. And when you're Taylor Swift, a star who refuses to protest or express an actual political opinion, triumphant displays of girl power are crucial to convincing the world that you're actually a feminist.'

THE DAILY BEAST AMY ZIMMERMAN

'Since Taylor's machinations have been so widely criticized in the past, it's strange that she would want to double down on her victimhood narrative, further portraying herself as maligned and misunderstood.'

'The problem with 'Look What You Made Me Do,' leaving aside its questionable musical merits, is that it continues to shift the blame. The very title implies that Swift's reinvention was forced on her by a cruel, conniving world.'

'The old Taylor Swift isn't dead and gone—she's just exploring new revenue streams.'

Kim Kardashian vs Taylor Swift: a battle of two PR styles

'West apologised.'

'During her transformation from underdog to top dog, Swift became representative of everything America privileges: thinness, wealth, a particular brand of blonde, white beauty. Simultaneously, she capitalised on the popularity of social justice movements by incorporating feminism into her appeal – calling herself a feminist in interviews, heavily publicising her female friendships online.'

NEW STATESMAN ANNA LESZKIEWICZ

'Now, instead, we get overly posed shots of her birthday and 4 July parties, crowded with famous faces. It feels colder, more try-hard, and more fake – to the extent that people are wondering if her current relationship is, in fact, an elaborate prank. (If it was intended as a distraction from this oncoming storm, it hasn't worked.)'

'Her latest Instagram post is a real case in point: a screenshot of the Notes app has, 'um, and seventh of all...' quality of someone who is rambling because they lack an obvious response, like a bad lie. The 'back to search' option also reveals that she has searched for the post in her phone, suggesting it was written a long time ago in preparation for this day, and revealing the PR machine whirring in the background. 'I would very much like to be excluded from this narrative.' Like any celebrity, Taylor Swift has long tried to control the media narrative surrounding her life. Now, she has lost some of that control. And she wants out.'

Kanye & Kim or Taylor Swift: Who Won the Feud? Media Critics Weigh In

'However, Swift denied approving the song and specified she was not made aware of the "I made that bitch famous line," which she deemed offensive and derogatory.'

Iyana Robertson, music editor, BET:

'and Taylor Swift got caught in a conversation she claims she didn't have.'

'Much can be said about where this all leaves artistic license, but the victim buck stops here. Sorry, Taylor Swift.'

Sylvia Obell, pop culture writer, BuzzFeed:

'But like, girl, those who have been paying close attention haven't forgotten your rep's statement saying that Ye 'did not call for approval' and that you cautioned him about releasing a song with "such a strong misogynistic message." Last I checked, saying you take something as compliment isn't very cautionary. And her attempt to play victim is a cheap shot because none of this would have happened if she hadn't lied about being blindsided by all of this in the first place. Kim did not start this, she just finished it. Taylor just needs to take her first big L like a G (the way Beyoncé, Kendrick, and all the other artists who didn't deserve to lose to her at various award shows did) and move on. People bounce back from bad videos everyday, just look at Kim.'

Sowmya Krishnamurthy, freelance music & pop culture contributor:

'Taylor Swift's doe-eyed, good girl facade has been effectively stripped. She lied about her approval of "Famous" and Kanye West has been vindicated.'

Stacy-Ann Ellis, assistant editor, Vibe:

BILLBOARD
ASHLEY MONAE

'So it (ashamedly) thrilled me to see Kimberly Kardashian-West pull all the receipts from the bottom of her Balenciaga bag to silence Taylor's nagging, victim-y ways. It made me admire Kim in a whole new way. Not only did she make the journalist in me smile by having all her sources handy, credible and downright undeniable, but she doled out a valuable lesson in patience.'

'...the footage was shared silently but widely via Kim's Snapchat after an episode of KUWTK— also made me tip my hat to Kimye in regards to their unwavering loyalty to each other. Even when no one believed 'Ye's claims that he received Swift's blessing, Kim stood by her husband's words and stepped out on a limb to clear his name in the pettiest, most public (but perfect) way possible. Salute, Kim.'

Michael Lewittes, founder, GossipCop.com

'From a perception standpoint, the win goes to Kim Kardashian and Kanye West because the public seems to believe Taylor Swift lied about ever having a conversation with West. But from a factual standpoint, Swift never denied they spoke. In fact, her rep very carefully told Gossip Cop back in February, 'Taylor was never made aware of the actual lyric, 'I made that bitch famous.' There was no denying — or her lying — about talking to West. Swift is the proper winner, while Kardashian is the more popular winner.'

Stephanie "Eleven8" Ogbogu, editor, Baller Alert:

'The faux tears and Grammy speeches become null and void because now the truth is out, Taylor was totally in on it. She even thanked Yeezy for having the decency to reach out to her before dropping the song. Do you know what this means? It means Taylor Swift will forever be known as a liar. It means that Calvin Harris, Katy Perry, and whoever else has beefed with her in the past, were right. It means that every time Taylor Swift pretended to be shocked that she won an award, she really wasn't shocked at all. If I can't trust Taylor Swift, who can I trust?'

'Now I'm torn because as much as I couldn't stand Kim Kardashian before, Taylor Swift made me like her. For that reason, I'll never forgive Taylor Swift."'

Swiftly to the alt-right: Taylor subtly gets the lower case kkk in formation

'But the most notable moment of the Taylor-as-an-innocent-victim narrative may have come when Kanye West interrupted her Best Female Video acceptance speech at the 2009 Video Music Awards to drunkenly ramble about how Beyoncé should have won.'

'... it also looked like the personification of many a long-standing white fear: a black man taking away a white woman's power. And Taylor has been playing off that narrative ever since, while America has embraced the notion of white victimhood — despite the reality.'

'Taylor's lyrics in 'Look What You Made Me Do' seem to play to the same subtle, quiet white support of a racial hierarchy.'

'At one point in the accompanying music video, Taylor lords over an army of models from a podium, akin to what Hitler had in Nazis Germany. The similarities are uncanny and unsettling.'

POPFRONT
ADMIN8

'Later in the song, there is another telling line: 'I don't like your kingdom keys. They once belonged to me. You asked me for a place to sleep. Locked me out and threw a feast (what?).' These lyrics are the most explicit in speaking to white anger and affirming white supremacy. The lyrics speak to the white people resentful of any non-white person having a position of power and privilege.'

'And considering Taylor's fan base is mostly young girls, does the song also serve as indoctrination into white supremacy?'

'It is hard to believe that Taylor had no idea that the lyrics of her latest single read like a defense of white privilege and white anger — specifically, white people who feel that they are being left behind as other races and groups start to receive dignity and legally recognized rights. 'We will not be replaced' and 'I don't like your kingdom keys' are not different in tone or message. Both are saying that whites feel threatened and don't want to share their privilege.'

'Quiet racism only needs subtle encouragement, and it seems that 'look what you made me do' fits the criteria perfectly.'

'Taylor is giving support to the white nationalist movements through lyrics that speak to their anger, entitlement, and selfishness.'

'it befits the movement to have a white, blonde, conservative pop star that has no doubt been 'bullied' by people of color in the media, singing their feelings out loud'

'So Taylor's silence is not innocent, it is calculated.'

'silence in the face of injustice means support for the oppressor.'

Taylor Swift tries to silence Popfront with cease and desist letter

POPFRONT ADMIN8

'At a time when the press is under constant attack from the highest branches of government, this cease and desist letter is far more insidious than Swift and her lawyer may understand. The press should not be bullied by legal action nor frightened into submission from covering any subject it chooses. Swift's scare tactics may have worked in the past, but PopFront refuses to back down because we believe the First Amendment is more important than preserving a celebrity's public image.'

Taylor Swift Has a Long History of Omitting Facts to Fit Her Own Narrative

'But for some Taylor Swift fans, like myself: fake friend who wants to destroy your image in the name of being nice and honest.'

'Swift has a habit of omitting details during these public disputes, in an attempt to frame a narrative of herself as a victim, even when she doesn't need to.'

'Swift then made a dig at her frenemy during the acceptance speech for Album of the Year at the Grammys later that month.'

COMPLEX NOLAOJOMU

'Proving that West and Swift did talk about her name being mention in the song, the video revealed that Taylor even gave her approval for him to rap about them having sex one day.'

'But the question remains: Why didn't she just say West had called, but he hadn't played her the full track? Or perhaps tell fans that he had failed to run the final version by her before release? Why lie entirely and claim he never contacted her when she knew he had? Why was she continuing to omit certain details from these disputes to fit her narrative?'

'Admitting the conversation took place wouldn't have stopped people from supporting her with regards to West's choice of lyrics, or for the music video he made for the song. But in her attempt to play the victim, Swift changed the narrative and allowed herself to get caught in a lie.'

'It's time for Taylor Swift to stop clinging to the victim narrative.'

The Delicious, Blinkered Hypocrisy of Taylor Swift's "Look What You Made Me Do"

COMPLEX

'She's greedy. She's a mean girl. She runs through Hollywood boyfriends like toilet paper. She's anti-feminist, reinforcing dated gender norms and 'playing the victim' whenever it suits her agenda. She embodies white womanhood in all its convoluted phases. Or, as The Read's Kid Fury puts it, 'a physical embodiment of white lies... walking around in beautiful gowns.''

LAUREN M.
JACKSON

'Swift 'continues to shift the blame,' says The Daily Beast's Amy Zimmerman on the single. Despite the social media cleanse, snake metaphors, and lyrics ('I'm sorry, the old Taylor can't come to the phone right now. Why? Oh, 'cause she's dead') that suggest schlepping off her old selves, 'Look What You Made Me Do' 'double[s] down on her victimhood narrative, further portraying herself as maligned and misunderstood.''

Taylor Swift, Kanye West And The Perpetuation Of The 'Intimidating Black Man' Myth

'But for whatever reason, Taylor Swift seems to be hellbent on perpetuating this narrative that Kanye West is the villain in her story. While I think Taylor is an exceptionally talented songwriter and artist, I can't stand the way she behaves in public. I shake my head when the camera insists on panning to her dancing awkwardly at award shows. I roll my eyes and kiss my teeth every time she acts shocked and stunned when she wins an award at these shows. And when she took the stage at this year's Grammys to accept and award of Album of the Year and slam Kanye for a lyric in his song, 'Famous,' I almost vomited.'

'Though she tried to play the victim in the incident, all of it came back to bite her in the butt when Kim Kardashian uploaded a few SnapChat videos of Kanye speaking to Taylor specifically about the line.'

'Taylor does not hold anything against Kim Kardashian as she recognizes the pressure Kim must be under and that she is only repeating what she has been told by Kanye West. However, that does not change the fact that much of what Kim is saying is incorrect. Kanye West and Taylor only spoke once on the phone while she was on vacation with her family in January of 2016 and they have never spoken since. Taylor has never denied that conversation took place. It was on that phone call that Kanye West also asked her to release the song on her Twitter account, which she declined to do. Kanye West never told Taylor he was going to use the term 'that bitch' in referencing her. A song cannot be approved if it was never heard. Kanye West never played the song for Taylor Swift. Taylor heard it for the first time when everyone else did and was humiliated. Kim Kardashian's claim that Taylor and her team were aware of being recorded is not true, and Taylor cannot understand why Kanye West, and now Kim Kardashian, will not just leave her alone.''

MADAME
NOIRE
VERONICA
WELLS

'One minute she's about love and light and forgiveness, taking pictures with Kanye, singing songs dedicated to him, ki-ki-ing on the phone and the next she's playing victim in the public eye.'

'She and her people could have easily said that while Taylor thought the 'have sex' or 'made her famous' line was tongue in cheek, she didn't appreciate being called 'that bitch.' It's still a valid concern. But it's the lies and half truths she tells that make me sick.'

'The narrative of the beautiful, frail, helpless White woman being bullied, attacked, or intimidated by the strong, overpowering Black man is one this country knows all too well. In fact, it's this narrative of the 'threatening' Black man that we're fighting against today.'

'but she's made it clear that she has been emotionally threatened by his words and thoughts.'

'But don't make it more than it really is to gain sympathy. Don't one minute call Kanye your friend, saying that you'll always respect him and then the next, when you're speaking to the public, wonder why Kanye and his wife won't leave you alone. They won't leave you alone because they thought y'all were cool. They won't leave you alone because you gassed him all the way up on the phone. Kim, specifically, won't leave you alone because you keep trying to make her husband the big, Black, bad guy because it suits your career.'

'And it's this narrative of the inherently threatening, intimidating, bullying, dangerous Black man that is causing so many innocent ones to lose their lives at the hands of police officers who, like Taylor, benefit from perpetuating such a story.'

'I'm never here for that. But at this time, when this narrative is causing us to literally lose our lives, Taylor can miss me with her sob stories.'

It's time to call out Taylor Swift's hypocrisy and privilege | Opinion

'It's time someone spoke out against Taylor Swift.'

'Media are afraid to do it;'

'the industry is afraid to do it'

'and even those artists who have feuded with her have never really questioned her motives'

'Because Swift has a large online presence'

'rabid fans and a big bank account'

'she has remained relatively immune to criticism'.

'No one even dares to criticize her lacking vocal talent'

TENNESSEAN BEAU DAVIDSON	'Big Machine Label Group, the label that gave Swift her start and, truly, her entire career'
	'yet her own father negotiated her original label deal because he was filthy rich. How many singers get that luxury?'

'Taylor's true privilege'

'Swift forgot where she came from and the people who made her a star'

'Her dad bought her way in, Borchetta got her on radio, and now, the label is the bad guy?'

'Notice that Swift never appears at the CMAs or any country events anymore. Ever wonder why?'

'She has bitten the hands that fed her'

'It's highly hypocritical for her to rally against bullying when that is precisely what she just did to her former label, resulting in death threats, using conflated, false information to do so.'

'Rarely does anyone speak out against Taylor Swift, but the time has come'

'She is a pandering phony and an even bigger bully who needs to mature rather quickly.'

It's Time for Taylor Swift to Denounce Her Neo-Nazi Admirers

THE DAILY
BEAST
AMY
ZIMMERMAN

'Swift condemned Kanye's lyrics, harnessed this victimhood for her public image, was thwarted by leaked footage of Kanye running the track by her in the studio and then reduced to a Notes app statement—are already the stuff of legend.'

'Not only did she refuse to endorse a presidential candidate—she wouldn't even denounce the candidate who was accused of serial sexual assault. Given Swift's history of failing to do the bare minimum.'

Kim Kardashian West and Kanye West Reignite Feud With Taylor Swift

NEW YORK
TIMES
JON
CARAMANICA

'Throughout this battle, each has accused the other of dishonesty'

'But her stern response to the song's release served as a reassertion of the old order. It also extended a narrative in which Kanye West, who is black, is painted as the predator and Taylor Swift, who is white, as the prey, a story with uncomfortable racial overtones.'

---

https://www.telltalesonline.com/20889/taylor-swift-liar-kanye-west-famous: (the link does not work, it was replaced with the link of the articles written in the next column; however, I saved the context of the article and it was used in this report)

'1. In her original statement, Taylor claimed – 'Kanye did not call for approval'. – LIE!
'We clearly heard Kanye seek approval for the song in the recording, and we heard Taylor give her full consent.'

'2. 'She cautioned him about releasing a song with such a strong misogynistic message. Taylor was never made aware of the actual lyric, 'I made that bitch famous.' – LIE!
If Taylor wasn't aware of the 'bitch' lyric in question, what 'misogynistic message' did she warn Kanye about, specifically? She'd already approved the line about 'Kanye having sex' with her, calling it a 'compliment', so what other line could it be? This ultimately proves that she was indeed knowledgeable of the 'bitch' lyric. It's also strange that Taylor approved the 'sex' line but not the 'bitch' line. We'd assume the former was more offensive.'

TELL TALES
NO NAME

'3. In her latest statement, Taylor said, 'Where is the video of Kanye telling me he was going to call me 'that bitch' in his song? It doesn't exist because it never happened.' – LIE!
Once again, it couldn't be more obvious that Taylor was WELL aware of this lyric. The proof lies in the phone call when she tells Kanye, 'Like, you obviously didn't know who I was before [the 2009 VMAs]. It doesn't matter if I sold 7 million of that album before you did that, which is what happened. You didn't know who I was before that...It's awesome that you're so outspoken and it's gonna be like, 'Yeah, she does, it made her famous.' In what other context would this comment make sense, except in regards to a line about him making her famous?'

'4. At the Grammy Awards, Taylor said she was upset with Kanye for trying to 'take credit for her accomplishments and her fame' – LIE!
If Taylor hates people taking credit for her accomplishments and fame, why then, in the phone call, did she agree that the 2009 VMAs incident helped make her famous? Why then, did she say her album sales were insignificant before Kanye stormed the stage that night? Taylor even admitted in the recording that she doesn't think anyone would find the song offensive. Her acceptance speech was based on nothing but lies, in an attempt to defame Kanye.'

'5. Taylor was upset with Kanye for calling her a 'bitch in front of the entire world' – LIE!
Like Kanye said, 'Bitch is an endearing term in hip hop'. Why is Taylor suddenly a stranger to the word 'bitch' when she claims to listen to rap and says that Kanye West's College Dropout was the 'first album she ever bought'? You'd think she was accustomed to hearing that word! Taylor Swift isn't just a liar, but a hypocrite, too.'

Kanye West and Taylor Swift: A Timeline of Their Feud

'Maybe Kanye had a right to call Taylor a 'fake ass'.'

'Remember when she denied ever approving Kanye's Famous lyrics? Well, in July 2016, Kim Kardashian published a recording of a telephone call between Kanye and Taylor, where she was HEARD fully approving the lyrics in question. Here is part of that conversation:

TELL TALES
ANGELA
STEPHANOU

Taylor Swift: Yeah. I mean, go with whatever line you think is better. It's obviously very tongue-in-cheek either way. And I really appreciate you telling me about it, that's really nice!

Kanye West: Yeah. I just felt I had a responsibility to you as a friend. I mean, thanks for being so cool about it.'

'After being exposed as a liar, Taylor took to Twitter to defend herself, insisting that she never knew Kanye would call her 'that bitch' in his song.'

'After dissecting her statement, however, we discovered that Taylor might indeed be a liar. It seems she was very much aware of all the lyrics in Kanye's song.'

Is Taylor Swift a hypocrite or just a really savvy songwriter?

'Swift, who at first gave the impression that she condemned the song, is now heard in a phone call with West (one that went viral when Kardashian leaked it on Snapchat Sunday) telling the rapper she knows he's being "tongue-in-cheek" and that she appreciated him giving her a heads-up. "I never would have expected you to tell me about a line in one of your songs," she said. "It's a really cool thing to do — and a really good show of friendship."'

THE
WASHINGTON
POST
EMILY YAHR

'It is a rare thing for an artist to do. As everyone knows, Swift's empire was fueled by her extremely successful songs that are — in part — so popular because she hints that they're written about real-life people, which generally sparks a media frenzy and more publicity. Yet there's no indication that she's given a warning to these subjects. So is Swift a hypocrite? Or is she just a really savvy songwriter who knows the best way to help sell millions of albums is to get fans invested in your personal life?

Look what you made me write, Taylor Swift

'Unfortunately, this single plays right into these claims with the title of the song itself literally discarding any sense of responsibility. Not to mention how cringy the lyrics are, with "The role you made me play/Of the fool, no, I don't like you" and "I'm sorry, the old Taylor can't come to the phone right now"/"Why?"/"Oh, 'cause she's dead!"' being by far the most infantile.'

'Also, it's been over a year since her beef with Kanye West and Kim Kardashian was blasted all over social media. This seems too late for a diss track, let alone a whole album dedicated to making Kanye West just roll his eyes once, probably.'

'There is a third theory but it's so abysmal that I desperately try to forget it. It's the 'Taylor Swift Just Sucks Now' theory.

FSUNEWS
MACKENZIE
JAMIESON

The 'Taylor Swift Just Sucks Now' theory:

She's a 27-year-old who can't seem to learn how to forgive and move on, despite her efforts to seem easy, breezy, beautiful covergirl in 'Shake It Off." She's perfectly capable of writing an album that isn't simply one giant 'heck off' to Kanye West and still being super successful and beloved, but she won't. Taylor Swift sucks now, but maybe she always has.'

'I don't like this new Taylor, I don't like this single and I definitely don't like that the album is set to drop on November 10th, the anniversary of Kanye West's mother's death. As anyone who's listened to *College Dropout* or *Graduation* knows, Donda West was the biggest influence on Kanye and his music. To drop a Kanye-diss album on the anniversary of the hardest day of his life is definitely too far by anyone's standards.'

'Taylor could claim ignorance before, but by now she's had to have heard this fact and if she doesn't move the album release date she's going to lose a lot of love from fans and defenders. Whether she does this and whether the rest of her album stands far above this garbage single is yet to be determined, but until then I think it's fair to say that Taylor is far, far from being out of the woods.'

In Kimye Vs. Taylor, No One Wins

'Swift's white victimhood complex and Kanye's gross misogyny are fueling this drama, and no one is a winner.'

'If Swift prefers the role of the innocent victim, West makes a perfect foil.'

ELLE
ANGELICA JADE
BASTIÉN

'It's the 2009 VMA stage, redux: the innocent white woman being bothered by the black man who doesn't know his place.'

'If Swift had chosen to focus on West's misogynistic desire to control the images and bodies of women, she might have garnered more public sympathy. But that would have required her to care about all women—particularly women of color—and not just her own interests.'

'With just a few Snapchats, the cracks in Swift's white victimhood complex have become more visible.'

Criticizing Taylor Swift Isn't About Negativity Towards Successful Women, It's About Vindication

'Kim Kardashian's big reveal doesn't "character assassinate" anyone; it liberates Kanye from the vilification that Taylor Swift has launched her career off.'

'Taylor was trapped in what seemed to be a complex and rotten lie.'

'Taylor was quick, almost too quick, to post a statement to her Instagram page'

'What we can unpack following Kim K's big reveal, is the way in which Taylor's team continually denied any claims that she had been approached for approval on "Famous" in any way.'

'The chronicle of Taylor, the innocent white girl, and Kanye, the bullying black demon.'

VICE
GRACE
MEDFORD

'When it suited, Taylor was a victim of Kanye. When that no longer suited, she endeavored to ingratiate herself with him – she invited him to dinner, she publicly thanked him for a gift of a floral arrangement, she stood side by side with his wife as he performed at the BRIT Awards – and when he received a Vanguard at the same awards show that started the drama, it wasn't one of his many friends or peers that handed it to him, it was Taylor Swift. This shifting narrative is one that Taylor has actively participated in, perpetuated and leveraged to her personal advantage. So that's perhaps why retconning herself as an unwilling passenger in light of the 'Famous' lyrics doesn't wash in an Internet age of eternal memory'

'But the reductionist notion that this is all about Taylor being a woman – rather than about her being manipulative or caught in a lie – simply underpins the lazy and prejudice 'victim and aggressor' narrative that has always been the mainstream media's portrayal of the Kanye West and Taylor Swift story.'

'When the shoe went to the other foot, Kanye called Taylor as 'a good person and a friend' to ask for her blessing regarding the lyrics on 'Famous'. Taylor appeared to give her approval, then turned her back on Kanye and her word, shifting the narrative back to her advantage. For seven years, she has relied on the fact that, historically, a white woman will always be taken at her word over a black man. You could say she was relying on it to ride her out on this 'Famous' controversy, and, until Kim put the receipts on the table, it was working. Don't get me wrong, there is no glee derived from tearing down women, but there is vindication in seeing someone – who has been disingenuous and hypocritical at best, manipulative at worst – being played at their own game.'

Taylor Swift Isn't Like Other Celebrities, She's Worse: this title is not available on their page, however, I saved the article. You can find the original article here.

'But when Kanye says 'Relationships are more important than punchlines', you can tell he means it.'

VICE RICHARD S. HE	'Secondly, Taylor isn't feigning politeness. Her press statements painted a picture of disgust, but in the video, her initial response is anything but emotional. 'I'm like, this close to overexposure', she says, a rational assessment of how the public will respond to the song. Everything else she says is positive, relaxed, spoken without hesitation. 'Go with whatever line you think is better. It's obviously very tongue in cheek either way. And I really appreciate you telling me about it, that's really nice!' By the end of the video, Kanye and Taylor agree on the song's intent, and she implicitly agrees to support him. 'It would be great for me to be like, 'Look, he called me and told me about the line before it came out.' Like, joke's on you guys, we're fine.''

'While the conversation's straightforward, Taylor's press statements since have been full of holes. What she objects to is, supposedly, being called 'that bitch' in public. So was it 'tongue in cheek' in their conversation, but misogynistic on the song itself? Memories distort, but the video's objective. Maybe her emotional response was authentic, maybe she manufactured it to claim a triumphant moment at the Grammys. But without acknowledging her and Kanye's conversation from day one, it's looked like she has something to hide. A truth told badly might as well be a lie.'

'Kanye's always practiced radical honesty, often to the detriment of his reputation: really? Why I can't trust you?'

'All Kim had to do was hang Taylor with her own rope, by releasing footage of her being really nice to Kanye. Is that so cruel?'

'She portrays herself as untouchable, above the bullshit of the tabloid media.'

'That's the beauty of being publicly shamed: it certainly can't get any worse.'

The Depressingly Predictable Downfall Of Taylor Swift

'It has been since last July, when Kim Kardashian West released videos of Swift approving the lyrics to Kanye West's 'Famous,' after Swift had sworn up and down she hated them, and claimed to have cautioned Kanye against the song's 'misogynistic message' to boot.'

'I should lay my cards on the table here: I am, to put it mildly, not a Swift fan.'

'She elevates herself by portraying herself as a perfect patriarchal subject—white, polite, and virginal, or at least 'romantic'—while bashing other women for their perceived impurity and carnality. Her racial politics are more than tone-deaf. She uses feminism to promote her work, but is not politically engaged when it doesn't benefit her financially.'

'The backlash is arriving right on schedule, and at the same epic scale.'

VICE
SADY DOYLE

'Make no mistake: There are serious and necessary critiques to be made of Taylor Swift. The lie she told about Kanye West was objectively wrong, and drew on a long history of white women perpetuating the idea that black men are predators.'

'Whether or not Swift was consciously aware of the structural racism she was playing into, people are right to be angry at her, and it's disturbing that she's never publicly apologized.

It's also troubling that she made it through an entire two-year election cycle without warning her young fans away from Trump.'

'The Swift backlash may be happening in part because, in the age of Ivanka, we're all sick of rich white women who mean well but remain complicit to protect their own profits.'

'The only next step that leaves for her, in a culture that's profoundly threatened by female visibility and power, is to fail, fall apart, or die. Swift knows this. It's why her single — and probably her album cover — both reference the best-known example of the phenomenon, Britney Spears.'

When Did the Media Turn Against Taylor Swift?

'In a concert review titled 'Taylor Swift Is Not Your Friend,' Evans wrote:

	To think of [Swift] as womanhood incarnate is to trick oneself into forgetting about 'Bad Blood' and 'Better Than Revenge.'
	Swift isn't here to help women — she's here to make bank. Seeing her on stage cavorting with World Cup winners and supermodels was not a win for feminism, but a win for Taylor
VULTURE NATE JONES	Swift. Her plan — to be as famous and as rich as she can possibly be — is working, and by using other women as tools of her self-promotion, she is distilling feminism for her own benefit.'
	'Swift became an embodiment of 'white feminism,' a brand of progressivism that centers wealthy white women at the expense of everyone else. (Like a hipster or a neoliberal, no one identifies as a white feminist.) Critics soon fell over themselves pointing out that Swift's clique was really just an exclusive group of mostly white actresses and supermodels. As Mic now put it, Swift's #squadgoals were 'totally disturbing.''
	'instead of a vague sense of Swift controlling events to make herself the victim, there's actual video proof'

Now That Taylor Swift Is Definitely Less Innocent Than She Pretends to Be, What's Next?

	'The only point that matters is that Taylor Swift has been exposed as mendacious and disingenuous'
THE CUT FRANK GUAN	
	'The sales for her next album won't suffer — spurred by the anticipation of more drama, they'll rise to new heights.'

The War Over 'That Bitch'

THE ATLANTIC SPENCER KORNHABER	'Why did the plan fall through? Swift has said she didn't know the call was recorded, and so maybe she simply misremembered its details when her reps put out her initial anti-'Famous' statement. Or maybe she just decided the risks of spinning a story were outweighed by the benefits of objecting to the song.'

'For Swift to allow herself to be called that term in a rap song really would be a betrayal of her own brand.'

What Do Kim Kardashian's Snapchat 'Receipts' Actually Prove About Taylor Swift and Kanye?

'Private Taylor is not really a person at all; there is only success robot Taylor.'

'Talking about how many likes an Instagram got is not cool—a cool person would pretend not to care about such things—but Taylor is numbers- and success-oriented. Later, when she cites the sales figures her album had before Kanye ever interrupted her ('It doesn't matter that I sold 7 million of that album before you did that, which is what happened,' she says—you can imagine her turning to a camera and winking for that last part), that number, too, is one she has at the ready. It's a little passive-aggressive, a reminder to Kanye that she doesn't think she needs him.'

SLATE
HEATHER
SCHWEDEL

'That's our Taylor: always thinking strategically about her image, how this will affect the big picture of her brand.'

'There are parts of the video where Taylor sounds resigned. 'You didn't know who I was before that, it's fine,' she says, when that is clearly not fine. Even the effusive thank yous and vows of friendship Taylor offers can be seen in this light—she's used to laying it on thick, weaponizing her sweet personality as a way to further her business interests. When she says, 'It's a really cool thing to do and a really good show of friendship,' you can hear a hint of falseness in her voice, her willing herself to say what she knows she's supposed to say.'

'No one can pretend to understand her motivations for insisting that Kanye is in the wrong here—Who cares if he called you 'that bitch'? Why make a big thing of it? Why continue to fight it?—but it seems like even after this umpteenth, mic drop of a chapter, there's probably still more to this story.'

How Keeping Up With the Kardashians Helps Kim Tell a Better Story Than Taylor

SLATE
KATHRYN
VANARENDONK

'Taylor is furious about something she apparently gave her full approval for. And maybe most importantly, Kim is merely trying to stand up for her husband, who is being publicly excoriated for something that's not his fault.'

'Plus, no matter how much you may wish to erase yourself from the narrative, posting a response to that effect sends a bit of a mixed message.'

Taylor Swift's Carefully Cultivated Image Is Starting To Crack

'Taylor Swift may have been a hard-working country star steadily making a name for herself in 2009, but prior to their now infamous MTV interaction, most of us hadn't a clue who she was. To the majority of the public, Taylor Swift came into being during that fateful moment where he stood on the stage beside her and claimed she was unworthy of the music award she'd worked so hard to win.'

FORBES DANI DI PLACIDO	'In what must've been, initially, a humiliating experience for Swift, a valuable lesson was learned. Controversy is just another word for attention.' 'Swift doesn't appear to give permission to use the phrase 'that bitch.' Name calling aside, however, it's clear that Swift is giving her blessing to Kanye to make fun of her, and planning to allow the public to believe that she is offended, until she corrects the situation. Later, she appears to have decided that a full-blown artificial feud would be more lucrative. This time, playing the victim appears to have blown up in her face.' 'In her public appearances and music videos, Swift behaves like a blond bundle of positive energy, all sparkling smile, and ruby-red lips. Beneath the sugar-coating, however, is an incredibly shrewd and intelligent businesswoman with a ruthless streak.'
VOX CONSTANCE GRADY	*Taylor Swift is cold-blooded and calculating. That's what makes her a great pop star.* 'Well, sure. We all knew she was fake. She's a celebrity. That's part of how being a celebrity works, yes?' 'But the video does seem to contradict much of Swift's original story, which is that West called to ask if he could release the song via her Twitter account, and that she not only declined but also cautioned him against "releasing a song with such a strong misogynistic message." It's within the realm of possibility that we didn't hear the whole phone call, and that West did indeed ask to release the song on Swift's Twitter and Swift told him not to be a misogynist, but there's no proof of that. And considering how chummy and ingratiating Swift sounds in the clips that Kardashian posted to Snapchat, it's difficult to imagine Swift saying something so confrontational within the span of the same conversation.' 'There's a lot to be said about Swift's reasons for (probably) lying in her initial statement, her history of presenting herself as the victim in every controversy involving her public life, and the racial and gendered nuances of her longstanding feud with West.' "Hearing Taylor Swift think out loud about how to spin the story, to me, is more damaging than learning that Taylor Swift lied about Kanye West," Vox's Alex Abad-Santos writes. "Kim Kardashian's Snapchat video ... confirms that underneath the thick coating of bubblegum pop known as Taylor Swift, there's a shrewd, savvy woman who puts a lot of effort into shaping and maintaining her public image." 'We have proof that Taylor Swift, one of the biggest celebrities in the world, thinks about the way the media perceives her. In the current state of news articles and the methods of interpretating evidence of the feud, it would be stupid not to think about how mass media perceives you.' 'Of course she curates the friends and boyfriends she's seen with in public; of course she thinks about how she'll spin this feud and that photo op into a good headline for the gossip mill. She does it because that's her job, and she's good at it.' 'But it's just as disingenuous for us, the audience, to pretend we're shocked to discover that Swift's persona is constructed — that when we look behind her mask, we're surprised to find she's put a lot of effort into cultivating her image. That's just us making the Taylor Swift Surprised Face at each other over and over again, into eternity.'

A unified theory of Taylor Swift's reputation

'And then Kim Kardashian West — Kanye West's wife and another celebrity who knows how to work a gossip cycle — released a series of videos that appeared to show Swift signing off on West's lyrics.'

'Swift tried to disavow the whole thing. 'I would very much like to be excluded from this narrative, one that I have never asked to be a part of, since 2009,' she wrote on Instagram in a now-deleted post. But the lie was too blatant to work. Because it was clear that Swift had asked to be a part of the narrative of her feud with Kanye West — had, if anything, amplified it by writing songs about it and talking about it in her Grammys speech — and that her public image had benefited as a result.'

VOX
CONSTANCE
GRADY

'But at this point, Swift's ability to hold on to her appeal without uniting both halves of her persona is in serious doubt. The controlling and manipulative side of her persona has come into view to an extent that much of her audience is having trouble believing in the authenticity and intimacy of the other side. So even though Taylor Swift knows exactly what you think of her, for the first time in her career, she seems to be at a loss as to how to change your mind.'

Taylor Swift's internet rulebook

THE VERGE
KAITLYN
TIFFANY

'she used the Grammys stage to call out men who wanted to take credit for her success. It was a cloying, cheap speech even before Kim Kardashian stepped up to say that West's phone call asking for permission for at least part of the lyric had been recorded, Swift's laughter and acquiescence included'

'And in the wake of the phone call's reveal on Snapchat, Swift's (since-deleted) tweeted screenshot from the Notes app — now a standard move for celebrities embroiled in controversy — only made things worse.'

The danger of Taylor Swift's privileged pop

'It's somewhat surprising to see the Kanye West vs. Taylor Swift saga reinvigorated by the pop star after West's wife — you may have heard of her, Kim (motherfucking) Kardashian — exposed Swift's conversation with West regarding 'Famous' before its release, a conversation Swift conveniently forgot in her reaction to the lyric, 'I feel like me and Taylor might still have sex / Why? I made that bitch famous.''

'But in practice, Swift's bid for feminism falls flat: leaving out women of color, women who aren't skinny, women who are poor, etc. etc.. She not only fails to acknowledge the possibility that her privilege as a skinny, attractive white woman has assisted in her rise to prominence, but basically refuses to acknowledge that the sociopolitical systems that benefit her make life and business more challenging for artists of color.'

'Additionally, when 1989 took Album of the Year over Kendrick Lamar's To Pimp A Butterfly'

MICHIGAN
DAILY

CHRISTIAN KENNEDY

'The privilege granted by their skin color that allows them to sacrifice the safety and peace of mind of Americans of color is the exact same privilege that allows Swift to 'stay out of politics' and post a non-committal 'make your voice heard' Instagram in one of the most critical elections in American history, guaranteeing that she is to lose no popularity or money due to the polarization of her audience.'

'While Beyoncé has the 'choice' to stay mum on political topics, the reality is that she lives in a Black body, married to a Black man, raising Black children in 2017. In that reality, today's political climate (and all of American history) presents tangible ways in which her family and friends can be harmed, dehumanized and killed. Political apathy isn't always a 'choice.''

'Swift's words and actions manipulate the truth and perpetuate the narrative of white-female victimhood at the hands of black, male villains at a time where it is especially dangerous. Whether she fails to see the sociopolitical tensions she is manipulating or she doesn't care, both of are equally unacceptable.'

FULCHER: Taylor Swift is creating trash, and we're letting it happen

'Between posting naked pictures of herself on Twitter (and embarrassing us all with her phenomenal hips) and defending racist makeup artists, there was only one time and one time alone Kim Kardashian did something that was actually important to me. Kim Kardashian ended Taylor Swift's 'America's Sweetheart' phase.'

'I have managed to be a Taylor Swift fan for more years than she deserved from me, but it looks that that may be coming to an end.'

'After Kanye West's drunken mic-stealing of 2009, she drew the incident out for as many years as possible — writing a song about it, referencing it whenever she possibly could and playing the victim, as she does so well.'

THE DAILY FREE PRESS NASHID FULCHER

'Over the years, Taylor Swift has played her 'fragile white feminist' card as often as possible.'

'Fairly recently, Kanye West dropped 'Famous,' in which he claims his 2009 MTV Awards stunt was what made Taylor Swift famous. It didn't. It did help her career.'

'Kanye West called to ask for permission and she said it was fine to put the line in the song and he did. Taylor Swift then said she wasn't aware of the line — that he never ran it past her. She accused him of trying to 'take credit' for her success.'

'Kim Kardashian was not having that. Kim posted snapchats showing Taylor Swift's conversation with Kanye West, where she approved the lyric. Swift's credibility was shattered in that moment. I was utterly dismayed. I'd always trusted her to never get caught being a liar, so I could enjoy 'We Are Never Ever Getting Back Together' and 'Dear John' in peace, pretending they weren't about actual people whom she may have actually humiliated by writing a song about.'

'Either way, one thing is clear: accepting white mediocrity in the name of supporting women has been the very basis of her career and it's truly time for it to come to an end.'

Taylor Swift won't stop talking about Kanye West

| CONSEQUENCE OF SOUND ALEX YOUNG | 'Taylor Swift's new album, Reputation, officially arrived today and one immediate takeaway is that the singer is still obsessed with Kanye West.'

'Upon the song's release in 2016, Swift claimed no prior knowledge of the lyrical content, but a phone call leaked by West's wife, Kim Kardashian, showed otherwise.' |
|---|---|
| HIP HOP DX KYLE EUSTICE | *Why is Taylor Swift still obsessed with Kanye West?*

'Whatever her ongoing obsession is with West, it's been nearly nine years since West.'

'Not to mention, the Graduation mastermind endured a mental breakdown last year. It looks more like little 'Tay Tay' is the bully in this case.'

'Word to the wise: just let it go.' |
| THE STANFORD DAILY UGUR DURSUN | *The business of Taylor Swift's 'Reputation'*

'As sincere as the letter might have been, there was a strategic reason behind the act. No, Taylor Swift did not care if Apple Music paid her for each of her listeners. She most likely did not care if they paid up-and-coming musicians, either, or any other ethical problem with streaming. Her earnings from the physical album and iTunes downloads, likely increased due to the album's inaccessibility on streaming platforms, did compensate for the lost streaming revenues and hence the lost streaming points on the multi-metric music charts like Billboard Hot 100 Singles Chart or Billboard 200 Albums Chart. '1989' ended up spending 11 weeks atop the albums chart and spawning five top-10 singles, three of which crowned the chart for a combined twelve weeks in 2014 and 2015; she calculated that she could survive without streaming and succeeded.' |
| MEDIUM DEVON MALONEY | *Just Like Us: The Rise, Fall, and Future of Taylor Swift, America's Relatable Sweetheart*

'When Kanye West and Kim Kardashian dared challenge that image by claiming Swift had signed off on West's song 'Famous' — 'I feel like me and Taylor might still have sex/Why? I made that bitch famous'—and then lied about it to portray herself as West's victim again, it seemed like sour grapes of the highest order. Until it wasn't. And things began falling apart.' |

There are also other unfair and hard critics about Taylor Swift, however, journalists does not bother to criticise the actions of Kanye West and Kim Kardashian toward and in reference to Taylor Swift.[671]

---

[671] Jennifer Gannon, 'Taylor Swift: Why is it so difficult to support her?', *Irish Times*, June 9, 2018, Available at: https://www.irishtimes.com/culture/music/taylor-swift-why-is-it-so-difficult-to-support-her-1.3520132, last accessed: January 15, 2022.

V. THE **FAMOUS** FEUD: STRATEGIES OF INTERPRETATION AND COMMUNICATION

In the next two sections of this chapter, I used the official statements from Kanye West, Kim Kardashian, Taylor Swift (all available in the table with the timeline of the feud), the extracts of the articles found in the last section, other information available online (such as albums released by the artists involved in the feud), with the purpose to find strategies of communication and interpretation of the events from the *Famous* feud.

V.2 Kanye West, Kim Kardashian West and Western Mass-Media

Based on this research, I found similarities of strategies of communication and interpretation used by Kanye West, Kim Kardashian, Taylor Swift and the Western mass-media. As I wrote before, overall, Western mass-media was neutral in presenting the *Famous* feud. Not all the journalists from this report are part of the following strategies of communication and interpretation, even if I used the word 'journalist', as it is an overall presentation of the strategies found.

1. *'Twist, Twist, Twist'* (Kanye West, Kim Kardashian and journalists):

Kanye West decided to release bits of information which included omitting parts of the conversation about the origins of the song, and it is valid at the time of publishing. Kanye West did not acknowledge publicly that he added a new line in the song, and Taylor Swift was not aware of it. This strategy had a big impact, and was used heavily by Taylor Swift's critics (negative) until in March 2020 (the telephone conversation was published on Youtube and Twitter) when, finally, the truth was out: Taylor Swift was not aware of the line 'I made that bitch famous.' This is a simple strategy, but with enough power to create confusion, and has the potential to create a view of a complicated situation; Taylor Swift was trapped with little effort by Kanye West (the lead actor of this strategy); this strategy was used also by journalists.

DIAGRAM 1. *Twist, Twist, Twist*

2. *'To Protect Kanye West from Taylor Swift'*: journalists and Kim Kardashian.

Kim Kardashian: 'I never talk [expletive] about anyone publicly, like, especially in interviews, but I was just, like, 'I've so had it'. […] 'I just felt, like, I wanted to defend him in it.' […] 'I feel like I've had it with people blatantly treating my husband a certain way and making him look a certain way.' […] 'At this point, I really don't give a [expletive], so I'll do whatever to protect my husband.'[672]

3. 'Passing the blame on Taylor Swift because she did not agree with Kanye and Kim's side of the story, and journalist's expectations of statements regarding her involvement in the making of the song': Kanye West, Kim Kardashian and journalists.

- Kim Kardashian, in an interview with GQ magazine, talked about the existence of a telephone conversation between Kanye West and Taylor Swift and said: 'She totally approved that.' […] 'She totally knew that that was coming out. She wanted to all of a sudden act like she didn't';
- during the MTV VMA from 2016, Kanye West mentioned Taylor Swift: 'You know, like, people come up to me like, 'Yeah, that's right! Take Taylor!' But bro, like, I love all y'all. That's why I called her.'

4. 50/50: more by journalists:

- shares Kanye West's mistake with Taylor Swift at the same level (a part of the journalists used in this report); however, for other journalists and bloggers, Taylor Swift is to blame for the promotion and the negative outcome of the *song Famous*.

DIAGRAM 2. *50/50*

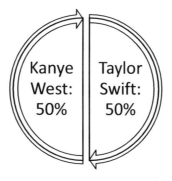

---

[672] Annie Martin, 'Kim Kardashian on GQ criticism of Taylor Swift: 'I'll do whatever to protect my husband', *UPI*, July 15, 2016, available at https://www.upi.com/Entertainment_News/2016/07/15/Kim-Kardashian-on-GQ-criticism-of-Taylor-Swift-Ill-do-whatever-to-protect-my-husband/7561468587941/#:~:text=%22At%20this%20point%2C%20I%20really,your%20accomplishments%20or%20your%20fame.%22, last accessed: October 24, 2020.

5. 'The Race Card: Black Man (Kanye West) Versus White Privileged Woman (Taylor Swift)' (journalists):

- in a country presented as being racist (USA), Kanye West has earned over a hundred million dollars[673], lived in multi-million dollars house built according to his own vision[674]; received a visible number of awards and nominations[675], and one of the highest reviews in the music industry; the last concert, *Saint Pablo Tour* based on his album *The Life of Pablo*, had a box office of 52.8 millions of dollars[676];
- a white woman (Taylor Swift) presented a bad image of a black man (Kanye West), and journalists need to speak the truth, even if Taylor Swift does not want the world to know; Kanye West cannot speak about it, because the general public does not believe a black man to tell his truth;
- in this feud the black man (Kanye West) is the victim of the white privileged woman (Taylor Swift);
- black man rejected by the society because of the persistent racism;
- black people are less appreciated than white people.

6. 'Stabbing in the Back While Shaking Her Hand' (Kanye West, Kim Kardashian, journalists):

- was nice on the telephone with Taylor Swift but, after the telephone conversation, he added new lyrics and Taylor was not aware of them, yet Kanye presented the song as she agreed and knew everything about the song; during the telephone conversation, Kanye asked Taylor to release his song on her Twitter account: 'Well, this is the thing where I'm calling you, because you're got an army. You own a country of mother–ing 2 billion people, basically, that if you felt that it's funny and cool and like hip-hop, and felt like just 'The College Dropout' and the artist like Ye that you love, then I think that people would be like way into it. And that's why I think it's super-genius to have you be the one that says, Oh, I like this song a lot. Like, yeah, whatever, this is cool, whatever';

---

[673] And in 2021 was valued at over 6 billion dollars, 'What is Kanye West's net worth in 2021?', *Capital Xtra*, March 19, 2021, available at: https://www.capitalxtra.com/artists/kanye-west/news/net-worth-full-breakdown/, last accessed: June 26, 2021.

[674] Andrew Court, 'Kim Kardashian takes fans inside $23M home she bought from Kanye West after split', *New York Post*, February 18, 2022, available at: https://nypost.com/2022/02/18/kim-kardashian-takes-fans-inside-23m-home-she-bought-from-kanye/, last accessed: June 26, 2022.

[675] 'List of awards and nominations received by Kanye West', *Wikipedia*, available at: https://en.wikipedia.org/wiki/List_of_awards_and_nominations_received_by_Kanye_West, last accessed: October 24, 2020.

[676] Pollstar, *Year End Top 100 Worldwide Tours, January 1, 2016 – December 31, 2016*, available at: https://www.pollstar.com/Chart/2017/01/2016YearEndTop100WorldwideTours_343.pdf, last accessed: October 24, 2020.

- during *The Saint Pablo Tour* he presented his side of the story, while people were chanting 'bitch' with reference to Taylor Swift;
- Kim Kardashian published a short video with her singing the line of the *song Famous*: 'I made that bitch famous.'

7. *'Behind the Curtains'* (Kanye West and journalists):

- doesn't include the fact that he added the line 'I made that bitch famous' without Taylor Swift's knowledge;
- the cover of his album is a picture with 'look like a white girl' (there is no evidence to support a clear causal link that the model if definitely a white person) wearing a bath suit and a black family which depicts a matrimony; also, on the cover is written 'Which/One ', the general meaning that readers may have is choosing between the white girl (which is lonely in the picture) or the black family; before the release of the album's cover, Kanye West released the song with the infamous line 'I made that bitch famous' about Taylor Swift (she is white and according with her dress style in music videos and private life -where there are pictures published on different websites about her in private life- is in opposition with the picture from Kanye West's album cover; Taylor Swift never pictured herself in the way that the white girl (?) is pictured on Kanye West's album cover); maybe the 'look like a white girl' picture on the album cover is a metaphor and artistic representation of Taylor Swift; maybe it's an alternate reality that exists in Kanye West's mind, meaning, to him, that Taylor Swift is just a 'bitch'; maybe it's Kanye West's way of saying about Taylor Swift that in reality she is different from what she promotes to the general public, and he managed to demonstrate her true personality;
- Kim Kardashian, in an interview with GQ magazine, talked about the existence of a telephone conversation between Kanye West and Taylor Swift: 'She totally approved that.' […] 'She totally knew that that was coming out. She wanted to all of a sudden act like she didn't': this interview (June 16, 2016) happened in the week that Kanye West started to sale tickets (June 14 for American Express cardholders, June 16 for Tidal members, June 18 for the general public) to his music tour named *Saint Pablo Tour*;
- Kim Kardashian presented a heavily edited video telephone conversation between Kanye West and Taylor Swift at a month after the start of Kanye West's sale of tickets for his music tour;
- a month before the start of Kanye West's *Saint Pablo Tour*, Kanye West and Kim Kardashian were on the cover of *Harper's Bazaar* September issue; during the interview editor Laura Brown asked them about their favourite Taylor Swift song, Kanye West replied, 'For me? I don't have one.' Kim Kardashian replied: 'I was such a fan of hers';
- journalists through their negative articles about Taylor Swift.

8. *'The Narrative Line'* (Kanye, Kim and journalists):

- interfered in Taylor Swift's narrative line with negative views about her skills and character, while ignoring Kanye's failure to keep his side of the bargain: he did not send her the final version of the song and the lyrics;
- did not analyse Taylor's statements and her true involvement in the making of the song.

9. *'The Balance of Image and Fame'* (Kim Kardashian, Kanye West and journalists):

- Kanye West is the good black man while Taylor Swift is the bad white woman.

DIAGRAM 3. *The Balance of Image and Fame*

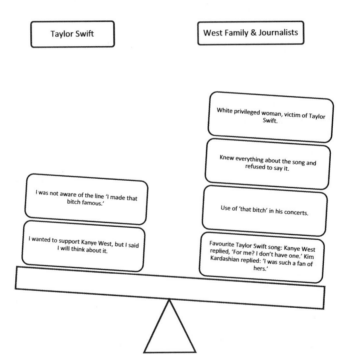

10. *'Til Her Sunshine Is Gone'* (Kanye West, Kim Kardashian and journalists):

DIAGRAM 4. *Til Her Sunshine is Gone*

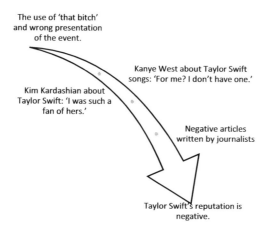

11. *'I Want to be Famous!'* (Kanye West):

- this strategy of communication is based on Kanye's conversation with Taylor Swift encouraging her to accept his deal to promote his song; in other words, Kanye, the black man that made Taylor famous, is asking her to promote his song with the purpose to make people to like his song; if he is the God of rap/hip hop music, then why this act of humiliation in front of Taylor, a white woman? why does the white woman who should not get the award from MTV in 2009, should not win the *Album of the Year* in 2010 and 2016, has to promote and use her fame to persuade people to like the song of a God in rap and hip hop?

DIAGRAM 5. *I Want to be Famous!*

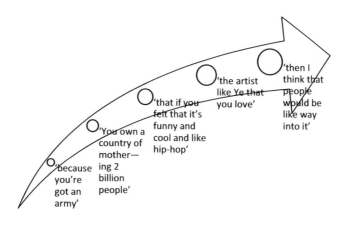

12. *'Controlling the Narrative Line'* (Kim and journalists):

- through music, Taylor Swift is trying to control the narrative line in her favour; fans and the general public should not believe her as she is not telling the truth: Kanye West is vindicated because Kim shared the edited conversation, and it is the final truth.

13. *'Shine and Die'* (Kanye, Kim and journalists):

- this strategy was done based on the two faces of Taylor Swift's career: good girl and bad events from her life.

DIAGRAM 6. *Shine and Die*

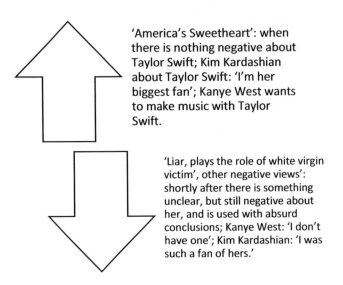

'America's Sweetheart': when there is nothing negative about Taylor Swift; Kim Kardashian about Taylor Swift: 'I'm her biggest fan'; Kanye West wants to make music with Taylor Swift.

'Liar, plays the role of white virgin victim', other negative views': shortly after there is something unclear, but still negative about her, and is used with absurd conclusions; Kanye West: 'I don't have one'; Kim Kardashian: 'I was such a fan of hers.'

14. *'Calculated'* (journalists):

- it is used because Taylor Swift does not allow the false narrative about her to circulate free without her version of the events; when Taylor Swift presented her version of the events, journalists wrote in a way to not trust her as she is *calculated* with the sole purpose to shift the narrative on her (the false white victim), while ignoring the truth delivered by journalists and bloggers who were not there to see what happened, and the evidence available is not enough to draw final conclusions, and pick the real perpetrator.

15. *'Impoverished people'* (Kanye West during the MTV VMA 2016 and journalists through negative articles):

- during the MTV VMA from 2016, Kanye West mentioned Taylor Swift: 'You know, like, people come up to me like, 'Yeah, that's right! Take Taylor!' But bro, like, I love all y'all. That's why I called her;' however, Kanye West failed to mention the full story behind the phone conversation; Kanye West shared only bits of information that put him as the owner of the truth;
- Kanye West said: 'My friend Zekiah [sp?] told me there's three keys to keeping people impoverished: that's taking away their esteem, taking away their resources, and taking away their role models;'[677] at the end of his speech Kanye West released the song *Fade* which contains lyrics: 'Your love is fadin', Know it ain't no wrong, I feel it's fadin', I think I think too much, I feel it's fadin;'[678] at this time in 2016, Taylor Swift's image is negative and Kanye West was the person behind it, digging her image with biased information about her true involvement in the *song Famous*;
- by presenting one biased side of the story, Kanye West matched at least one step of the strategy presented in his speech: he created a false narrative about Taylor Swift, which is a source of inspiration and model for millions of people; from the point of view of *only Taylor Swift*: through his negative actions, Kanye West maybe tried to take away her esteem; maybe Kanye tried to sabotage her character as a method of taking away the role model that she was/is for hundreds of thousands of fans; if we take the number of albums sold in the first week, over the years, and the number of sold tickets for concerts, it may exists around one million of people who look at Taylor as a role model.

DIAGRAM 7. *Impoverished people*

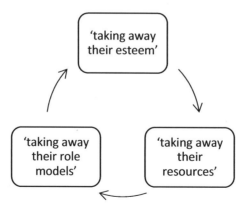

---

[677] For both quotes see: Patrick Hosken, 'Kanye West's 2016 VMA Speech – Here's the Full Transcript', *MTV*, September 28, 2016, available at: http://www.mtv.com/news/2925366/kanye-west-vmas-2016-full-speech-transcript/, last accessed: October 24, 2020.
[678] Kanye West, 'Fade'.

16. *The Spiral of Silence* (Kim Kardashian and journalists):

- it was used every time against Taylor Swift after she replied to people involved in the negative narrative, either by comments or through lyrics of various songs to expose her part of the story;
- *The Spiral of Silence* is a deadly strategy: whatever the victim says is never good enough to back up her side of the story, and the victim is for evermore the perpetrator.[679]

DIAGRAM 8. *The Spiral of Silence*

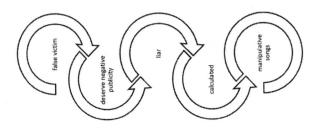

V.3 Taylor Swift

Based on this research, I found similarities of strategies of communication and interpretation used by Taylor Swift and Kanye West, Kim Kardashian and journalists. The difference between them and Taylor Swift, is that Taylor's strategies contain a more truthful side of the story. As I wrote before, overall, the Western mass-media is neutral in presenting the *Famous* feud. As in the first section of this chapter, with Kanye West, Kim Kardashian and journalists, here we have the same situation: not all the journalists from this report are part of the following strategies of communication and interpretation even if you find the word 'journalist', as it is an overall presentation of the strategies found, and the sources used in this report.

1. 'Long Story Short':

[679] More information about The Spiral of Silence, see: 'Spiral of Silence', *Wikipedia*, available at: https://en.wikipedia.org/wiki/Spiral_of_silence#:~:text=It%20states%20that%20an%20individual%27s,others%20to%20express%20their%20opinions., last accessed: October 24, 2020; 'The Spiral of Silence Theory', *Communication Theory*, available at: https://www.communicationtheory.org/the-spiral-of-silence-theory/, last accessed: October 24, 2020.

- posted short statements about her involvement in the *song Famous,* which were not good enough for mass-media to use as evidence of her innocence;
- replied only when her name was mentioned;
- let the story to unfold as Kanye and Kim wanted;
- stopped using social media to talk about the *song Famous*;
- this strategy was used to prove her innocence but, in 2016, it was not good enough for some journalists and people who rejected her evidence, and believed Kanye West and Kim Kardashian's side of the story.

DIAGRAM 9. *Long Story Short*

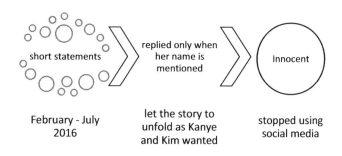

2. 'Meet Me Behind My Statements':

- Taylor Swift, from February 2016 until March 2020, released various statements about her involvement in the creation of the *song Famous*.

DIAGRAM 10. *Meet Me Behind My Statements*

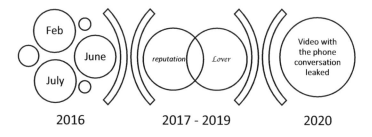

3. *'Teardrops On My Fame'*:

- Kanye West is the bad black man, Kim Kardashian is the bad white woman, while Taylor Swift is the good white woman.

DIAGRAM 11. *Teardrops On My Fame*

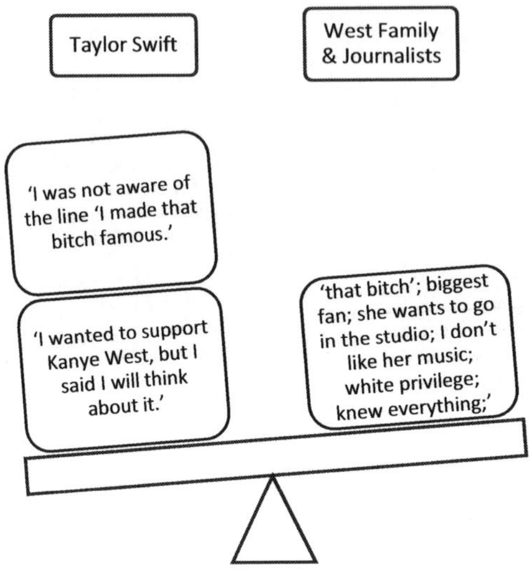

Taylor Swift

West Family & Journalists

'I was not aware of the line 'I made that bitch famous.'

'I wanted to support Kanye West, but I said I will think about it.'

'that bitch'; biggest fan; she wants to go in the studio; I don't like her music; white privilege; knew everything;

4. *'Speak Later'*:

- offered freedom of action to Kanye West and Kim Kardashian, and responded only when her name was mentioned by a participant in the *Famous* feud; this strategy may have its roots in the short feud she was involved with Nicki Minaj in 2015 before the MTV VMA, when Taylor Swift wrote: 'I thought I was being called out. I missed the point, I misunderstood, then misspoke. I'm sorry, Nicki'[680];
- did not post anything on social media accounts for more than a year;
- to promote *reputation* album from 2017: she created her own magazines, which were available in two copies, and only with the album at Target store;
- told her story through lyrics and videos more than a year after Kim Kardashian's post about the phone conversation between her and Kanye West;

---

[680] Jason Lipshutz, 'Taylor Swift & Nicki Minaj's Twitter Argument: A Full Timeline of the Disagreement', *Billboard*, July 23, 2015, available at: https://www.billboard.com/music/pop/taylor-swift-nicki-minaj-twitter-argument-timeline-6641794/, last accessed: January 22, 2022.

378

- in 2019 the album *Lover* is considered by critics and fans as the second answer (first is *reputation*) for Kanye West, and her involvement in the production of the *song Famous*.

DIAGRAM 12. *Speak Later*

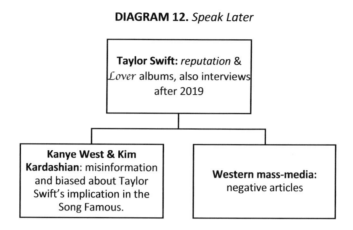

5. *'Out of the Woods'*:

- maybe the strategy of promoting her truth was made in two stages: the first stage through *reputation* and the darkest period of her musical life, and *Lover*: an album about her real personality;
- through *reputation* and *Lover* albums, Taylor Swift was caught in a journey from darkness (because Kanye West pushed and managed the feud in that direction) to light (through her own thinking and the power of writing songs); with *Lover* she returned stronger, and with the same well-being feeling and cool personality that she had before February 2016.

DIAGRAM 13. *Out of the Woods*

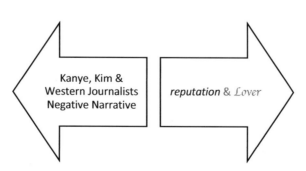

6. 'Controlling the Narrative of Truth':

- this strategy is on long term and it started in January 2016, when the phone conversation between Taylor Swift and Kanye West took place;

DIAGRAM 14. *Controlling the Narrative of Truth*

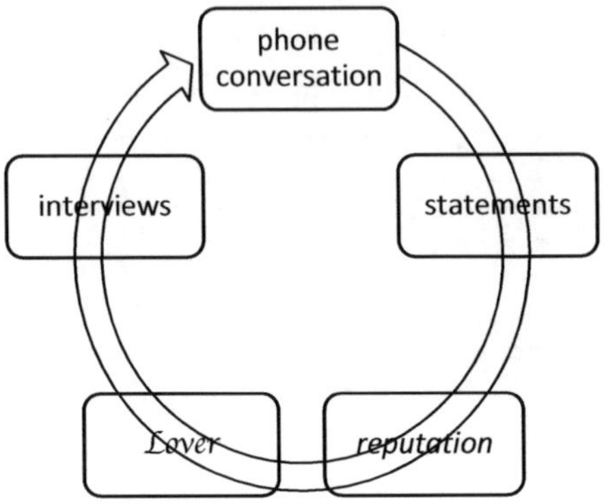

V.4 Kanye West, Beyoncé, Jay Z, Katy Perry and Taylor Swift: *The Dynamic Reaction Strategy* (DRS)

On August 21, 2017, more than a year after the post on Instagram about her participation in the song *Famous*, Taylor Swift returned on social media by revealing a new song and a new music album named *reputation*; on August 23, 2017 Taylor released the first song from the album, *Look What You Made Me Do*; two years later, on August 23, 2019 Taylor Swift released the album, *Lover*. According to fans and journalists, these two albums are considered to be Taylor Swift's response to the negative effects of the *Famous* feud with Kanye West.[681]

---

[681] Vogue, 'The Shadiest Shade Taylor Swift Throws at Kanye West on Reputation', November 10, 2017, available at: https://www.vogue.com/article/taylor-swift-shade-kanye-west-reputation; last accessed: November 11, 2017; Brittany Leitner, 'Is Taylor Swift's 'Reputation' Album About Kim Kardashian & Kanye West? Fans Think So', *Elite Daily*, August 23, 2017, available at: https://www.elitedaily.com/entertainment/taylor-swifts-reputation-album-kim-kardashian-kanye-west-fans-think/2052142, last accessed: November 11, 2017; 'Who are the songs on Taylor Swift's new album Lover about?', *Irish Times*, August 23, 2019, available at: https://www.irishnews.com/magazine/entertainment/2019/08/23/news/who-are-the-songs-on-taylor-swift-s-new-album-lover-about--1693146/; last accessed: August 27, 2019; Kelsie Gibson, 'Calvin or Kanye? Fans Guess Who Taylor Swift's "I

This strategy started in 2009 and may still exist as of today. *The Dynamic Reaction Strategy* is simple, but with serious consequences unleashed from the general public: each artist responded either by a statement on the official page, or through a song, video, album and interview.

In the next pages I explored different patterns which show Taylor Swift in defence mode toward Kanye West, while Kanye West initiated an offensive behaviour towards and in reference to Taylor Swift.

DIAGRAM 15. *The Dynamic Reaction Strategy: Kanye West and Taylor Swift*

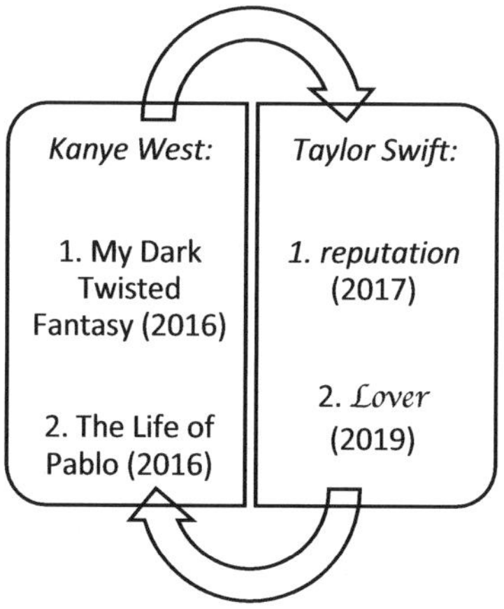

Kanye West:

1. My Dark Twisted Fantasy (2016)

2. The Life of Pablo (2016)

Taylor Swift:

1. *reputation* (2017)

2. *Lover* (2019)

Examples to support the *Dynamic Reaction Strategy* (DRS)

There are many examples that can support the *Dynamic Reaction Strategy*, but I used a number of examples that I found to be enough to understand how it works. Unfortunately, despite the use of examples, this report cannot confirm a clear causal link; the examples available in this section should not be seen as the final evidence that this strategy was created by the players of the feud with the sole purpose to answer to the allegations hold and promoted by all the parties involved in the feud, but have been illustrated by various fans on social media, articles published by Western mass-media, and my own interpretation based on lyrics, music videos and song titles.[682]

Forgot That You Existed" Is About', *Popsugar*, August 23, 2019, available at: https://www.popsugar.co.uk/entertainment/Who-Taylor-Swift-I-Forgot-You-Existed-About-46534507, last accessed: August 27, 2019.
[682] The examples of the *Dynamic Reaction* strategy were used/modified with new interpretation by the author of this report from the following sources: Christopher Rosa, '20 Taylor Swift 'Reputation' Fan Theories That Actually Make Sense', *Glamour*,

1. References in the song/album/video:

- Taylor Swift wrote lyrics in which she described key situations that the audience knew, and she confirmed them, refuted or added something unknown until the release of the song/album, for example:

Look What You Made Me Do[683]:

- Taylor Swift remade the scene with the phone conversation with Kanye West and added the lyrics: 'Taylor Swift can't come to the phone right now? Why? Oh, because she is dead:' this is a reference to the trend from July 2016, named *#TaylorSwiftOverParty*, where thousands of users tweeted that Taylor Swift is dead because the truth is out and she is guilty: a mural was created in Australia, and her birth and dead years were written on the left side: 1989 – 2016;

Endgame[684]:

- *'I'm one call away, whenever you need me'*: the phone call with Kanye West;

- *'Knew her when I was young'*: Kanye West met her at the age of 19 at the MTV VMA 2009;

September 8, 2017, available at: https://www.glamour.com/story/best-taylor-swift-reputation-fan-theories, last accessed: March 27, 2020; Rebecca Farley, 'Every Single Taylor Swift Clone That Appears In Reputation', *Refinery29*, November 10, 2017, available at: https://www.refinery29.com/en-gb/2017/11/180787/taylor-swift-reputation-taylors-theory, last accessed: March 27, 2020; Lauren Rearick, 'Taylor Swift's Reputation Sparks Multiple Fans Theories About Who She's Shading', *Teen Vogue*, November 10, 2017, available at: https://www.teenvogue.com/story/taylor-swifts-reputation-shade-fans-theories, last accessed: March 27, 2020; Dusty Baxter-Wright, '8 Fan Theories On What Taylor Swift's Reputation Lyrics Are About', *Cosmopolitan*, November 10, 2017, available at: https://www.cosmopolitan.com/uk/entertainment/a13514492/who-are-taylor-swift-reputation-lyrics-about/, last accessed: March 27, 2020; Nicole Pomarico, 'Fans Have Theories About Taylor Swift's '...Ready For It?' Video & It's Not Even Out Yet', *Bustle*, October 23, 2017, available at: https://www.bustle.com/p/theories-about-taylor-swifts-ready-for-it-video-from-kanye-references-to-reputation-connections-2971233, last accessed: March 27, 2020; Cady Lang, 'The 10 Most Convincing Theories About Taylor Swift's Album Reputation', *Time*, September 29, 2017, https://time.com/4944028/taylor-swift-reputation-album-theories/, last accessed: March 27, 2020; Alyssa Bailey, 'All The Hidden Messages Taylor Swift Wants You To Notice In Her "End Game" Music Video', *Elle*, January 12, 2018, available at: https://www.elle.com/culture/music/a15069497/taylor-swift-end-game-hidden-messages-easter-eggs/, last accessed: March 27, 2020; Ashley Hoffman, 'The Internet Is Freaking Out About These Details in Taylor Swift's 'End Game' Video', *Time*, January 12, 2018, https://time.com/5100657/taylor-swift-end-game-video-theories/, last accessed: March 27, 2020; Jill Gutowitz, 'What Is Every Song on Taylor Swift's Lover Actually About?', *Vulture*, August 23, 2019, last accessed: March 27, 2020; Emily Yahr, 'Taylor Swift's 'Lover': A Track-By-Track Breakdown, From Coded Lyrics to Leonardo DiCaprio and Drake References', *The Washington Post*, August 23, 2019, available at: https://www.washingtonpost.com/arts-entertainment/2019/08/23/taylor-swifts-lover-track-by-track-breakdown-coded-lyrics-leonardo-dicaprio-drake-references/, last accessed: March 27, 2020.

[683] Taylor Swift, 'Look What You Made Me Do Lyrics', *Genius*, available at: https://genius.com/Taylor-swift-look-what-you-made-me-do-lyrics, last accessed: March 20, 2020.

[684] Taylor Swift, 'Endgame Lyrics', *Genius*, available at: https://genius.com/Taylor-swift-end-game-lyrics, last accessed: March 20, 2020.

- *'Reconnected when we were little bit older'*: in 2015 Kanye West called Taylor Swift and asked her to present the *MTV Michael Jackson Video Vanguard Award*; eventually, Taylor accepted his request; during this event, Taylor Swift stayed next to his wife, Kim Kardashian; after the ceremony Kanye West sent flowers to Taylor Swift;

- *'And I can't let you go, your hand print's on my soul'*: Kanye West used the private conversation to blame Taylor for not accepting the final version of the song; Kim Kardashian released edited parts of the private conversation on Snapchat; Kanye West used a wax clone of Taylor Swift in the music video of the song *Famous* without her permission; during *Saint Pablo Tour,* in various places in the USA, Kanye West, through live speaking and by interpreting his song *Famous*, created a feeling of encouragement in his concerts where fans started shouting 'bitch' in reference to Taylor Swift; in the end, Kanye West, in his speech to MTV in 2016, presented his position as the man who is telling the truth while Taylor Swift is a liar: 'That's why I called her';

Gorgeous[685]:

- same title as Kanye West's song 'Gorgeous' from the album *My Beautiful Dark Twisted Fantasy* (2010)[686];

Getaway Car[687]:

'We were jet-set, Bonnie and Clyde[688] *(oh, oh)'*: possible reference to Beyoncé and Jay Z; '03 Bonnie & Clyde' is a song performed by Jay Z; there are also connections with the concert *On the Run* and the Tidal platform; let's see the possible connections with the lyrics and the title of the songs[689]:

- Kanye West released the song *Famous* (*The Life of Pablo*) where Taylor Swift is called 'that bitch';
- Kanye promised that his album, *The Life of Pablo*, will be available exclusively on the *Tidal* platform (the platform owned also by Jay Z); however, on April 1, 2016, his

[685] Taylor Swift, 'Gorgeous Lyrics', *Genius*, available at: https://genius.com/Taylor-swift-gorgeous-lyrics, last accessed: March 27, 2020.

[686] Kanye West, 'Gorgeous Lyrics', *Genius*, available at: https://genius.com/Kanye-west-gorgeous-lyrics, last accessed: March 27, 2020.

[687] Taylor Swift, 'Getaway Car Lyrics', *Genius*, available at: https://genius.com/Taylor-swift-getaway-car-lyrics, last accessed: March 27, 2020.

[688] Bonnie Elizabeth Parker (October 1, 1910 – May 23, 1934) and Clyde Champion Barrow[1][2] (March 24, 1909 – May 23, 1934) were an American criminal couple who travelled the Central United States with their gang during the Great Depression, known for their bank robberies, although they preferred to rob small stores or rural gas stations.

[689] The following connections are from *Black and White Music*, pp: 185-191;

album was made available on *Apple Music*, which led to the accusation that he cheated the audience; according to an article in Variety: 'By the time Mr. West changed course and broadly released 'The Life of Pablo,' the deceptive marketing ploy had served its purpose: Tidal's subscriber numbers had tripled, streaming numbers were through the roof, and Tidal had collected the personal information, credit card numbers, and social media information of millions of deceived consumers […] Instead, they just wanted to boost Tidal's subscriber numbers – which indeed did get a big bump from the release. Tidal may have signed up as many as two million new subscribers thanks to the album, claims the lawsuit, arguing that this could have added as much as $84 million to Tidal's valuation;'[690]

- Beyoncé released the surprise album *Lemonade* on April 23, 2016; Taylor Swift was caught in the negative narrative created and promoted by Kanye West; *Lemonade* enjoyed success from critics being considered the best album released by Beyoncé; on Tidal, *Lemonade* was streamed 115 million times, setting a record for the most-streamed album in a single week by a female artist; what if Kanye West, through the exclusivity strategy of his album, plus the use of Taylor in his song, spread the narrative that in his album there could be something more about Taylor, which led to the growth of curious users and, in the end, some users decided to stay on the platform? at the same time, maybe the new number of users were used to justify the record number of streaming of his album, *The Life of Pablo*, and Beyoncé's *Lemonade*?

- in 2018 Tidal was accused of intentionally falsifying the streaming number of *The Life of Pablo* and *Lemonade*, according to Variety: 'Tidal, which has rarely shared its data publicly, had a streaming exclusive on West's album for its first six weeks of release and continues to be the exclusive streamer for Beyoncé's album. It claimed that West's album had been streamed 250 million times in its first 10 days of release in February of 2016, while claiming it had just 3 million subscribers – a claim that would have meant every subscriber played the album an average of eight times per day; and that Beyoncé's album was streamed 306 million times in its first 15 days of release in April of 2016.' […] 'Today's report, according to MBW's translation, says that 'Beyoncé's and Kanye West's listener numbers on Tidal have been manipulated to the tune of several hundred million false plays… which has generated massive royalty payouts at the expense of other artists;[691'] what if Kanye West and Jay Z's

---

[690] Janko Roettgers, 'Kanye West Tricked Fans Into Subscribing to Tidal, Lawsuit Claims', *Variety*, April 18, 2016, available at: https://variety.com/2016/digital/news/kanye-west-tricked-fans-into-subscribing-to-tidal-lawsuit-claims-1201755580/, last accessed: February 25, 2021.

[691] Jem Aswad, 'Tidal Accused of Falsifying Beyoncé and Kanye West Streaming Numbers', *Variety*, May 9, 2018, available at: https://variety.com/2018/biz/news/jay-z-tidal-accused-of-falsifying-beyonce-and-kanye-west-streaming-numbers-1202804222/, last accessed: February 25, 2021; Andy Cush, 'Tidal Accused of Generating 300 Million Fake Streams for Kanye and Beyoncé', *Spin*, May 9, 2018, available at: https://www.spin.com/2018/05/tidal-fake-streams-kanye-beyonce-investigation-300-million/, last accessed: February 25, 2021; Tim Ingham, 'Tidal 'Fake Streams': Criminal Investigation Underway Over Potential Data Fraud In Norway, *Music Business Worldwide*, January 14, 2019, available at: https://www.musicbusinessworldwide.com/tidal-fake-streams-criminal-investigation-underway-over-potential-data-fraud-in-norway/, last accessed: February 25, 2021; Dagens Næringsliv's

strategy to use Taylor Swift was also to increase the number of users? what if Kanye West and Jay Z used the new subscribers to falsify the numbers of plays to make more money? let's not forget that in the conversation with Taylor Kanye admitted having big debts (millions of dollars); what if the false plays was done in order to increase Beyoncé's profile and the records obtained? what if the false plays were made this route as on the other streaming platforms (Apple and Spotify) Beyoncé would not make the numbers to have new records to celebrate, and maintain relevance in the music industry as Taylor Swift does? what if the false plays and the exclusive availability of her album, *Lemonade*, on Tidal was made to show the world that she is so loved that her fans follow her on the new platform, and set new records in the music industry? what if Tidal is being used to justify a false point of view that black artists are not safe on other platforms because they are ruled by white people? what if Kanye, Jay Z and Beyoncé used Tidal for their own benefit, therefore, cheating the music industry and their fans?

- Kanye West interfered in the narrative line of Taylor Swift with a negative story about her character, while Beyoncé has a positive image about her skills and character; Kanye West is behind the negative stories about Taylor Swift's character and skills in 2009 and in 2016; Kanye West in 2016 interfered in Taylor Swift's narrative line with a negative story, while Beyoncé's narrative line is involved in releasing a new album; Kanye West negative behaviour toward Taylor Swift is after Beyoncé released an album (2008) and before (2016, *Lemonade*) she is out with a new album;

Dress[692]:

- contains one word from the song 'Devil in a New Dress'[693] by Kanye West from the album *My Beautiful Dark Twisted Fantasy* (2010).

This is Why We Can't Have Nice Things[694]:

'This is why we can't have nice things, darling, Because you break them, I had to take them away, Did you think I wouldn't hear all the things you said about me?, It was so nice being friends again, There I was giving you a second chance, But you stabbed me in the back while shaking my hand, And therein lies the issue, friends don't try to trick you, Get you on the phone and mind-twist you.'

---

investigation can be found here:
https://www.musicbusinessworldwide.com/files/2018/05/NTNU_DigitalForensicsReport_DN_Final_Version.pdf, last accessed: February 25, 2021.

[692] Taylor Swift, 'Dress Lyrics', *Genius*, November 10, 2017, available at: https://genius.com/Taylor-swift-dress-lyrics, last accessed: February 25, 2021.

[693] Kanye West, 'Devil in New Dress Lyrics', *Genius*, November 22, 2010, available at: https://genius.com/Kanye-west-devil-in-a-new-dress-lyrics, last accessed: February 25, 2021.

[694] Taylor Swift, 'This Is Why We Can't Have Nice Things Lyrics', *Genius*, available at: https://genius.com/Taylor-swift-this-is-why-we-cant-have-nice-things-lyrics, last accessed: March 27, 2020.

- Kanye West misinformed the general public about the telephone conversation, and Taylor Swift cannot offer anymore her friendship and support;
- Kim Kardashian posted a video on her Snapchat while signing the part from the *song Famous,* which Taylor Swift did not approve: 'I made that bitch famous'; during Saint Pablo Tour in various places in the USA, Kanye West, through live speaking and by interpreting his song *Famous,* created a feeling of encouragement in his concerts where fans started shouting 'bitch' in reference to Taylor Swift; during the interview in 2016 for Harper's Bazaar, Kanye West said he does not have a favourite song made by Taylor, and Kim Kardashian said that she is not anymore a fan of Taylor;
- in 2015 Taylor accepted Kanye West's request to present the MTV Michael Jackson Video Vanguard Award; during this event, Taylor Swift sat next to his wife, Kim Kardashian; after the ceremony, Kanye West sent flowers to Taylor Swift;
- identic narrative of the song *Runaway* by Kanye West (from the album *My Beautiful Dark Twisted Fantasy*, 2010) and *This is Why We Can't Have Nice Things* by Taylor Swift (*reputation* album, 2017): in both songs there is a party.

Runaway (2010): it is a party with a ballerina (Taylor Swift played this role in *Shake It Off* song, from her blockbuster album, *1989*, released in October 2014):

'Let's have a toast for the douchebags, Let's have a toast for the assholes, Let's have a toast for the scumbags, Every one of them that I know, Let's have a toast for the jerk-offs, That'll never take work off, Baby, I got a plan, Run away fast as you can.'[695]

This is Why We Can't Have Nice Things: it is a party that in the end is ruined, but Taylor Swift offered her forgiveness, and concluded the party with a toast:

'Here's a toast to my real friends, They don't care about the he-said, she-said, And here's to my baby, He ain't reading what they call me lately, And here's to my mama, Had to listen to all this drama, And here's to you, 'Cause forgiveness is a nice thing to do, Haha, I can't even say it with a straight face'[696]

I Forgot That You Existed[697]:

'How many days did I spend, Thinkin' 'bout how you did me wrong, wrong, wrong?, Lived in the shade you were throwin', 'Til all of my sunshine was gone, gone, gone, And I couldn't get away from ya, In my feelings more than Drake, so yeah: , I forgot that you, Got out some popcorn, As soon as my rep starting going down, down, down, Laughed on the schoolyard, As soon as I tripped up and hit the ground,

---

[695] Kanye West, 'Runaway Lyrics', *Genius*, October 4, 2010, available at: https://genius.com/Kanye-west-runaway-lyrics, last accessed: March 27, 2020.
[696] Taylor Swift, 'This Is Why We Can't Have Nice Things Lyrics'.
[697] Taylor Swift, 'I Forgot That You Existed Lyrics', *Genius*, available at: https://genius.com/Taylor-swift-i-forgot-that-you-existed-lyrics, last accessed: March 27, 2020.

ground, ground, And I would've stuck around for ya, Would've fought the whole town, so yeah, Would've been right there, front row, Even if nobody came to your show'

- during the telephone conversation, Taylor agreed to support Kanye West and waited for him to send her the song, which never happened;
- during an interview for Harper's Bazaar, Kanye West said he does not like Taylor's music, while Kim Kardashian is not anymore a fan of Taylor Swift;
- during Saint Pablo Tour in various places around USA, Kanye West, through live speaking and by interpreting his song *Famous*, created a feeling of encouragement in his concerts where fans started shouting 'bitch' in reference to Taylor Swift;
- Kanye West made a guest appearance at Drake's concert in Chicago, and spoke out about Taylor Swift; Kanye West told his fans, 'All I gotta say is, I am so glad my wife has Snapchat!', 'Now y'all can know the truth and can't nobody talk s–t about 'Ye no more.' After his words, he performed the *song Famous* and people chanted 'bitch' in reference to Taylor Swift.[698]

Cruel Summer[699]: Kanye West has a compilation album with the same name released on September 14, 2012[700];

Lyrics:

'Shiny toy with a price, You know that I bought it': Kanye West wanted Taylor Swift's support by promoting his song on her Twitter account, which she declined; Taylor Swift wanted to hear the full song, and then to decide her next step; Kanye West told Taylor Swift that if she says the song is good and she likes it, the people will be into his song; Taylor Swift said to Kanye West that she will think about it, and was positive about his song.

Lover[701]:

- in 2015 Kanye West called Taylor Swift and asked her to present the *MTV Michael Jackson Video Vanguard Award,* and Taylor accepted his request; during this event, Taylor Swift sat next to his wife, Kim Kardashian; after the ceremony, Kanye West sent flowers to Taylor Swift;
- in 2016, at the MTV VMA, Kanye West was allowed to have a speech in which she mentioned the *song Famous*, by saying 'But bro, like, I love all y'all. That's why I called

[698] Elias Leight, idem.

[699] Taylor Swift, 'Cruel Summer Lyrics', *Genius*, available at: https://genius.com/Taylor-swift-cruel-summer-lyrics, last accessed: March 27, 2020.

[700] Kanye West, 'Cruel Summer (GOOD Music Album)', *Wikipedia*, available at: https://en.wikipedia.org/wiki/Cruel_Summer_(GOOD_Music_album), last accessed: March 27, 2020.

[701] Taylor Swift, 'Lover Lyrics', *Genius*, available at: https://genius.com/Taylor-swift-lover-lyrics, last accessed: March 27, 2020.

her'; however, at the same time, Kanye mislead all the people who says he loves so much by mentioning only parts that are in his benefit, not the whole and true story of the telephone conversation, and what Taylor Swift really knew; during his entrance on the stage, the *song Famous* was being played at the part where Kanye sings: 'I made that bitch famous', twice; at the end of his speech, Kanye presented the music video for *Fade*, a song from the album *The Life of Pablo*; *Fade* has the following lyrics: 'Your love is fadin', Know it ain't no wrong, I feel it's fadin', I think I think too much, I feel it's fadin', Ain't nobody watchin'[702]; in the video Teyana Taylor (born on December 10, 1990, one year after Taylor Swift) is the main dancer;

- in the song *Swish, Swish*, Nicki Minaj sings the lyrics 'Don't be tryna double back, I already despise you, All that fake love you showin', Couldn't even disguise you, Ran? When? Nicki getting' tan, Mirror mirror who's the fairest bitch in all the land, Damn, man, this bitch is a Stan, Muah, muah, the generous queen will kiss a fan, Ass goodbye, I'ma be riding by, I'ma tell my n- Biggz, yeah that's tha guy, A star's a star, da ha da ha, They never thought the swish god would take it this far, Get my pimp cup, this is pimp shit, baby, I only rock with Queens, so I'm makin' hits with Katy'[703];
- in 2019 Taylor Swift released the song *Lover* (also the name of the album) written by herself;
- in 2019 at the MTV VMA, Taylor Swift performed a live version of her song *Lover* and won (voted by fans) *Video of the Year Award* for *You Need to Calm Down* music video (a song from her album *Lover*), which is 10 years from the first *Famous* feud event.

Miss Americana & The Heartbreak Prince[704]:

- *80s & Heartbreak* is the name of Kanye West album released on November 24, 2008.
- 'I just wanted you to know': (lyrics from the song 'Famous', *The Life of Pablo*, Kanye West, 2016)[705];
- '[…] Just thought you should know' (lyrics from 'Miss Americana & The Heartbreak Prince', *Lover*, Taylor Swift, 2019).

False God[706]:

---

[702] Kanye West, 'Fade Lyrics', *Genius*, available at: https://genius.com/Kanye-west-fade-lyrics, last accessed: March 27, 2020.

[703] Katy Perry, 'Swish, Swish Lyrics'.

[704] Taylor Swift, 'Miss Americana & The Heartbreak Prince Lyrics', *Genius*, available at: https://genius.com/Taylor-swift-miss-americana-and-the-heartbreak-prince-lyrics, last accessed: March 27, 2020.

[705] Kanye West, 'Famous Lyrics', *Genius*, available at: https://genius.com/Kanye-west-famous-lyrics, last accessed: March 27, 2020.

[706] Taylor Swift, 'False God Lyrics', *Genius*, available at: https://genius.com/Taylor-swift-false-god-lyrics, last accessed: March 27, 2020.

V. THE **FAMOUS** FEUD: STRATEGIES OF INTERPRETATION AND COMMUNICATION

- Kanye West compared himself with many famous characters, including Jesus in his album *Yeezus* (close reference with Jesus);[707] Kanye West released various gospel songs before 2019, however, Taylor Swift used the following lyrics:

'Religion's in your lips, Even if it's a false god, We'd still worship, You're the West Village, You still do it for me, babe'.

- the lyrics may be a reference to the following idea: despite Kanye misleading the general public about her real implication in the *song Famous* and chanting 'bitch' in his concerts, there are still people who believe and bow their heads at Kanye's altar.

2. Songs/Album/Video music creation:

- she followed Kanye West steps to create the *song Famous*: phone call, samples, used the artwork created by other people.

Look What You Made Me Do (lyrics):

- she called the artists of the song that she sampled just as Kanye West called her; however, the difference is that she recognized the real artists, and the conversation between them was peaceful and true[708];
- the other side of the coin (translation into English of *Il Rovescio Della Medgalia*); Kanye West used a sample from the song *Mi Sono Svegliato E...Ho Chiuso Gli Occhi*, by Il Rovescio Della Medaglia[709];
- Taylor Swift is afraid of being recorded, however, Kanye West did it and Kim Kardashian released to the general public edited parts of their telephone

[707] Lyneka Little, 'Surprise! Kanye West Compares Himself to Jesus', *The Wall Street Journal*, June 14, 2013, available at: https://www.wsj.com/articles/BL-SEB-75185; last accessed: March 27, 2020; Michael Rothman, 'Kanye West's Most Egotistical Comparisons Ever', *ABC News*, October 10, 2013, available at: https://abcnews.go.com/Entertainment/kanye-wests-best-comparisons/story?id=20528936; last accessed: March 27, 2020; Emily Barker, 'Every Preposterous Comparison Kanye West Has Made Between Himself And These Cultural Icons', *NME*, October 2, 2015, available at: ; last accessed: March 27, 2020; Ben Grieco, 'Kanye Compares Himself To Jesus In New Christian-Inspired Album', *The Oswegonian*, October 31, 2019, available at: https://www.oswegonian.com/2019/10/31/kanye-compares-himself-to-jesus-in-new-christian-inspired-album/; last accessed: March 27, 2020; Press Association, 'Kanye West compares himself to Moses and rules out releasing new music', *Christian News*, September 15, 2020, available at: https://premierchristian.news/en/news/article/kanye-west-compares-himself-to-moses-and-rules-out-releasing-new-music, last accessed: September 14, 2021.
[708] Kory Grow, 'Right Said Fred on Taylor Swift's 'Cynical' 'Look What You Made Me Do', *Rolling Stone*, August 23, 2017, available at: https://www.rollingstone.com/music/music-features/right-said-fred-on-taylor-swifts-cynical-look-what-you-made-me-do-205808/, last accessed: March 27, 2020.
[709] Il Rovescio Della Medaglia, 'Mi Sono Svegliato E...Ho Chiuso Gli Occhi', *Genius*, available at: https://genius.com/Il-rovescio-della-medaglia-mi-sono-svegliato-e-ho-chiuso-gli-occhi-lyrics, last accessed: March 27, 2020.

conversation; in the music video Taylor used the scene of Kim's robbery from Paris in 2016, which is the worst event from Kim's life[710].

Endgame music video[711]:

In the *song Famous* Kanye West used a sample from the song *Rock the Boat* by Aaliyah[712]; in this song, Aaliyah is dancing on the boat with other girls; in the music video of *Endgame*, Taylor is dancing on a yacht with other girls[713].

...Ready for it? music video:

- in the music video[714], seconds 8-9, Taylor Swift opens her left eye: Kanye West used a sample from the song *Mi Sono Svegliato E...Ho Chiuso Gli Occhi*, by Il Rovescio Della Medaglia; translated into English, the title is close to: *I Woke Up, and I Closed My Eyes, by The Other Side of the Coin*; also, this opening scene and the sample used by Kanye West, could be linked with the reference to the trend from July 2016, named *#TaylorSwiftOverParty*: thousands of users tweeted that Taylor Swift is dead because the truth is out and she is guilty: a mural was created in Australia, and her birth and dead years were written on the left side: 1989 – 2016.

Delicate music video:

Kanye West used samples and ideas from other artists[715], then promoted himself as somehow the owner of those ideas; also, was accused of copying other artists without their

---

[710] Aurelie Corinthios, Julia Emmanuele, Lanford Beard, 'Everything We Know About Kim Kardashian West's Paris Heist', *People*, December 2, 2020, available at: https://people.com/tv/kim-kardashian-robbery-questions-answered/, last accessed: December 5, 2020.

[711] Taylor Swift, 'Engame', *Youtube*, January 12, 2018, available at: https://www.youtube.com/watch?v=dfnCAmr569k, last accessed: March 27, 2020.

[712] Aliyah, 'Rock the Boat', *Youtube*, September 10, 2021, available at: https://www.youtube.com/watch?v=3HSJU5fDg0A, last accessed: September 14, 2021.

[713] Taylor Swift, 'Endgame', *Youtube*.

[714] Taylor Swift, '...Ready for it?', *Youtube*, October 27, 2017, available at: https://www.youtube.com/watch?v=wIft-t-MQuE, last accessed: September 14, 2021.

[715] Some accusations: Wenn, 'West Accused Of Copying French Film In New Video', *Contact Music*, February 22, 2011, available at: https://www.contactmusic.com/kanye-west/news/west-accused-of-copying-french-film-in-new-video_1203310, last accessed: March 27, 2020; 'Kanye West accused of copyright theft by Hungarian rock singer', *BBC*, May 24, 2016, available at: https://www.bbc.co.uk/news/entertainment-arts-36367591, last accessed: March 27, 2020; Cassidy Mantor, 'Kanye West's Yeezy sued for copying camo print', *Fashion Network*, March 19, 2018, available at: https://ww.fashionnetwork.com/news/kanye-west-s-yeezy-sued-for-copying-camo-print,959797.html, last accessed: March 27, 2020; Susanna Heller, 'Kim Kardashian and Kanye West are being accused of copying famous designers with their new kids' clothing line', *Insider*, December 6, 2017, available at: https://www.insider.com/kim-kardashian-kanye-west-accused-of-copying-famous-designers-2017-12, last accessed: March 27, 2020; Clemence Michallon, 'Seeing double? Kanye West's fashion label Yeezy is SUED over accusations that it 'ripped off' another brand's camo designs', *The Daily Mail*, March 16, 2018, available at: https://www.dailymail.co.uk/femail/article-5506945/Kanye-Wests-Yeezy-accused-ripping-designs.html, last accessed: March 27, 2020; Samantha Ibrahim, 'Kanye West accused of stealing

permission; Taylor Swift maybe used the same strategy for *Delicate* music video: she was accused of copying and ripping off a Kenzo advert.[716]

However, maybe Taylor Swift did it before *Delicate* music video with *Shake It Off* music video in 2014: there is a similarity between her music video and Kanye West's music video *Runaway*: Taylor is dressed as a ballerina and she is dancing; in Kanye West's song ballerinas are also playing, while Kanye is using the piano. Also, the videos *Bad Blood* by Taylor Swift and *Stronger* by Kanye West have one similarity: in the beginning of the video, both artists are using technology to repair their bodies, and to become stronger (is like *Bad Blood* from 2014 is one video with two targets: Kanye West and Katy Perry, exactly like *Look What You Made Me Do* from 2017: references to Katy Perry and Kanye West, but also other people).

Use of sample from same category of music:

- Taylor Swift used samples from 'Humpty Dumpty' which is a character in an English nursery rhyme and one of the best known in the English-speaking world;[717]
- Kanye West used sample in the song 'Bad News' (from the album *808s & Heartbreak*, 2008) from 'Sea Lion Woman' which is a traditional African American folk song originally used as a children's playground song.[718]

3. Album theme: dark and light; Taylor Swift seems to followed the path of two albums released by Kanye West, and in which she was one of the characters who inspired songs from his albums:

- *Kanye West*:

    My Beautiful Dark Twisted Fantasy (2010): an album that tries to erase the mistakes of the past and an apology to Taylor Swift (I tried to find a specific, clear lyrics and song dedicated to Taylor Swift as apology, however, I did not find anything to support his statement'; from Taylor Swift there is a specific, clear lyrics and song dedicated to Kanye West about the incident and her forgiveness: 'Innocent' on *Speak Now* album); it is the album of a man with a

'Donda' logo from black-owned company', *New York Post*, August 31, 2021, available at: https://nypost.com/2021/08/31/kanye-west-accused-of-allegedly-stealing-donda-album-logo-design/, last accessed: September 12, 2021.

[716] 'Taylor Swift: Delicate Video Accused of Copying Kenzo Advert', *BBC*, March 13, 2018, available at: https://www.bbc.co.uk/news/newsbeat-43382742, last accessed: March 27, 2020; Diana Samson, 'Is Taylor Swift's 'Delicate' Music Video A Rip Off Of A Perfume Ad?', *Music Times*, March 13, 2018, available at: https://www.musictimes.com/articles/78315/20180313/is-taylor-swift-s-delicate-music-video-a-rip-off-of-a-perfume-ad.htm, last accessed: March 27, 2020.

[717] Lyrics: 'Humpty, Dumpty', *Genius*, available at: https://genius.com/Children-songs-humpty-dumpty-annotated, last accessed: February 25, 2020; 'Humpty Dumpty', *Wikipedia*, available at: https://en.wikipedia.org/wiki/Humpty_Dumpty; last accessed: February 25, 2020.

[718] 'Sea Lion Woman', *Wikipedia*, available at: https://en.wikipedia.org/wiki/Sea_Lion_Woman, last accessed: February 25, 2020.

negative reputation obtained after interrupting Taylor Swift's speech at the MTV VMA Awards in 2009; the album was created during self-imposed exile;

The Life of Pablo (2016): an album describing the overall life (family, love, faith, importance) of a man named Pablo (possible Kanye West);

- *Taylor Swift*:

    reputation (2017): an album with a dark theme and design that describes the life of a person with a negative reputation based on gossips and lies, and the search for love in a dark period of her life; the album was created during self-imposed exile which, according to fans and mass-media[719], it could be due to negative presentation to the general public of her side of the story in the creation of the song *Famous,* and her failure to respond according to the expectations of Kanye, Kim and some Western journalists who unjustly sanctioned her;

    Lover (2019): covers all facets of love and represents a character who loves life and comes to conclusions that help her to overcome the state of negativity, and she realises that 'is morning' and 'love is golden'.

    Through two albums, *reputation* and *Lover*, maybe Taylor Swift closed the circle started by Kanye West in 2009 and continued in 2016.

4. Marketing:

Taylor Swift and Kanye West:

- first, Kanye West used Taylor Swift in the *song Famous*, interviews and the musical tour, *Saint Pablo Tour* 2016; second, Taylor Swift used references in her songs, music videos and the musical tour, *Taylor Swift's Stadium Reputation Tour*, 2018;
- in 2018, Kanye West released his eight album, *ye,* which is stylized with lower letters as Taylor Swift's *reputation*; in 2020, on October 27 (same release date as Taylor Swift with *Speak Now* album in 2010) released the album *Jesus is King*, which has 27:04

---

[719] Laura Harding, 'Taylor Swift addresses self-imposed exile and Joe Alwyn romance in Netflix film', *Belfast Telegraph*, January 31, 2020, available at: https://www.belfasttelegraph.co.uk/entertainment/film-tv/news/taylor-swift-addresses-self-imposed-exile-and-joe-alwyn-romance-in-netflix-film/38913520.html, last accessed: October 30, 2020; Tobi Akingbade, 'Miss Americana: Taylor Swift opens up on self-imposed exile after Kanye West feud', *Evening Standard*, January 31, 2020, available at: https://www.standard.co.uk/showbiz/celebrity-news/taylor-swift-kanye-west-miss-americana-netflix-a4350226.html; last accessed: October 30, 2020.

minutes[720], which (based on how Taylor Swift includes easter eggs in her statements, lyrics and music video) calculated as individual numbers, we have the following maths calculation: 2+7+4=13 (the birth date of Taylor Swift and her lucky number);

- merchandise to promote her album, *reputation*: similarities between *reputation's* merch and Kanye West's merch for the album *The Life of Pablo*: fonts, colour palette, clothes category, album covers etc;[721]
- in July 2016 Kanye West and Kim Kardashian had an interview with Laura Brown for the Harper's Bazaar: both expressed an opinion about Taylor Swift[722]; in July 2018, Taylor Swift was interviewed by Pattie Boyd for the Harper's Bazaar; in this interview Taylor Swift did not mention Kanye West or Kim Kardashian, but instead she focused on speaking about her abilities as songwriter: this point is interesting, since in the first part of this investigation, *Black and White Music*, I exposed Kanye West being in partnership with more producers, lyricists, and his discography contains samples (title, lyrics, instruments) from other artists, which is in high negative contrast with Taylor Swift (she writes all the songs on her albums; the final songs and album belongs to her to a greater extent in comparison with Kanye West).

Taylor Swift and Katy Perry:

- Weeks before the release of the album, Katy Perry confessed about Taylor Swift's song *Bad Blood* being about her. Katy Perry said, according to American Songwriter:

'Honestly, [Swift] started it, and it's time for her to finish it.' […] 'It's about backing dancers. It's so crazy,' she continued. 'There [are] three backing dancers that went on tour with her tour, and they asked me before they went on tour if they could go. I was like, 'Yeah, of course. I'm not on a record cycle. Get the work. She's great. But I will be on a record cycle, probably, in about a year, so be sure to put a 30-day contingency in your contract so you can get out if you wanna join me when I say I'm going back on.' So that year came up, and I texted all of them because I'm very close with them. I said, 'Look, just FYI: I'm about to start. I want to put the word out there.' They said, 'Okay. We're gonna go talk to management about it.' They did, and they got fired. I tried to talk to [Swift] about it, and she wouldn't speak to me.' […] 'I do the right thing anytime that it feels like a fumble. It was a full shutdown, and then she writes a song about me. And I'm like 'Okay, cool, cool. That's how you wanna do it? Karma.'[723]

- *Swish, swish* song has the following lyrics which are considered by fans and mass-media to be about Taylor Swift:

---

[720] Kanye West, 'Jesus is King', *Wikipedia*, available at: https://en.wikipedia.org/wiki/Jesus_Is_King, last accessed: October 30, 2020.

[721] Susie Heller, 'Fans can't stop pointing out how much Taylor Swift's new merchandise looks like Kanye West's fashion line', *Insider*, August 25, 2017, available at: https://www.insider.com/taylor-swifts-merchandise-kanye-fashion-line-2017-8, last accessed: October 30, 2020.

[722] Carine Roitfeld, 'Icons: In Bed with Kim and Kanye'.

[723] Catherine Walthall, 'Behind the Beef: Katy Perry and Taylor Swift's Feud Explained Blow By Blow'.

'You're calculated, I got your number, 'Cause you're a joker, And I'm a courtside killer queen, And you will kiss the ring, You best believe, Your game is tired, You should retire, You're 'bout cute as, An old coupon expired, And karma's not a liar, She keeps receipts;'[724]

- on the day of her album release, the world witnessed Taylor Swift's decision to release her entire music catalogue on streaming services for the first time:

'In celebration of 1989 selling over 10 million albums worldwide and the RIAA's 100 million song certification announcement, Taylor wants to thank her fans by making her entire catalogue available to all streaming services tonight at midnight';

- furthermore, in August 2017, Taylor Swift released the first single, *Look What You Made Me Do*, from the new album, *reputation*; fans and mass-media think is also a reply through music to Katy Perry.

---

[724] Katy Perry, idem.

VI. **FAMOUS** REASONS FOR A **FAMOUS** FEUD[725]

In this chapter I wrote various hypothetical and negative reasons as possible answers to the following question: why *Famous* feud was created and supported for more than 10 years? The hypothetical reasons and answers are based on the information used in this report. Maybe the answers written below have the possibility to be true to some extent, and could help in making a better understanding of the events between Kanye West and Taylor Swift. There are more negative reasons for Kanye West, because he started the feud, and Taylor Swift was in defence mode.

Kanye West:

- wanted to have enough publicity to get customers for his album *The Life of Pablo*: Kanye West lost half of his popularity in the USA first week pure sales in 1 year (from 2007 to 2008, and after three successful albums and high increase), and remained low (in comparison with the first three albums); in September 2009 (the start of the feud) Taylor Swift was on the natural path of increasing as global pop artist, while Kanye West was decreasing as global rap artist;
- does not make enough money from music (used many samples from various artists), and has to share the money, which means less money for him to live up to the level he aspires to; if music doesn't help him to make enough money, he resorted to other methods, including the shoes business with Adidas;
- to maintain his presence (even negative) on the music market and business with clothes;
- played the victim's card to sell clothes, shoes and music to make money to pay his debts, and to become a free person;
- to distract the negative attention from him to Taylor Swift, so he can fulfil his dreams, while Taylor Swift had to fight the misleading narrative he told and credited/promoted by mass-media;
- what if 'bitch' lyric was based on Taylor Swift's word used in the telephone conversation: 'That stupid, dumb bitch'? did Kanye West changed his mind and used

---

[725] Parts of this chapter were used also in Casian Anton, *Black and White Music*.

Taylor Swift's word, because she refused him (until she thinks about the song), and his plan would have been ruined?

- what if Kanye West interfered in Taylor Swift's album release pattern a year earlier (2007), and then justified the release of the next album (2008) in the same timeframe as Taylor Swift? this strategy maybe was used with the purpose to create a racial comparison: Kanye West (black man) received better reviews than Taylor Swift (white woman), and that Taylor Swift success is because she is white, not because she has better music than him? yet, Taylor Swift came with her lyrics, and Kanye West came with samples from other artists;

- what if Kanye West accused Taylor Swift of doing what he did in order to cover his track, and other artists that he is supporting by creating a negative view about her? the end of this strategy is to create a negative wave about Taylor Swift, hoping that her fans will get sick of the negative stories that she is involved too often, and switch to his favourite artists, such as Beyoncé, because there are no negative stories about her?

- MTV VMA 2015: what if Kanye West tried to humiliate Taylor Swift by asking her (the girl who should not get the award, despite being voted by fans) to give him the award, even though he was the one who didn't give her the courtesy to end the speech of thanks to her fans?

- if *My Beautiful Dark Twisted Fantasy* was the apology album offered to Taylor Swift, then what are the specific lyrics with the necessary apologies dedicated to Taylor Swift? according to this research (by reading the lyrics of the songs from this album), Kanye West does not provide specific details of his apology that is easy to observe and understand by fans and the general public; on the contrary, Taylor Swift wrote the song 'Innocent' and her fans know (and maybe to a larger extent by the general public) that this song is addressed to Kanye West as a sign of forgiveness;

- what if Kanye West found out that Taylor Swift planned to release on July 24, 2020 the album *folklore,* and stepped in her narrative line of album release (once again) with the announcement that he on July 24th, 2020 will release the album *Donda* (in her mother's memory)[726], in order to create a negative narrative in Taylor Swift's line? the negative narrative is as follows: the purpose for which Taylor Swift intervenes in his narrative line is to show disrespect and lack of manners to the memory of his mother, *Donda*, as it happened on November 10, 2017? (this is the day of Kanye West's mother's death; also, this is the day of the release of her album *reputation*: some Kanye West's fans accused Taylor Swift, and the release of the album on the

[726] Saint, 'Tweet', *Twitter*, July 18, 2020, available at: https://twitter.com/saint/status/1284616155244703750?lang=en, last accessed: July 21, 2021; Bryan Rolli, 'Kanye West Is Apparently, Maybe, Releasing A New Album Called 'Donda' Next Week', *Forbes*, July 18, 2020, available at: https://www.forbes.com/sites/bryanrolli/2020/07/18/kanye-west-announces-new-album-donda/?sh=1dac593a1523, last accessed: July 21, 2021; Luke Morgan Britton, 'Kanye West's much-delayed 10th album 'DONDA': the story so far', *NME*, August 9, 2021, available at: https://www.nme.com/blogs/nme-blogs/kanye-wests-donda-album-everything-we-know-2898638, last accessed: August 11, 2021.

day of Donda's death, as being disrespectful and an insensitive method of attack on Kanye West; Big Machine's (Taylor Swift's label at that time) response was: 'It is standard practice that releases come out on Fridays and we locked in this release date based on other Universal Music Group releases' [...] There is no correlation.'[727]); Kanye West did not release the album in July 2020, but on August 29, 2021: what if the name *Donda* came to his mind after learning that Taylor Swift planned to release a new music album, that she is involved in a new musical genre for her, and he decided to intervene, so that people would hate her and give up listening to her music? well, if that was the plan, it didn't work: in the end, *folklore* album was a resounding worldwide success and won the *Album of the Year* at the Grammy Awards in 2021 (for Taylor Swift this is her third win, the only female in the music history of The Recording Academy to achieve this record); what if in July 2020 Kanye West had only the title of the album and no songs written, and no samples available to use, and that is why he released the album a year later in 2021? from July 2020 until August 28, 2021 Kanye West had enough time to create music and plans to justify the existence of the album, and not be considered a persistent liar (because he does not release the albums on the promised day)[728];

- what if Kanye West refused to publicly say that Taylor Swift has the right to publicly challenge the new line he added and without informing Taylor Swift, with the purpose of using the video recording to influence people to buy his concert tickets? after all, he is a black man who tells the truth and deserves to play concerts in the USA? Kim Kardashian spoke about the video evidence the week his concert tickets went on sale;

- what if Kanye West refused to publicly say that Taylor Swift has the right to publicly challenge the new line he added without informing Taylor Swift, because otherwise he would not have had a great source of publicity (Taylor Swift, America's Sweetheart) for at least 6 months before his *Saint Pablo Tour* started? Kanye West's public acknowledgment (of the topics during his conversation with Taylor Swift, immediately after the release of the song *Famous* in February 2016) would have been a per se erasure of any negative feeling towards Taylor Swift from the general public, a self-incrimination of his decision to record the telephone conversation, and using it against Taylor Swift; in the long run, Kanye West's self-admission of the actual phone conversation with Taylor Swift would not have helped him to create a high interest from his fans, the general public, and the Western mass-media in his music and tour:

[727] Roisin O'Conner, 'Taylor Swift: Reputation release date coinciding with anniversary of Donda West death is a 'coincidence', *The Independent*, August 26, 2017, available at: https://www.independent.co.uk/arts-entertainment/music/news/taylor-swift-donda-west-reputation-release-date-kanye-kim-kardashian-album-tour-dates-a7914191.html, last accessed: March 27, 2020.

[728] Bryan Rolli, 'Kanye West Is Apparently, Maybe, Releasing A New Album Called 'Donda' Next Week'; Morgan Britton, 'Kanye West's much-delayed 10th album 'DONDA': the story so far'. Rebecca Laurence, ''Did I miss something?!' Kanye West fans fuming as rapper DOESN'T release new album Donda (despite holding a streaming event) with lucky few attendees raving about new track', *Daily Mail*, July 23, 2021, available at: https://www.dailymail.co.uk/tvshowbiz/article-9818173/Kanye-West-fans-fuming-rapper-DOESNT-release-new-album-Donda.html; last accessed: August 11, 2021.

from February 2016 (the release of the song *Famous*) – to November 2016 (the last month of the tour);

- what if Kanye West has no mental health problems, but it is a long-term scam? the strategies used towards Taylor Swift and in his private life, published by various news agencies, offer the image of a man that is able to successfully follow and use a sense of rational thinking; moreover, he has too well thought out movements for a person facing mental problems;

- in 2015 Kanye West said that Taylor Swift wants to go with him in the studio, and he does not discriminate; however, in 2016 Kanye West said, in the interview for the Harper's Bazaar, that he does not have a favourite song of Taylor Swift, therefore: why Kanye West wanted to work with Taylor Swift although he does not have a favourite song from her catalogue? what if one of the album titles he had, namely SWISH, was actually planned with this name because Kanye wanted and expected Taylor Swift to work with him, and since Taylor Swift did not agree with him on the telephone (Taylor Swift said: 'I need to think about it') Kanye West had a reason to change his attitude about her music, turned against Taylor Swift's public character and added the infamous lyrics? Kanye West struggles to create titles for his songs and samples other artists, and is he capable of creating a song for Taylor Swift that he could have as favourite? if this was the plan, Kanye West had in mind to use other people's work to create a good song for Taylor Swift, or was willing to believe in the songwriting abilities of Taylor Swift to create original music, as she did before knowing Kanye West, and together to be awarded only based on their abilities to make music?

- what if his mental health problems is the ultimate strategy to cover up and justify the dirty tricks used on Taylor Swift, on the general public to forgive him for what he did/does to Taylor Swift and Kim Kardashian (maybe he forced her to publish the edited videos to hurt an innocent woman, which contradicts the pro-women ideas promoted by Kim Kardashian; to be able to sell albums and clothes, to hide behind the release of albums with poor quality, because his talent expired and used all the samples that could have brought him more financial and critical success than before, and now he has nothing valuable and real worthy of attention?

- what if his divorce from Kim Kardashian's is the second ultimate marketing strategy for both? both maintain their popularity and visibility in the Western mass-media, the world loves a scandal between famous people; what if in the end, both will end up together, a sort of family reunion due to Kanye West's mental problems: but now that is in the past, Kanye West is cured, Kim Kardashian is more mature than before, have a new story to present, new clothes, new music and new purchases by fans, and more money for both?

Kanye West, Beyoncé and Jay Z:

- what if Beyoncé and Jay Z were part of the plan in 2009 for the MTV Awards?
- what if Kanye West and Jay Z developed the plan for MTV Awards in 2009 without Beyoncé's knowledge?
- what if Kanye West played The Bad Man (interrupted the speech) and Beyoncé the Good Woman (offered the chance to Taylor Swift to thank the fans for the award) at the MTV Awards? And if that was the plan, let's see how it could have been done in practice:

   o *Step 1*. Kanye West (black man) entered the stage and interrupted Taylor Swift's speech (white woman) on the reason that she does not deserve the award, even if it was voted by the public, and that Beyoncé deserved the award;

   o *Step 2*. Taylor Swift does not end the speech to thank her fans;

   o *Step 3*. Beyoncé (black woman) fixed the narrative and gave Taylor Swift (white woman) her time to finish the speech (time that she received because she won *Video of the Year*), but first she mentioned her success: 'I remember being 17 years old, up for my first MTV Award with Destiny's Child, and it was one of the most exciting moments in my life, so, I'd like for Taylor to come out and have her moment '; this is a situation where the black artist, with the award of the year, offered the opportunity to the white artist (with the negative image that she does not deserve the award) to finish her speech; what if the staff behind the curtain knew that Beyoncé will get the award, and the plan was set up before the award ceremony?

- what if Taylor Swift's career and progress was closely watched by Kanye West and Jay Z (probably with other people in their circle), and came to the conclusion that Taylor Swift would be the next famous pop artist in the USA and in the world (because she has the power to write her songs), and interfered in her narrative to destroy it, or to insert in the audience's memory that Taylor Swift could not have been a successful artist without a black artist (through Kanye West)?
- what if the release of Beyoncé's album on November 12 was her idea, but also Jay Z and Kanye West were involved in making this decision (the day after the release of Taylor Swift's album, *Fearless*) and then November 18 (in the USA)?
- what if Kanye West's album release pattern (November 24, 2008) was made in order to block Taylor Swift (November 11) to reach number 1 for several weeks, to reduce the popularity she enjoyed and grew every year since her debut in 2006?
- what if Beyoncé (maybe got an idea from her husband Jay Z) changed her album name and included the word *Fierce*, which has a similar meaning to *Fearless*, and entered into direct and planned competition with Taylor Swift? in 2008 both artists

used the same theme, *fear*, and in 2009 both artists competed for an award at the MTV VMA;

- what if the albums released by Beyoncé (*I Am… Sasha Fierce*) a week later after Taylor Swift, then Kanye West (*808s & Heartbreak*) two weeks later than Taylor Swift and one week later than Beyoncé, were made in order to advance three strategies of promotion:

  4. to block Taylor Swift to create and have a strong influence in top charts around the USA for at least two weeks after her album release;

  5. Kanye West interfered in Taylor Swift's album release pattern a year earlier (2007), and then again with the next album (2008), which might have created (intentional or unintentional) a racial comparison: Kanye West (black man) received better reviews than Taylor Swift (white woman); Beyoncé interfered in Taylor Swift's album release pattern for the first time, but her high number of fans blocked Taylor Swift to reach number 1 for the second week, and Kanye West's fans blocked Taylor Swift on the third week;

  6. to create a sense of *leave Taylor in the past*, now focus on Beyoncé and Kanye West;

  however, if these 3 strategies of promotion for their album were actually put into practice, on long term they failed: Taylor Swift came with her own lyrics, and in 2008 had stronger albums sales in the USA than Beyoncé and Kanye West.[729]

- what if Beyoncé released the surprise album, *Beyoncé*, intentionally on Taylor Swift's birthday (December 13, 2013) as a sublime message: look who Beyoncé is and I'm coming after you (she did not win the Grammy Awards for the *Album of the Year*);
- what if Kanye West and Jay Z knew Taylor Swift is the winner of the *Best Female Video Award* before the ceremony, and Kanye West decided to bring a bottle of alcohol with him to cover his plan?[730] just as he probably knew Taylor Swift wrote a song for him, and said that he also wrote a song for her (I did not find information that he really wrote a song for Taylor Swift (maybe he said it as a marketing strategy, to not to

[729] Randy Lewis, Taylor Swift, 'Lil Wayne led music sales in 2008', *Seattle Times*, January 22, 2009, available at: https://www.seattletimes.com/entertainment/taylor-swift-lil-wayne-led-music-sales-in-2008/, last accessed: February 25, 2021.
[730] Atlien, '2009 MTV VMAs: Kanye West ~ Blame it on the ALCOHOL!', *Straight From the A*, September 14, 2009, available at: https://straightfromthea.com/2009/09/14/2009-mtv-vmas-kanye-west-blame-it-on-the-alcohol/, last accessed: February 25, 2021; Lauren McIver, 'KIM'S HELL Kanye West admits he was an 'alcoholic' who drank 'Grey Goose and orange juice' in the morning- but no longer drinks', *The Sun*, April 15, 2020, available at: https://www.thesun.co.uk/tvandshowbiz/11404128/kanye-west-alcoholic-drank-grey-goose-morning-no-longer/, last accessed: February 25, 2021; James Robertson, 'Kanye West: I needed God, booze and lots of sex after Taylor Swift scandal', *Mirror*, January 21, 2014, available at: https://www.mirror.co.uk/3am/celebrity-news/kanye-west-needed-sex-alcohol-3042866, last accessed: February 25, 2021.

be lower than Taylor Swift in the eyes of the general public)), and may have known some of the lyrics: CBS[731] wrote an article with content from Kanye West published on his Twitter account: 'When I woke up from the crazy nightmare I looked in the mirror and said GROW UP KANYE... '; after few days Taylor Swift sang the lyrics of the song *Innocent* written for Kanye West and played at the MTV Awards: '32 and still growin'up now'; what are the chances for Kanye West to use words so close to Taylor Swift's lyrics? if there was a leak about the lyrics written by Taylor Swift for Kanye West, who provided the information?

- what if the release of the album by Kanye West and Beyoncé in 2008, then the disagreement with the MTV award in 2009, and finally the release of the album in 2010 (for Kanye West), respectively in 2011 (for Beyoncé), was actually a long-term plan in order to present themselves as better than the white artist Taylor Swift, to diminish her popularity and creativity in the music industry?

- what if Jay Z and Kanye West are actually fighting Taylor Swift's influence over people and the music industry in which they do not accept her records, and do whatever it takes to keep Beyoncé on top?

- what if Kanye West, Jay Z and Beyoncé are too desperate to win the awards and be recognized more than they are in reality? what if they create all sorts of plans that in the end do not work, create more damage for themselves and blame other people?

- in 2017 the relationship between Kanye West and Jay Z was not so good, however, in 2019 it was reported that they are again on good terms[732]; what if this tension between them is false and was created as a solution to change the focus on a different topic considering *Tidal* was the platform where Kanye exclusively released his song with lyrics that put him and Taylor Swift in difficulty, also about the Tidal false plays? what if the new better terms of the relationship between Kanye and Jay Z (from December 2019) happened as a sublime and reply message to Taylor Swift, which she could have a line about their bad relationship in one of her songs from *reputation*, *This Is Why We Can't Have Nice Things*: 'but I'm not the only friend you've lost lately/if only you weren't so shady'?

- what if Kanye and Jay Z are behind these dark strategies, and everything that the album patterns show in this report? what if Beyoncé has no idea about the tricks, even if it benefits her by having a positive image?

- what if Beyoncé's *Lemonade* album (including Jay Z) were part of Kanye West's strategy against Taylor Swift in 2016? and if this was the plan, maybe it was put into motion based on the steps written below:

Step 1:

---

[731] Devon Thomas, 'Kanye West Writes Song in Honor of Taylor Swift', *CBS*, September 7, 2010, available at: https: // www. cbsnews.com/news/kanye-west-writes-song-in-honor-of-taylor-swift/, last accessed: February 25, 2021.
[732] Rianne Addo, 'Kanye West and Jay-Z are back on friendly terms two years after Tidal lawsuit left their complicated relationship on the rocks', *MailOnline*, December 17, 2019, available at: https://www.dailymail.co.uk/tvshowbiz/article-7800777/Kanye-West-Jay-Z-friendly-terms-two-years-Tidal-lawsuit.html, last accessed: February 25, 2021.

- Kanye West released the song *Famous* (The Life of Pablo) where Taylor Swift is called 'that bitch'; Taylor entered the narrative created and promoted by Kanye by writing the truth: she did not know the lyrics in which she was called 'that bitch';

Step 2:

- Taylor was assailed by negative comments on social media, and the preferred term to address and label her character was 'bitch';

Step 3:

- Kanye promised that his album, *The Life of Pablo*, will be available exclusively on the *Tidal* platform (the platform owned also by Jay Z); however, on April 1, 2016, his album was made available on *Apple Music*, which led to the accusation that he cheated the audience; according to an article in Variety: 'By the time Mr. West changed course and broadly released 'The Life of Pablo,' the deceptive marketing ploy had served its purpose: Tidal's subscriber numbers had tripled, streaming numbers were through the roof, and Tidal had collected the personal information, credit card numbers, and social media information of millions of deceived consumers […] Instead, they just wanted to boost Tidal's subscriber numbers – which indeed did get a big bump from the release. Tidal may have signed up as many as two million new subscribers thanks to the album, claims the lawsuit, arguing that this could have added as much as $84 million to Tidal's valuation;'[733]

Step 4:

- Beyoncé released the surprise album *Lemonade* on April 23, 2016; Taylor Swift was caught in the negative narrative created and promoted by Kanye West; *Lemonade* enjoyed success from critics being considered the best album released by Beyoncé; on Tidal, *Lemonade* was streamed 115 million times, setting a record for the most-streamed album in a single week by a female artist; what if Kanye West, through the exclusivity strategy of his album, plus the use of Taylor in his song, spread the narrative that in his album there could be something more about Taylor,

---

[733] Janko Roettgers, 'Kanye West Tricked Fans Into Subscribing to Tidal, Lawsuit Claims', *Variety*, April 18, 2016, available at: https://variety.com/2016/digital/news/kanye-west-tricked-fans-into-subscribing-to-tidal-lawsuit-claims-1201755580/, last accessed: February 25, 2021.

which led to the growth of curious users and, in the end, some users decided to stay on the platform? at the same time, maybe the new number of users were used to justify the record number of plays of his album, *The Life of Pablo*, and Beyoncé's *Lemonade*?

Step 5:

- in July 2016, the positive popular opinion was on Kanye's side, especially after Kim Kardashian (Kanye's wife at the time of the event) published edited parts of the phone conversation between Kanye and Taylor; the conclusion of the published videos is that Taylor knew about everything; at this time, the public image of Taylor Swift was negative;

Step 6:

- based on her previous pattern release, Taylor releases the first song in August or September, but the *Famous* feud and the negative image obtained as a result of Kanye's song, her strategy and public image do not allow her to release a new song every two years (the last album released was in the fall of 2014, so the next album should have been in the fall of 2016); all this time Beyoncé has no competition and a positive image, while Taylor does not release a new album and has a negative image;

Step 7 (unexpected shift of the plan, and not possible to change the course of their plan):

- although *Lemonade* received the most positive reviews in her career, Beyoncé does not win the *Album of the Year* (12 songs on the album), and lost in favour of the white artist, Adele;

Step 8 (unexpected shift of the plan, and not possible to change the course of their plan):

- in 2018 Tidal was accused of intentionally falsifying the streaming number of *The Life of Pablo* and *Lemonade*, according to Variety: 'Tidal, which has rarely shared its data publicly, had a streaming exclusive on West's album for its first six weeks of release and continues to be the exclusive streamer for Beyoncé's album. It claimed that West's album had been streamed 250 million times in its first 10 days of release in February of 2016, while claiming it had just 3 million subscribers – a claim that would have meant every subscriber played the album an average of eight times per day; and that Beyoncé's album was streamed 306 million times in its first 15 days of release in April of 2016.' [...] 'Today's report, according to MBW's translation, says that 'Beyoncé's and Kanye West's listener numbers on Tidal have been manipulated to the tune of several hundred million false plays... which has generated massive royalty payouts at the expense of other artists;[734]' what if Kanye West and Jay Z's strategy to use Taylor Swift was also to increase the number of users? what if Kanye West and Jay Z used the new subscribers to falsify the numbers of plays to make more money? let's not forget that in the conversation with Taylor Kanye admitted having big debts (millions of dollars); what if the false plays was done in order to increase Beyoncé's profile and the records obtained? what if the false plays were made this route as on the other streaming platforms (Apple and Spotify) Beyoncé would not make the numbers to have new records to celebrate, and maintain relevance in the music industry as Taylor Swift does? what if the false plays and the exclusive availability of her album, *Lemonade*, on Tidal was made to show the world that she is so loved that her fans follow her on the new platform, and set new records in the music industry? what if Tidal is being used to justify a false point of view that black artists are not safe on other platforms because they are ruled by white people? what if Kanye, Jay Z and Beyoncé used Tidal for their own benefit, therefore, cheating the music industry and their fans?

Taylor Swift:

- what if the telephone interview between Kanye West and Ryan Seacrest, where Kanye West said: 'She wants to get in the studio and we're definitely going to go in', [...] 'I don't have an elitism about music, I don't discriminate'[735] is a lie, and Taylor Swift was not aware of it? in an interview with Entertainment Tonight, Cameron Mathison asked Taylor Swift about the rumoured collaboration between her and Kanye West, to which Taylor Swift answered: 'He has said that...' *(was not so sure about it: author interpretation)*', and then she was nice about Kanye West? Taylor Swift: 'We're never been in the studio together, but he's got a lot of amazing ideas, he's one of those people who's just like idea, idea, idea, like what you think of this, what you think of that, he's very creative and like I've think

[734] Jem Aswad, 'Tidal Accused of Falsifying Beyoncé and Kanye West Streaming Numbers'; Andy Cush, 'Tidal Accused of Generating 300 Million Fake Streams for Kanye and Beyoncé'; Tim Ingham, 'Tidal 'Fake Streams': Criminal Investigation Underway Over Potential Data Fraud In Norway.

[735] 'Kanye and Taylor Swift 'definitely' going to record together', *BBC News*, February 11, 2015, available at: https://www.bbc.co.uk/news/newsbeat-31418378; last accessed: February 25, 2021; On Air with Ryan Seacrest, 'Kanye West Explains Grammys Stunt, Plans to Work With Taylor Swift'.

(*not so sure, author interpretation*) we've talked about it but we've also about so many other things, I think I completely respect his vision as a producer, so that's all I know now, I have no idea how the next album is gonna be though;'[736]

- what if Taylor Swift came up with the *1989* album (the year of her birth) to complete Beyoncé 's cycle, to reply and show who she is: an original lyricist and her first pure pop album, which eventually is the winner of the *Album of the Year* at the Grammy Awards in 2016?

- what if Taylor Swift used samples in her songs to prove to Kanye West that she can do it too, it is not something hard, and she does it better and has a higher popularity than him?

- what if the mole inside Taylor Swift's team leaked the lyrics of the song *Dear John* (dark twisted games) to Kanye West and he decided to use them to name his album *My Beautiful Dark Twisted Fantasy*? Kanye West has a long list of songs based on other's artists ideas[737];

- what if Taylor Swift found out the name of Kanye West's album, and she decided to use it slightly differently in her song *Dear John* in order to remind people of the person who ruined her moment, therefore, positioning herself as a long-term white victim of a black man?

- Taylor Swift mentioned that she wanted to use existing musical instruments in the 80's for her own music: is it possible to say this as a subtle hit to Kanye West? Kanye West said that he is inspired by the music of those years ('70, '80, '90, '00), but he used instruments that did not exist at that time, and Taylor Swift came to show him how the music should sound like in those years? Kanye West presented himself as a genius in music, but he wrongly combined the instruments for the years from which he is inspired? and Taylor Swift came and gave him a subtle lesson of the correct use of musical instruments specific to the period from which he is inspired?[738]

Kanye West, Taylor Swift, Beyoncé and Western mass-media:

- what if the prediction of the album sales for Kanye West in 2013, *Yeezus*, of 500,000 copies sold in the first week[739] was made with the purpose to encourage people to buy it as it will be popular anyway? what if the prediction of the album sales for Taylor

---

[736] Entertainment Tonight, 'Taylor Swift on Rumored Kanye West Collaboration: 'He's Got a Lot of Amazing Ideas'.

[737] See Casian Anton, *Black & White Music*.

[738] This is based on an interview of Taylor Swift, but I simply lost the link. Maybe it was deleted with other articles for the Music Review chapter that I wanted to create. However, this idea was still saved in my notebook.

[739] Edna Gundersen, 'Kanye West's 'Yeezus' could debut with 500K copies', *USA Today*, June 13, 2013, available at: https://eu.usatoday.com/story/life/music/2013/06/13/kanye-west-yeezus-expected-to-sell-half-million-copies-first-week/2420829/#:~:text=Kanye%20West%27s%20Yeezus%2C%20out%20Tuesday,associate%20director%20of%20charts%2Fretail, last accessed: October 23, 2017.

Swift in 2014 (album *1989*), of 600,000 to 750,000 copies sold in the first week[740] was made with the purpose to discourage people to buy it as is a lower number than the last album, and as subtle message that she lost her fans and popularity, so there is no need to bother with her album? if we look at the number of sales in the first week, before 2013 and 2014, Kanye West had a lower number of albums sales in 2010, 2011 and 2012 with below 500,000 albums in the first week[741], and yet in 2013 the prediction increased to half a million albums sold first week; for Taylor Swift is the opposite: in 2010 and 2012 the number of album sales was over one million[742], yet in 2014 the prediction decreased to half of the last number of albums from 2012: to 600,000 to 750,000. The common point of the two predictions is that both were not true: in 2013 Kanye West's final album sales was below the prediction (327.000[743]), while in 2014 Taylor's the albums sales were higher than the prediction (1.287.000[744]); the failed prediction for the first week sales happened first with Kanye West in 2005 when his album, *Late Registration*, was predicted to sale over 1.6 million copies in the first week, however, it sold over half of the prediction, 860,000 copies[745]; what if there are people who intentionally play with the prediction (maybe a person of interest (maybe from Kanye's team or Taylor's team; or unrelated to them), but could profit somehow from the outcome) paid the source of the prediction to write it according to a specific interest, such as to modify fans' intentions and get lower and higher album sales?

- what if the *Famous* event from February 2016 offered the opportunity for envious journalists and bloggers to take revenge on Taylor Swift for the success they do not have? what if there are journalists and bloggers who are being paid for negative articles, they do not have a permanent job, and this scandal gave them the chance to use their negative imagination (which is based on their own frustrations and dissatisfaction) to project it onto a woman who did not do anything wrong to them, nor to the general public to justify the high interest in the case?
- what if an unknown number of songs, and the name of the albums released by Kanye West, Beyoncé and Taylor Swift, are a subtle/behind the curtain message to each other, and the information we already know about the pattern of album release, and the interference in Taylor Swift's pattern is the real evidence available to see it?

---

[740] Steve Knopper, 'Can Taylor Swift's '1989' Save Ailing Music Industry?', *Rolling Stone*, October 21, 2014, available at: https://www.rollingstone.com/music/music-news/can-taylor-swifts-1989-save-ailing-music-industry-170217/, last accessed: October 21, 2014.

[741] Hao Nguyen, 'Can't Tell Me Nothing: Ranking Kanye West First Week Album Sales'.

[742] Ed Christmas, 'What Taylor Swift's Million-Selling Album Means for Music'; Keith Caulfield, 'Taylor Swift's 'Red' Sells 1.21 Million; Biggest Sales Week for an Album Since 2002'; Keith Caulfield, 'Official: Taylor Swift's '1989' Debuts With 1.287 Million Sold In First Week'.

[743] Hao Nguyen, idem.

[744] Keith Caulfield, 'Official: Taylor Swift's '1989' Debuts With 1.287 Million Sold In First Week'.

[745] Hao Nguyen, idem.

In the following table I found a pattern that is happening in 2008, 2009 and 2016 and involves Taylor Swift, Kanye West and Beyoncé. The pattern is exposed in Figure 27.

TABLE 49. A **FAMOUS** ATTACK ON TAYLOR SWIFT?

EVENT/ NAME OF THE ARTIST:	TAYLOR SWIFT	BEYONCÉ	KANYE WEST
RELEASE PATTERN	Fixed pattern	Fixed pattern Changing pattern Surprise pattern	Fixed pattern Changing pattern
ALBUM RELEASE NARRATIVE LINE	2008: She followed her fixed pattern and released her album in November 2008. 2016: Taylor releases the first song in August or September, but the *Famous* feud did not allow her to release a new song every two years (the last album released was in the fall of 2014, so the next album should have been in the fall of 2016). The *Famous* feud ruined Taylor's album release pattern.	2008: She released the album in the same month as Taylor Swift, the second day and a week after Taylor Swift; she followed this release pattern one time. 2016: Surprise album like in 2013 (December 13, Taylor Swift birthday); released exclusively on Tidal.	2008: A year before (2007), he changed his pattern and released the album in the same month as Taylor Swift; in 2008 he followed the new pattern for the last time. 2016: Released the album a couple of days before the Grammy Awards ceremony.
THE PUBLIC IMAGE NARRATIVE LINE	2008 - 2009: Positive before the MTV award ceremony from 2009; a little bit negative after the ceremony from 2009: Kanye told the whole world that she does not deserve the award, Beyoncé is better. Positive before the song *Famous* was released; she walked to Grammy Awards while being called in Kanye's song 'that bitch'; Negative at high level after the release by his wife, Kim, of edited parts of the telephone conversation between her and Kanye.	2008 - 2009: Positive, and also seen (through free promotion by Kanye West) as an artist that deserved the award won by Taylor Swift; the MTV ceremony was unfair with her talent and creativity. 2016: Positive at high levels, she received the highest reviews in life for her album *Lemonade*.	2008 - 2009: Positive image before the MTV award ceremony from 2009; Negative image after MTV award ceremony from 2009 because of his view about the 'true' winner of the MTV award. 2016: Little negative image, and more negative after the release of the song *Famous*, but with positive changes after the release by Kim Kardashian of edited parts of the telephone conversation between him and Taylor.

AWARDS LINE	Taylor's music was nominated for MTV, in 2010 she won the Grammy Award for the *Album of the Year* for *Fearless,* in 2016 she won the Grammy Award for *Album of the Year* for *1989*). In both years Kanye West interfered in her narrative with a negative view about her music and character.

Discussion about another pattern personal: meaning of the album

In 2013 Beyoncé and Kanye West released their albums (*Beyoncé* album by Beyoncé, and Kanye West with *Yeezus* (which is a combination of his last two letters 'Ye' with 'Jesus' (*Yeezus* from Kanye: himself, people in his circle and fans around the world call him 'Ye') to promote himself as 'Ye' (Kanye) the Jesus (God) = Yeezus as sort of God of rap music. In 2014 Taylor Swift released her album *1989* (year of birthday). What if these albums are actually connected and Beyoncé and Kanye West, through their albums, took a shot at Taylor Swift, while Taylor Swift with her year of birth, *1989*, is her response to Beyoncé and Kanye West? Beyoncé took the shot by releasing her surprise album on Taylor Swift's birthday (December 13, 2013), while Kanye West few days before the release of his album *Yeezus,* in June 2013, in a *New York Times* interview stated about Taylor Swift VMA's moment that he doesn't have any regret about his interruption, and that it was a situation where he gave into peer pressure to apologize. When asked if he'd take back the original action or the apology, if given the choice, he answered, 'You know what? I can answer that, but I'm – I'm just -- not afraid, but I know that would be such a distraction. It's such a strong thing, and people have such a strong feeling about it. *My Beautiful Dark Twisted Fantasy* was my long, backhanded apology. You know how people give a backhanded compliment? It was a backhanded apology. It was like, all these raps, all these sonic acrobatics. I was like: 'Let me show you guys what I can do, and please accept me back. You want to have me on your shelves.'[746]

CONCLUSIONS:

- Kanye West interfered in the narrative line of Taylor Swift with a negative story about her character, while Beyoncé has a positive image about her skills and character;
- Kanye West is behind the negative stories about Taylor Swift's character and skills in 2009 and in 2016;
- Kanye West in 2016 interfered in Taylor Swift's narrative line with a negative story, while Beyoncé's narrative line is involved in releasing a new album;
- Kanye West negative behaviour toward Taylor Swift is after Beyoncé released an album (2008) and before (2016, *Lemonade*) she is out with a new album.

---

[746] Jon Caramanica, 'Behind Kanye's Mask', *New York Times*, June 11, 2013, https://www.nytimes.com/2013/06/16/arts/music/kanye-west-talks-about-his-career-and-album-yeezus.html?_r=0, last accessed: May 28, 2018.

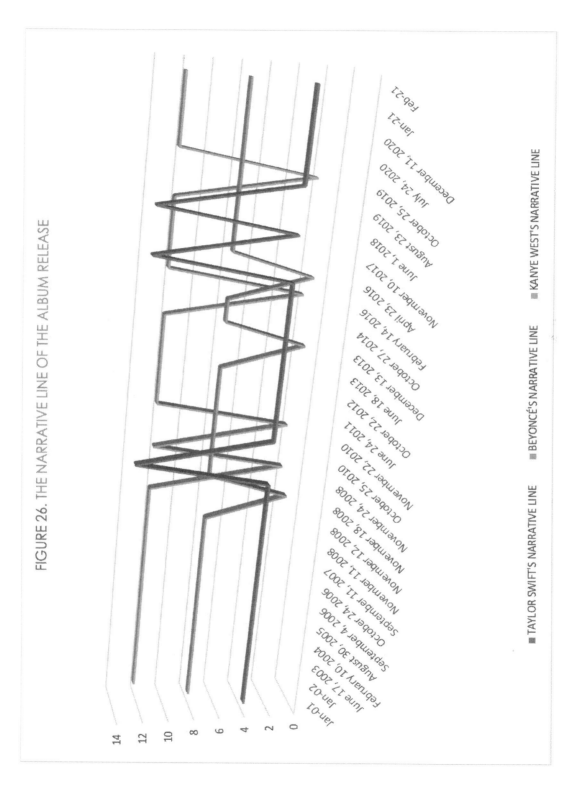

FIGURE 26. THE NARRATIVE LINE OF THE ALBUM RELEASE

VII. Conclusions: who is the **FAMOUS** victim and who is the **FAMOUS** perpetrator?

In this report I investigated the *Famous* feud between Kim Kardashian, Kanye West and Taylor Swift from the perspective of ten points of research. Below you find the conclusions I reached for each point of research.

1. To extract, to expose and to understand the role of the Western mass-media about:

a. key moments of the Famous feud: the Western mass-media, overall, was neutral and focused on the important elements and dates such as accusation, response to the accusation and evidence provided by the players of the feud; fortunately, there are few news agencies who delivered a more advanced view of the narrative line of the feud; the Western mass-media does not have any obligation toward the players of the feud (in the sense of creating an in-depth analysis of the events, and the narrative line of their feud) with the sole purpose to satisfy pretentious readers or anyone else interested in the feud; all of the events were available online on Twitter and Instagram ready to be consumed; some journalists and bloggers asked and encouraged the readers to make their own judgement about the feud;

b. specific information about the events from the Famous feud: as with the narrative line, the Western mass-media was overall neutral; however, there are negative articles with focus *only* on Taylor Swift while *ignoring* the acts of Kanye West and Kim Kardashian, which were the first and second to mislead the general public about Taylor Swift's intervention and the type, length, conditions and support for a song she never heard, but promised by Kanye West to send it to her after the telephone conversation; this report show a small (between 5%-10% of all the articles written about the feud in the Western mass-media that I was able to collect and read), yet visible, number of journalists and bloggers who spectacularly failed to show who is the real perpetrator, the real victim of the feud, and exaggerated with absurd interpretations that portrayed the participants of the feud in the wrong roles; few journalists ignored the neutrality role and sided with the perpetrators, presented final conclusions while the feud was in motion and with big gaps in the narrative, failed to hold Kanye West and Kim Kardashian accountable rightly at the same level they did wrongly with Taylor Swift; in March

2020, 25 minutes of the telephone conversation with Taylor Swift and Kanye West was leaked on Twitter and Youtube, and yet there are no negative articles about Kanye West with similar or identic language design and structure as it was used with Taylor Swift in July 2016 and onwards; why the Western mass-media failed to analyse Kanye West's behaviour toward and in reference to Taylor Swift for what he did in reality? Kanye West misled the general public with a negative view about Taylor Swift's character and skills (from this point of view, I can suggest that Kanye West enjoyed of a 'black privilege' by not being sanctioned by the Western mass-media at the same level they did with Taylor Swift); what if there is a 'black privilege' offered, supported and promoted by the Western mass-media against the white artists from the music industry?

c. what is missing from the Famous feud: the lack of Taylor Swift's opinion expressed during the interview in April 2016: is important in the timeline of the feud, because it shows a character that does not want to be part of the events put in motion by Kanye West, which is in strong relation with her expression on the telephone conversation with Kanye West about the song, 'I will think about it'; the Western mass-media should update the articles with the timeline of the feud and add the missing interview from April 2016, because it can help the readers to understand the point of view of Taylor Swift toward and in reference to Kanye West; also, Western mass-media should update the timeline and add the telephone conversation (25 minutes from Youtube) from March 2020 to January 2016, while keeping the short version of the telephone conversation published by Kim Kardashian on her Snapchat account to its original date, July 2016: doing this move, the readers can reach a better understanding of the strategies of communication and interpretation of each player, who is the real perpetrator and who is the real victim; finally, the addition of the telephone conversation in January 2016 it can help every person of interest in the feud to make a better judgement about Taylor Swift, and the negative treatment received for free from Kanye and Kim's camp, random people, journalists and bloggers..

2. To analyse the narrative line of the feud in order to identify patterns of behaviour: Kanye West's behaviour toward and in reference to Taylor Swift; Taylor Swift's behaviour toward and in reference to Kanye West; Kim Kardashian's behaviour toward and in reference to Taylor Swift; Taylor Swift's behaviour toward and in reference to Kim Kardashian:

- **for Kanye West to Taylor Swift**: I observed 10 patterns of an *overall negative behaviour* created, maintained and promoted worldwide toward and in reference to Taylor Swift since 2009; maybe he attempted to destroy a younger woman (character and skills, he was 32 years old when he actioned verbally against Taylor Swift, of 19 years old) that did nothing wrong against him before the start of the feud in 2009, and after 2009 to justify his actions;

411

- **for Taylor Swift to Kanye West:** I observed 8 patterns of an *overall defence mode behaviour* created, maintained and promoted worldwide toward and in reference to Kanye West's negative behaviour about her character and skills since 2009; she attempted to show that she is not guilty, does not deserve the negative behaviour of Kanye West, she was famous before he met her, and earned the awards because of the vote from her fans for the music she wrote and composed;
- **for Kim Kardashian to Taylor Swift:** I observed 7 patterns of an *overall negative behaviour* created, maintained and promoted worldwide toward and in reference to Taylor Swift since June 2016;
- **for Taylor Swift to Kim Kardashian**: I observed 7 patterns of an *overall defence mode behaviour* created, maintained and promoted worldwide toward and in reference to Kim Kardashian's negative behaviour about her character since June 2016.

3. To assess three points of view made by Kanye West, Kim Kardashian and Taylor Swift:

3.1 Kanye West wrote on Twitter: '3rd thing I called Taylor and had a hour long convo with her about the line and she thought it was funny and gave her blessings'; the information shared with the general public was partially true, biased, misleading and failed to mention the real discussion about the line that Taylor Swift disagreed with: 'I made that bitch famous'; the reason of this omission is because Taylor Swift was not aware of it; Kanye West used her verbal agreement for the two lyric lines: the one lyric line she heard over the phone and was good with it, and the second line 'I made that bitch famous' that she was not aware of; Kanye West failed to send her the full song and instead he published the song online; Taylor Swift heard the new lyrics at the same time with the general public;

3.2 Kim Kardashian in the interview with GQ magazine from 16 June 2016 and during her show *Keeping Up with The Kardashians* (season 12, episode 11): **'She totally approved that. [...] 'She totally knew that that was coming out;'** the information shared with the general public was partially true, biased, misleading and failed to mention that Taylor Swift was not aware of the full song and lyrics as she claimed in the interview; Taylor Swift said she will think about it, and Kanye West failed to keep his side of the bargain by sending her the full song as he said during the telephone conversation;

3.3 the affirmation made by Taylor Swift in July 2016: 'Being falsely painted as a liar when I was never given the full story *or played any part of the song* (underline by author) is character assassination'; this information is mostly true as Kanye West did not share with her the whole story of the song, failed to keep his side of the bargain and blamed her for his actions; however, the part **'played any part of the song':** she knew some lyrics and suggested a change of the lyrics; however, this support for the lyrics does not offer a clear causal link that she played a part because she *really* wanted, or because she tried to be *nice* and *supportive* with Kanye West; Taylor Swift was unaware of Kanye West's intention to record the telephone conversation and keeping it as evidence of her involvement, ready to be shared with the general public on his terms, without any information given to her; eventually, Taylor Swift found out at the same time as the general public that Kanye West had indeed recorded their telephone conversation, edited it and released it to show only the parts that benefited Kanye West and Kim Kardashian.

4. To analyse the song Famous to see how much Taylor Swift knew about the song before its release:

- by using various mathematical formulas (subtraction, percentage conversion, average method) Taylor Swift knew between **4.11(11)% to 7.94(44)%, respectively 8.05(22)% about the song *Famous*,** this level of knowledge about the song does not offer a clear causal link that she played a part because she *really* wanted, or because *she tried to be nice* and *supportive* with Kanye West.

5. To analyse the impact of the Famous feud on the albums sales and songs for Kanye West, Taylor Swift and Katy Perry:

- on long term, despite all the negative behaviour and attitude of Kanye West, then later Katy Perry, toward and in reference to Taylor Swift, there is a higher negative impact of the albums and songs sales for Kanye and Katy Perry than for Taylor Swift.

6. To identify and expose the mechanisms and strategies of interpretation and communication used by Kim Kardashian, Kanye West, Taylor Swift and the Western mass-media:

- **for Kanye West, Kim Kardashian, journalists and bloggers**: I found 16 strategies of communication and interpretation of the *Famous* feud, and all of them are against Taylor Swift's version of the story; each player used either their own strategy that was not used by other player, for example we have *The Race Card*: *Black Man versus White Privileged Woman* strategy used visible only by journalists, or all three players of the feud used the same strategy: *Stabbing in the Back While Shaking Her Hand* and *The Balance of Image and Fame*;

- **for Taylor Swift**: I found 6 strategies of communication and interpretation of the *Famous* feud; all of them are in defence mode toward and in reference to Kanye West, Kim Kardashian and journalists with the purpose to share her side of the story, which is mostly true (less true for the 'played any part of the song');

- **for all the players of the Famous feud**: there are similar strategies of communication and interpretation of the events, however, each part is presenting their own view; overall, Taylor Swift's strategies are mostly true in comparison with the strategies of the other players of the feud;

- **the most used strategy of communication and interpretation** was *The Dynamic Reaction Strategy*: each player of the feud responded by a statement on the official page, or through a song, video, music album or interview;

- **intelligence of the strategy**: all players have shown intelligence and creativity in their strategies of communication and interpretation of the feud;

- **side effects**: on long term, Taylor Swift's strategies of communication and interpretation of the feud were more powerful than Kanye West's strategies (because he started the feud), and the general public sided with her side of the story: we know this based on the high number of sales of her songs, albums and concert tickets in comparison with Kanye West since 2009 until today.

7. To explore possible reasons for creating, supporting and promoting the Famous feud by Kim Kardashian, Kanye West, Taylor Swift and Western mass-media:

- **for Kanye West:**

  o for free publicity;
  o to maintain his presence in the music industry and online;
  o to direct the negative attention from him to Taylor Swift;
  o to create headlines written and published by the Western mass-media;
  o to generate income from publicity and own businesses (music, clothes, shoes) even if it is done through negative publicity because, in the end, the only person that can sue him is Taylor Swift, the general public can only judge his actions and make a choice: on his side or Taylor Swift's side;

VII. CONCLUSIONS: who is the **FAMOUS** VICTIM and who is the **FAMOUS** PERPETRATOR?

- *for Kim Kardashian West:*

  - for free publicity;
  - to support the malicious actions of her husband Kanye West against Taylor Swift;
  - to maintain her presence online and in the mind of the general public which creates headlines written and published by the Western mass-media;
  - to generate income from publicity and own businesses even if it is done through negative publicity because, in the end, the only person that can sue her is Taylor Swift, the general public can only judge her actions and make a choice: on her side or Taylor Swift's side;

- *for Western mass-media:*

  - for income through incendiary and clickbait articles: being on the side of the perpetrators, Kanye West and Kim Kardashian, the reaction of Taylor Swift's fans was negative, with many of them being angry about the conclusions of the journalists, and engaged massively in the comment section of the articles, which, in return, generated views, increased the economic profile of the news agencies, and increased the profit from the taxes to run ads on their own websites;
  - possible to spread their own agenda: the comparison between two races, white and black (which generated a lot of interest through online debates (comments) and views of the articles);
  - to attract users to consume their services (online and print); to keep the number of users and their subscription, because there is content to read, so there is a reason to keep the subscription;
  - to show interest in various topics and create a profile of a diverse news agency capable of accommodating users with different interests;

- *for Taylor Swift:*

  - to present her side of the story;
  - because she is the victim of the *Famous* feud, and her behaviour was in defence mode toward and in reference to Kanye West, Kim Kardashian and Western mass-media, it is hard to suggest that Taylor Swift tried to profit from this feud for the sole purpose to earn money from fans, and to maintain a vivid and clean presence online.

8. To analyse the core argument of the false white victimhood attributed to Taylor Swift:

- this core argument was widely spread by the Western mass-media; indeed, the feud started because of Kanye West, however, there is no mention in his responses that the reason why he put in motion 'look-like-planned-negative-behaviour' toward and in reference to Taylor Swift is because Taylor Swift is white, and she is to blame for his poor choices, nor that his life suffered at the hand of Taylor Swift's actions (a white woman) before he interrupted her speech at the MTV Music Video Awards in 2009, and he wanted to get a sort of well-deserved justice;
- there is evidence to create at least a satisfactory argument that the core argument of the white victimhood attributed to Taylor Swift is a false creation of the Western mass-media, more precisely, by the authors mentioned in this research;
- based on Taylor Swift statements, music (all albums) and strategies of communication and interpretation, there is no clear causal link and evidence that she intentionally presented herself as a *white victim* of a *bad black man* for the specific reason to create a racial comparison, and that she is a white victim of the black man, Kanye West, because she planned this strategy before she met Kanye West in September 2009 and after, with the sole purpose to advance her career;
- the narrative line of Taylor Swift is the most advanced evidence to support the conclusions above: she interfered in Kanye West's narrative line only *after* his actions and with the purpose to *defend herself* from his negative accusations and opinions about her character and skills;
- the Western mass-media (based on the negative articles used in this report) interfered in Taylor Swift's narrative line with a false argument, and advanced their *own* worldview about Taylor Swift's strategies of communication and interpretation, *while totally ignoring* the reason of her responses: because of Kanye West.

9. To analyse the core argument of Ellie Woodward about the existence of a false worldview attributed to Kanye West which is that of a: 'black man terrorising the 'innocent' white woman' because of Taylor Swift:

- there are rich reasons and comments provided by Kanye West to create at least a good argument that he is the bad/evil black man of the feud (The Narrative Line, the patterns of negative behaviour, the strategies of communications and interpretations);
- based on Kanye West's patterns of negative behaviour in reference to Taylor Swift, I found Ellie Woodward statement false and lacks of substantial evidences

to support it; in contrast, Kanye West's patterns of negative behaviour in reference to Taylor Swift are a rich resource of creating at least a satisfactory argument that there could be a picture of a 'black man terrorising the innocent white woman': he started the feud, he continued the feud, he controlled the feud, while Taylor Swift's pattern of behaviour was to defend herself from his negative views about her character and skills; he called her 'bitch' in front of the entire world while falsely claiming that Taylor Swift approved it; Kanye West, through live speaking and by interpreting his song *Famous*, created a feeling of encouragement in his concerts where fans started shouting 'bitch' in reference to Taylor Swift; Kanye West spread the negative presentation toward and in reference to Taylor Swift's character through various statements during his concerts and interviews;

- **'black man terrorising':** this part of the statement, however, cannot be taken in the entirety written by Ellie Woodward, due to the issue regarding the acceptance from experts about the clear existence of a universal concept of 'terror', 'terrorism' and 'terrorising'[747]: to some extent the definition is in the eye of the beholder; for Ellie Woodward, despite the existence of a rich evidence of persistent patterns of negative behaviour, Kanye does not terrorise Taylor Swift, it is the other way around and we should not believe Taylor Swift; however, from the point of view of Taylor Swift and his patterns of negative behaviour toward and in reference to her character and skills (she presented all the time a positive image about him, and tried her best to support him), it may have a different view about him, it may be the view of a 'black man terrorising her' despite trying to help him out, he betrayed his word and misled the general public about her true implications in the creation of the *song Famous*, and about her character;

- **'black man terrorising':** this statement is exaggerated by Ellie Woodward in relation with Kanye West's worldview and added an unnecessary evil/bad view for him; his fans and the general public are capable of seeing and understanding the events of the feud, and can be influenced to reach conclusions, surprisingly, against Kanye West (because he started the feud against Taylor Swift which was in defence mode in relation to his patterns of negative behaviour); maybe through Ellie Woodward's opinion, and her lack of following the logical flow of Taylor Swift's statements about her involvement, Kanye West's negative public

---

[747] Andrew Heywood, *Global Politics*, Palgrave Macmillan, New York, 2011, p. 282; David Brown, 'Terrorism', in Trevor C. Salmon, Mark F. Imber (eds), *Issue in International Relations*, Second Edition. New York, Routledge, 2008, pp. 107-120; Colin Wight, 'Theorising Terrorism: The State, Structure, and History', *International Relations*, 23:1 (2009), p. 99; Thomas J. Badey, 'Defining international terrorism: A pragmatic approach', *Terrorism and Political Violence*, 10:1, 1998, p. 90; Ben Saul, 'Attempts to Define 'Terrorism' in International Law', *Netherlands International Law Review*, Vol. 52, No. 1, 2005, pp. 58-59; Myra Williamson, *Terrorism, War and International Law the Legality of the Use of Force Against Afghanistan in 2001*, The Ashgate International Law Series, Asgate, England, 2009, p. 49; Joshua Woods, 'What We Talk About When We Talk About Terrorism: Elite Press Coverage of Terrorism Risk from 1997 to 2005', *The Harvard International Journal of Press/Politics*, 12: 3, 2007, p.3.

image grew more than the effort and the reaction of fans on both camps, and of the general public;

- it is possible that Kanye West's worldview of a **'black man terrorising the 'innocent" white woman'** to exist more after Ellie Woodward's article than only by his actions, as the general public may attribute simple words to describe Kanye West's negative behaviour, such as 'bad/evil man' or 'perpetrator'; maybe thanks to Ellie Woodward's rich imagination his worldview image may have changed for the worst;

- **Ellie Woodward statement: 'The dominant reaction, however, was a reflection of what the world has been conditioned to see: the 'threat' of an 'angry" black man terrorising the 'innocent" white woman. Even their clothes reflected the racially fuelled victim/villain framework that would define the incident: The image of West, wearing dark shades and an entirely black outfit, accosting sweet Swift in her white and silver party dress, remains an iconic one':** I found it to be biased and misleading toward and in reference to Taylor Swift 'false white woman victimhood'; Kanye West initiated the events of the *Famous* feud (evidence: the patterns of behaviour and the strategies of communications and interpretations) for which Taylor Swift is not guilty; Taylor Swift interfered in the narrative line of Kanye West *only after he initiated* and *perpetuated* the events, she interfered to protect herself from his malicious, biased and misleading information spread to the general public in his own terms; there is nothing wrong for a white woman to reply to a black man who she did not nothing wrong to him to justify his malicious actions from 2009 until and after 2016;

- **'black man terrorising the 'innocent" white woman':** if this perception exist in the mind of fans on both camps and the general public about Kanye West, then Ellie Woodward should provide more strong examples and in-depth explanations about the reasons and evidence behind her statement, and the connections that she tried to create in reference to Taylor Swift 'white victimhood' and the 'black man terrorising';

- **'black man terrorising the 'innocent" white woman':** if this perception exist in the mind of the general public about Kanye West, then Kanye West is to blame because he initiated the events of the *Famous* feud in his own terms.

10. To find out who is the Famous victim and who is the Famous perpetrator of the Famous feud:

to find out the answer to this point of research, I used the strategy presented below:

- ***perpetrator points***:

VII. CONCLUSIONS: who is the **FAMOUS** VICTIM and who is the **FAMOUS** PERPETRATOR?

13 September 2009:

Kanye West: 1 point;
Taylor Swift: 0 points;

11 February 2016:

Kanye West: 1 point;
Kim Kardashian West: 1 point (because she interfered with misleading statements about the real role played by Taylor Swift in the feud and the background details of the song);
Taylor Swift: no points (because Kanye West initiated the new event of the feud);

- **final perpetrator points**:

Kanye West: 2 points;
Kim Kardashian West: 1 point;
Taylor Swift: 0 points.

- **conclusions:**

  - Kanye West was the first to misled the general public about Taylor Swift's involvement in the creation of the *song Famous*, then Kim Kardashian and Taylor Swift (for 'played any part of the song');
  - for Kanye West the advices and suggestions received by Taylor Swift (she sold millions of albums before he met him; she will think about the song) via the telephone conversation did not matter: he decided to record the telephone conversation and to continue with his plan; maybe Kim Kardashian or Kanye West edited the video with the telephone conversation posted on Kim's Snapchat account, but definitely was published online according with their needs;
  - Taylor Swift is the *Famous victim* of the *Famous perpetrators*: Kanye West and Kim Kardashian (due to their intentional interference in her narrative line with a negative view about her skills and character in front of the entire world);
  - **Kanye West is the real perpetrator in the *Famous* feud** because he had the power and the evidence to respond to Taylor Swift's publicly disputed lyric line, and he never did it; had plenty of chances to publicly acknowledge Taylor Swift's right to publicly challenge the song's final lyrics: they spoke on

the phone about the song, but not the new line 'I made that bitch famous' and he decided to add it; he did not send Taylor Swift the final version of the song; he is the author of the song and, therefore, it is his duty to say exactly what happened;

- Kanye West, Kim Kardashian and some Western journalists and bloggers own a deep, genuine and classic apology to Taylor Swift for publishing and spreading biased and misleading information about her character.

Other conclusions & discussions:

- **the cause of Kanye West's negative view about his personality:** based on the figure *The Narrative Line of the Famous Feud*, I found that **lack of manners** is to blame for everything bad that came for Kanye West from the general public since September 2009 until today, and forevermore: by walking on the stage and interrupting the speech of Taylor Swift, Kanye West showed **lack of manners** toward a person who did not do anything wrong to him; **lack of manners** may be the real reason of Kanye West's fall in the eyes of the general public;
- in the first event of the *Famous* feud, in September 2009, many artists expressed their personal opinion towards all participants, for example Pink and 50 Cents expressed a negative opinion about Kanye West's interruption of Taylor Swift's speech[748]; in 2016, Kanye West initiated a second major event, the *song Famous*, and in 2019 Wendy Williams (black woman; before 2008 she worked as radio DJ; since 2008 she has her own show, *The Wendy Williams Show*) had an interesting opinion about Kanye West and Taylor Swift: 'I didn't really know her until Kanye West brought her on stage all those years ago;'[749] Wendy Williams worked as a radio DJ while Taylor Swift started her musical career, and her albums (*Taylor Swift* in 2006; *Fearless* in 2008) were included for many weeks in the music charts like those published by Billboard and Nielson; is it possible that a former radio DJ, then her own public show, to miss all the news about the success of Taylor Swift, a new artist in the music industry who managed to sell more albums than other artists considered better than her? she did not read the Billboard charts? what if Wendy Williams sided with Kanye West because it was the right moment to pour out all her internal dissatisfaction accumulated over the years toward a person who did nothing wrong to her? what if Wendy Williams took advantage of

---

[748] Marianne Garvey, 'How Pink came to Taylor Swift's defense after that Kanye West stage-rush incident at the VMAs', *CNN*, August 23, 2019, available at: https://edition.cnn.com/2019/08/23/entertainment/pink-billboards-kanye-west-taylor-swift/index.html, last accessed: November 27, 2019; People Staff, '50 Cent Wants to Give Kanye West a Black Eye', *People*, September 15, 2009, available at: https://people.com/celebrity/50-cent-wants-to-give-kanye-west-a-black-eye/, last accessed: November 27, 2019.

[749] Celebs Today, 'Wendy Williams says it's 'unbelievable' Taylor Swift is named AMAs Artist of the Decade', *Youtube*, November 26, 2019, available at: https://www.youtube.com/watch?v=YUJbMnZ_qbU, last accessed: November 27, 2019.

the *Famous* feud to project her discriminatory attitude toward a white artist, towards a white woman with possible greater success than her and Kanye West? what we know for sure is that Wendy Williams decided to draw final conclusions while the event was in motion, and without having the whole story, which suggests a possible negative view about her state of mind (reasoning) and character; Wendy Williams said that Kanye West brought Taylor on the stage, but Taylor was already on the stage as an artist who sold millions of copies from her last two albums (Taylor definitely sold more copies than Kanye West, even though Kanye West released his album in the same timeframe and pattern of album release as Taylor: November 2008); Wendy Williams may have sided with the perpetrators, Kanye West and Kim Kardashian;

- surprisingly, the negative articles written about Taylor Swift did not have a negative effect on long term; in 2021 Taylor Swift won for the third time the *Album of the Year* with an album that she owns, *folklore*; the number of pure albums sales decreased in the last 14 years, however, she is still in top of various charts and world records;

- Taylor Swift (the victim) was criticised head to toe while Kanye West (the perpetrator) got away with it; imagine the reaction of the Western mass-media and Black Lives Matter, if Taylor Swift was indeed the perpetrator and Kanye West the victim;

- Taylor Swift is being accused that she is following 'only the money', yet, in this report, I showed and described the opposite picture: Kanye West, Jay Z and Beyoncé are involved in various strategies (such as Tidal false plays) where 'money' are involved in their narrative, and the end of their narrative;

- Kanye West interfered in Taylor Swift's increasing and positive narrative line, after and while his narrative line of success was decreasing;

- in this report I discovered that Fake News is real and it is happening to some extent inside the most prestigious news agencies of the Western world, and involves a white woman which contradicts the argument of the Black Lives Matter movement that white people have a higher privilege than black people[750]; from the point of view of the *Famous* feud and the sources used in this report, there is not enough evidence to create at least a satisfactory argument that Taylor Swift is the privileged white woman, and Kanye West is the exiled black man who does not deserve to be treated negatively by the Western mass-media, for example, although the leak of the conversation between Kanye West and Taylor Swift supported her side of the story more than Kanye's story, *The Wall Street Journal* decided to keep Kanye West on the main cover[751];

---

[750] Cory Collins, 'What is White Privilege, Really?', *Learning for Justice*, Fall 2018, available at: https://www.learningforjustice.org/magazine/fall-2018/what-is-white-privilege-really, last accessed: March 26, 2020.
[751] 'The Creation and the Myth of Kanye West', *The Wall Street Journal*, March 25, 2020, available at: https://www.wsj.com/articles/the-creation-and-the-myth-of-kanye-west-11585138241, last accessed: March 26, 2020.

- there are people involved in criminal organisations and activities and do not get the same malicious treatment as the one offered for free to Taylor Swift by the Western mass-media;
- Kanye West used the line 'I made that bitch famous', yet he was not cancelled, but he got support from American Express and Tidal with exclusive tickets for customers and other venue places; this a good reason to suggest that Kanye West does not experience discrimination in the USA from companies; the high number of tickets sold for his *Saint Pablo Tour* is another good evidence to suggest that people does not discriminate Kanye West because he is black; his public behaviour toward and in reference to Taylor Swift may weight more for people in making the decision to support or not his music and concerts;
- the 25-minute telephone conversation available on Youtube does not change the conclusion of the first version of this report from 2017, but confirms them: the evidence available is good to create at least a satisfactory argument that Kanye West and Kim Kardashian are the perpetrators, and Taylor Swift is the victim of the *Famous* feud;
- based on the information used in this report, and other events from the feud that were not included in this report, it is not possible to determine whether the feud is over or not;
- **Taylor Swift won the *Famous* feud by herself** against Kanye West, Kim Kardashian (possible Beyoncé and Jay Z), Western mass-media journalists and bloggers (only for the negative articles) and other supporters against her, and based on the events from 2009 until November 2017 (for the narrative line with Kanye West), and from June 2016 until March 2020 (for the narrative line with Kim Kardashian); the biggest war in her career was won only through her vision and naturally born abilities to write and compose music, plus a visible holder of common sense; Taylor Swift's power of a higher truthful storyline of the events is incredible and consistent on long term;
- despite all the information used in this research, I was unable to find genuine evidence with strong reasons that can justify the look-like-planned-hate-and-mean-strategies-and-feedback from Kanye West toward and in reference to Taylor Swift; why Kanye West was so deep involved in negative plans to advance a negative view about Taylor Swift's skills and character? we need an answer, considering that Kanye West presents himself as a man in the service of God;[752]
- in this report there is evidence to create a good suggestion regarding the following final conclusions: Kanye West is not the famous black artist who is fighting to calm the race problem in the USA and build a peaceful world; Kanye West interfered brutally and negatively in the narrative line of a famous white

---

[752] This statement is based on Kanye West participation on long term for Sunday Service. See for example: Jordan Darville, 'What exactly is Kanye West's Sunday Service?', *The Fader*, September 24, 2019, available at: https://www.thefader.com/2019/09/24/a-history-of-sunday-service-kanye-west, last accessed: March 26, 2020.

artist, and refused to accept the negative consequences towards other people due to his behaviour and, therefore, his attitude increases and continues the negative narrative line of the race problem in the USA; people who want a better world must look for another source of inspiration; Kanye West failed to promote a better world in the USA for black and white people; on long term, can Taylor Swift, through her music, influence black and white people to leave the past behind and to embrace a common and a brighter future forevermore?

Printed in Great Britain
by Amazon